AXIS SUBMARINE SUCCESSES 1939-1945

BY JÜRGEN ROHWER

Introductory material translated by John A. Broadwin

NAVAL INSTITUTE PRESS
Annapolis, Maryland

This book is an updated
translation of *Die U-Boot-Erfolge*
Der Achsenmachte 1939-1945, originally
published for the Bibliothek für Aeitgeschichte
by J.F. Lehmanns Verlag, Munich, 1968.

English language edition
Copyright © 1983 by the United States Naval Institute

Library of Congress Cataloging in Publication Data

Rohwer, Jürgen.
   Axis submarine successes, 1939-1945.

   Updated translation of: Die U-Boot Erfolge der
Achsenmächte, 1939-1945.
   Includes index.
   1. World War, 1939-1945--Naval operations--Submarine
--Tables. 2. World War, 1939-1945--Naval operations--
Submarine--Chronology. 3. World War, 1939-1945--Naval
operations, German--Tables. 4. World War, 1939-1945--
Naval operations, German--Chronology. I. Title.
D780.R5713 1983   940.54'5943   83-13103
ISBN 0-87021-082-3

Printed in the United States of America on acid-free paper ⊗

10 9 8 7 6 5 4 3 2

This volume is dedicated to
the many thousands of dead seamen
who met their fate on the ships listed within.

Contents

Preface to the English Edition

The 1968 German edition of this source book has been out of print for quite some time. After the recent accessibility of newly declassified records and documents--mainly on the Allied side--a large number of additions and corrections seemed necessary. Therefore we decided not to reprint the German edition but, instead, to undertake a complete revision.

Because of numerous inquiries, chiefly from English-speaking countries, we had to consider whether it might not be more useful to first publish a new edition in English. The United States Naval Institute kindly expressed its willingness to publish this translated and revised edition.

Even before 1968 we were able to check and verify reports on attacks and sinkings by lone U-boats against Allied reports on shipping losses. Therefore most of the information in the German edition was not in need of revision. However in 1968 we still had problems in dealing with coordinated U-boat attacks (wolf packs) against convoys which involved the sinking of several ships; in attributing sinkings to particular U-boat attacks, we depended in many cases on position information that was often questionable. Not until the release of the action reports of the escort commanders and the convoy commodores, housed in archives in London, Washington, and Ottawa, were we able to check the times in the patrol reports against those in the shipping loss reports and give credit for most convoy sinkings with greater certainty. Therefore most of the corrections and additions are to be found in this area.

Also, the gradual though still incomplete release of British and American Ultra signal descriptions that began in 1975 has enabled us to fill quite a few war-related gaps in Axis and, particularly, German U-boat command records.

As a result of my extensive correspondence during the past fourteen years with former staff officers of the Axis U-boat commands and Allied naval forces, as well as with a number of former U-boat captains, seamen in Allied convoys and merchant ships, and historians and many ship lovers, I have been able to check, correct, and add a number of details. Even though it is not possible to thank all my correspondents for their support individually, I would still like to cite a few particularly helpful persons whom I did not mention in the preface to the German edition and to whom I would like to express my gratitude for support that often involved great effort. On the German side: Archivdirektor Dr. Hans-Joseph Maierhöfer of the Bundesarchiv-Militärarchiv, Kapitän zur See (Ret.) Heinz Bonatz, for many years the chief of German naval radio intelligence, Jochen Ahme of the Verband Deutscher U-Bootfahrer (German Submariners Association), Kapitän zur See (Ret.) Klaus Corth and Horst Bredow of the U-boat Memorial in Möltenort, and two U-boat experts Bodo Herzog and Eberhard Rössler.

On the Italian side, Contralmirante Gino Galuppini, Director of the Ufficio Storico della Marina Militare, and Prof. Alberto Santo of the University of Rome were of assistance. In Japan Rear Admiral (Ret.) Prof. Saburo Toyama and Major Takeo Takai

of the Defence Academy provided help. In Great Britain my thanks
go to David Brown and, in particular, to Robert M. Coppock of the
Naval Historical Branch, to Mrs. Mary Z. Pain for her assistance
in the Public Record Office and Vice Admirals Brian B. Schofield,
Sir Norman Denning and Sir Peter Gretton as well as to Patrick
Beesly, who as participants in the events of the past were very
forthcoming with assistance in the present. In the U.S. I
would like to thank, above all, Dr. Dean Allard and Bernard
Cavalcante of the Operational Archives of the U.S. Navy for their
unflagging support, as well as Robert Wolfe, William H. Cunliffe
and John E. Taylor of the National Archives and Prof. Dr. Philip
Lundeberg, Curator of Naval History in the Smithsonian Institution.

In Canada my thanks go to Dr. W.A.B. Douglas and Philip Chaplin
of the Directorate of History and Prof. Dr. Michael Hadley of the
University of Victoria as well as the many participants in the
Battle of the Atlantic who gathered in 1980 for an historical con-
ference at the Royal Roads Military College.

Vice Admiral Arthur Oscar Saldanha Da Gama and Capital de Mar e
Guerra Max Justo Guedes provided valuable information on shipping
losses off the coast of Brazil.

To these and all my other unnamed helpers and, in particular,
my colleagues at the United States Naval Institute, go my many
thanks.

Preface to the German Edition

The Bibliothek für Zeitgeschichte (Library of Modern History) was founded in 1915 by the Swabian industrialist Richard Franck as the Weltkriegsbücherei (Library of the Great War). Franck commissioned the library to build the most complete collection possible of printed material on the First World War, starting with treatises, leaflets, and posters and extending to newspapers, journals, and comprehensive monographic works. Later the library was commissioned to list its holdings completely and systematically and expand its coverage to include the period before and after the war and--finally--the entire twentieth century.

Under its original mandate the Weltkriegsbücherei began to publish categorized lists of its new acquisitions as early as 1921. At first these lists appeared monthly. Later they developed into the annual *Bücherschau der Weltkriegsbücherei* (Bibliography of the Library of the Great War), which is currently in its forty-fourth year of publication, now under the title *Jahresbibliographie der Bibliothek für Zeitgeschichte* (Annual Bibliography of the Library of Modern History). The bibliography is categorized by subject area, and arranged alphabetically. Each year it contains an average of 8,000 entries comprising almost all internationally published books and journal articles dealing with the history of the twentieth century.

In 1934 the Weltkriegsbücherei began the publication of a second series--the *Bibliographische Vierteljahrshefte der Weltkriegsbücherei* (Bibliographic Quarterly of the Library of the Great War), which contained bibliographic reviews on specific topics in World War I history. When work on this series resumed in 1962 under the title *Schriften der Bibliothek für Zeitgeschichte* (Publications of the Library of Modern History), its scope was expanded to include the entire twentieth century, and recognized experts in the various subject areas wrote literature surveys or research articles covering large numbers of titles.

To complement its predominantly bibliographic publications, the Bibliothek für Zeitgeschichte with this volume begins a new series: Dokumentationen der Bibliothek für Zeitgeschichte (Sources in the Library of Modern History). The purpose of this new series is to make available to a wider public material originally prepared for the library's reference department, particularly material dealing with the history of World War II. The initial volumes planned in this series are the Shipping Losses File, compiled by Jürgen Rohwer, of which this book is the first, and a listing of the of the units of the German armed forces, their composition, commands, leaders, campaigns, and combat operations, compiled by Werner Haupt and Walter Straub. Similar studies by other scholars--for example, a study by Helmut Sander of naval and merchant marine losses during World War I--are also planned.

We therefore hope to offer the field of military history an additional aid for rapidly and reliably checking facts based on scarce source material that is often hard to assemble in one place.

Bibliothek für Zeitgeschichte

Introduction

This book is the outcome of more than twenty years of research. However it would not have been possible without the generous help given again and again by the many officers, historians, ship lovers and, last but not least, the many former U-boat crewmen and merchant seamen who share an interest in naval history, be they members of private or governmental naval history research institutes, or naval history buffs. A brief summary of the book's development should elaborate this, while giving me the chance to thank all my friends and associates, and identify the sources on which it is based.

Immediately after the end of World War II, I began to rebuild my naval records collection, part of which I had managed to keep intact during the war. At first I was interested mainly in the German Navy of World War II--its ships, data on their construction, technical specifications, and information on their fate. Often working under difficult circumstances, I copied plans and transcribed data from the remaining business records I found in the partly-dismantled shipyards of Hamburg, Kiel, Bremen, Bremerhaven, and Wilhelmshaven. In Hamburg's "Navy House", the headquarters of Germany's minesweeping force, I culled information from the official records on the operations and fate of the sea defense forces. And in the Allied office responsible for notifying families of the death of relatives who had died in combat, I searched for documents on the operations and fate of the other naval vessels, particularly U-boats. During the period 1946-1948, I came into contact with former German naval officers who were under Allied orders to do studies on various aspects of Germany's conduct of the war at sea: for example, with a group in Bremerhaven consisting of Generaladmiral Schniewind, Vizeadmiral Ruge, Vizeadmiral Heye, Konteradmiral Wagner, and Kapitän zur See Rösing, who were focusing on operations in the eastern theaters of the war at the behest of the Americans; and with Fregattenkapitän Hessler and Korvettenkapitän Hoschatt in Brunsbüttel, who were writing a detailed study of German submarine warfare for the British.

Offering the material I had collected at the various shipyards and other locations for use by these officers in their studies, I was able in return to gain access to other vital source material, including in particular the war diaries of the Commander-in-Chief of Submarines, the Chief of Submarines North Sea (Norway), and other commanders. The details recorded in these meticulously-kept diaries formed the basis of my initial compilation of the data on German U-boat attacks during World War II. These war diary records were supplemented by much information taken from the ships' logs of individual U-boats and, some time later, by torpedo data reports in which the U-boat captains carefully recorded each torpedo attack, including detailed firing data, figures, target observations, and plots. My many conversations and written correspondence--some of which extended over many years--with the former German Commander-in-Chief of Submarines Grossadmiral Karl Dönitz and his staff officers, especially Konteradmiral Eberhard Godt, Fregattenkapitän Günter Hessler, and Fregattenkapitän Adalbert Schnee, as well as with a number of

surviving U-boat captains and crewmembers, helped me resolve
many ambiguities and clarify doubtful information. Let me take
the occasion of the publication of this book to thank them all
for their unflagging support and constant encouragement in carrying out this project.

On the Allied side, List B.R. 1337--"British and Foreign Merchant Vessels Lost or Damaged by Enemy Action During the Second
World War"--issued on 1 October 1945 by the British Admiralty for
official use only, was the starting point for identifying ships
sunk or damaged by Axis U-boats. This list contains the names
of all the maritime nations' merchant ships then known to have
been lost or damaged in areas under Allied control. For several
years it was regularly revised and updated. The Brunsbüttel group
got their information on Allied warships sunk or damaged by U-boats
from this British Admiralty source.

To make comparisons easier, between 1948 and 1950 I entered on
index cards all the data on U-boat attacks contained in the U-boat
logs and in List B.R. 1337. Later I used lists of shipping losses
published by other maritime nations for comparison and to fill
gaps in my file. By the end of the 1950s I was able use these
data to account for a very large proportion of reported U-boat
successes, in particular when the U-boats operated individually.
When dealing with "wolf pack" attacks on convoys, however, I at
first encountered difficulties: there was still not enough data
available from German and Allied sources to enable me to correlate
the many and often rapid series of attacks by different U-boats
with loss statistics consisting mainly of just dates and locations.
I was also unable to correlate information on many ships listed
as missing--where dates were often wrong by one or two weeks, and
position reports off by several hundred miles--with the pertinent
success report, especially when particulars on the cause of the
loss were wrong as well. This explains why figures I published
in various places during the 1950s on sinkings by individual
U-boats (and that later found their way into other publications)
still contained errors. I therefore recommend that in the future
researchers consult this book, rather than use previously published
data.

Italian submarines operating at the same time and in the same
general vicinity as German U-boats were another problem. That
is why, as early as 1951, I began correspondence that has since
continued without interruption with the Ufficio Storico della
Marina Militare in Rome. Its chief at that time, Ammiraglio di
squadra Giuseppe Fioravanzo, for his part, ordered data compiled
on attacks and successes reported by Italian submarines. His
work enable me to make much progress in identifying the ships
attacked by Italian submarines. The correspondence since carried
on with Admiral Fioravanzo and his successors, Ammiraglio di
squadra Aldo Cocchia, Contrammiraglio Vittorio Emanuele Tognelli,
and Contrammiraglio Alberto Donato, gradually helped me to resolve
uncertainties about the Atlantic theater and, later, the Mediterranean.

Similarly, I tried to get data on Japanese submarine attacks.
To begin with, the last Chief of the Operations Section of the
Japanese Naval General Staff, Captain Toshikazu Ohmae, filled the
gaps in a list of ships that had been sunk in the Indian and
Pacific Oceans by neither Italian nor German submarines. Later,
the President of the Japanese-German Society, retired Rear Admiral
Kojima, the German military and naval attachés in Tokyo, Kapitän

zur See Poser, Kapitän zur See Bode and Dr. Schünemann, and particularly Rear Admiral Sakamoto of the Japanese Self-Defense
Force's Office for Military History, facilitated the updating
of that first list with the results of subsequent Japanese research.

Beginning in 1952, I obtained information from Lieutenant Commander Erkki Ainamo in Helsinki on operations and attacks by
Finnish submarines. The diaries of the German Naval Training
Detachment Rumania for 1941-42 and Admiral Black Sea for 1944
offered much basic data on the wartime operations of Rumanian
submarines.

In contrast, it was hard to identify Soviet ships reported as
sunk or damaged by Axis U-boats in the eastern maritime theaters
of the Baltic, the Black Sea, and the upper North Sea, since the
data in British List B.R. 1337 for these areas were generally
inexact and incomplete. A good deal could be inferred, however,
from the German records--especially when they contained details
from radio intelligence reports--and by exchanges of information
with experts both in and out of Germany, in particular Jürg Meister
(Zurich), Siegfried Breyer (Hanau), Claud Huan (Lorient), Rolf
Erikson (Kingman, Arizona), and Pierre Warneck (Brussels). In
the past ten years I have also been able to glean an increasing
number of details from Soviet publications. However, except for
a short exchange of letters in 1962, my many attempts to coor-
dinate lists with the Soviet Navy's Historical Section have been
fruitless. Therefore some gaps still exist, though their number
is insignificant when compared with the total number of listings
contained herein. One special case was resolved using information
supplied by Colonel Militaru of the Central Military Museum (Muzeul
Militar Central) in Bucharest.

The main focus of my work during the last ten years has been
on the investigation of U-boat successes in operations against
convoys, and on a reexamination of the fate of ships reported as
missing. The fact that I have been able to resolve all but a
negligible number of doubtful or uncertain cases is due in large
part to generous and tireless help received from the following
directors and staff members of the historical sections of the
navies that took part in the Battle of the Atlantic: Rear Admiral
R.M. Bellairs, Commander M.G. Saunders, Lieutenant Commanders P.K.
Kemp, H.C. Beaumont, J.D. Lawson, and lastly Rear Admiral P.N.
Buckley and Captain D. Macintyre of the Historical Section of the
Admiralty and the Naval Historical Branch of the Ministry of
Defence in London; Rear Admiral Ernest M. Eller and, especially,
Captain F. Kent Loomis of the Historical Division of the U.S.
Navy in Washington; Dr. G.N. Tucker and E.C. Russell of the Naval
Historical Section and Colonel C.P. Stacey and S.F. Wise of the
Division of History in the Department of Defence in Ottawa; Prof.
L.C.F. Turner, J.A.I. Agar-Hamilton and J.E. Betzler of the Union
War Histories Section in Pretoria; Contreadmiral Rostand, Médecin
en Chef Hervé Cras, Contreadmiral de Brossard and Contreadmiral
Fliche of the Service Historique de la Marine in Paris; and
Orlogskaptein E.A. Steen of the Forsvarets Krigshistoriske
Avdeling in Oslo. Equally helpful was the author of the official
history of British naval operations, Captain S.W. Roskill, as
well as the author of the corresponding history of U.S. naval
operations, Rear Admiral Samuel E. Morison and his colleagues
Dr. Roger Pineau and Dr. Jack Bauer. All of them responded with
never-ending patience to my many inquiries. Also not to be overlooked in this regard is my colleague Dr. Gerhard Hümmelchen, with

whose aid I was able to identify a number of successes wrongly credited to armed merchant cruisers or U-boats, and my many ship-lover friends throughout the world whose individual knowledge contributed to the success of this work, including particularly Erich Gröner, L.L. von Münching (Wassenaar) and Paul Scarceriaux (Brussels), as well as various veterans of and writers about the submarine war, especially David Irving (London) and Captain J.M. Waters (USCG). Finally, many shipping companies obliged me by answering my questions. To all who helped I would like to express my sincerest gratitude.

The extensive World War II Shipping Losses File in the Bibliothek für Zeitgeschichte contains the source material summarized heretofore, the results of the research done in the international literature that forms part of the Library's collection, and since 1960, the information supplied by the persons mentioned above. That file formed the foundation for this book.

The incorporation in this file of all the U-boat reports on torpedo attacks, regardless of whether they were erroneously considered successes or recognized at the outset as failures, led to an interesting finding. It has long been established that the figures on German U-boat successes contained in the reports of the German Armed Forces High Command--as was also true of the corresponding figures for the submarine forces of other navies-- greatly exceeded the actual numbers in many cases. Postwar studies invariably made it seem as though these extreme over- estimates of U-boat successes were the result of deliberately falsified reports by the U-boat captains, inflated estimates by Headquarters, or even fabrications by the various war- time propaganda agencies. However, an examination of every

German U-boat attack documented in this book and, further, of the attacks by submarines of the other navies, both Allied and Axis, shows that these are, with minor exceptions, false conclu- sions. The real cause of the large overestimates of successes was the difficulty the U-boats had in getting the necessary data following an attack. And here Allied antisubmarine forces played a crucial part. When single U-boats attacked solitary unescorted merchant ships, false reports of hits or sinkings were quite rare; and when conditions for visual observation were normal, gross misestimates of tonnage were relatively unusual. But when Allied antisubmarine efforts made visual observation of the results of an attack difficult or even impossible, the U-boats were much more apt to misinterpret acoustic phenomena. The U-boat captains were prone to classify almost all torpedo detonations heard as hits, and all manner of acoustic noise as "sinking" sounds, despite the fact that torpedoes often exploded for a wide variety of other reasons, including contact with a bottom feature such as a rock behind the target, failure of the detonating pistol, es- pecially in the case of the magnetic torpedoes used at the begin- ning of the war by both the German and U.S. navies, detonations of acoustic torpedoes in ships' wakes, and end-of-run detonations. Moreover, since almost all U-boats participating in coordinated operations against convoys calculated their hits on the basis of the explosions seen or heard, the claims of individual U-boats were often duplicated in the various reports. The U-boats also generally assumed that multiple detonations meant hits scored against more than one ship; whereas in fact several different torpedoes often struck the same ship. That is why the number of ships in a convoy reported as sunk or damaged by the members of a wolf pack was usually on the high side, and why reported tonnage could seldom be determined with precision in operations against convoys, even when the targets hit had been identified by name; the U-boat captains made estimates that could have large errors, depending on antisubmarine activity and prevailing light (most attacks took place at night). These factors were particularly true for convoys consisting mostly of smaller ships displacing between 800 and 2,000 GRT, such as the British Gibraltar convoys. The marked difference in the tonnage of these ships when sailing in ballast condition caused even experienced captains to make substantial overestimates.

With the foregoing sources of error in mind, detailed examination of all unsubstantiated success reports led to the conclusion that most of them were based on faulty evaluations and misinterpretations of the raw visual and acoustic data. Seldom was there found a wrong report for which there was no reasonable explanation. Most erroneous reports and overestimates resulted primarily from difficult external circumstances surrounding an attack, and consequent reduced chances for visual observation. A few resulted from the observer's overoptimistic temperament, or lack of experience. Only very rarely were they assessed to be solely the products of the captain's imagination. This applies even to instances often cited in the past as examples of out-and-out false reporting, such as the reports of the Italian submarine *Barbarigo* on the sinking of two American battleships in May and October 1942 (see p.97, note 26, and p.127, note 3).

I also found that Command Headquarters with few exceptions accepted and forwarded virtually intact all the U-boat reports, so that their unverified data was subsequently included in official communiqués at all levels, as well as in the official statistical reports used by Headquarters to formulate policy. Considering the information then available from the various intelligence sources, it might have been possible for the operational staffs in most navies to be much more critical in evaluating and verifying data used in decision-making. Today, of course, we should refrain from ever referring, as still happens occasionally both inside and outside of Germany, to outdated wartime statistics. The juxtaposition of the original U-boat reports and the actual losses as documented in this book should make it possible, by the way, for any researcher to analyze these matters in detail.

I have tried to arrange the material in this book in such a way that the historian and the ship buff can refer to it with maximum efficiency and ease, shipyards and shipping companies can quickly find information on the fate of their own vessels, and last but not least, so that the submariners and seamen of all nations can review events in which they themselves took part. Only by putting the data into tabular form was I able to present such a vast amount of information in a limited space. To make the information readable and usable internationally with a great deal of translating, I used easily understandable abbreviations. In order to consolidate all available data for each success listed, I placed the dates, times, positions, and particulars gleaned from the U-boat reports alongside the corresponding data from the loss reports by the other side. The listings are arranged chronologically by date and time of day within each of the main theaters of operation: North Sea/Atlantic, Northern Theater, Baltic, Black Sea, Mediterranean, and Indian and Pacific Oceans. Differentiation among warships, auxiliaries, and merchant ships is accomplished by the printing of warship data, including displacements tonnage, in italics, while auxiliaries and merchant ship data, with size stated in terms of gross registered tons (GRT), is printed in roman type.

To make it easier to locate particular U-boats, U-boat captains, convoys, or ships, I put all-inclusive indexes at the end of the book. Though I was able to list the captains by last name only in the tables, I did include in the index first and last name, last rank as commanding officer, and, for the German captains, the size of their crew. Messrs. H.H. Hildebrandt, G. Fioravanzo, and Sakamoto helped me determine the correct spellings. To check and where necessary to correct the spelling of merchant ship names, I used the wartime volumes of *Lloyd's Register* (formerly the property of the British Ministry of War Transport in Blackpool and acquired by the Bibliothek für Zeitgeschichte in 1963). The only exceptions were the names of Soviet ships; I transliterated them according to ISO Recommendation R 9, adopted by Unesco (see P.20), and so avoided the confusions and mistakes resulting from the very different systems in all languages for transliterating Cyrillic script. P. Scarceriaux and L.L. von Münching, in particular, as well as the office of *Lloyd's Register* in London, helped in the identification of ships I could not find because of printing or spelling errors in the sources. My son Jochen Rohwer helped with the laborious job of preparing the indexes. To all I wish to express my deep gratitude.

Despite all my efforts and the assistance of so many friends and government agencies inside and outside of Germany, this book probably still contains some errors and mistakes, be they due to gaps in the sources that could not be filled, unresolvable in-consistencies, misinterpreted data, overlooked spelling errors, or translation errors. Therefore I would be grateful for any recommendations for additional or revised material, no matter how trivial or insignificant it may seem.

September 1968   Jürgen Rohwer
                                            c/o Naval Institute Press
                                            Annapolis, Maryland 21402

Explanation of Table and Index Formats

In order to present the maximum amount of data in the minimum amount of space, the tables in Part I have been grouped into six main theaters of operation as explained in the introduction, with entries within each theater arranged chronologically. Each table contains columns numbered 1-15, with the information in each column presented in abbreviated form as described in the following pages.

Column 1 Date/Time of beginning of attack or first shot, according to the U-boat patrol report. The two numbers preceding the slash specify the date, and the four following the slash give the time according to the 24-hour clock (for German and Italian U-boats, in Central European time or in a few cases where applicable, Daylight Savings Time; for Japanese submarines, Tokyo Time). Dates in parentheses give the day and month the submarine laid a minefield.

Column 2 Nationality of submarine.
Abbreviations: dt = German
fi = Finnish
fr = French (Vichy)
it = Italian
jp = Japanese
ru = Rumanian

Column 3 Number or name of submarine.

Column 4 Family name of submarine's captain. For first name, rank, etc., see the Index of U-boat Captains.

Column 5 Position of attack according to U-boat patrol report. For German U-boats, positions are cited according to the grid system of the standard German naval chart used for reporting to U-boat Headquarters (see charts 1-10 in pocket). For other submarines, positions are rounded off to whole degrees: latitude/longitude: N = north, S = south, E = East, W = West. Punctuation between degrees and minutes of latitude and longitude conforms to the European system, ie, the use of a decimal point vice a degree symbol or dash. A series of dashes signifies that the U-boat did not return and stopped submitting reports.

Column 6 Target designation by attacking submarine.

Warship designations, together with estimated displacement in English tons, are printed in italics:

BB	*Battleship*
BC	*Battlecruiser*
BM	*Monitor*
CA	*Heavy Cruiser*
CB	*Large Cruiser*
CGC	*Coast Guard Cutter*
CL	*Light Cruiser*
CM	*Mine Cruiser (Minelayer)*
CV	*Fleet Carrier*
CVL	*Light Fleet Carrier*
CVE	*Escort Carrier*

DD	Destroyer		AG	Miscellaneous Auxiliary
DE	Destroyer Escort		AGL	Light House Tender
DL	Destroyer Leader		AGS	Survey Ship
LC	Landing Craft		AH	Hospital Ship
LCF	Landing Craft Flak (A/A)		AK	Cargo Ship
LCI	Landing Craft Infantry		AKA	Attack Cargo Ship
LCT	Landing Craft Tank		AKS	General Stores Issue Ship
LS	Landing Ship		AO	Fleet Oiler
LSD	Landing Ship Dock		AP	Troop Transport
LSI	Landing Ship Infantry		APA	Attack Transport
LST	Landing Ship Tank		APC	A/S Trawler
Mbt	Motor Boat		APG	Auxiliary Gunboat
PC	Patrol Craft (A/S)		APM	M/S Trawler
PE	Corvette		AR	Repair Ship
PF	Frigate		ARL	Repair Ship for Landing Craft
PG	Gunboat		AS	Submarine Tender
PM	Fleet Minesweeper		AV	Aircraft Tender/Seaplane Tender
PN	Netlayer		AVP	Small Aircraft Tender
PR	Coastal Minesweeper			
PT	Motor Torpedo Boat			
PY	Patrol Yacht			
SS	Submarine			
TB	Torpedo Boat			
Y	Harbor Craft			

Auxiliary ship designations, together with estimated size in gross registered tons (GRT), all begin with the letter "A", and are printed in roman type:

ACL	Armed Merchant Cruiser
AD	Destroyer Tender

Merchant ship designations, together with estimated size in gross registered tons (GRT), all begin with a dash, and are printed in roman type:

-Bg	Barge
-D	Steam Ship
-Df	Steam Trawler
-DP	Steam Passenger Ship/Liner
-DT	Steam Tanker
-Dt	Steam Tug
-DW	Whaling Factory
-Dw	Whaler

-M   Motorship

-Mf   Motor Trawler

-MP   Motor Liner

-MT   Motor Tanker

-S   Sailing Vessel

-T   Tanker

-TT   Turbine Tanker

A colon (:) following a type designator and preceding a tonnage number signifies that the attacked ship was identified by name by the attacking submarine.

The symbols following the tonnage numbers represent the following:

+   reported sunk

+?   probably sunk

=   damaged

=?   probably damaged

=§   damaged, towed to harbor, but not repaired, total loss

P   taken as a prize

Column 7   Weapons used by the attacking submarine.

A   Gunfire

AR   Gunfire/Ramming

AS   Gunfire/Scuttling charges

HM   magnetic mines

KT   Japanese suicide torpedo

KU   Midget Submarine

M   Mine

ma   "Chariots"

P   Prize crew

R   Ramming

S   Scuttling charges

T   Torpedo

T.   FAT (flächenabsuchender Torpedo) torpedo - a torpedo with pre-set course

T: LUT (lagen-unabhängiger Torpedo) torpedo - a torpedo with pre-set gyro-angle and zig-zag course

T'   acoustic homing torpedo (Gnat)

TA   Torpedo and Gunfire

Tf   Torpedo, coup de grâce

Column 8   Designation of Allied convoys (see Convoy Index, p.317). A capital letter behind the convoy designator (e.g., JW.56A) represents a part of a convoy [joiners/leavers]. Lower-case letters following the designator are explained below:

d   aufgelöst, dispersed

r   Vorausläufer, romper

s   Nachzügler, straggler

Column 9   Date/Time of hit, i.e., of first hit scored against vessel under attack. The two numbers preceding the slash give the day of the month (the name of the month comes above the days as the heading of a subsection); the four numbers following the slash give the hours and minutes according to the 24-hour clock. As far as possible, times have been converted to GMT. Since time zones were not always clearly discernible in the Allied reports, chronological data may differ substantially from those in the U-boat patrol reports.

Column 10   Nationality of vessel attacked. The key to the abbreviations follows:

äg	Egypt	ho	Honduras
al	Albania	in	India
am	United States of America (U.S.A.)	ir	Ireland
ar	Argentina	is	Iceland
au	Australia	it	Italy
be	Belgium	jp	Japan
br	United Kingdom	jg	Yugoslavia
bu	Bulgaria	kr	Croatia
bz	Brazil	lb	Lebanon
ca	Canada	le	Latvia
cl	Chile	li	Lithuania
ch	China	me	Mexico
co	Colombia	ni	Nicaragua
cr	Costa Rica	nl	Netherlands
cu	Cuba	nw	Norway
dä	Denmark	nz	New Zealand
do	Dominican Republic	pa	Panama
dt	Germany	pe	Peru
ec	Ecuador	pl	Palestine
es	Estland	po	Poland
fa	Faroes	ps	Persia/Iran
fi	Finland	pt	Portugal
fr	France	ru	Rumania
gö	Greenland	sa	South Africa
gr	Greece	sj	U.S.S.R.
gu	Guatemala	sp	Spain
ha	Haiti	sv	Swiss
		sw	Sweden
		sy	Syria

th   Thailand

tü   Turkey

un   Hungary

ur   Uruguay

ve   Venezuela

Column 11 Type of ship attacked.

Same designators as in Column 6 (see pp.

Column 12 Name of ship attacked.

Spelling of warships' names was based on spellings in the common naval handbooks. *Lloyd's Register* was used for merchant ships' names. Russian names were the only exception. To avoid errors resulting from the different systems used in the various European languages to transliterate Cyrillic script, Russian names were transliterated according to the system recommended by the International Standards Organization (ISO Recommendation R 9 and the German Standards Committee (Deutscher Normenausschuss DIN 1460).

Column 13 Actual tonnage

Warships in italics: displacement in standard (English) tons. Auxiliaries and merchant ships in gross registered tons (GRT). Symbols following numbers:

+   sunk

=§   damaged, towed to harbor or beached, not repaired, total loss

=   damaged

p   taken prize

-----ship attacked but not hit

Column 14 Position of attack according to report of ship attacked, i.e., according to data of Allied authorities. E.g., 21.35 N/ 45.12 W = 21 degrees 35 minutes north latitude, 45 degrees 12 minutes west longitude. As in Column 5, the decimal point indicates division between degrees and minutes of latitude and longitude, not fractions of a degree.

Column 15 Explanatory notes. Numbers refer to explanatory footnotes at the bottom of the page.

INDEX A. U-BOATS

U-boats that reported successful attacks against Allied ships or against neutral shipping in Allied-controlled waters are arranged in alphabetical order (abbreviations in parentheses stand for the U-boat's nationality; see p. xv, Column 2). The numbers refer to pages in the tables section, and are listed in the chronological order of the attacks. If a U-boat has several attacks listed on a single page of the tables, the number of those attacks is noted in parentheses.

INDEX B. U-BOAT CAPTAINS

The commanding officers of all U-boats that submitted success reports are listed in alphabetical order, along with the following information:

Family name, first name, either the number of crew ( ) in the
case of German captains or nationality ( ) of commanding
officer if other than German (for abbreviations see pp.
column 2), rank (or rank last reported), number or name of
U-boat(s), page reference(s) to main table.

Abbreviations of ranks:

dt, fi, jp, ru   it

L   Ensign   TV   Lieutenant
OL   Lieutenant j.g.   CC   Lieutenant Commander
KL   Lieutenant   CF   Commander
KK   Lieutenant Commander
FK   Commander
KzS Captain

For German U-boat captains, the decorations below, where
appropriate, are listed after rank:

R   Knight's Cross
RE   Knight's Cross with Oak Leaves
RES   Knight's Cross with Oak Leaves and Swords
RESB Knight's Cross with Oak Leaves, Swords and Diamonds

INDEX C. CONVOYS

All known Allied convoy designators are arranged in the alphabetical order of their designation letters and include a definition of
the designator as well as, in most cases, information on the
convoy's inception and duration. Beneath the designators the
convoys are listed in the order of their serial numbers, with
page references to the main tables.

Note: A dot in the tables designates a ship that sailed in a
convoy whose designator is not known, and a dash represents an
unescorted vessel.

INDEX D. SHIPS ATTACKED

The names of all warships and merchant ships attacked, damaged, or
sunk by U-boats and listed in the tables are arranged alphabetically. Ships renamed during the war after 1939 are listed
with their ex-names and the year of the name change in parentheses.
Below the ex-names and marked with an "s" are references to the
name at the time of the attack. For warships and auxiliaries,
hull numbers, when known, are included in parentheses behind
the name.

Column 1   Name of ship
Column 2   Nationality (For abbreviations see p. xviii, Column 10)
Column 3   Type (For abbreviations see pp. xv-xvi, Column 6)
Column 4   Year built
Column 5   Displacement in standard tons for warships and gross
           registered tons for merchant ships and auxiliaries
Column 6   Home port. The following abbreviations are used:

Aab	Denmark	And	Greece
Aal	Denmark	Ant	Belgium
Abe	Great Britain	Arc	Arkhangelsk/Soviet Union
Ale	Egypt	Ard	Great Britain
Alg	Algeria	Are	Norway
Ams	Netherlands	Arg	Greece

Ari	Sweden	Dra	Norway	Hau	Norway	Leb	Sweden
Ask	Denmark	Dub	Ireland	Hav	France	Lei	Great Britain
BAi	Argentina	Dun	France	Hbg	Germany	Len	Soviet Union
Ban	Dutch East Indies	Dur	South Africa	Hel	Sweden	Lim	Ireland
Bar	Spain	Els	Denmark	Hgö	Finland (leased to	Liv	Great Britain
Bat	Dutch East Indies	Esb	Denmark		Soviet Union)	Lla	Great Britain
Bdg	Bermuda	Fam	Cyprus	Hög	Sweden	Lon	Great Britain
Bel	Northern Ireland	Far	Norway	Hon	British Crown Colony	Lor	France
Ber	Norway	Fec	France	Hor	Norway	Lov	Finland
Bid	Great Britain	FFN	Free French Navy	Hsk	Finland	Man	Great Britain
Bil	Spain	Fle	Great Britain	Hul	Great Britain	Mar	Finland-Aaland Islands
Blu	Nicaragua	Fre	Denmark	Hvn	Havana	Mdf	Denmark
Bom	India	Frs	Denmark	Hyd	Greece	Mdv	Faroe Islands
Bor	Finland	Gdy	Poland	Ilo	Philippines	Mel	Australia
Bra	Finland	Gen	Italy	Ist	Turkey	Met	Great Britain
Bre	Germany	Gla	Great Britain	Ith	Greece	Mid	Great Britain
Bri	Great Britain	Gnt	Belgium	Jaf	Palestine	Mil	Great Britain
BzN	Brazilian Navy	Göt	Sweden	Jer	Channel Islands	Mnl	Philippines
Cad	Spain	Gra	Great Britain	Kal	Denmark	Mos	Norway
Cae	France	Gre	Great Britain	Kar	Sweden	Msl	France
Car	Great Britain	Gri	Great Britain	Käs	Estonia (Soviet Union)	Mur	Soviet Union
Chi	Greece	Grm	Norway	Koi	Finland	Nan	France
CTr	Dominican Republic	Gro	Netherlands	Kon	Constanta/Rumania	Nea	Italy
Cur	Dutch West Indies	Grt	Great Britain	Kop	Copenhagen/Denmark	New	Great Britain
Dbr	Yugoslavia	Gue	Channel Islands	Kra	Norway	Nor	Sweden
Dde	Great Britain	Hai	Palestine	Kri	Kristiansand-North/Norway	Npt	Great Britain
Dea	Great Britain	Ham	Bermuda	Ksd	Kristiansand-South/Norway	Nyh	Sweden
Dou	Great Britain	Hap	Sweden	Kur	Estonia (Soviet Union)	Ode	Soviet Union
Dov	Great Britain	Har	Great Britain	Lar	Norway	Odn	Denmark

ORP	Polish Navy	Sev	Spain		Ven	Italy
Osl	Norway	Shi	Great Britain		Ver	Mexico
Pal	Dutch Indies	Siv	Great Britain		Vig	Spain
Par	Brazil	SNF	Soviet Northern Fleet		Vla	Soviet Union
Pär	Estonia (Soviet Union)	Söl	Sweden		Was	Vaasa/Sweden
PDe	Azores	Sou	Great Britain		Whi	Sweden-Gotland
Per	Brazil	SPF	Soviet Pacific Fleet		Wil	Dutch West Indies
Pir	Piraeus/Greece	Spl	Yugoslavia		Yar	Great Britain
Ply	Great Britain	SSF	Soviet Black Sea Fleet			
Por	Norway	Sta	Norway	Column 7	Page reference to tables.
PTa	Great Britain	Std	Spain			
Pzc	Great Britain	Sto	Sweden			
Raa	Sweden	Sun	Great Britain			
Ram	Finland	Sus	Yugoslavia			
Rch	France	Sve	Sweden			
Rey	Iceland	Svt	Lithuania (Soviet Union)			
RFN	French Navy	Swa	Great Britain			
RHN	Royal Hellenic Navy	Syd	Australia			
Rig	Latvia (Soviet Union)	Syr	Greece			
Rio	Brazil	Tal	Estonia (Soviet Union)			
Ris	Denmark	Tam	Mexico			
RIt	Royal Italian Navy	Tho	Faroe Islands			
RNe	Royal Dutch Navy	T.N.	Turkish Navy			
RNo	Royal Norwegian Navy	Tön	Norway			
Rot	Netherlands	Tre	Sweden			
Rou	France	Tri	Italy			
Sam	Greece	Trn	West Indies			
San	Norway	Tro	Norway			
SBF	Soviet Baltic Fleet	Tua	Soviet Union			

North Sea - Atlantic

1	2	3	4	5	6	7	8	9	10	11	12	13	14	15
September 1939														
3/	dt	U 30	Lemp	AM 16	---------	T	-	3/1939	br	-D	Athenia	13581+	56.44 N/ 14.05 W	1)
5/0815	dt	U 47	Prien	BF 7225	-D: 2407+	TA	-	5/1040	br	-D	Bosnia	2407+	45.29 N/ 09.45 W	
5/1225	dt	U 48	Schultze	BE 6473	-D: 4053+	TA	-	5/1400	br	-D	Royal Sceptre	4853+	46.23 N/ 14.59 W	
6/0600	dt	U 38	Liebe	CG 5573	-D: 7242+	TA	-	6/0510	br	-D	Manaar	7242+	38.28 N/ 10.50 W	
6/1440	dt	U 47	Prien	BE 6689	-D: 4086+	TA	-	6/1425	br	-D	Rio Claro	4086+	46.30 N/ 12.00 W	
7/1330	dt	U 34	Rollmann	BF 1625	-D: 5809+	TA	-	7/1340	br	-D	Pukkastan	5809+	49.23 N/ 07.49 W	
7/1555	dt	U 33	v.Dresky	BE 2939	-D: 4060+	T	-	7/1424	br	-D	Olivegrove	4060+	49.05 N/ 15.58 W	
7/1747	dt	U 47	Prien	BF 4118	-D: 1777+	A	-	7/1800	br	-D	Gartavon	1777+	47.04 N/ 11.32 W	
8/0830	dt	U 48	Schultze	BE 2888	-D: 5055+	T	-	8/0744	br	-D	Winkleigh	5055+	48.06 N/ 18.12 W	
8/1215	dt	U 29	Schuhart	BE 3413	-T:10176+	T	-	8/1128	br	-MT	Regent Tiger	10176+	49.57 N/ 15.34 W	
8/1813	dt	U 34	Rollmann	BF 1673	-T: 5548+	TA	-	8/1758	br	-DT	Kennebec	5548+	49.18 N/ 08.13 W	2)
8/1815	dt	U 52	Barten	BE 50	-T 8826+	T	-					-----		3)
(6. 9.)	dt	U 15	Buchholz	AN 5856	---------	M	-	10/0610	br	-D	Goodwood	2796+	1m SE Flam-borough Head	
(4. 9.)	dt	U 13	Daublebsky v.Eichhain	AN 7691	---------	M	-	10/1725	br	-D	Magdapur	8641+	52.11 N/ 01.43 W	
11/0424	dt	U 30	Lemp	AM 4458	-D: 4425+	TA	-	11/0322	br	-D	Blairlogie	4425+	54.58 N/ 15.14 W	
11/1335	dt	U 48	Schultze	AM 1366	-D: 4863+	TA	-	11/1457	br	-D	Firby	4869+	59.40 N/ 13.50 W	
11/1350	dt	U 38	Liebe	BE 6337	-T: 9445+	TA	-	11/1355	br	-MT	Inverliffey	9456+	48.14 N/ 11.48 W	
13/	dt	U 27	Franz	-------	---------	A	-	13/1455	br	-Df	Davara	291+	21m NWzN Tory I.	
13/1530	dt	U 29	Schuhart	BE 3471	-Dt: 900+	TA	-	13/1455	br	-Dt	Neptunia	798+	49.20 N/ 14.40 W	
14/1000	dt	U 28	Kuhnke	AM 8966	ACL =	T	.	14/1106	br	-M	Vancouver City	4955+	51.23 N/ 07.03 W	

1) The sinking of the *Athenia* by *U 30*, accomplished by disobeying standing orders, was denied by the German side during the war.
   It is the only case when a war diary (KTB) of a U-boat was changed afterwards by higher order.
2) Parts of the wreck of the *Kennebec* were sunk by a British naval vessel on Sept.9th.
3) This attack by *U 52* was the first case--besides two attacks against enemy submarines in the Baltic--when a U-boat
   reported a hit but in reality the detonation was caused by a misfiring pistol.

1	2	3	4	5	6	7	8	9	10	11	12	13	14	15
September 1939, cont.														
14/1323	dt	U 30	Lemp	AM 19	-D: 5274+	TA	-	14/1225	br	-D	Fanad Head	5200+	56.43 N/ 15.21 W	
14/1415	dt	U 29	Schuhart	BE 3655	-T: 8431+	TA	-	14/1155	br	-MT	British Influence	8431+	49.43 N/ 12.49 W	
(8. 9.)	dt	U 26	Ewerth	BE 3147	---------	M	-	15/	be	-M	Alex van Opstal	5965+	near Shambles LV.	
15/1544	dt	U 53	Heinicke	BE 3261	-D: 8825+	TA	-	15/1446	br	-MT	Cheyenne	8825+	50.20 N/ 13.30 W	1)
15/1900	dt	U 36	Fröhlich	AN 4533	-D +	TA	-	15/1830	br	-D	Truro	974+	58.20 N/ 02.00 E	
16/0700	dt	U 33	v.Dresky	BF 4156	-D: 1567+	A	-	16/0900	br	-D	Arkleside	1567+	48.00 N/ 09.30 W	
16/0815	dt	U 31	Habekost	BE 3850	-D +	T	OB.4	16/0837	br	-D	Aviemore	4060+	49.11 N/ 13.38 W	
16/0815	dt	U 31	Habekost	BE 3850	-D =?	T	OB.4					-----		2)
(4. 9.)	dt	U 13	Daublebsky v.Eichhain	AN 7691	---------	M	-	16/	br	-D	City of Paris	10902=	52.14 N/ 01.43 E	
16/	dt	U 27	Franz	-------	---------	S	-	16/1553	br	-Df	Rudyerd Kipling	333+	53.50 N/ 11.10 W	
17/0505	dt	U 41	Mugler	AN 4639	-D: 1073p	P	-	17/	fi	-D	Vega	1073p	58.　 N/ 04.　 E	3)
17/0600	dt	U 41	Mugler	AN 4639	-D: 1096p	P	-	17/	fi	-D	Suomen Poika	1099p	58.　 N/ 04.　 E	3)
17/1540	dt	U 53	Heinicke	BE 2384	-D: 5193+	T	-	17/1548	br	-D	Kafiristan	5193+	50.16 N/ 16.55 W	
17/1950	*dt*	*U 29*	*Schuhart*	*BE 3198*	*CV:22500+*	*T*	*Task F.*	*17/2020*	*br*	*CV*	*Courageous*	*22500+*	*50.10 N/ 14.45 W*	
18/1238	dt	U 32	Büchel	BF 1341	-D: 4863+	A	-	18/1234	br	-D	Kensington Court	4863+	50.31 N/ 08.27 W	
18/1848	dt	U 35	Lott	AM 2823	-Df: 325+	A	-	18/1904	br	-Df	Arlita	326+	57.51 N/ 09.28 W	
18/1900	dt	U 35	Lott	AM 2823	-Df: 285+	A	-	18/1825	br	-Df	Lord Minto	295+	57.51 N/ 09.28 W	
(8. 9.)	*dt*	*U 26*	*Ewerth*	*BE 3147*	*---------*	*M*	*-*	*20/1900*	*br*	*PE*	*Kittiwake*	*530=*	*near Shambles LV.*	
21/1200	dt	U 35	Lott	BF 2451	-T 17200=	T	OA.7	21/1435	br	-DT	Teakwood	6014=	49.39 N/ 06.39 W	
22/1418	*dt*	*U 21*	*Frauenheim*	*AN 5182*	*DD =*	*T*	*-*					*-----*		*4)*

1) The abandoned wreck of the *Cheyenne* was sunk by a British destroyer on Sept.15th.
2) When U-boats attacked convoys with multiple shots or spread salvoes of torpedoes, they sometimes assumed multiple detonations to be hits on different ships, whereas in reality they were often hits only on one ship.
3) The *Vega* and *Soumen Poika* were brought by prize crews to German ports.
4) See footnote 1 on page 3.

North Sea - Atlantic

1	2	3	4	5	6	7	8	9	10	11	12	13	14	15
September 1939, cont.														
22/1430	dt	U 7	Heydel	AN 2473	-D: 2694+	T	-	22/1415	br	-D	Akenside	2694+	60.07 N/ 04.37 E	
22/2300	dt	U 4	v.Klot-Heydenfeldt	AN 33	-D: 2200+	S	-	22/	fi	-D	Martti Ragnar	2262+	5m S Arendal	
23/1120	dt	U 4	v.Klot-Heydenfeldt	AO 41	-D: 1300+	S	-	23/	fi	-D	Walma	1361+	58.15 N/ 11.00 E	
(4. 9.)	dt	U 13	Daublebsky v.Eichhain	AN 7691	---------	M	-	24/0100	fr	-D	Phryne	2660+	3,5m E Aldeburgh LV.	
24/	dt	U 14	Wellner	AN 18	SS +?	T	-					-----		1)
24/0800	dt	U 33	v.Dresky	AM 3228	-D: 600+	A	-	24/0700	br	-Df	Caldew	287+	60.47 N/ 06.20 W	
24/1030	dt	U 4	v.Klot-Heydenfeldt	AN 33	-D: 1500+	T	-	24/	sw	-D	Gertrud Bratt	1510+	58.40 N/ 09.52 E	
24/1250	dt	U 31	Habekost	AM 8858	-D: 4646+	T	-	24/1205	br	-D	Hazelside	4646+	51.17 N/ 09.22 W	
24/	dt	U 35	Lott	AM	-D 9000+	T	.					-----		
24/1430	dt	U 34	Rollmann	AN	-D: 2534p	P	-	24/	es	-D	Hanonia	2534p	near Norway	2)
24/	dt	U 24	Behrens	AN 21	DD =?	T	-					-----		1)
25/0555	dt	U 36	Fröhlich	AN 3181	-D: 1839+	T	-	25/0900	sw	-D	Silesia	1839+	45m WNW Ekkeröy	
28/0030	dt	U 16	Weingaertner	AN 31	-D: 3378+	T	-	28/1716	sw	-D	Nyland	3378+	45m SW Stavanger	
28/	dt	U 7	Heydel	AN	-D +	T	-	28/	nw	-D	Solaas	1368+	25m SW Lista LT.	
28/1537	dt	U 32	Büchel	AN 34	-D: 875+	S	-	28/1537	nw	-D	Jern	875+	65m W Skudenes	
29/0855	dt	U 7	Heydel	AF 87	-D: 1830+	T	-	28/	nw	-D	Takstaas	1830+	60.15 N/ 04.41 E	
29/	dt	U 22	Winter	AN 6277	SS =	T	-					-----		1)
30/1100	dt	U 3	Schepke	AN 3647	-D: 1150+	TA	-	30/	dä	-D	Vendia	1150+	35m NW Hanstholm	
30/2130	dt	U 3	Schepke	AN 36	-D: 1222+	S	-	30/	sw	-D	Gun	1198+	30m NW Hanstholm	

1) In the first phase of the war there were many hits against enemy vessels reported, when the torpedoes in reality were running deep or the magnetic pistol was misfiring. Such detonations were later called "Frühzünder" (early detonations). During submerged attacks only acoustic information was obtainable, so when there was a detonation at about the correct running time, the U-boats considered them to be hits.

2) The *Hanonia* was brought into a German port by a prize crew. The ship was used a short time later as a minelayer off the British east coast, using the name *Schiff 11*.

1	2	3	4	5	6	7	8	9	10	11	12	13	14	15
October 1939														
1/1845	dt	U 35	Lott	BE 2736	-D: 2239+	TA	-	1/1850	be	-D	Suzon	2239+	42m W Quessant	
3/1350	dt	U 35	Lott	BF 2479	-D: 4990+	T	-	3/1330	gr	-D	Diamantis	4990+	40m W Skellings	
4/0600	dt	U 23	Kretschmer	AN 2679	-D: 876+	TA	-	4/0550	br	-D	Glen Farg	876+	58.52 N/ 01.31 W	
(17. 9.)	dt	U 32	Büchel	AM 9869	---------	M	-	5/	br	-D	Marwarri	8063=	3,5m 190° Scar-weather LV.	
(17. 9.)	dt	U 32	Büchel	AM 9869	-D: 9462+	M	-	6/1620	br	-D	Lochgoil	9462+	51.24 N/ 04.00 W	
(8. 9.)	dt	U 26	Ewerth	BE 3147	---------	M	-	7/	nl	-D	Binnendijk	6873+	2,5m SE Shambles	1)
8/1400	dt	U 37	Hartmann	AF 7974	-D: 1018+	TA	-	8/	sw	-D	Vistula	1018+	45m N Muggle Flugga/Shetland	
12/1808	dt	U 48	Schultze	BE 3246	-T:14115+	A	KJ.2s	12/1930	fr	-MT	Emile Miguet	14115+	50.15 N/ 14.50 W	
12/1945	dt	U 37	Hartmann	AM 7241	-D: 4810+	A	-	12/	gr	-D	Aris	4810+	53.28 N/ 14.30 W	
12/2024	dt	U 48	Schultze	BE 3194	-D: 5202+	T	OB.17s	12/2300	br	-D	Heronspool	5202+	50.13 N/ 14.48 W	
13/	dt	U 42	Dau	-------	-D: 4803=	A	OB.17d	13/0730	br	-D	Stonepool	4803=	48.40 N/ 15.30 W	
13/0814	dt	U 48	Schultze	BE 3544	-D: 6903+	A	OA.17	13/0855	fr	-D	Louisiane	6903+	50.14 N/ 15.02 W	
13/2358	*dt*	*U 47*	*Prien*	*AN 1610*	*BB:32000=*	*T*	*-*	*14/0123*	*br*	*BB*	*Royal Oak*	*29150+*	*58.55 N/ 02.59 W*	*2)*
14/0116	*dt*	*U 47*	*Prien*	*AN 1610*	*BB:29150+*	*T*	*-*							
14/	dt	U 45	Gelhaar	BE 3366	-D groß+	T	KJF.3	14/0525	br	-M	Lochavon	9205+	50.25 N/ 13.10 W	
14/	dt	U 45	Gelhaar	BE 3366	-D groß+	T	KJF.3	14/0600	fr	-D	Bretagne	10108+	50.20 N/ 12.45 W	
14/	dt	U 45	Gelhaar	BE 3366	-D groß+	T	KJF.3	14/0630	br	-D	Karamea	-----	50.30 N/ 12.14 W	
14/1213	dt	U 48	Schultze	BE 3836	-D: 3677+	TA	-	14/1224	br	-D	Sneaton	3677+	49.05 N/ 13.05 W	
15/0818	dt	U 37	Hartmann	BE 5349	-D: 5186+	AS	-	15/0750	fr	-D	Vermont	5186+	48.01 N/ 17.22 W	

1) The heavily damaged *Binnedijk* sank on Oct.10th.
2) During the first attack at 2358, *U 47* fired 3 torpedoes from her bow tubes (a fourth was a dud) and after turning, one torpedo from an aft tube. Only one torpedo detonated near the bow of the *Royal Oak* without great effect. *U 47* assumed to have hit a ship behind the *Royal Oak*, misidentified for the battlecruiser *Repulse*. In reality this ship was the aircraft repair ship *Pegasus*, which was not damaged at all. During the second attack at 0116, *U 47* hit the *Royal Oak* with all three torpedoes that were fired. The battleship sank in only 13 minutes.

North Sea - Atlantic

1	2	3	4	5	6	7	8	9	10	11	12	13	14	15
October 1939, cont.														
17/	dt	U 46	Sohler	BE	-T 5000=	T	HG.3	17/0835	br	-D	Yorkshire	-----	44.54 N/ 12.40 W	
17/1631	dt	U 37	Hartmann	BE 9272	-D:10183+	T	HG.3	17/1640	br	-D	Yorkshire	10184+	44.52 N/ 14.31 W	
17/1640	dt	U 46	Sohler	BE 6789	-D 8000+	T	HG.3	17/1742	br	-D	City of Mandalay	7028+	44.57 N/ 13.36 W	
17/2035	dt	U 48	Schultze	BE 3835	-D 7014+	T	HG.3	17/	br	-D	Clan Chisholm	7256+	45. N/ 15. W	
20/0732	dt	U 34	Rollmann	AF 7975	-D: 935+	TA	-	21/	sw	-D	Gustav Adolf	926+	61.00 N/ 00.48 E	
20/1340	dt	U 34	Rollmann	AN 2131	-D 1200+	TA	-	20/	br	-D	Sea Venture	2327+	60.50 N/ 00.15 E	
(17.10.)	dt	U 19	Meckel	AN 7342	---------	M	-	21/0200	fr	-D	Capitaine Edmond Laborie	3087+	2m E Inner Dowsing LV.	
(6. 9.)	dt	U 15	Buchholz	AN 5856	---------	M	-	21/	br	-D	Orsa	1478+	15m 150° Flamborough Hd.	
(17.10.)	dt	U 19	Meckel	AN 7342	---------	M	-	21/	nw	-MT	Deodata	3295+	1,5m from Inner Dowsing LV.	
(17.10.)	dt	U 19	Meckel	AN 7342	---------	M	-	24/0900	gr	-D	Konstantinos Hadjipateras	5962+	b. Inner Dowsing LV.	
24/0616	dt	U 37	Hartmann	CG 9467	-D: 2474+	T	-	24/	br	-D	Menin Ridge	2474+	36.01 N/ 07.22 W	
24/0918	dt	U 37	Hartmann	CG 9454	-D: 3528+	A	-	24/	br	-D	Ledbury	3528+	36.01 N/ 07.22 W	
24/1119	dt	U 37	Hartmann	CG 9449	-D: 4413+	T	-	24/	br	-D	Tafna	4413+	35.44 N/ 07.23 W	
27/1930	dt	U 34	Rollmann	BE 1452	-D: 5317+	T	HX.5A	27/2150	br	-D	Bronte	5317+	49.30 N/ 12.15 W	1)
27/	dt	U 34	Rollmann	BE 1452	-D 4666+	T	HX.5A					-----		
28/0305	dt	U 59	Jürst	AN 1316	-Df +	AS	-	28/0315	br	-Df	St.Nidan	565+	59.50 N/ 04.20 W	
28/0655	dt	U 59	Jürst	AN 1316	-Df +	AS	-	28/0425	br	-Df	Lynx II	250+	59.50 N/ 04.20·W	
29/0150	dt	U 34	Rollmann	BF 1387	-D: 7976+	T	HX.5A	29/0315	br	-D	Malabar	7976+	49.57 N/ 07.37 W	
29/	dt	U 34	Rollmann	BF 1387	-T 6000+	T	HX.5A					-----		
30/1212	dt	U 37	Hartmann	BF 1711	-D: 3693+	T	-	30/1333	gr	-D	Thrasyvoulos	3693+	49.25 N/ 11.18 W	
30/2250	dt	U 13	Daublebsky v.Eichhain	AN 1863	-D +	T	HX.5B	30/2153	br	-D	Cairnmona	4666+	57.38 N/ 01.45 W	
30/2335	dt	U 59	Jürst	AN 1313	APC +	T	-	30/	br	APC	Northern Rover	655+	Kirkwall/Orkneys	
31/0525	dt	U 25	Schütze	BF 7832	-D =	T	20.K	31/0525	fr	-D	Baoulé	5874+	43.48 N/ 09.08 W	

1) The wreck of the *Bronte* was sunk on Oct.30th by the destroyers HMS *Walpole* and HMS *Whirlwind*.

1	2	3	4	5	6	7	8	9	10	11	12	13	14	15
November 1939														
(27.10.)	dt	U 24	Jeppener-Haltenhoff	AN 5492	---------	M	-	9/0720	br	-D	Carmarthen Coast	961+	3m E Seaham Harb.	
9/	dt	U 34	Rollmann	AN 30	-D: 3176p	P	-	9/	nw	-D	Snar	3176p	near Southern Norway	
12/0700	dt	U 41	Mugler	AM 3570	-Df: 275+	A	-	12/0800	br	-Df	Cresswell	275+	18m NWzW Flannan, Outer Hebrides	
12/0955	dt	U 41	Mugler	AM 3570	-MT11500+	T	-	12/	nw	-MT	Arne Kjöde	11019+	58.51 N/ 08.07 W	1)
/	dt	U 26	Ewerth	CH	-D +	T	-							2)
16/1407	dt	U 43	Ambrosius	BF 4157	-D +	T	SL.7A	16/1300	br	-D	Arlington Court	4915+	320m 248° from Start Point	
16/	dt	U 49	v.Goßler	CG 21	-D +?	T	KS.27	16/1429	fr	---	(Konvoi)	-----		
17/0020	dt	U 28	Kuhnke	AM 48	-T: 5130+	T	-	16/	nl	-MT	Sliedrecht	5133+	200m S Rockall	
17/2015	dt	U 57	Korth	AN 87	-D +	T	-	17/	li	-D	Kaunas	1566+	6,5m WNW from Noordhinder L.V.	
(17.11.)	dt	U 19	Müller-Warnecke	AN 7691	---------	M	-	18/1155	ju	-D	Carica Milica	6371+	3,5m 5° Shipwash L.V.	
18/2116	dt	U 18	Mengersen	AN 0167	-T +	T	I.F.C.	18/2330	br	-Df	Wigmore	345+	57.59 N/ 02.06 W	3)
18/2310	dt	U 22	Jenisch	AN 1821	-D 1000+	T	-	17/	br	-D	Parkhill	500+	58.07 N/ 02.18 W	
19/0043	dt	U 41	Mugler	BF 7538	-D: 1350+	T	-	19/0200	br	-D	Darino	1351+	44.12 N/ 11.07 W	
19/0213	dt	U 57	Korth	AN 87	-D +	T	-	18/	br	-D	Stanbrook	1383+	Antwerp-Tyne	
19/	dt	U 43	Ambrosius	BF 44	-D 6000+	TA	OG.7s	19/1145	br	-D	Pensilva	4258+	46.51 N/ 11.36 W	
20/0100	dt	U 18	Mengersen	AN 18	-T +	T	-	20/	br	DD	*Inglefield*	-----	*Rattray Head*	
(2210)	dt	U 16	Wellner	AN 7980	---------	M	-	20/	fr	-Df	Ste.Clair	57+	10m SE Folkestone	
20/1430	dt	U 33	v.Dresky	AM 5610	-Df +	A	-	20/	br	-Df	Thomas Hankins	276+	14m NW Tory Isl.	
20/1600	dt	U 33	v.Dresky	AM 5610	-Df +	A	-	20/1600	br	-Df	Delphine	250+	18m NzE Tory Isl.	
20/1705	dt	U 33	v.Dresky	AM 5530	-Df +	A	-	20/1700	br	-Df	Sea Sweeper	329+	25m NWzW Tory Isl.	
21/1250	dt	U 41	Mugler	BF 6778	-Df: 290+	A	-	21/1230	fr	-Df	Les Barges II	296+	45.35 N/ 03.22 W	
(4.11.)	*dt*	*U 21*	*Frauenheim*	*AN 0530*	---------	*M*	-	*21/*	*br*	*CL*	*Belfast*	*11500=*	*Firth of Forth*	

1) The wreck of the *Arne Kjöde* was sunk by British naval vessels.
2) *U 26* advanced for some days through the Straits of Gibraltar into the Mediterranean, and it was reported by the KTB B.d.U.
   of Dec.5th,1939, that there was one ship sunk during this advance. But this report is very dubious.
3) The *Wigmore* belonged to an Icelandic Fishing Convoy.

North Sea – Atlantic

1	2	3	4	5	6	7	8	9	10	11	12	13	14	15
November 1939, cont.														
21/0830	dt	U 33	v.Dresky	AM 53	-Df	+	A	-	21/0800	br	-Df	Sulby	287+	75m NW Rathlin
21/0920	dt	U 33	v.Dresky	AM 53	-Df	+	A	-	21/	br	-Df	William Humphries	276+	75m NW Rathlin
22/1605	dt	U 43	Ambrosius	BF 83	-T 10000+		T	14.BS	22/1607	fr	-D	Arijon	4374+	45.40 N/ 04.50 W
(0409)	dt	U 26	Ewerth	BE 3147	---------		M	-	22/2300	gr	-D	Elena R.	4576+	2m S Shambles L.V.
23/1530	dt	U 33	v.Dresky	AN 13	-D	+	TA	-	23/	dt	-D	Borkum	3670+	59.33 N/ 03.57 W 4)
(0511)	dt	U 33	v.Dresky	AM 6518	---------		M	-	24/1625	br	-M	Sussex	13647=	SE Southend, North Channel
25/1319	dt	U 28	Kuhnke	BF 1837	-D: 5144+		T	SL.8B	25/1323	br	-D	Royston Grange	5144+	49.15 N/ 09.00 W
25/2135	dt	U 43	Ambrosius	BF 77	-D: 2483+		TA	-	25/2310	br	-D	Uskmouth	2483+	43.22 N/ 11.27 W
26/2332	dt	U 48	Schultze	AM 14	-T: 6336+		T	-	27/0055	sw	-MT	Gustaf E.Reuter	6336+	14m WNW Fair I.
28/1334	*dt*	*U 47*	*Prien*	*AN 2250*	*CA 9850=*		*T*	*-*	*28/*		*br CA*	*Norfolk*	*-----*		*5)*
(22.11.)	dt	U 20	Moehle	AN	---------		M	FN.43	29/0130	br	-D	Ionian	3114+	1,5m 132° Newarp L.V.
December 1939														
1/0453	dt	U 21	Frauenheim	AN 1895	-D	5000+	T	-	1/	nw	-D	Arcturus	1277+	
1/0927	dt	U 31	Habekost	AN 4547	-D	+	T	-	1/	fi	-D	Mercator	4260+	57.39 N/ 00.36 E
2/2240	dt	U 56	Zahn	AN 5134	-D	3000+	T	-	2/2240	br	-D	Eskdene	3829=	56.30 N/ 01.40 W
2/2240	dt	U 56	Zahn	AN 5134	-D	5000+	T	-	2/2333	sw	-D	Rudolf	2119+	56.15 N/ 01.25 W
3/1320	dt	U 31	Habekost	AN 5196	-D: 2135+		T	-	3/	dä	-D	Ove Toft	2135+	55.36 N/ 00.46 E
4/0123	dt	U 31	Habekost	AN 5316	-D	2000+	T	-	4/	nw	-D	Gimle	1271+	57.15 N/ 01.50 E
(28.10.)	*dt*	*U 31*	*Habekost*	*AM 3826*	*---------*		*M*	*-*	*4/0752*	*br*	*BB*	*Nelson*	*33950=*	*Loch Ewe*
4/1542	dt	U 31	Habekost	AN 4598	-D	2000+	T	-	4/1400	nw	-D	Primula	1024+	57.15 N/ 01.50 E
5/1440	dt	U 47	Prien	BF 1125	-T 10000+		T	OB.46	5/1445	br	-D	Navasota	8795+	50.43 N/ 10.16 W
6/0754	dt	U 31	Habekost	AN 5341	-D	2000+	T	-	7/	nw	-D	Foina	1674+	Blyth-Norway

4) The German steamer *Borkum* was captured by British vessels on Nov.17th and taken by a prize crew to Kirkwall/Orkneys. After being hit by a torpedo, the ship was beached in Papa-Sound and abandoned.
5) The torpedo fired by *U 47* exploded in the wake of the cruiser *Norfolk*.

1	2	3	4	5	6		7	8	9	10	11	12	13	14	15
December 1939, cont.															
(0512)	dt	U 59	Jürst	AN 7635	---------		M	–	6/1032	br	APM	Washington	209+	Great Yarmouth	
6/2029	dt	U 47	Prien	BF 2473	-T	9000+	T	–	6/2030	nw	-MT	Britta	6214+	45m SW Long-ships L.T.	
6/2351	dt	U 31	Habekost	AN 4887	-D	6000+	T	–	6/	sw	-D	Vinga	1974+	56.25 N/ 01.08 E	
7/0524	dt	U 47	Prien	BF 2819	-D	12000+	T	–	7/0530	nl	-M	Tajandoen	8159+	49.09 N/ 04.51 W	
7/1709	dt	U 38	Liebe	AF 3640	-D:	4400+	T	–	7/1715	br	-D	Thomas Walton	4460+	67.52 N/ 14.28 E	
8/0004	dt	U 23	Kretschmer	AN 1837	-D	2500+	T	–	7/2339	dä	-D	Scotia	2400+	57.31 N/ 02.17 W	
8/1155	dt	U 48	Schultze	BF 1532	-D	8795+	T	OB.48	8/	br	-D	Brandon	6668+	50.28 N/ 08.28 W	
9/0644	dt	U 48	Schultze	BE 3933	-T:	7397+	T	OB.48	9/0630	br	-MT	San Alberto	7397+	49.20 N/ 09.45 W	1)
9/	dt	U 23	Kretschmer	AN 4450	-D	2500+	T	–							
9/1841	dt	U 20	Moehle	AN 44	-D	+	T	–	9/	dä	-D	Magnus	1339+	57.48 N/ 00.35 W	
(2211)	dt	U 20	Moehle	AN 7	---------		M	–	10/1600	br	-D	Willowpool	4815+	3m E Newarp L.V.	
11/0819	dt	U 38	Liebe	AF 6480	-D:	4700+	T	–	11/	gr	-D	Garoufalia	4708+	64.36 N/ 10.42 E	
(0512)	dt	U 59	Jürst	AN 7635	---------		M	–	12/0815	br	-D	Marwick Head	496+	0,5m S North Caister Buoy	
13/1528	dt	U 38	Liebe	AF 8540	-D:	4000+	T	–	13/1200	br	-D	Deptford	4101+	Honningsvaag	
13/1915	dt	U 57	Korth	AN 8447	-D	3000+	T	–	13/	sj	-D	Mina	1173+	Cross-Sand	
15/1740	dt	U 48	Schultze	BE 3334	-D:	5217+	T	–	15/1630	gr	-D	Germaine	5217+	51.00 N/ 12.18 W	
16/0028	dt	U 59	Jürst	AN 6416	-D	2000+	T	–	16/0030	sw	-D	Lister	1366+	55.13 N/ 01.33 E	
16/1249	dt	U 59	Jürst	AN 5321	-D	2500+	T	–	16/1230	nw	-D	Glittrefjell	1568+	56.14 N/ 01.04 E	
17/0234	dt	U 59	Jürst	AN 4723	-D	3000+	T	–	18/	dä	-D	Bogo	1214+	75m E May Island	
17/0536	dt	U 59	Jürst	AN 4723	-D	3000+	T	–							
(17.12.)	dt	U 60	Schewe	AN 7636	---------		M	FS.56	19/0335	br	-D	City of Kobe	4373+	52.35 N/ 01.59 E	
(15.12.)	dt	U 22	Jenisch	AN 5460	---------		M	–	20/1430	sw	-D	Mars	1877+	1m E St.Mary's L.V., Blyth	
21/0430	dt	U 46	Sohler	AN 4267	-D	3000+	T	–	21/	nw	-D	Rudolf	924+	58.07 N/ 01.32 E	

1) The wreck of the *San Alberto* was sunk by a British escort vessel on Dec.12th.

1	2	3	4	5	6		7	8	9	10	11	12	13	14	15
December 1939, cont.															
21/0725	dt	U 21	Frauenheim	AN 4577	-D	4000+	T	-	21/		sw -D	Mars	1475+	ENE May Iceland	
21/0735	dt	U 21	Frauenheim	AN 4577	-D	1500+	T	-	21/		sw -D	Carl Henckel	1352+	57. 00 N/ 00.17 E	
(4.11.)	dt	U 21	Frauenheim	AN 0530	---------		M	-	21/		br PN	Bayonet	605+	Firth of Forth	
(2.12.)	dt	U 61	Oesten	AN 5453	---------		M	-	22/1340		br -D	Gryfevale	4434+	3m E Tyne Pier	
(28.10.)	dt	U 31	Habekost	AM 3826	---------		M	-	23/		br APM	Glen Albyn	82+	Loch Ewe	
(28.10.)	dt	U 31	Habekost	AM 3826	---------		M	-	23/		br APM	Promotive	78+	Loch Ewe	
(5.11.)	dt	U 33	v.Dresky	AM 6518	---------		M	-	25/0745		br -D	Stanholme	2473+	51.20 N/ 03.39 W	
(22.12.)	dt	U 22	Jenisch	AN 5460	---------		M	-	25/0745		br APM	Loch Doon	534+	near Blyth	
28/0400	dt	U 30	Lemp	AM 3617	APC	+	A	-	28/0230		br APC	Barbara Robertson	325+	35m NW from Butt of Lewis	
(22.12.)	dt	U 22	Jenisch	AN 5460	---------		M	-	28/0932		dä -D	Hanne	1080+	1m E Blyth	
28/1545	dt	U 30	Lemp	AM 3540	BB 31100=		T	Task F.	28/1449		br BB	Barham	31100=	58.47 N/ 08.05 W	
(17.11.)	dt	U 15	Frahm	AN 7662	---------		M	-	28/2253		br -Df	Resercho	258+	6m SEzE Flamborough Hd.	
31/	dt	U 58	Kuppisch	AN 18	DD	1090+?	T	-					------		
31/1947	dt	U 32	Büchel	AN 0119	-D	965+	T	-	1/		nw -D	Luna	959+	58.48 N/ 03.20 E	
January 1940															
1/1058	dt	U 58	Kuppisch	AN 1692	-D	2000+	T	-	1/1028		sw -D	Lars Magnus Trozelli	1951+	58.14 N/ 01.36 W	
3/0911	dt	U 58	Kuppisch	AN 1866	-D	3000+	T	HN.6	3/0820		sw -D	Svartön	2475+	57.48 N/ 01.47 W	
9/0221	dt	U 19	Schepke	AN 1692	-D	+	T	-	8/2359		nw -D	Manx	1343+	58.30 N/ 01.33 W	
(6. 1.)	dt	U 30	Lemp	AM 9329	---------		M	HX.14B	11/1100		br -DT	El Oso	7267+	6m 280° Bar L.V., Liverpool	
11/1632	dt	U 23	Kretschmer	AN 4128	-D	3000+	T	-	11/1830		nw -D	Fredville	1150+	58.25 N/ 01.10 W	
12/0650	dt	U 23	Kretschmer	AN 1633	-T:10517+		T	-	12/		dä -MT	Danmark	10517+	58.59 N/ 02.53 W	
13/0430	dt	U 20	Moehle	AN 4141	-D	3000+	T	-	13/		sw -D	Sylvia	1524+	NE Aberdeen	

1	2	3	4	5	6	7	8	9	10	11	12	13	14	15
January 1940, cont.														
(6. 1.)	dt	U 30	Lemp	AM 9329	---------	M	OB.71	15/	br	-D	Gracia	5642=	5m WSW Bar L.V., Liverpool	
15/0013	dt	U 44	Mathes	BF 5181	-D 3000+	T	-	14/2359	nw	-D	Fagerheim	1590+	80m SW Quessant	
15/1010	dt	U 44	Mathes	BF 5414	-M: 7886+	T	-	15/1100	nl	-M	Arendskerk	7906+	46.55 N/ 06.34 W	
16/0611	dt	U 44	Mathes	BF 1886	-D 4220+	T	-	16/	gr	-D	Panachandros	4661+	W Brest	
(5.11.)	dt	U 33	v.Dresky	AM 6518	---------	M	-	16/1619	br	-MT	Inverdargle	9456+	51.16 N/ 03.43 W	
17/1255	dt	U 25	Schütze	AF 7887	-D 6000+	T	-	17/	br	-D	Polzella	4751+	Muckle Flugga	
17/1410	dt	U 25	Schütze	AF 7889	-D: 1140+	TA	-	17/1403	nw	-D	Enid	1140+	6-7m N Muckle Flugga, Shetland	
(6. 1.)	dt	U 30	Lemp	AM 9329	---------	M	OB.74	17/1700	br	-D	Cairnross	5494+	7m 276° Bar L.V.	
------	--	----	---------	-------	---------	T		18/	sw	-D	Foxen	1304+	58.52 N/ 00.22 W	1)
18/1126	dt	U 44	Mathes	CG 2228	-D: 1820+	T	-	18/	dä	-M	Canadian Reefer	1831+	25m NE C.Villano	
18/1625	dt	U 25	Schütze	AM 3488	-D 5600+	T	-	18/1715	sw	-M	Pajala	6873+	10m 72° North Rona, Hebriden	
18/2353	dt	U 9	Lüth	AN 6758	-D 4000+	T	-	18/2354	sw	-D	Flandria	1179+	54.00 N/ 03.40 E	
19/0145	dt	U 9	Lüth	AN 6725	-D 8000+	T	-	19/0120	sw	-D	Patria	1188+	54. N/ 03.30 E	
19/2100	dt	U 59	Jürst	AN 8417	-D 2500+	T	-	19/	fr	-D	Quiberon	1296+	near Great Yarmouth	
20/0415	dt	U 44	Mathes	CG 1963	-D: 5329+	T	-	20/0300	gr	-D	Ekatontarchos Dracoulis	5329+	40.20 N/ 10.07 W	
2o/2026	dt	U 57	Korth	AN 1819	-D 2500+	T								1)
21/0535	dt	U 22	Jenisch	AN 1684	DD 1600+	T	-	21/0444	br	DD	Exmouth	1475+	near Tarbett Ness, Moray Firth	
21/	dt	U 55	Heidel	AN	-D +	T	-	21/0500	dä	-D	Tekla	1469+	58.18 N/ 02.25 W	
21/0711	dt	U 22	Jenisch	AN 1681	-D 1500+	T	-	21/0540	nw	-D	Miranda	1328+	58.14 N/ 02.05 W	
..	dt	U 55	Heidel	AN		T	-	21 ?	sw	-D	Andalusia	1357+	North Sea	2)

1) The *Foxen* was sunk according to British reports by U-boat torpedo, according to Swedish reports by mine. There is no corresponding U-boat report. If the ship in reality sank two days later, there is the possibility that it might have been the ship reported sunk by *U 57* on January 20th. But it is more probable that the ship was sunk by a mine of the British flanking mine fields.
2) The *Andalusia* departed from Bordeaux on Jan.16th for Göteborg, and gave a last radio signal on Jan.21st. Probably it was the ship sunk by *U 55*. This U-boat did not return, so there are no exact reports on the position and time.

1	2	3	4	5	6		7	8	9	10	11	12	13	14	15
January 1940, cont.															
(13.11.)	dt	U 28	Kuhnke	AM 9863	---------		M	-	21/0836	br	-D	Protesilaus	9577+	51.31 N/ 04.04 W	
(11.12.)	dt	U 61	Oesten	AN 51	---------		M	-	21/1430	br	-D	Ferryhill	1086+	1,5m N St.Mary's Firth of Forth	
22/0933	dt	U 51	Knorr	AM 2689	-D	6500+	T	-	22/0945	sw	-M	Gothia	1640+	57.46 N/ 09.50 W	
22/1326	dt	U 25	Schütze	BE 3643	-D:	2977+	T	-	22/	nw	-D	Songa	2589+	220m W Scilly I.	
22/2127	dt	U 61	Oesten	AN 4158	-D	2000+	T	-	22/	nw	-D	Sydvold	2434+	58.40 N/ 00.30 W	
22/									22/	nw	-M	Segovia	1387+	North Sea	3)
23/0701	dt	U 18	Mengersen	AN 4219	-D	3000+	T	-	22/	nw	-D	Varild	1085+	North Sea	4)
23/0840	dt	U 19	Schepke	AN 5186	-D	4000+	T	-	23/0741	br	-D	Baltanglia	1523+	55.35 N/ 01.27 W	
23/0848	dt	U 19	Schepke	AN 5186	-D	5000+	T	-	23/0745	nw	-D	Pluto	1598+	55.35 N/ 01.27 W	
(8. 1.)	dt	U 56	Zahn	AN 8177	---------		M	-	23/2213	fi	-D	Onto	1333+	2,7m 251° Smith's L.V.,Cross Sand	
24/1140	dt	U 44	Mathes	CG 5552	-D	6000+	T	56.KS	24/1145	fr	-D	Alsacien	3819+	39.01 N/ 09.54 W	
24/1908	dt	U 23	Kretschmer	AN 1115	-D	1500+	T	-	23/	nw	-D	Bisp	1000+	North Sea	5)
25/0230	dt	U 14	Wohlfarth	AN 8462	-D	2500+	T	-	25/0100	nw	-D	Biarritz	1752+	52.39 N/ 04.15 E	
25/0411	dt	U 44	Mathes	CG 2839	-D	7000+	T	56.KS s	25/0400	fr	-D	Tourny	2769+	38.00 N/ 09.55 W	
25/2112	dt	U 19	Schepke	AN 5186	-D	7000+	T	-	25/2030	be	-D	Louvain/Everene	4434+	Longstone L.T.	6)
25/2130	dt	U 19	Schepke	AN 5186	-D	3000+	T	-	25/2040	nw	-D	Gudveig	1300+	4,5m E Longstone	
(22. 1.)	dt	U 57	Korth	AN 1752	---------		M	-	26/	br	-D	Durham Castle	8240+	near Cromarty	7)
27/2003	dt	U 20	v.Klot-Heydenfeldt	AN 1652	-D	750+	T	-	27/1930	nw	-D	Faro	844+	15m SE Copinsay, Orkneys	
27/2052	dt	U 20	v.Klot-Heydenfeldt	AN 1628	-D	1600+	T	-	27/1930	dä	-D	Fredensborg	2094+	58.25 N/ 01.53 W	
27/2124	dt	U 20	v.Klot-Heydenfeldt	AN 1651	-D	2300+	T	-	27/1930	dä	-D	England	2319+	58.25 N/ 01.53 W	
27/2313	dt	U 20	v.Klot-Heydenfeldt	AN 1643	-D	2200+	T	-	27/2300	nw	-D	Hosanger	1591+	58.25 N/ 01.53 W	

3) The *Segovia* departed Great Britain on Jan.22nd for Norway. There is no sinking report by a U-boat.
4) The *Varild* departed Horten on Jan.22nd for Sunderland and was reported missing thereafter.
5) The *Bisp* departed Sunderland on Jan.20th for Andalsnes and was reported missing thereafter.
6) The Latvian steamer *Everene* was sailing under Belgian flag as *Louvain*.
7) There is no final proof: The *Durham Castle* may have been sunk by a mine of *U 57* or of another barrage.

1	2	3	4	5	6	7	8	9	10	11	12	13	14	15
January 1940, cont.														
(20.12.) dt	U 22	Jenisch	AN 5460	---------		M	FN.81 s	28/	br	-D	Eston	1487+	near Blyth	
28/0421 dt	U 34	Rollmann	BF 1629	-D	7000+	T	-	28/p.m.	gr	-D	Eleni Stathatos	5625+	200m W Scilly I.	
28/2000 dt	U 44	Mathes	CG 1888	-D	4000+	T	-	28/	gr	-D	Flora	2980+	W Figuera la Foz	
29/früh dt	U 13	Schulte	AN 1856	-D	4000=	T	.							
29/1530 dt	U 51	Knorr	BF 1430	-D:	1503+	T	-	29/	nw	-D	Eika	1503+	50. N/ 10. W	
30/0700 dt	U 55	Heidel	-------	---------		T	0A.80G	30/0150	br	-MT	Vaclite	5026+	49.20 N/ 07.04 W	8)
30/1105 dt	U 55	Heidel	-------	---------		T	0A.80G	30/1105	gr	-D	Keramiai	5085+	48.37 N/ 07.46 W	8)
31/0043 dt	U 13	Schulte	AN 1846	-D	4000+	T	-	31/	nw	-D	Start	1168+	North Sea	9)
31/1954 dt	U 21	Stiebler	AN 4245	-D	1365+	T	-	31/1914	dä	-D	Vidar	1353+	58.39 N/ 02.00 E	
February 1940														
1/0143 dt	U 13	Schulte	AN 1558	-D	+	T	-	1/0100	sw	-D	Fram	2491+	57.43 N/ 02.06 W	
1/2044 dt	U 59	Jürst	AN 8418	-D	3000+	T	-	1/	br	-M	Ellen M.	498+	52.33 N/ 02.15 E	
2/0624 dt	U 59	Jürst	AN 8419	-T	2500+	T	-	2/	br	-DT	Creofield	838+	52.33 N/ 02.25 E	
2/2040 dt	U 59	Jürst	AN 8442	-D	3000+	T	-	2/2130	br	-D	Portelet	1064+	52.40 N/ 02.13 E	
2/2241 dt	U 59	Jürst	AN 8442	-D	2000+	T	-							
3/0413 dt	U 26	Scheringer	AN 6276	-D	5000=	T	-							
3/0936 dt	U 58	Kuppisch	AN 4241	-D	2500+	T	-	31/	es	-D	Reet	815+	North Sea	1)
3/1432 dt	U 25	Schütze	CG 5719	-D:	6805+	T	OG.16	3/1438	br	-D	Arministan	6805+	38.15 N/ 11.15 W	
4/0415 dt	U 37	Hartmann	AN 4126	-T	1200+	T	-	4/	nw	-D	Hop	1365+	58.55 N/ 00.14 W	2)
4/2104 dt	U 21	Stiebler	AN 4179	-D:	3000+	T	-	4/	jg	-D	Vid	3547+	58.15 N/ 00.48 W	

8) *U 55* could not report about attacks or successes against convoy OA.80G or OG.16 because she was herself sunk by the second attack of the escort.
9) The *Start* departed Sunderland on Jan.29th for Oslo and was reported missing thereafter.
1) The *Reet* departed Methil on Jan.31st for Gotenburg and was reported missing thereafter.
2) The *Hop* departed Bergen on Feb.2nd for Middlesborough and was reported missing thereafter.

1	2	3	4	5	6	7	8	9	10	11	12	13	14	15
February 1940, cont.														
4/2125	dt	U 37	Hartmann	AN 2184	-D 7000+	T	–	4/		br -D	Leo Dawson	4330+	60.10 N/ 00.39 W	
5/	dt	U 41	Mugler	-------	---------	T	–	5/0332		nl -MT	Ceronia	8096=	49.14 N/ 08.34 W	3)
5/	dt	U 41	Mugler	-------	---------	T	OA.84	5/1310		br -D	Beaverburn	9874+	49.20 N/ 10.07 W	3)
(12.12.)	dt	U 13	Scheringer	AN 0170	---------	M	–	6/		es -D	Anu	1421+	near River Tay	
(9. 1.)	dt	U 30	Lemp	AM 9329	---------	M	–	7/0600		br -M	Munster	4305+	53.36 N/ 03.24 W	
(9. 1.)	dt	U 30	Lemp	AM 9329	---------	M	–	9/0105		br -D	Chagres	5406+	5,5m 270° Bar L.V. Liverpool	
10/1845	dt	U 48	Schultze	BF 24	-D: 6853+	T	–	10/1835		nl -D	Burgerdijk	6853+	49.45 N/ 06.30 W	
10/2059	dt	U 37	Hartmann	AM 8744	-D 4563+	T	–	10/		nw -D	Silja	1259+	51.21 N/ 11.32 W	4)
11/0330	dt	U 37	Hartmann	BF 11	-Df: 290+	A	–	11/0500		br -Df	Togimo	290+	50.40 N/ 11.02 W	
11/	dt	U 53	Grosse	AM 1490	-D +	T	–	11/1100		nw -M	Snestad	4114+	58.40 N/ 13.40 W	
11/1820	dt	U 9	Lüth	AN 1769	-D 2000+	T	–	11/1800		es -D	Linda	1213+	58.51 N/ 01.54 E	
11/	dt	U 53	Grosse	AM 1490	-T +	T	–	11/2130		br -MT	Imperial Transport	8022=	59. N/ 12. W	
11/2354	dt	U 50	Bauer	AF 7837	-D 3500+	T	–	11/2230		sw -D	Orania	1854+	60m NE Shetlands	
12/1009	dt	U 26	Scheringer	BE 3261	-D: 3482+	TA	–	12/0930		nw -D	Nidarholm	3482+	50.50 N/ 14.10 W	
12/	dt	U 53	Grosse	AM 2970	-D +	T	–	12/0935		sw -D	Dalarö	3927+	56.44 N/ 11.44 W	
13/0155	dt	U 50	Bauer	AE 9977	-T: 8309=	T	–	13/		nw -MT	Albert L.Ellsworth	-----		5)
13/0716	dt	U 25	Schütze	AF 7953	-T: 5200+	TA	–	13/0645		dä -MT	Chastine Maersk	5177+	61.30 N/ 02.00 E	
13/	dt	U 53	Grosse	AM 51	-D +	T	–	14/		sw -D	Norna	1022+	55.30 N/ 11.00 W	6)
14/0135	dt	U 57	Korth	AN 1671	-T:10191+	T	HX.18 s	14/0100		br -DT	Gretafield	10191+	58.27 N/ 02.33 W	
14/	dt	U 53	Grosse	AM 4350	-D +	T	–	14/0500		dä -D	Martin Goldschmidt	2095+	55.53 N/ 12.37 W	

3) There was no sinking report by *U 44* because she was sunk by the second attack of the escort of convoy OA.84.
4) The *Silja* departed Gibraltar on Feb.5th for Bergen and was reported missing thereafter.
5) *U 50* fired two torpedoes. The first exploded near the bow of the *Albert L. Ellsworth*, but did not hit. The second torpedo exploded a few yards off the side amidship.
6) The *Norma* departed Gibraltar on Feb.7th and was reported missing thereafter.

1	2	3	4	5	6	7	8	9	10	11	12	13	14	15
February 1940, cont.														
14/0800 dt		U 26	Scheringer	BE 3332	-D: 4622+	T	–	13/0900	br	-D	Langleeford	4622+	70m NW Fastnet	
14/1655 dt		U 48	Schultze	BE 18	-D:12306+	T	–	14/1652	br	-D	Sultan Star	12306+	48.54 N/ 10.03 W	
15/0207 dt		U 50	Bauer	AM 2914	-D 5000+	T	–	10/	dä	-D	Maryland	4895+	57.09 N/ 12.00 W	7)
15/0545 dt		U 37	Hartmann	BF 1922	-D 6500+	T	–	17/	dä	-D	Aase	1206+	49.17 N/ 08.15 W	
15/0837 dt		U 26	Scheringer	AM 7391	-D: 2477+	T	–	15/a.m.	nw	-D	Steinstad	2476+	W Ireland	
15/1400 dt		U 48	Schultze	BF 43	-T: 8971+	T	–	15/1315	nl	-MT	Den Haag	8971+	48.02 N/ 08.26 W	
15/2355 dt		U 14	Wohlfarth	AN 1699	-D: 1060+	T	–	15/2259	dä	-D	Sleipner	1066+	58.18 N/ 01.46 W	
16/0000 dt		U 14	Wohlfarth	AN 1699	-D: 1060+	T	–	15/2359	dä	-D	Rhone	1064+	58.18 N/ 01.46 W	
16/2125 dt		U 14	Wohlfarth	AN 1853	-D 2000+	T	–	16/2030	sw	-D	Osmed	1526+	20m N Kinnaird Hd.	
16/2135 dt		U 14	Wohlfarth	AN 1853	-D 1000+	T	–	16/2030	sw	-D	Liana	1664+	24m N Kinnaird Hd.	
17/0205 dt		U 10	Preuß	AN 87	-D 1800+	T	–	17/	nw	-D	Kvernaas	1819+	51.50 N/ 03.19 E	
17/1553 dt		U 37	Hartmann	BF 7555	-D 7000+	T	OG.18	17/1600	br	-D	Pyrrhus	7418+	44.02 N/ 10.18 W	
17/2040 dt		U 48	Schultze	BF 16	-D 6000+	T	–	17/2040	fi	-D	Wilja	3396+	49.00 N/ 06.33 W	
18/0023 dt		U 61	Oesten	AN 2779	-D 3000+	T	–	18/	pa	-D	El Sonador	1406+	E Shetlands	8)
18/0045 dt		U 37	Hartmann	BF 7582	-D 10000+	T	–	17/2330	gr	-D	Ellin	4917+	25m NW Cape Finisterre	
18/0354 dt		*U 23*	*Kretschmer*	*AN 1692*	*DD: 1375+*	*T*	*HN.*	*18/0300*	*br*	*DD*	*Daring*	*1375+*	*58.40 N/ 01.40 E*	
18/0420 dt		U 53	Grosse	CG 31	-T +	T	–	18/0330	sp	-D	Banderas	2140+	8m NW Cape Villano 9)	
18/0609 dt		U 61	Oesten	AN 2747	-D 7000+	T	–	18/0500	nw	-M	Sangstad	4297+	59.00 N/ 00.25 E	
18/0823 dt		U 37	Hartmann	BF 7837	-T 6000+	T	10.RS	18/0830	fr	-D	P.L.M.15	3754+	43.37 N/ 09.15 W	
18/0926 dt		U 10	Preuß	AN 87	-D: 4537+	T	–	18/1041	nl	-D	Ameland	4537+	51.54 N/ 03.01 E	

7) The *Maryland* departed Madeira on Feb.7th for Copenhagen. She radioed her position on Feb.10th and was reported missing thereafter. One wrecked boat was found at North Uist.

8) The *El Sonador* was reported missing after Feb.17th in the area east of the Shetlands.

9) *U 53* at 17/2054 observed the convoy 10.RS - 65.KS and reported at 18/0420 to have sunk one tanker. In reality it was the *Banderas* at 10 miles distance from the convoy. At 1024 GCT *U 53* again attacked the convoy 10.RS, and one torpedo exploded a short distance from the side of the tanker *La Garonne*. With no torpedoes left the U-boat started its return journey but was sunk on Feb.23rd by HMS *Gurkha*.

1	2	3	4	5	6	7	8	9	10	11	12	13	14	15
February 1940, cont.														
20/0015	dt	U 19	Schepke	AN 1491	-T 5000=	T	–	19/2330	br	-MT	Daghestan	-----	59.21 N/ 01.48 W	10)
21/0254	dt	U 50	Bauer	CG 2133	-D: 4760+	T	–	21/0310	nl	-D	Tara	4760+	42.45 N/ 10.25 W	
21/0626	dt	U 22	Jenisch	AN 1437	-D 1500+	T	–	21/0530	br	-Df	Strathclova	----	N Fair Island	11)
21/1809	dt	U 57	Korth	AN 1654	-D 7000=	T	HX.19 s	21/1615	br	-D	Loch Maddy	4996+	70° 20m Copinsay, Orkneys	12)
22/0107	dt	U 23	Kretschmer	AN 1651	-D 7000+	Tf		22/						
22/0020	dt	U 50	Bauer	CG 1366	-T 10000+	T	OGF.19	22/0020	br	-DT	British Endeavour	4580+	42.11 N/ 11.35 W	
(3.11.)	dt	U 21	Frauenheim	AN 0530	---------	M	–	24/	br	-D	Royal Archer	2266+	56.06 N/ 02.55 W	
24/	dt	U 63	Lorentz	-------	---------	T	HN.14	24/2100	sw	-M	Santos	3840+	59.17 N/ 00.42 W	13)
29/2232	dt	U 20	v.Klot-Heydenfeldt	AN 8730	-D 4500+	T	–	29/	it	-D	Maria Rosa	4211+	52.24 N/ 01.59 E	
March 1940														
1/0315	dt	U 20	v.Klot-Heydenfeldt	AN 8730	-D 5400+	T	–	1/	it	-D	Mirella	5340+	52.24 N/ 02.02 E	
2/0112	dt	U 32	Jenisch	AM 3491	-T 4000+	T	–	2/	nw	-D	Belpamela	-----		1)
2/0810	dt	U 32	Jenisch	AM 34	-M: 2818+	A	–	2/	sw	-D	Lagaholm	2818+	59.34 N/ 05.10 W	
2/2159	dt	U 17	Behrens	AN 8753	-T 9000+	T	–	2/	nl	-D	Rijnstroom	695+	51.36 N/ 02.54 E	
(3. 3.)	dt	U 29	Schuhart	AM 9944	---------	M	–	3/	br	-D	Cato	710+	51.24 N/ 03.33 W	
4/0523	dt	U 29	Schuhart	BF 2137	-D 3000+	T	–	4/	br	-D	Thurston	3072+	32m W Trevose Hd.	
4/1208	dt	U 29	Schuhart	BF 2161	-D 6000+	T	–	4/1120	br	-M	Pacific Reliance	6717+	50.23 N/ 05.49 W	
4/1209	dt	U 29	Schuhart	BF 2161	-T 12000+?	T	–	4/	br	-DT	San Florentino	------		2)

10) The torpedo fired by *U 19* exploded a few yards off the side of the *Daghestan*.

11) The torpedo fired by *U 22* exploded a few yards off the side of the *Strathclova*.

12) The *Loch Maddy* was hit amidships by one torpedo from *U 57* and abandoned. After the final hit by *U 23* the wreck broke into two parts and sank.

13) *U 63* could not report its success because it was sunk by the escort of convoy HN.14.

1) Three torpedoes from *U 32* exploded a few yards off the side of the *Belpamela*.

2) *U 29* reported having fired two torpedoes against a tanker of 6000 gross tons, with only light detonations assumed to be ground explosions. After a report by the German xB-Dienst, the B.d.U. assumed the *San Florentino* sunk. But there was no hit at all.

1	2	3	4	5	6		7	8	9	10	11	12	13	14	15

March 1940, cont.

1	2	3	4	5	6a	6b	7	8	9	10-11	12	13	14	15
5/2038	dt	U 17	Behrens	AN 8753	-D	3500+	T	-	5/	nl -D	Grutto	920+	51.41 N/ 02.47 E	
7/0430	dt	U 14	Wohlfarth	AN 8734	-D	2000+	T	-	7/	nl -D	Vecht	1965+	51.45 N/ 03.05 E	
(7. 3.)	dt	U 32	Jenisch	AM 9328	---------		M	-	8/	br -D	Counsellor	5068+	53.38 N/ 03.23 W	
9/0542	dt	U 14	Wohlfarth	AN 8757	-D	1100+	T	-	9/	br -D	Borthwick	1097+	51.44 N/ 03.22 E	
9/2113	dt	U 38	Liebe	AM 52	-Df	+	A	-	10/	br -Df	Leukos	216+	NW Tory Island	
9/2317	dt	U 28	Kuhnke	BF 2129	-D	6000+	T	-	8/	gr -D	P.Margaronis	4979+	SW Landsend	3)
9/2330	dt	U 14	Wohlfarth	AN 8733	-D	3500+	T	-	11/	br -D	Abbotsford	1585+	North Sea	4)
9/2345	dt	U 14	Wohlfarth	AN 8733	-D	2000+	T	-	9/	br -D	Akeld	643+	51.44 N/ 03.22 E	
11/0317	dt	U 28	Kuhnke	BF 1669	-T	10000+	T	-	11/	nl -M	Eulota	6236+	48.35 N/ 08.22 W	
17/2325	dt	U 38	Liebe	AN 1129	-D	5000+	T	-	17/	dä -M	Argentina	5375+	North Sea	5)
19/2221	dt	U 19	Schepke	AN 1680	-D	3000+	TA	-	19/	dä -D	Minsk	1229+	58.07 N/ 02.39 W	
19/2237	dt	U 19	Schepke	AN 1680	-D	3000+	T	-	19/	dä -D	Charkow	1026+	58.07 N/ 02.39 W	
20/0457	dt	U 19	Schepke	AN 1680	-D	2000+	T	-	20/	dä -D	Viking	1153+	58.21 N/ 02.22 W	
20/0518	dt	U 19	Schepke	AN 1680	-D	3000+	T	-	20/	dä -D	Bothal	2109+	58.21 N/ 02.22 W '	
21/0111	dt	U 38	Liebe	AN 1283	-D	2000+	T	-	20/	dä -M	Algier	1654+	60.17 N/ 02.49 W	
21/	dt	U 57	Korth	AN 1680	-D	+	Tf	-	21/	nw -D	Svinta	1267+	4,75m E Copinsay, Orkney	6)
21/0326	dt	U 38	Liebe	AN 1342	-D	4000+	T	-	21/	dä -M	Christiansborg	3270+	60.17 N/ 02.49 W	
25/0540	dt	U 47	Prien	AN 1194	-D	5000+	T	-	25/	dä -D	Britta	1146+	60.00 N/ 04.19 W	
25/2011	dt	U 57	Korth	AN 1642	-T:	5742+	Tf	-	25/	br -MT	Daghestan	5742+	9m E Copinsay	7)
26/0220	dt	U 38	Liebe	AN 2624	-M:	3794+	T	-	26/	nw -M	Cometa	3794+	60.06 N/ 04.36 W	

3) The *P.Margaronis* was reported missing after March 8th.
4) The *Abbotsford* was reported missing after March 11th. No other ship could have been sunk by *U 14*.
5) The *Argentina* departed Copenhagen on March 13th for Las Palmas, and radioed on March 17th for the last time. She was reported missing thereafter.
6) The *Svinta* was damaged by a bomb hit from a German aircraft on March 20th.
7) The *Daghestan* was damaged by a bomb hit from a German aircraft on March 20th.

North Sea - Atlantic

1	2	3	4	5	6	7	8	9	10	11	12	13	14	15
April 1940														
2/0021 dt	U 38		Liebe	AN 1814	-D	5000+	T	.							1)
6/0316 dt	U 59		Jürst	AN 1537	-D	6000+	T	-	6/	nw	-D	Navarra	2118+	59. N/ 04. W	
10/0136 dt	U 37		Hartmann	AE 9273	-T	9000+	T	-	10/	sw	-MT	Sveaborg	9076+	62.52 N/ 07.34 W	
10/0213 dt	*U 4*		*Hinsch*	*AN 2989*	*SS*	*1500+*	*T*	*-*	*10/*	*br*	*SS*	*Thistle*	*1090+*	*near Skudesnes*	
10/0352 dt	U 37		Hartmann	AE 9273	-D	4000+	T	-	10/	nw	-M	Tosca	5128+	62.52 N/ 07.34 W	
11/2107 dt	*U 25*		*Schütze*	*AF*	*DD*	*1360=*	*T*	*Task F.*	*11/*				-----	*Ofot-Fjord*	
11/2107 dt	*U 25*		*Schütze*	*AF*	*DD*	*1360=*	*T*	*Task F.*	*11/*				-----	*Ofot-Fjord*	
12/0942 dt	U 37		Hartmann	AF 7834	-D	4600+	T	-	12/	br	-D	Stancliffe	4511+	45m NE Unst I.	
13/1234 dt	*U 37*		*Hartmann*	*AF 7835*	*CL*	*9100+*	*T*	*-*	*13/*				-----		
13/1858 dt	*U 34*		*Rollmann*	*AF 6775*	*CM*	*595+*	*Tf*	*-*	*13/*	*nw*	*CM*	*Fröya*	*595+*	*Drontheim Fjord*	2)
16/1519 dt	*U 13*		*Schulte*	*AF 7890*	*DD*	*1870=*	*T*	*-*	*16/*				-----		
17/1733 dt	U 13		Schulte	AF 7890	-D	5000+	T	-	17/	br	-D	Swainby	4935+	25m N Muckle Flugga, Shetlands	
20/1248 dt	*U 9*		*Lüth*	*AF 7945*	*DD*	*1975=*	*T*	*-*	*20/*				-----		
21/0748 dt	U 26		Scheringer	AE		-D	6000+	T	.	21/	br	-M	Cedarbank	5159+	62.49 N/ 04.10 E	
26/0117 dt	U 13		Schulte	AN 1524	-D	4000+	T	-							3)
28/0129 dt	U 13		Schulte	AN 15	-T	7400+	T	-	28/	br	-DT	Scottish American	6999=	58.41 N/ 04.40 W	
May 1940														
(9. 2.) dt	U 9		Lüth	AN 1728	---------		M	-	4/	br	-DT	San Tiburcio	5995+	4m 330° Tarbett Ness,Moray F.	
9/0014 dt	*U 9*		*Lüth*	*AN 8511*	*SS*	*1500+*	*T*	*-*	*9/*	*fr*	*SS*	*Doris*	*552+*	*53.40 N/ 04. E*	
11/0049 dt	U 9		Lüth	AN 8749	-T	6000+	T	-	11/	es	-D	Viiu	1908+	Westhinder Buoy	
11/1400 dt	U 9		Lüth	AN 8749	-D	4000+	T	-	11/	br	-D	Tringa	1930+	51.21 N/ 02.25 E	

1) *U 38* attacked a ship at the end of the convoy and observed a dense cloud of smoke and vapor.
2) The *Fröya* was already beached when *U 34* torpedoed the ship to prevent salvage operations.
3) *U 13* observed one hit at the bow which broke off the forecastle. The ship sank in 45 seconds.

1	2	3	4	5	6	7	8	9	10	11	12	13	14	15

May 1940, cont.

1	2	3	4	5	6	7	8	9	10 11	12	13	14	15
19/0631	dt	U 37	Oehrn	AM 2885	-D: 5066+	A	-	19/	sw -M	Erik Frisell	5066+	57.25 N/ 09.15 W	
22/23	dt	U 37	Oehrn	BF 1597	-M: 9494=	A	-	22/2157	br -M	Dunster Grange	9494=	49.20 N/ 08.40 W	
23/1254	dt	U 9	Lüth	AN 8757	-D: 3500+	T	-	23/	dt -D	Sigurds Faulbaums	3256+	51.29 N/ 02.38 E	1)
24/0248	dt	U 37	Oehrn	BF 1983	-D 5700+	T	-	24/	gr -D	Kyma	3994+	48.30 N/ 09.30 W	
27/1551	dt	U 37	Oehrn	BE 9912	-D 3700+	T	-	27/	br -D	Sheaf Mead	5008+	43.48 N/ 12.32 W	
27/2148	dt	U 37	Oehrn	BE 9926	-D: 3425+	S	-	27/	ar -D	Uruguay	3425+	160m C.Villano	
28/0924	dt	U 37	Oehrn	BF 7787	-M:10400+	T	.	28/0825	fr -M	Brazza	10387+	42.43 N/ 11.00 W	
28/1630	dt	U 37	Oehrn	CG 21	-Df: 177+	A	-	28/	fr -Df	Julien	177+	42.50 N/ 10.40 W	
29/0657	dt	U 37	Oehrn	CG 22	-D: 2500+	TA	-	29/0430	fr -D	Marie José	2477+	40m NW Vigo	
29/07	dt	U 37	Oehrn	CG 22	-D: 7406+	A	-	29/	br -MT	Telena	7406+	42.25 N/ 09.08 W	2)
29/	*dt*	*U 62*	*Michalowski*	*AN 8758*	*-D: 2954=*	*T*	*-*	*30/0358*	*br DD*	*Grafton*	*1350+*	*51.22 N/ 02.45 E*	*3)*
30/0517	dt	U 56	Harms	AM 3472	-D 12000=	T	.	30/0420	br -D	Ulster Prince	-----	59.32 N/ 06.23 W	4)
30/1925	dt	U 101	Frauenheim	BF 2733	-D 4427+	T	-	30/	br -D	Stanhall	4831+	48.59 N/ 05.17 W	
31/1402	dt	U 101	Frauenheim	BF 2655	-D 5000+	T	-	31/1305	br -D	Orangemoor	5775+	49.43 N/ 03.23 W	

June 1940

1	2	3	4	5	6	7	8	9	10 11	12	13	14	15
1/2304	dt	U 37	Oehrn	BF 9994	-D 1100+	A	-	1/	gr -D	Ioanna	950+	120m W Cape Finisterre	
1/2348	dt	U 58	Kuppisch	AN 1829	ACL:8400+	T	-	1/	br -D	Astronomer	8401+	58.01 N/ 02.12 W	
2/0505	dt	U 101	Frauenheim	BF 2495	-D 6000+	T	-	2/	br -D	Polycarp	3577+	49.19 N/ 05.35 W	
3/	dt	U 37	Oehrn		-D +	A	-	3/	fi -D	Snabb	2317+	Cape Finisterre	
6/	dt	U 48	Rösing	AM 3388	-D: 798+	A	-	5/	br -D	Stancor	798+	58.48 N/ 08.45 W	

1) The *Sigurds Faulbaums* was a German steamer on the way to England as a British prize.
2) The *Telena* was later salvaged by the Portuguese and renamed the *Gerona*.
3) Based on reports by the xB-Dienst, the B.d.U. assumed that *U 62* had sunk the French transport *Douaisien*. But by comparing the German and Allied sources we have come to the conclusion that in reality the *Grafton* was sunk.
4) The torpedo exploded a few yards off the side of the *Ulster Prince*.

1	2	3	4	5	6	7	8	9	10	11	12	13	14	15
June 1940, cont.														
6/1313	dt	U 46	Endraß	AM 5432	ACL22300+	T	-	6/	br	ACL	Carinthia	20277+	53.13 N/ 10.40 W	
7/0213	dt	U 48	Rösing	AM 5299	-D 4500+	T	-	6/	br	-D	Frances Massey	4212+	55.33 N/ 08.26 W	
7/0322	dt	U 48	Rösing	AM 5296	-D: 5900+	T	-	7/	br	-D	Eros	5888=	55.33 N/ 08.26 W	
9/1305	dt	U 46	Endraß	BF 6885	-D 3000+	T	-	9/	fi	-D	Margareta	2155+	45. N/ 14.30 W	
11/0110	dt	U 48	Rösing	BE 9397	-D 5500+	T	-	10/	gr	-D	Violando N.Goulandris	3598+	44.04 N/ 12.30 W	
11/1117	dt	U 101	Frauenheim	CG 1372	-D: 5820+	A	-	11/	gr	-D	Mount Hymettus	5820+	42.13 N/ 11.20 W	
11/2304	dt	U 46	Endraß	BF 7716	-T 11000+	T	.	11/2300	br	-MT	Athelprince	8782=	43.42 N/ 13.20 W	
12/1208	dt	U 101	Frauenheim	CG 1617	-D: 5250+	T	-	12/1010	br	-D	Earlspark	5250+	42.26 N/ 11.33 W	
12/1938	dt	U 46	Endraß	BE 9584	-D 6000+	T	.	12/	br	-D	Barbara Marie	4223+	44.16 N/ 13.54 W	
12/1946	dt	U 46	Endraß	BE 9584	-T 8000+	T	.	12/	br	-M	Willowbank	5041+	44.16 N/ 13.54 W	
13/0716	dt	U 25	Beduhn	AM 0217	ACL16800+	T	-	13/	br	ACL	Scotstoun	17046+	57.00 N/ 09.57 W	
14/0820	dt	U 101	Frauenheim	CF 3235	-D: 3557+	A	-	14/	gr	-D	Antonis Georgandis	3557+	NW Cape Finisterre	
14/1938	dt	U 38	Liebe	BF 1526	-D 5500+	TA	-	14/	gr	-D	Mount Myrto	5403+	50.03 N/ 10.05 W	
14/1944	dt	U 47	Prien	BF 1158	-D: 5834+	T	HX.48 s	14/	br	-D	Balmoralwood	5834+	50.19 N/ 10.28 W	
15/0101	dt	U 38	Liebe	BF 1347	-T 12000+	T	HX.48	15/	nw	-MT	Italia	9973+	50.37 N/ 08.44 W	
15/0105	dt	U 38	Liebe	BF 1347	-D 6500+	T	HX.48	15/	dä	-D	Erik Boye	2238+	50.37 N/ 08.44 W	
16/0027	dt	UA	Cohausz	AE 8287	ACL14000+	T	-	16/	br	ACL	Andania	13950+	62.36 N/ 15.09 W	
16/1302	dt	U 101	Frauenheim	CF 3224	-M:11400+	T	-	16/	br	-M	Wellington Star	13212+	42.39 N/ 17.01 W	
17/0115	dt	U 46	Endraß	BE 9498	-D 4500+	T	-	17/0109	gr	-D	Elpis	3651+	43.46 N/ 14.06 W	
18/1232	dt	U 28	Kuhnke	BF 1714	-D: 2417	T	-	18/	fi	-D	Sarmatia	2417+	49.04 N/ 12.05 W	
18/1902	dt	U 32	Jenisch	BF 1432	-D: 1522+	T	-	18/	nw	-D	Altair	1522+	49.39 N/ 11.15 W	
18/	dt	U 32	Jenisch	BF 1423	-Df: 108+	A	-	18/	sp	-Df	Sálvora	108+	49.39 N/ 11. W	
18/	dt	U 32	Jenisch	BF 1423	-Df: 108+	A	-	18/	sp	-Df	Faro-Ons	108+	49.39 N/ 11. W	
19/0125	dt	U 48	Rösing	BE 9359	-D 6500+	T	HGF.34	19/	nw	-M	Tudor	6607+	45.10 N/ 11.50 W	

1	2	3	4	5	6	7	8	9	10	11	12	13	14	15
June 1940, cont.														
19/0128	dt	U 25	Beduhn	BF 5151	-T 8000+	T								1)
19/0256	dt	U 48	Rösing	BE 9369	-D 5000+	T	HGF.34	19/	br	-D	Baron Loudoun	3164+	45. N/ 11.21 W	
19/0346	dt	U 48	Rösing	BE 7171	-D 7000+	T	HGF.34	19/	br	-D	British Monarch	5661+	45. N/ 11.21 W	
19/0457	dt	U 52	Salman	BF 5525	-T 6000+	T	-	19/	br	-D	The Monarch	824+	47.20 N/ 04.40 W	
19/1916	dt	U 32	Jenisch	AM 8898	-D: 5334+	T	-	19/	jg	-D	Labud	5334+	SW Fastnet	
19/1929	dt	U 28	Kuhnke	BF 1448	-D: 3443+	T	-	19/	gr	-D	Adamandios Georgandis	3443+	49.35 N/ 11.15 W	
19/2005	dt	U 52	Salman	BF 5589	-D 11400+	T	-	19/	be	-D	Ville de Namur	7463+	46.25 N/ 04.35 W	
20/	dt	U 122	Looff	-------	---------	T	.	20/	br	-D	Empire Conveyor	5911+	56.16 N/ 08.10 W	2)
20/1533	dt	U 51	Knorr	BF 1983	-D 3509=	T	HGF.34	20/1404	br	-D	Andalusian	-----		3)
20/1554	dt	U 51	Knorr	BF 1983	-D 4876=	T	HGF.34	20/	br	-D	Otterpool	-----		3)
20/1614	dt	U 38	Liebe	BF 5193	-D: 1800+	T	-	20/	sw	-D	Tilia Gorthon	1776+	48.32 N/ 06.20 W	
20/1730	dt	U 48	Rösing	BE 9574	-T: 7439+	T	HX.49 s	20/	nl	-MT	Moerdrecht	7493+	43.34 N/ 14.20 W	
20/2140	dt	U 30	Lemp	BF 1946	-D 7000+	T	-	20/1943	br	-D	Otterpool	4876+	48.45 N/ 08.13 W	
21/0411	dt	U 52	Salman	BF 6783	-D 3200+	T	-	21/	fi	-D	Hilda	1144+	45.46 N/ 03.17 W	
21/0817	dt	U 65	v.Stockhausen	BF 5559	-D:28124+	Tf	-	21/	fr	-D	Champlain	28124+	La Pallice Roads	4)
21/0846	dt	U 28	Kuhnke	BF 1562	-D 5000+	T	-	21/	br	-D	Prunella (SSV)	4443+	SW Approaches	
21/1630	dt	U 43	Ambrosius	CG 5415	-T 6000+	T	65.X	21/	br	-DT	Yarraville	8627+	39.40 N/ 11.34 W	
21/1753	dt	U 38	Liebe	BF 5276	-D 5300+	T	-	21/	be	-D	Luxembourg	5809+	47.25 N/ 04.55 W	
21/2007	dt	U 47	Prien	BF 1193	-T 12000+	T	HX.49	22/	br	-DT	San Fernando	13056+	50.20 N/ 10.24 W	
21/2007	dt	U 47	Prien	BF 1193	-D 7000+	T	HX.49							
21/2008	dt	U 47	Prien	BF 1193	-D 7000=	T	HX.49							
21/2356	dt	U 25	Beduhn	BF 4367	-D 10000=	T	-	21/	fr	-DT	Aragaz	-----	45.53 N/ 04.07 W	

1) *U 25*, which was rammed by the following ship after the attack, observed one stopped ship after surfacing. This heavily damaged tanker was not found again 45 minutes later.
2) The *Empire Conveyor* was probably sunk by *U 122*, which was lost after the attack and therefore did not report it.
3) *U 51* after the attacks against the *Andalusian* (reported as *Fellside* by the xB-Dienst) and *Otterpool* reported two detonations, but no other effects on the ships. The B.d.U. assumed hits on both ships according to the xB-Dienst-reports.
4) The *Champlain* settled on the bottom after being damaged by an air-laid magnetic mine on June 17th at La Pallice roads, and received a torpedo hit as a result of this attack.

North Sea - Atlantic

1	2	3	4	5	6	7	8	9	10	11	12	13	14	15
June 1940, cont.														
22/0217	dt	U 38	Liebe	BF 5568	-D 6000+	T	-	22/	gr	-D	Neion	5154+	47.09 N/ 04.17 W	
22/0336	dt	U 32	Jenisch	BF 1237	-T:12000+	T	HX.49	22/	nw	-MT	Eli Knudsen	9026+	50.36 N/ 08.44 W	
22/	dt	U 46	Endraß	BE 6378	CV 23000=	T	Task F.	22/	br	CV	Ark Royal	------		5)
22/1804	dt	U 65	vStockhausen	BF 5514	-T 7000+	T	-	21/	nl	-D	Berenice	1177+	47.10 N/ 03.35 W	
22/2240	dt	U 30	Lemp	BF 1264	-D: 4000+	T	HX.49	22/	nw	-M	Randsfjord	3999+	70m SSE Queenstown	
24/0241	dt	U 47	Prien	BE 3292	-D 2800+	A	-	24/	pa	-D	Cathrine	1885+	50.08 N/ 14. W	
25/1543	dt	U 51	Knorr	BE 3783	-D: 5395+	T	-	25/	br	-D	Windsorwood	5395+	48.31 N/ 14.50 W	
25/1619	dt	U 51	Knorr	BE 3783	-T:12049+	T	TA	25/	br	-DT	Saranac	12049+	48.24 N/ 15.05 W	
26/0228	dt	UA	Cohausz	CG 7168	-T: 3828+	T	-	26/	nw	-M	Crux	3828+	36.53 N/ 14. W	
26/0719	dt	U 62	Michalowski	AM 5615	-T 5000+	T	-	28/	br	-Df	Castleton	211+	Orkneys	6)
26/	dt	U 29	Schuhart	BE 96	-D: 5254+	TA	-	26/	gr	-D	Dimitris	5254+	44.23 N/ 11.41 W	
27/0338	dt	U 47	Prien	BE 3282	-D: 4005+	TA	-	27/	nw	-D	Lenda	4005+	150m SW Fastnet	
27/	dt	U 47	Prien	BE 32	-T: 2800+	A	-	27/	nl	-DT	Leticia	2580+	50.11 N/ 13.15 W	
28/0202	dt	U 30	Lemp	BF 4192	-D: 5053+	T	-	28/	br	-D	Llanarth	5053+	47.30 N/ 10.30 W	
29/0012	dt	U 51	Knorr	BE 3476	ACL14000+	T	-	29/	br	-D	Edgehill (SSV)	4724+	SW Approaches	
29/05	dt	U 47	Prien	BE 3821	-D: 7000+	TA	-	29/	br	-D	Empire Toucan	4421+	49.20 N/ 13.52 W	
30/	dt	U 102	v.Klot-Heydenfeldt	-------	---------	T	.	30/	nw	-D	Belmoira	3214+	48.15 N/ 10.30 W	7)
30/	dt	U 102	v.Klot-Heydenfeldt	-------	---------	T	.	30/	es	-D	Merkur	1291+	48.26 N/ 10.58 W	7)
30/	dt	U 26	Scheringer	-------	---------	T	-	30/	gr	-D	Frangoula Goulandris	6701+	49.59 N/ 11.24 W	8)

5) *U 46* observed during an orkan force 11 one carrier - identified as *Illustrious* - with two destroyers and heard after a three-torpedo salvo one explosion. In reality the carrier was the *Ark Royal* accompanied by the battlecruiser *Hood* and two destroyers on the way to Gibraltar. The carrier was not hit or damaged.
6) *U 62* heard a heavy explosion after 5 minutes and then sinking noises. The *Castleton* was reported missing after June 28th.
7) There is no sinking report for *Belmoira* and *Merkur*. But only the missing *U 102* could have been in this area.
8) There is no attack report for the *Fragoula Goulandris*. *U 26* sunk the following day in this area must have been the attacker.

1	2	3	4	5	6	7	8	9	10	11	12	13	14	15
June 1940, cont.														
30/1203	dt	U 65	vStockhausen	BE 6864	-D 6900=	T	.	30/	br	-D	Clan Ogilvy	5802=	46.17 N/ 14.35 W	
30/1203	dt	U 65	vStockhausen	BE 6864	-D 9600=	T	.	30/	br	-D		-----		
30/1445	dt	U 47	Prien	BE 3195	-D: 4201+	T	-	30/	gr	-D	Georgios Kyriakides	4201+	50.25 N/ 14.33 W	
30/2227	dt	U 43	Ambrosius	BE 6663	-D 14000+	T	.	30/	br	-D	Avelona Star	13376+	46.46 N/ 12.17 W	
July 1940														
1/0023	dt	U 30	Lemp	BF 4441	-D 7900+	T	-	1/	br	-D	Beignon	5218+	47.20 N/ 10.30 W	
1/0400	dt	U 30	Lemp	BF 4421	-D 8000+	T	-	1/	br	-D	Clearton	5219+	47.53 N/ 09.30 W	
1/	dt	U 26	Scheringer	-------	---------	T	-	1/	br	-D	Zarian	4871=	48.03 N/ 11.11 W	1)
1/	dt	U 29	Schuhart	BE 67	-D: 7466+	A	-	1/	gr	-D	Adamastos	5889+	46.20 N/ 14.30 W	
1/1351	dt	U 65	vStockhausen	BE 6292	-D 4900+	T	.	1/	nl	-D	Amstelland	8156=	47.53 N/ 13.23 W	
2/	dt	U 29	Schuhart	BE 64	-D: 4919+	A	-	2/	pa	-D	Santa Margarita	4919+	47. N/ 15.30 W	
2/0758	dt	U 47	Prien	AM 5116	-D:15501+	T	-	2/	br	-D	Arandora Star	15501+	55.20 N/ 10.33 W	
2/2354	dt	U 29	Schuhart	BE 5364	-T 9000+	T	-	2/	br	-MT	Athellaird	8999+	47.24 N/ 16.49 W	
5/1251	dt	U 99	Kretschmer	BF 1144	-D: 2053+	TA	HX.52s	5/	ca	-D	Magog	2053+	50.31 N/ 11.05 W	
5/1826	*dt*	*U 34*	*Rollmann*	*BF 1286*	*DD: 1100+*	*T*	*-*	*5/*	*br*	*DD*	*Whirlwind*	*1100+*	*50.17 N/ 08.48 W*	
6/0831	dt	U 30	Lemp	BF 4651	-D 2000+	T	-	11/	br	-D	Sea Glory	1964+	North Atlantic	2)
6/1058	dt	U 34	Rollmann	BF 1824	-D: 4549+	T	-	6/	es	-D	Vapper	4543+	49.30 N/ 09.15 W	
7/0053	dt	U 99	Kretschmer	BF 1464	-D 3600+	T	-							2)
7/0714	dt	U 34	Rollmann	BE 1563	-T 5600+	T	-	7/	nl	-DT	Lucrecia	2584+	49.50 N/ 08.07 W	
7/2312	dt	U 99	Kretschmer	BF 1191	-D 8401+	T	-	7/	sw	-D	Bissen	1514+	50.06 N/ 10.23 W	
8/0753	dt	U 99	Kretschmer	BF 1251	-D 10000+	T	HX.53	8/	br	-D	Humber Arm	5758+	50.36 N/ 09.24 W	

1) *U 26* could not report the attack. It was sunk immediately after the attack by one escort vessel.
2) The *Sea Glory* was reported as missing after July 11th. Probably she was sunk by the attack of *U 34* some days earlier, or possibly by the attack of *U 99*. There must have been a second smaller merchant vessel lost on July 6th or 7th, which has not been identified up to this time.

1	2	3	4	5	6	7	8	9	10	11	12	13	14	15
July 1940, cont.														
9/1232 dt	U 34	Rollmann	BE 3398	-D: 1865+	T	-		9/	es	-D	Tiiu	1865+	50.20 N/ 12. W	
9/2119 dt	U 43	Ambrosius	BE 3853	-T 15000+	T	-		9/	br	-D	Aylesbury	3944+	48.39 N/ 13.55 W	
10/1306 dt	U 61	Oesten	AM 1542	-D 8000=	T	OA.180		10/	nl	-D	Alwaki	4533+	58.46 N/ 04.46 W	
10/1425 dt	U 34	Rollmann	AM 8875	-D: 4596+	T	-		10/	fi	-D	Petsamo	4596+	51.08 N/ 09.22 W	
11/0706 dt	U 34	Rollmann	BE 3328	-D: 2197+	T	HX.54s		11/	nw	-D	Janna	2197+	50.34 N/ 12.10 W	
12/0206 dt	U 99	Kretschmer	BE 3274	-D: 4860+	T	-		12/	gr	-D	Ia	4860+	51. N/ 14. W	
12/1006 dt	U 56	Harms	AM 5349	-D 15000=?	T	-		12/	br	-D	Dunera	------	North Canal	1)
12/2231 dt	U 99	Kretschmer	BE 3224	-D: 2136p	P	-		12/	es	-D	Merisaar	2136p		2)
14/ dt	UA	Cohausz	EJ 42	-T: 5824+	T	-		14/	nw	-DT	Sarita	5824+	15.22 N/ 26.28 W	
14/1818 dt	U 52	Salman	BE 6556	-D: 4111+	T	-		14/	gr	-D	Thetis A	4111+	47.40 N/ 13.20 W	
15/0321 dt	U 34	Rollmann	AM 8784	-D 4000+	T	-		15/	gr	-D	Evdoxia	2018+	40m SW Bull Rock, SW-Ireland	
15/ dt	U 34	Rollmann	BF 41	-D: 3531+	A	-		15/	gr	-D	Naftilos	3531+	48.05 N/ 10.25 W	
15/2035 dt	U 58	Schonder	AM 3659	-T 9000+	T	-								3)
16/1223 dt	U 61	Oesten	AM 5216	-T 10000+	T	HX.55		16/	br	-MT	Scottish Minstrel	6998+	56.10 N/ 10.20 W	4)
17/0410 dt	U 57	Topp	AN 1368	-D 2560+	T	-		17/	sw	-D	O.A.Brodin	1960+	59.22 N/ 03.40 W	
17/1040 dt	U 43	Ambrosius	AM 4355	-D: 3509+	T	-		17/	br	-D	Fellside	3509+	56.09 N/ 12.30 W	
17/2222 dt	U 57	Topp	AM 3662	-D 9000+	T	HX.55A		17/	br	-D	Manipur	8652+	58.41 N/ 05.14 W	
18/0203 dt	U 99	Kretschmer	BE 3344	-D: 4434+	T	-		17/	br	-D	Woodbury	4434+	50.46 N/ 13.56 W	
18/1641 dt	U 58	Schonder	AM 5281	-D 5600+	T	-		18/	nw	-D	Gyda	1591+	56. N/ 10. W	
19/1828 dt	U 62	Michalowski	AM 5534	-D 6000+	T	-		19/	br	-D	Pearlmoor	4581+	55.23 N/ 09.18 W	
21/2239 dt	U 30	Lemp	CG 1316	-D: 1100+	TA	-		21/	br	-D	Ellaroy	712+	42.30 N/ 12.36 W	

1) The *Dunera* was glanced by a torpedo which did not detonate.
2) The *Merisaar* was given a route order by *U 99* to go to a French port. On the way she was sunk on July 15th by bombs of
   a German aircraft south of Queenstown.
3) *U 58* observed hit on this tanker which broke the back of the ship.
4) The *Scottish Minstrel* remained afloat for a time, but sank on July 17th.

1	2	3	4	5	6	7	8	9	10	11	12	13	14	15
July 1940, cont.														
26/1447 dt	U 34	Rollmann	AL 6394	-D	17000+	T	.	26/	br	-M	Accra	9337+	55.40 N/ 16.28 W	
26/1447 dt	U 34	Rollmann	AL 6394	-D	7000+	T	.	26/	br	-D	Vinemoor	4359+	55.43 N/ 16.25 W	
27/0258 dt	U 34	Rollmann	AL 3991	-D	8000+	T	.	27/	br	-D	Sambre	5260+	56.37 N/ 17.53 W	
27/0305 dt	U 34	Rollmann	AL 3991	-D	6000=	T	.							
27/0313 dt	U 34	Rollmann	AL 3991	-T	9000+	T	.	27/	br	-MT	Thiara	10364+	56.37 N/ 17.56 W	
28/0557 dt	U 99	Kretschmer	AM 7676	-M:	11400+	T	-	28/	br	-M	Auckland Star	13212+	52.17 N/ 12.32 W	
29/0215 dt	U 99	Kretschmer	AM 4977	-D:	7336+	T	.	29/	br	-D	Clan Menzies	7336+	54.10 N/ 12. W	
31/0138 dt	U 99	Kretschmer	AM 5226	-D:	5475+	T	-	31/	br	-D	Jamaica Progress	5475+	56.26 N/ 08.30 W	
31/1324 dt	U 99	Kretschmer	AM 5285	-D	8000+	T	.	31/	br	-D	Jersey City	6322+	55.47 N/ 09.18 W	
August 1940														
1/0345 dt	U 59	Matz	AM 5273	-D	6000+	T	-	1/	sw	-D	Sigyn	1981+	56.10 N/ 09.25 W	
1/1905 dt	*U 34*	*Rollmann*	*AN 4281*	*SS:*	*670+*	*T*	*-*	*1/*	*br*	*SS*	*Spearfish*	*670+*	*Cape Nose Head*	
2/0251 dt	U 99	Kretschmer	AL 6628	-T	9385+	T	.	2/	nw	-MT	Strinda	10973=	55.10 N/ 17.16 W	
2/0345 dt	U 99	Kretschmer	AL 6616	-T:	6556+	TA	.	2/	br	-MT	Lucerna	6556=	55.18 N/ 16.39 W	
2/0427 dt	U 99	Kretschmer	AL 6616	-T:	8016=	TA	.	2/	br	-MT	Alexia	8016=	55.30 N/ 15.30 W	
3/0810 dt	U 57	Topp	AM 5364	-D	5000+	T	-	3/	sw	-D	Atos	2161+	56. N/ 07. W	
3/2015 dt	UA	Cohausz	EJ 9583	-D:	4201+	TA	-	3/	jg	-D	Rad	4201+	11.20 N/ 21. W	
4/0335 dt	U 52	Salman	AL 0344	-D:	5272+	T	HX.60	4/0220	br	-D	King Alfred	5272+	56.59 N/ 17.38 W	
4/0338 dt	U 52	Salman	AL 0344	-D:	4600+	T	HX.60	4/0225	br	-D	Gogovale	4586+	56.59 N/ 17.38 W	
4/0922 dt	U 52	Salman	AL 0392	-D	7000+	T	HX.60	4/0720	br	-D	Geraldine Mary	7244+	56.46 N/ 15.48 W	
4/2120 dt	U 58	Schonder	AM 5198	-D	8724+	T	HX.60	4/1845	gr	-D	Pindos	4360+	55.22 N/ 08.50 W	
4/2138 dt	U 56	Harms	AM 5349	-T	8000+?		OB.193	4/2048	br	-D	Boma	5408+	55.44 N/ 08.04 W	
7/2140 dt	U 38	Liebe	AM 4525	-D	9400+	T	HX.61	7/	äg	-D	Mohamed Ali El-Kebir	7527+	55.22 N/ 13.18 W	
8/1314 dt	U 37	Oehrn	AM 7124	-M:	9130+	T	-	8/	br	-M	Upwey Grange	9130+	54.20 N/ 15.28 W	

1	2	3	4	5	6	7	8	9	10	11	12	13	14	15

August 1940, cont.

1	2	3	4	5	6	7	8	9	10 11	12	13	14	15
9/2032 dt	U 30	Lemp	AM 5424	-M: 5773+	T	-	9/	sw -M	Canton	5779+	Tory I.	
10/0100 dt	U 56	Harms	AM 5354	-D 7300+	T	-	10/	br ACL	Transylvania	16923+	55.50 N/ 08.03 W	
11/1519 dt	U 38	Liebe	AM 4585	-D 5000+	T	-	11/	br -D	Llanfair	4966+	54.48 N/ 13.46 W	
12/0550 it	MALASPINA	Leoni	38n/23w	-T:17500+	T	OB.193d	12/	br -MT	British Fame	8406+	37.44 N/ 22.56 W	
13/2147 dt	U 60	Schnee	AM 5373	-D 5000+	T	HX.62s	13/	sw -D	Nils Gorthon	1787+	25m NNE Malin Hd.	
14/2123 dt	U 60	Schnee	AM 5292	-D 7000+	T	-						
14/2234 dt	U 59	Matz	AM 5462	-D 4500+	T	-	14/	br -D	Betty	2339+	35m N Tory I.	
15/ dt	U 51	Knorr	AM 29	-T: 5709+	T	HX.62s	15/	br -MT	Sylvafield	5709+	56.39 N/ 11.16 W	
15/2200 dt	UA	Cohausz	CF 2164	-D 4500+	T	-	15/	gr -D	Aspasia	4211+	35. N/ 20. W	1)
16/0927 dt	U 100	Schepke	AM 4611	-D 6000+	T	-	16/	br -M	Empire Merchant	4864+	55.23 N/ 13.24 W	
16/1203 dt	U 48	Rösing	AL 3888	-D 4800+	T	-	16/	sw -D	Hedrun	2325+	57.10 N/ 16.37 W	
16/1302 dt	U 46	Endraß	AL 0312	-D 8000=	T	OB.197	16/	nl -M	Alcinous	6189=	57.16 N/ 17.02 W	
16/1932 dt	U 30	Lemp	AL 3783	-D: 6628+	T	-	16/	br -D	Clan Macphee	6628+	57.30 N/ 17.14 W	
19/0005 dt	U 48	Rösing	AM 4424	-D 10000+	T	-	18/	be -D	Ville de Gand	7590+	55.28 N/ 15.10 W	
19/0120 it	MALASPINA	Leoni	39n/21w	-D 8000+	T	-				-----	39.20 N/ 21.25 W	
19/0154 dt	U 101	Frauenheim	AM 4355	-D: 4576+	T	-	18/	br -D	Ampleforth	4576+	56.10 N/ 10.40 W	
19/0916 dt	UA	Cohausz	BE 1612	-D: 4300+	TA	-	19/	un -D	Kelet	4295+	50. N/ 22. W	
19/1400 it	BARBARIGO	Ghilieri	32n/13w	-D: 3255=	A	-	19/	br -D	Aguila	-----	31.15 N/ 13.02 W	2)
20/0027 dt	UA	Cohausz	AL 8723	-D: 4397+	T	-	20/	pa -D	Tuira	4397+	54.46 N/ 20.30 W	
20/2150 dt	U 46	Endraß	AM 2872	-D 6500=	T	-	20/	gr -D	Leonidas M.Valmas	2080=§	55.13 N/ 10.38 W	3)

1) The *Aspasia* was reported missing after August 12th. She was sunk without doubt by *UA*.
2) The *Aquila* was only identified by a xB-Dienst report about a U-boat attack. The *Barbarigo* reported 5 hits by her 4-inch gun.
3) The *Leonidas M. Valmas* was heavily damaged and towed into port, but was declared a total loss.

1	2	3	4	5	6	7	8	9	10	11	12	13	14	15

August 1940, cont.

1	2	3	4	5	6	7	8	9	10 11	12	13	14
21/0026	dt	U 48	Rösing	AM 4621	-D 4000=	T	.					
21/0027	dt	U 48	Rösing	AM 4621	-D 5000=	T	.					
21/2030	it	DANDOLO	Boris	37n/14w	-D:10000+	T	-	21/	nl -MT	Hermes	3768=	38.57 N/ 13.50 W
23/0222	dt	U 37	Oehrn	AL 5722	-D 4000+	T	-	22/	nw -D	Keret	1718+	54.16 N/ 23.08 W
23/1250	dt	U 37	Oehrn	AL 4722	-D: 5242+	T	-	23/	br -D	Severn Leigh	5242+	54.31 N/ 25.41 W
24/0042	dt	U 57	Topp	AM 5392	-D 9000+	T	OB.202	23/2344	br -D	Saint Dunstan	5681+	55.44 N/ 07.32 W
24/0042	dt	U 57	Topp	AM 5392	-D 5000+	T	OB.202	23/2344	br -D	Cumberland	10939+	55.44 N/ 07.32 W
24/0042	dt	U 57	Topp	AM 5392	-D 5000+	T	OB.202	23/2346	br -D	Havildar	5407=	55.39 N/ 07.18 W
24/0314	dt	U 37	Oehrn	AK 6698	-D: 5100+	TA	-	23/	br -D	Brookwood	5100+	54.40 N/ 27.57 W
24/1424	dt	U 48	Rösing	AM 2743	-T 8670+	T	HX.65s	24/	br -DT	La Brea	6665+	57.24 N/ 11.21 W
24/2038	*dt*	*U 37*	*Oehrn*	*AK 6333*	*DD +*	*T*	*SC.1*	*24/*	*br PS*	*Penzance*	*1025+*	*56.16 N/ 27.19 W*
25/0146	dt	U 37	Oehrn	AK 6327	-D 7000+	T	SC.1	24/	br -D	Blairmore	4141+	56. N/ 27.30 W
25/0245	dt	U 48	Rösing	AM 2583	-T 8000+	T	HX.65A	25/	br -MT	Athelcrest	6825+	58.24 N/ 11.25 W
25/0246	dt	U 48	Rösing	AM 2583	-D 6000+	T	HX.65A	25/	br -D	Empire Merlin	5763+	58.30 N/ 10.15 W
25/	dt	U 37	Oehrn	AL 44	-D: 2500+	A	-	25/	br -D	Yewcrest	3774+	55.10 N/ 25.02 W
25/1912	dt	U 100	Schepke	AM 2952	-D: 5500+	T	-	25/	br -D	Jamaica Pioneer	5471+	57.05 N/ 11.02 W
25/1948	dt	U 57	Topp	AM 5313	-T 9600+	T	HX.65s	25/	br -MT	Pecten	7468+	56.22 N/ 07.55 W
25/2350	dt	U 124	Schulz	AM 3645	-D 8000+	T	HX.65A	25/	br -D	Stakesby	3900=	23m N Butt of Lewis, Hebriden
25/2351	dt	U 124	Schulz	AM 3645	-D 6000+	T	HX.65A	25/	br -D	Harpalyce	5169+	58.52 N/ 06.34 W
25/2353	dt	U 124	Schulz	AM 3645	-D 6000+	T	HX.65A					
25/2356	dt	U 124	Schulz	AM 3645	-D 8000+	T	HX.65A	25/	br -D	Firecrest	5394+	58.52 N/ 06.34 W
26/1800	it	DANDOLO	Boris	37n/22w	-D 8000+	T	-	26/	br -D	Ilvington Court	5187+	37.14 N/ 21.52 W
27/1610	dt	U 28	Kuhnke	AM 2713	-D: 1599+	TA	SC.1	27/	nw -D	Eva	1599+	57.50 N/ 11.15 W
27/2147	dt	U 46	Endraß	AM 5482	ACL15007+	T	-	27/	br ACL	Dunvegan Castle	15007+	55. N/ 11. W
27/2231	dt	U 37	Oehrn	BE 2423	-D: 3409+	TA	-	27/	gr -D	Theodoros T.	3409+	50.10 N/ 19.50 W
28/0425	dt	U 101	Frauenheim	AM 1863	-D 6000+	T	-	28/	fi -D	Elle	3868+	57.43 N/ 12.18 W

North Sea — Atlantic

1	2	3	4	5	6		7	8	9	10	11	12	13	14	15

August 1940, cont.

28/2057	dt	U 28	Kuhnke	AM 1676	-D	6000+	T	HX.66	28/		br -D	Kyno	3946+	58.06 N/ 13.26 W	
29/0023	dt	U 100	Schepke	AM 4345	-D	9000+	T	OA.204	28/2330	br -D	Hartismere	5498=	56.04 N/ 13.06 W	
29/0023	dt	U 100	Schepke	AM 4345	-D	11000+	T	OA.204	28/2331	br -D	Dalblair	4608+	56.06 N/ 13.33 W	
29/0140	dt	U 100	Schepke	AM 2952	-D	3000+	T	OA.204	29/0007	br -D	Astra II	2393+	56.09 N/ 12.14 W	
29/0338	dt	U 100	Schepke	AM 2952	-D	3000+	T	OA.204s	29/0225	sw -D	Alida Gorthon	2373+	56.09 N/ 12.14 W	
29/0427	dt	U 100	Schepke	AM 2952	-D	5000+	T	OA.204s	29/0330	br -D	Empire Moose	6103+	56.06 N/ 13.33 W ?	
30/0220	dt	U 32	Jenisch	AM 3538	-D	8000+	T	HX.66A	30/0127	br -D	Mill Hill	4318+	58.48 N/ 06.49 W	
30/0232	dt	U 32	Jenisch	AM 3538	-D	7000+	T	HX.66A	30/0129	br -D	Chelsea	4804+	59.45 N/ 04.00 W ?	
30/0234	dt	U 32	Jenisch	AM 3538	-D	6000+	T	HX.66A	30/0129	nw -M	Norne	3971+	58.48 N/ 06.49 W	
30/2134	dt	U 59	Matz	AM 5245	-D	7000+	T	OB.205	30/	gr -D	San Gabriel	4943=§	56.04 N/ 09.54 W	4)
30/2153	dt	U 59	Matz	AM 5245	-T	12000+	T	OB.205	30/	br -MT	Anadara	8009=	56.15 N/ 09.10 W	
31/0000	dt	U 60	Schnee	AM 5217	-D	20000+	T	OB.205	30/	nl -D	Volendam	15434=	56.04 N/ 09.52 W	
31/0206	dt	U 59	Matz	AM 5157	-D	10000+	T	OB.205	31/	br -D	Har Zion	2508+	56.20 N/ 10. W	
31/	dt	U 38	Liebe	AM 5144	-D	5000+	T	OB.205						
31/1600	dt	U 46	Endraß	AM 0211	-D:	8000+	T	-	31/	be -D	Ville de Hasselt	7461+	57. N/ 09. W	

September 1940

1/0055	dt	U 101	Frauenheim	AM 4289	-D	5000+	T	-	31/	gr -D	Efploia	3867+	55.27 N/ 13.17 W	1)
1/1800	*dt*	*U 32*	*Jenisch*	*AM 1684*	*ACL*	*19700=*	*T*	*Task F.*	*1/*	*br CL*	*Fiji*	*8000=*	*58.25 N/ 13.10 W*	*2)*
2/1635	dt	U 47	Prien	AM 1685	-D:	7430+	T	-	2/	be -D	Ville de Mons	7463+	58.20 N/ 12. W	
2/2204	dt	U 46	Endraß	AM 4245	-T	8000+	T	OB.205d	2/	br -D	Thornlea	4261+	55.14 N/ 16.40 W	
2/2204	dt	U 46	Endraß	AM 4245	-D	5500+	T	OB.205d	2/	br -D	Bibury	4616+	North Atlantic	3)

4) The *San Gabriel* was damaged, towed into port, and was declared a total loss.
1) The wreck of the *Efploia* was sunk on Sept.1st by a British naval vessel.
2) *U 32* attacked the Dakar task force and reported torpedoing the AMC *Scythia*, but in reality the cruiser *Fiji* was hit
   and damaged.
3) The *Bibury* was missing after leaving the convoy OB.205 on Sept.1st. For a long time it was assumed that she was sunk by a
   German AMC. But there was one dead member of the crew swept ashore at Tobermory. So the report of the sinking on Sept.2nd
   seems correct.

1	2	3	4	5	6	7	8	9	10	11	12	13	14	15
September 1940, cont.														
3/0326	dt	U 60	Schnee	AM 5154	–D 7000+	T	–	3/		br –D	Ulva	1401+	55.45 N/ 11.45 W	
4/0128	dt	U 47	Prien	AL 3866	–D 5500+	T	OA.207	4/		br –D	Titan	9035+	58.14 N/ 15.50 W	
4/0129	dt	U 47	Prien	AL 3866	–D 4000=	T	OA.207							
4/	dt	U 46	Endraß	BF 1796	–D: 1074+	A	–	4/		br –D	Luimneach	1074+	47.50 N/ 09.12 W	
7/0404	dt	U 47	Prien	AL 3678	–D 10000+	T	SC.2	7/		br –D	Neptunian	5155+	58.27 N/ 17.17 W	
7/0515	dt	U 47	Prien	AL 3678	–D 5500+	T	SC.2	7/		br –D	Jose de Larrinaga	5303+	58.30 N/ 16.10 W	
7/0533	dt	U 47	Prien	AL 3678	–D 5000+	T	SC.2	7/		nw –D	Gro	4211+	58.30 N/ 16.10 W	
8/0030	it	FAA' DI BRUNO	Enrici	37n/21w	–D 4300=	T	–							
9/0024	dt	U 47	Prien	AM 0249	–T 7000+	T	SC.2	8/2330		gr –D	Possidon	3840+	56.43 N/ 09.16 W	
9/0447	dt	U 28	Kuhnke	AM 0294	–D 7000+	T	SC.2	9/0345		br –D	Mardinian	2434+	56.37 N/ 09. W	
9/1040.	it	FAA' DI BRUNO	Enrici	36n/22w	–D 8000=	A	–							
11/0326	dt	U 28	Kuhnke	AL 6369	–T 10000=	T	OA.210							
11/0327	dt	U 28	Kuhnke	AL 6369	–T 7000+	T	OA.210	11/		br –D	Harpenden	4678=	55.34 N/ 15.56 W	
11/0328	dt	U 28	Kuhnke	AL 6369	–D 6000+	T	OA.210	11/		nl –D	Maas	1966+	55.34 N/ 15.56 W	
11/0716	dt	U 99	Kretschmer	AM 0173	–D 2300+	T	–	11/		br –D	Albionic	2468+	North Atlantic	4)
14/0830	it	EMO	Liannazza	41n/22w	–D: 6000+	TA	SLS.46 d	14/		br –D	Saint Agnes	5199+	41.27 N/ 21.50 W	
15/0024	dt	U 48	Bleichrodt	AM 1998	–D 6000+	T	SC.3	14/2328		br –D	Empire Soldier	-----		4b)
15/0025	*dt*	*U 48*	*Bleichrodt*	*AM 1998*	*PS: 1060+*	*T*	*SC.3*	*14/2328*		*br PS*	*Dundee*	*1060+*	*56.45 N/ 14.14 W*	
15/0123	dt	U 48	Bleichrodt	AM 1998	–D: 4343+	T	SC.3	15/0045		gr –D	Alexandros	4343+	56.50 N/ 15.04 W	
15/0300	dt	U 48	Bleichrodt	AM 1998	–D 7000+	T	SC.3	15/0210		br –D	Empire Volunteer	5319+	56.43 N/ 15.17 W	
15/	dt	U 48	Bleichrodt	AM 1988	–D ?	T	SC.3s	15/		br –D	Kenordoc	1780+	57.42 N/ 15.02 W	4c)
16/0241	dt	U 99	Kretschmer	AM 1751	–D: 1327+	T	–	15/		nw –D	Lotos	1327+	15m NE Rockall	

4) The *Albionic* departed on Aug.31st from Wabana / New Foundland and was missing after Sept.11th. For a long time it was assumed she was sunk by a German AMC.

4b) The *Empire Soldier* was slightly damaged by a collision earlier, and was missed by the torpedoes.

4c) There are some doubts about the sinking of the *Kenordoc* by *U 48*. The ship may have been sunk by gunfire from another U-boat.

1	2	3	4	5	6	7	8	9	10 11	12	13	14	15
September 1940, cont.													
17/0832 dt		U 99	Kretschmer	AM 1734	-D: 2372+	TA	HX.71s	17/	br -D	Crown Arun	2372+	58.02 N/ 14.18 W	
17/1626 dt		U 65	vStockhausen	AM 1574	-D 5800+	T	HX.71	17/	br -D	Tregenna	5242+	58.22 N/ 15.42 W	
18/0001 dt		U 48	Bleichrodt	AL 2966	-D:11100+	T	.	17/	br -D	City of Benares	11081+	56.43 N/ 21.15 W	
18/0007 dt		U 48	Bleichrodt	AL 2966	-D: 5100+	T	.	17/	br -D	Marina	5088+	56.46 N/ 21.15 W	
18/1849 dt		U 48	Bleichrodt	AL 2881	-D: 3100+	T	.	18/	br -D	Magdalena	3118+	57.20 N/ 20.16 W	
18/	it	BAGNOLINI	Tosoni-Pittoni	Oporto	-D: 5000+	T	-	18/	sp -D	Cabo Tortosa	3302+	near Oporto	
19/0315 it		MARCONI	Chialamberto	43n/09w	-Df 500+	T	-	19/	sp -Df	Almirante Jose de Carranza	330+	16m NW C.Villano	
19/1720 it		FAA' DI BRUNO	Enrici	36n/22w	-D 5000=	T	-						
20/2120 dt		U 138	Lüth	AM 5365	-D 7500+	T	OB.216	20/	br -DT	New Sevilla	13801+	55.48 N/ 07.22 W	
20/2123 dt		U 138	Lüth	AM 5365	-D 6500+	T	OB.216	20/	pa -D	Boka	5560+	55.54 N/ 07.24 W	
20/2126 dt		U 138	Lüth	AM 5365	-D 6000+	T	OB.216	20/	br -D	Empire Adventure	5145+	Islay	
21/0227 dt		U 138	Lüth	AM 5318	-D 7500+	T	OB.216	21/	br -D	City of Simla	10138+	55.55 N/ 08.20 W	
21/0312 dt		U 99	Kretschmer	AL 5432	-T: 9154+	T	HX.72	21/	br -MT	Invershannon	9154+	55.40 N/ 22.04 W	5)
21/0419 dt		U 99	Kretschmer	AL 5438	-D: 3660+	T	HX.72	21/	br -D	Baron Blythswood	3668+	56. N/ 23. W	
21/0447 dt		U 99	Kretschmer	AL 5462	-D: 5156+	TA	HX.72	21/	br -D	Elmbank	5156+	55.20 N/ 22.30 W	6)
21/15 dt		U 47	Prien	AL 5462	-D: 5156=	A							
21/0614 dt		U 48	Bleichrodt	AL 5436	-D: 4409+	T	HX.72	21/	br -D	Blairangus	4409+	55.18 N/ 22.21 W	
21/2310 dt		U 100	Schepke	AL 6549	-D 5000+	T	HX.72	21/2220	br -D	Canonesa	8286+	54.55 N/ 18.25 W	
21/2310 dt		U 100	Schepke	AL 6549	-T:10380+	T	HX.72	21/2220	br -MT	Torinia	10364+	55. N/ 19. W	
21/2311 dt		U 100	Schepke	AL 6549	-D 5000+?	T	HX.72						
21/2313 dt		U 100	Schepke	AL 6549	-D 4000+	T	HX.72	21/	br -D	Dalcairn	4608+	55. N/ 19. W	
21/2338 dt		U 48	Bleichrodt	AL 6554	-D: 5800+	T	HX.72	21/	br -D	Broompark	5136=	55.08 N/ 18.30 W	
22/0022 dt		U 100	Schepke	AL 6551	-T 11000+	T	HX.72	22/	br -D	Empire Airman	6586+	54. N/ 18. W	
22/0050 dt		U 100	Schepke	AL 6553	-D 5000+	T	HX.72	22/	br -D	Scholar	3940+	55.11 N/ 17.58 W	7)

5) The *Invershannon* was sunk at 21/1142 by a coup de grâce from *U 99*.
6) The *Elmbank* was first damaged by torpedo, then from 21/0600 *U 99* fired 88 rounds of 88mm at her, many of which hit the ship.
In the afternoon the ship was set on fire by gunfire first from *U 47* and then from *U 99*, which finally administered the
coup de grâce.
7) The *Schilar* sank on Sept. 24th at 54.38 N/ 16.40 W.

1	2	3	4	5	6	7	8	9	10	11	12	13	14	15
September 1940, cont.														
22/0152	dt	U 100	Schepke	AL 6553	-T 14600+	T	HX.72	22/	br	-DT	Frederick S.Fales	10525+	55.30 N/ 13.40 W	
22/0214	dt	U 100	Schepke	AL 6553	-D 7500+	T	HX.72	22/	nw	-D	Simla	6031+	55.11 N/ 17.58 W	
22/0646	dt	U 32	Jenisch	AL 6626	-D: 7886=	TA	HX.72	22/	br	-D	Collegian	7886=	320m W Malin Head	
22/	dt	U 31	Prellberg	AM	-Df +	A	-	22/	fa	-Df	Union Jack	81+	100m NWzN Butt of Lewis	
25/	*fr*	*BÉVÉZIERS*	*Lancelot*	*Dakar*	*BB:29150=*	*T*	*Task F.*	*25/*	*br*	*BB*	*Resolution*	*29150=*	*near Dakar*	*8)*
25/0325	dt	U 32	Jenisch	AL 0158	-D: 6694+	T	-	25/	br	-D	Mabriton	6694+	56.12 N/ 23. W	
25/1330	dt	U 43	Ambrosius	AL 6784	-D: 4500+	T	OB.217d	25/	br	-D	Sulairia	5802+	53.43 N/ 20.10 W	
25/1402	dt	U 29	Schuhart	AL 9111	-D: 6300+	T	OB.217d	25/	br	-D	Eurymedon	6223+	53.34 N/ 20.23 W	
26/0050	dt	U 137	Wohlfarth	AM 5720	-D 5000+	T	.	26/	br	-D	Manchester Brigade	6042+	54.53 N/ 10.22 W	
26/0051	dt	U 137	Wohlfarth	AM 5720	-D 5000+	T	.	26/	br	-D	Ashantian	4917=	55.10 N/ 11. W	
26/0135	dt	U 137	Wohlfarth	AM 4960	-T 8000+	T	.	26/	br	-DT	Stratford	4753+	54.50 N/ 10.40 W	
26/0135	dt	U 46	Endraß	BE 3483	-D 3000+	T	OG.43s	26/	br	-D	Coast Wings	862+	North Atlantic	
26/0234	dt	U 32	Jenisch	AL 4885	-D: 6863=	T	OB.217d	26/	br	-D	Corrientes	6863+	53.49 N/ 24.19 W	9)
28/2140	dt	U 37	Oehrn	AL 5753	-D: 6800+	TA	OB.217d							
26/0410	dt	U 137	Wohlfarth	AM 4960	-D 7000+	T	.	27/	nw	-D	Asgerd	1308+	56.34 N/ 09.10 W	10)
26/0811	dt	U 32	Jenisch	AL 7217	-M: 6094+	T	OB.217d	26/	nw	-M	Tancred	6094+	53.32 N/ 24.35 W	
26/1337	dt	U 32	Jenisch	AL 7127	-D: 4084+	T	OB.217d	26/	br	-D	Darcoila	4084+	North Atlantic	
26/2120	dt	U 46	Endraß	BE 2272	-D 5000+	T	-	26/	sw	-D	Siljan	3058+	350m SW Ireland	
27/1113	dt	U 31	Prellberg	AL	-D: 4319+	T	-	27/	nw	-D	Vestvard	4319+	300m W Ireland	
27/2259	dt	U 37	Oehrn	AL 9731	-D 4000+	T	-	29/	äg	-D	Georges Mabro	2555+	52. N/ 19. W	11)
28/1609	dt	U 32	Jenisch	AL 5461	-D: 5758+	TA	-	28/	br	-D	Empire Ocelot	5759+	54.37 N/ 21.30 W	

8) The *Resolution* was participating in the British/Free French attack on Dakar, and was torpedoed by the Vichy-French submarine.
9) The *Corrientes* was torpedoed on Sept.26th by *U 32*, but remained afloat. The abandoned wreck was sunk on Sept.28th by *U-37* with torpedo and gunfire.
10) The Allied and German dates differ, but there was no other German U-boat in the area.

North Sea - Atlantic

1	2	3	4	5	6	7	8	9	10	11	12	13	14	15
September 1940, cont.														
29/0053 dt	U 32	Jenisch	AL 4587	-D: 5267+	T	-	29/	br	-D	Bassa	5267+	54.	N/ 21.	W
30/1013 dt	U 37	Oehrn	AL 6832	-D: 5300+	TA	-	30/	br	-D	Samala	5390+	46.	N/ 33.	W
30/2156 dt	U 37	Oehrn	AL 9267	-D: 2500+	T	-	30/	br	-D	Heminge	2499+	53.26 N/ 18.33 W	
October 1940														
1/ dt	U 32	Jenisch	AK 6987	-D: 3278+	A	-	1/	nl	-D	Haulerwijk	3278+	53.34 N/ 27.28 W	
1/0647 dt	U 38	Liebe	AL 9422	ACL14172+	T	-	1/	br	-M	Highland Patriot	14172+	52.20 N/ 19.04 W	
1/1615 it	BARACCA	Bertarelli	40n/17w	-D: 3980+	A	-	1/	gr	-D	Aghios Nicolaos	3687+	40.	N/ 16.55 W	
2/1825 dt	U 32	Jenisch	AL 7884	-D: 4606+	T	-	2/	br	-D	Kayeson	4606+	51.12 N/ 24.22 W	
3/0435 it	GLAUCO	Mellina	36n/06w	APC 1500=	T	-							
5/0413 it	NANI	Polizzi	36n/07w	-T 7000+	T	-	5/	br	APC	Kingston Sapphire	356+	W Gibraltar	
6/1304 dt	U 123	Moehle	AL 7124	-D: 5943+	T	-	6/	br	-D	Benlawers	5943+	53.20 N/ 26.10 W	
6/1809 dt	U 37	Oehrn	AL 8424	-T: 6989+	T	-	6/	br	-DT	British General	6989+	51.42 N/ 24.03 W	1)
6/2204 dt	U 103	Schütze	AL 7191	-T 10000+	T	-	6/	nw	-MT	Nina Borthen	6123+	54.	N/ 26.	W
7/1601 dt	U 59	Matz	AM 5445	-D 9500+	T	-	7/	nw	-M	Touraine	5811+	55.14 N/ 10.34 W	
8/2131 dt	U 58	Schonder	AM 29	-D 10528+	T	HX.76s	8/	br	-D	Confield	4956+	56.48 N/ 10.17 W	2)
9/2211 dt	U 103	Schütze	AL 1762	-D 7000+	T	SC.6	9/2015	gr	-D	Zannes Gounaris	4407+	58.11 N/ 13.57 W	
9/2212 dt	U 103	Schütze	AL 1762	-D 4500=	T	SC.6	9/2015	br	-D	Graigwen (s.u.)	3697=	58.11 N/ 13.57 W	3)
9/2213 dt	U 103	Schütze	AL 1762	-D 7000+	T	SC.6	9/2015	gr	-D	Delphin	3816+	58.11 N/ 13.57 W	
10/2144 dt	U 123	Moehle	AM 1848	-D 7500+	Tf	SC.6s	10/	br	-D	Graigwen (s.o.)	3697+	58.11 N/ 13.57 W	3)
11/2150 dt	U 48	Bleichrodt	AL 0378	-D 4721+	T	HX.77	11/	nw	-M	Brandanger	4624+	57.10 N/ 17.	W
11/2209 dt	U 48	Bleichrodt	AL 0378	-D: 8390+	T	HX.77	11/2100	br	-M	Port Gisborne	10144+	56.38 N/ 16.40 W	4)
12/0014 dt	U 48	Bleichrodt	AL 0381	-D 8000+	T	HX.77	11/	nw	-DT	Davanger	7102+	57.	N/ 19.10 W	
12/1252 it	TAZZOLI	Raccanelli	36n/10w	-D: 5135+	TA	-	12/	jg	₮D	Orao	5135+	35.34 N/ 10.35 W	

1) The *British General* sank only after four additional torpedoes were fired at her by *U 37* Oct.7th/0906.
2) The *Confield* was hit by one additional torpedo on Oct.8th and sank after a coup de grâce was administered the forenoon of Oct.9th.
3) The *Graigwen* was damaged by the first attack of *U 103*, and sank after a coup de grâce from *U 123*.

October 1940, cont.

1	2	3	4	5	6	7	8	9	10	11	12	13	14	15
12/1803	dt	U 59	Matz	AM 2973	-M: 6800+	T	HX.77	12/	br	-M	Pacific Ranger	6895+	56.20 N/ 11.43 W	
12/2325	dt	U 101	Frauenheim	AM 4214	-D: 5779+	T	HX.77s	12/	ca	-D	Saint Malô	5779+	57.58 N/ 16.32 W	
13/0846	dt	U 103	Schütze	AM 0127	-D: 1186+	T	-	13/	es	-D	Nora	1186+	57.02 N/ 13.11 W	
13/1532	dt	U 138	Lüth	AM 5329	-D: 4562=	T	-	13/	nw	-M	Dagrun	4562=	.	4)
13/1957	dt	U 37	Oehrn	AM 1694	-D: 5804+	T	HX.77	13/	br	-D	Stangrant	5804+	58.27 N/ 12.36 W	
14/2128	dt	U 137	Wohlfarth	AM 4561	ACL11275=	T	-	14/	br	ACL	Cheshire	10552=	NW Ireland	5)
15/0018	dt	U 93	Korth	AM 2563	-D 6000=	T	OB.227	14/	br	-D	Hurunui	9331+	58.58 N/ 09.54 W	6)
15/0510	dt	U 138	Lüth	AM 3941	-T 11000+	T	OB.228	15/	br	-D	Bonheur	5327+	57.10 N/ 08.36 W	
15/0515	dt	U 138	Lüth	AM 3941	-T 12000+	T	OB.228	15/	br	-MT	British Glory	6993=	57.10 N/ 08.36 W	
15/1933	dt	U 103	Schütze	AL 3639	-D: 4800+	T	OB.227	15/	br	-D	Thistlegarth	4747+	58.43 N/ 15. W	
15/2315	it	CAPPELLINI	Todaro	32n/31w	-D: 7545+	A	OB.223 d	15/	be	-D	Kabalo	5186+	32. N/ 31.20 W	
16/0350	dt	U 124	Schulz	AL 2876	-D: 1813+	T	SC.7 s	16/0235	ca	-D	Trevisa	1813+	57.28 N/ 20.30 W	
17/0317	dt	U 93	Korth	AE 8783	-D 6000=	T	OB.228	17/	nw	-D	Dokka	1168+	60.46 N/ 16.30 W	6)
17/0339	dt	U 93	Korth	AE 8783	-T 10000=	T	OB.228	17/	br	-D	Uskbridge	2715+	60.40 N/ 15.50 W	6)
17/0553	dt	U 48	Bleichrodt	AL 3388	-T 10000+	T	SC.7	17/0400	br	-MT	Languedoc	9512+	59.14 N/ 17.51 W	
17/0553	dt	U 48	Bleichrodt	AL 3388	-D 6000+	T	SC.7	17/0400	br	-D	Scoresby	3843+	59.14 N/ 17.51 W	
17/0553	dt	U 48	Bleichrodt	AL 3388	-D 5000=	T	SC.7	17/0400	br	-D	Haspenden	4678=	59.14 N/ 17.51 W	7)
17/0951	dt	U 38	Liebe	AM 1632	-D: 3554+	TA	SC.7 s	17/	gr	-D	Aenos	3554+	59. N/ 13. W	
18/0204	dt	U 38	Liebe	AM 1539	-D 6000=	T	SC.7	18/	br	-D	Carsbreck	3670=	58.46 N/ 14.11 W	
18/1025	dt	U 48	Bleichrodt	AL 2593	-D 4500+	T	OB.22.?	18/	br	-D	Sandsend	3612+	58.12 N/ 21.29 W	
18/2020	dt	U 123	Moehle	AM 1844	-D 11000+	T	SC.7 r	18/	br	-D	Shekatika (s.o.)	5458=	57.12 N/ 11.08 W	

4) The name *Dagrun* was only established by the xB-Dienst. There is no report about damage by enemy action in Allied documents.
5) The *Cheshire* was hit by one torpedo and had to be laid up for repairs for 6 months in Liverpool.
6) During 3 attacks by *U 93*, the torpedoes missed the target ships, but hit other ships in the convoy. The *Uskbridge* was sunk by a coup de grâce from *U 93*, but the U-boat claimed a ship of 2,500 gross tons.
7) Because of contradicting reports in the archives, it is very difficult to establish with certainty the U-boats responsible for the attacks against SC.7. The evaluation was made in a combined effort with Mr. Coppock and Vice Admiral Sir Peter Gretton (RN.ret), and is the most probable assessment from the available documents of both sides.

1	2	3	4	5	6	7	8	9	10	11	12	13	14	15

October 1940, cont.

1	2	3	4	5	6	7	8	9	10 11	12	13	14	15
18/2100 dt	U 46		Endraß	AM 2922	-D	7000=	T	SC.7					
18/2103 dt	U 46		Endraß	AM 2922	-D	4000+	T	SC.7(11) 18/	br -D	Beatus	4885+	57.31 N/ 13.10 W	
18/2104 dt	U 46		Endraß	AM 2922	-D	4000+	T	SC.7(12) 18/2015	sw -D	Convallaria	1996+	57.22 N/ 11.11 W	
18/2112 dt	U 101		Frauenheim	AM 2921	-D	6000+	T	SC.7(91) 18/2117	br -D	Creekirk	3971+	57.30 N/ 11.10 W	
18/2112 dt	U 101		Frauenheim	AM 2921	-D	5000+	T	SC.7					
18/2206 dt	U 99		Kretschmer	AM 2924	-D	6500+	T	SC.7(81) 18/2115	br -D	Empire Miniver	6055+	310° 250m Rathlin Head	
18/2225 dt	U 46		Endraß	AM 2929	-D	6000+	T	SC.7(33) 18/	sw -D	Gunborg	1572+	57.14 N/ 11. W	
18/2308 dt	U 101		Frauenheim	AM 2952	-D	6000+	T	SC.7(13) 18/	br -D	Blairspey (s.d.)	4155=	57.55 N/ 11.10 W	8)
18/2309 dt	U 101		Frauenheim	AM 2952	-D	3500+	T	SC.7					7)
18/2309 dt	U 101		Frauenheim	AM 2952	-D	6000=	T	SC.7					7)
18/2317 dt	U 100		Schepke	AM 2921	-D:	5458=	Tf	SC.7 s	18/2228 br -D	Shekatika (s.a.)	5458=	57.12 N/ 11.08 W	9)
18/2330 dt	U 99		Kretschmer	AM 2928	-D	7000+	T	SC.7(73) 18/	gr -D	Niritos	3854+	57.14 N/ 10.38 W	7)
18/2337 dt	U 100		Schepke	AM 2916	-D	3500+	T	SC.7 s	18/	nl -D	Boekolo (s.d.)	2118=	56.40 N/ 10.45 W	9a)
18/2355 dt	U 99		Kretschmer	AM 2928	-D	6000+	T	SC.7(62) 18/	br -D	Fiscus	4815+	57.29 N/ 11.10 W	7)
19/0122 dt	U 101		Frauenheim	AM 2958	-D	7000+	T	SC.7					7)
19/0122 dt	U 101		Frauenheim	AM 2958	-D	7000+	T	SC.7					7)
19/0122 dt	U 101		Frauenheim	AM 2958	-D	4000+	T	SC.7(51) 19/0030	br -D	Assyrian	2962+	57.12 N/ 10.43 W	
19/0124 dt	U 101		Frauenheim	AM 2958	-D	3000+	T	SC.7( ) 19/0030	nl -D	Soesterberg	1904+	57.12 N/ 10.43 W	
19/0131 dt	U 123		Moehle	AM 2950	-D	7000+	T	SC.7 s	18/2118 nl -D	Boekolo (s.a.)	2118+	57.14 N/ 10.38 W	9a)
19/0138 dt	U 99		Kretschmer	AM 2955	-D	6000+	T	SC.7(54) 19/0030	br -D	Empire Brigade	5154+	57.12 N/ 10.43 W	7)
19/0155 dt	U 99		Kretschmer	AM 2957	-D	7000+	T	SC.7(72) 19/	gr -D	Thalia	5875+	57.00 N/ 11.30 W	7)
19/0155 dt	U 123		Moehle	AM 2950	-D	4000+	T	SC.7(71) 19/0100	br -D	Sedgepool	5556+	57.20 N/ 11.22 W	7)
19/0250 dt	U 100		Schepke	AM 2919	-D:	4155=	T	SC.7 s	19/	br -D	Blairspey	4155=	57.55 N/ 11.10 W	8)
19/0302 dt	U 99		Kretschmer	AM 2981	-D	9500+	T	SC.7( ) 19/0138	nw -D	Snefjeld	1643+	57.28 N/ 11.10 W	7)
19/0311 dt	U 123		Moehle	AM 2950	-D	5500+	Tf	SC.7 s	19/	br -D	Shekatika (s.a.)	5458+	57.12 N/ 11.08 W	9)

8) The *Blairspey* was hit by one or two torpedoes from *U 101*, and two from *U 100*, but remained afloat because of its load of timber and was saved.
9) The *Shekatika* was a romper, hit by 3 torpedoes from *U 123*, then one from *U 100*, and finally sunk by *U 123*. Timber loaded.
9a) The *Boekolo* remained behind to rescue survivors of the *Beatus*, and was hit probably by *U 100* and *U 123*.
    The numbers in brackets behind SC.7 give the position of the ship in the convoy at the time of torpedoing.

1	2	3	4	5	6	7	8	9	10	11	12	13	14	15

October 1940, cont.

1	2	3	4	5	6	7	8	9	10 11	12	13	14	15
19/0358 dt	U 99	Kretschmer	AM 2981	-D: 3106=	T	SC.7	19/	br -D	Clintonia	3106+	57.10 N/ 11.20 W	10)
19/0504 dt	U 123	Moehle	AM 2981	-D: 3106+	A							
19/2213 dt	U 38	Liebe	AL 0357	-D	7000+	T	HX.79	19/2118 br -D	Matheran	7653+	57. N/ 17. W	
19/2219 dt	U 38	Liebe	AL 0357	-D	6000+	T	HX.79	19/2121 br -D	Uganda	4966+	56.37 N/ 17.15 W	
19/2227 dt	U 47	Prien	AL 0372	-D	5500+	T	HX.79	19/2145 nl -D	Bilderdijk	6856+	56.35 N/ 17.15 W	
19/2331 dt	U 47	Prien	AL 0346	-T	8000+	T	HX.79	19/2322 br -MT	Shirak	6023+	57.00 N/ 16.53 W	11)
20/0024 dt	U 48	Bleichrodt	AL 0355	-T	7000+	Tf	HX.79					
19/2346 dt	U 47	Prien	AL 0357	-D	7000+	T	HX.79	19/2322 br -D	Wandby	4947+	56.45 N/ 17.07 W	12)
19/2346 dt	U 46	Endraß	AL 6331	-D	4000+	T	HX.79					
19/2347 dt	U 46	Endraß	AL 6331	-D	5000+	T	HX.79	19/2323 br -D	Ruperra	4548+	57. N/ 16. W	
19/2354 dt	U 47	Prien	AL 0357	-D	4500+	T	HX.79					13)
20/0015 dt	U 100	Schepke	AL 0381	-T	12000+	T	HX.79	19/2315 br -MT	Caprella	8230+	56.37 N/ 17.15 W	
20/0016 dt	U 100	Schepke	AL 0381	-T	10000+	T	HX.79	19/2315 br -MT	Sitala	6218+	150m SW Rockall	
20/0037 dt	U 47	Prien	AL 0356	-D	7000+	T	HX.79	19/2340 br -D	La Estancia	5185+	57. N/ 17. W	14)
20/0043 dt	U 47	Prien	AL 0356	-D	5000+	T	HX.79					14)
20/0143 dt	U 124	Schulz	AL 1738	-D	8500+	T	OB.229	20/	nw -D	Cubano	5810+	57.55 N/ 25. W	
20/0148 dt	U 47	Prien	AL 0364	-D	4000+	T	HX.79	20/0124 br -D	Whitford Point	5026+	56.38 N/ 16.00 W	
20/0204 dt	U 47	Prien	AL 0365	-T	9000=	T	HX.79	20/0124 br -MT	Athelmonarch	8995=	56.45 N/ 15.58 W	
20/0229 dt	U 124	Schulz	AL 1738	-D	5000+	T	OB.229	20/	br -D	Sulaco	5389+	57.25 N/ 25. W	
20/0325 dt	U 46	Endraß	AM 4137	-T	12000+	T	HX.79 s	20/0200 sw -MT	Janus	9965+	56.36 N/ 15.03 W	
20/0720 dt	U 100	Schepke	AM 4149	-D: 5458+	TA	HX.79 s	20/0630 br -D	Loch Lomond	5452+	56.00 N/ 14.30 W	
20/	it MALASPINA	Leoni	59n/29w	-D	8000+	T	OB.229d					

---

10) The *Clintonia* remained afloat after the torpedo hit by *U 99*, and was sunk by gunfire from *U 123*.

11) *U 47* observed a column of fire shooting up. The *Shirak* then remained behind the convoy, and was stopped when *U 48* sank her by torpedo.

12) *U 46* and *U 47* attacked at the same time from the same side of the convoy. Both U-boats may have hit the *Wandby*, but it is more probable that only *U 47* hit the ship. The *Wandby* later sank on Oct.21st.

13) The torpedo missed the target. *U 47* assumed wrongly to have hit another ship behind the target.

14) There is a possibility that both torpedoes from *U 47* hit the same ship, the *La Estancia*.

1	2	3	4	5	6	7	8	9	10	11	12	13	14	15
October 1940, cont.														
26/0432 dt	U 28	Kuhnke	AL 3862	-D: 5389+	T	-	26/	br	-D	Matina	5389+	57.30 N/ 16.31 W	14)
29/2200 dt	U 31	Prellberg	AM	-D	+	Tf	-							
27/0000 it	NANI	Polizzi	37n/24w	-D: 4000+	A	-	27/	sw	-D	Meggie	1583+	60m E Azores	
28/ dt	U 32	Jenisch	AM 55	-D:42348+	T	2 DD's	28/	br	-D	Empreß of Britain	42348+	55.16 N/ 09.50 W	15)
31/2158 dt	U 124	Schulz	AL 3662	-D 6000+	T	HX.82s	31/	br	-D	Rutland	1437+	57.14 N/ 16. W	
November 1940														
1/0706 dt	U 124	Schulz	AL 3465	-D 8034+	T	HX.82s	1/	br	-D	Empire Bison	5612+	59.30 N/ 17.40 W	
3/2140 dt	U 99	Kretschmer	AM 4875	-D: 5376+	T	-	3/	br	-D	Casanare	5376+	53.58 N/ 14.13 W	
3/2250 dt	U 99	Kretschmer	AM 4796	ACL18724+	T	-	3/	br	ACL	Laurentic	18724+	54.09 N/ 13.44 W	1)
4/0002 dt	U 99	Kretschmer	AM 4796	ACL11314+	T	-	3/	br	ACL	Patroclus	11314+	53.43 N/ 14.41 W	1)
5/0255 dt	U 99	Kretschmer	AM 4577	-T 9000+	T	HX.83	5/0210	br	-MT	Scottish Maiden	6993+	54.36 N/ 14.23 W	
9/2105 it	MARCONI	Chialamberto	55n/18w	-D 10000+	Tf	HX.84	9/	sw	-M	Vingaland	2734+	55.41 N/ 18.24 W	2)
10/0618 it	*BARBARIGO*	*Ghiglieri*	*54n/18w*	*DD 1500+*	*T*	*.*							
13/2108 dt	U 137	Wohlfarth	AM 5429	-D 8000+	T	.	13/	br	-D	Cape St.Andrew	5094+	55.14 N/ 10.29 W	3)
15/1511 dt	U 65	vStockhausen	ET 9117	-D: 5168+	T	-	15/	br	-D	Kohinur	5168+	04.24 N/ 13.46 W	
15/1811 dt	U 65	vStockhausen	ET 9117	-T 8000+	T	-	15/	nw	-MT	Havbör	7614+	04.24 N/ 13.46 W	
16/1429 dt	U 65	vStockhausen	ET 8944	-D: 3059+	T	-	16/	br	-D	Fabian	3059+	02.49 N/ 15.29 W	
16/2015 dt	U 137	Wohlfarth	AM 5427	-D: 5880+	T	HG.	16/	br	-D	Planter	5887+	55.38 N/ 08.28 W	
17/2014 dt	U 137	Wohlfarth	AM 5289	-D 6000+	T	HG.	17/	sw	-D	Veronica	1316+	55.20 N/ 08.45 W	
17/2050 dt	U 137	Wohlfarth	AM 5289	-D 4000+	T	HG.	17/	br	-M	Saint Germain	1044+	55.40 N/ 08.40 W	

14) *U 28* did not observe the *Matina* going down. So the wreck sunk by *U 31* very probably was the *Matina*.

15) The *Empreß of Britain* was set on fire by bombs from German aircraft. During the salvage operation she was sunk by two torpedoes from *U 32*.

1) The *Laurentic* sank after two additional torpedoes were fired at 4/0453; the *Patroclus*, after five torpedoes were fired at 4/0525.

2) The *Marconi* reported having sunk one damaged ship. Probably it was the *Vingaland*, damaged by bombs from a Focke-Wulf "Condor" of K.G.40 on November 8th.

3) *U 137* reported the *Cape St. Andrew* to have been under tow and escorted by one destroyer.

1	2	3	4	5	6	7	8	9	10	11	12	13	14	15
November 1940, cont.														
18/1740	it	BARACCA	Bertarelli	53n/18w	-D: 4866+	T	SLS.53d	18/	br	-D	Lilian Moller	4866+	57. N/ 17. W	
18/1802	dt	U 65	vStockhausen	ET 2821	-T: 5065+	T	-	18/	br	-MT	Congonian	5056+	08.21 N/ 16.12 W	
21/0740	dt	U 103	Schütze	AM 4241	-D 6000+	T	OB.244	21/	br	-D	Daydawn	4768+	56.30 N/ 14.10 W	
21/0740	dt	U 103	Schütze	AM 4241	-D 5000=?	T	OB.244							4)
21/0750	dt	U 103	Schütze	AM 4241	-D 5000+	T	OB.244	21/	gr	-D	Victoria	6085+	56.17 N/ 14.12 W	
22/0021	dt	U 123	Moehle	AL 6572	-D: 4791+	T	-	22/	br	-D	Cree	4791+	54.39 N/ 18.50 W	
23/0018	dt	U 100	Schepke	AM 4568	-D 5000+	T	SC.11	23/	br	-D	Justitia	4562+	55. N/ 13.10 W	
23/0101	dt	U 100	Schepke	AM 4566	-D 4500+	T	SC.11	23/	br	-D	Bradfyne	4740+	55.04 N/ 12.15 W	
23/0117	dt	U 100	Schepke	AM 4566	-D 4500+	T	SC.11	23/	nw	-D	Bruse	2205+	55.04 N/ 12.15 W	
23/0414	dt	U 100	Schepke	AM 4641	-D 7500+	T	SC.11	23/	nl	-D	Cotmarsum	3628+	55. N/ 12. W	
23/0418	dt	U 123	Moehle	AL 3981	-D 6000+	T	OB.244	23/	br	-D	Oakcrest	5407+	53. N/ 17. W	
23/0436	dt	U 100	Schepke	AM 4642	-D 5500+	T	SC.11	23/	nw	-D	Salonica	2694+	55.16 N/ 12.14 W	
23/0553	dt	U 123	Moehle	AL 3958	-D 3300+	T	OB.244	23/	gr	-D	Kolchis	2219+	North Atlantic	5)
23/0712	dt	U 123	Moehle	AL 3958	-D 6000+	T	OB.244	23/	br	-D	King Idwal	5115+	56.44 N/ 19.13 W	
23/0802	dt	U 100	Schepke	AM 4662	-D 7000+	T	SC.11	23/	br	-M	Leise Maersk	3136+	55.30 N/ 11. W	
23/0815	dt	U 123	Moehle	AL 3958	-D: 5228+	T	OB.244	23/	br	-D	Tymeric	5228+	57. N/ 20.30 W	
23/0914	dt	U 123	Moehle	AL 3958	-D: 5123+	T	OB.244	23/	sw	-D	Anten	5135+	56.57 N/ 18.18 W	
23/2105	dt	U 100	Schepke	AM 5523	-D 7000+	T	SC.11	23/	nl	-D	Bussum	3636+	55.39 N/ 08.58 W	
27/	dt	U 104	Jürst	-------	---------	T	HX.88s	27/	br	-D	Diplomat	8240+	55.42 N/ 11.37 W	6)
27/	dt	U 104	Jürst	-------	---------	T	HX.87	27/	br	-MT	Charles F.Meyer	10516=	56. N/ 13.52 W	6)
27/0058	dt	U 95	Schreiber	AM 1986	-D 3000+	T	-	28/	br	-D	Irene Maria	1860+	North Atlantic	7)

4) *U 103* reported to have hit a steamer running directly for the U-boat, but the torpedo glanced off and did not explode.
5) The *Kolchis* was reported missing since Nov.23rd. Probably it was the ship identified by *U 123* as British S/S *Blairesk*.
6) The *Diplomat* and *Charles F. Meyer* must have been attacked by the missing *U 104*, because there is no other report.
7) The *Irene Maria* was reported missing since Nov.28th. There is no other ship reported to have been attacked by *U 95*.

1	2	3	4	5	6	7	8	9	10	11	12	13	14	15

November 1940, cont.

27/1956 dt		U 103	Schütze	AM 4818	-M: 4400+	T	-	27/		br -M	Glenmoor	4393+	54.35 N/ 14.31 W	
28/0827 dt		U 95	Schreiber	AL 6282	-D: 1298+	T	-	28/		nw -D	Ringhorn	1298=	55.29 N/ 18.01 W	
28/0842 dt		U 103	Schütze	AL 6698	-D: 3578+	T	-	28/		gr -D	Mount Athos	3578+	54.30 N/ 15.25 W	
28/2024 dt		U 103	Schütze	AL 6826	-D 7500+	T	-	28/		br -D	St.Elwyn	4940+	55.30 N/ 19.30 W	
30/0041 dt		U 101	Mengersen	AL 0245	-D 7000+	T	-	29/		br -D	Aracataca	5378+	57.08 N/ 20.50 W	

December 1940

1/0449 it		ARGO	Crepas	54n/17w	DD: 1337+	T	HG.47	1/		ca DD	Saguenay	1337=	54.40 N/ 15.50 W	
1/2022 dt		U 37	Clausen	CG 18	-D: 1578+	T	-	1/		br -D	Palmella	1578+	40.30 N/ 13.30 W	
1/2212 dt		U 101	Mengersen	AL 5883	-M 6000=	T	HX.90							
1/2213 dt		U 101	Mengersen	AL 5883	-T 12000+	T	HX.90	1/2014		br -MT	Appalachee	8826+	54.30 N/ 20. W	
1/2214 dt		U 101	Mengersen	AL 5883	-D 8000+	T	HX.90	1/2015		br -D	Loch Ranza	4958=	54.37 N/ 18.54 W	
2/0406 dt		U 101	Mengersen	AL 6492	-D 5000+	T	HX.90	2/		br -D	Kavak	2782+	55. N/ 19.30 W	
2/0406 dt		U 101	Mengersen	AL 6492	-D 5000=	T	HX.90							
2/0409 dt		U 47	Prien	AL 6492	-D 10000+	T	HX.90s	2/		be -D	Ville d'Arlon	7555+	North Atlantic	
2/0418 dt		U 37	Clausen	CF 3989	-D 3500+	T	-	1/		sw -D	Gwalia	1258+	39.22 N/ 14.22 W	
2/0440 dt		U 37	Clausen	CF 3989	-D 4000+	T	OG.46	2/		br -D	Jeanne M.	2465+	39.19 N/ 13.54 W	
2/0507 dt		U 101	Mengersen	AL 6571	-M 8000+	T	HX.90	2/0320		br -M	Lady Glanely	5497+	55 N/ 20 W	
2/0520 dt		U 37	Clausen	CF 3989	-T 7000+	T	-							
2/0525 dt		U 47	Prien	AL 6548	-T 8000=	T	HX.90	2/0330		br -MT	Conch (s.u.)	8376=	55.40 N/ 19.00 W	1)
2/0546 dt		U 99	Kretschmer	AL 6581	ACL16418+	T	HX.90	2/0350		br ACL	Forfar	16402+	54.35 N/ 18.18 W	2)
2/	dt	U 47	Prien	AL 65	-D =	A	HX.90s							3)

1) The *Conch* was stopped by one torpedo hit from *U 47*. From 2/0905 to 2/0932 she was hit by three additional torpedoes from
   U 95, two of which had only slight effect. On Dec.3rd at 1019 the *Conch* was finally sunk by a torpedo from *U 99*.
2) The AMC *Forfar* sank only after four additional torpedoes from *U 99* at 2/0657. *Forfar* left the convoy for OB.251.
3) *U 47* fired 11 rounds of 88mm, five of which hit, at an unknown steamer behind HX.90. Possibly it was the *Pennrose*.

1	2	3	4	5	6	7	8	9	10	11	12	13	14	15
December 1940, cont.														
2/0725	dt	U 52	Salman	AL 6558	-D 7000+	T	HX.90	2/0520	br	-D	Tasso	1586+	55.03 N/ 18.04 W	
2/0725	dt	U 52	Salman	AL 6558	-D 5000+	T	HX.90	2/0534	br	-D	Goodleigh	5448+	55.02 N/ 18.45 W	
2/0735	dt	U 52	Salman	AL 6558	-D 5500+	T	HX.90		br	-D	Dunsley	3862=	54.41 N/ 18.41 W	
2/0901	dt	U 43	Lüth	AL 6244	-D 9000+	T	OB.251	2/	br	-M	Pacific President	7113+	56.04 N/ 18.45 W	
2/0905	dt	U 95	Schreiber	AL 6582	-T 9000+	T	HX.90s	2/	br	-MT	Conch (s.o./s.u.)	8376=	55.40 N/ 19.00 W	1)
2/0941	dt	U 43	Lüth	AL 6244	-T:11180+	T	OB.251	2/	br	-MT	Victor Ross	12247+	56.04 N/ 18.30 W	
2/1825	dt	U 94	Kuppisch	AM 4416	-D 6000+	T	HX.90	2/1625	br	-M	Stirlingshire	6022+	55.36 N/ 16.22 W	
2/2050	dt	U 99	Kretschmer	AL 6885	-D: 4276+	TA	-	2/	nw	-D	Samnanger	4276+		4)
2/2143	dt	U 140	Hinsch	AM	-D 5200+	T	-	2/	br	-D	Victoria City	4739+	North Atlantic	5)
2/2216	dt	U 94	Kuppisch	AM 4432	-T 10000+	T	HX.90	2/2016	br	-D	Wilhelmina	6725+	55.43 N/ 15.06 W	6)
2/2217	dt	U 94	Kuppisch	AM 4432	-D: 4360+	T	HX.90	2/	nl	-D	W.Hendrik (?)	4360 ?		6)
3/1019	dt	U 99	Kretschmer	AL 6558	-T: 8376+	Tf	HX.90	3/	br	-MT	Conch (s.o._	8376+	55.40 N/ 19. W	1)
4/0147	dt	U 52	Salman	AL 6886	-D 8000+	T	-							7)
4/0457	dt	U 37	Clausen	CG 5840	-D 4000+	T	-	4/	sw	-D	Daphne	1513+	SW Coast of Spain	
5/0339	it	ARGO	Crepas	53n/17w	-D 12000+	T	OB.252 s	5/	br	-M	Silverpine	5066+	54.14 N/ 18.08 W	
6/2248	dt	U 43	Lüth	AL 8225	-D 6000+	T	-	5/	nw	-D	Skrim	1902+	North Atlantic	8)
7/2239	dt	U 99	Kretschmer	AL 8473	-D: 5273+	T	OB.252 s	7/	nl	-D	Farmsum	5237+	52.11 N/ 22.56 W	
8/1226	dt	U 140	Hinsch	AM 5511	-S: 2200+	T	-	8/	fi	-S	Penang (?)	1997+	North Atlantic	9)
8/2020	dt	U 140	Hinsch	AM 5511	-D: 7800+	T	-	8/	br	-D	Ashcrest	5652+	North Atlantic	10)
8/2058	dt	U 103	Schütze	AL 9612	-D: 9515+	T	-	8/	br	-D	Calabria	9515+	52.43 N/ 18.07 W	
9/0132	dt	U 103	Schütze	AL 9646	-D: 5000+	T	-	8/	br	-D	Empire Jaguar	5186+	51.34 N/ 17.35 W	

4) In BR.1337 the *Samnanger* is reported lost on Dec.21st at 08.26 N/ 16.50 W together with the *Charles Pratt*. But *U 65* which sank this tanker attacked only one ship. *U 99* identified the attacked ship as the *Samnanger*.

5) The *Victoria City* was reported missing after Dec.2nd. She could not send a message, because *U 140* reported that she sank in 12 min.

6) *U 94* reported two hits on a tanker and one hit on another ship, identified as *W.Hendrik*. But only the *Wilhelmina* was hit.

7) *U 52* attacked a single ship going east and observed the ship sinking by the bow after 38 minutes. Not identified.

8) *U 43* attacked a single ship going west and observed the ship sinking in 63 seconds. Possibly it was the *Skrim*, missing since Dec.5th.

9) *U 140* reported one hit on the Finnish sailing vessel *Lawhill*. Thirty minutes later the ship was gone. Possibly the ship hit was the only other missing Finnish sailing vessel, the *Penang*, which was on the way to Queenstown/Ireland. The *Lawhill* survived the war.

1	2	3	4	5	6	7	8	9	10	11	12	13	14	15

December 1940, cont.

11/1512	dt	U 96	Lehmann-Willenbrock	AM 2376	-D 11000+	T	HX.92	11/		br -D	Rotorua	10890+	58.56 N/ 11.20 W	
11/1912	dt	U 94	Kuppisch	AL 9616	-D: 4000+	T	-	5/		br -D	Empire Statesman	5306+	North Atlantic	11)
11/2052	dt	U 96	Lehmann-Willenbrock	AM 2618	-D 7000+	T	HX.92	11/		nl -D	Towa	5419+	55.50 N/ 10.10 W	
12/0156	dt	U 96	Lehmann-Willenbrock	AM 2618	-M 8000+	T	HX.92	11/		sw -M	Stureholm	4575+	North Atlantic	12)
12/0431	dt	U 96	Lehmann-Willenbrock	AM 2863	-D 4000+	T	HX.92	12/		be -D	Macedonier	5227+	57.52 N/ 08.42 W	
13/2047	dt	U 43	Lüth	BE 2442	-M:10350=	T	.	13/		br -M	Orari	10350=	49.50 N/ 20.55 W	
14/0816	dt	U 100	Schepke	AL 2977	-D: 4500+	T	-	14/		br -D	Kyleglen	3670+	58. N/ 25. W	
14/0855	dt	U 96	Lehmann-Willenbrock	AL 3337	-M:10926+	T	-	14/		br -M	Western Prince	10926+	59.32 N/ 17.47 W	
14/	dt	U 96	Lehmann-Willenbrock	AL	-D 5000=	A	-	14/		br -D	Empire Razorbill	5118=	59.31 N/ 13.15 W	
14/1955	dt	U 100	Schepke	AL 0165	-D 3500+	T	-	14/		br -D	Euphorbia	3380+	North Atlantic	
16/1950	dt	U 37	Clausen	DH 9590	-D 300+	A	-	16/		sp -S	San Carlos	223+	Cape Juby	
18/0515	it	VENIERO	Petroni	54n/20w	-D: 2883+	T	SC.15 d	18/		gr -D	Anastassia	2883+	54.24 N/ 19.04 W	
18/1615	dt	U 96	Lehmann-Willenbrock	AL 3568	-T:10746=	T	OB.259	18/		nl -MT	Pendrecht	10746=	59.05 N/ 17.47 W	
18/2020	dt	U 100	Schepke	AL 1653	-D:10000+	T	-	18/		br -D	Napier Star	10116+	58.58 N/ 23.13 W	
19/	dt	U 37	Clausen	DH 96	SS: 1379+	T	.	19/		fr SS	Sfax	1379+	Cape Juby	13)
19/	dt	U 37	Clausen	DH 96	-T +	T	.	19/		fr -DT	Rhone	2785+	Cape Juby	13)
19/1750	it	BAGNOLINI	Tosoni-Pittoni	54n/17w	-D: 3660+	T	SC.15 d	19/		br -D	Amicus	3660+	54.10 N/ 15.50 W	

10) The *Ashcrest* was reported missing after Dec.9th. *U 140* identified the ship as the *Ashcroft*.
11) The *Empire Statesman* was reported missing after Dec.5th. *U 94* reported this ship sunk.
12) The *Stureholm* departed Halifax on Nov.29th for England, and was reported missing after Dec.12th.
13) *U 37* attacked the two Vichy-French ships by mistake.

1	2	3	4	5	6	7	8	9	10	11	12	13	14	15

December 1940, cont.

1	2	3	4	5	6	7	8	9	10 11	12	13	14	15
20/1000	it	CALVI	Caridi	55n/19w	-D: 5000+	T	OB.260 d	20/	br -D	Carlton	5162+	54.30 N/ 18.30 W	
21/1605	dt	U 65	vStockhausen	ET 2753	-T: 8982+	T	-	21/	pa -DT	Charles Pratt	8982+	08.26 N/ 16.50 W	
21/2209	it	MOCENIGO	Agostini	41n/17w	-D 3700+	T	OG.47	21/	sw -D	Mangen	1253+	40.45 N/ 16.50 W	
21/2209	it	MOCENIGO	Agostini	41n/17w	-D 8500+	T	OG.47						
21/2214	it	MOCENIGO	Agostini	41n/17w	-D =	T	OG.47						
22/1550	it	MOCENIGO	Agostini	41n/15w	-D 3000=	A	OG.47 d		br -D	Sarastone	2473?		14)
24/1641	dt	U 65	vStockhausen	ET 2661	-T 10191+	T	-	24/	br -DT	British Premier	5872+	06.20 N/ 13.20 W	
26/1645	it	CALVI	Caridi	55n/19w	-D 10000+	T	-						
26/2003	dt	U 95	Schreiber	AL 3687	-M:12800+	T	-	26/	br -M	Waiotira	12823+	58.05 N/ 17.10 W	
27/0146	dt	U 38	Liebe	AL 3687	-D: 4980=	T		27/	br -D	Ardanbhan	4980+	59.16 N/ 20.27 W	15)
27/1445	it	TAZZOLI	Raccanelli	59n/20w	-D: 4980+	T	OB.263						
27/1131	dt	U 65	vStockhausen	EJ 9675	-D: 5455+	TA	-	27/	nw -D	Risanger	5455+	12.30 N/ 21.30 W	
31/2111	dt	U 38	Liebe	AL 2787	-M: 3739+	T	HX.97s	30/	sw -D	Valparaiso	3760+	60.01 N/ 23.00 W	16)
31/2300	dt	U 65	vStockhausen	EJ 6315	-T: 8532+?	T	-	31/	br -MT	British Zeal	8532=	15.40 N/ 20.43 W	

January 1941

1	2	3	4	5	6	7	8	9	10 11	12	13	14	15
1/2000	it	BAGNOLINI	Tosoni-Pittoni	54n/14w	ACL 1500+?	T	-	1/	br APC	Northern Pride	----		
2/2207	dt	U 65	vStockhausen	DT 6537	-D: 6579+	TA	-	2/	br -D	Nalgora	6579+	22.24 N/ 21.11 W	
5/1000	it	CAPPELLINI	Todaro	18n/21w	-D: 5029+	A	OB.262 d	5/	br -D	Shakespeare	5029+	18.05 N/ 21.10 W	
6/1137	dt	U 124	Schulz	AM 1497	-D: 6000+	T	-	6/	br -D	Empire Thunder	5965+	59.14 N/ 12.43 W	

14) The name of this ship was only reported by the German xB-Dienst. Probably the *Sarastone* was not damaged at all.
15) *U 38* reported one hit on the *Ardanbhan*. The ship was sunk by two torpedoes from the *Tazzoli*.
16) The *Valparaiso* departed Halifax on Dec.18th for England and was reported for the last time with the convoy on Dec.29th. She was reported missing thereafter.

1	2	3	4	5	6	7	8	9	10	11	12	13	14	15
January 1941, cont.														
9/0245	it	GLAUCO	Baroni	53n/17w	-D	8000=	A	-						1)
9/1814	dt	U 105	Schewe	AL 3850	-D	4500+	T	-	9/	br	-D	Bassano	4843+	57.57 N/ 17.42 W	
14/0830	it	CAPPELLINI	Todaro	09n/15w	-D:	7472+	TA	-	14/	br	-D	Eumaeus	7472+	08.55 N/ 15.03 W	
15/2120	it	TORELLI	Longobardo	53n/24w	-D	6000+	T	.	15/	gr	-D	Nemea	5101+	52.33 N/ 24.13 W	
15/2148	it	TORELLI	Longobardo	53n/24w	-D	3500+	T	.	15/	nw	-D	Brask	4079+	52.45 N/ 23.59 W	
16/0045	dt	U 106	Oesten	AL 2599	-D:	8443+	T	-	16/	br	-M	Zealandic	10578+	58.28 N/ 20.43 W	
16/0100	it	TORELLI	Longobardo	53n/24w	-D	6000+	TA	.	16/	gr	-D	Nicolaos Filinis	3111+	53. N/ 24. W	
16/0356	dt	U 96	Lehmann-Willenbrock	AM 0185	-D:	14118+	T	-	16/	br	-D	Oropesa	14118+	56.28 N/ 12. W	2)
17/0745	dt	U 96	Lehmann-Willenbrock	AM 1832	-D:	14936+	T	-	17/	br	-D	Almeda Star	14935+	58.16 N/ 13.40 W	2)
20/0042	dt	U 94	Kuppisch	AE 8956	-D	2500+	T	-	20/	br	-D	Florian	3174+	North Atlantic	3)
20/1220	it	MARCELLO	Teppati	50n/18w	-D	7000+	A	-	20/	be	-D	Portugal	1550+	50. N/ 19. W	4)
24/	dt	U 123	Moehle	AL 30	-D	6000+	T	-	24/	nw	-D	Vespasian	1570+	55. N/ 15. W	5)
26/0212	dt	U 105	Schewe	AL 6987	-D	7000+	Tf	SL.61s	21/	nl	-D	Heemskerck	6516+	53.43 N/ 16.07 W	6)
28/2100	it	TORELLI	Longobardo	55n/19w	-D:	5198+	T	HX.102s	28/	br	-D	Urla	5198+	54.54 N/ 19. W	
29/0348	dt	U 93	Korth	AM 4125	-D	6000+	T	SC.19	29/0250	br	-D	King Robert	5886+	56. N/ 15.23 W	
29/0355	dt	U 93	Korth	AM 4125	-T:	10468+	T	SC.19	29/0258	br	-DT	W.B.Walker	10468+	56. N/ 15.23 W	
29/0405	dt	U 93	Korth	AM 4125	-D	5000+	T	SC.19	29/0303	gr	-D	Aikaterini	4929+	56. N/ 15.23 W	
29/0618	dt	U 94	Kuppisch	AM 4137	-D	7500+	T	SC.19s	29/0615	br	-D	West Wales	4354+	56. N/ 15.23 W	
29/0715	dt	U 106	Oesten	AM 4131	-D	3500+	T	SC.19s	29/	äg	-D	Sesostris	2962+	56. N/ 15.23 W	

1) The *Glauco* reported two 100mm hits on the attacked ship. There was no significant damage.
2) The *Oropesa* sank only after one additional shot that missed, and two coups de grâce at 0616. The *Alameda Star* evaded three attacks before being hit, and sank only after three additional hits at 1355.
3) The *Florian* was reported missing after Jan.20th. She sank in 42 seconds, and could not send a distress message.
4) The *Portugal* was reported missing after Jan.20th. The *Marcello* attacked one ship, which was identified by the German xB-Dienst as the Greek *Eleni* of 5655 gross tons.
5) The *Vespasian* departed Oban on Jan.21st, and was reported missing thereafter at about 55 N/ 15 W.
6) *U 105* attacked one damaged and burning ship, possibly the *Heemskerck*, which was hit by bombs of German aircraft. She did not sink until Jan.26th.

1	2	3	4	5	6	7	8	9	10	11	12	13	14	15
January 1941, cont.														
30/0247	dt	U 94	Kuppisch	AM 2948	-D	9000+	T	SC.19s	30/0520	br	-D	Rushpool	5125+	56. N/ 15.42 W	
31/1918	it	DANDOLO	Boris	49n/19w	-T	6500+	T	-	31/	br	-D	Pizarro	1367+	49.03 N/ 19.40 W	
February 1941														
1/2125	dt	U 48	Schultze	AL 3616	-D:	4351+	T	-	1/	gr	-D	Nicolaos Angelos	4351+	59. N/ 17. W	
3/0145	dt	U 107	Hessler	AL 2714	-D:	4706+	T	OB.279	3/	br	-D	Empire Citizen	4683+	58.12 N/ 23.22 W	
3/2333	dt	U 107	Hessler	AL 0249	-D	7000+	T	OB.279d	3/	br	-D	Crispin	5051+	57. N/ 19.30 W	1)
4/0838	dt	U 52	Salman	AL 5132	-D	3500+	T	-	4/	nw	-D	Ringhorn	1298+	55.46 N/ 22.36 W	
4/	dt	U 93	Korth	AM	-D:	2660+	Af	SC.20s	4/	br	-D	Dione II	2660+	55.50 N/ 10.30 W	2)
4/1644	dt	U 123	Moehle	AL	-D	6000+	T	SC.20 s	2/	br	-D	Empire Engineer	5358+	54. N/ 34. W	3)
6/1732	dt	U 107	Hessler	AL 3871	-D	5000+	T	SC.20 s	6/	ca	-D	Maplecourt	3388+	55.39 N/ 15.56 W	
9/0430	dt	U 37	Clausen	CG 7555	-D	5000+	T	HG.53	9/0432	br	-D	Courland	1325+	35.53 N/ 13.13 W	
9/0430	dt	U 37	Clausen	CG 7555	-D	4500+	T	HG.53	9/0435	br	-D	Estrellano	1983+	35.53 N/ 13.13 W	
9/0545	dt	U 37	Clausen	CG 7554	-D	4000+	T	HG.53	9/0601	-----		No.61, No.31	-----		4)
10/0633	dt	U 37	Clausen	CF 9645	-T	+	T	HG.53	10/	br	-D	Brandenburg	1473+	36.10 N/ 16.38 W	5)
10/0633	dt	U 37	Clausen	CF 9645	-T	+	T	HG.53					-----		5)
10/1435	dt	U 52	Salman	AL 6269	-D	3500+	T	OG.52 s	8/	br	-D	Canford Chine	3364+	55. N/ 15. W	6)
13/1508	dt	U 96	Lehmann-Willenbrock	AE 8774	-T:	7987+	TA	HX.106s	13/	br	-MT	Clea	8074+	NW Approaches	
13/1625	dt	U 103	Schütze	AL 3245	-T:	10516+	T								
13/1950	dt	U 96	Lehmann-Willenbrock	AL 3281	-T:	10516+	Tf	HX.106s	13/	br	-MT	Arthur F.Corwin	10516+	60.25 N/ 17.11 W	7)

1) The *Crispin* was an "Ocean Boarding Vessel" and was escorted by one destroyer.
2) The *Dione II* was damaged by bombs of a German aircraft on Feb.3rd.
3) The *Empire Engineer* was last observed on Feb.2nd at about 54 N/34 W, and was reported missing thereafter.
4) This torpedo missed the ships in positions 61 and 31, but did not hit a ship behind them as *U 37* assumed.
5) *U 37* missed a big tanker in the convoy, but assumed hits on two other ships behind them. In reality the *Brandenburg* was hit twice.
6) The *Canford Chine* was last observed on Feb.8th at about 55 N/15 W and was reported missing thereafter.
7) The *Arthur F.Corwin* was hit by two torpedoes fired by *U 123*, and was sunk by *U 96* with two additional hits.

1	2	3	4	5	6		7	8	9	10 11	12	13	14	15
February 1941, cont.														
14/0145	it	BIANCHI	Giovannini	55n/19w	-D	6000+	T	SC.21 s	14/	br -D	Belcrest	4517+	54. N/ 21. W	
14/2257	dt	U 101	Mengersen	AL 6842	-D	5500+	T	-	15/	br -D	Holystone	5462+	North Atlantic	8)
15/0038	dt	U 123	Moehle	AL	-D	6500+	T	SC.21 s	15/	br -D	Alnmoor	6573+	55. N/ 13. W	9)
17/0008	dt	U 101	Mengersen	BE 3437	-D	6000+	T	SL.64 s	16/2030	br -D	Gairsoppa	5237+	300m SW Galway	
17/0633	dt	U 103	Schütze	AL 2299	-T:10455+		T	HX.107s	17/	br -MT	Edwy R.Brown	10455+	61. N/ 18. W	
17/2119	dt	U 69	Metzler	AM 1435	-D: 8456+		T	-	17/	br -M	Siamese Prince	8456+	59.53 N/ 12.12 W	
18/0227	dt	U 96	Lehmann-Willenbrock	AE 7988	-D: 5589+		T	HX.107s	18/	br -D	Black Osprey	5589+	61.30 N/ 18.10 W	
18/2133	dt	U 103	Schütze	AL 3488	-D	4199+	T	-	18/	br -M	Seaforth	5459+	58.48 N/ 18.17 W	
19/08	dt	U 69	Metzler	AL 3124	-D	7980+	T	HX.107s	18/	br -D	Empire Blanda	5693+	North Atlantic	10)
19/2222	dt	U 103	Schütze	AM 1377	-D: 7034+		T	HX.107s	19/	nw -M	Benjamin Franklin	7034+	58.50 N/ 16.30 W	
22/1549	dt	U 96	Lehmann-Willenbrock	AL 3668	-T	10000+	Tf	OB.287s	22/	br -DT	Scottish Standard	6999+	59.20 N/ 16.12 W	11)
22/2224	dt	U 108	Scholtz	AE 7261	-D	5600+	T	-	22/	nl -D	Texelstroom	1617+	63.15 N/ 20.30 W	
23/2242	dt	U 107	Hessler	AL 2598	-D: 5400+		T	-	23/	br -D	Manistee	5360+	59.30 N/ 21. W	12)
23/2256	it	BIANCHI	Giovannini	59n/21w	-D: 7000+		T	-						
23/2327	dt	U 96	Lehmann-Willenbrock	AL 2472	ACL 9000+		T	OB.288	24/0300	br -D	Huntingdon	10946+	58.25 N/ 20.23 W	
23/2339	dt	U 69	Metzler	AL 2362	-D	9500+	T	OB.288s	23/	br -D	Temple Moat	4427+	59.27 N/ 20.20 W	
24/0027	dt	U 95	Schreiber	AL 2362	-D	5000=	T	OB.288				-----		13)
24/0027	dt	U 95	Schreiber	AL 2362	-D	4000+	T	OB.288	23/2350	br -D	Cape Nelson	3807+	59.30 N/ 21.00 W	
24/0046	dt	U 95	Schreiber	AL 2362	-D	6000+	T	OB.288	23/2153	br -D	Anglo Peruvian	5457+	59.30 N/ 21.00 W	

8) The *Holystone* was reported missing after Feb.15th.
9) The *Alnmoor* was reported missing after Feb.15th at about 55 N/13 W. The ship attacked by *U 123* exploded.
10) The *Empire Blanda* was a straggler from convoy HX.107 since Feb.18th and was reported missing thereafter.
11) The *Scottish Standard* was damaged by bombs from a German FW-200 Condor of I./K.G.40 on Feb.21st.
12) The *Manistee* was an "Ocean Broading Vessel". The first hit by *U 107* slowed the ship down. The hit by *Bianchi* is not certain. The ship was sunk after several attacks by *U 107* at 07.58 hrs.
13) The torpedo missed the target, but *U 95* assumed that one other ship behind the target in the convoy was hit.

1	2	3	4	5	6	7	8	9	10 11	12	13	14	15

February 1941, cont.

1	2	3	4	5	6	7	8	9	10 11	12	13	14	15
24/0053	dt	U 123	Moehle	AL 0152	-D 14000+	T	-	?/	nl -D	Grootekerk	8685+	Atlantic	14)
24/0116	dt	U 96	Lehmann-Willenbrock	AL 2418	-D 4500+	T	-	24/	nw -D	Svein Jarl	1908+	59.30 N/ 21. W	
24/0145	dt	U 95	Schreiber	AL 2331	-D 8000+	T	OB.288d	24/	br -D	Marslew	4542+	59.18 N/ 21.30 W	
24/0212	dt	U 97	Heilmann	AE 8985	-D 7000+	T	OB.289 OB.289	24/0350 24/1016	br -D br -D	Mansepool Jonathan Holt	4894+ 4973+	61.01 N/ 12. W 61.10 N/ 11.55 W	15) 15)
24/0220	dt	U 96	Lehmann-Willenbrock	AL 2417	-D 8000+	T	OB.288d	24/	br -D	Sirikishna	5458+	58. N/ 21. W	
24/0345	it	BIANCHI	Giovannini	60n/21w	-D 7000+	T	OB.288d	24/	br -D	Linaria	3385+	61. N/ 25. w	16)
24/0419	dt	U 73	Rosenbaum	AL 2534	-D 6500+	T	OB.288d	24/0220	br -D	Waynegate	4260+	58.50 N/ 21.47 W	16)
24/0624	dt	U 97	Heilmann	AE 8893	-T 9000+	T	OB.289	24/0530	br -DT	British Gunner	6894+	61.09 N/ 12.04 W	
24/0818	dt	U 97	Heilmann	AE 8894	-T 10000+	T	OB.289	24/0755	nw -MT	G.C.Brovig	9718=	61.04 N/ 14.24 W	
24/2143	dt	U 48	Schultze	BF 1185	-D: 4289+	T	SLS.64s	24/	br -D	Nailsea Lass	4289+	60m SW Fastnet	
26/ 26/	dt dt	U 47 U 47	Prien Prien	AM 4236 AM 4236	-D + -D +	T T	OB.290 OB.290	26/0018 26/0025	be -D br -MT	Kasongo Diala	5254+ 8106=	55.50 N/ 14.20 W 55.50 N/ 14. W	17) 17)
26/	dt	U 47	Prien	AM 4236	-D +	T	OB.290	26/0110	sw -M	Rydboholm	3197+	55.32 N/ 14.24 W	17)
26/	dt	U 47	Prien	AM 4236	-D +	T	OB.290	26/0137	nw -M	Borgland	3636+	55.50 N/ 14. W	17)
/	dt	U 70 (?)	Matz	-------	---------	T	-	26/	sw -D	Göteborg	820+	SE Iceland	18)
27/0145	it	BIANCHI	Giovannini	54n/14w	-D: 7603=?	T	OB.290	27/	br -D	Empire Ability	?		19)
27/0447	it	BIANCHI	Giovannini	54n/14w	-D: 6800+	T	OB.290	27/	br -D	Baltistan	6803+	51.52 N/ 19.55 W	
28/	dt	U 47	Prien	-------	---------	A	OB.290d	28/	br -D	Holmelea	4223+	54.24 N/ 17.25 W	20)
28/2332	dt	U 108	Scholtz	AL 3264	-D: 6461+	T	-	28/	br -D	Effna	6461+	61.30 N/ 15.45 W	

14) The *Grootekerk* departed Swansea on Feb.18th for Freetown. It was assumed that she was sunk by a raider.
15) *U 97* assumed that she hit only one ship with two torpedoes, but in reality two ships were hit.
16) The Italian assumption that the *Waynegate* was sunk was very probably incorrect. It was the *Linaria*.
17) *U 47* reported to have sunk a ship of only 22,000 gross tons. But there was no other U-boat which could have attacked there.
18) The *Göteborg* departed Reykjavik on Feb.25th for Göteborg and was reported missing thereafter. Possibly she was attacked by *U 70*.
19) The *Bianchi* reported a probable hit on the *Empire Ability*, which in reality was not damaged at all.
20) The *Holmlea* was missed by one torpedo from *U 99* and was sunk by gunfire from *U 47*.

North Sea - Atlantic

1	2	3	4	5	6	7	8	9	10	11	12	13	14	15
March 1941														
1/2356	dt	U 552	Topp	AM 2175	-T 12250+	T	HX.109	1/		br	-DT Cadillac	12062+	59.44 N/ 11.16 W	
2/0046	dt	U 95	Schreiber	AM 1472	-D 4000+	T	HX.109	1/		br	-D Pacific	6034+	180m WSW Syderö	
2/2212	dt	U 147	Hardegen	AM 3353	-D 9000+	T	HX.109	2/		nw	-D Augvald	4811+	150m NW Loch Ewe	
5/0525	dt	U 95	Schreiber	AL 3534	-M 5070+	T	-	5/		sw	-M Murjek	5070+	North Atlantic	1)
7/	dt	U 99	Kretschmer	-------	-DW20638+	T	OB.293	7/		br	-DW Terje Viken	20638+	60. N/ 12.50 W	2)
7/	dt	U 70	Matz	-------	---------	T	OB.293	7/0607		br	-D Delilian	6423=	60.28 N/ 13.38 W	4)
7/	dt	U 70	Matz	-------	---------	T	OB.293	7/				-----		4)
7/	dt	U 70	Matz	-------	---------	T	OB.293	7/				-----		4)
7/	dt	U 70	Matz	-------	---------	T	OB.293	7/0632		nl	-MT Mijdrecht	7493=	60.31 N/ 13.52 W	5)
7/	dt	U 99	Kretschmer	-------	-T: 6568+	TA	OB.293	7/0747		br	-MT Athelbeach	6568+	60.30 N/ 13.30 W	3)
7/1047	dt	U 37	Clausen	AL 2587	-D: 3050+	T	-	7/		gr	-D Mentor	3050+	59.30 N/ 25. W	
8/0045	dt	U 74	Kentrat	AE 8999	-D 6000=	T	.							6)
8/0109	dt	UA	Eckermann	AL 3113	-D: 7524+	T	OB.293	8/0012		br	-D Dunaff Head	5258=	60.33 N/ 18.50 W	7)
8/0341	dt	U 105	Schewe	DT 9351	-D 10000+	T	SL.67	8/		br	-D Harmodius	5229+	20.35 N/ 20.40 W	
8/0547	dt	U 124	Schulz	DT 9352	-D 9000+	T	SL.67	8/		br	-D Nardana	7974+	20.51 N/ 20.32 W	8)
8/0550	dt	U 124	Schulz	DT 9352	-D 6000+	T	SL.67							8)
8/0556	dt	U 124	Schulz	DT 9352	-D 6000+	T	SL.67	8/		br	-D Hindpool	4897+	20.51 N/ 20.32 W	8)
8/0600	dt	U 124	Schulz	DT 9352	-D 7000+	T	SL.67	8/		br	-D Tielbank	5084+	20.51 N/ 20.32 W	8)
8/0602	dt	U 124	Schulz	DT 9352	-D 5000+	T	SL.67	8/		br	-D Lahore	5304+	21.03 N/ 20.38 W	8)
8/0608	dt	U 124	Schulz	DT 9352	-D 6000=	T	SL.67							8)
10/2052	dt	U 552	Topp	AM 2529	-Df 1000+	TA	-	10/		is	-Df Reykjaborg	687+	459m SE Iceland	
11/1546	dt	U 106	Oesten	DT 9252	-D: 7506+	T	-	11/		br	-D Memnon	7506+	20.41 N/ 21.00 W	

1) The *Murjek* departed Santos on Jan.25th for Göteborg and was reported missing thereafter.
2) The wreck of *Terje Viken* was finally sunk by two British destroyers and one corvette on March 14th.
3) The *Athelbeach* was first torpedoed in convoy, then attacked by gunfire, and finally sunk by torpedo.
4) *U 70* was sunk after an attack on this convoy. The commanding officer claimed hits on 4 ships in this convoy.
5) The *Mijdrecht* after being torpedoed by *U 70* rammed the U-Boat as it tried to deliver the coup de grâce. *U 70* was damaged.
6) *U 74* attacked a ship escorted by two destroyers, maybe a damaged ship of OB.293.
7) *UA* assumed that she hit a ship with two torpedoes, identified by the xB-Dienst as *Empire Attendant* (7524 gross tons). But at this time according to the convoy commodore's report, it was the *Dunaff Head* that was slightly damaged.
8) *U 124* observed four ships going down. Two other shots were seen to hit, and one other ship was in a sinking condition.

1	2	3	4	5	6	7	8	9	10	11	12	13	14	15
March 1941, cont.														
11/	dt	U 37 ?	Clausen			A	-	11/	is	-Df	Frodi	97=	200m SE Reykjavik	9)
12/	dt	U 37 ?	Clausen			A	-	12/	is	-Df	Petrusey	91+	S Iceland	9)
14/1307	it	EMO	Roselli-Lorenzini	59n/ 22w	-D		8000+ T	SC.24 s	14/	br	-D	Western Chief	5759+	58.52 N/ 21.13 W	
16/0018	dt	U 110	Lemp	AE 7959	-D		6000=? T	HX.112					-----		
16/0022	dt	U 110	Lemp	AE 7959	-T		8000+ T	HX.112	16/	br	-MT	Erodona	6207=	61.20 N/ 17. W	
16/0632	dt	U 110	Lemp	AE 8781	-T		8000+ T	HX.112							
16/1636	dt	U 106	Oesten	EJ 6983	-M:		6810+ T	-	16/	nl	-M	Almkerk	6810+	13.40 N/ 20.30 W	
16/	dt	U 99	Kretschmer	-------	-T	+	T	HX.112	16/	nw	-MT	Ferm	6593+	60.42 N/ 13.10 W	
16/	dt	U 99	Kretschmer	-------	-T	+	T	HX.112	16/	nw	-MT	Beduin	8136+	60.42 N/ 13.10 W	
16/	dt	U 99	Kretschmer	-------	-T	+	T	HX.112	16/	br	-MT	Franche Comte	9314=	61.15 N/ 12.30 W	
16/	dt	U 99	Kertschmer	-------	-D	+	T	HX.112	16/	br	-DT	Venetia	5728+	61. N/ 12.36 W	
16/	dt	U 99	Kretschmer	-------	-D	+	T	HX.112	16/	ca	-D	J.B.White	7375+	60.57 N/ 12.27 W	10)
17/	dt	U 99	Kretschmer	-------	-M	+	T	HX.112	17/	sw	-M	Korshamn	6673+	61.09 N/ 12.20 W	
17/2107	dt	U 106	Oesten	EJ 3895	-D		7000+ T	SL.68	17/	br	-D	Andalusian	3082+	14.33 N/ 21.06 W	
17/2108	dt	U 106	Oesten	EJ 3895	-D		7000+ T	SL.68	17/	nl	-D	Tapanoeli	7031+	15.56 N/ 20.49 W	
17/2109	dt	U 106	Oesten	EJ 3895	-D		7000+ T	SL.68							
17/2110	dt	U 106	Oesten	EJ 3895	-D		7000= T	SL.68							
18/0418	dt	U 105	Schewe	EJ 3852	-D		6000+ T	SL.68	18/	br	-D	Medjerda	4380+	17. N/ 21. W	
18/1619	it	EMO	Roselli-Lorenzini	58n/24w	-D:		4500= T	-		br	-D	Clan Maciver	-----		11)
19/0024	dt	U 105	Schewe	EJ 3254	-D		8000+ T	SL.68	19/	nl	-D	Mandalika	7750+	18.16 N/ 21.26 W	
19/0029	dt	U 105	Schewe	EJ 3254	-D		6000+ T	SL.68							
20/2323	*dt*	*U 106*	*Oesten*	*DT 7643*	*-D*		*8000+ T*	*SL.68*	*20/*	*br*	*BB*	*Malaya*	*31100=*	*20.02 N/ 25.50 W*	*12)*
20/2323	dt	U 106	Oesten	DT 7643	-D		7000= T	SL.68					-----		

9) The fishing vessels very probably were sunk by *U 37*, the only boat in the area that did not report otherwise.
10) The *J.B.White* was first torpedoed and later sunk by a coup de grâce from *U 99*.
11) The *Clan MacIver* (4,500 gross tons) radioed an SSS-signal from this position at the time, which was intercepted by the German xB-Dienst. But there was no hit in reality.
12) *U 106* attacked the shadow of a merchant ship in bad light conditions and did not realize that the torpedo hit the *Malaya*.

1	2	3	4	5	6	7	8	9	10	11	12	13	14	15
March 1941, cont.														
21/0046	dt	U 105	Schewe	DT 7653	-D: 5800+	T	SL.68	21/	br	-D	Clan Ogilvy	5802+	20.04 N/ 25.45 W	
21/0047	dt	U 105	Schewe	DT 7653	-D 7000+	T	SL.68	21/	br	-D	Benwyvis	5920+	20. N/ 26. W	
21/2159	dt	U 105	Schewe	DT 8151	-D 8000+	T	SL.68	21/	br	-D	Jhelum	4038+	21. N/ 25. W	
23/0427	dt	U 110	Lemp	AK 3162	-D 4000+	T	-	23/	nw	-D	Siremalm	2468=	60.35 N/ 28.25 W	
23/2326	dt	U 97	Heilmann	BE 2428	-T: 8028+	T	-	23/	br	-MT	Chama	8077+	49.35 N/ 19.13 W	
24/1609	it	VENIERO	Petroni	49n/23w	-D: 2088+	TA	OG.56 d	24/	br	-D	Agnete Maersk	2104+	49. N/ 22.55 W	
24/1643	dt	U 97	Heilmann	BE 1435	-D 4000+	T	-	24/	nw	-D	Hörda	4301+	49. N/ 23. W	
24/2258	dt	U 106	Oesten	EJ 1425	-D 5000+	T	-							13)
27/1350	dt	U 98	Gysae	AL 2518	-D 8000+	T	-	24/	br	-D	Koranton	6695+	59. N/ 27. W	14)
29/0619	dt	U 48	Schultze	AE 7844	-D: 5197+	T	HX.115	29/	br	-D	Germanic	5352+	61.18 N/ 22.05 W	15)
29/0624	dt	U 48	Schultze	AE 7844	-D 6000+	T	HX.115	29/	be	-D	Limbourg	2483+	61.18 N/ 22.05 W	15)
29/0627	dt	U 48	Schultze	AE 7844	-T: 8900+	T	HX.115			br	-MT	Athelprince	-----		15)
29/0655	dt	U 48	Schultze	AE 7844	-D: 5250+	T	HX.115	30/	br	-D	Eastlea	4267+	North Atlantic	15)
29/0806	dt	U 48	Schultze	AE 7844	-D 6000+	T	HX.115	29/	br	-D	Hylton	5197+	60.20 N/ 18.10 W	15)
29/1750	dt	U 46	Endraß	AL 1447	-D 6000+	T	OB.302	29/0615	sw	-D	Liguria	1751+	60. N/ 29. W	16)
30/0734	dt	U 69	Metzler	AK 3151	-D 7000+	T	OB.302	30/	br	-D	Coultarn	3759+	60.18 N/ 29.28 W	
30/2301	dt	U 124	Schulz	ET 5356	-D: 3767+	T	-	30/	br	-D	Umona	3767+	90m SW Freetown	
31/1033	dt	U 46	Endraß	AK 2836	-T: 8714+	T	-	31/	sw	-MT	Castor	8714+	57.59 N/ 32.08 W	

13) *U 106* observed from a distance of 600 yds one hit amidships on a steamer running north. The ship sank with a broken keel in ten minutes. For some time it was assumed to have been the Brazilian S/S *Santa Clara* (ex American S/S *Mahukona*) 2512 gross tons, but this ship radioed a SOS-signal on March 14th from 30.48 N/68.42 W after an explosion. USCGC *Bibb* found some wreckage of the *Santa Clara/Mahukona* but no survivors. There was no Axis U-Boat in the area.

14) The *Koranton* was reported missing after March 24th at about 59 N/27 W.

15) *U 48* reported one hit with her first torpedo on the *Hylton*. The second and the third torpedo did not hit the targets, but two ships behind. The hit assumed on the *Athelprince* was reported by the xB-Dienst, but the ship was not hit in reality. The fourth torpedo was reported as a hit on the British ship *Masunda* (5250 gross tons). Probably the ship hit and sunk was the *Eastlea* missing after March 30th. In reality first the two ships *Germania* and *Limbourg* were hit, and last the *Hylton*.

16) The *Liguria* first sailed in the convoy OG.56, but became a straggler. Later she joined OB.302. Ten survivors were picked up.

1	2	3	4	5	6	7	8	9	10	11	12	13	14	15

April 1941

1	2	3	4	5	6	7	8	9	10 11	12	13	14	15
2/2329	dt	U 46	Endraß	AK 3658	-T: 7000+	T	SC.26	2/	br -MT	British Reliance	7000+	58.21 N/ 28.30 W	1)
2/2330	dt	U 46	Endraß	AK 3658	-D 5000=	T	SC.26						
3/0042	dt	U 46	Endraß	AK 3659	-D: 4313+	T	SC.26	3/0141	br -D	Alderpool	4313+	58.21 N/ 27.59 W	1)
								3/0142	br -D	Thirlby	4887 ?		1)
								3/0142	br -D	Athenic	5351=		1)
3/0328	dt	U 73	Rosenbaum	AK 3672	-D 6000+	Tf	SC.26s	3/1856	br -D	Athenic (?)	5351+	58.32 N/ 20.13 W	1)
3/0500	dt	U 74	Kentrat	AK 3621	-D 12000+	T	SC.26	3/0405	be -D	Indier	5409+	58.12 N/ 27.40 W	2)
3/0501	dt	U 74	Kentrat	AK 3621	-D 8000+	T	SC.26	3/0406	gr -D	Leonidas Z.Cambanis	4274+	58.12 N/ 27.40 W	2)
3/0508	dt	U 73	Rosenbaum	AK 3687	-D 7000+	T	SC.26	3/0410	br -D	Westpool	5724+	58.12 N/ 27.40 W	2)
3/0512	dt	U 73	Rosenbaum	AK 3687	-D 5000+	T	SC.26						2)
3/0532	dt	U 73	Rosenbaum	AK 3687	-T 12000+	T	SC.26	3/0435	br -DT	British Viscount	6895+	58.15 N/ 27.30 W	
3/0539	dt	U 74	Kentrat	AK 3688	ACL12000=	T	SC.26	3/0445	br ACL	Worcestershire	11402=	58. N/ 27. W	3)
3/0601	dt	U 69	Metzler	AK 3785	-D 7000+	T	SC.26						
3/	dt	U 76	v.Hippel ?	AK	-D: 1939+	T	-	3/	fi -D	Daphne	1939+	North Atlantic	4)
4/0029	dt	U 98	Gysae	AL 1621	-D: 2500+	T	SC.26s	3/2330	nw -D	Helle	2467+	59. N/ 24.30 W	
4/0340	dt	U 94	Kuppisch	AL 1834	-D: 5122+	T	SC.26	4/0242	br -D	Harbledown	5414+	58.30 N/ 23. W	4a)
4/0344	dt	U 98	Gysae	AL 1486	-D: 5122+	T	SC.26	4/0256	br -D	Wellcombe	5122+	59.09 N/ 22. W	4a)
4/1819	dt	U 97	Heilmann	AK 6261	-T 9000+	T	-	4/	br -MT	Conus	8132+	56.14 N/ 31.19 W	
4/2302	dt	U 124	Schulz	ET 3749	-D: 6507+	T	-	4/	br -D	Marlene	6507+	08.15 N/ 14.19 W	
5/0338	dt	U 105	Schewe	FD 1644	-D: 5200+	T	-	5/0200	br -D	Ena de Larrinaga	5200+	01.10 N/ 26. W	
6/1530	dt	U 94	Kuppisch	AD 8259	-T: 5580+	T	-	6/	nw -MT	Lincoln Ellsworth	5580+	62.37 N/ 27.06 W	

1) During its first attack *U 46* hit the *British Reliance* and one freighter without being able to observe the ships sink. During its second attack *U 46* observed a hit on the *Alderpool*. There was no A/S escort with the convoy on April 3rd. From the report of the convoy commodore comes the information that at the time of *U 46*'s second attack at 0141 the *Alderpool* (pos.11) and at 0142 the *Thirlby* (pos.12) and *Athenic* (pos.22) were hit. From 0159 to 0321 there were two and three unsuccessful attacks by *U 46* and *U 73* against two damaged ships and one of them was sunk by *U 73* at 0328, possibly the *Athenic*.

2) *U 74* and *U 73* reported two ships sunk each during this attack. From the British times and the position in convoy it is very probable that the two first hits came from *U 74* and the third ship was hit by *U 73*.

3) *U 74* observed a hit by a surface running torpedo. The *Worcestershire* was identified by the xB-Dienst.

4) *U 69* observed the ship sink immediately after the hit. Because there was no other success reports on this ship from a U-boat, it is probable that the *Daphne* was sunk by this attack. The B.d.U. awarded this ship, identified by the xB-Dienst, to *U 76* which was lost on April 5th 0705 to 0920 by escorts from SC.26.

4a) *U 94* and *U 98* overheard the SOS signal of the *Wellcombe*, but from the times of hits, *U 94* must have sunk the *Harbledown*.

1	2	3	4	5	6	7	8	9	10	11	12	13	14	15
April 1941, cont.														
7/1730 dt	U 124	Schulz	ET 5321	-D: 1746+	T	-		7/	br	-D	Portadoc	1746+	07.17 N/ 16.53 W	
8/0402 dt	U 94	Kuppisch	AD 5611	-D 15000=	T	-								5)
8/0742 dt	U 107	Hessler	DG 3319	-D: 3800+	TA	-		8/	br	-D	Eskdene	3829+	34.43 N/ 24.21 W	
8/1225 dt	U 124	Schulz	ET 2672	-D: 2697+	T	-		8/	br	-D	Tweed	2697+	07.43 N/ 15.11 W	
8/1940 dt	U 107	Hessler	DG 3934	-D: 5000+	T	-		8/	br	-D	Helena Margareta	3316+	33. N/ 23.52 W	
9/0037 dt	U 107	Hessler	DG 3983	-D 8100+	T	-		8/	br	-D	Harpathian	4671+	32.22 N/ 22.53 W	6)
9/0216 dt	U 98	Gysae	AL 1443	-D 5500+	T	HX.117s		8/	nl	-D	Prins Willem II	1304+	59.50 N/ 24.25 W	
9/1920 dt	U 107	Hessler	DH 4416	-T: 8500+	T	-		9/	br	-MT	Duffield	8516+	31.13 N/ 23.24 W	
10/1912 dt	U 52	Salman	AK 2852	-D 7000+	T	OB.306d		10/	nl	-D	Saleier	6563+	58.04 N/ 30.48 W	
11/2059 dt	U 124	Schulz	ET 5635	-D: 5285+	T	-		11/	gr	-D	Aegeon	5285+	06.55 N/ 15.38 W	
12/0509 dt	U 124	Schulz	ET 6117	-D: 4313+	T	-		12/	br	-D	St.Helena	4313+	07.50 N/ 14. W	
12/0732 it	*TAZZOLI*	*Fecia di Cossato*	*45n/19w*	*DD 3500=*	*T*	.								
13/0743 dt	U 108	Scholtz	AD 5582	ACL10000+	T	-		13/	br	ACL	Rajputana	16444+	64.50 N/ 27.25 W	
13/2229 dt	U 124	Schulz	ET 3744	-D 7000+	T	-		13/	br	-D	Corinthic	4823+	08.10 N/ 14.40 W	
14/0117 dt	U 52	Salman	AK 3342	-D: 7463+	T	-		13/	be	-D	Ville de Liège	7430+	59.50 N/ 29.30 W	
15/2131 it	TAZZOLI	Fecia di Cossato	37n/19w	-D: 8000+	TA	-		15/	br	-D	Aurillac	4733+	37.09 N/ 18.42 W	
17/1550 dt	U 123	Moehle	AK 8936	-D: 6991+	T	-		17/	sw	-M	Venezuela	6991+	53. N/ 18. W	
20/0332 dt	U 73	Rosenbaum	AL 8424	-D 7000+	T	-		20/	br	-D	Empire Endurance	8570+	53.05 N/ 23.14 W	7)
21/0640 it	CAPPELLINI	Todaro	54n/18w	-D 9337=	T	-								8)
21/1420 dt	U 107	Hessler	DT 4249	-D:10300+	T	-		21/	br	-D	Calchas	10305+	23.50 N/ 27. W	

5) *U 94* heard a strong detonation, but could not observe a column of water. Probably it was a misfiring torpedo.
6) *U 107* identified this ship mistakenly as the British S/S *Malancha* (8124 gross tons).
7) With the *Empire Endurance* the two "motor launches" *ML 1003* and *ML 1037* were lost.
8) *Cappellini* attacked two big liners under escort of three destroyers. Three torpedoes were fired, one detonation heard. But it was impossible to identify the ship.

1	2	3	4	5	6	7	8	9	10	11	12	13	14	15
April 1941, cont.														
25/0038	dt	U 103	Schütze	EH 9356	-D 5000+	T	OG.60 d	23/	nw	-D	Polyana	2267+	24. N/ 27. W	9)
26/	dt	U 110	Lemp	-------	---------	T	-	27/	fr	-D	André Moyrant	2471+		10)
27/0210	dt	U 552	Topp	AE 8816	-Df 700+	T	-	26/	br	APC	Commander Horton	227+	62. N/ 16. W	
27/0242	dt	U 147	Wetjen	AM 2264	-D 3000+	T	-	27/	nw	-D	Rimfakse	1334+	60.10 N/ 08.54 W	
27/1612	dt	U 552	Topp	AL 3236	-D 10100+	T	-	27/	br	-M	Beacon Grange	10160+	62.05 N/ 16.20 W	
28/1615	dt	U 552	Topp	AL 3415	-T 9683+	T	HX.121	28/1520	br	-MT	Capulet (s.u.)	8190=	60.16 N/ 16.10 W	11)
28/1925	dt	U 96	Lehmann-Willenbrock	AL 3437	-T 10000+	T	HX.121	28/1829	br	-MT	Oilfield	8516+	60.05 N/ 17. W	
28/1925	dt	U 96	Lehmann-Willenbrock	AL 3437	-T 8000+	T	HX.121	28/1829	nw	-MT	Caledonia	9892+	60.03 N/ 16.10 W	
28/1925	dt	U 96	Lehmann-Willenbrock	AL 3437	-T 6000=	T	HX.121	28/1830	br	-D	Port Hardy	8897+	60.14 N/ 15.20 W	12)
29/0229	dt	U 75	Ringelmann	AL 7421	-D:10146+	T	-	29/	br	-D	City of Nagpur	10146+	52.30 N/ 26. W	
30/2155	dt	U 107	Hessler	EH 9315	-D: 7443+	T	-	30/	br	-M	Lassell	7417+	12.55 N/ 28.56 W	
May 1941														
1/0027	dt	U 552	Topp	AM 5162	-D 5500+	T	-	1/	br	-D	Nerissa	5583+	57.57 N/ 10.08 W	
1/1834	dt	U 103	Schütze	ET 2829	-D 1500+	T	-	1/	br	-D	Samsö	1494+	08.35 N/ 16.17 W	
2/2114	dt	U 201	Schnee	AL 3133	-T: 8200+	Tf	HX.121s	2/	br	-MT	Capulet (s.o.)	8190+	60. N/ 16. W	11)
3/0316	dt	U 95	Schreiber	AL 1137	-M: 4873+	TA	-	3/	nw	-M	Taranger	4873+	61.07 N/ 25.20 W	

9) The *Polyana* was last seen when the convoy was dispersed on April 14th and was reported missing thereafter.
10) It is not clear whether the attacked ship was the British *Henry Mory* (2564 gross tons), or the Vichy-French *André Moyrant*.
11) The *Capulet* was torpedoed by *U 552* and was abandoned burning. The wreck was sunk on May 2nd by *U 201*.
12) From the report of the convoy commodore, it is clear that all three ships were hit in the same attack by *U 96*. The *Port Hardy* was hit by chance after the torpedo missed the intended target. There is no evidence that *U 65* (Hoppe) made an attack before being sunk by the escorts.
 1) The *Malaspina* reported one hit on the *Lycaon*, but the ship was not significantly damaged.

1	2	3	4	5	6	7	8	9	10	11	12	13	14	15

May 1941, cont.

1	2	3	4	5	6	7	8	9	10 11	12	13	14	15
4/1915	dt	U 38	Liebe	ET 2137	-D: 5230+	T	OB.310d	4/	sw -D	Japan	5230+		
5/1105	dt	U 38	Liebe	ET 2871	-D 8000+	T	-	5/	br -M	Queen Maud	4976+	07.54 N/ 16.41 W	
6/0240	dt	U 97	Heilmann	BE 1372	APC 6000=	T	.	6/	br -D	Camito	6833+	50.42 N/ 21.20 W	2)
6/0353	dt	U 97	Heilmann	BE 1348	-T 6000=	T	.	6/	it -DT	Sangro	6466+	50.42 N/ 21.22 W	2)
6/0515	dt	U 103	Schütze	ET 2954	-D 5500+	T	-	6/	br -M	Surat	5529+	08.23 N/ 15.13 W	
6/	dt	U 556	Wohlfarth	AE 95	APC +	A	-	6/	fa -Df	Emanuel	166+	62.06 N/ 08.10 W	
6/1152	dt	U 105	Schewe	ES 4440	-D: 4300+	T	-	6/	br -D	Oakdene	4255+	06.19 N/ 27.55 W	
6/1717	dt	U 103	Schütze	ET 2485	-D 3800+	T	-	6/	br -M	Dunkwa	4752+	08.43 N/ 17.13 W	
7/0900	it	TAZZOLI	Fecia di Cossato	10n/20w	-D: 4310+	T	-	7/	nw -M	Fernlane	4310+	10.02 N/ 20.17 W	
7/2310	dt	U 94	Kuppisch	AE 7744	-D 5000+	T	OB.318	7/2122	br -D	Ixion	10263+	61.29 N/ 22.40 W	3)
7/2310	dt	U 94	Kuppisch	AE 7744	-D 5000+	T	OB.318	7/			-----		3)
7/2311	dt	U 94	Kuppisch	AE 7744	-D 5000+	T	OB.318	7/2123	nw -D	Eastern Star	5658+	61.29 N/ 22.40 W	3)
7/2312	dt	U 94	Kuppisch	AE 7744	-D 5000+	T	OB.318	7/			-----		3)
8/1547	dt	U 201	Schnee	AD 8843	-D 6000=?	T	-						4)
8/1813	dt	U 97	Heilmann	BD 5533	-D 7000+	T	-	8/	br -D	Ramillies	4553+	48.05 N/ 32.26 W	
9/1158	dt	U 110	Lemp	-------	---------	T	OB.318	9/1159	br -D	Esmond	4976+	60.45 N/ 33.02 W	
9/1158	dt	U 110	Lemp	-------	---------	T	OB.318	9/1201	br -D	Bengore Head	2609+	60.45 N/ 33.02 W	
9/1426	dt	U 201	Schnee	AK 2181	-D 12000+	T	OB.318	9/1428	br -D	Gregalia	5802+	60.24 N/ 32.37 W	
9/1428	dt	U 201	Schnee	AK 2181	-D 6000+	T	OB.318	9/1429	br -D	Empire Cloud	5969=	61.00 N/ 32.30 W	
9/2016	it	TAZZOLI	Fecia di Cossato	03n/21w	-T: 8817+	TA	-	9/	nw -MT	Alfred Olsen	8817+	02.59 N/ 20.26 W	
9/2309	dt	U 103	Schütze	ES 1951	-D: 7120+	T	-	9/	br -D	City of Winchester	7120+	08.20 N/ 26.14 W	

2) The *Camito* was an "ocean boarding vessel" and escorted the Italian tanker *Sangro*, taken prize during her journey from Brazil to France. *U 97* regarded the *Camito* as a U-Boat trap.

3) *U 94* interpreted two depth charges dropped by the escorts HMS *Bulldog* and HMS *Rochester* immediately after the torpedo hits as hits on additional ships.

4) *U 201* attacked a passenger liner and observed the torpedo hit the ship without detonating. It is possible that the French steamer *Kervegan* (2018 gross tons) missing after May 5th was sunk by this attack.

May 1941, cont.

1	2	3	4	5	6	7	8	9	10	11	12	13	14	15
10/0442	dt	U 556	Wohlfarth	AK 1470	-D	8000+	T	OB.318	10/0248	br	-D	Aelybryn	4986=	59.23 N/ 35.25 W 5)
10/0443	dt	U 556	Wohlfarth	AK 1470	-D:	2085+	T	OB.318	10/0248	br	-D	Chaucer	-----	5)
10/0752	dt	U 556	Wohlfarth	AK 1390	-D	7000+	T	OB.318d	10/0445	br	-D	Empire Caribou	4861+	59.28 N/ 35.44 W
10/2037	dt	U 556	Wohlfarth	AK 4640	-D:	5086+	TA	OB.318d	10/1750	be	-D	Gand	5086+	57.54 N/ 37.34 W
11/0148	dt	U 103	Schütze	ES 4473	-D:	5828+	TA	-	11/	br	-D	City of Shanghai	5828+	06.40 N/ 27.50 W
13/0725	dt	U 98	Gysae	AJ 3825	ACL	20000+	T	SC.30	13/	br	ACL	Salopian	10549+	59.04 N/ 38.15 W 6)
13/0748	dt	U 105	Schewe	FD 36	-D:	6434+	T	-	13/	br	-D	Benvrackie	6434+	00.49 N/ 20.15 W
13/1141	dt	U 111	Kleinschmidt	AL 1119	-D	8000+	T	SC.30 s	13/	br	-D	Somersby	5170+	60.39 N/ 26.13 W
15/0138	it	BARBARIGO	Ghilieri	54n/22w	-D:	5464=	T	-		br	-D	Manchester Port	?	
15/0415	dt	U 43	Lüth	BE 6167	-S	800+	A	-	15/0220	fr	-S	Notre Dame du Chatelet	488+	48 N/ 14 W 6a)
15/2029	dt	U 105	Schewe	ET 72	-D:	5920+	T	-	15/	br	-D	Benvenue	5920+	04.27 N/ 18.25 W
16/0548	dt	U 105	Schewe	ET 47	-D:	11900+	TA	-	16/	br	-D	Rodney Star	11803+	05.03 N/ 19.02 W
17/0036	dt	U 107	Hessler	ET 4568	-T	8100+	T	-	16/	nl	-MT	Marisa	8029+	06.10 N/ 18.09 W
18/2227	dt	U 107	Hessler	ET 2988	-D:	8300+	T	-	18/	br	-D	Piako	8286+	07.52 N/ 14.57 W
19/0324	dt	U 96	Lehmann-Willenbrock	AM 5474	-T	9000+	Tf	-	19/	br	-D	Empire Ridge	2922+	90m W Bloody Foreland
20/0013	it	OTARIA	Vocaturo	52n/21w	-D	12000+	T	SL.73	20/0419	br	-D	Starcross	4662+	51.45 N/ 20.45 W 6b)
20/0458	dt	U 94	Kuppisch	AJ 3796	-D	6000+	T	HX.126	20/	br	-D	Harpagus	5173+	56.47 N/ 40.55 W 7)
20/0458	dt	U 94	Kuppisch	-------	---------		T	HX.126	20/	br	-D	Norman Monarch	4718+	56.41 N/ 40.52 W 7)
20/1450	dt	U 556	Wohlfarth	AJ 3482	-T	14000+	T	HX.126	20/	br	-MT	San Felix	13037=	57.32 N/ 40.21 W
20/1448	dt	U 556	Wohlfarth	AK 3482	-T	8000+	T	HX.126	20/	br	-MT	British Security	8470+	57.28 N/ 41.07 W
20/1516	dt	U 556	Wohlfarth	AK 3482	-D	5000+	T	HX.126	20/	br	-M	Darlington Court	4974+	57.28 N/ 41.07 W

5) The *Aelybryn* reached Reykjavik in damaged condition on May 17th. The second ship was not the Dutch steamer *Hercules* (2095 gross tons), as assumed by the xB-Dienst from a SSS-signal. The torpedo missed in reality the British steamer *Chaucer* (5792 gross tons).

6) The *Salopian* was hit only after three missed shots, and sank after another torpedo hit at 10.45 hrs.

6a) The *Notre Dame du Chatelet* was enroute from St.Malo to the Grand Banks of Newfoundland when she was sunk by a U-boat by gunfire. The day before she was met by the Italian U-boat *Cappellini* at 47.42 N/13.56 W. Two survivors were rescued by the Italian *Otaria* on May 23rd.

7) *U 94* fired two torpedoes at one steamer which missed, but hit two ships in an inner column. *U 94* reported only one hit.

1	2	3	4	5	6	7	8	9	10	11	12	13	14		15
May 1941, cont.															
20/1638	dt	U 103	Schütze	ET 6937	-D: 3500+	T	-	25/	äg	-D	Radames	3575+	06.	N/ 12. W	8)
20/1644	dt	U 111	Kleinschmidt	AJ 3542	-T: 7500+	T	HX.126	20/	br	-D	Cockaponset	5995+	57.28	N/ 41.07 W	9)
20/1729	dt	U 98	Gysae	AJ 3455	-D: 5356+	T	HX.126	20/	·br	-D	Rothermere	5356+	57.48	N/ 41.36 W	
20/1817	dt	U 94	Kuppisch	AJ 3454	-T: 6128+	T	HX.126	20/	nw	-MT	John P.Pedersen	6128+	57.	N/ 41. W	
20/2124	dt	U 138	v.Gramitzky	AM 2338	-D 12000+	T	-	20/	br	-M	Javanese Prince	8593+	59.46	N/ 10.45 W	
20/2320	dt	U 109	Fischer	AJ 3256	-D 7000+	T	HX.126	20/	br	-D	Marconi	7402+	58.	N/ 41. W	
21/0512	dt	U 98	Gysae	AJ 6252	-D 10000+	T	HX.126?								10)
21/0522	dt	U 93	Korth	AJ 3255	-T 10000+	T	HX.126	21/	nl	-MT	Elusa	6235+	59.	N/ 38.05 W	
21/1005	dt	U 69	Metzler	ES 4670	-D: 4999+	TA	-	21/	am	-D	Robin Moor	4999+	06.10	N/ 25.40 W	11)
21/2341	dt	U 69	Metzler	ES 5550	-D: 4601+	TA	-	21/	br	-D	Tewkesbury	4601+	05.49	N/ 24.09 W	
22/1340	dt	U 111	Kleinschmidt	AK 1236	-D 6500+	T	-	22/	br	-D	Barnby	4813+	60.30	N/ 34.12 W	
22/2252	dt	U 103	Schütze	ET 6852	-T: 6800+	T	-	22/	br	-MT	British Grenadier	6857+	06.15	N/ 12.59 W	
23/1951	dt	U 38	Liebe	ET 2178	-D 8000+	T	OB.318d	23/	nl	-M	Berhala	6622+	09.50	N/ 17.50 W	
24/0249	dt	U 38	Liebe	ET 2281	-D 4000+	T	-	23/	br	-D	Vulcain	4362+	09.20	N/ 15.35 W	
24/0356	dt	U 103	Schütze	EU 7116	-D: 4214+	T	-	23/	gr	-D	Marionga	4236+	05.42	N/ 10.29 W	
25/2213	dt	U 103	Schütze	ET 6999	-D 8800+	T	-	25/	nl	-D	Wangi Wangi	7789+	05.24	N/ 12. W	
27/0101	dt	U 107	Hessler	ET 26	-D: 5108+	T	-	27/	br	-D	Colonial	5108+	09.13	N/ 15.09 W	
28/1452	dt	U 107	Hessler	ET 27	-D: 3748+	T	-	28/	gr	-D	Papalemos	3748+	08.06	N/ 16.18 W	
29/2043	dt	U 557	Paulshen	AK 4441	-D 8000+	T	HX.128s	29/	br	-D	Empire Storm	7290+	55.	N/ 39.50 W	

8) According to the war diary of *U 103*, the *Radames* was sunk on May 20, not on May 25th.
9) *U 111* submerged and could not observe the hit. The torpedo missed the target, but hit the *Cockaponset* behind.
10) *U 98* observed one hit aft of the funnel, but no column of water. The vessel was going down after 33 minutes.
11) The *Robin Moor* was stopped by *U 69* and sunk according to the rules of prize law.

1	2	3	4	5	6	7	8	9	10	11	12	13	14	15
May 1941, cont.														
29/2350	dt	U 38	Liebe	ET 5535	-D 6500+	T	-	29/	br	-D	Tabaristan	6251+	06.32 N/ 15.23 W	
30/0036	dt	U 106	Oesten	EJ 1933	-D 4000+	T	-	30/	br	-M	Silveryew	6373+	16.42 N/ 25.29 W	
30/0116	*it*	*VENIERO*	*Petroni*	*36n/10w*	*DD*	*=*	*T*	*.*						
30/0800	it	MARCONI	Pollina	35n/09w	-T 12000+	T	.	30/	br	-DT	Cairndale	8129+	170m WSW Trafalgar	
30/1311	dt	U 38	Liebe	ET 5694	-D 6500+	T	-	30/	br	-D	Empire Protector	6181+	06. N/ 14.25 W	
31/0024	dt	U 38	Liebe	ET 5386	-D: 6025+	T	-	30/	nw	-D	Rinda	6029+	06.52 N/ 15.14 W	
31/0025	dt	U 69	Metzler	EV 5760	-D: 4124+	T	-	30/	br	-M	Sangara	5445=	Hafen v.Accra	12)
31/0313	dt	U 106	Oesten	EJ 1931	-M: 6843+	T	-	31/	br	-M	Clan Macdougall	6843+	16.50 N/ 25.10 W	
31/0739	dt	U 107	Hessler	ET 26	-D: 5664+	T	-	30/	br	-D	Sire	5664+	08.50 N/ 15.30 W	
31/	dt	U 147	Wetjen	-------	---------	T	HX.127a	31/	br	-D	Gravelines	2491+	56. N/ 11.13 W	
June 1941														
1/0022	dt	U 105	Schewe	EJ 71	-D: 4719+	T	-	31/	br	-D	Scottish Monarch	4719+	12.58 N/ 27.20 W	
1/	dt	U 204	Kell	AE	-Df +	A	-	1/	is	-Df	Holmsteinn	16+	NNW Dyrafjorden	
1/1409	dt	U 107	Hessler	ET 29	ACL:4227+	T	-	1/	br	-M	Alfred Jones	5013+	08. N/ 15. W	
1/1452	it	MARCONI	Pollina	36n/11w	-D 1500+	A	-	1/	pt	-Df	Exportador I.	318+	137m SW Cape St.Vincent	
2/	dt	U 147	Wetjen	-------	---------	T	.	2/	be	-M	Mokambo	4996+	56.38 N/ 10.24 W	
2/1332	dt	U 46	Endraß	BD 1723	-D 5000=?	T	-							1)
2/2043	dt	U 108	Scholtz	BD 3815	ACL14000+	T	-	2/	br	-D	Michael E.	7628+	48.50 N/ 29. W	2)
3/0101	dt	U 48	Schultze	BD 6131	-T: 9456+	TA	-	2/	br	-DT	Inversuir	9456+	48.28 N/ 28.20 W	
3/0345	dt	U 75	Ringelmann	BD 6622	-D: 4801+	T	OB.327d	3/	nl	-D	Eibergen	4801+	48.02 N/ 25.06 W	

12) The *Sangara* sank to the bottom in harbor, but was later salvaged and repaired.
1) *U 46* observed a torpedo hit the ship, but it did not explode.
2) *U 108* reported the *Michael E.* as a merchant cruiser because there was a catapult observed on the forecastle (C.A.M.ship).

1	2	3	4	5	6	7	8	9	10 11	12	13	14	15

June 1941, cont.

1	2	3	4	5	6	7	8	9	10 11	12	13	14	15
4/0503	dt	U 101	Mengersen	BD 5682	-D: 5271+	T	-	4/	br -D	Trecarrell	5271+	47.10 N/ 31. W	
(27. 5.)	dt	U 69	Metzler	Lagos	---------	M	-	4/	br -Bg	Robert Hughes	2879+	Lagos-Einfahrt	
4/1357	dt	U 73	Rosenbaum	BD 4236	-D 7000=?	T	-						3)
5/0131	dt	U 48	Schultze	BD 5185	-T: 6054+	T	-	4/	br -MT	Wellfield	6054+	48.34 N/ 31.34 W	
6/0215	it	VENIERO	Petroni	34n/11w	-T 7000+	T	HG.64	6/0015	br -D	Ariosto	-----		4)
6/0215	it	VENIERO	Petroni	34n/11w	-D 6000+	T	HG.64						4)
6/0422	it	MARCONI	Pollina	35n/11w	-T 5742+	T	OG.63						4)
6/0425	it	MARCONI	Pollina	35n/11w	-D 6000+	T	OG.63	6/	br -D	Baron Lovat	3395+	35.30 N/ 11.30 W	
6/0427	it	MARCONI	Pollina	35n/11w	-D 6000+	T	OG.63	6/	sw -D	Taberg	1392+	35.36 N/ 11.12 W	
6/0427	it	MARCONI	Pollina	35n/11w	-D 8000=	T	OG.63						4)
6/0503	dt	U 106	Oesten	EH 3429	-D 4000+	T	-	6/	br -D	Sacramento Valley	4573+	17.10 N/ 30.10 W	
6/0555	it	VELELLA	Terra	35n/11w	-T 14000+	T	OG.63						4)
6/0555	it	VELELLA	Terra	35n/11w	-D 7500+	T	OG.63						4)
6/1004	dt	U 46	Endraß	BC 3556	-T 9000=	T	-						5)
6/1232	it	EMO	Roselli-	36n/09w	-D 7000+	T	OG.63						4)
6/1232	it	EMO	Lorenzini	36n/09w	-D 4000+	T	OG.63						4)
6/2024	dt	U 43	Lüth	BC 3486	-D 4700+	T	OB.328 d	6/	nl -D	Yselhaven	4802+	49.25 N/ 40.54 W	
6/2325	dt	U 48	Schultze	BD 4827	-D: 5201+	T	-	6/	br -D	Tregarthen	5201+	46.17 N/ 36.20 W	
7/	dt	U 38	Liebe	ER	-D 10000+	T	-	7/	br -D	Kingston Hill	7628+	09.35 N/ 29.40 W	
8/0006	dt	U 108	Scholtz	BC 6378	-D 5600+	T	-	7/	br -D	Baron Nairn	3164+	47.35 N/ 39.02 W	
8/0442	dt	U 107	Hessler	ET 2930	-D: 7818+	T	-	8/	br -D	Adda	7816+	08.30 N/ 14.39 W	
8/0604	dt	U 108	Scholtz	BC 6521	-D: 4240+	T	-	8/	gr -D	Dirphys	4240+	47.44 N/ 39.02 W	
8/1234	dt	U 103	Schütze	ET 2724	-D 4800+	T	-	8/	br -D	Elmdene	4853+	08.16 N/ 16.50 W	

3) *U 73* observed a torpedo hit the ship, but it did not explode.
4) The British S/S *Ariosto* in position 41 observed torpedoes going by at the time of *Veniero's* attack. During this operation only the *Baron Lovat* and *Taberg* were lost most probably by the attack of *Marconi*.
5) *U 46* heard a very heavy detonation, but did not observe a hit. It was rammed while submerged by the tanker running in a circle.

1	2	3	4	5	6	7	8	9	10	11	12	13	14	15
June 1941, cont.														
8/1325	dt	U 46	Endraß	BD 3748	-T 7000+	T	-	8/	br	-MT	Ensis	6207=	48.46 N/ 29.14 W	6)
8/1325	dt	U 46	Endraß	-------	---------	T	-	8/	br	-D	Trevarrack	5270+	48.46 N/ 29.14 W	6)
8/1545	dt	U 48	Schultze	BD 7212	-T:10746+	T	OB.329d	8/	nl	-MT	Pendrecht	10746+	45.18 N/ 36.40 W	
9/0001	dt	U 46	Endraß	BD 6242	-D 5000+	TA	-	8/	br	-D	Phidias	5623+	48.25 N/ 26.12 W	7)
9/1835	dt	U 101	Mengersen	BC	-D 7500+	T	-	9/	br	-M	Silverpalm	6373+	51. N/ 26. W	
10/0248	dt	U 204	Kell	BC 6129	-D: 7886+	T	-	10/	be	-D	Mercier	7886+	48.30 N/ 41.30 W	
10/0723	dt	U 108	Scholtz	BC 6452	-D 3500+	T	OB.328	8/	nw	-D	Christian Krohg	1992+	45. N/ 36.30 W	8)
10/1055	dt	U 552	Topp	AM 4386	-D 6000+	T	-	10/	br	-D	Ainderby	4860+	55.30 N/ 12.10 W	
11/2051	dt	U 79	Kaufmann	AD 8218	-D: 1524+	TA	-	11/	nw	-D	Havtor	1524+	63.35 N/ 28.05 W	
12/0115	dt	U 553	Thurmann	BD 9389	-D 5100+	T	-	13/	br	-D	Susan Maersk	2355+	North Atlantic	9)
12/0326	dt	U 371	Driver	AL 1997	-D 9833+	T	-							10)
12/0252	dt	U 48	Schultze	AK 9784	-D 10000+	T	-	12/	br	-D	Empire Dew	7005+	51.09 N/ 30.16 W	
12/0414	dt	U 552	Topp	AM 4243	-M: 8593+	T	-	12/	br	-M	Chinese Prince	8593+	56.12 N/ 14.18 W	
12/1505	dt	U 553	Thurmann	BD 9814	-T: 5590+	T	OG.64	12/	nw	-DT	Ranella	5590+	43.39 N/ 28. W	
13/0404	dt	U 77	Schonder	BC 85	-D: 4743+	T	-	12/	br	-D	Tresillian	4743+	44.40 N/ 45.30 W	
13/0440	it	BRIN	Longanesi-	39n/23w	-D 4000∓	T	SL.75							11)
13/0450	it	BRIN	Cattani	39n/23w	-D 4000+	T	SL.75	13/	br	-D	Djurdjura	3460+	38.53 N/ 23.11 W	
13/0450	it	BRIN	Longanesi-	39n/23w	-D 4000+	T	SL.75	13/	gr	-D	Eirini Kyriakides	3781+	38.53 N/ 23.11 W	
13/0500	it	BRIN	Cattani	39n/23w	-D 4000+	T	SL.75							11)
13/1157	dt	U 107	Hessler	ES 5313	-D: 4981+	T	-	13/	gr	-D	Pandias	4981+	07.49 N/ 23.28 W	
14/0346	dt	U 751	Bigalk	BD 4144	-D 5500+	T	-	13/	br	-D	St.Lindsay	5370+	51. N/ 30. W	12)

6) *U 46* assumed one hit and one additional hit by a dud on the *Ensis*. *U 46* sank her later by a coup de grâce.
7) The *Phidias* was hit by a dud torpedo and then sunk by gunfire.
8) The *Christian Krong* was missed with one torpedo by *U 108* on Jun 9th, and sunk on Jun.10th.
9) The ship hit by *U 553* sank in 60 seconds; it must have been the *Susan Maersk*, reported missing after Jun.13th.
10) The ship of the type *Kent* or *Tongario* was attacked by *U 371*. The ship received two hits and sank after 38 minutes.
11) The *Brin* attacked five ships in different columns of the convoy and reported four ships hit. But only two were hit in reality.
12) The ship hit by *U 751* exploded. Probably it was the *St.Lindsey* reported missing after Jun.13th.

1	2	3	4	5	6	7	8	9	10	11	12	13	14	15
June 1941, cont.														
16/0806	dt	U 141	Schüler	AM 50	−D 21000=?	T	−							13)
17/0315	dt	U 43	Lüth	BD 3933	−D 4500+	T	.	17/		br	−M Cathrine	2727+	49.30 N/ 16. W	
18/0328	dt	U 552	Topp	AM 2912	−D:10948+	T	−	18/		br	−D Norfolk	10948+	57.17 N/ 11.14 W	
18/1607	dt	U 75	Ringelmann	CC 6534	−D 10000=?	T	−							13)
20/2019	dt	U 123	Hardegen	DJ 1169	−D: 4333+	TA	−	20/		pt	−D Ganda	4333+	34.10 N/ 11.40 W	
22/0329	dt	U 141	Schüler	AM 50	−D 4000+	T	SL.75	22/		sw	−D Calabria	1277+	100m v. Inishtrabull	
22/2236	dt	U 77	Schonder	BC 64	−D 4355+	T	−	23/		br	−D Arakaka	2379+	47. N/ 40. W	14)
24/0331	dt	U 203	Mützelburg	AK 4710	−T 15000=?	T	HX.133							15)
24/0331	dt	U 203	Mützelburg	AK 4710	−D 5000+	T	HX.133	24/0133	nw	−M Solöy	4402+	54.39 N/ 39.43 W	15)
24/0333	dt	U 203	Mützelburg	AK 4710	−D 8000=	T	HX.133							15)
24/1108	dt	U 203	Mützelburg	AK 4770	−D 6000+	T	OB.336	24/0913	br	−M Kinross	4956+	55.23 N/ 38.49 W	
24/1110	dt	U 203	Mützelburg	AK 4770	−D 5000+	T	OB.336	24/	nl	−D Schie	1967+	55.23 N/ 38.49 W	
24/1132	dt	U 371	Driver	AK 4455	−D 7000+	T	HX.133s	24/0740	nw	−M Vigrid	4765+	55. N/ 41. W	
24/2106	dt	U 651	Lohmeyer	AK 1973	−−−−−−−−−	T	HX.133	24/1906	br	−D Brockley Hill	5297+	58.30 N/ 38.20 W	
25/0456	dt	U 77	Schonder	BC 23	−D: 4603+	T	−	24/	gr	−D Anna Bulgaris	4603+	55. N/ 38. W	
25/0620	dt	U 108	Scholtz	AJ 9976	−D 5000+	T	−	24/	gr	−D Ellinico	3059+	55. N/ 38. W	
25/1135	dt	U 75	Ringelmann	AL 9259	−D 4000+	T	−							16)
25/1614	dt	U 108	Scholtz	AJ 9587	−D: 4362+	T	OB.336s	24/	gr	−D Nicolas Pateras	4362+	55. N/ 38. W	
27/0056	dt	U 79	Kaufmann	AK 2434	−T 10000=	T	HX.133	26/2258	nl	−MT Tibia	10356=	59.55 N/ 30.49 W	
27/0119	dt	U 69	Metzler	DT 3800	−D 6000=	T	SL.76							17)
27/0149	dt	U 69	Metzler	DT 3897	−D 9500+	T	SL.76	26/	br	−D Empire Ability	7603+	23.50 N/ 21.10 W	

13) The torpedoes of *U 141* and *U 75* hit their targets but did not explode.
14) The weather-reporting ship *Arakaka* was reported by *U 77* as the Greek steamer *Alexandra*.
15) *U 203* fired two torpedoes against a ship of 15,000 gross tons. The first hit but did not explode, the second missed but hit a target behind. A third torpedo was heard to detonate. Only the *Solöy* was hit and sunk at this time.
16) *U 75* attacked an empty steamer going east. The ship sank by the stern after only 4 minutes.
17) *U 69* missed the target but assumed a hit on a ship behind in the convoy.

1	2	3	4	5	6	7	8	9	10	11	12	13	14	15
June 1941, cont.														
27/0155	dt	U 564	Suhren	AK 2432	-D 8000+	T	HX.133	26/2353	nl	-D	Maasdam	8812+	60. N/ 30.35 W	
27/0156	dt	U 564	Suhren	AK 2432	-D 5000+	T	HX.133	26/2353	br	-M	Malaya II	8651+	59.56 N/ 30.35 W	
27/0157	dt	U 564	Suhren	AK 2432	-D: 5000=	T	HX.133	26/2354	nw	-MT	Kongsgaard	9467=	60. N/ 30.42 W	
27/0237	dt	U 69	Metzler	DT 3898	-D 8000+	T	SL.76	26/	br	-D	River Lugar	5423+	24. N/ 21. W	
27/0310	dt	U 552	Topp	AK 2816	-D 3000=?	T								18)
27/2357	dt	U 123	Hardegen	DT 2626	-T 10000+	T	SL.76	27/	br	-D	P.L.M.22	5646+	25.43 N/ 22.47 W	
27/2358	dt	U 123	Hardegen	DT 2626	-D 6000+	T	SL.76	27/	nl	-D	Oberon	1996+	25.43 N/ 22.47 W	
27/2400	dt	U 123	Hardegen	DT 2626	-D 4000+	T	SL.76							19)
28/0207	dt	U 146	Ites	AM 3381	-D 8000+	T	-	28/	fi	-D	Pluto	3496+	100m NNW Butt of Lewis	
28/1254	it	DA VINCI	Calda	34n/12w	-T: 8000+	T	-	28/	br	-MT	Auris	8030+	34.27 N/ 11.57 W	
29/0051	dt	U 103	Schütze	DG 9541	-D: 6600+	T	-	28/	it	-D	Ernani	6619+	450m W Las Palmas	20)
29/	dt	U 651	Lohmeyer	-------	---------	T	HX.133	29/0030	br	-D	Grayburn	6342+	59.30 N/ 18.07 W	
29/1146	dt	U 66	Zapp	DG 9240	-D: 4345+	T	SL.76s	29/	gr	-D	George J.Goulandris	4345+	29.05 N/ 25.10 W	
29/1850	dt	U 66	Zapp	DG 60	-D 6300+	T	SL.76s	29/	gr	-D	Kalypso Vergotti	5686+	29. N/ 25. W	
29/1936	dt	U 123	Hardegen	DG 8316	ACL:4088+	T	SL.76	29/	br	-D	Rio Azul	4088+	29. N/ 25. W	
29/1958	dt	U 564	Suhren	AD 9891	-D 3500+	T	-	29/	is	-D	Hekla	1215+	58.20 N/ 43. W	
30/0559	dt	U 66	Zapp	DG	-D: 5614+	TA	-	30/	br	-D	St.Anselm	5614+	31. N/ 26. W	21)
July 1941														
1/1825	dt	U 108	Scholtz	BD 5654	-D: 2486+	T	-	1/	br	-D	Toronto City	2486+	47.03 N/ 30. W	1)
4/	dt	U 69	Metzler	DH 19	-D 5000+	A	-	4/	br	-D	Robert L.Holt	2918+	24.15 N/ 20.00 W	

18) The torpedo fired by *U 552* hit the ship but did not detonate.
19) The third torpedo fired by *U 123* missed the target but was assumed to have hit a ship behind her in the convoy.
20) The *Ernani* was an Italian blockade runner going from Teneriffa to Bordeaux. She sailed under cover as the Dutch *Enggano* and was sunk by *U 103* by mistake.
21) The *St.Anselm* evaded four torpedoes and was hit by two duds before being sunk.
 1) The *Toronto City* was a weather observation ship.

1	2	3	4	5	6	7	8	9	10	11	12	13	14	15
July 1941, cont.														
4/0355	dt	U 123	Hardegen	DS 3622	-D: 5444+	T	-	4/	br	-D	Auditor	5444+	25.33 N/ 28.23 W	
5/0829	dt	U 96	Lehmann-Willenbrock	BD 9419	-D 12000+	T	-	5/	br	-D	Anselm	5954+	44.25 N/ 28.35 W	2)
5/0829	dt	U 96	Lehmann-Willenbrock	BD 9419	-PY 5000=	T	-					-----		2)
9/0155	dt	U 98	Gysae	CE 1344	-D: 5945+	T	-	9/	br	-D	Designer	5945+	42.59 N/ 31.40 W	
9/0528	dt	U 98	Gysae	CE 1315	-D: 4900+	T	-	9/	br	-D	Inverness	4897+	42.46 N/ 32.45 W	
14/1607	it	MOROSINI	Fraternale	36n/21w	-D: 5358+	T	OG.67d	14/	br	-D	Rupert de Larrinaga	5358+	36.18 N/ 21.11 W	
14/2215	it	MALASPINA	Prini	36n/21w	-D 7000+	T	OG.67d	14/	gr	-D	Nikoklis	3576+	105m SW Azores	
15/0344	it	MOROSINI	Fraternale	37n/21w	-D: 8194+	T	-	15/	br	-D	Lady Somers	8194+	36. N/ 21. W	3)
17/1645	it	MALASPINA	Prini	31n/17w	-D 5000+	T	-	17/	br	-D	Guelma	4402+	30.44 N/ 17.33 W	
19/1042	dt	U 66	Zapp	DT 95	-D 7600+	T	-	19/	br	-D	Holmside	3433+	19. N/ 21.30 W	
19/1355	dt	U 98	Gysae	AL 8824	-M 6000=?	T	-							4)
20/	dt	U 203	Mützelburg	BE 19	-D =	A	-	20/	br	-M	Canadian Star	8293=	49.15 N/ 21. W	5)
20/0505	dt	U 95	Schreiber	BE 2294	-M =	A	-	20/0335	br	-M	Palma	5419=	50.14 N/ 17.53 W	6)
21/2134	it	TORELLI	de Giacomo	35n/14w	-T 7000+	T	-	21/	nw	-MT	Ida Knudsen	8913+	34.34 N/ 13.14 W	
23/2018	it	BAGNOLINI	Chialamberto	36n/14w	-T 8500+	T	OG.68 ?							7)
23/2134	it	BAGNOLINI	Chialamberto	36n/14w	-D 5000=	T	OG.68 ?							7)
25/0034	it	BARBARIGO	Murzi	32n/26w	-D: 9000+	T	-	25/	br	-D	Macon	5135+	32.48 N/ 26.12 W	

2) *U 96* fired a four-torpedo salvo and assumed hits on a big steamer (the armed merchant cruiser HMS *Cathay*) and a yacht (the surveying ship HMS *Challenger*). But both torpedoes hit the *Anselm*. The ships were escorted by 3 destroyers.
3) The *Lady Somers* was an "ocean boarding vessel."
4) *U 98* fired two torpedoes and assumed one hit on this motorship, but the torpedo did not explode.
5) The *Canadian Star* at 02.42 evaded a two-torpedo-salvo of *U 126* (Bauer).
6) *U 95* missed the *Palma* with two torpedoes and had to break off a subsequent gun duel after 3 hits.
7) The *Bagnolini* assumed to have hit in the convoy one tanker with two and a freighter with one torpedo. It must have been the convoy OG.68, but there are no reports about this attack.

1	2	3	4	5	6	7	8	9	10	11	12	13	14	15

July 1941, cont.

1	2	3	4	5	6	7	8	9	10 11	12	13	14	15
26/0328 dt	U 141	Schüler	AM 5276	-D	6000+	T	OS.1	26/	br -D	Botwey	5106+	55.42 N/ 09.53 W	8)
26/0330 dt	U 141	Schüler	AM 5276	-D	5000+	T	OS.1	26/	br -D	Atlantic City	5133=	55.42 N/ 09.58 W	8)
26/0335 dt	U 141	Schüler	AM 5276	-D	10000+	T	OS.1						8)
26/2239 it	BARBARIGO	Murzi	33n/23w	-T:	8272+	T	-	26/	br -MT	Horn Shell	8272+	33.23 N/ 22.18 W	
27/0021 dt	U 79	Kaufmann	BE 8345	-D	6000+	T	OG.69	26/	br -D	Hawkinge	2475+	44.55 N/ 17.44 W	9)
27/0021 dt	U 79	Kaufmann	BE 8345	-D	12000+	T	OG.69						9)
27/0021 dt	U 79	Kaufmann	BE 8345	-D	6000+	T	OG.69						9)
27/0022 dt	U 79	Kaufmann	BE 8345	-D	=?	T	OG.69						9)
27/0024 dt	U 79	Kaufmann	BE 8345	-D	=?	T	OG.69						9)
27/0254 dt	U 203	Mützelburg	BE 8295	-D	8000+	T	OG.69	26/	br -D	Kellwyn	1459+	43. N/ 17. W	10)
27/0254 dt	U 203	Mützelburg	BE 8295	-D	6000+	T	OG.69						10)
27/2351 dt	U 126	Bauer	CF 3180	-D	8000+	T	OG.69	27/	br -D	Erato	1335+	43.10 N/ 17.30 W	11)
27/2351 dt	U 126	Bauer	CF 3180	-D	3000+	T	OG.69						11)
27/2351 dt	U 126	Bauer	CF 3180	-D	6000+	T	OG.69						11)
27/2351 dt	U 126	Bauer	CF 3180	-D	3000+	T	OG.69	27/	nw -D	Inga I	1304+	43.10 N/ 17.30 W	11)
28/0243 dt	*U 68*	*Merten*	*CF 3159*	*PE*	*+*	*T*	*OG.69*						*12)*
28/0424 dt	U 561	Bartels	CF 3513	-T	12000+	T	OG.69						13)
28/0424 dt	U 561	Bartels	CF 3513	-D	4000+	T	OG.69	28/	br -D	Wrotham	1884+	43. N/ 17. W	13)
28/0427 dt	U 561	Bartels	CF 3513	ACL	5000=	T	OG.69						13)
28/2127 dt	U 203	Mützelburg	CG 1784	-D	8000+	T	OG.69	28/	sw -D	Norita	1516+	40.10 N/ 15.30 W	14)
28/2127 dt	U 203	Mützelburg	CG 1784	-D	5000+	T	OG.69	28/	br -D	Lapland	1330+	40.36 N/ 15.30 W	14)
28/2128 dt	*U 203*	*Mützelburg*	*CG 1784*	*DD*	*+?*	*T*	*OG.69*						*14)*
28/2128 dt	U 203	Mützelburg	CG 1784	-D	4000+	T	OG.69						14)

8) *U 141* observed one hit on each of three ships. The first was seen being abandoned, the second exploded, and the third which had four masts was seen to develop a heavy list. The abandoned *Atlantic City* was later reboarded and salvaged.

9) *U 79* had to dive because a destroyer was running in, and could see only one column of fire. The later detonations must have been the depth charges from the escorts.

10) *U 203* observed one ship sinking immediately. The second ship was abandoned and sank after about 20 minutes.

11) *U 126* first fired four bow torpedoes and then two stern torpedoes. One ship exploded and one small ship behind that one was hit. The stern torpedoes hit two different ships aft and amidships. The last one was observed sinking.

12) *U 68* observed a red jet of flame on the side of a corvette, but could not hear a detonation or observe the ship sink.

13) *U 561* hit a big tanker which burst into flames. A freighter sank in only 30 seconds.

14) *U 203* had to dive after the attack and could only hear the detonations. The escorts dropped depth charges, so mistakes are possible.

1	2	3	4	5	6	7	8	9	10	11	12	13	14	15
July 1941, cont.														
30/0138	dt	U 371	Driver	CF 7866	-D	7000+	T	OS.1	30/		br -D	Shahristan	6935+	35.19 N/ 23.53 W	
30/0246	dt	U 371	Driver	CF 7945	-D	7000+	T	OS.1	30/		nl -D	Sitoebondo	7049+	35.19 N/ 23.53 W	
August 1941														
4/	dt	U 126	Bauer	CF 85	-S	171+	A	-	4/		br -Df	Robert Max	172+	36.47 N/ 21.15 W	
5/0150	dt	U 372	Neumann	AL 9392	-D	7500+	T	SL.81	5/0150		br -D	Belgravian	3136+	53.03 N/ 15.54 W	1)
5/0154	dt	U 372	Neumann	AL 9392	-D	7000=	T	SL.81	5/0159		br -D	Volturo	-----		1)
5/0159	dt	U 372	Neumann	AL 9392	-D	5000+	T	SL.81	5/0159		br -D	Swiftpool	5205+	53.03 N/ 16.00 W	1)
5/0416	dt	U 204	Kell	AM 7173	-D	14000=	T	SL.81							2)
5/0520	dt	U 75	Ringelmann	AM 7151	-D	6000+	T	SL.81	5/0524		br -D	Harlingen	5415+	53.26 N/ 15.40 W	3)
5/0520	dt	U 75	Ringelmann	AM 7151	-D	6000+	T	SL.81	5/0524		br -D	Cape Rodney	4512+	53.26 N/ 15.40 W	3)
5/0540	dt	U 74	Kentrat	AM 7156	-D	8000=	T	SL.81							4)
5/0540	dt	U 74	Kentrat	AM 7156	-D	8000+	T	SL.81	5/0528		br -D	Kumasian	4922+	53.26 N/ 15.40 W	4)
5/0541	dt	U 74	Kentrat	AM 7156	-D	8000=	T	SL.81							4)
5/0542	dt	U 74	Kentrat	AM 7156	-D	8000=	T	SL.81							4)
9/0528	dt	U 206	Opitz	AE 8525	-Df	groß+	T	-							5)
11/0335	it	MARCONI	Pollina	37n/10w	DD	1690+	T	.	11/		br PS	Deptford	-----		
12/0311	dt	U 568	Preuß	AE 7665	PE	+	T	ON.5	12/		br PE	Picotee	925+	S Iceland	
12/0311	dt	U 568	Preuß	AE 7665	-T	7000=?	T	.							6)
12/2110	it	TAZZOLI	Fecia di Cossato	04n/09w	-D:	5449=?	T	-			br -D	Sangara	-----		7)
14/1201	it	MARCONI	Pollina	41n/18w	-D:	4200+	TA	-	14/		jg -D	Sud	2589+	41.　N/ 17.41 W	8)
14/1601	dt	U 126	Bauer	CF 3733	-D:	2545+	Tf	-							

1) *U 372* reported one hit on a steamer with the first torpedo. The ship burned out. The second torpedo missed the target but exploded against a ship behind her. The fourth torpedo hit a ship loaded with ammunition, which exploded and sank in 50 seconds.
2) *U 204* observed two hits on a steamer which stopped under heavy smoke. Because of ASW operations there was no observation of
   the ship sinking.
3) *U 75* observed a fire and water column after the first hit, a water column only after the second hit, and then had to dive.
4) *U 74* observed a hit with the second torpedo. The other detonations were heard and not observed because the boat had to dive.
5) *U 206* met an armed fishing trawler on an easterly course which sank following a heavy detonation.
6) The hit was not observed very clearly.
7) The *Sangara* was not hit in reality.
8) The *Sud* was hit by the *Marconi* with about 25 rounds of 100mm shells and damaged, but was sunk only after a coup de grâce by
   U 126.

1	2	3	4	5	6	7	8	9	10	11	12	13	14	15

August 1941, cont.

1	2	3	4	5	6	7	8	9	10 11	12	13	14	15
18/0250	dt	U 38	Schuch	AD 7969	-D 6000+	T	-	17/	pa -D	Longtaker	1700+	61.26 N/ 30.50 W	
19/0205	*dt*	*U 204*	*Kell*	*BE 2647*	*DD 1870+*	*T*	*OG.71s*	*19/0114 nw*	*DD*	*Bath*	*1060+*	*49. N/ 17. W*	
19/0208	dt	U 559	Heidtmann	BE 2593	-D 14000+	T	OG.71						9)
19/0208	dt	U 559	Heidtmann	BE 2593	-D 8000+	T	OG.71	19/0115 br	-D	Alva	1584+	49. N/ 17. W	9)
19/0208	dt	U 559	Heidtmann	BE 2593	-D 8000=	T	OG.71						9)
19/0406	dt	U 201	Schnee	BE 2567	-D 4000+	T	OG.71	19/0309 br	-D	Ciscar	1809+	49.10 N/ 17.40 W	10)
19/0406	dt	U 201	Schnee	BE 2567	-DT 12000+	T	OG.71						10)
19/0406	dt	U 201	Schnee	BE 2567	-D 4000+	T	OG.71	19/0309 br	-D	Aguila	3255+	49.23 N/ 17.56 W	10)
19/0528	dt	U 204	Kell	BE 2599	-D 6000+	T	OG.71						11)
19/0528	dt	U 204	Kell	BE 2599	-D 10000+	T	OG.71						11)
19/2259	it	TAZZOLI	Fecia di Cossato	05n/13w	-T groß+	T	-	19/	nw -MT	Sildra	7313+	05.30 N/ 12.50 W	
22/2331	dt	U 564	Suhren	CG 1953	-D 5000+	T	OG.71	22/2228 br	-Dt	Empire Oak	484+	40.43 N/ 11.39 W	12)
22/2331	dt	U 564	Suhren	CG 1953	-D 5000+	T	OG.71	22/2228 br	-D	Clonlara	1203+	40.43 N/ 11.39 W	12)
22/2331	dt	U 564	Suhren	CG 1953	-D 5000=	T	OG.71						12)
22/2331	dt	U 564	Suhren	CG 1953	-D 5000=	T	OG.71						12)
23/0214	dt	U 201	Schnee	CG 2771	-D 4000+	T	OG.71	23/0116 br	-M	Stork	787+	40.43 N/ 11.39 W	13)
23/0214	dt	U 201	Schnee	CG 2771	-D 8000=	T	OG.71						13)
23/0214	dt	U 201	Schnee	CG 2771	-D 5000+	T	OG.71	23/0116 br	-D	Aldergrove	1974+	40.43 N/ 11.39 W	13)
23/0216	dt	U 201	Schnee	CG 2771	-D 4000=	T	OG.71						13)
23/0335	dt	U 564	Suhren	CG 2772	-D 5000=	T	OG.71	23/0245 nw	-D	Spind (s.u.)	2129=	40.43 N/ 11.39 W	14)
23/0335	dt	U 564	Suhren	CG 2772	-D 5000=?	T	OG.71						14)

9) *U 559* fired a 4-torpedo salvo and observed one hit and heard in addition one double and one single detonation. The assessment of the B.d.U. was two ships of 17,000 gross tons sunk and one additional ship of 7,000 gross tons damaged.

10) *U 201* fired a 4-torpedo salvo and observed two detonations on a tanker and two additional detonations on two ships behind her. The B.d.U. assumed (together with No.13) 4 ships of 20,000 gross tons sunk and 3 ships of 17,000 gross tons damaged.

11) *U 204* fired a 4-torpedo salvo and observed columns of fire on two ships. The first sank after 19 minutes and 25 seconds, the second after 43 minutes. Two torpedoes missed.

12) *U 564* fired a 4-torpedo salvo and observed four different detonations and three fire-columns. Rescue boats were observed.

13) *U 201* fired a four torpedo salvo and observed one hit on a freighter and two hits on a tanker which sank immediately in flames. Another detonation was heard.

14) *U 564* fired four single shots and heard one detonation and one possible detonation. The *Spind* was torpedoed and was sunk later by a coup de grâce (surface runner) and gunfire from *U 552*.

1	2	3	4	5	6		7	8	9	10	11	12	13	14	15

August 1941, cont.

1	2	3	4	5	6a	6b	7	8	9	10	11	12	13	14	15
23/0525	dt	U 564	Suhren	CG 2783	-D	5000+	T	OG.71							15)
23/0525	dt	U 564	Suhren	CG 2783	-D	5000+	T	OG.71							15)
23/0525	*dt*	*U 564*	*Suhren*	*CG 2783*	*PE*	*+*	*T*	*OG.71*	*23/0428*	*br*	*PE*	*Zinnia*	*900+*	*40.43 N/ 11.39 W*	*15)*
23/0648	dt	U 552	Topp	CG 5114	-D:	2129+	Af	OG.71	23/	nw	-D	Spind (s.o.)	2129+	40.43 N/ 11.39 W	14)
23/2347	dt	U 143	Gelhaus	AM 3523	-D	6000+	T	.	23/	nw	-D	Inger	1418+	58.58 N/ 07.50 W	
26/0044	dt	U 652	Fraatz	AE 9185	-M	9000=	T	.	25/						16)
27/0125	dt	U 557	Paulshen	AM 4774	-D	4000+	T	OS.4	27/	nw	-M	Segundo	4414+	53.36 N/ 16.40 W	17)
27/0133	dt	U 557	Paulshen	AM 4774	-D	5000=	T	OS.4							17)
27/0134	dt	U 557	Paulshen	AM 4774	-D	5000+	T	OS.4	27/	br	-D	Saugor	6303+	53.36 N/ 16.40 W	17)
27/0205	dt	U 557	Paulshen	AL 6996	-D	4000+	T	OS.4	27/	br	-D	Tremoda	4736+	53.36 N/ 16.40 W	17)
27/0426	dt	U 557	Paulshen	AL 6998	-D	4000+	T	OS.4	27/	br	-D	Embassage	4954+	54. N/ 13. W	17)
27/1435	dt	U 202	Linder	AE 8439	APC	800+	T	-	30/	br	-Df	Ladylove	230+	near Iceland	18)
28/1641	dt	U 558	Krech	AL 9284	-D	7000+	T	OS.4	28/	br	-M	Otaio	10298+	52.16 N/ 17.50 W	

September 1941

1	2	3	4	5	6a	6b	7	8	9	10	11	12	13	14	15
3/2042	dt	U 567	Fahr	AL 8563	-M:	3485+	T	-	3/	br	-M	Fort Richepanse	3485+	52.15 N/ 21.10 W	
4/1439	*dt*	*U 652*	*Fraatz*	*AD 8526*	*DD*	*1090/*	*T*	*-*	*4/*	*am*	*DD*	*Greer*	-----		*1)*
5/	dt	U 501	Förster	AK		---------	TA	SC.41 s	5/	nw	-D	Einvik	2000+	60.38 N/ 31.18 W	
5/	it	BARACCA	Viani (?)	-------		---------	A	-	5/	pa	-M	Trinidad	434+	46.06 N/ 17.04 W	2)
5/2337	dt	U 141	Schüler	AM 2522	APC	800+	T	-							3)
6/2330	dt	U 141	Schüler	AE 8996	APC	500+	T	-	8/	br	-Df	King Erik	228+	near Iceland	4)

15) *U 564* fired three single shots and observed one ammunition ship sinking immediately and one other ship sinking shortly
    afterwards. The corvette exploded. The B.d.U. assumed altogether three ships of 20,000 gross tons sunk and four ships of
    20,000 gross tons damaged. In addition one corvette was assumed sunk.
16) *U 652* observed one hit on a ship in a convoy running SSE with a black smoke column.
17) The second torpedo of *U 557* missed its target and hit a ship behind it.
18) The *Ladylove* was reported missing after Aug.30th. She sank in 15 seconds, and could not report being hit.
 1) The *Greer* was attacked by *U 652* when a British aircraft cooperating with the *Greer* dropped two depth charges which the
    U-boat misidentified as coming from the destroyer.

1	2	3	4	5	6		7	8	9	10	11	12	13	14	15

September 1941, cont.

1	2	3	4	5	6		7	8	9	10 11	12	13	14	15
9/0655	dt	U 81	Guggenberger	AD 6886	-D	5000+	T	SC.42s	9/2140?br	-D	Empire Springbuck	5591+	61.38 N/ 40.40 W	5)
9/1359	dt	U 85	Greger	AD 9259	-D	7000/	T	SC.42	9/0904 br	-D	Jedmoor	-----		5a)
10/0230	dt	U 432	Schultze	AD 6857	-D	8000+	T	SC.42						
10/0230	dt	U 432	Schultze	AD 6857	-D	6000+	T	SC.42	9/2130 br	-D	Muneric	5229+	61.38 N/ 40.40 W	6)
10/0303	dt	U 81	Guggenberger	AD 6851	-D	5000=	T	SC.42						7)
10/0303	dt	U 81	Guggenberger	AD 6851	-D	6000=	T	SC.42						7)
10/0304	dt	U 81	Guggenberger	AD 6851	-D	6000+	T	SC.42						7)
10/0452	dt	U 652	Fraatz	AD 6828	-DT	7000+?	T	SC.42	9/2355 br	-DT	Tahchee	6508=	61.15 N/ 41.05 W	8)
10/0453	dt	U 652	Fraatz	AD 6828	-D	4000+?	T	SC.42	9/2354 br	-D	Baron Pentland(su)	3410=	61.15 N/ 41.05 W	8)
10/0708	dt	U 432	Schultze	AD 6526	-D	4000+	T	SC.42	10/0210 nl	-D	Winterswijk	3205+	61.38 N/ 40.40 W	8a)
10/0709	dt	U 432	Schultze	AD 6526	-D	6000+	T	SC.42	10/0211 nw	-D	Stargard	1113+	61.30 N/ 40.30 W	8a)
10/0728	dt	U 81	Guggenberger	AD 6851	-M	7000+	T	SC.42						9)
10/0729	dt	U 81	Guggenberger	AD 6836	-D	6000+?	T	SC.42						9)
10/0753	dt	U 81	Guggenberger	AD 6835	-M	7000+?	T	SC.42	10/0247 br	-D	Sally Maersk	3252+	61.40 N/ 40.30 W	9)
10/0957	dt	U 82	Rollmann	AD 6830	-D	4000+	T	SC.42	10/0504 br	-D	Empire Hudson	7465+	61.28 N/ 39.46 W	10)
10/1640	dt	U 85	Greger	AD 6628	-D	7000+	T	SC.42	10/1143 br	-D	Thistleglen	4748+	61.59 N/ 39.46 W	11)
10/1640	dt	U 85	Greger	AD 6628	-D	=?	T	SC.42						11)
10/1718	dt	U 85	Greger	AD 6628	-D	4000+	T	SC.42						11)
10/1719	dt	U 85	Greger	AD 6628	-D	4000+	T	SC.42						11)
10/	dt	U 111	Kleinschmidt	FB 3354	-D	10000+	T	-	10/	nl -M	Marken	5719+	01.36 N/ 36.55 W	

2) The *Trinidad* was reported missing. The only U-boat in the area was the *Baracca* which did not return and could not report a success.
3) *U 141* hit a trawler amidships which exploded. 4) This trawler exploded too. One of the trawlers might have been the *King E.*
5) The *Empire Springbuck* was a straggler from SC.42 and exploded after two hits. 5a) The *Jedmoor* observed the attack but was not hit.
6) The *Muneric* was hit by two torpedoes from *U 432* which claimed to have hit two different ships.
7) *U 81* observed fire columns and detonations after 2 min 30 sec and 3 min 30 sec on three ships, but in reality there were no hits.
8) The *Tahchee* was towed by HMCS *Orillia* to Reykjavik. The *Baron Pentland* was abandoned, but remained floating because of its lumber load and was finally sunk on Sept.19th by *U 372* (see p.66). 8a) There are some discrepancies in the time of torpedoing of the two ships.
9) *U 81* observed one ship sinking after two hits and heard two other detonations. The fifth torpedo probably was a dud.
10) The *Empire Hudson* was a C.A.M.ship. 11) *U 85* made two attacks. In the first one hit was observed, and one detonation heard beyond. In the second attack two detonations were heard, but these must have been depth charges dropped by HMCS *Skeena*.

1	2	3	4	5	6		7	8	9	10 11	12	13	14	15
September 1941, cont.														
11/0151	dt	U 82	Rollmann	AD 7140	-T	8000+	T	SC.42	10/2057	br -MT	Bulysses	7519+	62.40 N/ 38.50 W	11a)
11/0212	dt	U 82	Rollmann	AD 7140	-T	10000+	T	SC.42	10/2119	br -D	Gypsum Queen	3915+	63.05 N/ 37.50 W	11a)
11/0406	dt	U 432	Schultze	AD 6644	-D	6000+	T	SC.42	10/2312	sw -D	Garm	1231+	63.02 N/ 37.51 W	12)
11/0408	dt	U 433	Ey	AD 7147	-D	4000=	Tf	SC.42s	10/2316	nw -D	Bestum	2215=	63. N/ 37. W	12)
11/	dt	U 207	Meyer	-------	--------		T	SC.42	11/0045	br -D	Stonepool	4815+	63.05 N/ 37.50 W	13)
11/	dt	U 207	Meyer	-------	--------		T	SC.42	11/0050	br -D	Brerury	4924+	62.40 N/ 38.50 W	13)
11/	dt	U 207	Meyer	-------	--------		T?	SC.42	11/0050	ca -D	Randa	1558??	63. N/ 37. W	13)
11/0705	dt	U 82	Rollmann	AD 7140	-D	4000+	T	SC.42	11/0210	sw -D	Scania (s.u.)	1980=	63.14 N/ 37.12 W	14)
11/0705	dt	U 82	Rollmann	AD 7140	-D	4000+	T	SC.42	11/0210	br -D	Empire Crossbill	5463+	63.14 N/ 37.12 W	14)
11/1332	dt	U 202	Linder	AD 7154	-D:	1629+	Tf	SC.42s	11/	sw -D	Scania (s.o.)	1980+	63.14 N/ 37.12 W	14)
11/1650	dt	U 105	Schewe	AD 7195	-D	5000+	T	-	11/	pa -D	Montana	1549+	63.40 N/ 35.50 W	
12/0129	dt	U 84	Uphoff	AD 4917	-D	6000=	T	SC.42						15)
15/0816	dt	U 94	Ites	AK 6682	-D:	5102+	T	-	15/	br -D	Newbury	5102+	54.39 N/ 28.04 W	
15/2038	dt	U 94	Ites	AK 6735	-D:	5762+	T	ON.14	15/	gr -D	Pegasus	5762+	54.40 N/ 29.50 W	16)
15/2348	dt	U 94	Ites	AK 6764	-D:	5613+	T	-	15/	br -D	Empire Eland	5613+	54. N/ 28. W	
16/2311	dt	U 98	Gysae	AM 2476	-D	big +	T	SC.42	16/2115	br -M	Jedmoor	4392+	59. N/ 10. W	17)
16/2316	dt	U 98	Gysae	AM 2476	-D	big =	T	SC.42						17)

11a) The first three torpedoes of *U 82* missed, and the fourth hit the *Bulysses* which exploded. The stern shot hit the *Gypsum Queen* which sank in 1 minute. 12) *U 432* fired two torpedoes. The first hit was observed, and it may have been the *Garm* which was torpedoed at this time according to the report of the S.O.E.- *U 433* first attacked two escorts but missed, and then a burning ship. At this time the S.O.E. reported the Norwegian S/S *Bestum* to have been torpedoed, which is not included in BR.1337.
13) There are no attack reports for this time. The attacking U-boat must have been the *U 207* which was sunk a few hours later by the escort. The Canadian S/S *Randa* was reported lost by the S.O.E. at this time in pos.113 (the other two ships were in pos.111, 112). But it is probable that the *Randa* became a straggler after staying behind to rescue survivors.
14) The *Scania* was first hit by one torpedo from *U 82*, and then sunk by two torpedoes from *U 202*.
15) *U 84* fired a four torpedo salvo against four ships, and heard one detonation.
16) The *Pegasus* sank on Sept.17th, two days after the coup de grâce by *U 94*.
17) *U 98* fired four torpedoes against an eastgoing convoy and observed two hits.

1	2	3	4	5	6	7	8	9	10	11	12	13	14	15

September 1941, cont.

1	2	3	4	5	6	7	8	9	10 11 12	13	14	15
19/0603	dt	U 74	Kentrat	AD 9458	-D	8000+	T	SC.44				18)
19/0603	dt	U 74	Kentrat	AD 9458	-D	6000+	T	SC.44	19/0210 ca PE Levis	925+	60.05 N/ 38.48 W	18)
19/1433	dt	U 372	Neumann	AJ 3278	-D:	3410+	Tf	SC.42s	19/ br -D Baron Pentland(so)	3410+	61.15 N/ 41.05 W	19)
20/0113	dt	U 74	Kentrat	AD 7851	-D	7000+	T	SC.44	19/2120 br -D Empire Burton	6966+	61.34 N/ 35.05 W	20)
20/0113	dt	U 74	Kentrat	AD 7851	-D	5000+	T	SC.44				20)
20/0113	dt	U 74	Kentrat	AD 7851	-D	=?	T	SC.44				20)
20/0138	dt	U 552	Topp	AD 7583	-DT	5000+	T	SC.44	19/2138 br -DT T.J.Williams	8212+	61.34 N/ 35.11 W	21)
20/0151	dt	U 552	Topp	AD 7583	-D	5000+	T	SC.44				21)
20/0151	dt	U 552	Topp	AD 7583	-D	7000+	T	SC.44	19/2149 pa -D Pink Star	4150+	61.36 N/ 35.07 W	21)
20/0327	dt	U 552	Topp	AD 7583	-T	10000+	T	SC.44	19/2330 nw -MT Barbro	6325+	61.30 N/ 35.00 W	22)
20/0430	dt	U 69	Zahn	AD 7800	-T	6000+?	Tf	SC.44s				22)
20/	dt	U 111	Kleinschmidt	FD 45	-M:	8474+	T	-	20/ br -M Cingalese Prince	8474+	02. S/ 25.30 W	
20/2332	dt	U 124	Mohr	BE 4232	-D	5000+	T	OG.74	20/ br -D Baltallinn	1303+	48.07 N/ 22.07 W	23)
20/2333	dt	U 124	Mohr	BE 4232	-T	8000=	T	OG.74				23)
20/2334	dt	U 124	Mohr	BE 4232	-D	10000+	T	OG.74	20/ br -D Empire Moat	2922+	48.07 N/ 22.05 W	23)
21/2250	dt	U 201	Schnee	BE 4866	-D	6000+	T	OG.74	21/ br -D Runa	1575+	46.20 N/ 22.23 W	
21/2320	dt	U 201	Schnee	BE 4944	-D	4000+	T	OG.74	21/ br -D Lissa	1511+	47. N/ 22. W	
21/2321	dt	U 201	Schnee	BE 4944	-D	4000+	T	OG.74	21/ br -D Rhineland	1381+	47. N/ 22. W	
22/0222	dt	U 68	Merten	DT 2595	-D	8000+	T	SL.87	22/0226 br -M Silverbelle	5302+	25.45 N/ 24. W	24)
22/0223	dt	U 68	Merten	DT 2595	-D	6000+	T	SL.87				24)
22/0224	dt	U 68	Merten	DT 2595	-T	7000=	T	SL.87				24)

18) *U 74* fired a 4-torpedo salvo and observed two hits on each of two ships. The first ship sank immediately. The second ship flashed a lamp signal "help" and sank in one minute. It must have been the corvette *Levis*.

19) The *Baron Pentland* was torpedoed by *U 652* on Sept.10th and drifted abandoned on her lumber cargo when sunk by *U 372*.

20) *U 74* fired a 4-torpedo salvo. The first ship was hit by two, the second by one and reported sunk. The fourth torpedo was a dud. There was only one ship hit and sunk.

21) *U 552* first missed two ships and then hit the *T.J.Williams*. Then a 2-torpedo salvo was fired. The first hit a ship behind the target, the second the *Pink Star*. 22) *U 552* hit the *Barbro* with two torpedoes, and *U 69* fired a coup de grâce that did not detonate.

23) *U 124* fired 3 torpedoes and heard one detonation, then one tanker was observed to be hit (burst cloud). One other ship was hit and sank immediately after a heavy explosion.

24) *U 68* observed two hits on the first ship with a boiler explosion, a fire column on a second ship with only a small detonation, and a hit on a tanker which was observed with a heavy list on the next day, supported by two escorts.

1	2	3	4	5	6	7	8	9	10	11	12	13	14	15
September 1941, cont.														
22/0244 dt		U 562	Hamm	AD 7835	-D	5000+	T	–	25/	br	-D	Erna III	1590+	61.45 N/ 35.15 W	25)
22/2346 dt		U 103	Winter	DG 9922	-D	7000+	T	SL.87	22/	br	-D	Niceto de Larrinaga	5591+	27.32 N/ 24.26 W	26)
22/2346 dt		U 103	Winter	DG 9922	-D	6000+	T	SL.87							26)
22/2347 dt		U 103	Winter	DG 9922	-D	6000+	T	SL.87							26)
22/2347 dt		U 103	Winter	DG 9922	-D	6000=	T	SL.87							26)
22/2347 dt		U 103	Winter	DG 9922	-D	5000+	T	SL.87	22/2152	br	-M	Edward Blyden	5003+	27.36 N/ 24.29 W	26)
24/0028 dt		U 67	Müller-Stöckheim	DG 6695	-D	7000+	T	SL.87	23/2235	br	-D	St.Clair II	3753+	30.25 N/ 23.35 W	
24/	it	MALASPINA	Prini	44n/22w	-D	+	T	.							27)
24/	it	MALASPINA	Prini	44n/22w	-D	25000+	T	.							27)
24/	it	MALASPINA	Prini	44n/22w	-D	+?	T	.							27)
24/0631 dt		U 107	Hessler	DH 4178	-D	8000+	T	SL.87	24/0441	br	-D	John Holt	4975+	31.12 N/ 23.32 W	
24/0633 dt		U 107	Hessler	DH 4178	-D	5000+	T	SL.87	24/0441	br	-D	Lafian	4876+	31.12 N/ 23.32 W	
24/0633 dt		U 107	Hessler	DH 4178	-DT	13000+	T	SL.87	24/0441	br	-M	Dixcove	3790+	31.12 N/ 23.41 W	
25/0744 dt		U 124	Mohr	BE 4165	-T	12000+	T	HG.73	25/0548	br	-D	Empire Stream	2922+	46.03 N/ 24.40 W	
26/0031 dt		U 203	Mützelburg	BE 4156	-D	8000+	T	HG.73	25/2233	nw	-D	Varangberg	2842+	47.50 N/ 24.50 W	28)
26/0031 dt		U 203	Mützelburg	BE 4156	-T	12000+	T	HG.73	25/2233	br	-D	Avoceta	3442+	47.57 N/ 24.05 W	28)
26/0031 dt		U 203	Mützelburg	BE 4156	-D	=	T	HG.73	26/0036	br	-D	Cortes	1374+	47.48 N/ 23.45 W	28)
26/0223 dt		U 124	Mohr	BE 4165	-D	6000+	T	HG.73	26/0036	br	-D	Petrel	1354+	47.40 N/ 23.28 W	
26/0223 dt		U 124	Mohr	BE 4165	-D	5000+	T	HG.73	26/0036	br	-D	Lapwing	1348+	47.40 N/ 23.30 W	
26/2310 dt		U 66	Zapp	FK 67	-T	12000+	T	–	26/	pa	-DT	I.C.White	7052+	10.26 S/ 27.30 W	
26/2335 dt		U 124	Mohr	BE 2711	-D	3000+	T	HG.73	26/	br	-D	Cervantes	1810+	48.37 N/ 20.01 W	

25) From British reports, the *Erna III* sank on Sept.25th. There are no other attack reports in the area.
26) *U 103* observed a ship capsizing after a weak detonation, then after two other detonations saw two ships going down by the stern. The fourth torpedo was a shallow hit with a big water column, and the fifth exploded with a blue-green flash.
27) This data about the successes of the *Malaspina*, which was lost during the operation, is based on the report of a German aircraft.
28) *U 203* fired four torpedoes and observed one hit and heard three additional detonations after diving. Later, lifeboats were observed and a damaged tanker was sunk by a coup de grâce at 06.34.

1	2	3	4	5	6		7	8	9	10	11	12	13	14	15
September 1941, cont.															
27/0208	dt	U 201	Schnee	BE 1939	-D	5000+	T	HG.73	27/		br -D	Springbank (CAM)	5155+	49.10 N/ 20.05 W	29)
27/0208	*dt*	*U 201*	*Schnee*	*BE 1939*	*PE*	*+*	*T*	*HG.73*							*29)*
27/0211	dt	U 201	Schnee	BE 1939	-D	3000+	T	HG.73	27/		nw -D	Siremalm	2468+	49.05 N/ 20.10 W	29)
27/2303	dt	U 201	Schnee	BE 2378	-D	5000+	T	HG.73	27/		br -D	Margareta	3103+	50.15 N/ 17.27 W	30)
27/2303	dt	U 201	Schnee	BE 2378	-D	3000+	T	HG.73			br -D				30)
October 1941															
1/2357	dt	U 94	Ites	AK 8168	-T:12842+		TA	-	1/1945 2/0130		br -DT	San Florentino	12842+	52.50 N/ 34.40 W 52.42 N/ 34.51 W	1) 1)
2/0652	dt	U 562	Hamm	AK 2717	-D	10000+	T	ON.19	2/		br -D	Empire Wave	7463+	59.08 N/ 32.26 W	
2/0709	dt	U 575	Heydemann	AK 6920	-D	6000+	T	.	2/		nl -M	Tuva	4652+	54.16 N/ 26.36 W	2)
2/0711	dt	U 575	Heydemann	AK 6920	-D	4000+?	T	.							2)
2/2345	dt	U 431	Dommes	AJ 9863	-D	5000+	T	-	2/		br -D	Hatasu	3198+	600m E Cape Race	
5/	dt	U 204 ?	Kell	-------	---------		T	-	5/		pa -D	C.Jon	744+	48.30 N/ 13.00 W	3)
7/1617	dt	U 502	v.Rosenstiel	AL 2211	-DW14795=		T	HX.152s	7/		br -DW	Svend Foyn	14795=	60.37 N/ 21.44 W	
10/0543	dt	U 126	Bauer	ES 3223	-D	8000+	T	.	10/		br -D	Nailsea Manor	4926+	18.45 N/ 21.18 W	
12/1654	dt	U 83	Kraus	CG 5445	-D:	2044+	Tf	-	12/		pt -D	Corte Real	2044+	80m W Lisbon	4)
14/0336	*dt*	*U 206*	*Opitz*	*CG 9592*	*DD*	*1870+*	*T*	*OG.75*	*14/*		*br PE*	*Fleur de Lys*	*925+*		

29) *U 201* fired five torpedoes. The first detonated with a big flash and the ship was seen sinking. The second exploded near an escort. Then two torpedoes hit one ship. Then *U 201* had to dive, and could not observe any further effects.
30) The first ship broke in two parts after being hit and sank; the second was seen sinking by the stern.
 1) *U 94* first hit the tanker with three torpedoes without great effect, then a fourth torpedo hit and the tanker broke into two parts and a boiler explosion was observed.
 2) *U 575* fired three torpedoes against four ships. After diving, two detonations on one ship and one on another ship were heard.
 3) There are no attack reports for *C.Jon* and *Inverlee*, so they must have been sunk by the lost *U 204*.
 4) The *Corte Real* was stopped and sunk after a search had established that she was transporting contraband.

1	2	3	4	5	6	7	8	9	10	11	12	13	14	15

October 1941, cont.

1	2	3	4	5	6	7	8	9	10 11	12	13	14	15
15/0815	dt	U 553	Thurmann	AK 9222	-D 6000+	T	SC.48	15/0630	br -M	Silvercedar (83)	4354+	53.36 N/ 29.57 W	
15/0817	dt	U 553	Thurmann	AK 9222	-D 4000+?	T	SC.48						5)
15/0823	dt	U 553	Thurmann	AK 9222	-D 5000+	T	SC.48	15/0650	nw -D	Ila (73)	1583+	53.34 N/ 30.10 W	
15/2317	dt	U 558	Krech	AL 7123	-D: 7000+	T	-	15/2057	ca -M	Vancouver Island	9472+	53.37 N/ 25.37 W	
16/0114	dt	U 568	Preuß	AK 6673	-D 4000+	T	SC.48	15/2330	br -D	Empire Heron(114)	6023+	54.05 N/ 27.15 W	
17/0007	dt	U 553	Thurmann	AL 1922	-T 6000+	T	SC.48	16/2220	pa -D	Bold Venture(94)	6595+	56.10 N/ 24.30 W	6)
17/0128	dt	U 558	Krech	AL 1966	-T 7000=?	T	SC.48						7a)
17/0131	dt	U 558	Krech	AL 1966	-T 7000+	T	SC.48	16/2345	br -DT	W.C.Teagle (103)	9552+	57. N/ 25. W	7a)
17/0149	dt	U 558	Krech	AL 1966	-D 6000+	T	SC.48	16/2345	nw -MT	Erviken (104)	6595+	56.10 N/ 24.30 W	7a)
17/0214	dt	U 558	Krech	AL 1966	-D 4000+	T	SC.48	16/	nw -D	Rym	1369+	57.01 N/ 24.20 W	7a)
17/0342	dt	U 432	Schultze	AL 0143	-D 6000+	T	SC.48	17/0145	gr -D	Evros (63)	5283+	57. N/ 24.30 W	7b)
17/0343	dt	U 432	Schultze	AL 0143	-D 5000=?	T	SC.48						7b)
17/0346	dt	U 432	Schultze	AL 0143	-D 7000+	T	SC.48						7b)
17/0400	dt	U 432	Schultze	AL 0143	-T 12000+	T	SC.48	17/	nw -MT	Barfonn (53)	9739+	56.58 N/ 25.04 W	7b)
17/0415	dt	U 568	Preuß	AL 0146	DD 14000	T	SC.48	17/0242	am DD	Kearny	1630=	57. N/ 24. W	8)
							SC.48	17/0320	br PE	Gladiolus	925+		7c)
18/0420	dt	U 101	Mengersen	AL 3951	DD 1190+	T	SC.48	18/0225	br DD	Broadwater	1190+	57.01 N/ 19.08 W	
19/0614	dt	U 206	Opitz	CG 9583	-D 6000+	T	-	19/	br -D	Baron Kelvin	3081+	14m 100° Tarifa	
19/1051	dt	U 126	Bauer	ET 2937	-D 7000+	T	-	19/	am -D	Lehigh	4983+	08.26 N/ 14.37 W	
19/	dt	U 204	Kell	-------	---------	T	-	19/	br -MT	Inverlee	9158+	30m 240° C.Spartel 3)	
20/0554	dt	U 126	Bauer	ET 6111	-T 8000+	T	-	20/	br -DT	British Mariner	6996+	07.43 N/ 14.20 W	
20/	?	?	?	?	? ?	?	-	20/	pa -D	Indra	2032+	W.Gibraltar ?	9)
21/0012	dt	U 84	Uphoff	BE 2167	-D =	T	-						10)

5) *U 553* missed the target but assumed a hit on a ship behind. - 6) The assessment of the attacks on SC.48 is difficult for the night of 16/17th Oct. These are the most probable hits, from a combined analysis by Mr.Coppock and V.Adm.Sir P.Gretton.
7a) *U 558* attacked from the starboard quarter, so it's probable she hit the ships in positions 103 and 104, and maybe the *Rym*.
7b) *U 432* attacked from inside the convoy between the 7th and 8th columns, so she probably first hit the ship in position 63. The fourth torpedo hit the *Barfonn*, which was finally sunk by a coup de grâce at 04.48 hrs. - 7c) The *Gladiolus* was reported missing after about 0100 hrs. At 03.20 hrs. British time there was a heavy explosion behind the convoy. This could have been a corvette hit by a stray torpedo, or the exploding *Barfonn*. The *Gladiolus* must have been sunk by the attacks of *U 558* or *U 432*.
8) The *Kearny* belonged to the Escort Group 4.1.4 which was sent to assist SC.48 from convoy ON.24.
9) The *Indra* departed Bari for Huelva and was reported missing after Oct.20th. - 10) *U 84* observed two detonations, maybe end runners.

1	2	3	4	5	6	7	8	9	10	11	12	13	14	15
October 1941, cont.														
21/0420	dt	U 123	Hardegen	BE 2136	ACL13984=	T	SL.89 s	21/	br	ACL	Aurania	13984=	50. N/ 19. W	
21/1435	*dt*	*U 83*	*Kraus*	*CG 9493*	*DD*	*+*	*T*	*Task F.*						*11)*
21/2203	dt	U 82	Rollmann	AL 9841	-D	4000+	T	SL.89	21/2105	br	-D	Serbino	4099+	51.10 N/ 19.20 W	
21/2231	dt	U 82	Rollmann	AL 9818	-D	6000+	T	SL.89	21/	br	-D	Treverbyn	5218+	51. N/ 19. W	
22/0142	dt	U 68	Merten	FU 7350	-T	8100+	T	-	21/	br	-DT	Darkdale	8145+	St.Helena	
24/0030	dt	U 563	Bargsten	CG 8813	-D	+	T	HG.75							12)
24/0038	*dt*	*U 563*	*Bargsten*	*CG 8813*	*DD*	*+*	*T*	*HG.75*	*23/2337*	*br*	*DD*	*Cossack*	*1870+*	*35.56 N/ 10.04 W*	*12)*
24/0636	dt	U 564	Suhren	CG 8492	-D	5000=	T	HG.75	24/0548	br	-D	Carsbreck	3670+	36.20 N/ 10.50 W	13)
24/0637	dt	U 564	Suhren	CG 8492	-D	5000=	T	HG.75	24/0550	br	-D	Ariosto	2176+	36.20 N/ 10.50 W	13)
24/0637	dt	U 564	Suhren	CG 8492	-D	5000=	T	HG.75	24/0552	br	-D	Alhama	1352+	35.42 N/ 10.58 W	13)
24/0638	dt	U 564	Suhren	CG 8492	-D	5000=	T	HG.75							13)
24/0638	dt	U 564	Suhren	CG 8492	-D	5000=	T	HG.75							13)
26/0354	dt	U 83	Kraus	CF 6945	-D	8000+	T	HG.75	26/0300	br	-D	Ariguani	6746=	37.50 N/ 16.10 W	14)
26/0354	dt	U 83	Kraus	CF 6945	-D	5000+	T	HG.75							14)
26/0354	dt	U 83	Kraus	CF 6945	-D	5000+	T	HG.75							14)
28/0639	*dt*	*U 563*	*Bargsten*	*CF 6918*	*DD*	*+*	*T*	*-*	*26/*	*br*	*PE*	*Heliotrope*	*-----*		*15)*
26/2142	dt	U 563	Bargsten	CF 6418	-D	=	T	HG.75							15)
26/2143	dt	U 563	Bargsten	CF 6418	-D	=	T	HG.75							15)
27/0205	dt	U 564	Suhren	CF 5360	-D	3000+	T	HG.75							16)

11) *U 83* fired a 4-torpedo salvo against two carriers in a task force, identified as *Eagle* and *Furious*. One detonation was heard.

12) *U 563* fired one torpedo against a steamer which seemed to hit after running 4 min 44 sec., and a twin salvo against a turning destroyer which missed. But there were detonations behind. In reality only the *Cossack* was hit, but she did not sink until Oct.27th. - 13) *U 564* fired five torpedoes. The first three exploded with red fire columns on different ships after 41 sec, 31 sec and 21 sec. The last two were heard to detonate after 3 min 14 sec and 3 min 56 sec.

14) *U 83* fired three torpedoes and observed three detonations and fire columns after 4 min 28 sec to 5 min. In reality there was only one hit.

15) *U 563* fired a two-shot salvo against a destroyer and heard a detonation after 5 min 20 sec. In the evening *U 563* fired five torpedoes and heard two detonations on one ship after 1 min 30 sec., and one detonation after 1 min 28 sec.on another ship. The last torpedo seemed to be a dud.

16) *U 564* assumed a hit after 15 min 25 sec. But after so long a time the torpedo could not have been a hit.

North Sea − Atlantic

1	2 3	4	5	6		7	8	9	10 11	12	13	14	15
October 1941, cont.													
28/0343 dt	U 68	Merten	GG 2637	-D	10400+	T	-	28/	br -D	Hazelside	5297+	23.10 S/ 01.36 E	
28/0508 dt	U 432	Schultze	CF 2483	-D	6000+	T	HG.75						17)
28/0509 dt	U 432	Schultze	CF 2483	-D	4000+	T	HG.75	28/0408	br -D	Ulea	1574+	41.17 N/ 21.40 W	17)
28/0719 dt	U 106	Rasch	AK 9985	-D	5000+	T	-						18)
30/0707 dt	U 106	Rasch	BD 4458	-T	8000+	T	ON.28	30/	am -DT	Salinas (AO)	8246=	700m E Newfoundland	
31/0834 dt	*U 552*	*Topp*	*AK 9922*	*DD*	*1190+*	*T*	*HX.156*	*31/*	*am DD*	*Reuben James*	*1190+*	*51.59 N/ 27.05 W*	*19)*
31/0903 dt	U 374	v.Fischel	BC 4163	-D	6000+	T	-	31/	br -M	King Malcolm	5120+	47.40 N/ 51.50 W	20)
31/2247 dt	U 96	Lehmann-Willenbrock	BE 1125	-D	8000+	T	OS.10	31/	nl -D	Bennekom	5998+	51.20 N/ 23.40 W	
31/2248 dt	U 96	Lehmann-Willenbrock	BE 1125	-D	5000+	T	OS.10						21)
November 1941													
1/0654 dt	U 68	Merten	GH 2638	-D	5000+	T	-	1/	br -M	Bradford City	4953+	22.59 S/ 09.49 E	
1/0723 dt	U 552	Topp	AL 5771	-D	8000=	T	HX.156						1)
1/0902 dt	U 567	Endraß	AL 4866	-D	5000=	T	HX.156						2)
2/0526 dt	U 208	Schlieper	BC 4885	-D	6000+	T	-	2/	br -D	Larpool	3872+	250m ESE C.Race	
3/0057 dt	U 569	Hinsch	BC 1121	-D	5000+	T	SC.52	2/	br -D	Rose Schiaffino	3349+	Newfoundland	
3/0454 dt	U 202	Linder	AJ 7849	-D	4000+	T	SC.52	3/	br -D	Flynderborg	2022+	51.21 N/ 51.45 W	
3/0458 dt	U 202	Linder	AJ 7849	-D	5000+	T	SC.52	3/	br -D	Gretavale	4586+	51.21 N/ 51.45 W	
3/0505 dt	U 202	Linder	AJ 7849	-D	4000+	T	SC.52						3)
3/0844 dt	U 202	Linder	AJ 7849	-D	4000+	Tf	SC.52						3)

17) *U 432* observed hits on two ships, one of which sank by the stern, and the other was seen to break into two parts.
18) *U 106* observed from close by one hit and the ship sinking after 3 minutes.
19) The *Reuben James* was escorting the convoy HX.156 with the U.S. Escort Group 4.1.3.
20) The *King Malcolm* was seen for the last time in this position. The ship was hit by *U 374* and sank in 30 seconds.
1, 2) *U 552* and *U 567* heard only one or two detonations, with no observation.
3) *U 202* observed hits on two ships, the first of which sank. A third hit was heard. The coup de grâce fired at 08.44 was against a capsized wreck, possibly one of the ships hit during the first attack.

1	2	3	4	5	6	7	8	9	10	11	12	13	14	15
November 1941, cont.														
3/1828	dt	U 203	Mützelburg	AJ 7442	-D 5000+	T	SC.52	3/	br	-D	Empire Gemsbuck	5626+	52.18 N/ 53.05 W	
3/1828	dt	U 203	Mützelburg	AJ 7442	-D 5000+	T	SC.52	3/	br	-D	Everoja	4830+	80m 77° Belle I.	
7/2234	dt	U 74	Kentrat	AK 5998	-M: 6000+	T	-	7/	br	-M	Nottingham	8532+	53.24 N/ 31.51 W	
11/2335	dt	U 561	Bartels	AK 8822	-D 6000+	T	SC.53 s	10/	pa	-D	Meridian	5592+	North Atlantic	4)
13/0042	dt	U 126	Bauer	FE 3514	-D: 6961+	T	-	12/	br	-M	Peru	6961+	01.30 N/ 13.20 W	
14/0337	dt	U 561	Bartels	BD 1542	-D 6000+	T	SC.53 s	26/	pa	-D	Crusader	2939+	North Atlantic	5)
24/1521	*dt*	*U 124*	*Mohr*	*ES 7985*	*CL: 4850+*	*T*	*-*	*24/*	*br*	*CL*	*Dunedin*	*4850+*	*03. S/ 26. W*	
29/0411	dt	U 43	Lüth	CE 2526	-D 8000+	T	OS.12	29/0115	br	-D	Thornliebank	5569+	41.50 N/ 29.48 W	
30/1926	dt	U 43	Lüth	CE 8234	-D 5000+	T	WS.13	30/	br	-D	Ashby	4868+	36.54 N/ 29.51 W	
December 1941														
2/0030	it	CAPPELLINI	Lenzi	35n/30w	-D: 5231+?	T	-		br	-D	Miguel de Larrinaga	?		1)
2/0924	dt	U 43	Lüth	CF 7588	-T 12300+	T	-	2/	am	-DT	Astral	7542+	35.40 N/ 24.00 W	2)
3/2146	dt	U 124	Mohr	FU 7887	-D: 6285+	T	-	3/	am	-D	Sagadahoc	6275+	21.50 S/ 07.50 W	3)
6/	dt	U 131	Baumann	AL 2830	-D 6000+	T	-	6/	br	-D	Scottish Trader	4016+	S Iceland	
10/2354	dt	U 130	Kals	AL 3962	-D 7000+	T	SC.57	10/2206	äg	-D	Star of Luxor	5298+	56.57 N/ 16.35 W	4)
10/2357	dt	U 130	Kals	AL 3962	-T 8000+	T	SC.57	10/2209	br	-D	Kurdistan	5844+	56-51 N/ 16.36 W	4)
10/2357	dt	U 130	Kals	------- ---------		T	SC.57	10/2210	br	-D	Kirnwood	3829+	56.57 N/ 16.35 W	4)
14/2157	dt	U 108	Scholtz	CG 8778	-D 7000+	T	-	14/	pt	-D	Cassequel	4751+	35.08 N/ 11.14 W	
15/0410	dt	U 77	Schonder	CG 9843	-D 5000+	T	HG.76	15/	br	-D	Empire Barracuda	4972+	35.30 N/ 06.17 W	5)
15/0430	dt	U 77	Schonder	CG 9843	-T 9000=	T	HG.76							5)

4) The *Meridian* was last seen by HMCS *Chambly* on Nov.11th at 17.30 and was reported missing thereafter.
5) The *Crusader* was supposed to sail with convoy CS.53, but failed to report and was reported missing thereafter.
1) *Cappellini* reported two hits on this ship, identified by the xB-Dienst. But there is no confirmation.
2) The *Astral* was reported missing after Dec.2nd.
3) The *Sagadahoc* was stopped and sunk after a search disclosed she was transporting contraband.
4) *U 130* fired a 4-torpedo salvo and observed two hits on one ship which sank in flames. Then a 2-torpedo salvo was fired which seemed to both explode on one ship, but in reality two ships were hit.
5) *U 77* observed one freighter in sinking condition after one hit and one tanker stopped after two hits.

1	2	3	4	5	6	7	8	9	10	11	12	13	14	15
December 1941, cont.														
17/2121	dt	U 108	Scholtz	CF 9991	-D 5000+	T	HG.76							6)
19/0615	dt	U 108	Scholtz	CF 6815	-D 5000+	T	HG.76	19/	br	-D	Ruckinge	2869+	38.20 N/ 17.15 W	7)
19/0615	dt	U 108	Scholtz	CF 6815	-D 5000+	T	HG.76							7)
19/	*dt*	*U 574*	*Gengelbach*	-------	---------	*T*	*HG.76*	*19/0415*	*br*	*DD*	*Stanley*	*1190+*	*38.12 N/ 17.23 W*	
20/2357	dt	U 573	Heinsohn	CF 9913	-D 8000+	T								8)
21/	dt	U 567	Endraß	-------	---------	T	HG.76	21/2032	nw	-D	Annavore	3324+	43.55 N/ 19.50 W	
21/2137	*dt*	*U 751*	*Bigalk*	*BE 8719*	*CV 23000+*	*T*	*HG.76*	*21/2035*	*br*	*CVE*	*Audacity*	*11000+*	*44. N/ 20. W*	
31/1954	dt	U 87	Berger	AM 2574	-T: 8237+	T	-	31/	br	-MT	Cardita	8237+	59.18 N/ 12.50 W	
January 1942														
6/1627	dt	U 701	Degen	AK 2816	-D: 3391+	T	-	10/	br	-D	Baron Erskine	3657+	59.15 N/ 18.30 W	1)
12/0149	dt	U 123	Hardegen	CB 2424	-D: 9076+	T	-	12/0002	br	-D	Cyclops	9076+	41.51 N/ 63.48 W	
12/0802	dt	U 43	Lüth	AL 1938	-D 6000+	T	HX.168 s	12/0400	sw	-M	Yngaren	5246+	57. N/ 26. W	
13/0118	dt	U 130	Kals	BB 58	-T 6000+	T	-	12/2200	nw	-D	Frisco	1582+	44.50 N/ 60.20 W	
13/0948	dt	U 130	Kals	BB 5898	-D 7000+	T	-	13/1000	pa	-D	Friar Rock	5427+	45.30 N/ 50.40 W	
14/0254	dt	U 43	Lüth	AL 2691	-D 6000+	T	ON.55 s	14?	gr	-D	Maro	3838+	North Atlantic	2)
14/0304	dt	U 43	Lüth	AL 2691	-D 4000+	T	ON.55	14/0100	br	-D	Empire Surf	6641+	58.42 N/ 19.16 W	
14/0453	dt	U 43	Lüth	AL 2659	-D 5000+	T	ON.55	14/0255	pa	-D	Chepo	5582+	58.30 N/ 19.40 W	

6) *U 108* heard one detonation and observed a black smoke cloud rising from the target.

7) *U 108* observed a flash on one ship after a two-torpedo salvo, and a large black smoke column, and heard two detonations.

8) *U 573* fired a 3-torpedo salvo and observed two black columns, but heard only one detonation.

1) *U 701* reported the British S/S *Baron Haig*, 3391 gross tons, as sunk, but it must have been the *Baron Erskine* because there is no other loss report or success report from the area.

2) *U 43* heard only two light detonations, but observed the sinking of the target ship after 10 minutes. The *Maro* departed England on Jan.2nd for Halifax. She may have been in the area. The ship did not arrive in Halifax on Jan.23rd as scheduled.

1	2	3	4	5	6	7	8	9	10	11	12	13	14	15
January 1942, cont.														
14/0835	dt	U 123	Hardegen	CA 3775	-T: 9577+	T	-	13/0630	pa	-MT	Norness	9577+	40.28 N/ 70.50 W	
15/0138	dt	U 552	Topp	BB 6673	-D: 4113+	T	-	14/2344	br	-D	Dayrose	4113+	46.32 N/ 53.00 W	
15/0941	dt	U 123	Hardegen	CA 2896	-T 10000+	T	-	15/0800	br	-DT	Coimbra	6768+	40.25 N/ 72.21 W	
15/1134	dt	U 203	Mützelburg	BB 6652	-D 6000+	T	-	15/	pt	-Mf	Catalina	632+	47. N/ 52. W	3)
15/2317	dt	U 553	Thurmann	BC 8524	-T 10000+	T	ON.52 d	19/2100	br	-MT	Diala	8106+	44.50 N/ 46.50 W	
16/1115	dt	U 402	v.Forstner	BE 5716	-D 10000=	T	-	16/0817	br	-M	Llangibby Castle	12053=	46.04 N/ 19.06 W	
16/1358	dt	U 86	Schug	BB 63	-T 8000+	T	ON.52 d	16/1310	br	-DT	Toorak	8627=	47.54 N/ 52.11 W	
17/0359	dt	U 87	Berger	BB 9855	-T 8000+	TA	ON.52 d	17/	nw	-MT	Nyholt	8087+	45.46 N/ 54.18 W	
17/1121	dt	U 203	Mützelburg	BB 6655	-D 4000+	T	-	16/	nw	-D	Octavian	1345+	45. N/ 60. W	4)
17/1304	dt	U 123	Hardegen	CA 5756	-D 4000+	T	-	17/	am	-D	San José	1932+	39.15 N/ 74.09 W	
18/0613	dt	U 86	Schug	BC 4110	-D: 4271+	T	SC.63 s	18/0422	gr	-D	Dimitrios G.Thermiotis	4271+	51. N/ 62. W	5)
18/0644	dt	U 552	Topp	BB 6679	-D 4000+	T	-	18/	am	-D	Frances Salman	2609+	Newfoundland	6)
18/0833	dt	U 66	Zapp	CA 8779	-T 9200+	T	-	18/0638	am	-DT	Allan Jackson	6635+	35.57 N/ 74.20 W	
18/1315	dt	U 333	Cremer	BC 65	-D 8000+	T	SC.63	18/	br	-D	Caledonian Monarch	5851+	57. N/ 26. W	
19/0516	dt	U 123	Hardegen	CA 7668	-D 4000+	T	-	18/	am	-D	Brazos	4497+	Cape Hatteras	
19/0624	dt	U 109	Bleichrodt	BA 9965	-D 4000+	T	-	19/	br	-M	Empire Kingfisher	6082+	43.26 N/ 65.40 W	
19/0743	dt	U 66	Zapp	CA 8997	-D 9000+	T	-	18/0645	ca	-D	Lady Hawkins	7988+	35. N/ 72.30 W	
19/0909	dt	U 123	Hardegen	CA 7962	-D: 4000+	T	-	19/0707	am	-D	City of Atlanta	5269+	35.42 N/ 75.21 W	
19/1201	dt	U 123	Hardegen	CA 7938	-D: 5000+	T	-	19/1000	le	-D	Ciltvaira	3779+	35.25 N/ 75.23 W	
19/1244	dt	U 123	Hardegen	CA 7938	-T: 8206=	TA	-	19/1100	am	-DT	Malay	8206=	35.40 N/ 75.20 W	

3) *U 203* assumed that she sank an ammunition ship. The *Catalina* was sunk at this time by an underwater detonation.
4) The *Octavian* was reported missing after Jan.16th in this area.
5) The SSS-signal of the *Dimitrios G.Thermiotis* was overheard by both *U 86* and *U 552* and correlated with attacks by each boat.
6) *U 552* did not attack the *Dimitrios G.Thermiotis*, but rather the *Frances Salman* which departed St.John's on Jan.17th for Corner Brook (New Foundland) and was reported missing after Jan.21st.

1	2	3	4	5	6	7	8	9	10	11	12	13	14	15
January 1942, cont.														
21/1843	dt	U 203	Mützelburg	BB 6628	-D	8000+	T	-	22/0200	ca	-M	North Gaspe	888=	46.33 N/ 53.04 W	7)
21/1847	dt	U 85	Greger	BD 8793	-D	9000+	T	-							8)
21/1922	dt	U 754	Oestermann	BB 6628	-D	3000+	T	-	22/	nw	-M	Belize	2153+	47.21 N/ 58.08 W	9)
21/2143	dt	U 754	Oestermann	BB 6682	-D	4000+	T	-	22/0231	nw	-D	William Hansen	1344+	46.56 N/ 52.47 W	
21/2221	dt	U 130	Kals	CB 1831	-T:	8248+	T	-	21/1700	nw	-MT	Alexandra Höegh	8248+	40.53 N/ 65.56 W	
22/0116	dt	U 203	Mützelburg	BB 6624	APC	+	T	-	22/	br	APC	Rosemonde	364+	Cape Race	
22/0411	dt	U 588	Vogel	AM 3555	-D	6000+	T	-							10)
22/1239	dt	U 66	Zapp	DC 1295	-D	7500+	T	-	21/	am	-D	Norvana	2677+	U.S. East Coast	11)
22/2045	dt	U 333	Cremer	BB 9600	-D:	6069+	T	ON.53 s	22/1930	gr	-D	Vissilios A.Polemis	3429+	42.32 N/ 52.38 W	12)
22/2221	dt	U 135	Praetorius	BC 9159	-D	5000+	T	ON.54 s	22/	be	-D	Gandia	9626+	42.45 N/ 53.00 W	
22/2243	dt	U 553	Thurmann	CB 3141	-T	6000+	T	-	22/2100	nw	-MT	Inneröy	8260+	42.30 N/ 59.54 W	
22/	dt	U 82	Rollmann	BC 22	-T:	11999+	T	-	22/2310	br	-MT	Athelcrown	11999+	45.06 N/ 40.56 W	
22/	dt	U 130	Kals	CA	-T	+	T	-	22/	pa	-DT	Olympic	5335+	36.01 N/ 75.30 W	
23/	it	BARBARIGO	Grossi	36n/15w	-D:	5473+	T	-	23/	sp	-D	Navemar	5473+	36.48 N/ 15.26 W	13)
23/0812	dt	U 109	Bleichrodt	BA 9956	-D:	6566+	T	-	23/0700	br	-D	Thirlby	4887+	43.20 N/ 66.15 W	14)
23/	dt	U 82	Rollmann	BB 87	-T:	6118+	T	ON.56	23/1340	nw	-MT	Leiesten	6118+	45.27 N/ 43.19 W	
24/0240	dt	U 66	Zapp	CA 7968	-T	14300+	T	-	24/0045	br	-MT	Empire Gem	8139+	35.06 N/ 74.58 W	
24/0243	dt	U 66	Zapp	CA 7968	-D	10000+	T	-	24/0040	am	-D	Venore	8017+	34.50 N/ 75.20 W	

7) The *North Gaspe* was a U.S.Army transport. The torpedo possibly missed the ship, but exploded in the vicinity.
8) *U 85* heard two detonations and after 10 minutes observed the damaged ship in sinking condition with a heavy list.
9) The *Belize* departed New York on Jan.15th for St.John's. HMCS *Spikenard* found a water-filled lifeboat on Jan.24th.
10) *U 588* sank the ship by a coup de grâce after 35 minutes.
11) The *Norvana* was proceeding from Curacao to Baltimore and was reported missing thereafter.
12) *U 333* reported this ship to be the British S/S *Burdwan*, 6069 gross tons, based on an xB-report.
13) The *Navemar* departed Cadiz at the end of July 1941 with 1120 Jewish refugees from France on board, and arrived by way of Bermuda and Cuba at New York on Sept.12th. In January this ship was returning empty to Spain.
14) *U 109* reported this ship as the Greek S/S *Andreas*, 6566 gross tons, based on an xB-report.

1	2	3	4	5	6	7	8	9	10	11	12	13	14	15
January 1942, cont.														
24/0653 dt	U	106	Rasch	CB 6192	-D 6000+	T	-	24/0558	br	-D	Empire Wildebeeste	5631+	39.30 N/ 59.54 W	
24/1525 dt	U	333	Cremer	BC 4700	-D 11000+	T	ONS.55	24/1333	nw	-M	Ringstad	4765+	45.50 N/ 51.04 W	
25/0325 dt	U	754	Oestermann	BB 6359	-D: 3876+	T	-	25/0725	gr	-D	Mount Kitheron	3876+	47.32 N/ 52.31 W	
25/1002 dt	U	130	Kals	CA 5435	-T 9500+	T	-	25/0810	nw	-MT	Varanger	9305+	38.58 N/ 74.06 W	
25/ dt	U	123	Hardegen	CC 79	-D: 3044+	A	-	17/	br	-D	Culebra	3044+	35.30 N/ 53.25 W	15)
25/2025 dt	U	125	Folkers	CA 8279	-T 7000=	T	-	28/	am	-DT	Olney	-----	37.55 N/ 74.56 W	16)
26/0842 dt	U	106	Rasch	CB 5172	-D: 3963+	T	-	26/	br	-D	Traveller	3963+	40. N/ 61.45 W	
26/0604 dt	U	125	Folkers	CA 8883	-D 7000+	T	-	24/	am	-D	West Ivis	5666+	U.S. East Coast	17)
26/1821 dt	U	754	Oestermann	BB 6958	-D 6000+	T	-	26/	gr	-D	Icarion	4013+	46.02 N/ 52.22 W	
26/1858 dt	U	582	Schulte	CC 2125	-T 6000+	T	ON.56	26/1410	br	-D	Refast	5189+	42.41 N/ 53.02 W	
26/ dt	U	123	Hardegen	CC 86	-T: 9231+	A	-	26/2400	nw	-MT	Pan Norway	9231+	35.56 N/ 50.27 W	
27/0943 dt	U	130	Kals	CA 5743	-T 7500+	T	-	27/0545	am	-DT	Francis E.Powell	7096+	38.05 N/ 74.53 W	
27/1358 dt	U	130	Kals	CA 7952	-T: 6986=	A	-	27/1358	am	-DT	Halo	6986=	35.23 N/ 75.20 W	
29/1610 dt	*U*	*132*	*Vogelsang*	*AE 4756*	*DD 2000+*	*T*	*-*	*29/1435*	*am*	*CGC*	*Alexander Hamilton*	*2216+*	*64.10 N/ 22.56 W*	
30/1805 dt	U	106	Rasch	CA 8241	-T: 6836+	TA	-	30/1609	am	-DT	Rochester	6836+	37.10 N/ 73.58 W	
31/1645 dt	U	107	Gelhaus	CB 5478	-T: 7419+	T	-	31/	br	-MT	San Arcadio	7419+	38.10 N/ 63.50 W	
31/1650 dt	U	333	Cremer	BE 7100	-D 8000+	T	-	31/	dt	-M	Spreewald	5083+	45. N/ 25. W	18)
31/2331 dt	*U*	*105*	*Schuch*	*BE 2784*	*-D +*	*T*	*SL.98*	*31/2035*	*br*	*-PS*	*Culver*	*1546+*	*48.43 N/ 20.14 W*	*19)*
31/ dt	*U*	*82*	*Rollmann*	*BB 8873*	*DD +*	*T*	*-*	*31/2212*	*br*	*DD*	*Belmont*	*1190+*	*42.02 N/ 57.18 W*	

15) Based on the report of *U 123*, the *Culebra* was sunk on Jan.25th, not on Jan.17th.
16) *U 125* heard one detonation after firing one torpedo against a stopped tanker. The *Olney* reported a U-boat attack without a hit.
17) The *West Ivis* departed New York on Jan.24th headed in a southerly direction. She was reported lost in February at 16.30 N/ 71.45 W. But the ship must have been sunk earlier by *U 125*'s attack.
18) The *Spreewald* was a German blockade runner operating ahead of schedule and was sunk by mistake by *U 333*.
19) *U 105* fired a 4-torpedo salvo and observed two hits with a big explosion. She assumed a hit on an ammunition freighter, but in reality the *Culver* exploded. She was equipped with the first operational automatic HF/DF-set.

1	2	3	4	5	6	7	8	9	10	11	12	13	14	15
February 1942														
1/0330 dt	U	109	Bleichrodt	CB 4842	-D: 7924+	T	–	1/	br	-D	Tacoma Star	7924+	37.33 N/ 69.21 W	
2/0746 dt	U	751	Bigalk	BB 7356	-T: 8096=	T	HX.173	2/	nl	-MT	Corilla	8096=	44.49 N/ 61.37 W	
2/1940 dt	U	103	Winter	CA 5640	-T: 6182+	TA	–	2/	am	-DT	W.L.Steed	6182+	38.25 N/ 73.00 W	
3/0323 dt	U	106	Rasch	CA 8458	-M:15355+	T	–	3/	sw	-M	Amerikaland	15355+	36.36 N/ 74.10 W	
3/0654 dt	U	86	Schug	CD 21	-D 14000=	T	.							1)
4/0427 dt	U	751	Bigalk	BB 7488	-T: 4535+	T	–	4/	br	-M	Silveray	4535+	43.54 N/ 64.16 W	
4/0643 dt	U	103	Winter	CA 5764	-D: 3627+	TA	–	4/	pa	-D	San Gil	3627+	38.05 N/ 74.40 W	
5/0142 dt	U	109	Bleichrodt	CB 9713	-T:11309+	T	–	5/	ca	-MT	Montrolite	11309+	35.14 N/ 60.05 W	
5/0153 dt	U	103	Winter	CA 5813	-T: 8327+	T	–	4/	am	-DT	India Arrow	8327+	38.48 N/ 72.43 W	
5/1808 dt	U	103	Winter	CA 5868	-T: 8403+	TA	–	5/	am	-DT	China Arrow	8403+	37.44 N/ 73.18 W	
5/2236 dt	*U*	*136*	*Zimmermann*	*AL 6146*	*DD +*	*T*	*ONS.63*	*5/*	*br*	*PE*	*Arbutus*	*925+*	*55.05 N/ 18.43 W*	
6/0241 dt	U	109	Bleichrodt	DD 3118	-D: 3531+	A	–	6/	pa	-D	Halcyon	3531+	34.20 N/ 59.16 W	
6/1210 dt	U	106	Rasch	CB 5682	-D 8000+	T	–	6/	br	-M	Opawa	10354+	38.21 N/ 61.13 W	
6/1608 dt	U	107	Gelhaus	DC 2134	-D 4500+	T	–	5/	am	-D	Major Wheeler	3431+	U.S. East Coast	2)
7/0552 dt	U	751	Bigalk	BB 7494	-D: 8000+	T	–	7/	br	-D	Empire Sun	6952+	43.55 N/ 64.22 W	
8/1035 dt	U	108	Scholtz	CA 8112	-D: 7174+	T	–	8/	br	-D	Ocean Venture	7174+	37.05 N/ 74.46 W	
9/0034 dt	U	654	Forster	BC 5947	-D 7000=	T	ONS.61							3)
9/0036 dt	*U*	*654*	*Forster*	*BC 5947*	*PE +*	*T*	*ONS.61*	*9/*	*fr*	*PE*	*Alysse*	*900+*	*46. N/ 44. W*	
9/0538 dt	U	586	v.d.Esch	AM 2364	-T 8500+	T	.	9/	nw	-MT	Anna Knudsen	9057=	59.50 N/ 09.40 W	
9/2020 dt	U	85	Greger	BC 8179	-D 6000+	T	–	9/	br	-D	Empire Fuselier	5408+	44.45 N/ 47.25 W	
9/2118 dt	U	108	Scholtz	DC 2118	-D 4000+	T	–	10/	nw	-D	Tolosa	1974+	U.S. East Coast	4)

1) *U 86* fired a 3-torpedo salvo against a convoy and heard two detonations after 10 minutes. Possibly there were detonations at the ends of the runs.
2) The *Major Wheeler* departed Puerto Rico on Jan.31st for Philadelphia and was reported missing after Feb.9th when she failed to arrive.
3) *U 654* fired three single torpedoes against a westbound convoy. At the same time when a corvette was hit, a second explosion took place beyond. A freighter was stopped and later missed by a coup de grâce.
4) The *Tolosa* departed Kingston/Jamaica on Feb.1st and was to arrive in Chester, Pa on Feb.10th.

1	2	3	4	5	6	7	8	9	10	11	12	13	14	15
February 1942, cont.														
11/0135	*dt*	*U 136*	*Zimmermann*	*AL 5235*	*PE*	*+*	*T*	*SC.67*	*10/0033*	*ca*	*PE*	*Spikenard*	*925+*	*56. N/ 21.*	*W 5)*
11/0135	dt	U 136	Zimmermann	AL 5235	-D	5000=	T	SC.67	10/						5)
11/	dt	U 591	Zetzsche	AL 6121	-M:	4028+	T	SC.67	10/0035	nw	-M	Heina	4028+	56.10 N/ 21.07 W	6)
11/	dt	U 591	Zetzsche	AL 6121	-D	8000=	T	SC.67							6)
11/	dt	U 591	Zetzsche	AL 6121	-D	5000=	T	SC.67							6)
11/0328	dt	U 564	Suhren	CB 7455	-T:	11410+	TA	-	10/		ca -MT	Victolite	11410+	36.12 N/ 67.14 W	
11/1334	dt	U 136	Zimmermann	AL 5235	-D	5000=	T	SC.67							6)
12/0241	dt	U 108	Scholtz	DC 2139	-D	4000+	T	-	11/		nw -D	Blink	2701+	35.00 N/ 72.27 W	
14/0337	dt	U 576	Heinicke	BB 8851	-D	8000+	T	-	15/		br -M	Empire Spring	6946+	42. N/ 55. W	7)
14/1150	dt	U 502	v.Rosenstiel	EC 9436	-T	2600+	T	-							8)
15/0026	dt	U 98	Gysae	CC 3675	-D:	7000+	T	-	14/		br -D	Biela	5298+	42.55 N/ 45.40 W	
15/0434	dt	U 566	Borchert	BB 7544	-D	9000+	T	ON.60 s	15/0245		gr -D	Meropi	4181+	44.14 N/ 62.41 W	
15/0443	dt	U 432	Schultze	CA 8448	-D	7000+	T	-	15/		bz -D	Buarque	5152+	36.35 N/ 75.20 W	
16/0801	dt	U 156	Hartenstein	Aruba	-T	3080+	T	-	16/0131		br -DT	Pedernales	4317=	San Nicholas	
16/0803	dt	U 156	Hartenstein	Aruba	-T	2730+	T	-	16/0133		br -DT	Oranjestad	2396+	San Nicholas	
16/0943	dt	U 156	Hartenstein	Aruba	-T	4500=	T	-	16/		am -DT	Arkansas	6452=	San Nicholas	
16/0944	dt	U 502	v.Rosenstiel	EC 9465	-T	3100+	T	-	16/0230		br -DT	Tia Juana	2395+	25m SW Pt.Macolla	
16/1028	dt	U 502	v.Rosenstiel	EC 9453	-T	2700+	T	-	16/0330		ve -DT	Monagas	2650+	Gulf v.Venezuela	
16/1035	dt	U 67	Müller-Stöckheim	EC 9625	-T	3177+	T	-	16/		nl -DT	Rafaela	3177=	1m v.Curacao	
16/1134	dt	U 502	v.Rosenstiel	EC 9438	-T	2600/	T	-	16/0400		br -DT	San Nicolas	2391+	25m SW Pt.Macolla	
16/1556	dt	U 108	Scholtz	CB 7858	-D	5000+	T	-	18/		pa -D	Ramapo	2968+	W Bermuda	9)

5) *U 136* observed after the hit on the corvette an additional fire column, and later on, debris and two life boats. During the second attack there was only one detonation heard, but not observed.
6) *U 591* reported the sinking of the *Heina* and in addition hits on two other ships.
7) The *Empire Spring* was due at Halifax on Feb.15th but did not arrive.
8) *U 502* reported a hit on a tanker. The tanker was seen sinking in flames.
9) The *Ramapo* departed Bermuda on Feb.12th for Philadelphia, but she did not arrive on time, and was reported missing.

1	2	3	4	5	6	7	8	9	10	11	12	13	14	15
February 1942, cont.														
16/1830	dt	U 564	Suhren	CB 4798	-T: 6195=	A	-	16/1915	br	-MT	Opalia	6195=	37.38 N/ 66.07 W	10)
17/2217	dt	U 136	Zimmermann	AM 1811	-D 8000+	T	HX.174s	19/	br	-M	Empire Comet	6914+	58.15 N/ 17.10 W	11)
18/1807	dt	U 432	Schultze	CA 5817	-D: 4053+	TA	-	18/	bz	-D	Olinda	4053+	37.30 N/ 75. W	
18/2327	dt	U 108	Scholtz	CB 8926	-D: 5265+	T	-	16/	br	-D	Somme	5265+	40. N/ 55. W	12)
19/0318	dt	U 432	Schultze	CA 5288	-D 4000+	T	-	20/	br	-D	Miraflores	2158+	U.S. East Coast	13)
19/0345	*dt*	*U 108*	*Scholtz*	*CB 1711*	*PC ? =*	*T*	*-*							*14)*
19/0532	dt	U 161	Achilles	Port of	-D 6000+	T	-	19/	am	-D	Mokihana	7460=	10.38 N/ 60.30 W	15)
19/0532	dt	U 161	Achilles	Spain	-T 4000+	T	-	19/	br	-DT	British Consul	6940=	10.37 N/ 61.34 W	15)
19/1945	dt	U 128	Heyse	DB 9546	-T 3000+	T	-	19/	am	-DT	Pan Massachusetts	8202+	28.27 N/ 80.08 W	
19/2329	dt	U 96	Lehmann-Willenbrock	BB 7753	-D 8000+	T	-	19/	br	-M	Empire Seal	7965+	43.14 N/ 64.45 W	
20/0027	it	TORELLI	de Giacomo	13n/50w	-D: 7224+	T	-	20/	br	-D	Scottish Star	7224+	13.24 N/ 49.36 W	
20/0359	dt	U 129	Clausen	EO 1518	-D 5500+	T	-	20/	nw	-D	Nordvangen	2400+	10.50 N/ 60.54 W	16)
20/0453	dt	U 96	Lehmann-Willenbrock	BB 7884	-D 6000+	T	-	19/	am	-M	Lake Osweya	2398+	43.14 N/ 64.45 W	
20/1131	dt	U 156	Hartenstein	ED 6452	-D: 5127+	T	-	20/	am	-D	Delplata	5127+	14.55 N/ 62.10 W	
21/0123	dt	U 432	Schultze	CA 5867	-D 5000+	T	-	16/	am	-D	Azalea City	5529+	38 N/ 73 W	17)
21/1044	dt	U 107	Gelhaus	CC 2731	-T 8000=	T	-	21/	nw	-MT	Egda	10068=	41.12 N/ 52.55 W	
21/1532	dt	U 67	Müller-Stöckheim	EC 9379	-T 9608+	T	-	21/	am	-DT	J.N.Pew	9033+	12.40 N/ 74.00 W	

10) The *Opalia* was only slightly damaged by gunfire.
11) The *Empire Comet* was a straggler from convoy HX.174 and was reported missing after Feb.19th.
12) The *Somme* was identified clearly by *U 108*. She was sunk on Feb.18th, not on Feb.16th.
13) The *Miraflores* departed Port au Prince on Feb.14th for New York, but had not arrived by Feb.20th.
14) *U 108* attacked a flat vessel without a bridge and heard a detonation after 8 minutes.
15) *U 161* torpedoed a freighter on the approaches to Port of Spain, Trinidad. This ship broke in two, and only the bow was visible above the waterline. A tanker exploded. But both ships were salvaged.
16) Wreckage of the *Nordvangen* was found at the given position.
17) The *Azalea City* departed Port of Spain on Feb.11th for Philadelphia, but never arrived. She must have been sunk after Feb.16th.

1	2	3	4	5	6	7	8	9	10	11	12	13	14	15

February 1942, cont.

1	2 3	4	5	6	7	8	9	10 11 12	13	14	15
21/2113 dt	U 161	Achilles	ED 9739	-T 5000+	TA	-	21/	br -MT Circe Shell	8207+	11.03 N/ 62.03 W	
22/0159 dt	U 502	v.Rosenstiel	EC 8279	-T 10200+	T	-	21/	nw -MT Kongsgaard	9467+	7m N Pt.Curacao	
22/0244 dt	U 96	Lehmann-Willenbrock	BB 7746	-D: 1948+	TA	-	22/	nw -D Torungen	1948+	44.00 N/ 63.30 W	18)
22/0455 dt	U 504	Poske	DB 9765	-T 6000+	T	-	22/	am -DT Republic	5287+	27.05 N/ 80.15 W	
22/0703 dt	U 155	Piening	BD 1455	-T 7000=	T	ON.67		br -MT Adellen	7984+	49.20 N/ 38.15 W	19)
22/0703 dt	U 155	Piening	BD 1455	-T 9000+	T	ON.67	22/0505	br -MT Adellen	7984+	49.20 N/ 38.15 W	19)
22/0704 dt	U 155	Piening	BD 1455	-D 6000+	T	ON.67	22/0505	nw -M Sama	1799+	49.20 N/ 38.15 W	19)
22/0845 dt	U 504	Poske	DB 9739	-D 10846+	T	-					20)
22/1151 dt	U 128	Heyse	DB 9439	-T 12000+	T	-	22/	am -DT Cities Service Empire	8103+	28.25 N/ 80.02 W	
22/2220 dt	U 129	Clausen	EO 1525	-D 6000+	T	-	22/	ca -D George L.Torain	1754+	09.13 N/ 59.04 W	
22/2257 dt	U 96	Lehmann-Willenbrock	BB 7557	-T: 8888+	T	-	22/	br -MT Kars	8888+	44.15 N/ 63.25 W	
22/2343 dt	U 129	Clausen	EO 1524	-D 9000+	T	-	23/	am -D West Zeda	5658+	09.13 N/ 59.04 W	
23/0132 dt	U 504	Poske	DB 1713	-T 12510+	T	-	22/	am -DT W.D.Anderson	10227+	27.09 N/ 79.56 W	
23/0643 dt	U 161	Achilles	ED 5955	-D: 7000=	TA	-	26/	am -D Lihue	7001+	14.30 N/ 64.45 W	21)
23/1032 dt	U 502	v.Rosenstiel	EC 9153	-T 8300+	T	-	23/	pa -MT Thalia	8329+	13.00 N/ 70.45 W	
23/ dt	U 587	Borcherdt	BC 9424	APC ? =	T	-					22)
23/1504 dt	U 129	Clausen	EO 1655	-D 3400+	T	-	23/	ca -D Lennox	1904+	09.15 N/ 58.30 W	
23/1643 dt	U 502	v.Rosenstiel	EC 9217	-T 6500=	T	-	24/0928	am -DT Sun	9002=	13.02 N/ 70.41 W	
24/0145 dt	U 94	Ites	BC 9296	-D: 7000+	T	-	23/	br -D Empire Hail	7005+	44.48 N/ 40.21 W	

18) *U 96* identified the *Torungen* clearly. So she was sunk on Feb.22nd and not on Feb.26th.
19) *U 155* observed no effects after the first detonation, but the other two ships exploded.
20) *U 504* heard two detonations but could not observe any effect. The ship stopped after 5 minutes. Twenty minutes later
   it was gone.
21) The *Lihue* fought back after the first hit, and dodged one torpedo. She finally sank on Feb.26th.
22) *U 587* reported that she hit a Q-ship.

1	2	3	4	5	6	7	8	9	10	11	12	13	14	15
February 1942, cont.														
24/0428	dt	U 558	Krech	BC 9446	-D	7000+	T	ON.67	24/0030	br	-DT Inverarder	5578+	44.34 N/ 42.37 W	23)
24/0651	dt	U 558	Krech	BC 8698	-D	5000+	T	ON.67	24/0255	nw	-MT Eidanger	9432∓	44.11 N/ 43.25 W	24)
24/0757	dt	U 752	Schroeter	AL 0345	-T	8000+	T	HX.175						25)
24/0835	dt	U 162	Wattenberg	BD 4148	-D	8000+	T	ON.67	24/0445	br	-DT Empire Celt	8032+	43.50 N/ 43.38 W	26)
24/0855	dt	U 158	Rostin	BC 9475	-T	10000+	T	ON.67						
24/0950	dt	U 558	Krech	BC 8932	-D	5000+	T	ON.67	24/	br	-MT Anadara	8009+	43.45 N/ 42.15 W	27)
24/0951	dt	U 558	Krech	BC 8932	-T	9000+	T	ON.67	24/	br	-MT Finnanger	9551+	43.45 N/ 42.15 W	27)
24/0952	dt	U 558	Krech	BC 8932	-D	5000+	T	ON.67	24/	br	-D White Crest	4365+	43.45 N/ 42.15 W	27)
24/1035	dt	U 158	Rostin	BC 8926	-T	4000+	T	ON.67	24/0642	br	-MT Diloma	8146=	43.51 N/ 43.41 W	28)
24/	dt	U 587	Borcherdt	BC 8590	-T	10000=	T	ON.67						27)
24/1540	dt	U 558	Krech	BC 8689	-T:	9432+	Tf	ON.67	24/	br	-MT Eidanger (s.a.)	9432+	44.11 N/ 43.25 W	24)
24/	dt	U 432 ?	Schultze				T	-	24/1632	am	-D Norlavore	2713+	35.05 N/ 75.20 W	29)
25/0218	dt	U 156	Hartenstein	ED 1834	-T:	5685+	T	-	24/	br	-DT La Carriere	5685+	16.53 N/ 67.05 W	30)
									?/	bz	-D Cabedelo	3557+	16. N/ 49. W	31)
25/	it	DA VINCI	Longanesi-Cattani	15n/53w	-D	8000+	T	-						31)
25/0043	it	TORELLI	de Giacomo	10n/54w	-T	10500+	TA	-	26/	pa	-MT Esso Copenhagen	9245+	10.32 N/ 53.20 W	
26/1913	dt	U 504	Poske	DC 7220	-T	7000+	T	-	26/	nl	-MT Mamura	8245+	29. N/ 76. W	
27/0636	dt	U 578	Rehwinkel	CA 5211	-T	10000+	T	-	26/	am	-DT R.P.Resor	7451+	39.47 N/ 73.26 W	

23) *U 558* observed two hits on a freighter which sank in 15 min. by the bow. - 24) *U 558* heard two detonations and observed one smoke cloud rising near the bow.
25) *U 752* heard two detonations on a tanker in the convoy that was sailing east. No effect observed, only a short glare of fire.
26) *U 162* observed two hits on a freighter which sank in 8 min. - *U 158* observed two hits on a tanker with fire- and water columns. Sinking not observed. - Possibly both U-boats hit the *Empire Celt*, or one of the boats mistook hits of the other boat for her own.
27) *U 558* fired three torpedoes and observed three hits. Two ships stopped, the third continued on. Probably all three ships were hit but one that stayed afloat was sunk later by *U 587*, which reported one tanker torpedoed.
28) *U 158* heard one detonation, but could not observe any effect because she had to dive.
29) The *Norlavore* departed Norfolk for Puerto la Cruz on Feb.22nd. There is no attack report, but *U 432* was in the area.
30) The *La Carriere* sank only after two additional hits and some other missed shots on Feb.25th, 08.39 (German time).
31) The *Cabedelo* departed Philadelphia on Feb.14th and was reported missing thereafter. The *Da Vinci* reported one ship sunk by torpedo: there is a vague possibility that the ship sunk was the *Cabedelo*.

1	2	3	4	5	6	7	8	9	10	11	12	13	14	15
February 1942, cont.														
27/0700	dt	U 432	Schultze	CA 7936	-D	10000+	TA	-	27/	am	-D	Marore	8215+	35.33 N/ 74.58 W	
27/1035	dt	U 156	Hartenstein	DN	-D	2500+	A	-	27/	br	-D	Macgregor	2498+	19.50 N/ 69.40 W	
28/0103	dt	U 129	Clausen	EO 3774	-D	4000+	T	-	27/	pa	-D	Bayou	2605+	08.08 N/ 55.14 W	
28/1130	it	DA VINCI	Longanesi-Cattani	17n/53w	-D	12000+	TA	-	28/o9oo	le	-D	Everasma	3644+	17. N/ 48. W	
28/0844	dt	U 653	Feiler	CA 9971	-M	7000+	T	-	28/	nw	-M	Leif	1582+	34.45 N/ 69.20 W	
28/1057	*dt*	*U 578*	*Rehwinkel*	*CA 5458*	*DD*	*1190+*	*T*	*-*	*28/*	*am*	*DD*	*Jacob Jones*	*1090+*	*38.37 N/ 74.32 W*	
28/	dt	U 156	Hartenstein	DO 71	-T	4500+	A	-	28/	am	-DT	Oregon	7017+	20.44 N/ 67.52 W	
March 1942														
1/0200	dt	U 588	Vogel	CB 4110	-D:	4800+	T	-	1/	br	-D	Carperby	4890+	39.57 N/ 55.40 W	
1/1133	dt	U 158	Rostin	CB 6591	-T	8000+	TA	-							1)
2/0428	dt	U 588	Vogel	CB 64	-T:	4850+	TA	-							2)
2/	*dt*	*U 587*	*Borcherdt*	*BB 8282*	*PC*	*+*	*T*	*-*							*3)*
2/2047	dt	U 126	Bauer	DO 1218	-D:	2362+	T	-	2/	nw	-D	Gunny	2362+	27.09 N/ 66.33 W	
3/1205	dt	U 129	Clausen	EO 3655	-D:	5104+	T	-	3/	am	-D	Mary	5104+	08.25 N/ 52.50 W	
3/1721	dt	U 68	Merten	ET 6685	-D	6000+	T	-	3/	br	-D	Helenus	7366+	06.01 N/ 12.02 W	
4/	dt	U 587	Borcherdt	BB 60	-D	=	T	-						St.Johns Hafen	4)
4/	dt	U 587	Borcherdt	BB 60	-D	=	T	-						St.Johns Hafen	4)
5/1135	dt	U 404	v.Bülow	BB 7528	-D:	5112+	T	HX.178s	5/	am	-D	Collamer	5112+	44.19 N/ 63.09 W	
5/1533	dt	U 128	Heyse	DN 1215	-T:	11007+	TA	-	5/	nw	-MT	O.A.Knudsen	11007+	26.17 N/ 75.50 W	
5/2244	dt	U 126	Bauer	DN 5695	-D:	3110+	T	-	6/	am	-D	Mariana	3110+	27.45 N/ 67. W	

1) *U 158* observed two hits. The tanker fired her guns at the U-boat and was herself sunk by gunfire after 4 hours and 45 min.
2) *U 588* hit an empty tanker with one torpedo, and sank this ship after firing 200 rounds of 88mm in 4 hours. It was identified as the *Consuelo* (Brit, 4847 gross tons), which gave an SSS-report on March 1st at 10.06 hrs, but arrived at New York on the 3rd without heavy damage.
3) *U 587* reported sinking a submarine-chaser.
4) *U 587* fired two torpedoes into the harbor of St.John's which probably detonated against the docks.

1	2	3	4	5	6	7	8	9	10	11	12	13	14	15
March 1942, cont.														
5/2307	dt	U 505	Loewe	ET 6480	-D: 5920+	T	-	5/	br	-D	Benmohr	5920+	06.05 N/ 14.15 W	
6/	dt	U 587	Borcherdt	BB 6759	-D:　　+	T	-	4/	gö	-D	Hans Egede	900+	Canadian Coast	5)
6/0235	it	TAZZOLI	Fecia di Cossato	29n/63w	-D: 1406+	TA	-	6/	nl	-D	Astrea	1406+	29.12 N/ 64.29 W	
6/0308	it	FINZI	Giudice	24n/62w	-T: 7011+	T	-	6/	br	-MT	Melpomene	7011+	23.35 N/ 62.39 W	
7/0500	it	TAZZOLI	Fecia di Cossato	30n/67w	-M 5000+	TA	-	6/	nw	-M	Tönsbergfjord	3156+	31.22 N/ 68.05 W	
6/1131	dt	U 505	Loewe	ET 8320	-T 8000+	T	-	6/	nw	-MT	Sydhav	7587+	04.47 N/ 14.57 W	
6/2220	dt	U 129	Clausen	EO 6625	-D: 6188+	T	-	6/	am	-D	Steel Age	6188+	06.45 N/ 53.15 W	
6/2306	dt	U 701	Degen	AE 8895	APC 1000+	T	-	6/	fa	-Df	Nyggjaberg	272+	South Coast Iceland	
7/0150	it	FINZI	Giudice	23n/60w	-D: 4528+	TA	-	7/	sw	-D	Skane	4528+	20.50 N/ 62.05 W	
7/0350	dt	U 94	Ites	CB 4498	-D 6000+	T	-	7/	br	APC	Northern Princess	655+	West Atlantic	
7/0835	dt	U 126	Bauer	DN 8423	-D 5500+	T	-	7/	am	-D	Barbara	4637+	20.10 N/ 73.05 W	
7/1144	dt	U 126	Bauer	DN 8454	-D 8000+	TA	-	7/	am	-D	Cardonia	5104+	19.53 N/ 73.27 W	
7/1614	dt	U 161	Achilles	ED 6891	-D 6000+	T	-	7/1605	ca	-DT	Uniwaleco	9755+	13.23 N/ 62.04 W	6)
7/1800	dt	U 161	Achilles	ED 68	-D 6000+	T	-							6)
7/2110	dt	U 155	Piening	CA 8786	-D 6000+	T	-	7/1910	bz	-D	Arabutan	7874+	35.15 N/ 73.55 W	
7/2314	dt	U 701	Degen	AE 8265	-D 1500+	T	-							7)
8/0039	dt	U 701	Degen	AE 8268	APC 800+	T	-	7/	br	APC	Notts Country	541+	South Iceland	
8/1117	dt	U 126	Bauer	DN 7921	-T:10389+	TA	-	8/	pa	-DT	Esso Bolivar	10389=	19.38 N/ 74.38 W	
8/1241	dt	U 68	Merten	EU 8196	-D: 6992+	TA	-	8/	br	-D	Baluchistan	6992+	04.13 N/ 08.32 W	
8/1917	dt	U 569	Hinsch	AM 2417	-D 5000+	T	-	8/	br	-D	Hengist	984+	59.31 N/ 10.15 W	

5) *U 587* erroneously reported the name of the ship as the *Hawse Gude*, but this must have been the *H.Egede*.
6) *U 161* observed during the first attack one ship sinking 3 min. after the hit. During the second attack, two detonations
　were heard and one smoke cloud was observed. The *Uniwaleco* was hit two times in 5-8 minutes, and broke in two.
7) *U 701* observed one ship sinking two minutes after being hit.

1	2	3	4	5	6	7	8	9	10	11	12	13	14	15
March 1942, cont.														
9/	dt	U 587	Borcherdt	BB 9812	-D 5800+	T	ONS.68	9/	gr	-D	Lily	5719+	43.32 N/ 54.14 W	
9/0200	it	TAZZOLI	Fecia di Cossato	29n/70w	-D 7000+	TA	-	8/	ur	-D	Montevideo	5785+	29.13 N/ 69.35 W	
9/0225	dt	U 94	Ites	CA 5654	-D: 5152+	T	-	7/	bz	-D	Cayrú	5152+	39.10 N/ 72.02 W	
9/1317	dt	U 126	Bauer	DN 7399	-T: 7932+	TA	-	9/	pa	-MT	Hanseat	8241+	20.25 N/ 74.07 W	
9/2109	dt	U 96	Lehmann-Willenbrock	BB 7965	-D: 4265+	T	-	9/	nw	-M	Tyr	4265+	43.40 N/ 61.10 W	
10/0124	it	FINZI	Giudice	23n/60w	-T: 9957+	T	-	10/	nw	-MT	Charles Racine	9957+	23.10 N/ 60.28 W	
10/0449	dt	U 161	Achilles	Port	-D 8000+	T	-	9/	ca	-D	Lady Nelson	7970=	Port Castries,	8)
10/0449	dt	U 161	Achilles	Castries-D	5000+	T	-	9/	br	-D	Umtata	8141=	Santa Lucia	8)
10/0632	dt	U 588	Vogel	CA 5156	-T: 6800+	T	-	10/	am	-DT	Gulftrade	6676+	39.50 N/ 73.52 W	
11/0056	it	TORELLI	de Giacomo	13n/57w	-M:10530=	T	-	10/	br	-M	Orari	------		
11/0211	dt	U 701	Degen	AE 5568	APC 800+	T	-	19/	br	APC	Stella Capella	440+	64.48 N/ 13.20 W	9)
11/0316	dt	U 94	Ites	CA 5489	-D 5000+	T	-	11/	nw	-D	Hvosleff	1630+	38.27 N/ 74.54 W	
11/0758	dt	U 158	Rostin	DC 1136	CGC 1500+	T	-	11/0200	am	-D	Caribsea	2609+	34.40 N/ 76.10 W	10)
11/	dt	U 126 ?	Bauer			T	-	11/nm	am	-DT	Halo	6986=	San Antonio Bay	11)
11/2250	it	TAZZOLI	Fecia di Cossato	24n/73w	-D: 3530+	TA	-	11/	pa	-D	Cygnet	3628+	5m San Salvador, Bahamas	
12/0138	it	MOROSINI	Fraternale	23n/58w	-D: 5966+	T	-	11/	br	-D	Stangarth	5966+	22.00 N/ 65.00 W	
12/0234	dt	U 126	Bauer	DN 4745	-D: 7005+	TA	-	12/	am	-D	Texan	7005+	21.34 N/ 76.28 W	
12/0611	dt	U 126	Bauer	DN 6959	-D: 2496+	T	-	12/	am	-D	Olga	2496+	21.32 N/ 76.24 W	
12/1536	dt	U 578	Rehwinkel	CC 2644	-D 2000+	T	-	18/	nw	-D	Ingerto	3089+	29.35 N/ 66.30 W	12)

8) *U 161* fired two torpedoes into the harbor. One ship was sinking by the stern in burning condition and a second exploded. But both ships were later salvaged and repaired.

9) *U 701* observed one ship sinking 2 min 30 sec after being hit. There were no other known losses besides the *Stella Capella*.

10) *U 158* assumed to have sunk a Coast Guard ship. In reality, the *Caribsea* had been hit and sank in 3 min.

11) The *Halo* was damaged 25 miles from San Antonio Bay (West Cuba). Only *U 128* was in the area, but there is no report of it from her.

12) The *Ingerto* departed the Clyde for Mobile and was reported missing after Feb.26th. The report of *U 578* may match this loss.

1	2	3	4	5	6	7	8	9	10 11	12	13	14	15
March 1942, cont.													
13/0441	dt	U 126	Bauer	DM 6599	-D: 5518+	T	-	13/0240	am -D	Colabee	5518=	22.10 N/ 77.30 W	13)
13/0505	dt	U 158	Rostin	DB 3999	-T 12000+	T	-	13/	am -DT	John D.Gill	11641+	33.55 N/ 77.39 W	
13/0643	dt	U 404	v.Bülow	CA 5241	-D 6000+	T	-	13/	cl -D	Tolten	1858+	40.10 N/ 73.50 W	14)
13/0720	dt	U 332	Liebe	CA 8681	-S 1000+	T	-	13/	am -S	Albert F.Paul	735+	26. N/ 72. W	15)
13/1747	dt	U 332	Liebe	CA 8654	-D: 5042+	T	-	13/	jg -D	Trepca	5042+	37. N/ 73.25 W	
13/1805	it	TAZZOLI	Fecia di Cossato	27n/75w	-D: 6434+	TA	-	13/	br -D	Daytonian	6434+	26.33 N/ 74.43 W	
14/0200	dt	U 67	Müller-Stöckheim	EC 5345	-T: 8436+	T	-	14/	pa -MT	Penelope	8436+	15. N/ 64.20 W	
14/0230	dt	U 161	Achilles	ED 90	-T 5000+	T	-	15/	ca -D	Sarniadoc	1940+	15.45 N/ 65. W	16)
14/0758	dt	U 404	v.Bülow	CA 5176	-D 6000+	T	-	14/	am -D	Lemuel Burrows	7610+	39.21 N/ 74.33 W	
14/2118	dt	U 124	Mohr	CB 7593	-T: 7209+	T	-	14/	br -MT	British Resource	7209+	36.04 N/ 65.38 W	
15/	dt	U 161	Achilles	ED 2955	CGC:1130+	A	-	15/	am AGL	Acacia	1130+	S Haiti	
15/0406	dt	U 158	Rostin	DC 1164	-T: 7118+	T	-	15/	am -DT	Olean	7118=	34.22 N/ 76.29 W	
15/0725	dt	U 158	Rostin	DC 1159	-T: 6952+	T	-	15/	am -DT	Ario	6952+	34.37 N/ 76.20 W	
15/2135	it	TAZZOLI	Fecia di Cossato	27n/76w	-T: 8782+	TA	-	15/	br -MT	Athelqueen	8780+	26.50 N/ 75.40 W	
16/0503	it	MOROSINI	Fraternale	19n/61w	-T: 6321+	TA	-	16/	nl -MT	Oscilla	6341+	19.15 N/ 60.25 W	
16/1824	dt	U 504	Poske	DO 5450	-D 7000+	T	-	15/	br -D	Manaqui	2802+	17.15 N/ 61.00 W	17)
16/1955	dt	U 332	Liebe	CA 7959	-T 9974+	T	-	16/	am -MT	Australia	11628+	35.43 N/ 75.22 W	
16/2317	dt	U 68	Merten	EU 8143	-D 5000+	T	-	16/	br -D	Baron Newlands	3386+	04.35 N/ 08.32 W	

13) The *Colabee* was beached and later salvaged.
14) The *Tolten* was running zig-zag in darkened condition, and was identified as Chilean only after the attack.
15) *U 332* reported the sinking of a 4-masted schooner. It may have been the *Albert F.Paul*.
16) *U 161* reported a tanker sunk after 30 sec from the hit. It must have been the *Sarniadoc*.
17) The *Manaqui* departed Loch Ewe on Feb.18th for Kingston and was reported missing after March 15th.

1	2	3	4	5	6	7	8	9	10	11	12	13	14	15
March 1942, cont.														
17/0216	dt	U 404	v.Bülow	CA 8163	-T: 8073+	T	-	16/		br -MT	San Demetrio	8073+	37.03 N/ 73.50 W	
17/0226	dt	U 124	Mohr	CA 8585	-D: 1698+	T	-	16/		ho -D	Ceiba	1698+	35.43 N/ 73.49 W	
17/0635	dt	U 68	Merten	EU 8511	-D: 5755+	TA	-	17/		br -D	Ile de Batz	5755+	04.04 N/ 08.04 W	
17/1326	dt	U 68	Merten	EU 8513	-D: 4917+	TA	-	17/		br -M	Scottish Prince	4917+	04.10 N/ 08. W	
17/1508	dt	U 373	Loeser	CB 3818	-D 5000+	T	-	14/		gr -D	Mount Lycabettus	4292+	40.15 N/ 61. W	18)
17/1858	dt	U 71	Flachsenberg	CB 4941	-T 8500+	T	-	16/		nw -MT	Ranja	6355+	32. N/ 72.30 W	19)
17/2153	dt	U 68	Merten	EU 8523	-D: 5081+	T	-	17/		br -D	Allende	5081+	04. N/ 07.44 W	
17/2352	dt	U 124	Mohr	CA 7966	-D 3000+	T	-	17/		am -DT	Acme	6878=	35.05 N/ 75.20 W	20)
18/0114	dt	U 124	Mohr	CA 7993	-D 3000+	T	-	17/		gr -D	Kassandra Louloudi	5106+	35.05 N/ 75.25 W	
18/0827	dt	U 124	Mohr	CA 7997	-T 8000+	T	-	18/		am -DT	E.M.Clark	9647+	34.50 N/ 75.35 W	
19/0137	dt	U 507	Schacht	AL 8918	-D 4000=	T	ONS.76							21)
19/0138	dt	U 507	Schacht	AL 8918	-D 6000=	T	ONS.76							21)
19/0141	dt	U 507	Schacht	AL 8918	-D 6000+	T	ONS.76							21)
19/0431	dt	U 124	Mohr	DC 1167	-T: 5939+	T	-	19/		am -DT	Papoose	5939+	34.17 N/ 76.39 W	
19/0538	dt	U 124	Mohr	DC 1183	-T: 7076+	T	-	19/		am -DT	W.E.Hutton	7076+	34.25 N/ 76.50 W	
19/1619	dt	U 332	Liebe	CA 7959	-D: 6000+	T	-	19/		am -D	Liberator	7720+	35.05 N/ 75.30 W	
20/2139	dt	U 71	Flachsenberg	CA 9618	-D: 5766+	TA	-	20/		am -D	Oakmar	5766+	36.22 N/ 68.50 W	
21/0608	dt	U 124	Mohr	DC 1418	-T 10000+	TA	-	21/		am -DT	Esso Nashville	7934=	33.35 N/ 77.22 W	22)
21/1005	dt	U 124	Mohr	DC 1441	-T:11000+	T	-	21/		am -DT	Atlantic Sun	11355=	33.34 N/ 77.25 W	
22/0045	dt	U 202	Linder	CC 5497	-T 10000+	T		21/		br -MT	Athelviscount	8882=	38.46 N/ 55.44 W	

18) The *Mount Lycabettus* departed Baltimore on March 13th for Lisbon and was reported missing after March 14th.

19) The *Ranja* was listed as sunk on March 16th, but it must have been this ship which was sunk by *U 71*.

20) The *Acme* was grounded by the stern but later salvaged.

21) *U 507* fired a 4-torpedo salvo and heard two detonations, and a short time later a third. No effects observed. Then a stern 2-torpedo salvo was fired. One detonation and a boiler explosion was heard, but no observation was made.

22) The *Esso Nashville* broke in two. The after part was salvaged and fitted with a new bow section.

1	2	3	4	5	6	7	8	9	10	11	12	13	14	15

March 1942, cont.

1	2	3	4	5	6	7	8	9	10/11	12	13	14	15
22/0509 dt	U 373	Loeser	CA 6593	-D: 6000+	T	-	22/	br -D	Thursobank	5575+	38.05 N/ 68.30 W	
22/1757 dt	U 123	Hardegen	CB 8314	-T: 7034+	T	-	19/	am -DT	Muskogee	7034+	28. N/ 58. W	23)
23/1023 dt	U 124	Mohr	DC 1189	-T 7000+	T	-	23/	am -DT	Naeco	5373+	33.59 N/ 76.40 W	
23/1531 dt	U 754	Oestermann	BB 8631	-T 10000+	T	-	23/	br -MT	British Prudence	8620+	45.28 N/ 56.13 W	
23/2038 it	MOROSINI	Fraternale	25n/57w	-T: 9300+	TA	-	23/	br -DT	Peder Bogen	9741+	24.41 N/ 57.44 W	
24/0300 dt	U 123	Hardegen	CB 8173	-T: 8150+	TA	-	23/	br -MT	Empire Steel	8138+	37.45 N/ 63.17 W	
25/0413 dt	U 552	Topp	CB 1363	-T: 6356+	T	-	25/	nl -MT	Ocana	6256+	42.36 N/ 65.30 W	24)
25/0610 dt	U 105	Schuch	CB 7779	-T:10389+	T	-	25/	br -MT	Narragansett	10389+	34.46 N/ 67.40 W	
25/0616 dt	U 94	Ites	BC 6763	-D 8000+	T	ON.77	25/					25)
25/0616 dt	U 94	Ites	BC 6763	-T 9000+	T	ON.77	25/0435	br -MT	Imperial Transport	8022=	46.26 N/ 41.30 W	25)
25/ dt	U 587	Borcherdt	BD 4226	-T 12000+	Tf	ON.77 s	25/					26)
26/1459 dt	U 71	Flachsenberg	CA 7995	-T 7000+	T	-	26/	am -DT	Dixie Arrow	8046+	34.55 N/ 75.02 W	
27/0237 dt	U 123	Hardegen	CA 9578	APC:3209+	TA	-	27/	am APC	Atik (Carolyn)	3209+	36. N/ 70. W	27)
27/0138 dt	U 160	Lassen	CA 84	-D +	T	-	26/2334	pa -D	Equipoise	6210+	36.36 N/ 74.45 W	
27/0256 dt	U 105	Schuch	DC 3126	-D 3000=	T	-						28)
27/0920 dt	U 105	Schuch	CA 9945	-T 7000+	TA	-	27/	nw -MT	Svenör	7616+	35.55 N/ 69.20 W	
29/0745 it	CALVI	Olivieri	12n/43w	-D 10946+	T	-	25/	br -D	Tredinnick	4589+	27.15 N/ 49.15 W	29)
29/1936 dt	U 160	Lassen	CA 8781	-M 4500+	T	-	29/	am -M	City of New York	8272+	35.16 N/ 74.25 W	
29/2058 dt	U 571	Möhlmann	CB 2753	-D:11785+	T	-	29/	br -D	Hertford	10923+	40.50 N/ 63.31 W	

23) The *Muskogee* was identified by *U 123*. The Allied reports about the date and position are wrong.
24) The wreck of the *Ocana* was burned out and sunk by British ships on April 15th.
25) *U 94* fired four torpedoes and observed one hit at the bow of a freighter, and two hits on a tanker. The *Imperial Transport* was hit by two torpedoes and abandoned, but remained afloat, and was reboarded and towed into St.John's. - 26) The attacked ship was probably the abandoned *Imperial Transport*.
27) The *Atik* (ex *Carolyn*) was a Q-ship. She was sunk after two torpedo hits and a gun duel by *U 123*.
28) *U 105* heard one detonation and observed the target ship with a slight list. Possibly the torpedo hit but did not detonate.
29) The *Tredinnick* departed New York on March 18th for Capetown, and made a last signal on March 25th from 27°15'N/49°15'W.

1	2	3	4	5	6	7	8	9	10	11	12	13	14			15

March 1942, cont.

1	2	3	4	5	6	7	8	9	10/11	12	13	14	15
30/2243	dt	U 68	Merten	FE 3366	-D: 5853+	T	-	30/	br -M	Muncaster Castle	5853+	02.02 N/ 12.02 W	
31/	dt	U 754	Oestermann	CA 4997	-Dt +	A	-	31/1535	am -Dt	Menominee	441+	37.34 N/ 75.25 W	
31/	dt	U 754	Oestermann	CA 4997	-Bg +	A	-	31/	am -Bg	Ontario	490=	37.34 N/ 75.25 W	
31/	dt	U 754	Oestermann	CA 4997	-Bg +	A	-	31/	am -Bg	Barnegat	914+	37.34 N/ 75.25 W	
31/	dt	U 754	Oestermann	CA 4997	-Bg +	A	-	31/	am -Bg	Alleghany	914+	37.34 N/ 75.25 W	
31/2105	it	CALVI	Olivieri	07n/45w	-T 10000+	TA	-	31/	am -DT	T.C.McCobb	7452+	07.10 N/ 45.20 W	
31/2222	dt	U 71	Flachsenberg	CA 6995	-T 8000+	T	-	31/	br -DT	San Gerardo	12915+	36. N/ 67. W	

April 1942

1	2	3	4	5	6	7	8	9	10/11	12	13	14	15
1/0453	dt	U 71	Flachsenberg	CA 6997	-D 6000+	T	-	31/	br -D	Eastmoor	5812+	37.33 N/ 68.18 W	
1/0618	dt	U 754	Oestermann	CA 7381	-D 7000+	T	-	1/0300	am -DT	Tiger	5992+	36.50 N/ 74.18 W	
1/1622	dt	U 160	Lassen	CA 8776	-D 6000+	T	-	1/1320	br -D	Rio Blanco	4086+	35.16 N/ 74.18 W	
1/2314	dt	U 202	Linder	CB 8387	-D: 5249+	T	-	1/2123	br -M	Loch Don	5249+	37.05 N/ 61.40 W	
2/0718	dt	U 123	Hardegen	DC 1196	-T: 7057+	TA	-	2/0532	am -DT	Liebre	7057=	34.11 N/ 76.08 W	
3/0340	dt	U 552	Topp	CA 5714	-D: 2438+	A	-	3/0118	am -D	David H.Atwater	2438+	37.57 N/ 75.10 W	
3/1149	dt	U 754	Oestermann	CA 8618	-D 5000+	T	-	3/0939	am -D	Otho	4839+	36.25 N/ 72.22 W	
3/2131	dt	U 505	Loewe	FU 9781	-D: 5775+	T	-	3/1935	am -D	West Irmo	5775+	02.10 N/ 05.35 W	
4/0110	dt	U 572	Hirsacker	CB 7588	-T: 6207=	A	-	4/0000	br -MT	Ensis	6207=	35.43 N/ 66.08 W	1)
4/2129	dt	U 505	Loewe	FF 2242	-D: 5759+	T	-	4/1910	nl -D	Alphacca	5759+	01.50 N/ 07.40 W	
4/2135	dt	U 154	Kölle	DO 7296	-D 4000+	T	-	4/1906	am -DT	Comol Rico	5034+	20.46 N/ 66.46 W	
5/0447	dt	U 552	Topp	CA 7652	-T 10000+	T	-	5/0301	am -DT	Byron T.Benson	7953+	36.08 N/ 75.32 W	
5/2318	dt	U 154	Kölle	DO 7471	-D 6000+	T	-	5/2127	am -DT	Catahoula	5030+	19.16 N/ 68.12 W	
6/0807	dt	U 160	Lassen	DC 1246	-T 12510+	T	-	6/0600	am -MT	Bidwell	6837=	34.25 N/ 75.57 W	
6/1700	dt	U 571	Möhlmann	CA 9922	-T:10044+	TA	-	6/1430	nw -MT	Koll	10044+	34.39 N/ 68.25 W	

1) The *Ensis* was only slightly damaged by 20mm gunfire.

1	2	3	4	5	6	7	8	9	10	11	12	13	14	15
April 1942, cont.														
6/2058	dt	U 754	Oestermann	CA 9986	-T:13000+	T	-	6/1850	nw	-MT	Kollskegg	9858+	34.58 N/ 68.38 W	
7/0417	dt	U 552	Topp	CA 7969	-T: 7138+	T	-	7/0215	br	-MT	British Splendour	7138+	35.07 N/ 75.19 W	
7/1052	dt	U 552	Topp	CA 7991	-D 14000+	T	-	7/0835	nw	-DW	Lancing	7866+	35.08 N/ 75.22 W	
8/0457	dt	U 84	Uphoff	CB 4269	-D: 5200+	T	-	8/0225	jg	-D	Nemanja	5226+	40.30 N/ 64.50 W	
8/0752	dt	U 123	Hardegen	DB 6177	-T 9500+	TA	-	8/0700	am	-DT	Oklahoma	9264=	31.18 N/ 80.59 W	2)
8/0844	dt	U 123	Hardegen	DB 6177	-T:10500+	T	-	8/0715	am	-DT	Esso Baton Rouge	7989=	31.02 N/ 80.53 W	3)
8/2357	it	CALVI	Olivieri	03s/39w	-T: 7138+	TA	-	9/0035	am	-DT	Eugene V.R.Thayer	7138+	02.12 S/ 39.55 W	
9/0938	dt	U 552	Topp	DC 1163	-T 8000+	T	-	9/0750	am	-DT	Atlas	7137+	34.27 N/ 76.16 W	
9/0716	dt	U 123	Hardegen	DB 5663	-D: 3365+	T	-	9/0525	am	-D	Esparta	3365+	30.46 N/ 81.11 W	4)
9/0758	dt	U 160	Lassen	DC 1227	-D 6000+	T	-	9/0558	am	-D	Malchace	3516+	34.28 N/ 75.56 W	4)
10/0220	dt	U 654	Forster	CB 6788	-D: 7000+	T	-	10/	br	-D	Empire Prairie	7010+	35. N/ 60. W	5)
10/0347	dt	U 203	Mützelburg	CA 7965	-T 13467+	T	-	10/0215	br	-MT	San Delfino	8072+	35.35 N/ 75.06 W	
10/0627	dt	U 552	Topp	DC 1246	-T 10000+	T	-	10/0429	am	-DT	Tamaulipas	6943+	34.25 N/ 76.00 W	4)
10/	dt	U 85	Greger	-------	---------	T	-	10/	nw	-M	Chr.Knudsen	4904+	U.S. East Coast	6)
11/0024	it	CALVI	Olivieri	02s/38w	-M +	TA	-	10/2230	nw	-M	Balkis	2161+	02.30 S/ 38.00 W	
11/0422	dt	U 123	Hardegen	DB 5699	-T 12500+	TA	-	11/0230	am	-DT	Gulfamerica	8081+	30.10 N/ 81.15 W	
11/	dt	U 252	Lerchen	AE 4112	-D 2000+	T	-	?	nw	-D	Fanefjeld	1355+		7)
11/1320	dt	U 203	Mützelburg	DC 1193	-T 8482+	T	-	11/1121	am	-DT	Harry F. Sinclair, Jr.	6151=	34.25 N/ 76.30 W	
11/1855	dt	U 130	Kals	DP 5418	-M: 5393+	TA	-	11/1600	nw	-M	Grenager	5393+	22.45 N/ 57.13 W	
11/2231	dt	U 160	Lassen	DC 1259	-D:14647+	T	-	11/2030	br	-D	Ulysses	14647+	34.23 N/ 75.35 W	

2) The *Oklahoma* was hit by one torpedo and five gun shots. She was beached and later salvaged and repaired.
3) The *Esso Baton Rouge* was beached in damaged condition but later salvaged.
4) The *Esparta*, *Malchace*, and *Tamaulipas* were sunk in shallow water, but were total losses.
5) *U 654* reported this ship erroneously as *Empire Lightning*.
6) The *Chr. Knudsen* departed from New York on April 8th for Capetown. It must have been the ship sunk by *U 85* April 14th.
7) *U 252* reported the sinking of a steamer off the Northwest Cape of Iceland. The *Fanefjeld* departed Isafjord on Apr.8th and was reported missing thereafter. One life ring was later found.

1	2	3	4	5	6	7	8	9	10	11	12	13	14	15
April 1942, cont.														
12/0657	dt	U 154	Kölle	EC 2586	-D 8300+	T	-	12/0502	am	-D	Delvalle	5032+	16.51 N/ 72.25 W	
12/0626	dt	U 203	Mützelburg	DC 1175	-D 5032+	T	-							8)
12/0706	dt	U 203	Mützelburg	DC 1177	-T:10444+	T	-	12/0513	pa	-MT	Stanvac Melbourne	10013=	33.53 N/ 77.29 W	8)
12/1921	dt	U 130	Kals	DP 4754	-T: 7699+	TA	-	12/1950	am	-DT	Esso Boston	7699+	21.42 N/ 60.00 W	9)
12/2320	it	CALVI	Olivieri	O4s/36w	-T +	TA	-	12/2215	pa	-MT	Ben Brush	7691+	04.32 S/ 35.03 W	
13/0511	dt	U 123	Hardegen	DB	-D 5500+	T	-	13/0230	am	-D	Leslie	2609+	28.35 N/ 80.19 W	10)
13/0552	dt	U 154	Kölle	EC 6299	-T 12000+	T	-	13/	br	-DT	Empire Amethyst	8032+	17.40 N/ 74.50 W	
13/0745	dt	U 123	Hardegen	DB 90	-D 8000+	A	-	13/0540	sw	-M	Korsholm	2647+	28.21 N/ 80.22 W	
13/2326	dt	U 402	v.Forstner	CC 2855	-D 5000+	T	-	13/2130	br	-D	Empire Progress	5249+	40.29 N/ 52.35 W	
14/1515	dt	U 203	Mützelburg	CA 7968	-D 5000+	T	-	14/1326	br	-D	Empire Thrush	6160+	35.08 N/ 75.18 W	
14/1636	dt	U 66	Zapp	ED 9619	-D 3100+	T	-	14/1430	gr	-D	Korthion	2116+	12.50 N/ 60.30 W	
14/2102	dt	U 571	Möhlmann	CA 8754	-D 8000+	T	-	14/	am	-D	Margaret	3352+	U.S. East Coast	11)
16/0338	dt	U 575	Heydemann	CB 44	-D 7000+	TA	-	15/	am	-D	Robin Hood	6887+	38.45 N/ 66.45 W	
16/1745	dt	U 66	Zapp	ED 9455	-T 8000+	T	-	16/1545	nl	-DT	Amsterdam	7329+	12.00 N/ 62.45 W	
16/1800	dt	U 572	Hirsacker	CA 8915	-D 4889+	T	-	16/1655	pa	-D	Desert Light	2368+	35.35 N/ 72.48 W	
17/0523	dt	U 123	Hardegen	DC 3179	-D: 4834+	A	-	17/0210	am	-D	Alcoa Guide	4834+	35.34 N/ 70.08 W	12)
17/0523	dt	U 66	Zapp	ED 8617	-T:11020+	T	-	17/0336	pa	-MT	Heinrich v.Riedemann	11020+	11.55 N/ 63.47 W	
18/0046	dt	U 201	Schnee	CA 9375	-T 10000+	T	-	17/2257	ar	-MT	Victoria	7417=	36.41 N/ 68.48 W	13)
19/0034	dt	U 136	Zimmermann	CA 7936	-D 6000+	T	.	18/2235	am	-DT	Axtell J.Byles	8955=	35.32 N/ 75.19 W	
20/0306	dt	U 572	Hirsacker	DC 3248	-M 9278+	T	-	19/2355	br	-D	Empire Dryden	7164+	34.21 N/ 69.00 W	

8) The torpedo fired by *U 203* against the *Delvalle* (identified by the B-Dienst) detonated on hitting the bottom beneath the stern of the *Stanvac Melbourne*, which was heavily damaged by the next torpedo. The *Delvalle* was sunk later by *U 154*.
9) The *Esso Boston* was beached while aflame and became a total loss.
10) The *Leslie* went down in shallow water (15 meters) but nevertheless was a total loss.
11) The *Margaret* departed Puerto Rico on March 28th for Baltimore, and was reported missing thereafter.

1	2	3	4	5	6	7	8	9	10	11	12	13	14	15

April 1942, cont.

1	2	3	4	5	6	7	8	9	10 11	12	13	14	15
20/0428 dt	U 654	Forster	CA 98	-D 10000+	T	-		20/0230 am	-D	Steelmaker	6176+	33.48 N/ 70.36 W	
20/0524 dt	U 109	Bleichrodt	DC 3225	-D 7500+	T	-		20/0315 br	-D	Harpagon	5719+	34.35 N/ 65.50 W	
20/2103 dt	U 154	Kölle	DN 5615	-D 3500+	TA	-		20/1825 br	-D	Vineland	5587+	23.05 N/ 72.20 W	
20/2323 dt	U 654	Forster	CA 9892	-D 4600+	T	-		20/2120 sw	-M	Agra	4569+	34.40 N/ 69.35 W	
21/0030 dt	U 84	Uphoff	DC 1314	-D 4000+	T	-		20/2300 pa	-D	Chenango	3014+	36.25 N/ 74.55 W	
21/0236 dt	U 201	Schnee	DC 3456	-D 4000+	T	-		21/0045 nw	-D	Bris	2027+	34. N/ 69. W	
21/0448 dt	U 752	Schroeter	CB 1677	-D: 5751+	TA	-		21/0250 am	-D	West Imboden	5751+	41.14 N/ 65.55 W	
21/1845 dt	U 576	Heinicke	DB 4872	-D: 5102+	T	-		21/1657 am	-D	Pipestone County	5102+	37.43 N/ 66.16 W	
22/0329 dt	U 201	Schnee	DC 5631	-D 6700+	TA	-		22/0030 am	-D	San Jacinto	6069+	31.10 N/ 70.45 W	
22/0905 dt	U 201	Schnee	DC 6178	-D 9500+	T	-		22/0730 br	-D	Derryheen	7217+	31.20 N/ 70.35 W	
23/1120 dt	U 752	Schroeter	CA 5394	-D: 7000=	A	-		23/0900 am	-M	Reinholt	4799+	39.10 N/ 72.00 W	14)
23/2053 dt	U 125	Folkers	DD 9585	-D 4000+	TA	-		23/1920 am	-D	Lammot Du Pont	5102+	27.10 N/ 57.10 W	
24/1409 dt	U 576	Heinicke	CA 3975	-D 5000=	T	-		24/1230 nw	-D	Tropic Star	-----	40.50 N/ 68.42 W	15)
24/2348 dt	U 136	Zimmermann	CA 9521	-D 7000+	T	-		24/2200 br	-M	Empire Drum	7244+	37.00 N/ 69.15 W	
25/0831 dt	U 108	Scholtz	DD 2447	-D: 3830+	T	-		25/0615 br	-D	Modesta	3849+	33.40 N/ 63.10 W	
25/2258 dt	U 130	Kals	EC 5425	-D 5500=	T	-							16)
26/0830 dt	U 66	Zapp	ED 4793	-D 9500+	T	-		26/0530 am	-D	Alcoa Partner	5513+	13.32 N/ 67.57 W	
28/1535 dt	U 136	Zimmermann	CA 2878	-D 5000+	T	-		28/1330 nl	-D	Arundo	5163+	40.10 N/ 73.44 W	
29/0412 dt	U 66	Zapp	ED 8696	-T:10350+	T	-		29/	pa	-MT	Harry G.Seidel	10354+	11.50 N/ 62.50 W	

12) *U 123* reported the former name of the ship sunk: *Point Brava*.
13) The *Victoria* was towed into New York by USS *Owl* on Apr.21st, escorted by the U.S. destroyers *Nicholson* and *Swanson*.
14) The *Reinholt* was hit by about 20-25 rounds of 88mm. She answered by firing 14 shots.
15) *U 576* heard the torpedo hit the ship, but it was a dud and did not explode. The *Tropic Sea* was not damaged.
16) *U 130* heard two torpedoes hit the ship without detonating: two duds.

1	2	3	4	5	6	7	8	9	10	11	12	13	14	15
April 1942, cont.														
29/0857	dt	U 108	Scholtz	DO 1389	-T: 9925+	TA	-	29/0759	am	-DT	Mobiloil	9925+	25.35 N/ 66.18 W	
30/0152	dt	U 162	Wattenberg	EE 8226	-T: 8941+	TA	.	29/2324	br	-MT	Athelempress	8941+	13.21 N/ 56.15 W	
30/0336	dt	U 402	v.Forstner	DC 1221	-D: 5284+	T	-	30/0113	sj	-D	Aschabad	5284+	34.19 N/ 76.31 W	
30/0737	dt	U 576	Heinicke	CA 3357	-D 5000+	T	-	30/0600	nw	-D	Taborfjell	1339+	41.52 N/ 67.43 W	
30/1440	dt	U 576	Heinicke	CA 3358	-D 5000=	T	.	/						17)
30/1810	dt	U 507	Schacht	DM 7131	-T: 2900+	A	-	30/1400	am	-DT	Federal	2881+	21.13 N/ 76.05 W	
May 1942														
1/0543	dt	U 752	Schroeter	CA 5265	-D: 4956+	T	-	1/	nw	-M	Bidevind	4956+	40.13 N/ 73.46 W	
1/1136	dt	U 109	Bleichrodt	DB 9429	-D: 6548+	T	-	1/0940	br	-M	La Paz	6548=	28.15 N/ 80.20 W	1)
1/	dt	U 109	Bleichrodt	DB 94	-M: 433+	A	-	1/0958	ni	-M	Worden	555+	10m SE C.Canaveral	
1/1540	dt	U 136	Zimmermann	CA 5346	-D: 5041=	T	-	1/	am	-D	Alcoa Leader			2)
1/1728	dt	U 69	Gräf	CB 9468	-S: 671+	A	-	1/	am	-S	James E.Newsom	671+	35.50 N/ 59.40 W	
1/2046	dt	U 162	Wattenberg	EO 2121	-D: 6692+	T	-	1/1852	bz	-D	Parnahyba	6692+	10.12 N/ 57.16 W	3)
2/0641	dt	U 402	v.Forstner	DC 1591	PY: 850+	T	-	2/	am	PY	Cythera	602+	Atlantic Coast	
2/2253	dt	U 66	Zapp	ED 9643	-T: 7600+	T	-	2/2056	nw	-MT	Sandar	7624+	11.42 N/ 61.10 W	
3/0638	dt	U 455	Gießler	BB 9663	-T: 6994+	T	-	3/0515	br	-DT	British Workman	6994+	44.07 N/ 51.53 W	
3/0812	dt	U 506	Würdemann	DM 2650	-D 3500+	T	-	3/	ni	-D	Sama	567+	26.04 N/ 79.45 W	
3/0824	dt	U 564	Suhren	DB 9434	-D 6000+	T	-	3/0515	br	-D	Ocean Venus	7174+	28.23 N/ 80.21 W	
3/1023	dt	U 66	Zapp	ED 9839	-T:12500+	TA	ON.87 s	3/0827	br	-MT	Geo W.McKnight	12502=	11.18 N/ 61.19 W	
3/1054	dt	U 109	Bleichrodt	DB 9423	-D 9050+	T	-	3/1010	nl	-D	Laertes	5825+	28.21 N/ 80.23 W	

17) *U 576* fired two torpedoes against four ships overlapping each other, and heard one detonation after 6 min 4 sec without optical observation.

1) *U 109* observed the *La Paz* sink to the bottom, but she was later salvaged and repaired.

2) *U 136* heard after 6 min one detonation without observing anything. The B-Dienst reported a hit on the *Alcoa Leader*.

3) The *Parnahyba* (or *Parnaíba* in Brazilian) was armed with one 127mm gun and identified only after the attack as Brazilian.

1	2	3	4	5	6		7	8	9	10	11	12	13	14	15

May 1942, cont.

1	2	3	4	5	6	7	8	9	10	11	12	13	14	15
3/1723	dt	U 125	Folkers	DM 8938	-D: 1937+	TA	-	3/	do	-D	San Rafael	1973+	18.36 N/ 79.12 W	
4/0943	dt	U 162	Wattenberg	EO 4391	-D 3000+	T	-	4/0745	am	-D	Eastern Sword	3785+	07.10 N/ 57.58 W	
4/	dt	U 162	Wattenberg	EO 1999	-S: 119+	A	-	4/	am	-S	Florence M.Douglas	119+	07.55 N/ 58.10 W	
4/1742	dt	U 507	Schacht	DM 1739	-D 2493+	T	-	4/1540	am	-D	Norlindo	2686+	24.57 N/ 84.00 W	
4/1904	dt	U 564	Suhren	DM 2318	-T 7000+	T	-	4/2210	br	-DT	Eclipse	9767=	26.30 N/ 80.00 W	4)
4/2220	dt	U 125	Folkers	EB 2128	-D: 5687+	T	-	4/2021	am	-D	Tuscaloosa City	5687+	18.25 N/ 81.31 W	
4/	dt			ED	-T: 6460=	T	-	5/	am	-D	Mokihana	7460=	16.40 N/ 65.12 W	5)
5/0132	dt	U 507	Schacht	DM 1467	-T 9900+	T	-	4/2345	am	-DT	Munger T.Ball	5104+	25.24 N/ 83.46 W	
5/0305	dt	U 106	Rasch	CB 7922	-D: 7985+	T	-	5/	ca	-D	Lady Drake	7985+	35.43 N/ 64.43 W	
5/0415	dt	U 507	Schacht	DM 1433	-T: 6950+	T	-	5/0228	am	-DT	Joseph M.Cudahy	6950+	25.57 N/ 83.57 W	
5/0453	dt	U 564	Suhren	DB 9762	-D 4000+	T	-	5/1900	am	-D	Delisle	3478=	27.06 N/ 80.03 W	
5/0830	dt	U 103	Winter	DD 2265	-D: 8000+	T	-	5/	br	-D	Stanbank	5966+	34.55 N/ 61.47 W	
5/2327	dt	U 108	Scholtz	DN 8440	-D 5500+	T	-	5/2240	am	-D	Afoundria	5010+	20.00 N/ 73.30 W	
6/0543	dt	U 333	Cremer	DB 9763	-T 12500+	T	-	6/0350	am	-DT	Java Arrow	8327=	27.35 N/ 80.08 W	6)
6/0935	dt	U 333	Cremer	DB 9763	-D 6000+	T	-	6/0900	nl	-D	Amazone	1294+	27.21 N/ 80.04 W	
6/1125	dt	U 333	Cremer	DB 9763	-T 10000+	T	-	6/0945	am	-DT	Halsey	7088+	27.20 N/ 80.03 W	
6/1430	dt	U 125	Folkers	DM 8779	-M 1200+	T	-	6/1215	am	-M	Green Island	1946+	18.25 N/ 81.30 W	
6/1943	dt	U 507	Schacht	DA 9393	-D 8000+	T	-	6/0800	am	-D	Alcoa Puritan	6759+	28.35 N/ 88.22 W	
6/2211	dt	U 108	Scholtz	DN 8190	-D 5000+	T	-	6/2012	le	-D	Abgara	4422+	20.45 N/ 72.55 W	
6/2225	dt	U 125	Folkers	DM 7937	-D: 6404+	T	-	6/2042	br	-D	Empire Buffalo	6404+	19.14 N/ 82.34 W	
7/0800	dt	U 162	Wattenberg	EO 5656	-D 7000+	T	-	7/0630	nw	-D	Frank Seamans	4271+	06.21 N/ 55.38 W	
8/0330	dt	U 507	Schacht	DB 7426	-D 5225+	A	-	8/0130	ho	-D	Ontario	3099+	28.11 N/ 87.32 W	

4) *U 564* observed the tanker grounded by the stern, but she was salvaged.
5) The xB-Dienst picked up a SOS from the *Mokihana* in Qu.ED 27. It is not clear which U-boats may have been responsible.
6) *U 333* observed the tanker sink to the bottom, but the ship was salvaged.

1	2	3	4	5	6	7	8	9	10	11	12	13	14	15
May 1942, cont.														
8/0133	dt	U 136	Zimmermann	CC 4254	-S	500+	A	-	1 ?	ca	-S	Mildred Pauline	300+	Nova Scotia	7)
8/1445	dt	U 507	Schacht	DB 7888	-D:	2424+	T	-	8/0240	nw	-D	Torny	2424+	26.40 N/ 86.40 W	
8/1812	dt	U 564	Suhren	DM 2316	-D	5000+	T	-	8/1714	am	-D	Ohioan	6078+	26.31 N/ 79.59 W	
9/0212	dt	U 162	Wattenberg	EO 1973	-D:	1905+	T	-	9/1205	ca	-D	Mont Louis	1905+	08.23 N/ 58.44 W	
9/0327	dt	U 588	Vogel	BB 7500	-D:	7460+	T	-	9/0115	am	-D	Greylock	7460=	10m Halifax L.V.	
9/1002	dt	U 564	Suhren	DM 2343	-T	8000+	T	-	9/0915	pa	-MT	Lubrafol	7138+	26.26 N/ 80.00 W	
9/2012	dt	U 125	Folkers	DM 7919	-T:	11941+	TA	-	9/1815	ca	-MT	Calgarolite	11941+	19.24 N/ 82.30 W	
10/0310	dt	U 588	Vogel	BB 7810	-D	8000+	T	-	10/0220	br	-D	Kitty's Brock	4031+	42.56 N/ 63.59 W	
10/0905	dt	U 333	Cremer	DC 6111	-D	6000+	T	-	10/0800	br	-D	Clan Skene	5214+	31.43 N/ 70.43 W	
10/0931	dt	U 506	Würdemann	DA 9288	-T:	7050+	T	-	10/0830	am	-MT	Aurora	7050=	28.35 N/ 90.00 W	8)
11/	dt	U 502	v.Rosenstiel	DP 46	-D:	4963+	TA	-	11/1943	br	-D	Cape of Good Hope	4963+	22.48 N/ 58.43 W	
12/0156	dt	U 124	Mohr	AK 9435	-D	6600+	T	ONS.92	12/0001	br	-D	Empire Dell	7065+	53.00 N/ 29.57 W	
12/0159	dt	U 124	Mohr	AK 9435	-D	4000+	T	ONS.92	12/0007	br	-D	Llanover	4959+	52.50 N/ 29.04 W	
12/0206	dt	U 124	Mohr	AK 9435	-D	2500+	T	ONS.92	12/						9)
12/0222	dt	U 124	Mohr	AK 9435	-D	3000+	T	ONS.92	12/						9)
12/0313	dt	U 569	Hinsch	AK 9195	-D	5000+	T	ONS.92	12/						10)
12/0340	dt	U 94	Ites	AK 9198	-D	7000+	T	ONS.92	12/0143	pa	-D	Cocle	5630+	52.37 N/ 29.13 W	
12/0355	dt	U 124	Mohr	AK 9429	-D	3000+	T	ONS.92	12/0153	gr	-D	Mount Parnes	4371+	52.31 N/ 29.20 W	
12/0358	dt	U 124	Mohr	AK 9429	-D	3500+	T	ONS.92	12/0203	br	-D	Cristales	5389+	52.55 N/ 29.50 W	11)
12/0540	dt	U 558	Krech	DC 1183	APC:	913+	T	-	12/	br	APC	Bedfordshire	913+	Cape Lookout,N.C.	
12/0552	dt	U 553	Thurmann	BB 1485	-D	5000ß	T	-	12/0355	br	-D	Nicoya	5364+	49.19 N/ 64.51 W	

7) The *Mildred Pauline* was reported missing after May 1st, but there is no U-boat success report in this area.
8) *U 506* left the *Aurora* in sinking condition after two hits. But she was towed into port.
9) *U 124* observed during her attack hits on three ships which obviously sank. During the second attack on 02.22 hrs, there was one hit after 1 min 56 sec amidships. The ship was assumed sunk.
10) *U 569* observed a hit after 3 min and then there was a column of fire. The ship was observed to be sinking.
11) The *Cristales* was finally sunk by an escort vessel.

1	2	3	4	5	6	7	8	9	10	11	12	13	14	15
May 1942, cont.														
12/08..	dt	U 69	Gräf	ED 4726	-T 11400+	TA	-	12/	nw	-MT	Lise	6826+	13.53 N/ 68.20 W	
12/0828	dt	U 553	Thurmann	BB 1476	-D 6000+	T	-	12/0640	nl	-D	Leto	4712+	49.32 N/ 65.19 W	
12/0944	dt	U 553	Thurmann	BB 1476	-D 3000+	T	-	/						12)
12/2203	dt	U 507	Schacht	DA 9347	-T 10000+	T	-	12/2130	am	-DT	Virginia	10731+	28.53 N/ 89.29 W	
13/0028	dt	U 128	Heyse	DS 6699	-D 5000+	T	SL.109	13/	br	-D	Denpark	3491+	22.28 N/ 28.10 Q	
13/0028	dt	U 128	Heyse	DS 6699	-D 8000=	T	SL.109	/						13)
13/0234	dt	U 162	Wattenberg	EE 8465	-T: 7699+	T	-	13/0030	am	-DT	Esso Houston	7699+	12.12 N/ 57.25 W	
13/0252	dt	U 108	Scholtz	DN 5214	-DP10544=	T	.	/						14)
13/0351	dt	U 94	Ites	AK 8494	-D 6000+	T	ONS.92	13/0053	br	-D	Batna	4399+	52.09 N/ 33.56 W	
13/0358	dt	U 156	Hartenstein	EE 6353	-D 6000+	T	-	13/0225	nl	-M	Koenjit	4551+	15.30 N/ 52.40 W	
13/0408	dt	U 69	Gräf	ED 7325	-D 5000+	TA	-	13/0100	am	-D	Norlantic	2606+	12.13 N/ 66.30 W	
13/0618	dt	U 94	Ites	AK 8734	-D 5000+	T	ONS.92	13/0510	sw	-D	Tolken	4471+	51.50 N/ 33.35 W	
13/2138	dt	U 506	Würdemann	DA 9536	-T 6000+	T	-	13/2050	am	-DT	Gulfpenn	8862+	28.29 N/ 89.17 W	
13/2205	dt	U 156	Hartenstein	EE 3797	-D: 6630+	TA	-	13/	br	-D	City of Melbourne	6630+	15.00 N/ 54.40 W	
14/0202	dt	U 162	Wattenberg	EE 7331	-T: 6817+	T	-	13/	br	-DT	British Colony	6917+	13.12 N/ 58.10 W	
14/0440	dt	U 155	Piening	ED 9489	-D 5000+	T	-	14/	be	-M	Brabant	2483+	11.32 N/ 62.43 W	
14/0547	dt	U 506	Würdemann	DA 9536	-T 7000+	T	-	14/0345	am	-DT	David McKelvy	6821+	28.30 N/ 89.55 W	
14/0717	dt	U 564	Suhren	DM 2643	-T 5000+	T	-	14/0620	me	-DT	Potrero del Llano	4000+	25.35 N/ 80.06 W	
14/1357	dt	U 593	Kelbling	CA 5344	-D: 4853+	T	-	14/1215	gr	-D	Stavros	4853=	39.45 N/ 72.35 W	15)
14/1812	dt	U 125	Folkers	DM 8727	-D: 2196+	T	-	14/	ho	-D	Comayagua	2493+	19.00 N/ 81.37 W	16)
15/0254	dt	U 156	Hartenstein	EE 6355	-M: 4301+	T	-	15/	nw	-M	Siljestad	4301+	15.20 N/ 52.40 W	

12) *U 553* observed one explosion aft, but could not observe the ship sink.
13) *U 128* fired a 4-torpedo salvo, and observed one detonation after 3 min 25 sec accompanied by a smoke pillar, and one other detonation.
14) *U 108* heard one detonation after 3 min on a passenger-freighter of the type *President Grant*.
15) *U 593* observed two hits but did not wait for the ship to sink. The *Stavros* was a Swiss charter and was salvaged.
16) *U 125* reported the ship erroneously as the British steamer *Cayuga*.

1	2	3	4	5	6	7	8	9	10	11	12	13	14	15
May 1942, cont.														
15/2057	dt	U 156	Hartenstein	EE 6621	-D: 4382+	T	-	15/	jg	-D	Kupa	4382+	14.50 N/ 52.20 W	
16/0012	dt	U 507	Schacht	DL 2211	-D: 4148+	AS	-	15/2305	ho	-D	Amapala	4148+	26.30 N/ 89.12 W	17)
16/0415	dt	U 751	Bigalk	DN 1656	-D 5000+	T	-	16/0315	am	-D	Nicarao	1445+	25.20 N/ 74.19 W	
16/1101	dt	U 506	Würdemann	DA 9521	-T 8000=	T	-	16/0912	am	-DT	William C. McTarnahan	7302=	28.52 N/ 90.20 W	18)
16/1110	dt	U 506	Würdemann	DA 9521	-T 9000=	TA	-	16/1000	am	-MT	Sun	9002=	28.41 N/ 90.19 W	
17/	dt	U 103	Winter	EB 1930	-D: 2612+	A	-	16/2300	am	-D	Ruth Lykes	2612+	16.37 N/ 82.25 W	
17/0217	dt	U 155	Piening	ED 9573	-T 11000+	T	-	17/	br	-MT	San Victorio	8136+	11.40 N/ 62.33 W	
17/0454	dt	U 135	Praetorius	CB 5156	-D 10000+	T	-	17/0235	br	-D	Fort Qu'Appelle	7127+	59.50 N/ 63.30 W	
17/0534	dt	U 506	Würdemann	DA 9561	-T 7000+	T	-	17/0441	am	-DT	Gulf Oil	5189+	28.08 N/ 89.46 W	
17/0952	dt	U 155	Piening	ED 9575	-D: 7667+	T	-	17/0800	am	-M	Challenger	7667+	12.11 N/ 61.18 W	
17/	dt	U 432	Schultze	BB 78	-Df: 308+	A	-	17/	am	-Df	Foam	324+	43.20 N/ 63.08 W	
17/1802	dt	U 588	Vogel	BA 9899	-D 7000+	T	-	17/1600	nw	-D	Skottland	2117+	43.07 N/ 67.18 W	
17/1901	dt	U 653	Feiler	CB 7233	-D 4500+	T	-	17/1700	br	-M	Peisander	6225+	37.24 N/ 65.38 W	
17/2104	dt	U 156	Hartenstein	EE 6377	-D: 5072+	T	-	17/1935	br	-D	Barrdale	5072+	15.15 N/ 52.27 W	
17/2240	dt	U 566	Borchert	CB 1145	-D 3000=?	T	-	17/						19)
18/0210	dt	U 162	Wattenberg	EE 7338	-T: 6852+	T	-	18/0020	br	-MT	Beth	6852+	11.48 N/ 57.32 W	
18/0356	dt	U 588	Vogel	BA 9944	-D: 4000=	A	-	18/0100	br	-D	Fort Binger	-----		20)
18/0605	dt	U 125	Folkers	DM 9633	-T 9000+	T	-	18/0500	am	-MT	Mercury Sun	8893+	20.01 N/ 84.26 W	
18/0615	dt	U 558	Krech	DN 5825	-D: 5419+	T	-	17/	nl	-D	Fauna	1254+	22.20 N/ 72.20 W	21)
18/1018	dt	U 156	Hartenstein	EE 6237	-D: 4961+	T	-	18/	am	-D	Quaker City	4961+	14.55 N/ 51.40 W	

17) *U 507* fired some machine-gun salvoes to stop the *Amapala*. She was sunk by opening of the sea valves.
18) *U 506* reported one torpedo hit on the ship and left her sinking after some gunfire.
19) *U 566* heard two torpedoes hit after 48 sec, but they did not detonate.
20) *U 588* missed with two torpedoes and had to forgo her gunfire attack. From the xB-Dienst the ship attacked was identified as the *Fort Binger*.
21) *U 558* reported to have sunk the Dutch vessel *Towa* (5419 gross tons), but this ship had been sunk already on Dec.12th, 1940 by *U 94*.

1	2	3	4	5	6	7	8	9	10 11 12	13	14	15

May 1942, cont.

1	2	3	4	5	6	7	8	9	10 11	12	13	14	15
18/1837 dt	U 455	Gießler	CA 5479	-DP12000=	T	-	/						22)
18/1852 dt	U 156	Hartenstein	EE 6165	-T 8000=	T	-	18/ 19/0225	br -MT	San Eliseo	8042=	15.30 N/ 54.16 W	23)
18/2150 dt	U 125	Folkers	DM 7460	-D 2592+	T	-	18/2100	am -D	William J.Salman	2616+	20.08 N/ 83.46 W	
18/2230 it	BARBARIGO	Grossi	02s/34w	-T 12000+	TA	-	18/2014	bz -D	Comandante Lyra	5052=	02.59 S/ 34.10 W	24)
19/0031 it	CAPPELLINI	Revedin	03n/32w	-M 10000+	TA	-	18/2230	sw -M	Tisnaren	5747+	03.38 N/ 32.01 W	
19/0155 dt	U 593	Kelbling	CA 2874	-D 7000=	T	-	/					25)
19/0856 dt	U 506	Würdemann	DA 97	-D 5200+	T	-	19/0750	am -D	Heredia	4732+	28.53 N/ 91.03 W	
19/1040 dt	U 751	Bigalk	EC 1355	-D 5000+	T	-	19/0900	am -D	Isabela	3110+	17.50 N/ 75.00 W	
19/2024 dt	U 103	Winter	DL 6271	-D: 5028+	T	-	19/1926	am -D	Ogontz	5037+	23.30 N/ 86.37 W	
20/0250 it	BARBARIGO	Grossi	04s/34w	BB 31500+	T	Task F.	20/	am CL	Milwaukee	-----		26)
20/0758 dt	U 506	Würdemann	DA 9553	-T 8000+	T	-	20/0715	am -DT	Halo	6986+	28.42 N/ 90.08 W	
20/ dt	U 158	Rostin	DE 7227	-T: 6303+	T	ON.93	20/2200	br -MT	Darina	8113+	29.17 N/ 54.25 W	
20/1321 dt	U 155	Piening	ED 9817	-T 8400+	T	OT.1	20/1120	pa -DT	Sylvan Arrow	7797+	11.25 N/ 62.18 W	
20/1839 dt	U 108	Scholtz	DE 4177	-T 8000+	TA	ON.93	20/1858	nw -MT	Norland	8134+	31.22 N/ 55.47 W	
20/1908 dt	U 753	v.Mannstein	DL 6639	-D: 6000+	T	-	20/2014	am -D	George Calvert	7191+	22.55 N/ 84.26 W	
20/ dt	U 753	v.Mannstein	DL 66	-S +	AS	-	20/	br -S	E.P.Theriault	326=	24.30 N/ 83.55 W	
21/0323 dt	U 159	Witte	CF 7389	-D 7000+	T	OS.28	21/	br -D	New Brunswick	6529+	36.53 N/ 22.55 W	27)
21/0323 dt	U 159	Witte	CF 7389	-D 5000+	T	OS.28	21/					27)
21/0324 dt	U 159	Witte	CF 7389	-D 3000+	T	OS.28	21/	br -DT	Montenol	2646+	36. N/ 22. W	27)
21/0325 dt	U 159	Witte	CF 7389	-D 5000+	T	OS.28	21/					27)

22) *U 455* fired a four-torpedo salvo and heard one detonation after 4 min. No optical observation was made.

23) The *San Eliseo* escaped after two additional hits at 04.39/19 and 07.39/19.

24) The *Commandante Lyra* was hit by one torpedo and 16 100mm rounds. She was towed into Fortaleza under cover of a U.S. task force.

25) *U 593* fired two torpedoes and heard one detonation after 5 min 32 sec.

26) *Barbarigo* happened upon a U.S. tank force in a dark night, and assumed to have hit a battleship of the *Maryland*-type with two torpedoes. In reality the torpedoes missed the cruiser *Milwaukee* and the destroyer *Moffet*.

27) *U 159* fired four torpedoes against a group of five ships. After run times of 1 min 45 sec, 1 min 46 sec, 1 min 50 sec and 1 min 55 sec, there were detonations and one column of fire was observed. Three ships were seen sinking, one of them burning. One of the damaged ships was hit by one more torpedo from a two-shot salvo.

1	2	3	4	5	6	7	8	9	10	11	12	13	14	15
May 1942, cont.														
21/0348	dt	U 103	Winter	DM 4747	-D: 3372+	T	-	21/1346	am	-D	Clare	3372+	21.35 N/ 84.43 W	
21/0421	dt	U 106	Rasch	DM 4157	-T 9000+	TA	-	21/0225	me	-DT	Faja de Oro	6067+	23.30 N/ 84.24 W	
21/0435	dt	U 103	Winter	DM 4771	-D: 4727+	TA	-	21/0238	am	-D	Elizabeth	4727+	21.35 N/ 84.48 W	
21/0753	dt	U 69	Gräf	ED 6871	-D: 1927+	T	-	21/	ca	-D	Torondoc	1927+	14.45 N/ 62.15 W	
21/1822	dt	U 558	Krech	EB 3111	-D: 1926+	T	-	21/2130	br	-D	Troisdoc	1925+	18.15 N/ 79.20 W	
21/1829	dt	U 156	Hartenstein	ED 66	-D: 1668+	T	-	21/1645	do	-D	Presidente Trujillo	1668+	14.38 N/ 61.11 W	
21/2010	dt	U 588	Vogel	CA 6650	-D: 6000+	T	-	21/1830	am	-D	Plow City	3282+	38.53 N/ 69.57 W	
22/	dt	U 158	Rostin	DD 94	-D: 1276+	A	-	22/	br	-D	F.B.Baird	1748+	28.03 N/ 58.50 W	
23/0024	dt	U 432	Schultze	CB 1928	-D: 4500+	T	-	22/	br	-D	Zurichmoor	4455+	39.30 N/ 66.00 W	
23/0053	dt	U 558	Krech	EB 3855	-T: 7061=	T	-	22/2305	am	-DT	William Boyce Thompson	7061=	16.26 N/ 77.51 W	
23/0926	dt	U 103	Winter	DM 7174	-T: 6625+	T	-	23/0745	am	-DT	Samuel Q.Brown	6625+	20.15 N/ 84.37 W	
23/0938	*it*	*ARCHIMEDE*	*Gazzana*	*02s/36w*	*CA 9100=*	*T*	-	*23/*	*am*	*DD*	*Moffett*	-----	*02.10 S/ 35.55 W*	*28)*
23/2203	dt	U 588	Vogel	CB 4750	-D: 4500+	TA	-	23/2040	br	-D	Margot	4545+	39. N/ 68. W	
23/2204	dt	U 155	Piening	ED 9314	-D 3000+	T	-	23/	pa	-D	Watsonville	2220+	13.12 N/ 61.20 W	
24/1640	dt	U 103	Winter	DM 8421	-D: 1828+	T	-	24/1010	nl	-M	Hector	1828+	19.50 N/ 81.53 W	
24/	dt	U 502	v.Rosenstiel	EC 6148	-D: 4996+	T	-	24/1315	bz	-D	Gonçalves Dias	4996+	16.09 N/ 70.00 W	29)
25/0134	dt	U 558	Krech	EC 1471	-D: 3451+	A	-	25/0030	am	-D	Beatrice	3451+	17.21 N/ 76.07 W	30)
25/0416	dt	U 753	v.Mannstein	DA 92	-T: 6582+	T	-	25/0320	nw	-MT	Haakon Hauan	6582=	28.45 N/ 90.03 W	

28) *Archimede* attacked a big vessel escorting the damaged and burning *Commandante Lyra* under tow by a U.S. tug. A hit on a heavy cruiser of the *Pensacola*-class was assumed, but in reality the detonation might have been a depth charge from the *Moffett*, dropped against a U-boat located by sonar.

29) *U 502* attacked an armed ship without neutrality markings. The *Gonçalvo Dias* was armed with one 120mm gun and identified as Brazilian only after the attack.

30) The *Beatrice* was first hit by a dud torpedo and then was sunk by gunfire.

1	2	3	4	5	6	7	8	9	10 11	12	13	14	15
May 1942, cont.													
25/1552 dt		U 156	Hartenstein	ED 66	DD	1190=	T	–	25/	am DD	Blakely	1190=	14.36 N/ 61.11 W	
25/2053 dt		U 593	Kelbling	CA 5165	-T	6000+	T	.	25/2000	pa -MT	Persephone	8426+	39.44 N/ 73.53 W	
26/0416 dt		U 103	Winter	EB 2313	-D:	7000+	T	–	26/0215	am -D	Alcoa Carrier	5588+	18.45 N/ 79.50 W	
26/1134 dt		U 106	Rasch	DL 2168	-D:	5030+	TA	–	26/0945	am -DT	Carrabulle	5030+	26.18 N/ 89.21 W	
27/0018 dt		U 578	Rehwinkel	CB 5731	-M:	6300+	T	–	26/2215	nl -M	Polyphemus	6269+	38.12 N/ 63.22 W	
27/	dt	U 106 ?	Rasch	DL 25			A	–	27/0409	am -D	Atenas	4639=	25.50 N/ 89.05 W	31)
27/0319 dt		U 172	Emmermann	DE 9654	-T:	8940+	TA	–	27/	br -MT	Athelknight	8940+	27.50 N/ 46.00 W	
27/1051 dt		U 558	Krech	EC 2574	-D	4000+	T	–				?		31a)
27/1103 dt		U 753	v.Mannstein	DA 9423	-T:	6578+	T	–	27/1010	nw -MT	Hamlet	6578+	28.32 N/ 91.30 W	
28/	dt	U 506	Würdemann	DC 5844	-D:	4457+	A	–	28/0215	br -D	Yorkmoor	4457+	29.30 N/ 72.29 W	
28/	dt	U 502	v.Rosenstiel	ED 1769	-D:	6750+	T	–	28/	am -D	Alcoa Pilgrim	6759+	16.28 N/ 67.37 W	
28/0029 it		BAGNOLINI	Tei	05s/31w	-T	11309=	T	–						32)
28/0208 dt		U 106	Rasch	DL 3746	-D	5318+	T	–	28/0222	br -D	Mentor	7383+	24.11 N/ 87.02 W	
28/0630 dt		U 155	Piening	EE 4646	-D	5000+	T	–	28/0948	am -D	Jack	2622+	Caribbean	33)
28/1142 dt		U 103	Winter	EB 2135	-T:	6414+	TA	–	28/0910	am -DT	New Jersey	6414+	19.10 N/ 81.50 W	
28/2220 it		BARBARIGO	Grossi	07s/29w	-D	groß+	TA	–	29/	br -D	Charlbury	4836+	06.22 S/ 29.44 W	
29/0103 dt		U 156	Hartenstein	ED 6483	-D	5000+	T	–	28/2304	br -D	Norman Prince	1913+	14.40 N/ 62.15 W	
29/0217 dt		U 107	Gelhaus	DN 7686	-D	5000+	T	–	29/0025	br -D	Western Head	2599+	19.57 N/ 74.18 W	
29/2137 dt		U 504	Poske	EB 2120	-D:	1597+	T	–	29/	br -D	Allister	1597+	18.23 N/ 81.13 W	
30/0651 dt		U 155	Piening	EE 6467	-D:	2200+	T	–	30/	nw -M	Baghdad	2161+	14.15 N/ 54.30 W	
30/1024 dt		U 404	v.Bülow	CB 4765	-D:	5491+	T	–	30/0825	am -D	Alcoa Shipper	5491+	37.49 N/ 65.15 W	
31/	dt	U 506	Würdemann	DD 57	-D:	2292+	A	–	31/	br -D	Fred W.Green	2292+	30.20 N/ 62.00 W	
31/0140 dt		U 432	Schultze	BA 9978	-D:	3000+	T	–	30/	ca -D	Liverpool Packet	1188+	43.20 N/ 66.20 W	
31/0230 it		CAPPELLINI	Revedin	01s/30w	-T	12000+	T	–	31/	br -DT	Dinsdale (AO)	8214+	00.45 S/ 29.50 W	

31) Only *U 106* was in this area, but there is no attack report. – 31a) *U 558* reported to have attacked a Soviet steamer of the
   type *Sibir* (3767 gross tons) and to have seen the ship sink.
32) *Bagnolini* attacked a tanker of the type *Canadolite* with a 4-torpedo salvo and heard one detonation.
33) The *Jack* was reported missing after May 27th in the Caribbean. Only *U 155* was in the area.

1	2	3	4	5	6	7	8	9	10	11	12	13	14	15
June 1942														
1/0354	dt	U 107	Gelhaus	EB 2137	-D 7000+	T	-	31/	pa	-D	Bushranger	4536+	19.15 N/ 81.25 W	
1/0836	dt	U 566	Borchert	CB 8466	-D: 9000+	TA	-	1/0610	br	-D	Westmoreland	8967+	35.55 N/ 63.35 W	
1/1146	dt	U 106	Rasch	DL 6538	-D: 2689+	T	-	1/1030	am	-D	Hampton Roads	2689+	22.45 N/ 85.13 W	
1/	dt	U 404	v.Bülow	DC 3212	-D: 5492+	S	-	1/1030	am	-D	West Notus	5492+	34.10 N/ 68.20 W	1)
1/2351	dt	U 156	Hartenstein	ED 6851	-D: 5970+	TA	-	1/2256	bz	-D	Alegrete	5970+	13.40 N/ 61.30 W	
2/	dt	U 558	Krech	DP 1432	-D: 2056+	A	-	1/0050	nl	-D	Triton	2078+	26. N/ 59.34 W	
2/0718	dt	U 553	Thurmann	CB 1895	-D: 6919+	T	-	2/0519	br	-M	Mattawin	6919+	40.14 N/ 66.01 W	
2/	dt	U 158	Rostin	DM 7132	-D 6000+	T	-	2/	am	-D	Knoxville City	5686+	21.25 N/ 83.50 W	
2/2027	dt	U 578	Rehwinkel	CA 6287	-D: 6826+	T	-	2/1930	nw	-M	Berganger	6826+	39.22 N/ 70.00 W	2)
2/2250	it	DA VINCI	Longanesi-Cattani	07n/13w	-S: 1087+	TA	-	2/1500	pa	-S	Reine Marie Stewart	1087+	07.16 N/ 13.20 W	
3/0410	dt	U 172	Emmermann	DO 6724	-D 5000+	T	-	3/0400	am	-D	Illinois	5447+	24. N/ 60. W	3)
3/	dt	U 404	v.Bülow	DC	-D: 1345+	T	-	3/0730	sw	-D	Anna	1345+	34.10 N/ 68.22 W	4)
3/	dt	U 156	Hartenstein	EE 71	-S 150+	A	-	3/	br	-S	Lillian	80+	12.25 N/ 59.30 W	
3/	dt	U 432	Schultze	BA 9976	-Df +	A	-	3/2100	am	-Mf	Ben and Josephine	102+	43.50 N/ 67.00 W	
3/	dt	U 432	Schultze	BA 9896	-Df +	A	-	3/2130	am	-Mf	Aeolus	41+	43.50 N/ 67.00 W	
3/1124	dt	U 126	Bauer	EP 6334	-D:10990+	TA	-	4/0005	nw	-MT	Höegh Giant	10990+	06.52 N/ 42.43 W	
3/	dt	U 502	v.Rosenstiel	ED 8692	-T: 6940+	T	-	4/0400	am	-DT	M.F.Elliott	6940+	12.04 N/ 63.49 W	3)
4/0253	dt	U 159	Witte	DO 63	-D 6200+	T	-	3/1410	am	-D	City of Alma	5446+	23.00 N/ 62.30 W	
4/	dt	U 158	Rostin	DL 9331	-D 4000+	T	-	4/0310	nw	-D	Nidarnes	2647+	21.17 N/ 85.07 W	
5/0608	dt	U 172	Emmermann	DO 7436	-D: 3480+	T	-	5/1210	am	-D	Delfina	3480+	20.20 N/ 67.07 W	

1) The *West Notus* was stopped by one shot of artillery and sunk by demolition charges.
2) The *Berganger* was missed by five torpedoes from *U 213* (v.Varendorff) at June 2nd/03.33-07.03 hrs.
3) *U 172* and *U 159* observed the sinking of one ship. It is not possible to establish exactly which ship was sunk by which U-boat, because the *Illinois* and the *City of Alma* both were the "Hog Island"-type.
4) The *Anna* was zigzagging without neutrality marks or lights.

1	2	3	4	5	6	7	8	9	10	11	12	13	14	15
June 1942, cont.														
5/	dt	U 159	Witte	EC 3593	-S 300+	A	-	5/	bz	-S	Paracury	265=	17.30 N/ 68.34 W	5)
5/2000	dt	U 159	Witte	EC 3811	-S: 150+	A	-	5/	ho	-S	Sally	150+		5)
5/				BD 23		A	-	5/1730	pt	-S	Maria da Gloria	270+	50.14 N/ 30.12 W	6)
5/	dt	U 69	Gräf	EE	-Dt +	A	-	5/						7)
				CA 94		T ?	-	5/	nl	-D	Poseidon	1928+	36. N/ 71. W	8)
5/2049	dt	U 68	Merten	ED 1749	-T 9000+	T	-	4/	am	-DT	L.J.Drake	6693+	Aruba-San Juan	9)
6/0307	dt	U 68	Merten	ED 1484	-T 12000+	T	-	6/0215	pa	-MT	C.O.Stillman	13006+	17.33 N/ 67.55 W	
5/	dt	U 158	Rostin	DL 6796	-D 4000+	T	-	6/0232	am	-D	Velma Lykes	2572+	21.21 N/ 86.36 W	
7/0237	dt	U 504	Poske	DL 9640	-D 6000=?	T	-							10)
7/0408	dt	U 107	Gelhaus	DM 7521	-D: 3910+	T	-	7/0310	ho	-D	Castilla	3910+	21.03 N/ 83.30 W	
7/0420	*dt*	*U 653*	*Feiler*	*CB 7636*	*PY =?*	*T*	*-*							*11)*
7/0742	*dt*	*U 653*	*Feiler*	*CB 7875*	*AVP 3000+*	*T*	*-*	*7/*	*am*	*AVP*	*Gannet*	*840+*	*35.50 N/ 65.38 W*	*12)*
7/	dt	U 158	Rostin	DM 4174	-D +	T	-	7/	pa	-D	Hermis	5234+	23.08 N/ 84.42 W	
7/2224	dt	U 159	Witte	EC 4644	-D: 3382+	T	-	7/2130	am	-D	Edith	3382+	14.33 N/ 74.35 W	
7/2328	it	DA VINCI	Longanesi-Cattani	04n/13w	-M 9000+	T	-	7/	br	-M	Chile	6956+	04.17 N/ 13.48 W	
8/0316	dt	U 135	Praetorius	DC 3244	-D: 4500+	T	-	8/0145	nw	-M	Pleasantville	4549+	34. N/ 68. W	
8/0458	dt	U 172	Emmermann	EC 3198	-M: 1654+	T	-	8/0302	am	-M	Sicilien	1654+	17.30 N/ 71.20 W	
8/0659	dt	U 504	Poske	EA 3320	-D 8000+	T	-	8/0601	ho	-D	Tela	3901+	18.15 N/ 85.20 W	
8/1419	dt	U 128	Heyse	EF 7392	-T: 9234+	T	-	8/1200	nw	-MT	South Africa	9234+	12.47 N/ 49.44 W	
8/	dt	U 504	Poske	DL 9980	-D 3000+	A	-	8/1809	br	-D	Rosenborg	1512+	18.47 N/ 85.05 W	

5) The *Paracury* was salvaged. - 6) There is no attack report by a German or Italian U-boat.
7) *U 69* sank a small abandoned tug. - 8) The *Poseidon* was reported missing after June 6th between New York and Trinidad.
9) The *L.J.Drake* was reported missing after June 4th between Aruba and San Juan. She was probably sunk by *U 68*.
10) *U 504* heard a torpedo hit after 67 sec, but it did not detonate.
11) *U 653* attacked a big patrol yacht at 04.20 hrs. The *Gannet* was not hit by this torpedo, which detonated after 100 sec.
12) *U 653* fired again at the same ships at 07.42 hrs. The *Gannet* was sunk and the patrol yacht was hit at the stern after 58
    sec, but the results could not be observed.

1	2	3	4	5	6	7	8	9	10	11	12	13	14	15

June 1942, cont.

1	2	3	4	5	6	7	8	9	10 11	12	13	14	15
8/0119	dt	U 107	Gelhaus	DL 9635	-D: 3243+	T	–	7/1830	am -D	Suwied	3249+	20.05 N/ 85.35 W	
9/0410	*dt*	*U 124*	*Mohr*	*AK 8659*	*DD 1350+*	*T*	*ONS.100*	*9/0213*	*fr PE*	*Mimose*	*925+*	*52.12 N/ 31.25 W*	
9/day	dt	U 502	v.Rosenstiel	ED 8499	-D 7000+	T	TA.5	9/	be -D	Bruxelles	5085+	11.05 N/ 66.41 W	
9/day	dt	U 502	v.Rosenstiel	ED 8499	-DT 6000+	T	TA.5	9/	am -DT	Franklin K.Lane	6589+	11.12 N/ 66.39 W	
9/1301	dt	U 432	Schultze	CB 1122	-D 8000+	T	.	9/	nw -M	Kronprinsen	7073=	42.53 N/ 67.11 W	
9/1302	dt	U 432	Schultze ᴣ	CB 1122	-D 8000=	T	.	9/					13)
10/0340	dt	U 94	Ites	AK 7991	-D 5000+	T	ONS.100	10/0135	br -D	Ramsay	4855+	51.53 N/ 34.59 W	
10/0340	dt	U 94	Ites	AK 7991	-D 6000+	T	ONS.100	10/0134	br -D	Empire Clough	6147+	51.50 N/ 35.00 W	
10/0501	dt	U 107	Gelhaus	DL 9564	-D 4000+	T	–	9/spät	am -D	Merrimack	2606+	S Yucatan Canal	14)
10/0617	dt	U 68	Merten	EB 8294	-D: 8581+	T	–	10/	br -D	Surrey	8581+	12.45 N/ 80.20 W	
10/0628	dt	U 68	Merten	EB 8294	-D: 5025+	T	–	10/	br -M	Ardenvohr	5025+	12.45 N/ 80.20 W	
10/1158	dt	U 68	Merten	EB 8582	-D: 5882+	T	–	10/	br -M	Port Montreal	5882+	12.17 N/ 80.20 W	
10/2006	dt	U 129	Witt	DD 7675	-D: 4362+	T	–	10/1750	nw -M	L.A.Christensen	4362+	27.44 N/ 63.54 W	
10/2333	it	DA VINCI	Longanesi-Cattani	OOs/18w	-M: 5483+	TA	–	10/	nl -M	Alioth	5483+	00.08 N/ 18.52 W	
11/0210	dt	U 504	Poske	EB 1140	-D 13241+	T	–	11/0020	nl -D	Crijnssen	4282+	18.14 N/ 85.11 W	15)
11/0445	dt	U 159	Witte	EL 2262	-D 9000+	T	.	11/	br -D	Fort Good Hope	7130+	10.19 N/ 80.16 W	
11/0445	dt	U 159	Witte	EL 2262	-D 8000+	T	.	11/					16)
11/0526	dt	U 455	Gießler	BE 7217	-T 8621+	T	–	11/	br -DT	Geo.H.Jones	6914+	45.40 N/ 22.40 W	
11/	dt	U 157	Henne	-------	---------	T	–	11/1010	am -DT	Hagan	6401+	22.00 N/ 77.30 W	
11/	dt	U 158	Rostin	DA 9180	-T 12000+	TA	–	11/1155	pa -MT	Sheherazade	13467+	28.41 N/ 91.20 W	
11/1455	dt	U 569	Hinsch	BC 3426	-D 6000+	T	ONS.100						
11/1606	dt	U 94	Ites	BC 3542	-D: 4457+	Tf	ONS.100	11/	br -D	Pontypridd	4458+	49.50 N/ 41.37 W	17)
11/1707	dt	U 569	Hinsch	BC 3426	-D 6000+	T	ONS.100						

13) *U 432* fired four torpedoes. The first hit after 92 sec. The fourth missed target but hit another vessel of 8000 gross tons after 2 min 5 sec. - 14) The *Merrimack* was reported missing after June 9th near Cozumel I. off the Yucatan Strait, where *U 107* attacked.
15) *U 504* sank a liner of the *Van Dyck*-type by two torpedoes followed by a coup de grâce. The *Crijnssen* was a passenger liner.
16) *U 159* observed two hits on a freighter of the *Empire Rowan*-type which sank after 30 min, and one hit on a freighter of the *Port Alma*-type which sank after 45 min. - 17) The *Pontypridd* was first hit by *U 569* near the bow, buckled in the middle after one other hit, and was finally sunk by a coup de grâce by *U 94* and *U 569*.

North Sea - Atlantic

1	2	3	4	5	6		7	8	9	10	11	12	13	14	15

June 1942, cont.

1	2	3	4	5	6		7	8	9	10 11	12	13	14	15
11/1801	dt	U 504	Poske	EB 1140	-D:	4846+	T	-	11/1604	am -D	American	4846+	17.58 N/ 84.28 W	
12/0612	dt	U 124	Mohr	BC 3419	-D	7000+	T	ONS.100	12/0423	br -D	Dartford	4093+	49.19 N/ 41.33 W	
12/0854	dt	U 129	Witt	DO 2713	-D:	9005+	TA	-	12/	br -D	Hardwicke Grange	9005+	25.45 N/ 65.45 W	
12/	dt	U 158	Rostin	DA 8368	-T	7000+	T	-	12/0750	am -DT	Cities Service Toledo	8192+	29.02 N/ 91.59 W	
13/0412	dt	U 159	Witte	EL 2184	-D:	4700+	TA	-	13/0215	am -D	Sixaola	4693+	09.41 N/ 81.10 W	
13/0830	it	DA VINCI	Longanesi-Cattani	05n/26w	-D	8000+	TA	-	13/0630	br -D	Clan Macquarrie	6471+	05.30 N/ 23.30 W	
13/1938	dt	U 159	Witte	EL 2264	-D	7000+	T	-	13/1835	am -D	Solon Turman	6762+	10.45 N/ 80.24 W	
14/0834	dt	U 172	Emmermann	EB 8281	-D:	8289+	T	-	14/0650	am -D	Lebore	8289+	12.53 N/ 80.40 W	
14/1755	dt	U 373	Loeser	CA 8491	APC	4000=?	T	-						18)
14/1912	dt	U 504	Poske	EB 1420	-D	4500+	T	-	14/1715	le -D	Regent	3280+	17.50 N/ 84.10 W	
15/0012	dt	U 161	Achilles	ED 7397	-D	4000+	T	-	14/2300	am -D	Scottsburg	8001+	11.51 N/ 62.56 W	
15/0058	dt	U 552	Topp	BE 8839	-D	4000+	T	HG.84	14/	br -D	Etrib	1943+	43.18 N/ 17.38 W	
15/0058	dt	U 552	Topp	BE 8839	-D	4000+	T	HG.84	14/	br -M	Pelayo	1346+	43.18 N/ 17.38 W	
15/0059	dt	U 552	Topp	BE 8839	-T	4000+	T	HG.84	14/	nw -MT	Slemdal	7374+	43.18 N/ 17.38 W	
14/	dt	U 172 ?	Emmermann	EB 59			A	-	15/0030	br -S	Dutch Princess	125+	13.46 N/ 80.06 W	
15/0410	dt	U 502	v.Rosenstiel	ED 9471	-D	6500+	T	-						
15/	dt	U 502	v.Rosenstiel	ED 9444	-D	6000+	T	-	15/0210	pa -D	Cold Harbor	5010+	11.40 N/ 62.55 W	27)
15/0433	dt	U 552	Topp	BE 8589	-D	4000+	T	HG.84	15/	br -D	City of Oxford	2759+	43.42 N/ 18.12 W	
15/0433	dt	U 552	Topp	BE 8589	-D	4000+	T	HG.84	15/	br -D	Thurso	2436+	43.41 N/ 18.02 W	
15/0433	dt	U 552	Topp	BE 8589	-D	4000=	T	HG.84	15/					19)
15/0718	dt	U 373	Loeser	CA 8544	-D	5000=	T	-	/					20)
15/	dt	U 126	Bauer	ED 6953	-S	+	A	-	16/	do -S	Nueva Alta Gracia	30+	13.27 N/ 67.35 W	

18) *U 373* heard one torpedo hit but not detonate after 1 min 38 sec. It was a dud.
19) *U 552* fired three torpedoes and observed hits after 1 min 32 sec and 45 sec, and heard one detonation after 1 min 55 sec.
20) *U 373* observed one detonation after 1 min 6 sec, but the ship only stopped without any damage.

1	2	3	4	5	6	7	8	9	10	11	12	13	14	15

June 1942, cont.

1	2	3	4	5	6	7	8	9	10 11	12	13	14	15
(12. 6.)	dt	U 701	Degen	CA 73	--------	M	-	15/2304	am -DT	Robert C.Tuttle	11615=	36.52 N/ 75.51 W	21)
(12. 6.)	dt	U 701	Degen	CA 73	--------	M	-	15/2333	am -MT	Esso Augusta	11237=	36.52 N/ 75.51 W	
(12. 6.)	dt	U 701	Degen	CA 73	--------	M	-	15/	br APC	Kingston Ceylonite	448+	36.52 N/ 75.51 W	
(12. 6.)	*dt*	*U 701*	*Degen*	*CA 73*	--------	*M*	*-*	*15/*	*am DD*	*Bainbridge*	*1190=*	*36.52 N/ 75.51 W*	
15/1630	it	ARCHIMEDE	Gazzana	04n/42w	-D: 6000+	TA	-	15/1445	pa -D	Cardina	5586+	04.45 N/ 40.55 W	
15/2000	dt	U 172	Emmermann	EB 8741	-D: 2438+	T	-	15/1800	nw -D	Bennestvet	2438+	10.47 N/ 82.12 W	
15/2015	dt	U 502	v.Rosenstiel	ED 8669	-D 5500+	T	-	15/1815	am -D	West Hardaway	5702+	11.50 N/ 62.15 W	24/7)
15/2034	dt	U 68	Merten	EC 8445	-T: 9242+	T	-	15/	pt -DT	Frimaire	9242+	Caribbean	22)
16/0158	dt	U 575	Heydemann	BE 8311	-D =?	T	HG.84	16/			-----		23)
16/0230	dt	U 126	Bauer	ED 9412	-D 7000+	T	-	16/0028	am -D	Arkansan	6997+	12.07 N/ 62.51 W	
16/0320	dt	U 126	Bauer	ED 9412	-D: 6062+	TA	-	16/0120	am -D	Kahuku	6062+	11.54 N/ 63.07 W	
16/0401	dt	U 67	Müller-Stöckheim	DM 5136	-D: 2500+	T	-	16/0245	ni -D	Managua	2220+	24.05 N/ 81.40 W	
16/0417	dt	U 87	Berger	CA 3268	-D 7000+	T	XB.25	16/0325	br -D	Port Nicholson	8402+	42.11 N/ 69.25 W	
16/0421	dt	U 87	Berger	CA 3268	-D 7000+	T	XB.25	16/	am -D	Cherokee	5896+	42.25 N/ 69.10 W	
17/	dt	U 158	Rostin	DK 3445	-D 6800+	T	-	17/0350	pa -D	San Blas	3601+	25.26 N/ 95.33 W	
17/	dt	U 158	Rostin	DK 2566	-DT:1560+	T	-	17/1300	nw -DT	Moira	1560+	25.35 N/ 96.20 W	
(12. 6.)	dt	U 701	Degen	CA 73	--------	M	-	17/1348	am -D	Santore	7117+	36.52 N/ 75.51 W	
18/0245	dt	U 159	Witte	EC 8553	-D: 5551+	T	-	17/0115	nl -D	Flora	1417+	11.55 N/ 72.36 W	25)
18/0500	dt	U 172	Emmermann	EL 2163	-T: 3500+	A	-	18/0200	am -MT	Motorex	1958+	10.10 N/ 81.30 W	
18/0621	dt	U 124	Mohr	BC 3157	-D 7000+	T	ONS.102	18/0426	am -D	Seattle Spirit	5627+	50.24 N/ 42.37 W	26)
18/0622	dt	U 124	Mohr	BC 3157	-D 6000+	T	ONS.102	18/			-----		26)
18/0622	dt	U 124	Mohr	BC 3157	-D 6000=	T	ONS.102	18/			-----		26)

21) The *Robert C.Tuttle* was grounded but later salvaged and repaired.
22) The *Frimaire* was a Vichy-French tanker, operating under Portuguese charter.
23) *U 575* fired a 4-torpedo spread and heard one hit without detonation after 2 min 16 sec, probably a dud.
24) *U 502* reported three ships sunk on June 15th; the third ship may have been the *Tillie Lykes*. (See note 27).
25) *U 159* misidentified this ship as the American steamer *Flomar*.
26) *U 124* observed two hits on the first ship and heard two other detonations, possibly depth charges.

1	2	3	4	5	6	7	8	9	10	11	12	13	14	15

June 1942, cont.

1	2	3	4	5	6	7	8	9	10 11	12	13	14	15
18/	dt	U 502	v.Rosenstiel			T	-	18/	am -D	Tillie Lykes	2572+	19. N/ 85. W	27)
18/2303	dt	U 129	Witt	DM 5375	-D: 3270+	T	-	18/2106	am -D	Millinocket	3274+	23.12 N/ 79.28 W	
19/früh	dt	U 701	Degen	CA 79	APC +	A	-	19/	am YP	YP 389	+	10m from Diamond Head	
19/	dt	U 159	Witte	EC 8524	-D: 2710+	A	-	19/1635	jg -D	Ante Matkovic	2710+	12.05 N/ 72.30 W	
20/	dt	U 161	Achilles	EC 6993	-S +	A	-	20/0630	am -S	Cheerio	35+	18.02 N/ 67.40 W	28)
20/1125	dt	U 67	Müller-Stöckheim	DA 9296	-T 8000=	T	-	20/1030	nw -MT	Nortind	8221=	28.41 N/ 89.34 W	
21/0401	dt	U 128	Heyse	EE 8186	-D: 5681+	T	-	21/0200	am -D	West Ira	5681+	12.28 N/ 57.05 W	
22/1234	dt	U 202	Linder	CA 5651	-D: 4866+	T	-	22/1045	ar -D	Rio Tercero	4864+	39.15 N/ 72.32 W	29)
22/	dt	U 159	Witte	ED 4161	-T: 9639+	AS	-	22/2035	am -DT	E.J.Sadler	9639+	15.36 N/ 67.52 W	30)
23/0611	dt	U 67	Müller-Stöckheim	DA 9349	-T 8600+	T	-	23/	am -DT	Rawleigh Warner	3664+	28.53 N/ 89.15 W	
23/0720	dt	U 128	Heyse	EE 7432	-T 14000+	TA	-	23/0530	nw -MT	Andrea Brövig	10173+	12.10 N/ 59.10 W	
23/	dt	U 172	Emmermann	EB 8234	-S +	A	-	23/	co -S	Resolute	35+	13.15 N/ 80.30 W	
23/	dt	U 158	Rostin	DL 2918	-D: 5000+	T	-	23/0640	am -D	Henry Gibbons	5766+	24. N/ 89. W	
23/1629	dt	U 84	Uphoff	CD 5194	-D: 6568+	T	-	23/	nw -D	Torvanger	6568+	39.40 N/ 41.30 W	
23/1933	dt	U 68	Merten	EC 8233	-T: 5000+	TA	-	23/1735	pa -MT	Arriaga	2469+	13.08 N/ 72.16 W	
24/0821	dt	U 156	Hartenstein	DQ 1188	-D: 4857+	A	-	24/0750	br -D	Willimantic	4558+	25.55 N/ 51.58 W	
24/0937	dt	U 404	v.Bülow	DC 1223	-D 6000+	T	-	24/0738	jg -D	Ljubica Matkovic	3289+	34.30 N/ 75.40 W	
(11. 6.)	dt	U 373	Loeser	CA 54	---------	M	-	24/2005	am -Dt	John R.Williams	396+	38.45 N/ 74.50 W	
25/0116	dt	U 404	v.Bülow	DC 1228	-D 10000+	T	.	24/1127	am -D	Manuela	4772+	34.30 N/ 75.40 W	
25/0120	dt	U 404	v.Bülow	DC 1228	-D 7000+	T	.	24/2323	pa -D	Nordal	3845+	34.30 N/ 75.40 W	

27) The *Tillie Lykes* was reported missing after June 18th. *U 158*, later lost, was in the area but made no report. So it is more probable that *U 502* was the attacker.
28) The position reported by *U 161* and the Allied report of the loss of the *Cheerio* do not correlate, but there was no other loss of a sailing vessel reported during this time.
29) *U 202* reported that the *Rio Tercero* displayed no neutrality signs, and was recognized as Argentine only after the attack.
30) The *E.J.Seiler* was set on fire by 37mm gunfire, and was sunk after four hours by demolition charges.

1	2	3	4	5	6	7	8	9	10	11	12	13	14	15
June 1942, cont.														
25/	dt	U 153	Reichmann	DP 2655	-D: 5268+	T	-	25/	br	-M	Anglo Canadian	5268+	25.12 N/ 55.31 W	
/						?	-	25/	br	-Df	Bromelia	242+	near Iceland	31)
26/0544	dt	U 203	Mützelburg	DO 3862	-D: 5216+	TA	-	26/0300	br	-M	Putney Hill	5216+	24.20 N/ 63.16 W	
26/	dt	U 701	Degen	DC-1281	-D =	T	-	26/0110	nw	-M	Tamesis	7256=	34.59 N/ 75.41 W	
26/1500	dt	U 107	Gelhaus	DE 1737	-D:10083+	T	-	26/0155	nl	-D	Jagersfontein	10083+	31.56 N/ 54.48 W	
26/2317	dt	U 203	Mützelburg	DO 9195	-D: 3666+	TA	-	26/2015	bz	-D	Pedrinhas	3666+	23.07 N/ 62.06 W	32)
27/0724	dt	U 129	Witt	DK 8259	-T: 7008+	TA	-	27/0515	me	-DT	Tuxpam	7008+	20.15 N/ 96.20 W	
27/1055	dt	U 126	Bauer	ED 9331	-T: 9952+	T	-	27/0845	nw	-MT	Leiv Eiriksson	9952+	13.18 N/ 59.57 W	
27/1525	dt	U 129	Witt	DK 8299	-T: 2000+	TA	-	27/1330	me	-DT	Las Choapas	2005+	20.15 N/ 96.20 W	
27/1552	dt	U 128	Heyse	EE 8747	-D: 7041+	T	-	27/1400	am	-D	Polybius	7041+	10.55 N/ 57.40 W	
27/	dt	U 701	Degen	DC 1231	-T +	T	.	27/1507	br	-MT	British Freedom	6985=	34.45 N/ 75.22 W	
27/	dt	U 153	Reichmann	DP 7110	-D: 6085+	T	-	27/1952	am	-D	Potlatch	6065+	19.20 N/ 53.18 W	33)
27/22	dt	U 404	v.Bülow	CA 6970	-M: 6827+	T	-	27/2050	nw	-M	Moldanger	6827+	38.03 N/ 70.52 W	
28/0350	dt	U 154	Kölle	DO 6262	-D 3200+	T	-	/						34)
28/1050	dt	U 332	Liebe	DD 4786	-D: 6027+	T	-	28/0833	am	-D	Raphael Semmes	6027+	29.30 N/ 64.30 W	
28/mitt	dt	U 701	Degen	DC 1246	-T 12000+	T	.	28/1816	am	-DT	William Rockefeller	14054+	35.07 N/ 75.07 W	
28/1538	dt	U 203	Mützelburg	DO 9734	-D: 7200+	TA	-	28/1245	am	-D	Sam Houston	7176+	19.21 N/ 62.22 W	
28/1855	dt	U 505	Loewe	DO 6646	-D 7000+	T	-	29/0100	am	-D	Sea Thrush	5447+	22.38 N/ 60.59 W	
28/2236	dt	U 128	Heyse	EE 9724	-D: 6687=	T	-	28/	am	-D	Steel Engineer	=?		35)
29/0750	dt	U 67	Müller-Stöckheim	DB 4987	-T 8400+	T	-	29/0545	br	-DT	Empire Mica	8032+	29.25 N/ 85.17 W	

31) The *Bromelia* was reported missing after June 25th, but there is no report about a U-boat attack on her.
32) The *Pedrinhas* was armed with one 120mm gun, as was reported by *U 203*.
33) *U 153* reported the *Potlatch* under her old name *Narcissus*.
34) *U 154* observed one hit amidship after 18 sec and observed the ship sink after 2 min 30 sec.
35) *U 128* observed two detonations after 7 min 30 sec. The ship stopped for a short time and then proceeded albeit with a list.

1	2	3	4	5	6	7	8	9	10	11	12	13	14	15
June 1942, cont.														
29/	dt	U 126	Bauer	ED 90	-S +	A	–	28/	ca	-S	Mona Marie	126+	12.22 N/ 60.10 W	
29/	dt	U 153	Reichmann	DP 4769	-D: 4781+	T	–	29/0355	am	-D	Ruth	4833+	21.44 N/ 74.05 W	
29/	dt	U 754	Oestermann	BD 4983	-D:12435+	T	–	29/0410	br	-M	Waiwera	12435+	45.49 N/ 34.29 W	
29/1355	dt	U 505	Loewe	DP 4457	-D: 7400+	TA	–	29/1120	am	-D	Thomas McKean	7191+	22. N/ 60. W	
29/	dt	U 158	Rostin	DC 5626	-D: 3950+	AS	–	29/1545	le	-D	Everalda	3950+	31. N/ 70. W	36)
30/0840	it	MOROSINI	d'Alessandro	26n/58w	-M 10000+	TA	–	30/1930	nl	-M	Tysa	5327+	25.33 N/ 57.53 W	
30/1626	dt	U 458	Diggins	AL 4224	-M: 2740+	TA	–	30/	nw	-M	Mosfruit	2714+	56.10 N/ 23.40 W	
July 1942														
1/0127	dt	U 202	Linder	CA 9758	-D 9000+	T	–	30/2330	am	-D	City of Birmingham	5861+	35.10 N/ 70.53 W	
1/1744	dt	U 129	Witt	DK 6636	-D: 1885+	T	–	1/	nw	-D	Cadmus	1855+	22.50 N/ 92.30 W	
1/1831	dt	U 126	Bauer	ED 9951	-D: 7551+	T	–	1/	am	-D	Warrior	7551+	10.54 N/ 61.02 W	
2/0616	dt	U 129	Witt	DK 4146	-D: 1841+	TA	–	2/	nw	-M	Gundersen	1841+	23.33 N/ 92.35 W	
3/	dt	U 215	Hoeckner	-------	---------	T	BA.2	3/	am	-D	Alexander Macomb	7191+	41.48 N/ 66.35 W	
3/0401	dt	U 161	Achilles	EL 1265	-D: 3305+	T	–	3/	pa	-D	San Pablo	3305=	Porto Limon	1)
3/	dt	U 126	Bauer	ED 9691	-T: 7104=	T	–	3/0422	am	-DT	Gulfbelle	7104+	11.40 N/ 60.39 W	
4/0342	dt	U 575	Heydemann	DN 96	-D: 2648+	T	–	4/0140	am	-D	Norlandia	2689+	19.33 N/ 68.39 W	2)
4/2325	dt	U 129	Witt	DL 6819	-T: 6326+	T	–	4/1800	sj	-MT	Tuapse	6320+	22.13 N/ 86.06 W	
6/0039	dt	U 201	Schnee	CF 4953	-D:14443+	T	–	5/2100	br	-D	Avila Star	14443+	38.04 N/ 22.48 W	
6/0521	dt	U 132	Vogelsang	BA 3911	-D 4000+		QS.15	6/	br	-D	Dinarić	2555+	49.30 N/ 66.30 W	
6/0521	dt	U 132	Vogelsang	BA 3911	-D 4000+		QS.15	6/0723	gr	-D	Anastassios Pateras	3382+	49.30 N/ 66.30 W	
6/0522	dt	U 132	Vogelsang	BA 3911	-D 5000+	T	QS.15	6/0735	be	-D	Hainaut	4312+	49.30 N/ 66.30 W	

36) The *Everalda* was stopped by gunfire and sunk by opening the sea valves. The captain was taken prisoner.
1) The *San Pablo* was sunk at the pier in Porto Limon, Costa Rica.
2) The *Norlandia* was erroneously reported by *U 575* as the Panamanian *Portland*.

1	2	3	4	5	6	7	8	9	10	11	12	13	14	15
July 1942, cont.														
6/0646	dt	U 132	Vogelsang	BA 3911	-D 7000+	T	QS.15	6/						3)
6/	dt	U 67	Müller-Stöckheim	DA 9326	-M 4000+	T	-	6/	nw	-M	Bayard	2160+	29.35 N/ 88.44 W	
6/	dt	U 154	Kölle	DL 6471	-Df +	A	-	6/1800	pa	-Mf	Lalita	65+	21.45 N/ 86.40 W	
7/0902	dt	U 571	Möhlmann	DM 2646	-D 10000+	T	.	7/0705	br	-D	Umtata	8141+	25.35 N/ 80.02 W	
7/1016	dt	U 67	Müller-Stöckheim	DA 6997	-T: 6610+	T	.	7/	am	-DT	Paul H.Harwood	6610=	29.26 N/ 88.38 W	
8/0616	dt	U 571	Möhlmann	DM 2824	-T: 9788+	TA	-	8/	am	-DT	J.A.Moffett Jr.	9788=§	24.47 N/ 80.42 W	4)
9/0247	dt	U 575	Heydemann	ED 9679	-D: 5985+	TA	-	9/0052	br	-D	Empire Explorer	5345+	11.40 N/ 60.55 W	5)
9/	dt	U 571	Möhlmann	DM 4328	-D: 1051+	A	-	9/1350	ho	-D	Nicholas Cuneo	1051+	23.54 N/ 82.33 W	
9/1624	dt	U 172	Emmermann	DP 2367	-D: 8400+	TA	-	9/1425	am	-D	Santa Rita	8379+	26.11 N/ 55.40 W	
9/2042	dt	U 66	Markworth	DE 9785	-D: 6363+	T	-	9/	jg	-D	Triglav	6363+	26.47 N/ 48.10 W	
9/2305	dt	U 203	Mützelburg	EE 7475	-D: 6914+	T	-	9/2100	br	-M	Cape Verde	6914+	11.32 N/ 60.17 W	
10/0619	dt	U 67	Müller-Stöckheim	DA 9252	-T 8000+	T	-	10/	am	-DT	Benjamin Brewster	5950+	20.05 N/ 90.05 W	
10/	dt	U 576	Heinicke	-------	---------	T	-	10/2125	pa	-MT	J.A.Mowinckel	11147=	33.44 N/ 75.19 W	
11/0352	dt	U 203	Mützelburg	ED 9694	-T:10444+	TA	-	11/0200	pa	-DT	Stanvac Palembang	10013+	11.28 N/ 60.23 W	
11/	dt	U 166	Kuhlmann	ED 11	-S +	A	-	11/	do	-S	Carmen	84+	19.43 N/ 70.12 W	
12/0022	dt	U 116	v.Schmidt	DG 6311	-D 4500+	T	OS.33 d	11/	br	-D	Cortona	7093+	32.45 N/ 24.45 W	6)
12/0025	dt	U 201	Schnee	DG 6317	-D: 7100+	T	OS.33 d							
12/0147	dt	U 582	Schulte	DG 6397	-D 8000+	T	OS.33 d	12/	br	-D	Port Hunter	8826+	31. N/ 24. W	
12/0413	dt	U 201	Schnee	DG 9296	-D 7000+	TA	OS.33 d	12/	br	-D	Siris	5242+	31.20 N/ 24.48 W	

3) *U 132* observed one hit amidships after 1 min 35 sec, with a big column of fire.

4) The *J.A.Moffett* was towed into harbor, but was so heavily damaged by two torpedoes and 20 hits by 88mm that she was a total loss.

5) *U 575* reported this ship erroneously to be the British *Inanda*.

6) The *Cortona* was hit at about the same time by torpedoes from *U 116* and *U 201*, and was later sunk by a coup de grâce from *U 201*.

1	2	3	4	5	6	7	8	9	10	11	12	13	14	15
July 1942, cont.														
12/0945	dt	U 116	v.Schmidt	DG 6257	-D: 4300+	T	OS.33 d	12/		br	-D Shaftesbury	4284+	31.42 N/ 25.30 W	
12/2346	dt	U 129	Witt	EB 2143	-D: 2325+	T	-	12/2145		am	-D Tachirá	2325+	18.15 N/ 81.45 W	
13/0221	dt	U 201	Schnee	DG 9552	-D: 6700+	T	OS.33 d	13/		br	-D Sithonia	6723+	29. N/ 25. W	
13/0408	dt	U 84	Uphoff	DM 5283	-D 7500+	T	-	13/0230		am	-D Andrew Jackson	5990+	23.32 N/ 81.02 W	
13/0735	dt	U 67	Müller-Stöckheim	DA 9198	-T 10000+	T	-	13/0540		am	-DT R.W.Gallagher	7989+	28.50 N/ 91.05 W	
13/	dt	U 166	Kuhlmann	DN	-D 3000+	T	-	13/1610		am	-D Oneida	2309+	20.17 N/ 74.06 W	
15/0146	dt	U 201	Schnee	DG 9975	-T: 7000+	TA	-	14/		br	-DT British Yeoman	6990+	26.42 N/ 24.20 W	
15/0330	dt	U 582	Schulte	DT 6153	-D: 8441+	T	OS.33 d	15/		br	-D Empire Attendant	7524+	23.48 N/ 21.51 W	7)
15/0749	dt	U 571	Möhlmann	DM 1976	-T 15000+	T	-	15/0545		am	-MT Pennsylvania Sun	11394+	24.05 N/ 83.42 W	
15/	dt	U 576	Heinicke	-------	---------	T	.	15/2020		am	-D Chilore	8310+	34.47 N/ 75.22 W	8)
15/	dt	U 576	Heinicke	-------	---------	T	.	15/2020		ni	-D Bluefields	2063+	34.46 N/ 75.22 W	
16/0934	dt	U 160	Lassen	ED 9946	-T: 9974+	T	-	16/0713		pa	-DT Beaconlight	6926+	10.59 N/ 61.05 W	9)
16/	dt	U 166	Kuhlmann	-------	---------	A	-	16/0900		am	-Df Gertrude	16+	23.32 N/ 82.00 W	
16/1543	dt	U 161	Achilles	DD 7862	-D 9000+	T	AS.4	16/1345		am	-D Fairport	6165+	27.10 N/ 64.33 W	
16/1544	dt	U 161	Achilles	DD 7862	-D 5000=?	T	AS.4							10)
18/0242	dt	U 437	Schulz	DN 8378	-D 10000+	T	.	18/						11)
18/0243	dt	U 437	Schulz	DN 8378	-D 10000=	T	.	18/						11)
18/0625	dt	U 575	Heydemann	EE 7778	-T:12910+	T	-	18/		br	-DT San Gaspar	12910=	10.30 N/ 60.27 W	
18/	dt	U 575	Heydemann	EE 78	-S: 130+	A	-	18/		br	-S Glacier	130+	10.50 N/ 58.58 W	
18/	dt	U 575	Heydemann	EE 75	-S: 110+	A	-	18/		br	-S Comrade	110+	11.20 N/ 58.50 W	
18/1633	dt	U 160	Lassen	ED 9865	-D 9000+	T	-	18/1427		pa	-D Carmona	5496+	10.58 N/ 61.20 W	

7) *U 582* reported this ship erroneously to be the *Domala*.
8) The *Chilore* was damaged and sank later under tow. *U 576* was sunk a short time later.
9) *U 160* reported this ship erroneously as the *Gallia*.
10) *U 161* observed two hits on the first ship after 2 min 32 sec and heard a third detonation after 3 min 35 sec.
11) *U 437* heard one detonation after 3 min 20 sec and a second one a short time later. There were sinking noises.

1	2	3	4	5	6	7	8	9	10	11	12	13	14	15

July 1942, cont.

1	2	3	4	5	6	7	8	9	10/11	12	13	14	15
19/0230	dt	U 564	Suhren	CE 3341	-D 5000+	T	OS.34	19/0035	br -D	Empire Hawksbill	5724+	42.29 N/ 25.56 W	12)
19/0230	dt	U 564	Suhren	CE 3341	-D 5000+	T	OS.34	19/0037	br -M	Lavington Court	5372+	42.38 N/ 25.28 W	12)
19/0230	dt	U 564	Suhren	CE 3341	-D 5000=	T	OS.34				-----		12)
19/0230	dt	U 564	Suhren	CE 3341	-D 8000=	T	OS.34				-----		12)
19/0339	dt	U 108	Scholtz	CE 3352	-D 5000+?	T	OS.34	19/0140			-----		13)
19/0339	dt	U 108	Scholtz	CE 3352	-D 5000+?	T	OS.34	19/0140			-----		13)
19/0343	dt	U 108	Scholtz	CE 3352	-D 5000=	T	OS.34	19/0140			-----		13)
19/0645	dt	U 84	Uphoff	DM 1651	-D 500+	T	-	19/0345	ho -D	Baja California	1648+	25.14 N/ 82.27 W	
19/1655	dt	U 332	Liebe	CC 8279	-D: 4573+	TA	-	19/1510	gr -D	Leonidas M.	4573+	37.01 N/ 52.04 W	
19/1912	dt	U 129	Witt	DM 4153	-D: 1266+	T	-	19/1615	nw -D	Port Antonio	1266+	23.39 N/ 84.00 W	
20/1724	dt	U 437	Schulz	DN 8199	-D 15000=	T	-	/					14)
20/1839	dt	U 132	Vogelsang	BB 1475	-D 4500+	T	QS.	20/1635	br -D	Frederika Lensen	4367+	49.22 N/ 65.12 W	15)
21/0907	dt	U 84	Uphoff	DM 1994	-D 9000+	T	.	21/0708	am -D	William Cullen Bryant	7176=	24.08 N/ 82.23 W	16)
21/0908	dt	U 84	Uphoff	DM 1994	-T 12000=	T	.	21/					16)
21/1029	dt	U 160	Lassen	ED 9946	-T: 8150+	T	-	21/0840	br -MT	Donovania	8149+	10.56 N/ 61.10 W	
22/	dt	U 505	Loewe	EB 8197	-S: 110+	A	-	22/	co -S	Roamar	110+	12.24 N/ 81.28 W	
22/2012	dt	U 582	Schulte	ES 3488	-D: 7493+	T	-	22/1814	am -D	Honolulan	7493+	08.41 N/ 22.04 W	
23/	dt	U 752	Schroeter	ET 5967	-D 5000+	T	-	23/	br -D	Garmula	5254+	05.32 N/ 14.45 W	
23/1347	*dt*	*U 89*	*Lohmann*	*CB 1497*	*PG 2000=?*	*T*	.	/					*17)*
23/2222	dt	U 129	Witt	DM 6464	-D 4000+	T	-	23/2030	am -D	Onondaga	2310+	22.40 N/ 78.44 W	
24/1640	it	GIULIANI	Bruno	22n/60w	-M 10000=	T	-	/					18)

12) *U 564* observed four detonations between 1 min 15 sec and 1 min 27 sec, after firing. There were probably two hits each on the two ships.
13) *U 108* heard four detonations after 2 min 50 sec and a fifth from a stern spread after 3 min. Probably were depth charges.
14) *U 437* heard two heavy detonations after a 3-shot spread. The target was a ship of the *President*-class.
15) The *Frederika Lensen* was beached heavily damaged and was declared a total loss.
16) *U 84* observed an explosion on the tanker after 4 min 35 sec, and a black cloud rising after 4 min 36 sec from the tanker.
17) *U 89* heard two detonations from a two-shot spread fired against an *Erie*-class gunboat, possibly premature detonations.
18) *Giuliani* heard one detonation after firing a two-shot spread against a two-funnel freighter.

1	2	3	4	5	6		7	8	9	10	11	12	13	14		15

July 1942, cont.

1	2	3	4	5	6	7	8	9	10 11	12	13	14	15
25/0114	dt	U 160	Lassen	EO 1424	-D 7500+	T	-	24/2355	nl -D	Telamon	2078+	09.15 N/ 59.54 W	
25/0352	dt	U 552	Topp	BC 3829	-T 9000+	T	ON.113	25/0159	br -MT	British Merit	8093=	49.03 N/ 40.36 W	
25/0409	dt	U 552	Topp	BC 3829	-D 7000+	T	ON.113	25/0212	br -D	Broompark	5136+	49.02 N/ 40.26 W	
25/0955	dt	U 89	Lohmann	CB 1295	-S +	A	-	25/	ca -Mf	Lucille M.	54+	42.02 N/ 65.38 W	
25/1653	dt	U 130	Kals	ES 5564	-T:10095+	TA	-	25/	nw -MT	Tankexpress	10095+	10.05 N/ 26.31 W	
25/2305	dt	U 201	Schnee	ET 5962	APC 1000+	T	-	25/	br APC	Laertes	545+	06.00 N/ 14.17 W	
26/0757	dt	U 607	Mengersen	BC 5693	-D 8000=	T	ON.113	26/	br -M	Empire Rainbow	6942+	47.08 N/ 42.57 W	19)
26/0757	dt	U 607	Mengersen	BC 5693	-D =	T	ON.113	26/		Empire Rainbow	-----		19)
26/0811	dt	U 704	Keßler	BC 6415	-D 5000=	T	ON.113	26/		Empire Rainbow			19)
26/0815	dt	U 66	Markworth	ED 9697	-D 10836+	T	-	26/0600	bz -D	Tamandaré	4942+	11.34 N/ 60.30 W	19a)
26/	dt	U 171	Pfeffer	DA 7625	-D 4500+	T	-	26/0945	me -D	Oaxaca	4351+	28.23 N/ 96.08 W	
27/0845	dt	U 582	Schulte	ES 5555	-D: 8500+	TAS	-	27/	am -D	Stella Lykes	6801+	06.40 N/ 25.05 W	20)
27/1414	dt	U 752	Schroeter	ET 7374	-D 6000+	T	FN.20	27/	nw -D	Leikanger	4003+	04. N/ 18. W	
27/1740	dt	U 130	Kals	ES 1541	-D: 7357+	T	-	27/	br -D	Elmwood	7167+	04.48 N/ 22.00 W	21)
28/0040	dt	U 66	Markworth	EE 7584	-D 6500+	T	-	27/2335	br -M	Weirbank	5150+	11.29 N/ 58.51 W	
28/0715	dt	U 155	Piening	EE 8133	-D 7500+	T	-	28/0535	bz -D	Barbacena	4772+	13.10 N/ 56.00 W	19a)
28/	dt	U 754	Oestermann	BB 7768	-Df +	A	-	28/0800	am -Mf	Ebb	260+	43.18 N/ 63.50 W	
28/2230	dt	U 155	Piening	EE 8296	-D: 2347+	TA	-	28/	bz -D	Piave	2347+	12.30 N/ 55.49 W	
29/1019	dt	U 160	Lassen	EO 1576	-D 12000+	T	-	29/0840	ca -D	Prescodoc	1938+	08.50 N/ 59.05 W	
(20. 7.)	*dt*	*U 66*	*Markworth*	*ED 69*	*---------*	*M*	-	*29/*	*am CGC*	*Port Castries*	=		
29/2000	dt	U 155	Piening	EE 8626	-D: 2445+	T	-	29/1810	nw -D	Bill	2445+	11.58 N/ 55.02 W	
30/0110	dt	U 132	Vogelsang	BB 8719	-D 8000+	T	ON.113	30/	br -M	Pacific Pioneer	6734+	43.30 N/ 60.35 W	
30/	dt	U 166	Kuhlmann	-------	---------	T	-	30/2230	am -D	Robert E.Lee	5184+	28.40 N/ 88.42 W	

19) *U 607* observed two hits on a freighter and heard one detonation beyond. *U 704* observed one detonation: probably both hit the same ship. - 19a) The *Tamandaré* and *Barbacena* were armed with one 120mm gun each.
20) The *Stella Lykes* was hit by two torpedoes and gunfire, but sank only after some demolition charges were exploded at 15.15 hrs.
21) *U 130* reported the ship erroneously as the *Almwood*.

1	2	3	4	5	6	7	8	9	10	11	12	13	14	15
July 1942, cont.														
30/1958	dt	U 155	Piening	EE 8634	-D: 6096+	T	-	30/	am	-D	Cranford	6096+	12.17 N/ 55.11 W	
30/2048	dt	U 130	Kals	ES 5185	-D: 8400+	TA	-	30/	br	-M	Danmark	8391+	07.00 N/ 24.19 W	
August 1942														
1/0220	dt	U 155	Piening	EE 8639	-D 6900+	T	-	1/0030	nl	-D	Kentar	5878+	11.52 N/ 57.30 W	
1/1758	dt	U 155	Piening	EE 9456	-D: 6088+	T	-	1/1620	br	-D	Clan Macnaughton	6088+	11.54 N/ 54.25 W	
1/2014	*dt*	*U 254*	*Gilardone*	*AE 7137*	*DD 1630=*	*T*	.	/						*1)*
1/2259	it	TAZZOLI	Fecia di Cossato	11n/59w	-D: 1880+	T	-	1/	gr	-D	Kastor	5497+	11.06 N/ 59.05 W	
2/0612	dt	U 510	Neitzel	DD 8417	-D: 5300+	TA	-	2/0445	ur	-D	Maldonaldo	5285+	28.20 N/ 63.10 W	
2/0927	dt	U 254	Gilardone	AE 7664	-D 4500+	T	-	2/	br	-D	Flora II	1218+	62.45 N/ 19.07 W	
(20. 7.)	*dt*	*U 66*	*Markworth*	*ED 69*	*---------*	*M*	-	*2/*	*br*	*PT*	*MTB 339*	*32=*	*Port Castries,*	
(2o. 7.)	*dt*	*U 66*	*Markworth*	*ED 69*	*---------*	*M*	-	*2/*	*br*	*PT*	*MTB 342*	*32=*	*Santa Lucia*	
2/1818	dt	U 160	Lassen	EE 8783	-D: 4694+	T	-	2/1620	br	-D	Treminnard	4694+	10.40 N/ 57.07 W	
2/1918	dt	U 71	Rodler v.Roithberg	BC 5887	-D 6000=	T	ON.115	2/						2)
3/0305	dt	U 552	Topp	BC 5775	-D 8000+	T	ON.115	3/	br	-MT	G.S.Walden	10627=	45.45 N/ 47.17 W	
3/0305	dt	U 552	Topp	BC 5775	-D 8000+	T	ON.115	3/	be	-D	Belgian Soldier	7167+	45.52 N/ 47.13 W	3)
3/0401	dt	U 553	Thurmann	BC 5771	-D 7000+	T	ON.115	3/0105	br	-M	Lochkatrine	9419+	45.52 N/ 46.44 W	
3/1654	dt	U 605	Schütze	AE 68	-Df 700+	T	-	6/	br	-Df	Bombay	229+	62. N/ 18. W	4)
3/2032	dt	U 155	Piening	EE 9773	-T 8000=?	T	-	/						5)
3/2220	dt	U 108	Scholtz	EE 9476	-T 10000+	T	-	3/2020	br	-MT	Tricula	6221+	11.35 N/ 56.51 W	
4/0159	dt	U 160	Lassen	EE 8950	-T: 6161+	TA	-	4/0015	nw	-MT	Havsten (s.u.)	6161=	11.18 N/ 54.45 W	6)

1) *U 254* heard detonations after 4 min 22 sec and 4 min 27 sec, after firing at a destroyer of the *Gleaves* class.
2) *U 71* heard one detonation after 3 min 17 sec.
3) *U 552* observed one hit each on a freighter with machinery aft (*G.S.Walden*) and another freighter at the bow. Both stopped. The last one was probably sunk by a coup de grâce from *U 607* at 02.29/Aug.4th.
4) The *Bombay* was reported missing after Aug.5th. Only the report of *U 605* may correlate with this loss.

1	2	3	4	5	6		7	8	9	10 11	12	13	14	15
August 1942, cont.														
4/0229	dt	U 607	Mengersen	BC 5746	-D	8000+	T	ON.115	4/	be -D	Belgian Soldier (s.o.)	7167+	45.52 N/ 47.13 W	3)
4/	dt	*U 134*	*Schendel*	*DN 7550*	*DD*	*1630+*	*T*	*-*	/					7)
4/1558	dt	U 176	Dierksen	BD 1647	-M:	7800+	T	-	4/	br -M	Richmond Castle	7798+	50.25 N/ 25.05 W	
4/1615	dt	U 155	Piening	EF 7784	-D:	7049+	T	-	4/1317	br -D	Empire Arnold	7045+	10.45 N/ 52.30 W	
4/2115	dt	U 66	Markworth	EE 7961	-D	5000=?	T	-	4/					8)
5/	dt	U 155	Piening	EE 98	-D:	389+	A	-	5/1145	nl -M	Draco	389+	11.05 N/ 53.30 W	
5/1613	dt	U 458	Diggins	BB 8682	-T	3000+	T	-	5/1520	br -DT	Arletta	4870+	44.44 N/ 55.22 W	
5/1848	dt	U 593	Kelbling	AJ 9191	-D	5000+	T	SC.94	5/1650	nl -D	Spar	3616+	53.05 N/ 43.38 W	9)
5/1849	dt	U 593	Kelbling	AJ 9191	-D	4000=	T	SC.94	5/			-----		
6/0155	dt	U 508	Staats	DM 4336	-D	5000=	T	.	/					10)
6/0155	dt	U 508	Staats	DM 4336	-D	5000=	T	.	/					10)
6/1031	it	TAZZOLI	Fecia di Cossato	10n/57w	-T:	6161+	T	-	6/	nw -MT	Havsten	6161+	11.18 N/ 54.45 W	6)
6/1719	dt	U 66	Markworth	EE 8717	-D	766+	T	-	6/	pl -D	Rozewie			11)
7/0133	dt	U 108	Scholtz	EO 2276	-D:	2687+	TA	-	6/2335	nw -M	Breñas	2687+	10.20 N/ 56.10 W	
7/0225	dt	U 572	Hirsacker	ES 5466	-D	8000+	T	-	6/	nl -D	Delfshaven	5281+	07.24 N/ 25.37 W	
7/2147	dt	U 109	Bleichrodt	ER 1839	-T:	6035+	TA	-	7/1930	nw -MT	Arthur W.Sewall	6030+	08.28 N/ 34.21 W	12)
7/2238	dt	U 86	Schug	CC 4559	-S:	500+	A	-	7/2000	am -S	Wawaloam	342+	39.18 N/ 55.44 W	

5) *U 155* heard one torpedo hit but did not detonate, probably a dud.
6) The *Havsten* was torpedoed by *U 160* and hit by gunfire. The U-boat left the ship burning. On Aug.8th the damaged *Havsten* was sunk by two torpedoes from *Tazzoli*.
7) *U 134* reported the sinking of one destroyer of the *Gleaves* class.
8) *U 66* heard one torpedo hit after 2 min 14 sec but did not detonate, probably a dud.
9) *U 593* observed one hit on the ship in pos.12 (*Spar*) and heard one detonation on the ship in pos.11.
10) *U 508* heard heavy detonations after 3 min and 3 min 20 sec, probably depth charges.
11) *U 66* reported the sinking of the armed steamer *Rosewie* (1 152mm, 3 MGs) after one torpedo hit. This ship is not mentioned in Allied sources.
12) The *Arthur W.Sewall* sank on Aug.8th.

1	2	3	4	5	6	7	8	9	10	11	12	13	14	15
August 1942, cont.														
8/0531 dt	U 704	Keßler	AK 0183	-D 7000=	T	SC.94		8/	br	-D	Duchess of Bedford	-----		13)
8/1155 dt	U 660	Baur	AK 2916	-D 8000=?	T	SC.94		8/				-----		14)
8/1518 dt	U 176	Dierksen	AK 0247	-D 9000+	T	SC.94		8/1325	br	-D	Trehata	4817+	56.30 N/ 32.14 W	15)
8/1518 dt	U 176	Dierksen	AK 0247	-D 7000+	T	SC.94		8/1325	br	-D	Kelso	3956+	56.30 N/ 32.14 W	15)
8/1518 dt	U 176	Dierksen	AK 0247	-D 4000+	T	SC.94		8/1325	gr	-D	Mount Kassion	7914+	56.30 N/ 32.14 W	15)
8/ dt	U 379	Kettner	-------	--------	T	SC.94		8/1325	am	-D	Kaimoku	6367+	56.30 N/ 32.14 W	15)
8/ dt	U 379	Kettner	-------	--------	T	SC.94		8/1325	br	-D	Anneberg	2537+	56.30 N/ 32.14 W	15)
9/ dt	U 155	Piening	EO 6134	-T 9000+	T	-		8/	br	-MT	San Emiliano	8071+	07.22 N/ 54.08 W	
9/0231 dt	*U 595*	*Quaet-Faslem*	*AK 3944*	*DD =*	*T*	*SC.94*						-----		*16)*
9/0649 dt	U 176	Dierksen	AK 0240	-D 7000+	Tf	SC.94 s		9/	br	-D	Radchurch	3701+	56.15 N/ 32.00 W	17)
9/2113 dt	U 752	Schroeter	ET 7385	-D: 6047+	T	-		9/	nl	-D	Mendenau	6047+	04.45 N/ 18. W	
9/2209 dt	U 704	Keßler	AL 4772	-D 15000=?	T	-		/				-----		18)
9/2237 dt	U 130	Kals	ES 5143	-T: 7078+	T	-		9/	nw	-DT	Malmanger	7078+	07.13 N/ 26.30 W	
10/0215 dt	U 510	Neitzel	ED 3927	-T 14000+	T	-		9/	br	-MT	Alexia	8016=	16.50 N/ 60.40 W	19)
10/0635 dt	U 597	Bopst	AL 0155	-D 8000=	T	SC.94		/				-----		20)
10/0636 dt	U 597	Bopst	AL 0155	-D 8000=	T	SC.94		/				-----		20)
10/0704 it	GIULIANI	Bruno	10n/38w	-M: 5445+	TA	-		10/0545	br	-M	Medon	5444+	09.26 N/ 38.28 W	

13) *U 704* heard one detonation after 1 min 20 sec. The *Duchess of Bedford* observed the detonation, but was not hit.

14) *U 660* heard one torpedo hit after 1 min 6 sec, but it did not detonate.

15) *U 176* fired three two-torpedo spreads. There were hits heard after 1 min 20 sec (2), 1 min 34 sec, and 2 min 11 sec. Then sinking noises were heard. Probably hit the ships in pos.51, 52 and 53: *Trehata*, *Kelso* and *Mount Kassion*. The last one did not sink until the forenoon of Aug.9th. The ships in pos.73 and 64, *Kaimoku* and *Anneberg*, probably were hit by the *U 379*, sunk by HMCS *Dianthus* before sending off a report. The *Anneberg* was sunk by an escort on Aug.8th.

16) *U 595* heard one heavy detonation after 36 sec. Probably a premature detonation.

17) *U 176* reported one damaged ship sunk. In reality the *Radchurch* was abandoned by the crew at 13.25/Aug.8th without being damaged.

18) *U 704* attacked one passenger steamer of the *Ormonde*-type and heard one detonation after 38 sec. Probably a premature detonation.

19) *U 510* observed three hits in sequence and assumed the tanker sank after 10 min.

20) *U 597* heard detonations after 1 min 32 sec (2) and 1 min 40 sec. Possibly depth charges.

1	2	3	4	5	6	7	8	9	10	11	12	13	14	15
August 1942, cont.														
10/	dt	U 155	Piening	EO 62	-D:	383+	A	-	10/		nl -M	Strabo	383+	07.29 N/ 54.05 W	21)
10/	dt	U 600	Zurmühlen	DN 6937	-S	+	A	-	10/		br -S	Vivian P.Smith	130+	21.50 N/ 68.40 W	
10/1220	dt	U 660	Baur	AL 2913	-D	6000+	T	SC.94	10/1023	gr	-D	Condylis (33)	4439+	57. N/ 22.30 W	22)
10/1221	dt	U 438	Franzius	AL 2913	-D	5000+	T	SC.94	10/1023	br	-D	Oregon (52) (61)	6008=	57.05 N/ 22.41 W	22)
10/1221	dt	U 660	Baur	AL 2913	-D	5000=	T	SC.94	10/1023	br	-D	Empire Reindeer	6259+	57.00 N/ 22.30 W	22)
10/1221	dt	U 660	Baur	AL 2913	-D	5000=	T	SC.94	10/1023	br	-D	Cape Race (62)	3807+	56.45 N/ 22.50 W	22)
10/1222	dt	U 660	Baur	AL 2913	-D	6000=	T	SC.94	10/1023	br	-D				
10/1547	dt	U 438	Franzius	AL 2910	-D	6000+	Tf	SC.94 s	10/	br	-D	Oregon (s.o.)	6008+	57.05 N/ 22.41 W	22)
11/1427	dt	U 130	Kals	ES 5198	-T:	7455+	T	-	11/	nw	-DT	Mirlo	7455+	06.04 N/ 26.50 W	
11/1913	dt	U 109	Bleichrodt	ER 3611	-T:	5728+	TA	-	11/	br	-DT	Vimeira	5728+	10.03 N/ 28.55 W	
12/1355	dt	U 508	Staats	DM 2748	-D	5000+	T	Spec.	12/1200	cu	-D	Santiago de Cuba	1685+	24.20 N/ 81.50 W	
12/1355	dt	U 508	Staats	DM 2748	-D	4000+	T	Conv.12	12/1200	cu	-D	Manzanillo	1025+	24.20 N/ 81.50 W	
13/0507	dt	U 658	Senkel	DN 7656	-T	13000+	T	WAT.13					-----		23)
13/0507	dt	U 658	Senkel	DN 7656	-D	8000+	T	WAT.13	12/2310	nl	-D	Medea	1311+	19.54 N/ 74.16 W	23)
13/0510	dt	U 658	Senkel	DN 7656	-D	6000=	T	WAT.13					-----		23)
13/0740	dt	U 752	Schroeter	ET 7317	-D	8000+	T	-	13/0500	am	-D	Cripple Creek	6347+	04.55 N/ 18.30 W	
13/0805	dt	U 658	Senkel	DN 7667	-D	5000=	T	WAT.13	/				-----		23)
13/0948	dt	U 600	Zurmühlen	DN 7663	-D	=	T	TAW.12	/				-----		24)
13/0948	dt	U 600	Zurmühlen	DN 7663	-T	=	T	TAW.12	/				-----		24)
13/0948	dt	U 600	Zurmühlen	DN 7663	-D	7000+	T	TAW.12	13/0751	le	-D	Everelza	4520+	19.55 N/ 73.49 W	24)
13/0958	dt	U 600	Zurmühlen	DN 7663	-D	7000+	T	TAW.12	13/0800	am	-D	Delmundo	5032+	19.55 N/ 73.49 W	24)

21) *U 155* reported this ship erroneously as the *Curacao*.
22) *U 660* fired one single shot, a two torpedo spread, and another single shot. There was one detonation after 47 sec, two after 1 min 30 sec, and one after 50 sec. *U 438* observed a detonation after 2 min 30 sec. The *Condylis* was hit by a torpedo both on the starboard and port side, so it must have been hit by both U-boats. The other ships were hit only on the starboard side, and so must have been hit by *U 660*. The damaged ship sunk by *U 438* must have been the *Oregon*.
23) *U 658* observed after two 2-torpedo spreads columns of fire after 3 min 58 sec (2) and 2 min 15 sec. Only the *Medea* was lost.
24) *U 600* fired three torpedoes which missed the targets but hit some ships beyond after 2 min 15 sec and 2 min 9 sec. The third torpedo hit after 58 sec and the target exploded with a 200m column of fire. The commodore's ship, the *Delmundo*, sank in 5 min after being hit by the stern torpedo.

1	2	3	4	5	6	7	8	9	10	11	12	13	14	15
August 1942, cont.														
13/	dt	U 171	Pfeffer	DA 9192	-T 11000+	TA	-	13/0750	am	-DT	R.M.Parker Jr.	6779+	28.50 N/ 90.42 W	
13/2030	it	GIULIANI	Bruno	09n/34w	-D: 5441+	TA	-	13/1925	am	-D	California	5441+	09.21 N/ 34.35 W	
14/1154	dt	U 598	Holtorf	DN 4782	-D 10000/	T	TAW.12	14/0950	br	-D	Michael Jebsen	2323+	21.45 N/ 76.10 W	25)
14/1155	dt	U 598	Holtorf	DN 4781	-T 8000/	T	TAW.12J	14/1000	br	-MT	Standella	6197=	21.41 N/ 76.09 W	25)
14/1157	dt	U 598	Holtorf	DN 4781	-T 12000+	T	TAW.12J	14/0950	br	-DT	Empire Corporal	6972+	21.45 N/ 76.10 W	25)
14/1930	it	GIULIANI	Bruno	11n/34w	-D 8000+	T	-	14/	br	-D	Sylvia de Larrinaga	5218+	10.49 N/ 33.35 W	
15/0358	dt	U 705	Horn	AL 4527	-D groß=	T	SC.95	15/0145	am	-D	Balladier	3279+	55.23 N/ 24.32 W	
16/0012	dt	U 507	Schacht	FJ 8285	-D 6000+	T	-	15/	bz	-D	Baependy	4801+	11.50 S/ 37.00 W	
16/0203	dt	U 507	Schacht	FJ 8495	-D 5000+	T	-	16/	bz	-D	Araraquara	4872+	12.00 S/ 37.19 W	
16/0913	dt	U 507	Schacht	FJ 8495	-D 3500+	T	-	16/0200	bz	-D	Annibal Benevolo	1905+	11.41 S/ 37.21 W	
16/1308	dt	U 596	Jahn	AL 4189	-D: 3740+	T	SC.95 s	16/	sw	-M	Suecia	4966+	55.43 N/ 25.58 W	26)
17/0619	dt	U 658	Senkel	DN 7892	-D 8000+	T	PG.6	17/0426	br	-D	Fort la Reine	7133+	18.80 N/ 75.20 W	
17/0619	dt	U 658	Senkel	DN 7892	-D 5000+	T	PG.6	17/0426	br	-M	Laguna	6466=	18.45 N/ 75.04 W	27)
17/0620	dt	U 658	Senkel	DN 7892	-D 6000+	T	PG.6	17/0426	äg	-D	Samir	3702+	18.30 N/ 75.20 W	
17/1549	dt	U 507	Schacht	FJ 8749	-D: 2200+	T	-	17/	bz	-D	Itagiba	2169+	13.20 S/ 38.40 W	
17/1657	dt	U 108	Scholtz	EP 4138	-T: 8587+	T	-	17/1501	am	-MT	Louisiana	8587+	07.24 N/ 52.33 W	
17/1756	dt	U 566	Remus	CF 4353	-D: 6710+	T	SL.118	17/	nw	-M	Triton	6607+	39.31 N/ 22.43 W	28)
17/1756	dt	U 566	Remus	CF 4353	-D 5000+	T	SL.118	17/						28)
17/1803	dt	U 507	Schacht	FJ 8749	-D 3000+	T	-	17/	bz	-D	Arará	1075+	13.20 S/ 38.49 W	
17/2237	dt	U 507	Schacht	FJ 8745	-D 4000=?	T	-							29)
18/0534	dt	U 510	Neitzel	EP 5161	-D 8000=	T	-	/						30)

25) *U 598* reported misses after two 2-torpedo spreads, but there was no other attack, and the first two torpedoes must have hit the *Michael Jebsen* which sank immediately. The second spread missed the *Empire Corporal* but one torpedo hit the *Standella*, which was subsequently towed to Key West. The stern shot sank the commodore's ship, the *Empire Corporal*.
26) *U 596* reported this ship erroneously as the Swedish *Suevia*.
27) The *Laguna* was damaged but towed into Guantanamo.
28) *U 566* fired a 3-torpedo spread against two ships and observed hits after 1 min 24 sec, 1 min 26 sec, and 1 min 27 sec.
29) *U 507* heard one hit without detonation after 35 sec: a premature. - 30) *U 510* heard three detonations after 1 min 30 sec.

North Sea - Atlantic

1	2	3	4	5	6	7	8	9	10	11	12	13	14	15

August 1942, cont.

1	2	3	4	5	6	7	8	9	10 11 12	13	14	15
18/0559 dt	U 553		Thurmann	DN 7472	-D	5000+	T	TAW.13	18/0405 sw -M Blankaholm	2845+	19.41 N/ 76.50 W	31)
18/0559 dt	U 553		Thurmann	DN 7472	-D	6000+	T	TAW.13		-----		31)
18/0603 dt	U 553		Thurmann	DN 7472	-DT	6000=	T	TAW.13				31)
18/0606 dt	U 553		Thurmann	DN 7472	-D	5000+	T	TAW.13	18/0415 am -D John Hancock	7176+	19.41 N/ 76.50 W	31)
18/0913 dt	U 553		Thurmann	DM 9691	-D	5000+	T	TAW.13		-----		32)
18/0913 dt	U 553		Thurmann	DM 9691	-D	5000+	T	TAW.13	18/0716 br -M Empire Bede	6959+	19.41 N/ 76.50 W	32)
18/0913 dt	U 553		Thurmann	DM 9691	-D	6000+	T	TAW.13		-----		32)
18/1125 dt	U 508		Staats	DM 2747	-T	8000=	T	.				33)
18/1125 dt	U 508		Staats	DM 2747	-D	5000=	T	.				33)
18/1852 dt	U 214		Reeder	CF 2569	-D	4000+	T	SL.118	18/ nl -D Balingkar	6318+	41.34 N/ 19.49 W	34)
18/1852 dt	U 214		Reeder	CF 2569	-D	5000+	T	SL.118	18/ br -D Hatarana	7522+	41.07 N/ 20.32 W	34)
18/1852 dt	U 214		Reeder	CF 2569	-D	5000+	T	SL.118	18/ br ACL Cheshire	10552=	41.30 N/ 19.49 W	34)
18/1852 dt	U 214		Reeder	CF 2569	-D	6000+	T	SL.118				
19/0025 dt	U 217		Reichenbach	EC 9625	-T	6000+	T	-	19/ am -DT Esso Concord	-----		35)
19/0437 dt	U 162		Wattenberg	ED 9467	-D	6000+	T	TAW.(S)	19/0240 am -D West Celina	5722+	11.45 N/ 62.30 W	
19/0907 dt	U 510		Neitzel	EP 6162	-D	11600+	T	-	19/0700 br -M Cressington Court	4971+	07.58 N/ 46.00 W	
19/1007 dt	U 564		Suhren	ED 9453	-T	8000=	T	TAW.(S)	19/0810 br -DT British Consul	6940+	11.58 N/ 62.38 W	36)
19/1007 dt	U 564		Suhren	ED 9453	-T	8000+	T	TAW.(S)	19/0810 br -D Empire Cloud	5969+	11.58 N/ 62.38 W	36)
19/1008 dt	U 564		Suhren	ED 9453	-D	7000+	T	TAW.(S)	19/	-----		36)
19/1010 dt	U 564		Suhren	ED 9453	-D	5000=	T	TAW.(S)	19/			36)
19/1356 dt	U 564		Suhren	ED 9416	-D	=?	T	TAW.(S)	/	-----		37)

31) *U 553* fired two 2-torpedo spreads and one stern shot. Two of the first spread probably hit the *Blankaholm*. One of the second spread or the stern shot hit the *John Hancock*.
32) *U 553* observed hits from a 4-torpedo spread after 56 sec, 63 sec and 66 sec, but only the *Empire Bede* was hit by one torpedo and later sunk by the corvette HMS *Pimpernel* with gunfire.
33) *U 508* missed the targets but heard detonations in the convoy after 8 min.
34) *U 214* fired four torpedoes and heard detonations after 4 min 31 sec, 4 min 37 sec, 3 min 10 sec and 2 min 27 sec. Probably one ship was hit by two torpedoes, the other by one. The AMC was salvaged.
35) *U 217* heard three detonations. The torpedoes probably hit the mole of Willemstad.
36) *U 564* observed three hits after 12 sec and 1 hit after 170 sec. The tanker was probably hit by several torpedoes.
37) *U 564* heard torpedoes hit after 59 sec and 79 sec, probably prematures or duds.

1	2	3	4	5	6	7	8	9	10	11	12	13	14	15

August 1942

1	2	3	4	5	6	7	8	9	10 11	12	13	14	15
19/	dt	U 217	Reichenbach	ED 75	-S 150+	A	-	19/2000	br -S	Seagull D.	75+	11.38 N/ 67.42 W	
19/	dt	U 507	Schacht	FQ 1330	-S: 150+	A	-	19/	bz -S	Jacyra	90+	14.30 S/ 38.40 W	
19/1622	dt	U 406	Dieterichs	BE 8977	-D 6000+	T	SL.118	19/	br -D	City of Manila	7452+	43.21 N/ 18.20 W	
21/2243	dt	U 506	Würdemann	ET 5328	-D 7000+	T	-	21/	br -D	City of Wellington	5733+	07.29 N/ 14.40 W	
22/0957	dt	U 507	Schacht	FJ 8724	-D 6000+	ATf	OS.36 d	22/	sw -M	Hamaren	3220+	13. S/ 38.15 W	38)
23/2337	dt	U 506	Würdemann	ET 5973	-D 5000+	T	-	18/	br -D	Hamla	4416+	04. S/ 24. W	39)
24/	dt	U 162	Wattenberg	EE 5745	-D 5000+	T	-	24/	nl -D	Moena	9286+	13.30 N/ 57.30 W	
25/0138	dt	U 605	Schütze	BD 1676	-D 5000=	T	ON.122						40)
25/0139	dt	U 605	Schütze	BD 1676	-D 5000+	T	ON.122	24/2345	br -D	Katvaldis	3163+	48.55 N/ 35.10 W	40)
25/0140	dt	U 605	Schütze	BD 1676	-D 5000=	T	ON.122	24/2345	br -D	Sheaf Mount	5017+	48.55 N/ 35.10 W	40)
25/0157	dt	U 176	Dierksen	BD 1667	-D: 7454+	T	ON.122						41)
25/0157	dt	U 438	Franzius	BD 1672	-D 7000+	T	ON.122	25/0013	br -D	Empire Breeze	7457+	49.22 N/ 35.52 W	41)
25/0201	dt	U 438	Franzius	BD 1672	-D 6000=	T	ON.122	25/0013	nw -D	Trolla	1598+	48.55 N/ 35.10 W	41)
25/0205	dt	U 438	Franzius	BD 1672	-D 5000=	T	ON.122						41)
25/0448	dt	U 604	Höltring	AK 9458	-D 12000+	T	-	25/0245	nl -M	Abbekerk	7906+	52.05 N/ 30.50 W	
25/1034	dt	U 558	Krech	EC 1196	-D 3500+	T	TAW.15s	25/	br -D	Amakura	1987+	17.46 N/ 75.52 W	
25/1830	dt	U 164	Fechner	EC 2728	-D 6000+	T	TAW.15s	25/	nl -D	Stad Amsterdam	3780+	16.39 N/ 73.15 W	
25/1944	dt	U 130	Kals	ET 6446	-D: 6455+	T	-	25/	br -D	Viking Star	6445+	06.00 N/ 14.00 W	
26/	dt	U 162	Wattenberg	EE 7312	-T 10000+	T	-	26/0323	nw -MT	Thelma	8297+	13.20 N/ 58.10 W	
26/1124	dt	U 130	Kals	ET 6715	-D: 4897+	T	-	26/	br -D	Beechwood	4897+	05.30 N/ 14.04 W	
27/0100	dt	U 156	Hartenstein	CF 8913	-D: 5941+	T	SL.119s	27/	br -D	Clan Macwirter	5941+	35.45 N/ 18.45 W	

38) *U 507* missed the *Hamaren* with four single torpedoes, then attacked with gunfire and finally fired a coup de grâce.
39) The *Hamla* departed Rio on Aug.18th for Freetown. It was assumed that she was sunk by a raider.
40) *U 605* fired five torpedoes. There was one detonation from the second after 4 min 56 sec, a double detonation after the third at 7 min 15 sec., and a fire shot up after the fourth at 6 min 50 sec. One burning and one sinking ship were observed.
41) *U 176* fired one 2-torpedo spread and heard detonations after 93 sec and 96 sec. At the same time *U 438* fired her first torpedo and heard one detonation after 91 sec and observed one ship sinking after 3 min. The second torpedo hit below the bridge of another ship, and the third missed and hit a ship beyond. Probably one ship was hit by both U-boats.

1	2	3	4	5	6	7	8	9	10	11	12	13	14	15
August 1942, cont.														
27/0254	dt	U 516	Wiebe	AL 8728	-D:11206=?	A	–	27/	br	-D	Port Jackson	9687 ?		42)
27/0620	dt	U 511	Steinhoff	EC 1299	-D 8000+	T	TAW.15	27/0535	br	-DT	San Fabian	13031+	18.09 N/ 74.38 W	
27/0623	dt	U 511	Steinhoff	EC 1299	-T 9000+	T	TAW.15	27/0535	nl	-MT	Rotterdam	8968+	18.09 N/ 74.38 W	
27/0623	dt	U 511	Steinhoff	EC 1299	-D =	T	TAW.15	27/0540	am	-DT	Esso Aruba	8773=	18.09 N/ 74.38 W	
27/1348	dt	U 517	Hartwig	AH 9823	-D 5000+	T	SG.6F	27/0846	am	-D	Chatham	5649+	51.53 N/ 55.48 W	
28/0232	dt	U 165	Hoffmann	AH 9823	-D 5000+	T	SG.6	27/2132	am	-DT	Laramie (AO)	7252=	51.44 N/ 55.40 W	
28/0232	dt	U 165	Hoffmann	AH 9823	-D 5000+	T	SG.6	27/2132	am	-D	Arlyn (s.u.)	3304+	51.53 N/ 55.48 W	
28/0232	dt	U 165	Hoffmann	AH 9823	-D 5000=	T	SG.6							43)
28/0844	dt	U 517	Hartwig	AH 9589	-D 3000+	Tf	SG.6	27/	am	-D	Arlyn (s.o.)	3304	51.53 N/ 55.48 W	43)
28/1908	dt	U 566	Remus	CF 6315	-D 7000+	T	SL.119	28/1713	nl	-D	Zuiderkerk	8424+	40.20 N/ 16.02 W	44)
28/1908	dt	U 566	Remus	CF 6315	-D 5000+	T	SL.119	28/1713	br	-D	City of Cardiff	5661+	40.20 N/ 16.02 W	44)
29/0237	dt	U 66	Markworth	ED 3323	-D: 5356+	T	–	29/0000	am	-D	Topa Topa	5356+	10.16 N/ 51.30 W	
30/0612	dt	U 564	Suhren	EE 9933	-T 9000+	TA	–	30/	nw	-MT	Vardaas	8176+	11.35 N/ 60.40 W	
30/	dt	U 162	Wattenberg	EE 74	-D: 7735+	TA	–	30/0628	am	-D	Star of Oregon	7176+	11.48 N/ 59.45 W	45)
30/0926	dt	U 66	Markworth	EE 9840	-D: 5200+	T	–	30/0844	pa	-M	Sir Huon	6049+	10.52 N/ 54.00 W	
30/1930	dt	U 66	Markworth	EE 9586	-D 4500+	T	–	30/	am	-D	West Lashaway	5637+	10.30 N/ 55.10 W	
30/	dt	U 705	Horn	BD 6852	-T 10000=?	T	–	30/	am	-DT	Jack Carnes	-----		46)
31/0154	dt	U 516	Wiebe	CE 2458	-T:12000+	TA	–	31/	am	-DT	Jack Carnes	10907+	41.35 N/ 29.01 W	46)
31/1004	dt	U 609	Rudloff	AK 2916	-D 6000+	T	SC.97	31/0905	pa	-D	Capira	5625+	57.13 N/ 33.40 W	
31/1005	dt	U 609	Rudloff	AK 2916	-D 4000+	T	SC.97	31/0905	nw	-M	Bronxville	4663+	57.13 N/ 33.40 W	
31/1417	dt	U 66	Markworth	EE 9590	-T 7000+	T	–	31/	br	-DT	Winamac	8621+	10.36 N/ 54.34 W	
/						A	–	31/	ho	-S	Sande	60+	21.22 N/ 76.00 W	
31/2104	dt	U 756	Harney	AK 2686	-------- ?		SC.97	/				-----		47)

42) *U 516* missed the *Port Jackson* with a 4-torpedo spread and hit her with two rounds of 105mm, but had to break off then.
43) The *Arlyn* was torpedoed by *U 165* and sunk by a coup de grâce from *U 517* at 08.44.
44) The *Zuiderkerk* was sunk by a British escort. The *City of Cardiff* sank on Aug.29th.
45) *U 162* reported the ship erroneously as the *Star of Orania*.
46) *U 705* heard one detonation, but observed no effect. *U 516* sank the ship with six torpedoes and gunfire.
47) *U 756* reported one attack without any details. The U-boat was sunk on Sept.1st.

1	2	3	4	5	6	7	8	9	10	11	12	13	14			15
September 1942																
1/0328	dt	U 604	Höltring	AK 2839	–D	5000=	T	SC.97	/								1)
1/0544	dt	U 609	Rudloff	AK 3727	–D	=	T	SC.97	/								2)
1/2206	dt	U 125	Folkers	EV 8123	–D	820+	T	–	1/		br –D	Ilorin	815+	05.	N/ 01.	W	
3/0050	dt	U 109	Bleichrodt	FF 3658	–D:10000+		T	–	2/		br –D	Ocean Might	7173+	00.57	N/ 04.11	W	
3/0552	dt	U 107	Gelhaus	CG 5944	–D: 4172+		T	–	3/		br –D	Hollinside	4172+	38.	N/ 09.	W	
3/0603	dt	U 107	Gelhaus	CG 5944	–D: 4393+		T	–	3/		br –D	Penrose	4393+	38.	N/ 09.	W	
3/0756	dt	U 517	Hartwig	BB 2273	–D	5000+	T	.	3/				-----				3)
3/0757	dt	U 517	Hartwig	BB 2273	–D	6500+	T	.	3/0700	ca –D		Donald Stewart	1781+	50.32	N/ 58.46	W	
4/	dt	U 171	Pfeffer	DK 5165	–T 12062+		T	–	4/0430	me –DT		Amatlan	6511+	23.27	N/ 97.30	W	
5/0233	dt	U 506	Würdemann	FF 2938	–D	5000+	T	.	5/		br –M	Myrmidon	6278+	00.45	N/ 06.27	W	
5/1615	dt	U 513	Rüggeberg	BB 6381	–D	7000+	T	–	5/0807	br –D		Saganaga	5454+	47.35	N/ 52.59	W	4)
5/1646	dt	U 513	Rüggeberg	BB 6381	–D	9000+	T	–	5/1230	ca –D		Lord Strathcona	7335+	47.35	N/ 52.59	W	4)
6/	dt	U 514	Auffermann	DD 9282	–S:	167+	A	–	6/		br –S	Helen Forsey	167+	28.35	N/ 57.35	W	
6/	dt	U 165	Hoffmann	BA 3836	–D	6000+	T	QS.33	6/2200	gr –D		Aeas	4729+	49.10	N/ 66.50	W	
6/2227	dt	U 164	Fechner	EC 5659	–D	2000+	T	–	6/2045	ca –D		John A.Holloway	1745+	14.10	N/ 71.30	W	
6/	dt	U 165	Hoffmann	BA 3836	–D	7000+	T	QS.33	6/2400				-----				5)
6/	dt	U 165	Hoffmann	BA 3836	–D	6000+	T	QS.33	6/2400	ca PY		Raccoon	358+	49.01	N/ 67.17	W	
6/2350	dt	U 109	Bleichrodt	FF 1149	–M:11449+		T	–	6/		br –M	Tuscan Star	11449+	01.34	N/ 11.39	W	
7/2157	dt	U 617	Brandi	AE 7672	–D	1500+	T	–	7/		fa –Df	Tor II	292+	62.30	N/ 18.30	W	
7/2301	dt	U 517	Hartwig	BB 1842	–D	6000+	T	QS.33	7/2100	gr –D		Mount Pindus	5729+	48.50	N/ 63.46	W	
7/2301	dt	U 517	Hartwig	BB 1842	–D	6000+	T	QS.33	7/2105	br –D		Oakton	1727+	48.50	N/ 63.46	W	
7/2302	dt	U 517	Hartwig	BB 1842	–D	6000+	T	QS.33	7/2105	gr –D		Mount Taygetus	3286+	48.50	N/ 63.46	W	

1) *U 604* heard one detonation after 1 min 15 sec, then depth charges were dropped.
2) *U 609* heard one detonation after 4 min 30 sec.
3) *U 517* heard one detonation after 2 min 35 sec and later observed burning parts of the superstructure, possibly of *D.Stewart*.
4) The *Saganaga* and *Lord Strathcona* were anchored at Wabana roads, Conception Bay, New Foundland.
5) *U 165* reported two hits on three ships of 19,000 gross tons combined.

North Sea - Atlantic

1	2	3	4	5	6	7	8	9	10	11	12	13	14	15
September 1942, cont.														
9/1516	dt	U 755	Göing	AJ 9727	AG 3000+	T	-	9/	am	PY	Muskeget (AG 48)	1827+	Norfolk - Island	6)
9/1528	dt	U 66	Markworth	DQ 1895	-M: 6390+	T	-	9/1305	sw	-M	Peiping	6390+	23.50 N/ 50.10 W	
10/0859	dt	U 513	Rüggeberg	BB 6381	-D 7000+	T	.	/						7)
10/1631	dt	U 96	Hellriegel	AK 9929	-D 5000+	T	ON.127	10/1435	be	-D	Elisabeth van Belgie	4241+	51.30 N/ 28.25 W	
10/1632	dt	U 96	Hellriegel	AK 9929	-D 5000+	T	ON.127	10/1435	br	-MT	F.J.Wolfe	12190=	51.30 N/ 28.25 W	8)
10/1633	dt	U 96	Hellriegel	AK 9929	-D 6000+	T	ON.127	10/1435	nw	-MT	Sveve	6313+	51.28 N/ 28.30 W	
10/2110	dt	U 659	Stock	AK 9893	-T 8000+	T	ON.127							
10/2110	dt	U 659	Stock	AK 9893	-D =	T	ON.127	10/1915	br	-DT	Empire Oil (s.u.)	8029=	51.23 N/ 28.13 W	9)
11/0016	dt	U 404	v.Bülow	AK 9876	-T 6000+	T	ON.127	10/2225	nw	-MT	Marit II	7417=	51.16 N/ 29.08 W	10)
11/0016	dt	U 404	v.Bülow	AK 9876	-D 5000=	T	ON.127					-----		10)
11/0020	dt	U 608	Struckmeier	AK 9885	-D 5000=	T	ON.127					-----		10)
11/0137	dt	U 218	Becker	AK 9678	-D 4000+	T	ON.127	10/2345	nw	-DT	Fjordaas	7361=	51.16 N/ 29.08 W	11)
11/0140	dt	U 218	Becker	AK 9678	-D 6000+	T	ON.127					-----		11)
11/0147	dt	U 584	Deecke	AK 9881	-T 9000+	Tf	ON.127	10/	br	-DT	Empire Oil (s.o.)	8029+	51.23 N/ 28.13 W	9)
11/0227	dt	U 92	Oelrich	AK 9875	-D 4000=?	T	ON.127					-----		12)
11/	dt	U 96	Hellriegel	BD 2394	-S +	A	-	11/	pt	-Mf	Belaes	415+	50.03 N/ 29.32 W	
11/1258	*dt*	*U 517*	*Hartwig*	*BA 3912*	*APC 3500+*	*T*	*SQ.30*	*11/*	*ca*	*PE*	*Charlottetown*	*900+*	*49.10 N/ 66.50*	
11/1925	dt	U 584	Deecke	BD 2491	-M 9000+	T	ON. 127	11/1755	nw	-M	Hindanger	4884+	49.32 N/ 32.21 W	13)

6) The weather-reporting ship *Muskeget* was reported missing after Sept.9th, en route from Norfolk to Iceland.

7) *U 513* heard one detonation after 2 min 26 sec and observed a red glare.

8) The *F.J.Wolfe* continued in a damaged state in the convoy and arrived at St.John's on Sept.19th.

9) The *Empire Oil* was hit by two torpedoes from *U 659* at the bow and stern and stopped. She was sunk by two coups de grâce from *U 584*.

10) *U 404* observed hits after 3 min 12 sec and 3 min 32 sec with water columns. *U 608* observed one hit after 28 sec. Probably only one torpedo of *U 404* hit the *Marit II*. She was damaged but joined the convoy again on Sept.12th and port on Sept.16th.

11) The *Fjordaas* was damaged and had to return to the Clyde.

12) *U 92* heard one torpedo hit without detonation, probably a dud.

13) The damaged *Hindanger* was sunk at 23.12 CGT by HMCS *Amherst* by gunfire and depth charges.

1	2	3	4	5	6	7	8	9	10	11	12	13	14	15
September 1942, cont.														
11/2237 dt	U 514	Auffermann	EE 7135	-D	7500+	T	-	11/	ca	-D	Cornwallis	5458=	13.05 N/ 59.36 W	14)
11/2237 dt	U 514	Auffermann	EE 7135	-D	4500+	T	-	11/						14)
12/0021 dt	U 380	Röther	BD 2752	-D	5000=	T	ON.127	11/						15)
12/0021 dt	U 380	Röther	BD 2752	-T	9000=	T	ON.127	11/						15)
12/0021 dt	U 380	Röther	BD 2752	-D	5000=	T	ON.127	11/						15)
12/0105 dt	U 211	Hauser	BD 2756	-T	5000+	T	ON.127	11/2314	br	DW	Hektoria (s.u.)	13797=	48.55 N/ 33.38 W	16)
12/0105 dt	U 211	Hauser	BD 2756	-D	5000=	T	ON.127	11/2313	br	-D	Empire Moonbeam	6849=	48.55 N/ 33.38 W	16)
12/0215 dt	*U 92*	*Oelrich*	*BD 2743*	*DD*	*1350=*	*T*	*ON.127*	*12/*	*ca*	*DD*	*Ottawa (?)*	*-----*		*17)*
12/0332 dt	U 68	Merten	FF 8588	-D:	5296+	TA	-	12/	br	-M	Trevilley	5296+	04.30 S/ 07.50 W	
12/0351 dt	U 608	Struckmeier	BD 2744	-DW	13797+	Tf	ON.127s	12/	br	DW	Hektoria (s.o.)	13797+	48.55 N/ 33.38 W	16)
12/0459 dt	U 608	Struckmeier	BD 2744	-D	10000+	Tf	ON.127s	12/0423	br	-D	Empire Moonbeam	6849+	48.55 N/ 33.38 W	16)
12/0534 dt	U 608	Struckmeier	BD 2744	-D	5000+	Tf	ON.127s	/						18)
12/0617 dt	U 404	v.Bülow	BD 1994	-D	5000+	T	ON.127	12/0624	nw	-MT	Daghild	9272=	49.02 N/ 33.30 W	19)
12/0617 dt	U 404	v.Bülow	BD 1994	-D	6000+	T	ON.127	/						19)
12/0617 dt	U 404	v.Bülow	BD 1994	-D	6000+	T	ON.127	/						19)
12/1000 dt	U 515	Henke	ED 9992	-T:	10444+	T	-	12/0705	pa	-MT	Stanvac Melbourne	10013+	10.30 N/ 60.20 W	
12/1041 dt	U 515	Henke	ED 9992	-D:	4668+	T	-	12/1000	nl	-MT	Woensdrecht	4668=§	10.27 N/ 60.17 W	20)
12/nm dt	U 512	Schultze	DQ 6417	-T:	10600+	A	-	12/2335	am	-DT	Patrick J.Hurley	10865+	22.59 N/ 46.15 W	
12/2207 dt	U 156	Hartenstein	FF 7721	AP:	19695+	T	-	12/	br	AP	Laconia	19695+	05.05 S/ 11.38 W	21)

14) The *Cornwallis* and one unidentified ship were sunk by three torpedoes each on the sealanes off Barbados.

15) *U 380* fired a 4-torpedo spread and heard three detonations after 4 min 40 sec - No optical observations.

16) *U 211* hit the *Hektoria* with two, and the *Empire Moonbeam* with one torpedo, but both ships were finally sunk by *U 608*.

17) *U 92* fired a 4-torpedo spread and heard two detonations after 46 sec on a destroyer of the *A-I*-class.

18) *U 608* sank a third damaged ship with two coups de grâce. Possibly the *Hindanger* (see note 13) was not really sunk before.

19) *U 404* heard detonations after single shots at 2 min 56 sec, 2 min 15 sec, and 3 min 30 sec. There were sinking noises.

20) The *Woensdrecht* was taken into port with four torpedo hits. She was a total loss.

21) The *Laconia* transported about 1500 Italian POWs. When U-boats tried to save as many survivors as possible, they were attacked by American planes from Ascension: the "Laconia" Incident.

1	2	3	4	5	6	7	8	9	10	11	12	13	14	15

September 1942, cont.

1	2	3	4	5	6	7	8	9	10 11	12	13	14	15
13/0058 dt	U 506	Würdemann	EU 7877	-D: 5244+	T	-	12/	sw -M	Lima	4959+	02.35 N/ 11.22 W	
13/0227 dt	U 515	Henke	EE 7772	-D: 8000+	T	-	13/0040 br -D		Ocean Vanguard	7174+	10.43 N/ 60.11 W	
13/0622 dt	U 558	Krech	ED 8375	-D 7000+	T	TAG.5	13/0440 nl -D		Suriname	7915+	12.07 N/ 63.32 W	
13/0623 dt	U 558	Krech	ED 8375	-T 7000=	T	TAG.5	13/					22)
13/0623 dt	U 558	Krech	ED 8375	-D 5000=	T	TAG.5	13/0441 br -M		Empire Lugard	7241+	12.07 N/ 63.32 W	
13/0634 dt	U 515	Henke	EE 7778	-D: 3785+	T	-	13/0405 pa -D		Nimba	1854+	10.41 N/ 60.24 W	23)
13/0828 dt	U 558	Krech	ED 8296	-T 8000+	T	TAG.5	13/0600 nw -MT		Vilja	6672+	12.15 N/ 62.52 W	
13/1436 dt	U 594	Mumm	BD 6316	-D: 6131+	T	ON.127s	13/	pa -D	Stone Street	6074+	48.18 N/ 39.43 W	
14/0205 dt	*U 91*	*Walkerling*	*BC 6191*	*DD 1375+*	*T*	*ON.127*	*14/0003 ca DD*		*Ottawa*	*1375+*	*47.55 N/ 43.27 W*	*24)*
14/0215 dt	*U 91*	*Walkerling*	*BC 6191*	*DD +*	*T*	*ON.127*	*14/ ca DD*		*Ottawa*			*24)*
14/0255 dt	U 92	Oelrich	BC 6145	-D 8000=	T	ON.127	14/			-----		25)
14/0255 dt	U 92	Oelrich	BC 6145	-D 6000=	T	ON.127	14/			-----		25)
14/0255 dt	U 92	Oelrich	BC 6145	-D 3000=	T	ON.127	14/			-----		25)
14/1410 dt	U 515	Henke	EO 1121	-D 6000+	TA	-	14/1220 br -D		Harborough	5415+	10.03 N/ 60.20 W	
15/0058 dt	U 68	Merten	FF 8479	-D: 6811+	T	-	14/	nl -D	Breedijk	6861+	05.05 S/ 08.54 W	
15/0714 dt	U 515	Henke	EO 1129	-D: 4801+	T	-	15/0530 nw -M		Sörholt	4801+	10.45 N/ 60.00 W	
15/1517 dt	U 514	Auffermann	ED 9952	-D: 3297+	TA	-	15/1525 br -D		Kioto	3297+	11.05 N/ 60.46 W	
15/1833 dt	U 517	Hartwig	BB 1763	-D 5500+	T	SQ.36	15/1630 nl -D		Saturnus	2741+	48.49 N/ 64.06 W	
15/1833 dt	U 517	Hartwig	BB 1763	-D 5500=	T	SQ.36	15/1636 nw -D		Inger Elisabeth	2166+	48.49 N/ 64.06 W	
16/0625 dt	U 515	Henke	EO 4320	-D: 7000+	TA	-	16/0325 am -D		Mae	5607+	08.03 N/ 58.13 W	23)
16/früh dt	U 165	Hoffmann	BA 3883	-D 6000+	T	SQ.36	16/0910 br -D		Essex Lance	6625=	49.03 N/ 67.08 W	
16/früh dt	U 165	Hoffmann	BA 3883	---------	T	SQ.36	16/0915 gr -D		Joannis	3667+	49.10 N/ 67.05 W	
16/früh dt	U 165	Hoffmann	BA 3883	---------	T	SQ.36	16/	am -D	Pan York	4570=	49.10 N/ 67.05 W	

22) *U 558* observed hits on three ships after 1 min 50 sec, 2 min 40 sec, and 1 min 59 sec. No optical confirmation because of ASW operations.
23) *U 515* reported the *Nimba* erroneously as Norwegian *Senta*, the *Mae* as the American *Mary*.
24) *U 91* assumed that she hit two destroyers, but in reality only the *Ottawa* was hit by two torpedoes.
25) *U 92* heard detonations after 2 min 32 sec, 2 min 35 sec, and 3 min 47 sec.

1	2	3	4	5	6	7	8	9	10 11	12	13	14	15

September 1942, cont.

1	2	3	4	5	6	7	8	9	10 11	12	13	14	15
16/1059	dt	U 558	Krech	ED 9995	-D 2000+	T	-	16/0900	am -D	Commercial Trader	2606+	10.30 N/ 60.15 W	
17/1314	dt	U 109	Bleichrodt	EH 3258	-D: 5221+	T	-	17/	br -D	Peterton	5221+	18.45 N/ 29.15 W	
18/0121	dt	U 380	Röther	BC 9777	-D: 3000+	T	ON.129	18/	nw -M	Olaf Fostenes	2994+	44.56 N/ 41.05 W	
18/1352	dt	U 175	Bruns	EO 1815	-T 3000+	T	-	18/1200	ca -D	Norfolk	1901+	08.36 N/ 58.13 W	
19/0301	dt	U 552	Popp	CG 5832	APC +	T	-	19/	br APC	Alouette	520+	75m W Sesimbra	
19/0648	dt	U 516	Wiebe	EE 7545	-D 6000+	T	-	15/	am -M	Wichita	6174+	15. N/ 54. W	26)
19/	dt	U 512	Schultze	EE 4423	-D 7500+	T	-	19/	sp -D	Monte Gorbea	3720+	14.55 N/ 60.00 W	
19/1546	dt	U 156	Hartenstein	FE 4925	-D: 4745+	TA	-	19/	br -D	Quebec City	4745+	02.12 S/ 17.36 W	
20/0815	dt	U 515	Henke	EO 2470	-D: 4838+	T	-	20/	br -D	Reedpool	4838+	08.58 N/ 57.34 W	
(10. 9.)	dt	U 69	Gräf	CA 8153	---------	M	KN.201	20/	am -DT	Petrofuel	-----	37.10 N/ 74.21 W	27)
20/1510	*dt*	*U 373*	*Loeser*	*AK 4215*	*-D =? *	*T*	*SC.100*	*20/*	*ca PE*	*Rosthern*	*------*		*28)*
20/1517	dt	U 596	Jahn	AK 4218	-D 6000+	T	SC.100	20/	br -D	Empire Hartlebeeste	5676+	56.20 N/ 38.10 W	28)
20/1518	dt	U 596	Jahn	AK 4218	-D 5000=	T	SC.100	/			-----		28)
21/0640	dt	U 175	Bruns	EO 1865	-D 5000+	T	-	21/	jg -D	Predsednik Kopajtić	1798+	08.30 N/ 59.30 W	
23/0019	dt	U 617	Brandi	AK 2565	-T 9000+	T	SC.100	22/	br -MT	Athelsultan	8882+	58.42 N/ 33.38 W	
23/0026	dt	U 211	Hauser	AK 7114	-T 10000+	T	-	22/	am -MT	Esso Williamsburg	11237+	53.12 N/ 41.00 W	
23/0142	dt	U 617	Brandi	AK 2565	-D 5500+	T	SC.100s	22/	br -D	Tennessee	2342+	58.40 N/ 33.41 W	
23/früh	dt	U 582	Schulte	BD 5959	-D: 2993+	T	ON.131 ?	24/	nw -M	Vibran	2993+	42.45 N/ 42.45 W	
23/0619	dt	U 515	Henke	EO 1410	-D: 2412+	T	-	23/	nw -D	Lindvangen	2412+	09.20 N/ 60.10 W	

26) The *Wichita* was reported missing after Sept.15th. The ship sunk was on course 220°, and sank in a few seconds.

27) The *Petrofuel* reported a detonation of a mine but was not damaged. Her signal was intercepted by the German B-Dienst.

28) *U 373* fired a 3-torpedo spread against the corvette HMCS *Rosthern*, which missed. After 3 min 55 sec a detonation was heard, and *U 373* assumed one hit on a ship in the convoy. In reality this was probably the hit of *U 596* against the *Empire Hartlebeeste*. One additional hit was heard after 2 min 07 sec and then sinking noises.

1	2	3	4	5	6	7	8	9	10	11	12	13	14	15

September 1942, cont.

23/1103	dt	U 515	Henke	EO 1490	-D	4500+	T	-	23/0912	am	-D	Antinous	6034=	0858 N/ 59.33 W	29)
24/	dt	U 512	Schultze	EO 1419	-D	8000+	Tf	-	23/1645	am	-D	Antinous	6034+		
23/1358	dt	U 617	Brandi	AK 2257	-D:	3600+	T	SC.100s	22/	be	-D	Roumanie	3563+	58.10 N/ 28.20 W	
23/2334	dt	U 125	Folkers	ET 7333	-D:	5335+	T	-	23/	br	-D	Bruyere	5335+	04.55 N/ 17.16 W	
24/0031	dt	U 356	Wallas	AK 2864	-D	5000+	T	ON.131s	/						30)
24/0037	dt	U 258	Mässenhausen	AK 3561	-D	5000=	T	SC.100	/						31)
24/0037	dt	U 258	Mässenhausen	AK 3561	-D	5000=	T	SC.100	/						31)
24/0144	dt	U 432	Schultze	AK 2721	-D:	5868+	T	SC.100s	23/2351	am	-D	Pennmar	5868+	58.25 N/ 32.15 W	
24/	dt	U 619	Makowski	AK 6119	-D	8000+	TA	ON.131s	24/	am	-D	John Winthrop	7176+	56. N/ 31. W	
24/0924	dt	U 175	Bruns	EO 1396	-D	6000+	T	-	24/0730	am	-D	West Chetac	5627+	08.45 N/ 57.00 W	
25/1616	dt	U 442	Hesse	AE 8519	-D	7000+	T	.	25/	br	-D	Empire Bell	1744+	62.19 N/ 15.27 W	
25/1637	dt	U 216	Schultz	AK 6656	-D	19000+	T	RB.1	25/	br	-D	Boston	4989+	54.23 N/ 27.54 W	32)
25/2357	dt	U 96	Hellriegel	AL 4483	-D	17702+	T	RB.1	25/	br	-D	New York	4989+	54.34 N/ 25.44 W	32)
26/0125	dt	U 91	Walkerling	AL 4499	-D	5000=	T	RB.1	/				-----		33)
26/1036	*dt*	*U 404*	*v.Bülow*	*AL 5472*	*DD*	*+*	*T*	*RB.1*	*26/*	*br*	*DD*	*Veteran*	*1120+*	*54.34 N/ 25.44 W*	
26/1036	dt	U 404	v.Bülow	AL 5472	-D	=?	T	RB.1	/				-----		34)
26/1225	dt	U 175	Bruns	EO 1495	-D	3000+	T	-	26/1006	pa	-D	Tambour	1811+	08.50 N/ 59.50 W	
26/1613	dt	U 617	Brandi	AK 6382	-D	5000=?	T	ON.131	/				-----		35)
26/1618	dt	U 617	Brandi	AK 6382	-D	5000+	T	ON.131	/						35)
26/1621	dt	U 617	Brandi	AK 6382	-D	3000+	T	ON.131	/						35)

---

29) The *Antinous* was hit by one torpedo from *U 515*, and was subsequently abandoned and then sunk by a coup de grâce of *U 512*.
30) *U 356* torpedoed a ship steaming independently, but the coup de grâce missed, and the ship was lost from sight after six hours.
31) After firing a 4-torpedo spread, *U 258* heard detonations after run times of 5 min 15 sec, 6 min 5 sec, and 6 min 25 sec.
32) The Great Lakes ships *Boston* and *New York* were erroneously reported as passenger liners of the *Viceroy of India*- and *Reina del Pacifico*-type because of their high superstructure and two funnels.
33) *U 91* heard one heavy detonation after 4 min 30 sec near the target.
34) *U 404* fired a 3-torpedo spread at the *Veteran*. She was hit after 53 sec and 57 sec. After 1 min 54 sec there was one additional detonation, and a hit on another ship in the convoy was assumed.
35) *U 617* heard the torpedo hit after 62 sec but it did not detonate (dud). Then after 42 sec and after 65 sec there were two certain detonations and sinking noises.

1	2	3	4	5	6	7	8	9	10	11	12	13	14	15
September 1942, cont.														
26/2325 dt		U 619	Makowski	AL 6527	-D	10000+	T	RB.1	26/		br -D	Yorktown	1547+	55.10 N/ 18.50 W	36)
28/0110 dt		U 514	Auffermann	FA 2948	-D	4000+	T	*Roe*	27/2010		bz -D	Ozório	2730+	00.03N/ 47.45 W	37)
28/0215 dt		U 514	Auffermann	FA 2831	-D	6000+	T	*Roe*	27/2115		bz -D	Lages	5472+	00.17 N/ 47.53 W	37)
28/0915 dt		U 516	Wiebe	EO 6595	-D	1500+	A	-	28/0430		bz -D	Antonico	1223+	05.30 N/ 53.30 W	
28/1152 dt		U 175	Bruns	EO 1446	-D	4500+	T	-	28/0850		am -D	Alcoa Mariner	5590+	08.57 N/ 60.08 W	38)
29/0112 dt		U 332	Liebe	EE 8184	-D:	5886+	T	-	29/2228		br -D	Registan	6008+	12.37 N/ 57.10 W	
29/0337 dt		U 202	Poser	ED 9652	-D	6000=?	T	-	/						39)
29/1020 dt		U 517	Hartwig	BB 1872	-D		=	T	-	/					40)
29/1255 dt		U 125	Folkers	ET 8986	-D:	3391+	T	-	29/		br -D	Baron Ogilvy	3391+	02.30 N/ 14.30 W	
29/2058 dt		U 610	v.Freyberg	AL 4244	-D	4000+	T	SC.101s	28/		br -D	Lifland	2254+	56.40 N/ 30.30 W	
29/2225 dt		U 513	Rüggeberg	BB 6386	-D	6000+	T	-	29/		br -D	Ocean Vagabond	7174=	47.31 N/ 52.27 W	
30/0055 dt		U 125	Folkers	ET 9439	-D:	5963+	T	-	29/		br -D	Empire Avocet	6015+	04.05 N/ 13.23 W	
30/0410 dt		U 516	Wiebe	EO 5367	-D	5000+	TA	-	30/0131		br -D	Alipore	5273+	07.09 N/ 54.23 W	
30/0055 dt		U 125	Folkers	ET 9434	-D:	5963+	TA	-	29/2200		br -D	Empire Avocet	6015+	04.05 N/ 13.23 W	
30/2347 dt		U 506	Würdemann	ET 8831	-D:	6637+	T	-	30/		br -D	Siam II	6637+	03.25 N/ 15.46 W	
October 1942														
1/0938 dt		U 175	Bruns	EO 1452	-D	6000+	T	-	1/0740		br -D	Empire Tennyson	2880+	09.27 N/ 60.05 W	1)
1/2241 dt		U 202	Poser	EO 1465	APC	3000+	T	-	1/2200		nl -D	Achilles	1815+	09.06 N/ 59.48 W	
2/0833 dt		U 201	Rosenberg	EO 1472	-D	3000+	T	-	2/0635		am -D	Alcoa Transport	2084+	09.03 N/ 60.10 W	

---

36) The Great Lakes steamer *Yorktown* was erroneously reported as a passenger steamer of the *Derbyshire* type (s.note 32).
37) The *Ozório* and *Lages* (armed with a single 120mm gun) settled to the bottom and were considered total losses. They were under escort by USS *Roe*.
38) The *Alcoa Mariner* sank to the bottom after two hits and was considered a total loss.
39) *U 202* heard a hit without detonation after 1 min 40 sec. Probably a dud.
40) *U 517* heard one detonation after 9 min 40 sec and assumed a hit, but in reality it was probably a detonation at the end of the run.
 1) *U 175* reported the ship erroneously as the *Tennessee*.

North Sea - Atlantic

1	2	3	4	5	6	7	8	9	10	11	12	13	14	15
October 1942, cont.														
2/1054	dt	U 175	Bruns	EO 1455	-D 5000+	T	-	2/0800	pa	-D	Aneroid	5074+	08.24 N/ 59.12 W	
3/1432	dt	U 254	Loewe	AK 5561	-T 8000+	T	HX.209	3/1640	am	-DT	Robert H.Colley	11651+	59.06 N/ 26.18 W	
4/1111	dt	U 175	Bruns	EO 1829	-D 3500+	T	-	4/0800	am	-D	Caribstar	2592+	08.35 N/ 59.37 W	2)
5/0606	dt	U 175	Bruns	EO 1575	-D 4000+	TA	-	5/0410	am	-D	William A.McKenney	6153+	08.35 N/ 59.20 W	
6/0220	it	BARBARIGO	Grossi	02n/14w	BB 33000+	T	-	6/	br	PE	Petunia	------		3)
6/	dt	U 333	Cremer	ET 2989	PE =	A	-	6/	br	PE	Crocus	925=	60m SW Freetown	4)
7/0029	dt	U 202	Poser	EP 1347	-D:10800+	T	-	8/0030	am	-D	John Carter Rose	7191+	10.27 N/ 45.37 W	5)
8/0232	dt	U 201	Rosenberg	EF 9795	-D:10800+	TA	-							
7/0080	dt	U 107	Gelhaus	ET 5562	-D:14943+	T	-	6/	br	-D	Andalucia Star	14943+	06.38 N/ 15.46 W	
8/1725	dt	U 125	Folkers	ET 7357	-D: 4412+	T	-	8/	br	-D	Glendene	4412+	04.29 N/ 17.41 W	
9/0123	dt	U 201	Rosenberg	EF 9773	-D 8300+	TA	-	8/2225	nl	-D	Flensburg	6421+	10.45 N/ 46.48 W	
9/0607	dt	U 69	Gräf	BA 3845	-D 5000=	T	.	9/						6)
9/0609	dt	U 69	Gräf	BA 3845	-D 4000+	T	.	9/0413	ca	-D	Carolus	2375+	48.47 N/ 68.10 W	
9/0705	it	ARCHIMEDE	Saccardo	04n/21w	-D:20000+	T	-	9/	br	-D	Oronsay	20043+	04.29 N/ 20.52 W	
9/2101	dt	U 254	Loewe	AK 3589	-D 6000+	T	-	9/	br	-D	Pennington Court	6098+	58.18 N/ 27.55 W	
10/0014	it	ARCHIMEDE	Saccardo	04n/20w	-D:16991=	T	-	10/	br	-D	Nea Hellas	------	04.05 N/ 20.15 W	
10/0819	dt	U 178	Ibbeken	FM 3734	-D:20119+	T	-	10/	br	-D	Duchess of Atholl	20119+	07.03 S/ 11.12 W	
11/0458	dt	U 87	Berger	ET 5558	-D: 7392+	T	-	11/	br	-D	Agapenor	7392+	06.53 N/ 15.23 W	
11/1147	dt	U 106	Rasch	BB 5437	-D 5000+	T	-	11/1500	br	-D	Waterton	2140+	47.07 N/ 59.54 W	
11/1959	dt	U 615	Kapitzky	AJ 8898	-D: 4219+	T	ONS.136s	11/	pa	-D	El Lago	4221+	44. N/ 40. W	
11/2240	dt	U 597	Bopst	AK 6321	-D 7000+	T	ON .	11/						7)

2) The *Caribstar*'s stern sank to the bottom and was considered a total loss. - 3) The *Barbarigo* reported the corvette HMS
  Petunia erroneously as a battleship of the U.S. *Mississippi* class, and assumed detonations of depth charges as hits.
4) *U 333* had a gun duel with the corvette HMS *Crocus*. Both ships had slight damages and personnel losses.
5) The *John Carter Rose* was first hit by a dud from *U 201*, and was then hit by two torpedoes from *U 202*. She finally sank after
  a second dud-hit by a torpedo coup de grâce and gunfire from *U 201*.
6) *U 69* heard one detonation after 6 min. - 7) *U 597* heard two detonations and sinking noises.

1	2	3	4	5	6	7	8	9	10	11	12	13	14	15
October 1942, cont.														
12/0010	dt	U 514	Auffermann	EP 4761	-D: 5700+	T	-	11/2212	am	-D	Steel Scientist	5688+	05.48 N/ 51.50 W	
12/1637	*dt*	*U 382*	*Juli*	*AK 6211*	*DD 1190+*	*T*	*ON.*							*8)*
12/0338	dt	U 706	v.Zitzewitz	AL 4478	-D: 4300+	T	ONS.136	13/	br	-D	Stornest	4265+	54.25 N/ 27.42 W	
13/0556	dt	U 221	Trojer	AJ 9145	-D 4000+	T	SC.104	13/0425	nw	-D	Fagersten	2342+	53.05 N/ 44.06 W	9)
13/0622	dt	U 221	Trojer	AJ 9146	-D 6000+	T	SC.104	13/0508	br	-D	Ashworth	5227+	53.05 N/ 44.06 W	9)
13/0623	dt	U 221	Trojer	AJ 9146	-D 5000+	T	SC.104	13/0508	nw	-D	Senta	3785+	53. N/ 44. W	9)
13/0710	dt	U 221	Trojer	AJ 9154	-D 5000+	T	SC.104							9)
14/0004	dt	U 221	Trojer	AJ 9327	-D 3000+	T	SC.104							10)
14/0012	dt	U 221	Trojer	AJ 9327	-D 6000+	T	SC.104	13/2215	am	-D	Susana	5929+	53.41 N/ 41.23 W	10)
14/0013	dt	U 221	Trojer	AJ 9327	-D 4000+	T	SC.104							10)
14/0032	dt	U 221	Trojer	AJ 9327	-DW14547+	T	SC.104	13/2230	br	-DW	Southern Empress	12398+	53.40 N/ 40.40 W	10)
14/0040	dt	U 607	Mengersen	AJ 9321	-D 7000+	T	SC.104	13/2330	gr	-D	Nellie	4826+	53.41 N/ 41.23 W	
14/	dt	U 661	v.Lilienfeldt	-------	---------	T	SC.104	13/2337	jg	-D	Nikolina Matković	3672+	53.41 N/ 41.23 W	
14/0429	dt	U 618	Baberg	AJ 9323	-D 6000+	T	SC.104	14/0230	br	-D	Empire Mersey	5791+	54. N/ 40.15 W	11)
14/0429	dt	U 618	Baberg	AJ 9323	-D 5000+	T	SC.104							11)
14/0429	dt	U 618	Baberg	AJ 9323	-D 5000=	T	SC.104							11)
14/0821	dt	U 69	Gräf	BB 5198	-D 6500+	T	.	14/	br	-D	Caribou	2222+	47.19 N/ 59.29 W	
15/0025	dt	U 129	Witt	DQ 1153	-D: 5542+	T	-	15/0220	nw	-M	Trafalgar	5542+	25.30 N/ 52.00 W	
15/1029	dt	U 410	Sturm	AK 5733	-D 3000+	Tf	SC.104s							12)
16/1321	dt	U 704	Keßler	AL 7129	-D 5000+	T	ONS.136	16/	br	-D	Newton Pine	4212+	55. N/ 30. W	

8) *U 382* fired a 3-torpedo spread against a "flush-deck" destroyer and heard a detonation after 1 min 50 sec and a boiler explosion after 14 min. 9) *U 221* observed the sinking of two ships after 10 and 20 min. The third ship was burning, and the fourth was down by the stern. It's not clear which torpedoes hit the first three ships.

10) *U 221* observed the first ship to have a broken back and be sinking after 10 min. The second had developed a list, and sinking noises were heard from the third. If the Allied times are correct, only the *Susana* was hit during these attacks, but the positions indicated show that in addition the *Nellie* and *N.Matković* were hit by *U 221*. The *Southern Empress* was later sunk by a coup de grâce from *U 221*.

11) *U 618* observed three hits from a 4-torpedo spread. Probably all three torpedoes hit the *E.Mersey*.

12) *U 410* sank one damaged ship, probably one of the ships torpedoed by *U 221*.

1	2	3	4	5	6	7	8	9	10	11	12	13	14	15
October 1942, cont.														
16/2120 dt	U 160		Lassen	ED 9954	-D 4000+	T	.	16/1920	br	-D	Castle Harbour	730+	11.00 N/ 61.10 W	
16/2120 dt	U 160		Lassen	ED 9954	-D 6000+	T	.	16/2320	am	-D	Winona	6197=	11. N/ 61.10 W	
18/0336 dt	U 618		Baberg	BD 3441	-D 9000+	T	ON.137s	18/0145	am	-D	Angelina	4772+	49.39 N/ 30.20 W	
19/0823 dt	U 332		Liebe	EE 6782	-D: 4996+	T	-	19/	br	-M	Rothley	4996+	13.34 N/ 54.34 W	
19/1446 dt	U 610		v.Freyberg	BD 2862	-D: 5700+	T	ON.137s	19/1750	am	-D	Steel Navigator	5719+	49.45 N/ 31.20 W	
20/0056 dt	U 69		Gräf	BB 6498	-D: 7800=?	T	-	20/	am	-D	Rosa Castle	-----	BB 6730	13)
22/2145 dt	U 443		v.Puttkamer	BD 3544	-D 5000=?	T	ON.139							14)
22/2148 dt	U 443		v.Puttkamer	BD 3544	-D 10528+	T	ON.139	22/2100	br	-D	Winnipeg II	9807+	49.51 N/ 27.58 W	
22/2150 dt	U 443		v.Puttkamer	BD 3544	-T 8000+	T	ON.139	22/2100	br	-MT	Donax	8036+	49.51 N/ 27.58 W	
23/0053 dt	U 621		Schünemann	AK 6922	-D 5600+	T	ONS.136s	22/	br	-D	Empire Thurnstone	6113+	54.40 N/ 28.00 W	
23/0540 dt	U 129		Witt	EE 5629	-D: 6870+	T	-	23/0430	am	-D	Reuben Tipton	6829+	14.33 N/ 54.51 W	
23/0756 dt	U 161		Achilles	FH 9678	DD 1806=	T	-	23/	br	CL	Phoebe	5450=	6m 282°Pt.Noire	15)
23/1021 dt	U 87		Berger	ET 5241	CL 4000=?	T	-					-----		16)
23/1852 dt	U 615		Kapitzky	BD 3984	-D:12656+	T	-	23/1613	br	-M	Empire Star	12656+	48.14 N/ 26.22 W	
24/ dt	U 516		Wiebe	EF 8353	-D: 5780+	T	-	24/0510	br	-D	Holmpark	5780+	13.11 N/ 47.00 W	
24/1324 dt	U 383		Kremser	AE 8449	-D 1500+	T	-							17)
25/1519 dt	U 67		Müller-Stöckheim	EE 6847	-M 5000+	T	-	25/	nw	-M	Primero	4414+	13.38 N/ 53.55 W	
26/1740 dt	U 509		Witte	DH 7555	-T 4000=	T	SL.125	26/1443	br	-MT	Anglo Maersk	7705=	27.50 N/ 22.15 W	18)
27/2106 dt	U 604		Höltring	DH 8547	-T 9000+	T	SL.125s	27/1810	br	-MT	Anglo Maersk	7705+	27.15 N/ 17.55 W	18)

13) U 69 reported a probable dud. The B-Dienst intercepted a SSS-report from the *Rosa Castle*.
14) U 443 heard after firing the first 2-torpedo spread two hits without detonations after 1 min 14 sec. Probably duds.
15) U 161 reported one destroyer of the *Balch* type torpedoed and observed the lowering of boats.
16) U 87 heard after 2 min 45 sec hits without detonations, probably duds fired against an unidentified naval vessel.
17) U 383 heard after 60 sec a detonation on an assumed Icelandic steamer and then sinking noises. Later wreckage was observed.
    Possibly the British trawler *Northern Spray* was hit (see Oct.30th).
18) U 509 observed a hit after 1 min 33 sec, but without significant effect. The ship was later sunk by U 604.

1	2	3	4	5	6	7	8	9	10	11	12	13	14	15
October 1942, cont.														
27/2233	dt	U 509	Witte	DH 7531	–D	9000+	T	SL.125	27/1935	br	–D	Pacific Star	7951+	29.15 N/ 20.57 W	
27/2238	dt	U 509	Witte	DH 7531	–D	6500+	T	SL.125	27/1935	br	–M	Stentor	6148+	29.13 N/ 20.53 W	
27/2303	dt	U 436	Seibicke	AK 6725	–D	6000+	T	HX.212	27/	nw	–DT	Frontenac	7350=	54.20 N/ 31.40 W	19)
27/2308	dt	U 436	Seibicke	AK 6725	–D	4000=	T	HX.212							19)
27/2308	dt	U 436	Seibicke	AK 6725	–DT	10000+	T	HX.212	27/2010	br	–DT	Sourabaya	10107+	54.32 N/ 31.02 W	19)
27/2309	dt	U 436	Seibicke	AK 6725	–D	7000=	T	HX.212	27/2010	am	–DT	Gurney E.Newlin	8225=	54.32 N/ 31.02 W	19)
27/2311	dt	U 436	Seibicke	AK 6725	–D	7000=	T	HX.212				(s.u.)			19)
28/0125	dt	U 621	Schünemann	AK 6498	–D	6000=	T	HX.212							20)
28/0128	dt	U 621	Schünemann	AK 6498	–D	5000=	T	HX.212							20)
28/0537	dt	U 606	Döhler	AK 6578	–DW	13600+	T	HX.212	28/	nw	–DW	Kosmos II (s.u.)	16966=	54.40 N/ 29.00 W	21)
28/0902	dt	U 606	Döhler	AK 6584	–T	6000+	T	HX.212	27/	am	–DT	Gurney E.Newlin	8225+	54.32 N/ 31.02 W	19)
28/2200	dt	U 509	Witte	DH 4958	–T	9000=?	T	SL.125							22)
28/2200	dt	U 509	Witte	DH 4958	–D	6000=?	T	SL.125							22)
28/2206	dt	U 509	Witte	DH 4958	–D	7000+	T	SL.125	28/1905	br	–D	Nagpore	5283+	31.30 N/ 19.35 W	22)
28/2209	dt	U 509	Witte	DH 4958	–D	5000+	T	SL.125	28/1910	br	–M	Hopecastle(s.u.)	5178=	31.39 N/ 19.35 W	22)
29/0015	dt	U 224	Kosbadt	AL 4552	–D	4000+	T	HX.212s	29/	ca	–D	Bic Island	4000+	55.05 N/ 23.27 W	
29/0305	dt	U 624	Graf v.Soden	AL 5441	–DW	14547≠	T	HX.212s	29/	nw	–DW	Kosmos II (s.o.)	16966+	54.40 N/ 29.00 W	21)
29/0452	dt	U 203	Kottmann	DH 5142	–D:	5283+	T	SL.125s	29/	br	–M	Hopecastle(S.o.)	5178+	31.39 N/ 19.35 W	22)
29/0757	dt	U 624	Graf v.Soden	AL 5428	–DT	6000+	T	HX.212	29/0525	am	–DT	Pan New York	7701+	54.58 N/ 23.56 W	
29/	dt	?							29/0920	pa	–D	Macabi	2802+	off Trinidad	23)
29/2118	dt	UD 5	Mahn	DS 9835	–D:	8000+	T	–	29/	br	–D	Primrose Hill	7628+	18.58 N/ 28.40 W	

19) *U 436* heard detonations after 59 sec, 2 min 24 sec, 1 min 16 sec, 1 min 1 sec, and 60 sec. Hits 1, 3, and 4 were observed.
The *Frontenac* reached port, and the *Gurney E.Newlin* was damaged and later sunk by coup de grâce of *U 606*.
20) *U 621* missed the targets and heard detonations at the end of the run at 11 min 8 sec and 12 min 5 sec, assumed to be hits on
ships behind the targets. - 21) The *Kosmos II* was burning after *U 606*'s hit and later sunk by *U 624*.
22) *U 509* heard detonations after 1 min 34 sec and 1 min 28 sec on unintended targets and then observed two hits on two ships.
One had its back broken, and one exploded. From British records, the *Nagpore* sank and the *Hopecastle* was left damaged and was
sunk later on by a second attack. But *U 203* identified its target during its torpedo and gunfire attack as the *Nasoore*.
23) The *Macabi* was reported missing after Oct.29th in the area off Trinidad. There is no report from a U-boat confirming this
attack.

1	2	3	4	5	6	7	8	9	10	11	12	13	14	15
October 1942, cont.														
29/2118	dt	U 436	Seibicke	AL 5482	-D	7000+	T	HX.212	29/		br -D	Barrwhin	4998+	55.02 N/ 22.45 W	
29/2213	dt	U 575	Heydemann	BD 3761	-D:11330+		T	-	29/		br -M	Abosso	11330+	48.30 N/ 28.50 W	
29/2216	dt	U 509	Witte	DH 5146	-D	8000+	T	SL.125	29/1930		br -D	Corinaldo (s.u.)	7131=	33.20 N/ 18.12 W	24)
30/0000	dt	U 509	Witte	DH 5152	-D	10000+	T	SL.125	29/2115		br -M	Brittany	4772+	33.29 N/ 18.32 W.	
30/0011	dt	U 129	Witt	EE 6413	-D: 5620+		T	-	29/2215		am -D	West Kebar	5620+	14.57 N/ 53.37 W	
30/0021	dt	U 409	Maßmann	DH 2521	-T	8000+	T	SL.125	29/2115		br -MT	Bullmouth (s.u.)	7519=	33.20 N/ 18.25 W	25)
30/0140	dt	U 659	Stock	DH 2545	-D	10000+	Tf	SL.125s	29/		br -MT	Bullmouth (s.o.)	7519+	33.20 N/ 18.25 W	25)
30/0207	dt	U 659	Stock	DH 2545	-D	7000+	Tf	SL.125s	29/		br -D	Corinaldo (s.o.)	7131=	33.20 N/ 18.12 W	24)
30/0416	dt	U 203	Kottmann	DH 2549	-D: 7133+		TfA	SL.125s	29/		br -D	Corinaldo (s.o.)	7131+	33.20 N/ 18.12 W	24)
30/							T	-	30/		br -Df	Northern Spray	655=	60.14 N/ 14.38 W	26)
30/1732	*dt*	*U 522*	*Schneider*	*BB 6943*	*DD*	*1190+*	*T*	*SC.107*	*30/1505*		*ca DD*	*Columbia*	*-----*		*27)*
30/2129	dt	U 604	Höltring	CF 9868	-D	11000+	T	SL.125	30/1830		br -M	Président Doumer	11898+	35.08 N/ 16.44 W	
30/2153	dt	U 659	Stock	CF 9948	-D	6000+	T	SL.125	30/1855		br -M	Tasmania (s.u.)	6405=	36.06 N/ 16.59 W	28)
30/2154	dt	U 659	Stock	CF 9948	-D	4000=	T	SL.125							28)
30/2302	dt	U 604	Höltring	CF 9865	-D	5000+	T	SL.125	30/1950		br -D	Baron Vernon	3642+	36.06 N/ 16.59 W	29)
30/2319	dt	U 604	Höltring	CF 9865	-D	4500+	T	SL.125							29)
30/2328	dt	U 409	Maßmann	CF 9864	-D	6000+	T	SL.125	30/2015		br -M	Silverwillow	6373+	35.08 N/ 16.44 W	
31/0003	dt	U 510	Neitzel	CF 9882	-D	6000+	T	SL.125	30/2115		nw -D	Alaska	5681=	36.06 N/ 16.59 W	
31/0012	dt	U 103	Janssen	CF 9856	-D	6000+	T	SL.125	30/		br -M	Tasmania (s.o.)	6405+	36.06 N/ 16.59 W	30)
31/0012	dt	U 103	Janssen	CF 9856	-D	9000+	T	SL.125							30)
31/0014	dt	U 174	Thilo	FC 5125	-D: 4555+		T	-	31/		br -D	Marylyn	4555+	00.46 S/ 32.42 W	

24) The *Corinaldo* was damaged by one torpedo from *U 509* and two attempted coups de grâce from *U 659*, and was finally sunk by a
    torpedo and gunfire from *U 203*. 25) The *Bullmouth* was damaged by one torpedo from *U 409* and sunk by two hits from *U 659*.
26) The *Northern Spray* was damaged by one torpedo. The only report from this area came from *U 383* on Oct.24th. (See note 17).
27) *U 522* reported one hit on a "flush-deck" destroyer. HMCS *Columbia* dropped depth charges at the same time.
28) The *Tasmania* was damaged and later sunk. (See note 30).
29) *U 604* observed one ship in sinking condition and heard one hit without detonation, probably a dud, after 52 sec.
30) *U 103* observed two hits after 2 min 3 sec and 1 min 57 sec on two ships. But only the *Tasmania* is known to have been sunk.

1	2	3	4	5	6	7	8	9	10	11	12	13	14	15

November 1942

1	2	3	4	5	6	7	8	9	12	13	14	15
1/2004	dt	U 126	Bauer	FH 5578	-D	8297+	T	–	1/ am -D George Thacher	7176+	01.45 S/ 07.40 W	
1/2307	dt	U 174	Thilo	FC 1855	-D:	4920+	T	–	1/2120 br -D Elmdale	4872+	00.17 N/ 34.55 W	
2/0200	dt	U 402	v.Forstner	AJ 8836	-D	7000=	T	SC.107	2/0052 (No.53)	-----		31)
2/0205	dt	U 402	v.Forstner	AJ 8836	-D	8000+	T	SC.107	2/0012 br -D Empire Sunrise	7459=	51.50 N/ 46.25 W	31)
2/0410	dt	U 402	v.Forstner	AJ 8674	-D	7000+	T	SC.107	2/0310	-----		32)
2/0411	dt	U 402	v.Forstner	AJ 8674	-D	6000+	T	SC.107	2/0314 br -D Dalcroy	4558+	52.30 N/ 45.30 W	
2/0413	dt	U 402	v.Forstner	AJ 8674	-D	5000+	T	SC.107	2/0316 gr -D Rinos	4649+	52.30 N/ 45.30 W	
2/0452	dt	U 522	Schneider	AJ 8599	-D	4163+	T	SC.107		-----		33)
2/0452	dt	U 522	Schneider	AJ 8599	-T	6230+	T	SC.107		-----		33)
2/0452	dt	U 522	Schneider	AJ 8599	-D	4350+	T	SC.107	2/0357 br -D Hartington (s.u.)	5496=	52.30 N/ 45.30 W	33)
2/0521	dt	U 84	Uphoff	AJ 8674	-D	8000+	Tf	SC.107	2/ br -D Empire Sunrise	7459+	51.50 N/ 46.25 W	31)
2/0606	dt	U 438	Franzius	AJ 8674	-D	4000+	Tf	SC.107	2/ br -D Hartington (s.o.)	5496=	52.30 N/ 45.30 W	33)
2/0703	dt	U 518	Wißmann	BB 6371	-D	3000+	T	–				34)
2/0703	dt	U 518	Wißmann	BB 6371	-D	6000+	T	–	2/ ca -D Rose Castle	7803+	47.36 N/ 52.28 W	34)
2/0706	dt	U 518	Wißmann	BB 6371	-D	5000+	T	–	2/ br -D P.L.M.27	5633+	47.36 N/ 52.28 W	34)
2/0713	it	DA VINCI	Gazzana	00n/31w	-D:	7009+	TA	–	2/0255 br -D Empire Zeal	7009+	00.30 S/ 30.45 W	
2/0746	*dt*	*U 521*	*Bargsten*	*AJ 8672*	*PE*	*=?*	*T*	*SC.107*	*2/0650 ca PE Moosejaw*	*-----*		*35)*
2/0803	dt	U 402	v.Forstner	AJ 8658	-D	6000+	T	SC.107	2/0709 br -D Empire Leopard	5676+	52.26 N/ 45.22 W	
2/0804	dt	U 402	v.Forstner	AJ 8658	-D	8000+	T	SC.107	2/0710 br -D Empire Antelope	4945+	52.26 N/ 45.22 W	
2/0807	dt	U 522	Schneider	AJ 8673	-T	12062+	T	SC.107	2/0715 br -D Maritima	5801+	52.20 N/ 45.40 W	36)
2/0807	dt	U 522	Schneider	AJ 8673	-D	7500+	T	SC.107	2/0725 gr -D Mount Pelion	5655+	52.20 N/ 45.30 W	36)
2/0807	dt	U 522	Schneider	AJ 8673	-D	7500+	T	SC.107				36)
2/0807	dt	U 522	Schneider	AJ 8673	-D	3660+	T	SC.107		-----		36)

31) U 402 heard after 2 min 30 sec a possible hit. In reality the torpedo detonated near the ship in pos.53 of the convoy. The Empire Sunrise was hit by one torpedo from U 402 and later sunk by a coup de grâce from U 84.
32) U 402 observed one hit on the ship of the Geraldine Mary type in pos.11. Possibly it was a detonation near but not on the ship.
33) U 522 observed one hit each on a munitions ship and a heavy oil tanker after 1 min 25 sec and 1 min 24 sec, and reported the ships in sinking condition. The detonations occurred in reality between the 8th and 9th columns. The Hartington in pos.63 was hit by U 522 and sunk after an additional hit by U 438 and a coup de grâce from U 521.
34) U 518 observed the sinking of three ore carriers. In reality the first torpedo probably also hit the Rose Castle.

1	2	3	4	5	6		7	8	9	10	11	12	13	14	15

November 1942, cont.

1	2	3	4	5	6		7	8	9	10	11	12	13	14	15
2/0840	dt	U 521	Bargsten	AJ 8672	-D	6000+	Tf	SC.107s	2/	br	-D	Hartington (s.o.)	5496+	52.30 N/ 45.30 W	33)
2/0847	dt	U 442	Hesse	AJ 8626	-D	=?	T	SC.107	2/0743	gr	-D	Parthenon	-----		37)
2/1743	dt	U 522	Schneider	AJ 9179	-D	3178+	T	SC.107	2/1645	gr	-D	Parthenon	3189+	53.30 N/ 42.15 W	38)
2/1744	dt	U 522	Schneider	AJ 9179	-D	3000+	T	SC.107					-----		38)
2/1817	dt	U 174	Thilo	FB 3622	-M:10909+		T	-	2/1627	nl	-M	Zaandam	10909+	01.25 N/ 36.22 W	
3/0105	it	DA VINCI	Gazzana	01s/32w	-D:10000+		T	-	2/2315	nl	-D	Frans Hals	-----		39)
3/0202	dt	U 160	Lassen	ED 9426	-D	7500+	T	TAG.18	3/0200	ca	-D	Chr.J.Kampmann	2260+	12.06 N/ 62.42 W	
3/0630	dt	U 160	Lassen	ED 8631	-D	5000+	T	TAG.18	3/0626	br	-MT	Thorshavet	11015+	12.16 N/ 64.06 W	
3/0630	dt	U 160	Lassen	ED 8631	-D	6000+	T	TAG.18	3/						40)
3/1137	dt	U 160	Lassen	ED 8298	-D	5000+	T	TAG.18	3/1130	br	-D	Gypsum Empress	4034+	12.27 N/ 64.04 W	
3/1137	dt	U 160	Lassen	ED 8298	-T	8000+	T	TAG.18	3/1143	pa	-MT	Leda	8546+	12.16 N/ 64.06 W	
3/1139	dt	U 521	Bargsten	AJ 6657	-T:	7115+	T	SC.107	3/1042	am	-DT	Hahira	6855+	54.15 N/ 41.57 W	41)
3/1139	dt	U 521	Bargsten	AJ 6657	-D	4000+	T	SC.107	3/				-----		41)
3/1703	it	CAGNI	Liannazza	02n/18w	-M:	3845+	T	TS.23 d	3/	br	-M	Dagomba	3845+	02.30 N/ 19.00 W	
3/2148	dt	U 89	Lohmann	AJ 6632	-D	6000=	T	SC.107	3/	nl	-D	Titus	-----		42)
3/2149	dt	U 89	Lohmann	AJ 6632	-D	5000+	T	SC.107	3/2048	br	-D	Jeypore	5318+	55.30 N/ 40.16 W	42)
4/0015	dt	U 132	Vogelsang	-------	---------		T	SC.107	3/2310	nl	-DT	Hobbema	5507+	55.30 N/ 40.00 W	43)
4/0015	dt	U 132	Vogelsang	-------	---------		T	SC.107	3/2315	br	-D	Empire Lynx	6379+	55.20 N/ 40.01 W	43)
4/0015	dt	U 132	Vogelsang	-------	---------		T	SC.107	3/2315	br	-D	Hatimura (s.u.)	6690=	55.38 N/ 39.52 W	43)
4/0159	dt	U 71	Rodler v.Roithberg	AK 5484	-D	5000=?	T	SC.107	/				-----		44)

35) *U 521* heard one detonation after 8 min 5 sec. The torpedo in reality detonated near the corvette HMCS *Moosejaw*.
36) *U 522* observed one heavy oil tanker sinking, saw two freighters sink and heard one detonation with sinking noises.
37) *U 442* heard detonations after 3 min 5 sec. The detonations were near the *Parthenon*.
38) *U 522* reported having observed and heard one hit on each of two ships, but in reality probably both torpedoes hit the *Parthenon*.
39) The *Frans Hals* observed five torpedoes go by without hitting her. - 40) *U 160* observed one ship going down and another about to.
41) *U 521* fired a 3-torpedo spread. One of them hit the *Hahira*, later sunk by two additional torpedoes.
42) The crew of the *Titus* first abandoned ship, thinking they had been hit, later they reboarded and brought her in undamaged.
43) The three ships must have been hit by *U 132*, lost in a big detonation later on. The *Hatimura* was later sunk by *U 442*.
44) *U 71* heard a hit without detonation after 8 min 30 sec. Probably detonations at the end of the run.

1	2	3	4	5	6	7	8	9	10	11	12	13	14	15

November 1942, cont.

1	2	3	4	5	6	7	8	9	10 11	12	13	14	15
4/0322 dt	U 442	Hesse	AK 4411	-D	7000+	T	SC.107	4/	br -D	Hatimura (s.o.)	6690+	55.38 N/ 39.52 W	43)
4/0334 dt	U 381	Graf v.Pück-	AK 4182	-D	7000+	T	SC.107	4/			-----		45)
4/0335 dt	U 381	ler und	AK 4182	-D	6000=	T	SC.107	4/			-----		45)
4/0337 dt	U 381	Limpurg	AK 4182	-D	=	T	SC.107	4/			-----		45)
4/0815 dt	U 126	Bauer	EW 7431	-D:	792+	T	-	4/	br -D	Oued Grou	792+	04.53 N/ 04.49 E	
4/1910 dt	U 437	Schulz	BD 4145	-D	7000+	T	-						46)
4/2208 it	DA VINCI	Gazzana	01s/29w	-D:	6566+	TA	-	4/	gr -D	Andreas	6566+	02.00 S/ 30.30 W	
4/2235 dt	U 89	Lohmann	AL 1926	-D	4000+	T	SC.107	4/2137	br -D	Daleby	4640+	57.24 N/ 35.54 W	
5/0807 dt	U 129	Witt	EC 8296	-T	9000+	T	TAG.18	5/0803	am -DT	Meton	7027+	12.21 N/ 69.21 W	47)
5/0807 dt	U 129	Witt	EC 9296	-D	5000+	T	TAG.18	5/					47)
5/0807 dt	U 129	Witt	EC 9296	-D	4000+	T	TAG.18	5/					47)
5/0811 dt	U 129	Witt	EC 9296	-T	7000+	T	TAG.18	5/					47)
5/0811 dt	U 129	Witt	EC 9296	-T	6000+	T	TAG.18	5/0803	nw -MT	Astrell	7595+	12.21 N/ 69.21 W	47)
5/1650 dt	U 163	Engelmann	EE 7329	-D:	6865+	T	-	5/1600	br -M	La Cordillera	5185+	12.02 N/ 58.04 W	
5/2059 dt	U 126	Bauer	EV 6734	-D:	6568+	T	-	5/	br -D	New Toronto	6568+	05.57 N/ 02.30 E	
6/1008 dt	U 183	Schäfer	BB 8146	-T	5000+	T	.	6/					48)
6/1915 dt	U 160	Lassen	ED 9952	-D	7000+	T	.	6/1820	br -D	Arica	5431+	10.58 N/ 60.52 W	
6/1915 dt	U 160	Lassen	ED 9952	-D	6000+	T	.	6/			-----		49)
7/0016 dt	U 505	Zschech	EO 1122	-D	5500+	T	-	6/2300	br -D	Ocean Justice	7173+	10.06 N/ 60.00 W	
7/0427 dt	U 508	Staats	ED 9474	-D	9000+	T	.	7/0330	am -D	Nathaniel Hawthorne	7176+	11.34 N/ 63.26 W	
7/0635 dt	U 508	Staats	ED 8667	-D	8000+	T	.	7/0620	br -D	Lindenhall	5248+	11.34 N/ 63.26 W	

45) *U 381* observed two detonations with columns of fire on the first target after 3 min and 3 min 5 sec, on the second after 3 min. After 3 min 4 sec there was an additional detonation. There were no observations on the Allied side.

46) *U 437* observed two hits after 2 min and after 10 min heard a boiler explosion.

47) *U 129* observed hits from bow shots after 1 min 29 sec, 1 min 29 sec and 1 min 27 sec. All torpedoes hit the *Meton*. Two stern shots hit the *Astrell* after run times of 1 min 9 sec and 1 min 4 sec.

48) *U 183* fired a two-torpedo spread at a tanker and a destroyer. After 2 min 56 sec two detonations were heard.

49) *U 160* fired two torpedoes and heard detonations after 1 min 54 sec and 7 min. The second shot probably detonated at the end of its run.

1	2	3	4	5	6	7	8	9	10	11	12	13	14	15

November 1942, cont.

1	2	3	4	5	6	7	8	9	10 11	12	13	14	15
7/1436	dt	U 566	Remus	BD 2922	-D: 4252+	T	ON.143s	7/1340	br -D	Glenlea	4252+	50. N/ 30. W	
7/1540	dt	U 613	Köppe	BD 2598	-D 4500+	T	-	7/	br -D	Roxby	4252+	49.35 N/ 30.32 W	
8/	dt	U 154	Schuch	EE 5193	-D 6000+	T	-	7/	br -D	D'Entrecasteaux	7291+	15.30 N/ 57.00 W	
8/1039	dt	U 67	Müller-Stöckheim	ED 9863	-D 4000+	T	-	8/0940	br -D	Capo Olmo	4712=	10.56 N/ 61.14 W	
8/1845	dt	U 128	Heyse	EJ 7443	-D 4000+	TA	-	8/	nw -M	Maloja	6400+	11.25 N/ 27.00 W	
8/2347	dt	U 161	Achilles	EV 7278	-D 6000+	T	.	8/2254	am -D	West Humhaw	5527+	04.19 N/ 02.44 W	
8/2347	dt	U 161	Achilles	EV 7278	-D 7000+	T	.	8/2254	br -D	Benalder	5161=	04.19 N/ 02.44 W	50)
9/	dt	U 154	Schuch	EE 5386	-D 7000+	T	-	9/	br -D	Nurmahal	5419+	14.45 N/ 55.45 W	51)
9/1243	dt	U 67	Müller-Stöckheim	ED 9624	-D 6000+	T	-	9/1205	nw -D	Nidarland	6132+	11.41 N/ 60.42 W	
9/1257	dt	U 704	Keßler	AK 6553	-D 85000=?	T	-	9/	br -D	Queen Elizabeth	------		52)
10/0002	dt	U 128	Heyse	EJ 7117	-T 10000+	TA	-	9/	br -DT	Cerinthus	3878+	12.27 N/ 27.45 W	
10/0012	it	DA VINCI	Gazzana	05s/33w	-D:10000+	TA	-	10/	am -D	Marcus Whitman	7176+	05.40 S/ 32.41 W	
10/1402	dt	U 128	Heyse	EJ 4787	-D: 5293+	T	-	10/	br -D	Start Point	5293+	13.12 N/ 27.27 W	
11/0611	it	DA VINCI	Gazzana	04s/29w	-D: 5291+	TA	-	11/	nl -D	Veerhaven	5291+	03.51 S/ 29.22 W	
11/0801	dt	U 160	Lassen	EO 1574	-D: 6368+	T	-	11/	br -D	City of Ripon	6368+	08.40 N/ 59.20 W	
11/	dt	U 173	Schweichel	DJ 2519	-D =	T	UGF.1	11/1948	am AP	Joseph Hewes	9359+	35.10 N/ 04.00 W	53)
11/	dt	U 173	Schweichel	DJ 2519	---------	T	UGF.1	11/1955	am AO	Winooski	10600=	33.45 N/ 07.22 W	53)
11/	dt	U 173	Schweichel	DJ 2519	---------	T	UGF.1	11/1956	am DD	Hambleton	1630=	33.40 N/ 07.35 W	53)
12/0015	dt	U 515	Henke	CG 8830	CL 9100+	T	Task F.	12/	br AD	Hecla	10850+	35.43 N/ 09.54 W	54)
12/0211	dt	U 515	Henke	CG 8850	DD 1690+	T	Task F.	12/	br DD	Marne	1920=	35.50 N/ 09.57 W	54)

50) The *Benalder* was hit by an additional coup de grâce but was later brought into harbor.
51) The *Nurmahal* finally sank on Nov.11th.
52) *U 704* fired a 4-torpedo spread at the *Queen Elizabeth*, and heard one detonation after 2 min 4 sec.
53) *U 173* heard three detonations and assumed one hit. No optical observations were made because of ASW operations.
54) *U 515* hit a ship assumed to be a cruiser of the *Birmingham* class, but which was in reality the depot ship.

1	2	3	4	5	6	7	8	9	10	11	12	13	14	15
November 1942, cont.														
12/1828 dt	U 130	Kals		DJ 2524	-D: 9400+	T	UGF.1	12/		am AP	Edward Rutledge	9360+	33.40 N/ 07.35 W	55)
12/1828 dt	U 130	Kals		DJ 2524	-D:12568+	T	UGF.1	12/		am AP	Tasker H.Bliss	12568+	33.40 N/ 07.35 W	55)
12/1833 dt	U 130	Kals		DJ 2524	-D:12579+	T	UGF.1	12/		am AP	Hugh L.Scott	12479+	33.40 N/ 07.35 W	55)
12/1839 dt	U 163	Engelmann		EC 9668	-D 5000+	T	TAG.20	/						56)
12/1839 dt	U 163	Engelmann		EC 9668	-D 6000=	T	TAG.20	/						56)
12/2135 dt	U 224	Kosbadt		AL 7481	-D 7000+	T	-	12/		pa -D	Buchanan	5614+	52.06 N/ 25.54 W	
12/2200 dt	*U 163*	*Engelmann*		*EC 9628*	*DD 1850+*	*T*	*TAG,20*	*12/*		*am PG*	*Erie*	*2000+*	*12.04 N/ 68.57 W*	*57)*
14/0844 dt	U 413	Poel		CG 4546	-D:20107+	T	MKF.1	14/		br -M	Warwick Castle	20107+	38.44 N/ 13.00 W	
14/1658 dt	U 134	Schendel		EH 9464	-D: 4836+	T	-	14/		pa -D	Scapa Flow	4827+	12. N/ 30. W	
15/0414 dt	*U 155*	*Piening*		*CG 8665*	*-D 10000=*	*T*	*MK.1*	*15/*		*br CVE*	*Avenger*	*13785+*	*36.15 N/ 07.45 W*	*58)*
15/0414 dt	U 155	Piening		CG 8665	-D 10000=	T	MK.1	15/		am AK	Almaak	6736=	36.19 N/ 07.52 W	58)
15/0417 dt	U 155	Piening		CG 8665	-D 15000=	T	MK.1	15/		br AP	Ettrick	11279+	36.13 N/ 07.54 W	58)
15/0519 dt	U 67	Müller-Stöckheim		EE 7888	-D: 5224+	T	-	15/		br -M	King Arthur	5224+	10.30 N/ 59.50 W	
15/ dt	U 173	Schweichel		DJ 2284	-D 6000=	T	.	15/0640		am AK	Electra (AK 21)	8113=	34.00 N/ 07.24 W	
15/2240 dt	U 521	Bargsten		AK 6215	-D 6000+	T	ONS.144	15/21				-----		59)
15/2241 dt	U 521	Bargsten		AK 6215	-D 5000=	T	ONS.144	15/21				-----		59)
15/2253 dt	U 521	Bargsten		AK 6215	-D 6000=	T	ONS.144	15/				-----		59)
16/0014 dt	U 608	Struckmeier		BB 8898	-D 5000+	T	-	15/		br -D	Irish Pine	5621+	near New York	
16/0549 dt	U 92	Oelrich		CG 9457	-D 12000+	T	-	16/		br -D	Clan Mactaggart	7662+	36.08 N/ 07.23 W	
17/0854 dt	U 508	Staats		ED 9949	-D 5500+	T	-	17/		br -D	City of Corinth	5318+	10.55 N/ 61.01 W	

55) *U 130* attacked the heavily guarded ships on the Fedala roads. The ships were reported by their former names *Exeter*, *President Cleveland*, and *President Pierce*.

56) *U 163* heard two detonations after 60 sec, but was forced to submerge before anything could be observed. Sinking noises were heard.

57) The *Erie* was reported as a destroyer of the *Somers* class. The gunboat was beached in burning condition, and was a total loss.

58) *U 155* fired a 4-torpedo spread against a convoy of 10,000-15,000 gross tons ships, and heard detonations after 3 min 20 sec, 3 min 25 sec, and 3 min 24 sec. No optical observations.

59) *U 521* heard after two 2-torpedo spreads two double detonations after 10 min 55 sec and 10 min 38 sec. The torpedoes detonated in the convoy. Two detonations from stern shots reported after 7 min 31 sec were in reality depth charges from HMS *Rose*.

November 1942, cont.

1	2	3	4	5	6	7	8	9	10	11	12	13	14	15
17/2110	dt	U 262	Franke	AK 5251	-D 7000=	T	ONS.144	17/				-----		60)
17/2300	dt	U 264	Looks	AK 4831	-D 6000+	T	ONS.144	17/2203	gr	-D	Mount Taurus	6696+	54.30 N/ 37.30 W	
17/2300	dt	U 264	Looks	AK 4831	-D 4000=	T	ONS.144	17/				-----		61)
17/2346	dt	U 184	Dangschat	AK 4690	-D 5000+	T	ONS.144	17/2245	br	-D	Widestone	3192+	54.30 N/ 37.10 W	62)
17/2346	dt	U 184	Dangschat	AK 4690	-D 8000+	T	ONS.144	17/				-----		62)
17/2346	dt	U 184	Dangschat	AK 4690	-D 5000+?	T	ONS.144	17/				-----		62)
18/0324	dt	U 752	Schroeter	CG 8887	-D 12000=	T								63)
18/0407	dt	U 521	Bargsten	AK 4858	-D 6000+	T	ONS.144	18/				-----		64)
18/0409	dt	U 521	Bargsten	AK 4858	-D 5000=	T	ONS.144	18/				-----		64)
18/0413	dt	U 521	Bargsten	AK 4858	-D 5000=	T	ONS.144	18/				-----		64)
18/0456	dt	U 224	Kosbadt	AK 4853	-D 5000=	T	ONS.144	18/				-----		65)
18/0456	dt	U 224	Kosbadt	AK 4853	-D 5000=	T	ONS.144	18/				-----		65)
18/0548	dt	U 224	Kosbadt	AK 4855	-D 8000=	T	ONS.144	18/				-----		65)
18/0537	dt	U 383	Kremser	AK 4825	-D 5000=?	T	ONS.144	18/				-----		66)
18/0556	dt	U 454	Hackländer	AK 4857	-D 5000+	T	ONS.144	18/				-----		67)
18/0559	dt	U 454	Hackländer	AK 4857	-D 5000=	T	ONS.144	18/				-----		67)
18/0603	dt	U 624	Graf v.Soden	AK 4858	-T 6000+	T	ONS.144	18/0500	br	-DT	President Sergent	5344+	54.07 N/ 38.26 W	68)
18/0603	*dt*	*U 624*	*Graf v.Soden*	*AK 4858*	*PE +*	*T*	*ONS.144*	*18/*	*nw*	*PE*	*Montbretia*	-----		*68)*
18/0604	dt	U 624	Graf v.Soden	AK 4858	-D: 5432+	T	ONS.144	18/0500	am	-D	Yaka (s.u.)	5432=	54.07 N/ 38.26 W	68)
18/0604	dt	U 624	Graf v.Soden	AK 4858	-D 5000=	T	ONS.144	18/0500	am	-D	Parismina	4732+	54.07 N/ 38.26 W	68)

60) *U 262* fired a 3-torpedo spread and heard detonations after 1 min 50 sec. No record on the Allied side.

61) *U 264* fired a 3-torpedo spread and heard detonations after 3 min 56 sec, 3 min 40 sec, and 4 min 31 sec. Only one hit the *M.Taurus*.

62) *U 184* reported one ship sunk, one ship probably sunk, and one ship possibly sinking.

63) *U 752* observed after run time of 2 min 45 sec a detonation and a bright column of fire near the stern of a passenger steamer.

64) *U 521* heard two detonations after 8 min 10 sec, one after 12 min 2 sec, and one after 9 min 50 sec.

65) *U 224* heard detonations after 8 min 56 sec (4) and 7 min 20 sec (1). Probably end-of-run detonations or depth charges.

66) *U 383* heard a possible detonation after 4 min. Probably a depth charge.

67) *U 454* observed after run times of 7 min 15 sec and 7 min 52 sec water-columns and detonations. In reality these were hits by *U 624*. The detonations reported by the U-boats came from depth charges of the Norwegian corvettes *Rose* (6 DC from 0327 on), *Montbretia* (39 DC from 0415 on), and *Potentilla* (from 0426).

68) *U 624* observed the damaged tanker four hours after the hit to have a heavy list and observed its sinking after seven hours, probably sunk by a corvette. The *Montbretia* was missed. The *Yuka* was damaged and sunk by *U 522*. The *Parismina* sank in 9 min.

1	2	3	4	5	6	7	8	9	10	11	12	13	14	15

November 1942, cont.

1	2	3	4	5	6	7	8	9	10 11	12	13	14	15
18/	dt	U 154	Schuch	EP 5423	-D	8000+	T	–	18/0548 br -M	Tower Grange	5226+	06.20 N/ 49.10 W	
18/0805	dt	U 522	Schneider	AK 4874	-D	4500+	T	ONS.144	18/0714 am -D	Yaka (s.o.)	5432+	54.07 N/ 38.26 W	68)
18/0805	dt	U 522	Schneider	AK 4874	-D	6000+	T	ONS.144			-----		69)
18/0851	*dt*	*U 262*	*Franke*	*AK 4877*	*DD*	*2200+*	*T*	*ONS.144*	*18/0755 nw PE*	*Montbretia*	*925+*	*53.37 N/ 38.15 W*	*70)*
18/0857	*dt*	*U 262*	*Franke*	*AK 4877*	*DD*	*2200+*	*T*	*ONS.144*	*18/0805*				*70)*
18/0956	dt	U 43	Schwantke	BC 2241	-D	5000+	T	SC.109	18/				71)
18/0956	dt	U 43	Schwantke	BC 2241	-D	5000+	T	SC.109	18/				71)
18/0956	dt	U 43	Schwantke	BC 2241	-T	7000=	T	SC.109	18/0845 am -MT	Brilliant	9132=+	50.45 N/ 45.53 W	71)
18/1000	dt	U 753	v.Mannstein	AK 4841	-D	3000+	Tf	ONS.144s	18/ br -D	Perth	-----		72)
18/1423	dt	U 264	Looks	AK 4875	-D	4000+	T	ONS.144	18/		-----		73)
18/2030	dt	U 67	Müller-Stöckheim	EE 6721	-D:	4697+	T	–	18/2015 nw -M	Tortugas	4697+	13.24 N/ 55.00 W	
19/0825	dt	U 184	Dangschat	AJ 9830	-D	7000+	T	ONS.144	19/0725		-----		74)
19/0825	dt	U 184	Dangschat	AJ 9830	-D	7000=	T	ONS.144	19/0725		-----		74)
19/0825	dt	U 184	Dangschat	AJ 9830	-D	7000=?	T	ONS.144	19/0725		-----		74)
20/1000	dt	U 263	Nölke	CG 8731	-D	5000=	T	KRS.3	20/		-----		75)
20/100	dt	U 263	Nölke	CG 8731	-D	6000+	T	KRS.3	20/ nw -M	Prins Harald	7244+	35.55 N/ 10.14 W	75)
20/100	dt	U 263	Nölke	CG 8731	-D	5000+	T	KRS.3	20/ br -D	Grangepark	5132+	35.55 N/ 10.14 W	75)
20/100	dt	U 263	Nölke	CG 8731	-D	6000=	T	KRS.3	20/		-----		75)
21/0416	dt	U 518	Wißmann	BB 9515	*PE*	/	T	ON.145	21/0315 br -MT	British Renown	6997=	43.53 N/ 55.02 W	76)
21/0416	dt	U 518	Wißmann	BB 9515	-T	8000+	T	ON.145	21/0315 br -MT	British Promise	8443=	43.53 N/ 55.02 W	76)
21/0423	dt	U 518	Wißmann	BB 9515	-D	10000+	T	ON.145	21/0325 br -M	Empire Sailor	6140+	43.53 N/ 55.12 W	76)

69) *U 522* observed after 2 min 47 sec one hit between bridge and funnel, and observed the ship burning heavily.

70) *U 262* assumed to have hit two destroyers of different size. But in reality both torpedoes hit the *Montbretia*.

71) *U 43* observed two hits on a munitions freighter after 1 min 44 sec, which exploded with a column of fire rising 200 m. The next shot missed a tanker and hit a ship beyond, and the third shot hit and stopped the tanker. The *Brilliant* sank under tow on Jan.25th.

72) *U 753* missed the rescue ship *Perth* and the corvette HMS *Rose*.

73) *U 264* heard two detonations after 6 min 44 sec. No record on the Allied side.

74) *U 184* reported one ship sunk, one ship torpedoed, and one ship possibly hit. Three detonations were observed in the convoy.

75) *U 263* observed hits after 13 sec, 1 min 47 sec, 1 min 27 sec, 47 sec. Two ships were seen to be sinking, one ship burning.

76) *U 518* assumed a miss of a corvette with one stern torpedo, but hit on a tanker behind. In reality both torpedoes hit the tanker. The freighter was sunk by two torpedoes fired at a 4-min interval.

1	2	3	4	5	6	7	8	9	10	11	12	13	14	15
November 1942, cont.														
21/0926 dt		U 160	Lassen	EO 3364	-D 5000+	T	-	21/0830	nl	-M	Bintang	6481+	10.30 N/ 51.00 W	
21/2237 dt		U 163	Engelmann	EE 8229	-D: 6060+	T	-	21/	br	-D	Empire Starling	6060+	13.05 N/ 56.20 W	
22/0018 dt		U 160	Lassen	EF 7715	-D 4000=?	T	-							77)
22/2217 dt		U 163	Engelmann	EE 9151	-D 4000+	T	BRN.3	22/1820	bz	-D	Apaléide	3766+	13.28 N/ 54.42 W	
23/0636 dt		U 518	Wißmann	CC 3215	-T:10172+	T	-	23/0550	am	-DT	Caddo	10172+	42.25 N/ 48.27 W	
23/1410 dt		U 172	Emmermann	FC 1138	-D: 6630+	T	-	23/	br	-D	Benlomond	6630+	00.30 N/ 38.45 W	
26/1657 dt		U 262	Franke	BC 2217	-D 6000+	T	-	26/1555	br	-D	Ocean Crusader	7178+	50.30 N/ 45.30 W	
26/1735 dt		UD 3	Rigele	ER 9833	-M: 5041+	T	-	26/	nw	-M	Indra	5041+	02.10 N/ 28.52 W	
26/1917 dt		U 663	Schmid	BC 8844	-D: 6471+	T	-	26/	br	-D	Barberrys	5170+	50.36 N/ 47.10 W	78)
27/0002 dt		U 508	Staats	EO 1431	-D 6000+	T	-	26/	br	-D	Clan Macfadyen	6191+	08.57 N/ 59.48 W	
27/0450 dt		U 176	Dierksen	ES 1659	-D: 6300+	T	-	27/	nl	-D	Polydorus	5922+	09.01 N/ 25.38 W	
28/0217 dt		U 508	Staats	EO 1590	-D: 7090+	T	-	28/0150	br	-D	Empire Cromwell	5970+	09.00 N/ 58.30 W	
28/0716 dt		U 172	Emmermann	ER 9427	-D: 5364+	TA	-	28/0650	am	-D	Alaskan	5364+	03.58 N/ 26.19 W	
28/ dt		U 67	Müller-Stöckheim	EF 2463	-D: 7000=	A	-	28/0753	br	-M	Empire Glade	7006=	17.16 N/ 48.44 W	
29/0037 dt		U 161	Achilles	ES 7693	-D: 5760+	T	-	28/	nl	-D	Tjileboet	5760+	05.34 N/ 25.02 W	
December 1942														
2/0025 dt		U 508	Staats	EO 1271	-M: 5299+	T	-	30/	br	-M	Trevalgan	5299+	09.40 N/ 59.15 W	
2/0143 dt		U 508	Staats	EO 1276	-D: 5079+	T	-	2/	br	-D	City of Bath	5079+	09.29 N/ 59.30 W	
2/2018 dt		U 604	Höltring	BE 1739	-DP16000+	T	MKF.3	9/	am	-DP	Coamo	7057+	Bermuda	1)
2/2317 dt		U 174	Thilo	ER 9798	-M: 4977+	T	-	2/2230	nw	-M	Besholt	4977+	03.20 N/ 30.30 W	
3/0037 dt		U 552	Popp	DT 8413	-D 3500+	T	-	2/	br	-D	Wallsend	3157+	20.08 N/ 25.50 W	

77) *U 160* heard one hit without detonation after 56 sec. Probably a dud.
78) The ship was reported by *U 663* as the *Clan MacQuarrie*, which had already been sunk on June 13th, 1942, by the Italian U-boat *Da Vinci*.
1) *U 604* sank one passenger steamer with one funnel. The one-funnel passenger liner *Coamo* was reported missing after Dec.9th in the area of Bermuda. Probably the ship sunk was this passenger vessel.

1	2	3	4	5	6	7	8	9	10	11	12	13	14	15
December 1942, cont.														
3/0949	dt	U 183	Schäfer	BB 8896	-D: 6000+	T	ONS.146	3/	br	-D	Empire Dabchink	6089+	43.00 N/ 58.17 W	
3/2356	dt	U 508	Staats	EO 5225	-D: 4561+	T	-	2/	br	-D	Solon II	4561+	07.45 N/ 56.30 W	
5/0546	dt	U 128	Heyse	ER 9814	-D: 5136+	T	-	5/	br	-M	Teesbank	5136+	03.33 N/ 29.35 W	
?							-	5/	am	-DT	Frederick R.Kellogg	7127=	off Venezuela	2)
6/2206	dt	U 155	Piening	CD 2658	-D 7000+	T	ON.149d	7/	nl	-D	Serooskerk	8456+	37. N/ 38. W	
6/2359	dt	U 103	Janssen	CD 2611	-D: 5025+	T	-	7/	br	-M	Henry Stanley	5025+	40.35 N/ 39.40 W	
7/0000	dt	U 515	Henke	CD 2927	-D:18800+	T	-	6/	br	-D	Ceramic	18713+	40.30 N/ 40.20 W	
7/0340	dt	U 185	Maus	CD 5283	-D: 5476+	T	-	7/	br	-M	Peter Maersk	5476+	39.47 N/ 41.00 W	
7/0945	dt	U 524	v.Steinäcker	AJ 6663	-D =	T	HX.217					-----		3)
7/0948	dt	U 524	v.Steinäcker	AJ 6663	-D =	T	HX.217					-----		3)
8/0005	dt	U 508	Staats	EO 1537	-D: 5423+	T	-	8/	br	-D	Nigerian	5423+	09.17 N/ 59.00 W	
8/0139	dt	U 600	Zurmühlen	AL 1853	-D: 9000+	T	-	8/	am	-D	James McKay	6762+	57.50 N/ 23.10 W	
8/0217	dt	U 524	v.Steinäcker	AK 1959	-D 9462=	T	HX.217	8/0125	br	-MT	Empire Spenser	8194=	57.04 N/ 36.01 W	4)
8/0217	*dt*	*U 524*	*v.Steinäcker*	*AK 1959*	*DD =*	*T*	*HX.217*	*8/*	*br*	*DD*	*Fame*	-----		4)
8/0219	dt	U 524	v.Steinäcker	AK 1959	-D 8000=	T	HX.217					-----		4)
8/0221	dt	U 524	v.Steinäcker	AK 1959	-D 6000=	T	HX.217					-----		4)
8/0553	dt	U 524	v.Steinäcker	AK 1959	-D 9000+	Tf	HX.217s	8/	br	-MT	Empire Spenser	8194+	57.04 N/ 36.01 W	4)
8/0821	dt	U 758	Manseck	AK 1795	-D 5000=?	T	HX.217					-----		5)
9/0910	dt	U 553	Thurmann	AK 3510	-DT 7000+	T	HX.217	9/0811	br	-M	Charles L.D.	5273+	59.02 N/ 30.45 W	
10/0021	dt	U 758	Manseck	AK 3635	-M 8700+	T	HX.217					-----		6)
10/0024	dt	U 758	Manseck	AK 3635	-D 5000=	T	HX.217					-----		6)
10/0240	dt	U 758	Manseck	AK 1515	-D 7000=	T	HX.217					-----		7)

2) There is no U-boat report for this attack, and no U-boat was operating off Venezuela at the time. *U 154* was operating near Trinidad.

3) *U 524* fired a 4-torpedo spread and heard two detonations without optical confirmation. - 4) *U 524* fired two 2-torpedo spreads. A column of fire was observed on a freighter of the *Lochgoil* type, sunk by a coup de grâce at 05.53. A black smoke column was seen rising from a destroyer. Then a freighter exploded.

5) *U 758* heard a detonation after 2 min 38 sec. - 6) *U 758* heard four detonations after 2 min 8 sec, and a heavy explosion after 5 min 28 sec after a stern shot. - 7) *U 758* observed a column of fire on a ship after 4 min 2 sec.

1	2	3	4	5	6	7	8	9	10	11	12	13	14	15
December 1942, cont.														
11/2116	dt	U 172	Emmermann	ER 2413	-D	8000+	T	.	11/					8)
11/2116	dt	U 172	Emmermann	ER 2413	-D	4000=	T	.	11/					8)
12/0050	it	TAZZOLI	Fecia di Cossato	05n/39w	-D:	5033+	TA	-	12/	br -D	Empire Hawk	5032+	05.56 N/ 39.50 W	
12/1424	dt	U 161	Achilles	FG 5247	-D:	4997+	T	-	12/	br -M	Ripley	4997+	00.35 S/ 32.17 W	
12/1825	it	TAZZOLI	Fecia di Cossato	07n/39w	-D:	5658+	T	-	12/1730 nl -D		Ombilin	5658+	07.25 N/ 39.19 W	
13/	dt	U 176	Dierksen	FC 2515	-D:	1980+	S	-	13/1500 sw -D		Scania	1629+	01.36 N/ 32.22 W	9)
13/1842	dt	U 103	Janssen	CE 1521	-D	12614=	T	-	13/	br -D	Hororata	13945=	42.03 N/ 34.33 W	
13/2205	dt	U 159	Witte	FC 6863	-D:	7140+	TA	-	13/	br -D	City of Bombay	7140+	02.43 S/ 29.06 W	
14/								-	14/	am -S	Thomas B.Schall	62+	Caribbean	10)
14/0414	dt	U 105	Nissen	EF 1952	-D:	6578+	T	-	14/0301 br -D		Orfor	6578+	16. N/ 50. W	
14/0451	dt	U 217	Reichenbach	EF 3517	-D:	2619+	S	-	14/1545 sw -D		Etna	2619+	17.50 N/ 46.20 W	9)
15/0200	dt	U 174	Thilo	FC 8185	-D	6500+	T	-	15/	am -D	Alcoa Rambler	5500+	03.51 S/ 33.08 W	
15/1420	dt	U 159	Witte	FC 3725	-D:	4999+	T	-	15/1225 äg -D		Star of Suez	4999+	00.42 S/ 29.34 W	
16/0115	dt	U 356	Ruppelt	AL 7594	-T	5000+	T	ON.153				?		11)
16/0637	dt	U 124	Mohr	EP 2178	-T	8000+	T	.				?		12)
16/0639	dt	U 124	Mohr	EP 2178	-T	6000+	T	.				?		12)
16/0836	dt	U 610	v.Freyberg	AL 7837	-T	8400+	T	ON.153	16/0742 nw -MT		Bello	6125+	51.45 N/ 23.50 W	13)
16/0838	dt	U 610	v.Freyberg	AL 7837	-D	5000+	T	ON.153	16/0742 br -MT		Regent Lion	9551=	50.49 N/ 24.07 W	13)
16/1233	dt	U 621	Kruschka	AL 7539	-D	5000+	T	ON.153				?		14)

8) *U 172* heard detonations after 3 min 5 sec and 3 min 35 sec. Probably depth charges from a destroyer.
9) The *Scania* and *Etna* were searched by boarding parties. Both ships were then abandoned and scuttled.
10) The *Thomas B.Schall* was reported missing after Dec.14th. There is no U-boat report involving her.
11) *U 356* reported one tanker exploded after three detonations. In reality these were end-of-run detonations and depth charges.
12) *U 124* observed two hits on a tanker that went down by the bow, and one hit on a second tanker that sank in 5 min with a broken back.
13) *U 610* observed one tanker sink in 4 min, and a column of fire on a second tanker, which sank after 9 hours.
14) *U 621* reported two detonations on a freighter.

1	2	3	4	5	6	7	8	9	10	11	12	13	14	15
December 1942, cont.														
16/2013	dt	U 664	Graef	BD 3338	-D	4000=	T	ON.153	16/1915	be -D	Emile Francqui	5859+	50.58 N/ 24.42 W	15)
16/2039	dt	U 159	Witte	FC 2911	-D: 4358+		T	-	16/1925	br -D	East Wales	4358+	00.24 N/ 31.27 W	
16/2127	dt	U 176	Dierksen	FC 8474	-D: 5881+		T	-	16/	br -D	Observer	5881+	05.30 S/ 31.00 W	
17/0115	*dt*	*U 211*	*Hause*	*BD 3335*	*DD*	*1350+*	*T*	*ON.153*	*17/0010*	*br DD*	*Firedrake*	*1350+*	*50.50 N/ 25.15 W*	
17/2101	dt	U 432	Schultze	DJ 2479	-Df	500+	T	-	17/	fr APC	Poitou	310+	33.23 N/ 08.30 W	
18/0226	dt	U 621	Kruschka	BD 3288	-D	5000=	T	-	21/	gr -D	Oropos	4474+	51. N/ 37. W	16)
18/	dt	U 563	v.Hartmann	BE 8691	-D	5094+	T	MKS.3Y s	18/	br -D	Bretwalda	4906+	44.35 N/ 16.28 W	
20/0931	dt	U 217	Reichenbach	EF 8931	-D	6000+	T	-						17)
20/2021	dt	U 621	Kruschka	BD 5226	-T	8100+	T	-	20/	br -MT	Otina	6217+	47.40 N/ 33.06 W	
21/0043	dt	U 185	Maus	CF 6383	-D	5300=?	T	-						18)
21/0356	dt	U 591	Zetzsche	BD 1167	-D: 3077+		T	ONS.152	21/0310	br -D	Montreal City	3066+	50.23 N/ 38.00 W	
21/1959	it	TAZZOLI	Fecia di Cossato	01s/42w	-D: 4814+		TA	-	21/	br -D	Queen City	4814+	00.49 S/ 41.34 W	
25/1000	it	TAZZOLI	Fecia di Cossato	02s/36w	-M: 5011+		T	-	25/	am -M	Dona Aurora	5011+	02.02 S/ 35.17 W	
27/	dt	U 507	Schacht	FB 6583	-M: 5154+		T	-	27/	br -M	Oakbank	5154+	00.46 S/ 37.58 W	
27/	dt	U 356	Ruppelt	-------	---------		T	ONS.154	27/0240	br -D	Empire Union	5952+	47.30 N/ 24.30 W	19)
27/	dt	U 356	Ruppelt	-------	---------		T	ONS.154	27/0241	br -D	Melrose Abbey	2473+	47.30 N/ 24.30 W	19)
27/	dt	U 356	Ruppelt	-------	---------		T	ONS.154	27/0310	nl -D	Soekaboemi(s.u.)	7051=	47.25 N/ 25.20 W	19)
27/	dt	U 356	Ruppelt	-------	---------		T	ONS.154	27/0315	br -D	King Edward	5224+	47.25 N/ 25.20 W	19)
27/1937	dt	U 441	Hartmann	BD 66	-D	5000+	Tf	ONS.154s	27/	nl -D	Soekaboemi (s.o.)	7051+	47.25 N/ 25.20 W	19)

15) *U 664* heard a probable hit, and sinking noises after 15 min.
16) *U 621* heard a dull hit, and a detonation after 25 min. Later observed dark smoke and a burning smell. The *Oropos* was reported missing after Dec.21st.
17) *U 217* observed a hit at the stern and observed the freighter suddenly sink after 36 min following two detonations.
18) *U 185* fired a 3-torpedo spread against a *Mokambo*-type freighter, and heard a detonation after 63 sec. The ship continued on course.
19) There is no other success report from a U-boat, so the four ships must have been hit by *U 358*. The *Soekaboemi* was only damaged, and was later sunk by a coup de grâce from *U 441*.

1	2	3	4	5	6	7	8	9	10	11	12	13	14	15

December 1942, cont.

27/2135 dt	U 225	Leimkühler	BD 6835	-T	8000+	T	ONS.154s	27/2040 br		-DT	Scottish Heather	7087=	46.15 N/ 26.20 W	20)
28/0946 dt	U 124	Mohr	ED 9963	-D	4000+	T	-	28/0845 br		-D	Treworlas	4692+	10.52 N/ 60.45 W	
28/1328 dt	U 217	Reichenbach	EO 5258	-DP	7527=	T	-							21)
28/2152 dt	U 591	Zetzsche	BD 9888	-D	5000=	T	ONS.154	28/2104 nw		-D	Norse King (s.u.)	5701=	43.27 N/ 27.15 W	22)
28/2202 dt	U 225	Leimkühler	BD 9869	-D	9000+	T	ONS.154					-----		22)
28/2202 dt	U 225	Leimkühler	BD 9869	-D	5000+?	T	ONS.154	28/2115 br		-D	Melmore Head	5273+	43.27 N/ 27.15 W	22)
28/2202 dt	U 225	Leimkühler	BD 9869	-D	4000+?	T	ONS.154							22)
28/2205 dt	U 225	Leimkühler	BD 9869	-D	5000+	T	ONS.154	28/2120 br		-D	Ville de Rouen(u.)	5083+	43.25 N/ 27.15 W	22)
28/2235 dt	U 260	Purkhold	BD 9881	-D	5000+	T	ONS.154					-----		23)
28/2236 dt	U 260	Purkhold	BD 9881	-D	4000+	T	ONS.154	28/2145 br		-D	Empire Wagtail	4893+	43.17 N/ 27.22 W	23)
28/2237 dt	U 260	Purkhold	BD 9881	-D	4000=	T	ONS.154					-----		23)
28/2246 dt	U 203	Kottmann	BD 9854	-DP	9000=	T	ONS.154					-----		24)
28/2317 dt	U 406	Dieterichs	BD 9340	-D	6000+	T.	ONS.154	28/2215 br		-D	Baron Cochrane(u.)	3385=	43.23 N/ 27.14 W	25)
28/2317 dt	U 406	Dieterichs	BD 9340	-D	5000+	T.	ONS.154	28/2217 br		-D	Lynton Grange(u.)	5029=	43.23 N/ 27.14 W	25)
28/2317 dt	U 406	Dieterichs	BD 9340	-D	6889=	T	ONS.154	28/2220 br		-D	Zarian (s.u.)	4871=	43.23 N/ 27.14 W	25)
28/2317 dt	U 406	Dieterichs	BD 9340	-D	5000=	T	ONS.154					-----		25)
28/2353 dt	U 225	Leimkühler	BD 9869	-D	4000=	T	ONS.154	28/2313 be		-MT	President Francqui	4919=	43.23 N/ 27.14 W	26)
28/2355 dt	U 225	Leimkühler	BD 9869	-D	7000+	T	ONS.154	28/2300 br		-D	Empire Shackleton	7068=	43.23 N/ 27.14 W	26)
28/2356 dt	U 225	Leimkühler	BD 9869	-D	4000=	T	ONS.154					-----		26)
29/0001 dt	U 591	Zetzsche	BD 9887	-D	5000+	Tf	ONS.154s	28/2245 br		-D	Zarian (s.o.)	4871+	43.23 N/ 27.14 W	25)
29/0053 dt	U 123	v.Schroeter	BD 9849	-D	5000+	Tf	ONS.154s	28/2250 br		-D	Baron Cochrane(o.)	3385+	43.23 N/ 27.14 W	25)
29/0103 dt	U 628	Hasenschar	BD 9854	-D	5000+	Tf	ONS.154s	28/2255 br		-D	Lynton Grange (o.)	5029+	43.23 N/ 27.14 W	25)

20) The *Scottish Heather* was a straggler 8nm behind a convoy and was supplying oil to HMCS *Chilliwack*. She was brought in to the Clyde.

21) *U 217* heard one detonation after 7 min 56 sec. The ship stopped and then continued on course making black smoke.

22) *U 591* hit the *Norse King* in pos.112 which was finally sunk on 29/1507 by *U 435* while making for the Azores. *U 225* hit the *Melmore Head* in pos.113 with two torpedoes. She blew up. The *Ville de Rouen* was hit by a stern torpedo and damaged. On 29/0130 she was sunk by *U 662*.

23) *U 260* reported one ship sunk with one torpedo, and a second sunk with three. A third ship was damaged by one torpedo.

24) *U 203* observed a big smoke column after 2 min 16 sec, but the torpedo was a surface runner.

25) *U 406* reported two ships sunk and two ships damaged by two FAT torpedoes and three T-3s. In reality ships were stopped. *U 591* sank the *Zarian* and missed the *Baron Cochrane* with a coup de grâce. *U 123* sank the *Baron Cochrane* and missed the *Lynton Grange*, which was finally sunk by *U 628*.

1	2	3	4	5	6	7	8	9	10	11	12	13	14	15
December 1942, cont.														
29/0055 dt	U	435	Strelow	BD 9845	DD	1800+	T	ONS.154 29/				-----		27)
29/0101 dt	U	628	Hasenschar	BD 9854	PE	1000+	T	ONS.154 29/				-----		27)
29/0130 dt	U	662	Hermann	BD 9770	-D	5000+	T	ONS.154s 29/	br	-D	Ville de Rouen(o.)	5083+	43.25 N/ 27.15 W	22)
29/0148 dt	U	662	Hermann	BD 9770	-D	=	T	ONS.154s				-----		22)
29/0500 dt	U	123	v.Schroeter	BD 9882	-D	9419+	T	ONS.154s 29/	br	-D	Empire Shackleton	7068=	43.20 N/ 27.18 W	26)
29/0543 dt	U	435	Strelow	BD 98	-D:	5952+	A	ONS.154s 29/	br	-D	Empire Shackleton	7068+	43.20 N/ 27.18 W	26)
29/früh dt	U	217	Reichenbach	EF	-D	12390=	T	-						28)
29/0813 dt	U	225	Leimkühler	CE 2332	-T:	4990+	T	ONS.154s 29/	be	-MT	President Francqui	4919=	43.23 N/ 27.14 W	26)
29/1025 dt	U	336	Hunger	CE 3142	-T:	4900+	T	ONS.154s 29/	be	-MT	President Francqui	4919+	43.23 N/ 27.14 W	26)
29/1507 dt	U	435	Strelow	BD 9878	-D	6000+	TA	ONS.154s 29/	nw	-D	Norse King	5701+	43.27 N/ 27.15 W	22)
29/2356 dt	U	631	Krüger	AL 2357	-D	4000+	T	ONS.156s 30/	nw	-D	Ingerfem	3987+	59. N/ 21. W	
30/0819 dt	U	214	Reeder	EE 7747	-D	6000+	TA	- 30/	po	-D	Paderewski	4426+	10.52 N/ 60.25 W	
30/1638 dt	U	435	Strelow	CE 3178	-D	3500+	T	ONS.154s 30/	br	-D	Fidelity	2456+	43.23 N/ 27.07 W	29)
											LCV 752, LCV 754	10+	each	

26) *U 225* fired four single torpedoes. One hit the *President Francqui* without great effect, and two hit the *Empire Shackleton*. The fourth torpedo detonated after 2 min 15 sec without visual observation. The *Empire Shackleton* was missed two times by *U 435* at 02.55 and 02.59, and hit by *U 123* at 05.00 with one torpedo and sunk by gunfire by *U 435* at 05.43. *U 336* attacked the *President Francqui* with three torpedoes which were duds. The ship was stopped by a torpedo from *U 225* at 08.13. After two additional duds hit at 09.16 and 10.10, the ship was sunk by a torpedo from *U 336* at 10.25.

27) The attacks by *U 435* and *U 628* missed escorts picking up survivors of *Baron Cochrane*, *Lynton Grange* and *Zarian*. The hit reported by *U 435* was probably the detonation of *U 591*'s hit on *Zarian*. *U 628* observed a hit after 1 min 22 sec, and the corvette lying with a broken back.

28) *U 217* reported two hits on a ship of the *Martava* (?)-type.

29) The *Fidelity* was a fighter catapult ship with the British naval flag and a Free-French crew (ex *Le Rhone*). She was missed by *U 225* at 29/2138 and by *U 615* with five torpedoes from 29/2200-2300. Then she was sunk by two torpedoes from *U 435*.

1	2	3	4	5	6	7	8	9	10	11	12	13	14	15
January 1943, cont.														
1/	dt	U 164	Fechner	FB 3815	-D: 2608+	T	-	1/0735	sw	-M	Brageland	2608+	00.19 N/ 37.28 W	1)
3/	dt	U 507	Schacht	FB 9141	-D: 3675+	T	-	3/	br	-D	Baron Dechmont	3675+	03.11 S/ 38.41 W	
3/2252	dt	U 514	Auffermann	DQ 9325	-DW:16966+	T	TM.1	3/2146	br	-MR	British Vigilance	80933	20.58 N/ 44.40 W	2)
8/	dt	U 507	Schacht	FC 7416	-D: 5401+	T	-	8/	br	-D	Yorkwood	5401+	04.10 S/ 35.30 W	
8/2237	dt	U 436	Seibicke	DG 8565	-T 12000+	T	TM.1	8/2139	nw	-MT	Albert L. Ellsworth (s.u.)	8309=	27.59 N/ 28.50 W	3)
8/2237	dt	U 436	Seibicke	DG 8565	-T: 8309+	T	TM.1							
8/2237	dt	U 436	Seibicke	DG 8565	-T: 6394+	T	TM.1	8/2140	br	-DT	Oltenia II	6394+	27.59 N/ 28.50 W	3)
9/0003	dt	U 575	Heydemann	DG 8672	-T (3?) =	T	TM.1	8/2301				-----		4)
9/0433	dt	U 124	Mohr	EO 5354	-T: 7719+	T	TB.1	9/0340	am	-DT	Broad Arrow	7718+	07.35 N/ 55.45 W	
9/0436	dt	U 124	Mohr	EO 5354	-D: 6194+	T	TB.1	9/0340	am	-D	Birmingham City	6194+	07.23 N/ 55.48 W	
9/0557	dt	U 124	Mohr	EO 5266	-D: 5101+	T	TB.1	9/0459	am	-D	Collingsworth	5101+	07.12 N/ 55.37 W	5)
9/0557	dt	U 124	Mohr	EO 5266	-D 5000+	T	TB.1							
9/0559	dt	U 124	Mohr	EO 5266	-D: 4553+	T	TB.1	9/0500	am	-D	Minotaur	4554+	07.12 N/ 55.37 W	5)
9/0619	dt	U 522	Schneider	DG 8636	-T 8000+	T	TM.1	9/0515	nw	-MT	Minister Wedel(u)	6833=	28.08 N/ 28.20 W	6)
9/0619	dt	U 522	Schneider	DG 8636	-T 8000+	T	TM.1	9/0516	pa	-MT	Norvik (s.u.)	10034=	28.08 N/ 28.20 W	6)
9/0619	dt	U 522	Schneider	DG 8636	-T 8000+	T	TM.1							6)
9/0636	dt	U 575	Heydemann	DG 8683	-T 7000+	T	TM.1	9/0535				-----		6)
9/0638	dt	U 575	Heydemann	DG 8683	-T (2?) =	T	TM.1	9/0542				-----		6)
9/0727	dt	U 442	Hesse	DG 9411	-T 7000+	T	TM.1	9/0625	br	-DT	Empire Lytton	9807=	28.08 N/ 28.20 W	7)
9/0727	dt	U 442	Hesse	DG 9411	-T 7000+	T	TM.1	9/0627				-----		7)
9/	dt	U 441	Hartmann	AL 1628	-D 6000+	T	TB.1d ?	9/	br	-M	King James (?)	5122+	(?)	8)

1) The *Brageland* was stopped, searched, and sunk according to the prize regulations.
2) The *British Vigilance* was damaged and abandoned. The drifting wreck was sunk by *U 105* on Jan.24th with two torpedoes.
3) Two torpedoes of the three single shots of *U 436* hit the *Oltenia II* which exploded and sank, and the third hit the *Albert L.Ellsworth* which dropped behind and was sunk the next day by gunfire from *U 436*.
4) *U 575* fired a spread of four FAT and heard three detonations after 4 min 30 sec. At this time HMS *Pimpernel* dropped depth charges.
5) *U 124* assumed hits on two ships, but only the *Collingsworth* was hit by both torpedoes of this spread.
6) *U 522* reported three hits, also observed by *U 575*. Probably two hit the *Min.Wedel* which started to burn fiercely, one the *Norvik*. HMS *Havelock* tried unsuccessfully to sink both by gunfire. They were sunk on the next day by torpedoes from *U 522*. *U 575* about 30 min later fired 1 stern shot and a spread of four FAT and assumed one tanker sunk and two damaged. Again the depth charges dropped at this time by HMS *Pimpernel* were misinterpreted as torpedo hits.
7) *U 442* assumed to have hit two tankers, but only one torpedo hit the *Emp.Lytton*, later sunk by two attacks of *U 442*.
8) *U 441* sank an east-bound ship. The *King James* was reported missing after Jan.9th in this area.

1	2	3	4	5	6	7	8	9	10	11	12	13	14	15
January 1943, cont.														
9/1450	dt	U 442	Hesse	DG 8635	-T 7000+	Tf	TM.1s	9/1230	br	-DT	Empire Lytton(o.)	9807=	28.08 N/ 28.20 W	7)
9/1515	dt	U 522	Schneider	DG 9510	-T:10034+	Tf	TM.1s	9/1415	pa	-MT	Norvik	10034+	28.08 N/ 28.20 W	6)
9/1533	dt	U 134	Schendel	DG 9270	-T: 9807+	T	TM.1	9/1431	nw	-MT	Vanja	-----		9)
9/1650	dt	U 522	Schneider	DG 9510	-T: 6833+	Tf	TM.1s	9/1550	nw	-MT	Minister Wedel (0)	6833+	28.08 N/ 28.20 W	6)
9/1730	dt	U 522	Schneider	DG 9510	-T 8000=	Tf	TM.1s							10)
9/1938	dt	U 442	Hesse	DG 8635	-T 7000+	Tf	TM.1s	9/	br	-DT	Empire Lytton	9807+	28.08 N/ 28.20 W	7)
9/2043	dt	U 436	Seibicke	DG 8565	-T: 8309+	A	TM.1s	9/1945	nw	-MT	Albert L. Ellsworth(s.o.)	8309+	27.59 N/ 28.50 W	3)
9/2037	dt	U 384	v.Rosenberg-Gruszczynski	AL 0149	-D 10000+	T	-	10/	am	-D	Louise Lykes	6155+	56-15 N/ 22. "	11)
9/2042	dt	U 511	Schneewind	DG 9116	-D: 5004+	T	-	9/	br	-M	William Wilberforce	5004+	29.20 N/ 26.53 W	
10/1552	dt	U 632	Karpf	AL 1725	-DT15000=	T	UGS.3s	/	pa	-DT	C.J.Barkdull	6773+	North Atlantic	12)
10/2015	dt	U 620	Stein	DH 5110	-T 8000=	T	TM.1	10/2000				-----		13)
10/2015	dt	U 620	Stein	DH 5110	-T 8000=	T	TM.1	10/2000				-----		13)
11/0033	dt	U 186	Hesemann	AL 2882	-D 6000+	T	-	10/	br	-D	Ocean Vagabond	7174+	57.17 N/ 20.11 W	
11/0040	dt	U 522	Schneider	DH 5110	-T 9000+	T	TM.1	10/2340	br	-DT	British Dominion	6983=	30.30 N/ 19.55 W	14)
11/0040	dt	U 522	Schneider	DH 5110	-T =	T	TM.1					-----		14)
11/0053	dt	U 571	Möhlmann	DH 5724	-T 9000+	T	TM.1	10/2353	nw	-MT	Cliona	-----		15)
11/03	dt	U 620	Stein	DH 5119	-T: 6983+	TfA	TM.1 s	11/0222	br	-DT	British Dominion	6983+	30.30 N/ 19.55 W	14)
11/	dt	U 105	Nissen	ED 5956	-S +	A	-	11/2025	br	-S	C.S.Flight	67+	12.25 N/ 63. W	

9) *U 134* reported one tanker sunk by three hits. The *Vanja* evaded the torpedoes, and the detonations were depth charges from HMS *Godetia*.

10) *U 522* reported the wrecks of *Norvik* and *Min.Wedel* sunk and assumed to have sunk a third tanker, but probably it was again the *Min.Wedel*. - 11) The *Louise Lykes* was reported missing after Jan.10th, but it is probable the munitions-freighter was sunk by two hits from *U 384*. - 12) *U 632* fired a three-torpedo spread against a tanker of the *Abbeydale*-type and heard one hit without detonation and then a detonation after a stern shot. The *C.J.Barkdull* was reported missing after leaving New York on Dec.12th.

13) *U 620* reported hits on two overlapping tankers. HMS *Saxifrage* heard underwater detonations at this time, probably end-of-run detonations.

14) *U 522* reported one tanker sunk, one damaged. The *British Dominion* received three hits, and was abandoned and later sunk by *U 620* with a coup de grâce and gunfire.

15) *U 571* heard two detonations but missed the *Cliona*, and mistook depth charges by HMS *Havelock* for torpedo hits.

1	2	3	4	5	6	7	8	9	10	11	12	13	14	15
January 1943, cont.														
15/	dt	U 182	Clausen	EJ 8994	-D 6000+	T	–		15/0215	br -D	Ocean Courage	7173+	10.52 N/ 23.28 W	
17/1600	dt	U 268	Heydemann	AD 8947	-T:14547+	T	HX.222		17/1044	pa -DW	Vestfold	14547+	61.25 N/ 26.12 W	16)
17/	dt	U 268	Heydemann	-------	---------	–	"		17/1044	br LC	LCT 2239	143+	alongside Vestfold	16)
17/	dt	U 268	Heydemann	-------	---------	–	"		17/1044	br LC	LCT 2267	143+	alongside Vestfold	16)
17/	dt	U 268	Heydemann	-------	---------	–	"		17/1044	br LC	LCT 2344	143+	alongside Vestfold	16)
22/0626	dt	U 358	Manke	AE 8575	-D 3500+	T	UR.59	22/	sw -D		Neva	1456+	61.35 N/ 14.15 W	
22/2351	dt	U 413	Poel	AJ 7592	-D 5000+	T	SC.117 s	22/	gr -D		Mount Mycale	3556+	55. N/ 47. W	
23/0300	dt	U 175	Bruns	EU 8627	-D: 7000+	T	–	23/	am -D		Benjamin Smith	7177+	04.05 N/ 07.50 W	
24/1005	dt	U 105	Nissen	DQ 7345	-T:10000+	Tf	(s.o.)	24/	br -MT		British Vigilance	8093+		2)
25/	dt	U 624	Graf v.Soden	AK 4557	-D 6000+	T	SC.117s	23/	br -D		Lackenby	5112+	55. N/ 47. W	17)
25/2205	dt	U 575	Heydemann	DG 1326	-D: 4963+	T	UGS.4 s	25/	am -D		City of Flint	4963+	34.47 N/ 31.10 W	18)
26/1533	dt	U 358	Manke	AK 1660	-T 9900+	T	HX.223s	26/	nw -MT		Nortind	8221+	59. N/ 39. W	19)
26/0450	dt	U 607	Mengersen	AJ 3197	-T: 8259+	Tf	HX.223s	24/	nw -MT		Kollbjörg	(8259+)		20)
26/1609	dt	U 594	Mumm	AJ 3284	-T: 8259+	Tf	HX.223s							
27/0925	dt	U 105	Nissen	DQ 5634	-D: 8000+	T	–	27/0651	am -M		Cape Decision	5106+	22.57 N/ 47.28 W	
27/	dt	U 514	Auffermann	CE 8157	-D: 6800+	T	UGS.4 s	27/	am -D		Charles C.Pinckney	7177+	36.37 N/ 30.55 W	
27/	dt	U 442	Hesse	CE 8487	-D: 6800+	T	UGS.4 s	27/	am -D		Julia Ward Howe	7176+	35.29 N/ 29.10 W	

16) The *Vestfold* was carrying the lend-lease landing vessels *LCT 2239*, *LCT 2267* and *LCT 2344* which were also lost.
17) The *Lackenby* was reported missing after Jan.23rd. She was probably sunk by *U 624* which reported an independent ship sunk.
18) The *City of Flint* was taken as a prize by the pocket battleship *Deutschland* in the North Atlantic. Returning to Germany by way of Norway she was stopped by the minelayer *Olav Tryggvason* and released at Bergen on Nov.14th, 1939.
19) The *Nortind* was reported missing after leaving the convoy HX.223 on Jan.26th. She was sunk by *U 358*.
20) The *Kollbjörg* was in convoy HX.223 when she broke in two during a heavy storm. The stern part sank. *U 607* hit the drifting fore part with two coups de grâce, but it sank only after one more torpedo from *U 594*.

1	2	3	4	5	6		7	8	9	10	11	12	13	14	15

February 1943

1	2	3	4	5	6		7	8	9	10 11	12	13	14	15
1/	dt	U 66	Markworth	DH 9665	-D	500+	A	-	1/	fr -Mf	Joseph Elise	113+		1)
2/0304	dt	U 456	Teichert	AK 6461	-D	8000+	T	HX.224	2/0200	am -D	Jeremiah van Rensselaer	7177+	55.13 N/ 28.53 W	
3/0257	dt	U 456	Teichert	AL 4131	-T	7000+	T	HX.224	2/2201	br -MT	Inverilen	9456+	56.35 N/ 23.30 W	
3/0452	dt	U 223	Wächter	ÄA 3852	-D	7000+	T	SG.19	3/0355	am -D	Dorchester	5649+	59.22 N/ 48.42 W	2)
3/0452	dt	U 223	Wächter	ÄA 3852	-D	4000=	T	SG.19	3/	nw -D	Biscaya	-----		2)
3/0452	dt	U 223	Wächter	ÄA 3852	-D	4000/	T	SG.19	3/	nw -D	Lutz	-----		2)
3/1050	dt	U 217	Reichenbach	DR 1478	-D:	7957+	TA	-	3/0845	br -D	Rhexenor	7957+	24.59 N/ 43.37 W	
3/2154	dt	U 632	Karpf	AL 6119	-T:	8190+	T	HX.224 s	3/	br -MT	Cordelia	8190+	56.37 N/ 22.58 W	
5/0655	dt	U 262	Franke	AK 8443	-T	12000+	T	SC.118						3)
5/1707	dt	U 413	Poel	AK 8134	-D	5000+	T	SC.118 s	5/1300	am -D	West Portal	5376+	53. N/ 33. W	
6/1917	dt	U 266	v.Jessen	AK 9142	-D:	4077+	T	SC.118 s	6/	gr -D	Polyktor	4077+	53.04 N/ 33.04 W	
6/2255	dt	U 262	Franke	AK 6676	-T	8000=?	T	SC.118						3)
6/2305	dt	U 262	Franke	AK 6684	-T	9000+	T	SC.118	9/	po -D	Zagloba	2864+	56.32 N/ 16. W	3)
7/0347	dt	U 402	v.Forstner	AK 6668	-D	6000+	T	SC.118	7/0250	br -D	Toward	1571+	55.13 N/ 26.22 W	4)
7/0352	dt	U 402	v.Forstner	AK 6668	-T	10000+	T	SC.118	7/0248	am -DT	Robert E.Hopkins	6625+	55.13 N/ 26.22 W	4)
7/0411	dt	U 614	Sträter	AK 66	-D	8000+	T	SC.118	7/0315	br -D	Harmala	5730+	55.14 N/ 26.37 W	5)
7/0411	dt	U 614	Sträter	AK 66	-D	=	T	SC.118				-----		5)
7/0438	dt	U 402	v.Forstner	AK 6666	-T	12200+	T	SC.118	7/0350	nw -MT	Daghild (s.u.)	9272=	55.25 N/ 26.12 W	6)
7/0438	*dt*	*U 402*	*v.Forstner*	*AK 6666*	---------		*T*	*"*	*7/0350*	*br LC*	*LCT 2335*	*143+*	*alongside Daghild*	*6)*
7/0636	dt	U 402	v.Forstner	AL 4441	-D	8000+	T	SC.118	7/0540	br -M	Afrika	8597+	55.16 N/ 26.31 W	

1) The recorded position of the sinking of the *Joseph Elise* at 55.18 N/ 29.20 W probably is wrong.

2) *U 223* fired five single shots. Two hit the U.S.Army transport *Dorchester*, and a second ship was missed.

3) *U 262* observed three hits on a tanker, which burned and broke in two and sank in 20 min. It is possible that the Polish freighter *Zagloba* which had its machinery aft, was also lost during this attack. During the second attack *U 262* heard two duds hit the tanker, and heard a detonation after 75 sec on a second ship.

4) The *Toward* was a rescue ship that had dropped behind. The *R.E.Hopkins* sank in 20 min after a coup de grâce by *U 402*.

5) *U 614* observed two detonations on the target and one additional one on a ship beyond. The *Harmala* was straggling a short distance behind.

6) The *Daghild* received one hit by *U 402* and later sank after coups de grâce by *U 614* and *U 608* with *LCT 2335* on board.

1	2	3	4	5	6		7	8	9	10	11	12	13	14	15
February 1943, cont.															
7/0659	dt	U 402	v.Forstner	AL 4441	-D	6200+	T	SC.118	7/0400	am	-D	Henry R.Mallory	6063+	55.18 N/ 26.29 W	
7/0735	dt	U 402	v.Forstner	AL 4418	-D	8900+	T	SC.118	7/0600	gr	-D	Kalliopi	4965+	55.27 N/ 26.08 W	
7/	dt	U 614	Sträter	AK 6480	-T	8000+	Tf	SC.118 s	7/0713	nw	-MT	Daghild (s.o.)	9272=	55.25 N/ 26.12 W	6)
(1. 2.)	dt	U 118	Czygan	CG 85	---------		M	MKS.7	7/2359	br	-D	Baltonia	2013+	35.58 N/ 05.59 W	
(1. 2.)	dt	U 118	Czygan	CG 85	---------		M	MKS.7	7/2359	br	-M	Mary Slessor	5027+	35.58 N/ 05.59 W	
(1. 2.)	dt	U 118	Czygan	CG 85	---------		M	MKS.7	7/2359	br	-D	Empire Mordred	7024+	35.58 N/ 05.59 W	
8/0142	dt	U 402	v.Forstner	AL 5134	-D	10900+	T	SC.118	7/	br	-D	Newton Ash	4625+	56.25 N/ 22.26 W	
8/0213	dt	U 160	Lassen	GF 2224	-D:	6800+	T	-	7/	am	-D	Roger B.Taney	7191+	22.00 S/ 07.45 W	
8/0237	dt	U 608	Struckmeier	AL 5143	-T	12000+	Tf	SC.118 s	7/	br	-MT	Daghild (s.o.)	9272+	55.25 N/ 26.12 W	6)
8/0757	dt	U 521	Bargsten	DH 6863	-T	10000+	T	Gibr.2	8/				-----		7)
8/0758	dt	U 521	Bargsten	DH 6863	*PE*	÷	*T*	*Gibr.2*	8/	br	APC	Bredon	750+	29.49 N/ 14.05 W	7)
8/0758	dt	U 521	Bargsten	DH 6863	-D	8000=	T	Gibr.2	8/				-----		7)
(1. 2.)	dt	U 118	Czygan	CG 85	---------		M	-	10/	sp	-D	Duero	2008+	35.55 N/ 05.50 W	
11/							.	-	11/	pa	-D	Portland	2648+	S Cape Hatteras	8)
15/	dt	U 607	Mengersen	BC 5163	-T:	11355+	T	.	s 15/	am	-MT	Atlantic Sun	11355+	51. N/ 41. W	
(. .)					---------		M	-	16/	fr	-Dt	Geir	323+	Fedhala	9)
18/	dt	U 518	Wißmann	FJ 8577	-D	8000+	T	-	18/0315	bz	-M	Brasiloide	6075+	12.47 S/ 37.33 W	
19/0817	dt	U 403	Clausen	BC 2696	-D	7600+	T	ONS.165	19/	gr	-D	Zeus	5961+	49.28 N/ 44.50 W	
20/0508	dt	U 525	Drewitz	BC 3424	-D	6000+	T	ONS.165s	21/	br	-D	Radhurst	3454+	49.50 N/ 41.50 W	
21/	dt	U 106	? Rasch	BE 98	---------		T	KMS.							

6) The *Daghild* was torpedoed by *U 402*. A corvette failed to sink her after rescuing the crew. The ship was sunk by torpedoes from *U 614* and *U 608*.
7) *U 521* observed two fire columns on a tanker which sank in 2 min. The *Bredon* was hit by the spread fired at the tanker.
8) The *Portland* was reported missing after Feb.11th. There is no U-boat report on the sinking.
9) The *Geir* possibly hit an Allied defensive mine barrage and not mines laid by a U-boat.

1		2 3	4	5	6		7	8	9	10 11	12	13	14	15

February 1943, cont.

1		2 3	4	5	6		7	8	9	10 11	12	13	14	15
21/1659 dt	U 332	Hüttemann	BD 2931	-T: 5964+		T	ON.166	21/1600	nw -MT	Stigstad	5964+	49.26 N/ 29.08 W	11)
21/1705 dt	U 603	Bertelsmann	BD 2925	-T: 5964+		T	ON.166						
21/2135 dt	U 664	Graef	BE 1171	-D	5000+	T	ONS.167	21/2037	am -D	Rosario	4659+	50.30 N/ 24.38 W	
21/2135 dt	U 664	Graef	BE 1171	-T	8000+	T	ONS.167	21/2140	pa -DT	H.H.Rogers	8807+	50.30 N/ 24.38 W	
21/2226 dt	U 92	Oelrich	BD 5326	-D	7000+	T	ON.166	21/2135	br -D	Empire Trader	9990+	48.25 N/ 30.10 W	12)
22/0436 dt	U 92	Oelrich	BD 5328	-D	5000+	T.	ON.166	22/0351	nw -MW	N.T. Nielsen Alonso	9348=	48. N/ 31.24 W	13)
22/0436 dt	U 92	Oelrich	BD 5328	-D	6000+	T.	ON.166				-----		13)
22/0446 dt	U 92	Oelrich	BD 5328	-D	=	T.	ON.166			"			13)
22/0729 dt	U 753	v.Mannstein	BD 5253	-D	5000+	T	ON.166s	22/	nw -MW	N.T. Nielsen Alonso	9348+	48. N/ 31.24 W	13)
(1. 2.) dt	U 118	Czygan	CG 85	---------		M	-	22/	nw -MT	Thorsholm	9937=	14° 15m Cape Espartel	
(*1. 2.*) *dt*	*U 118*	*Czygan*	*CG 85*	---------		*M*	-	*22/*	*br DD*	*Wivern*	*1120=*	*Cape Espartel*	
22/	dt	U 107	Gelhaus	CE 6837	-D: 7801+		T	-	22/	br -M	Roxborough Castle	7801+	38.12 N/ 26.22 W	
22/2220 dt	U 606	Döhler	BD 5441	---------		T	ON.166	22/2125	br -D	Empire Redshank	6615+	47. N/ 34.30 W	14)
22/2220 dt	U 606	Döhler	BD 5441	---------		T	ON.166	22/2126	am -D	Chattanooga City	5687+	46.53 N/ 34.32 W	14)
22/2220 dt	U 606	Döhler	BD 5441	---------		T	ON.166	22/2125	am -D	Expositor (s.u.)	4959=	46.53 N/ 34.32 W	14)
23/0312 dt	U 604	Höltring	BD 4633	-D	7000+	T	ON.166s	23/0212	br -D	Stockport	1683+	45. N/ 44. W	15)
23/0331 dt	U 303	Heine	BD 4646	-D	5000+	Tf	ON.166s	23/	am -D	Expositor (s.o.)	4959=	46.53 N/ 34.32 W	14)
23/0714 dt	U 628	Hasenschar	BD 4564	-D	5000+	T.	ON.166	23/0610	pa -MT	Winkler (s.u.)	6907=	46.48 N/ 36.18 W	16)
23/0714 dt	U 628	Hasenschar	BD 4564	-T	=	T.	ON.166	23/0615	nw -MT	Glittre (s.u.)	6409=	47.00 N/ 36.20 W	16)

11) The *Stigstad* was hit by *U 332* with one torpedo and then by two torpedoes from *U 603*, and sank in 15 min.
12) The *E.Trader* was damaged and en route to the Azores, escorted by HMCS *Dauphin*. At 22/2000 GCT the ship was sunk on order of the Admiralty at 48.27 N/29.47 W by the corvette.
13) The *N.T.Nielsen Alonso* was hit by the first and third of *U 92*'s FAT-torpedoes and later by one torpedo from *U 753*. The wreck was sunk at 22/1215 GCT by the Polish destroyer ORP *Burza*.
14) *U 606* was sunk after the attack. The *Empire Redshank* was sunk at 22/2350 by the corvette HMCS *Trillium*. The *Chatanooga City* sank in 9 min. The *Trillium* failed to sink the *Expositor* which was sunk by *U 303*.
15) The *Stockport* was a rescue ship that had fallen behind the convoy after rescuing survivors of the *E.Trader* at 22/0100 GCT.
16) The two tankers received one FAT-torpedo each from *U 628*. The *Winkler* was sunk by three hits from *U 223*, the *Glittre* by two torpedoes from *U 603*.

1	2	3	4	5	6	7	8	9	10	11	12	13	14	15

February 1943, cont.

1	2 3	4	5	6	7 8	9	10 11 12	13	14	15
23/0735 dt	U 186	Hesemann	BD 4835	–D 6000+	T ON.166	23/0635 am –D	Hastings	5401+	46.30 N/ 36.30 W	17)
23/0735 dt	U 186	Hesemann	BD 4835	–D 7000+	T ON.166			–––––		17)
23/0740 dt	U 186	Hesemann	BD 4835	–D 5000=	T ON.166	23/0656 br –MT	Eulima (s.u.)	6207=	46.48 N/ 36.18 W	17)
23/0740 dt	U 186	Hesemann	BD 4835	–D 4000=	T ON.166			–––––		17)
23/0741 dt	U 522	Schneider	DG 6239	–T groß+	T UC.1	23/0638 br –MT	Athelprincess	8882+	32.02 N/ 24.38 W	
23/0842 dt	U 603	Bertelsmann	BD 4583	–T 6000+	Tf ON.166s	23/ nw –MT	Glittre (s.o.)	6409+	47.00 N/ 36.20 W	16)
23/0951 dt	U 223	Wächter	BD 4559	–T 6000+	T ON.166s	23/0859 pa –MT	Winkler (s.o.)	6907+	46.48 N/ 36.18 W	16)
23/1130 dt	U 186	Hesemann	BD 4835	–T: 6207+	TfA ON.166s	23/ br –MT	Eulima (s.o.)	6207+	46.48 N/ 36.18 W	17)
(1. 2.) dt	U 118	Czygan	CG 85	–––––––––	M –	23/ ca PE	Weyburn	1060+	35.46 N/ 06.02 W	
23/1438 dt	U 456	Teichert	BE	–D 3000+	T –	23/ br –D	Kyleclare	700+	48.50 N/ 13.20 W	18)
23/2021 dt	U 621	Kruschka	BD 4716	–D 5963=	T ON.166	23/		–––––		19)
23/2214 dt	U 382	Juli	DG 5624	–D =?	T˙ UC.1	23/		–––––		20)
23/2214 dt	U 382	Juli	DG 5624	–D 8000+	T. UC.1	23/1920 nl –MT	Murena	8252=	31.10 N/ 27.30 W	20)
23/2214 dt	U 382	Juli	DG 5624	–D 8000+	T UC.1	23/1920 nw –MT	(Pos.42)	–––––	31.15 N/ 27.22 W	20)
23/2217 dt	U 202	Poser	DG 5624	–T 6000+	T UC.1	23/1920 br –DT	Empire	9811=	31.18 N/ 27.20 W	20)
23/2217 dt	U 202	Poser	DG 5624	–T 6000+	T UC.1		Norseman (s.u.)			20)
23/2217 dt	U 202	Poser	DG 5624	–T 6000=	T UC.1	23/1920 br –MT	British Fortitude	8482=	31.10 N/ 27.30 W	20)
23/2221 dt	U 202	Poser	DG 5624	–T 6000=	T UC.1	23/1920 am –DT	Esso Baton Rouge	7989+	31.15 N/ 27.22 W	20)
23/2230 dt	U 569	Johannsen	DG 5388	–T 10000=	T UC.1	23/1900 br –DT	Empire Marvel	–––––	32.15 N/ 29.50 W	20)
23/2345 dt	U 558	Krech	DG 5389	–T 9000+	Tf UC.1	24/0014 br –DT	Empire Norseman	9811+	31.18 N/ 27.20 W	20)

17) *U 186* observed one hit after 2 min 32 sec on the ship in pos.12, *Hastings*, which was recorded as the *Hassop (?)* erroneously. The second hit after 2 min 35 sec possibly hit the same ship, which sank in 7 min. The third hit after 2 min 41 sec was only heard. After the stern spread two detonations on different targets were heard, but only the *Bulina* was hit. The second detonation was a depth charge of USCGC *Spencer*. The *Bulina* was sunk by a coup de grâce of *U 186*.

18) *U 456* observed two hits and a huge column of fire. The ship disappeared. Possibly she was the *Kyleclare*.

19) *U 621* heard one detonation on a ship of the *Dalgoma* type. But there is not report of a hit.

20) *U 382* fired one acoustic "Falke"-torpedo, one FAT, and two G7e-torpedoes, and heard detonations. One torpedo hit the *Murena* which continued in pos.41, one torpedo detonated near the ship in pos.42. *U 202* fired a four-torpedo spread. The first two hit the *Emp.Norseman*, later sunk by a coup de grâce from *U 558*. A third torpedo hit the *British Fortitude* which continued in damaged condition. The *Esso Baton Rouge* was sunk by a stern shot. *U 569* fired a three-torpedo spread and heard without optical confirmation three detonations on different targets. But there were no hits in reality.

1	2	3	4	5	6	7	8	9	10 11	12	13	14	15
February 1943, cont.													
24/0111 dt	U 707	Gretschel	BC 9328	-D	6000+	T	ON.166s	23/2220 am	-D	Jonathan Sturges	7176+	46.15 N/ 38.11 W	21)
24/0114 dt	U 707	Gretschel	BC 9328	-D	8000+	T	ON.166s				-----		21)
24/0116 dt	U 653	Feiler	BC 6956	-D	6000+	T	ON.166	24/0021 br	-D	Delilian	-----		22)
24/0116 dt	U 653	Feiler	BC 6956	-D	5000+	T	ON.166	24/0021 nl	-M	Madoera	9382=	46.02 N/ 39.20 W	22)
24/0116 dt	U 653	Feiler	BC 6956	-D	=	T	ON.166				-----		22)
24/0754 dt	U 600	Zurmühlen	BC 9359	-D	5000=	T.	ON.166	24/0655	nw -M	Ingria	4391+	45.12 N/ 39.17 W	23)
24/0813 dt	U 628	Hasenschar	BC 9353	-D	7000+	T.	ON.166	24/0733					23)
24/0813 dt	U 628	Hasenschar	BC 9353	-D	4000+	T	ON.166				-----		23)
24/0814 dt	U 628	Hasenschar	BC 9353	-D	5000=	T	ON.166				-----		23)
24/1044 dt	U 92	Oelrich	BC 9372	-D	8000+	T	ON.166				-----		24)
24/1225 it	BARBARIGO	Rigoli	04s/32w	-D:	3453+	T	-	24/	sp -D	Monte Igueldo	3453+	04.46 S/ 31.55 W	
24/1930 dt	U 621	Kruschka	BC 9370	-D	5000=	T	ON.166	24/2040			-----		25)
25/0032 dt	U 521	Bargsten	DF 9228	-D	=	T	.				-----		26)
25/0817 dt	U 628	Hasenschar	BC 8230	-D	5000+	T.	ON.166	25/0720 br	-D	Manchester Merchant	7264+	45.10 N/ 43.23 W	
25/0838 dt	U 600	Zurmühlen	BC 8230	-D	5000+	T.	ON.166	25/0743			-----		27)
25/2118 dt	*U 66*	*Markworth*	*DE 9264*	*DD*	=	*T*	*UC.1*				——		*28)*
25/2118 dt	U 66	Markworth	DE 9264	-D	5000=	T	UC.1				-----		28)
25/2118 dt	U 66	Markworth	DE 9264	-D	=	T	UC.1				-----		28)
27/1731 dt	U 66	Markworth	DF 7587	-D:	4312+	T	-	27/	br -D	St.Margaret	4312+	27.38 N/ 43.23 W	

21) *U 707* observed two hits on the first ship which sank, and heard an additional detonation on another ship behind.
22) *U 653* fired a stern shot which missed the target, but the torpedo detonated near the *Delilian*. After a four-torpedo spread several detonations were heard, but only the *Madoera* was hit, on the bow. She was taken into St.John's on March 2nd.
23) *U 600* and *U 628* hit the *Ingria* with one FAT each. *U 628* fired a two-torpedo spread and a stern shot, and heard three detonations. But this must have been depth charges from HMCS *Rosthern*.
24) *U 92* heard after 5 min 30 sec run time one detonation and then probably a boiler explosion and sinking noises.
25) *U 621* reported the observation of two hits. USCGC *Spencer* observed the track of the torpedoes and dropped depth charges.
26) *U 521* fired a two-torpedo spread against a destroyer which evaded the torpedoes. After 7 min 5 sec two detonations were heard.
27) *U 600* fired 3 FAT torpedoes and 1 G7e torpedo and heard three detonations. These must have been depth charges from USCGC *Spencer*.
28) *U 66* reported one hit on a destroyer, other possible hits on two additional ships.

1	2	3	4	5	6	7	8	9	10	11	12	13	14	15
February 1943, cont.														
28/1930 dt	U 757		Deetz	BE 1991	-D groß=	T	-							29)
28/2133 dt	U 405		Hopmann	AK 1384	-D 9000+	T	HX.227	28/		br -D	Wade Hampton	7176+	59.49 N/ 34.43 W	30)
28/2133 dt	*U 405*		*Hopmann*	-------	---------	-	*"*	*28/*		*sj PT*	*RPT-1 (ex PT 85)*	*35+*	*on Wade Hampton*	*30)*
28/2133 dt	*U 405*		*Hopmann*	-------	---------	-	*"*	*28/*		*sj PT*	*RPT-3 (ex PT 87)*	*350*	*on Wade Hampton*	*30)*
March 1943														
1/0039 dt	U 405		Hopmann	AK 1359	-D 9000+	T	HX.227							30)
1/0652 dt	U 518		Wißmann	FJ 9411	-D 7000+	T	BT.6	1/0340		am -D	Fitz-John Porter	7176+	12.24 S/ 36.56 W	31)
2/0643 dt	U 634		Dahlhaus	AD 8264	-D: 6800+	T	HX.227s	1/		am -D	Meriwether Lewis	7176+	62.10 N/ 28.25 W	1)
2/2301 it	BARBARIGO		Rigoli	17s/36w	-D: 3540+	TA	-	3/		bz -D	Afonso Pena	3540+	17.10 S/ 35.58 W	
3/2156 dt	U 43		Schwantke	DF 9329	-D 12891+	T	-	3/		dt -M	Doggerbank	(5154+)	29. N/ 34. W	2)
3/2313 it	BARBARIGO		Rigoli	17s/37w	-M 12000+	T	-	4/		am -M	Stag Hound	8591+	16.44 S/ 36.33 W	
4/0609 dt	U 172		Emmermann	CD 3239	-D 9000+	T	-	3/		br -D	City of Pretoria	8049+	41.45 N/ 42.30 W	
4/ dt	U 515		Henke	CD 3245	-D: 8300+	T	-	4/		br -M	California Star	8300+	42.32 N/ 37.20 W	
5/1745 dt	U 130		Keller	BE 9495	-D 2500+	T	XK.2	5/		br -D	Fidra	1574+	43.50 N/ 14.46 W	
5/1745 dt	U 130		Keller	BE 9495	-D 2500+	T	XK.2	5/		br -D	Empire Tower	4378+	43.50 N/ 14.46 W	
5/1745 dt	U 130		Keller	BE 9495	-D 5000+	T	XK.2	5/		br -D	Trefusis	5299+	43.50 N/ 14.46 W	
5/1745 dt	U 130		Keller	BE 9495	-D 3000+	T	XK.2	5/		br -D	Ger-Y-Bryn	5108+	43.50 N/ 14.45 W	
6/1520 dt	U 410		Fenski	CG 8511	-D 6000=	T	KMS.10	6/		br -D	Fort Battle River	7133+	36.33 N/ 10.22 W	
6/1520 dt	U 410		Fenski	CG 8511	-D 7000=	T	KMS.10	6/		br -D	Fort Paskoyac	7134=	36.27 N/ 10.17 W	
6/1520 dt	U 410		Fenski	CG 8511	-D =?	T	KMS.10	6/						3)
6/2307 dt	U 172		Emmermann	CD 1675	-D: 3041+	T	-	6/2210		nw -M	Thorstrand	3041+	41.23 N/ 42.59 W	

29) *U 757* reported one possible hit by a FAT torpedo.
30) *U 405* first attacked at 28/2133 and missed the target, but heard two detonations after 7 min on a ship behind. During the second attack at 1/0039, two hits on a ship of the *Pertshire* type were observed. At 1/2056 the sinking of one of the ships was observed. Possibly both ships were the same. On board the *Wade Hampton* there were two lend-lease PT boats for the Soviet Northern Fleet.
31) *U 518* reported during the attack against BT.6 from 28/1400 to 2/1000 in addition to the sinking of one ship six missed shots and eight duds and deep running torpedoes. The escort consisted of the Brazilian corvettes *Carioca*, *Caraveles*, and *Rio Branco*.
 1) The *Meriwether Lewis* was first missed by *U 759* (Friedrich), and this boat led *U 634* to the straggler from HX.227.

1	2	3	4	5	6	7	8	9	10	11	12	13	14	15

March 1943, cont.

1	2	3	4	5	6	7	8	9	10	11	12	13	14	15
7/0210	dt	U 230	Siegmann	AK 4224	-D	5000+	T	SC.121	6/2349	br -D	Egyptian	2868+	56.25 N/ 37.38 W	
7/0906	dt	U 591	Zetzsche	AK 1929	-D	8000+	T	SC.121s	11/ ?	br -D	Empire Impala	6116+	58. N/ 15. W	4)
7/0925	dt	U 230	Siegmann	AK 4224	-D	5000+	T	SC.121						4a)
7/	dt	U 221	Trojer	BE 1571	-D	4500+	T	-	7/	nw -M	Jamaica	3015+	48. N/ 23.30 W	
7/1820	dt	U 638	Bernbeck	AJ 5897	-D	5000/	T	ON.168s	7/1839	br -DT	Empire Light	6537=		5)
8/	dt	U					SC.121r	8/0855	br -D	Guido	3921+	58.08 N/ 32.20 W	6)
8/1823	dt	U 527	Uhlig	AK 2841	-D	6000+	T	SC.121s	8/1530	br -D	Fort Lamy	5242+	58.30 N/ 31.00 W	7)
8/1823	*dt*	*U 527*	*Uhlig*	-------	--------	-	"	*8/1530*	*br LC*	*LCT 2480*	*143+*	*on Fort Lamy*	7)
8/2119	dt	U 591	Zetzsche	AK 3594	-D	7000+	Tf	SC.121 s	8/1621	jg -D	Vojvoda Putnik	5879+	58.42 N/ 31.25 W	8)
8/2158	dt	U 190	Wintermeyer	AK 3814	-D	6500+	T	SC.121 s	11/	br -D	Empire Lakeland	7015+	58. N/ 15. W	9)
8/2303	dt	U 642	Brünning	AK 3857	-D	3500+	T	SC.121 s	11/	br -D	Leadgate	2125+	58. N/ 15. W	10)
9/0306	dt	U 510	Neitzel	EP 4168	-D	7000+	T	BT.6	9/	am -D	George Meade	7176=	07.11 N/ 52.30 W	
9/0307	dt	U 510	Neitzel	EP 4168	-T	8000+	T	BT.6	9/	br -M	Kelvinbank	3872+	07.24 N/ 52.11 W	
9/0310	dt	U 510	Neitzel	EP 4168	-D	5000+	T	BT.6	9/	am -D	Tabitha Brown	7176=	07.11 N/ 52.30 W	
9/0310	dt	U 510	Neitzel	EP 4168	-D	6000+	T	BT.6	9/	am -D	Joseph Rodman Drake	7181=	07.11 N/ 52.30 W	
9/0604	dt	U 510	Neitzel	EP 4128	-D	10000+	T	BT.6	9/0506	am -D	Mark Hanna	7176=	07.40 N/ 52.07 W	
9/0607	dt	U 510	Neitzel	EP 4128	-D	6000+	T	BT.6	9/0507	am -D	James Smith	7181=	07.40 N/ 52.07 W	
9/0608	dt	U 510	Neitzel	EP 4128	-D	6000+	T	BT.6	9/0510	am -D	Thomas Ruffin	7191+	07.40 N/ 52.07 W	
9/0611	dt	U 510	Neitzel	EP 4128	-D	7000+	T	BT.6	9/0510	am -D	James K.Polk	7177+	07.40 N/ 52.07 W	
9/2136	dt	U 530	Lange	AL 1763	-D	6000+	T	SC.121 s	11/	sw -D	Milos	3058+	58. N/ 15. W	11)

2) The German blockade-runner *Doggerbank* was reported by *U 43* as steamer of the *Dunedin Star* type, and erroneously sunk.
3) *U 410* reported one possible hit on a third ship.
4) The *Empire Impala* was stopped to pick up survivors from the *Egyptian* and *U 591* attacked and sank the ship. 4a) *U 230* heard a detonation and observed a fire and smoke column 1500m distant. - 5) *U 638* assumed to have missed the target, but the *Empire Light* was damaged and abandoned. The drifting wreck was sunk on March 12/2212 by *U 468*.
6) The *Guido* was a romper 10nm off the starboard bow of the convoy. There is no attack report, but possibly the ship was sunk by *U 432*, herself sunk March 11th, or by *U 526*. - 7) *U 527* reported one ship of the *Alphacca* type sunk, possibly the straggler *Fort Lamy* with one LCT on board. - 8) The *Vojvoda Putnik* was straggling with steering troubles since morning and was abandoned at 1621. *U 591* sank a stopped ship. - 9) *U 190* sank an independent with two torpedoes, probably the straggler *Empire Lakeland*. - 10) *U 642* sank an independent ship, probably the straggler *Leadgate*.
11) *U 530* sank an independent ship, probably the straggler *Milos*.

1	2	3	4	5	6	7	8	9	10	11	12	13	14	15
March 1943, cont.														
9/2226	dt	U 409	Massmann	AL 1690	-D 5000+	T	SC.121	9/2128	am	-D	Malantic	3837+	58.37 N/ 22.32 W	12)
9/2235	dt	U 405	Hopmann	AL 1759	-D 6000+	T	SC.121	10/0007	nw	-M	Bonneville	4665+	58.45 N/ 21.57 W	12)
9/2235	*dt*	*U 405*	*Hopmann*	-------	---------	-	*"*	*10/0007*	*br*	*LC*	*LCT 2341*	*143+*	*alongside Bonneville*	
9/2241	dt	U 409	Massmann	AL 1690	-T 8000+	T	SC.121	9/2145	br	-DT	Roosewood	5989+	58.37 N/ 22.32 W	
9/2244	dt	U 409	Massmann	AL 1690	-T 8000=	T	SC.121					-----		13)
10/0104	dt	U 229	Schetelig	AL 2537	-D 5000+	T	SC.121	10/0005	br	-D	Nailsea Court	4946+	58.45 N/ 21.57 W	14)
10/0105	dt	U 229	Schetelig	AL 2537	-D 5000+	T	SC.121	10/0007	br	-D	Coulmore	3670=	58.48 N/ 22.00 W	14)
10/0105	dt	U 229	Schetelig	AL 2537	-D 3500=	T	SC.121							
10/morg	dt	U 185	Maus	DN 76	-T 8000+	T	KG.123	10/0530	am	-DT	Virginia Sinclair	6151+	19.49 N/ 74.38 W	
10/morg	dt	U 185	Maus	DN 76	-D 8000+	T	KG.123	10/0910	am	-D	James Sprunt	7177+	19.49 N/ 74.38 W	
10/1115	dt	U 229	Schetelig	AL 2622	-D 5000=	T	SC.121	10/	br	-D	Scorton	-----		15)
10/1116	dt	U 229	Schetelig	AL 2622	-T 7000=?	T	SC.121					-----		15)
10/1500	dt	U 616	Koitschka	AL 2495	-D 5000+	T	SC.121					-----		16)
10/2126	dt	U 221	Trojer	BD 3115	-D 8580+	T	HX.228	10/2024	br	-D	Tucurinca	5412+	51.00 N/ 30.10 W	17)
10/2131	dt	U 221	Trojer	BD 3118	-D 10923+	T.	HX.228	10/2024	am	-D	Andrea F. Luckenbach	6565+	51.20 N/ 29.29 W	17)
10/2131	dt	U 221	Trojer	BD 3118	-D 8697+	T.	HX.228	10/2024	am	-D	Lawton B.Evans	7197=	?51.20 N/ 29.25 W	17)
10/2332	dt	U 336	Hunger	AK 9874	-T 10000=	T	HX.228							18)
11/	dt	U 444	Langfeld	-------	---------	T	HX.228	11/0115	am	-D	William M.Gorgas (s.u.)	7197=	51.35 N/ 28.30 W	19)
11/	dt	U 86	Schug	AK 9920	-D =	T.	HX.228	11/0115	br	-D	Jamaica Producer	5464=	?51.14 N/ 29.18 W	20)
11/	dt	U 406	Dieterichs	AK 9920	-T 8000+	T.	HX.228							20)

12) *U 409* assumed one ship sunk after one hit. At this time the *Malantic* sank in 15 min. *U 405* observed two hits from starboard on one ship which sank. From Allied sources the *Bonneville* was sunk at the time of *U 229*'s attack, but this boat attacked from port, and the B. was hit on stb. - 13) *U 409* torpedoed the *Rosewood* which broke into two parts which were sunk by USCGC *Bibb*. There was another detonation heard. - 14) The hits of *U 229* all must have been in the 1st and 2nd column from the running times, but the commodore's ship *Bonneville* was in pos.81, so she must have been hit by *U 405*.
15) *U 229* heard detonations after 2 min 45 sec and 4 min 15 sec. The freighter *Scorton* (pos.52) observed a torpedo that missed.
16) *U 616* heard a detonation after 6 min 40 sec. It was a depth charge dropped by HMCS *Dianthus*.
17) *U 221* observed hits on three munitions freighters of the types *Wyndham*, *Hertford*, and *Kent*. The S.O.E. reported a hit on the *Lawton B.Evans*, but this ship arrived undamaged at the Clyde.
18) *U 336* heard two detonations after 2 min 50 sec. - 19) The *Wm.M.Gorgas* must have been hit by the *U 444*, later sunk.
20) *U 86* and *U 406* reported hits by FATs. The *Jamaica Producer* was damaged by an internal explosion but was brought into harbor.

1	2	3	4	5	6	7	8	9	10	11	12	13	14	15
March 1943, cont.														
11/0325	dt	U 757	Deetz	AK 9872	-D	7600+	T HX.228	11/0240	nw	-D	Brant County	5001+	52.05 N/ 27.35 W	21)
11/0438	dt	U 757	Deetz	"		"	Tf HX.228 s	11/0330	am	-D	William C.Gorgas (s.o.)	7197+	51.35 N/ 28.30 W	22)
11/1052	dt	U 228	Christophersen	BD 2142	-D	6000=	T HX.228					-----		23)
11/1112	dt	U 359	Förster	AK 9655	-D	8000=	T HX.228 s					-----		24)
11/	*dt*	*U 432*	*Eckhardt*	-------	---------		*T HX.228*	*11/12*	*br*	*DD*	*Harvester*	*1340+*	*51.23 N/ 28.40 W*	
11/	dt	U 183	Schäfer	DL 6921	-D	7000+	T -	11/	ho	-D	Olancho	2493+	22.08 N/ 85.14 W	
11/1917	dt	U 621	Kruschka	AK 7174	-D	6000+	Tf ONS.169s	9/	br	-D	Baron Kinnaird	3355+	50. N/ 40. W	25)
11/2040	dt	U 440	Geißler	AL 7453	-D	=	T HX.228s					-----		26)
12/0215	dt	U 590	Müller-Edzards	AL 7158	-D	6000+	T HX.228s					-----		27)
12/0316	dt	U 440	Geißler	AL 7524	-D	=	T HX.228s					-----		28)
12/	dt	U 653	Feiler	AJ 9154	-D	4000+	Tf ONS.169s	9/	am	-D	Thomas Hooker	7176+	53. N/ 43. W	29)
12/2212	dt	U 468	Schamong	AJ 9585	-T	10000+	Tf ON.168	7/	br	-MT	Empire Light(s.o.)	6537+	53.57 N/ 46-14 W	30)
13/0530	dt	U 107	Gelhaus	CG 1218	-D	+	T OS.44	13/0439	br	-D	Clan Alpine	5442+	42.45 N/ 13.31 W	
13/0530	dt	U 107	Gelhaus	CG 1218	-D	+	T OS.44	13/0440	br	-D	Marcella	4592+	42.45 N/ 13.31 W	
13/0530	dt	U 107	Gelhaus	CG 1218	-D	+	T OS.44	13/0440	br	-D	Oporto	2352+	42.45 N/ 13.31 W	
13/0530	dt	U 107	Gelhaus	CG 1218	-D-------		T OS.44	13/0442	nl	-D	Sembilangan	4990+	42.45 N/ 13.31 W	

21) *U 757* hit a munitions ship which exploded and damaged the U-boat heavily. It was the *Brant County*.

22) *U 757* sank a wreck. From survivors it was learned that the name was *William P.Palmer*, but this was a mix-up with *William M.Gorgas*, torpedoed earlier by *U 444*. - 23) *U 228* fired two torpedoes and heard a detonation after 7 min.

24) *U 359* heard a detonation after 3 min 6 sec and observed smoke and a listing ship.

25) The *Baron Kinnaird* was straggling after March 6th and reported missing after March 7th. *U 621* sank an independent ship steering SW.

26) *U 440* heard two end-of-run detonations of G7es after 9 min 48 sec, and a FAT end-of-run detonation after 12 min 30 sec.

27) *U 590* reported one ship sunk. - 28) *U 440* reported one end-of-run detonation after 8 min 38 sec.

28) The *Thomas Hooker* reported breaking up in heavy storm on March 7th; the crew was taken off by HMS *Pimpernel*. The drifting wreck was sunk by *U 653*. - 30) *U 468* torpedoed and later sank one tanker of the *Cadillac* type by two coups de grâce. It must have been the abandoned wreck of the *Empire Light*.

1	2	3	4	5	6	7	8	9	10	11	12	13	14	15
March 1943, cont.														
13/	dt	U 68	Lauzemis	EC 5299	-D 7886+	T	GAT.49	13/	nl	-D	Ceres	2680+	14.50 N/ 71.46 W	
13/	dt	U 68	Lauzemis	EC 5299	-T: 7506+	T	GAT.49	13/	am	-DT	Cities Service Missouri	7506+	14.50 N/ 71.46 W	
13/2322	dt	U 172	Emmermann	CD 6823	-D: 5565+	T	UGS.6	13/	am	-D	Keystone	5565+	37.59 N/ 37.40 W	31)
14/0100	it	DA VINCI	Gazzana	01s/10w	-D:21517+	T	-	13/2359	br	-D	Empreß of Canada	21517+	01.13 S/ 09.57 W	
15/2100	dt	U 524	v.Steinaecker	CE 5326	-D 6000+	T	UGS.6	15/	fr	-D	Wyoming	8062+	40.18 N/ 28.56 W	
16/2040	dt	U 524	v.Steinaecker	CF 4515	-D ?	T	UGS.6					-----		32)
16/2048	dt	U 172	Emmermann	CF 4515	-D 6000+?	T	UGS.6					-----		32)
16/2048	dt	U 172	Emmermann	CF 4515	-D 6000+?	T	UGS.6					-----		32)
16/2048	dt	U 172	Emmermann	CF 4515	-D 8000+	T	UGS.6					-----		32)
16/2050	dt	U 172	Emmermann	CF 4515	-D 10000+	T	UGS.6	16/	am	-D	Benjamin Harrison	7191+	39.09 N/ 24.15 W	32)
16/2300	dt	U 603	Bertelsmann	BD 1539	-D 5000=	T.	HX.229	16/2200	nw	-M	Elin K.	5214+	50.38 N/ 34.46 W	33)
16/2300	dt	U 603	Bertelsmann	BD 1539	-D =?	T	HX.229							
17/0023	dt	U 758	Manseck	BD 1378	-D 6000+	T.	HX.229	16/2330	nl	-D	Zaanland	6813+	50.38 N/ 34.46 W	34)
17/0024	dt	U 758	Manseck	BD 1378	-D 7000+	T	HX.229	16/2330	am	-D	James Oglethorpe (s.u.)	7176=	50.38 N/ 34.46 W	34)
17/0025	dt	U 758	Manseck	BD 1378	-T 8000+	T	HX.229	16/	nl	-MT	Magdala	-----		34)
17/0032	dt	U 758	Manseck	BD 1378	-D 4000=	T	HX.229	16/				-----		34)
17/0122	dt	U 435	Strelow	BD 1379	-T 7000=	T.	HX.229	17/0030	am	-D	William Eustis (s.u.)	7196=	50.10 N/ 35.02 W	35)
17/0305	dt	U 338	Kinzel	AK 8599	-D 5000+	T	SC.122	17/0203	br	-D	Kingsbury	4898+	51.55 N/ 32.41 W	36)
17/0305	dt	U 338	Kinzel	AK 8599	-D 5000+	T	SC.122	17/0204	br	-D	King Gruffydd	5072+	51.55 N/ 32.41 W	36)
17/0306	dt	U 338	Kinzel	AK 8599	-D 8500+	T	SC.122	17/0204	nl	-D	Alderamin	7886+	52.14 N/ 32.15 W	36)
17/0307	dt	U 338	Kinzel	AK 8599	-D 4000/	T	SC.122	17/0215	br	-D	Fort Cedar Lake (s.u.)	7134=	52.14 N/ 32.15 W	36)

31) *U 172* reported the old name of the *Keystone* and *Sage Brush*. - 32) *U 172* attacked at the same time as *U 524* and heard ten detonations. *U 524* didn't report hits. *U 172* fired a four-torpedo spread and heard detonations after 2 min 50 sec, 3 min 10 sec, and 3 min 20 sec (2). After a stern spread, hits after 56 sec and 58 sec were observed. Probably both torpedoes hit the *B.Harrison*. Other detonations must have been depth charges by the American escorts.
33) *U 603* fired three FAT- and one G7e-torpedo, and heard one certain detonation and one possible.
34) *U 758* fired two FAT- and two G7e-torpedoes. The *J.Oglethorpe* was sunk by *U 91* at 0839 with a coup de grâce.
35) *U 435* fired a two-torpedo FAT spread, and heard two detonations after 13 min 46 sec. The *W.Eustis* was sunk by *U 91*.

1	2 3	4	5	6	7	8	9	10 11	12	13	14	15

March 1943, cont.

1	2 3	4	5	6	7	8	9	10 11	12	13	14	15
17/0330 dt	U 435	Strelow	BD 1386	-D	7000+	T.	HX.229	17/		-----		37)
17/0332 dt	U 435	Strelow	BD 1386	-D	6000+	T	HX.229	17/		-----		37)
17/0333 dt	U 435	Strelow	BD 1386	-D	4500=	T	HX.229	17/		-----		37)
17/0337 dt	U 91	Walkerling	BD 1353	-D	8000+	T·	HX.229	17/0250 am -D	Harry Luckenbach	6366+	50.38 N/ 34.46 W	37)
17/0355 dt	U 435	Strelow	BD 1386	-T	7000+	T	HX.229	17/		-----		37)
17/0556 dt	U 600	Zurmühlen	BD 1361	-D	7000+	T.	HX.229	17/0459 br -D	Nariva (s.u.)	8714=	50.40 N/ 34.10 W	38)
17/0556 dt	U 600	Zurmühlen	BD 1361	-D	5000+	T.	HX.229	17/0459 am -D	Irenée Du Pont(u.)	6125=	50.36 N/ 34.30 W	38)
17/0556 dt	U 600	Zurmühlen	BD 1361	-D	5000+	T.	HX.229					38)
17/0556 dt	U 600	Zurmühlen	BD 1361	-D	5000=	T.	HX.229	17/0500 br -DW	Southern Princess	12156+	50.36 N/ 34.30 W	38)
17/0738 dt	U 558	Krech	CF 4694	-D		=? T	UGS.6			-----		39)
17/0839 dt	U 91	Walkerling	BD 1334	-D:	5000+	Tf	HX.229s	17/	am -D	James Oglethorpe	7176+	50.38 N/ 34.46 W	34)
17/0839 dt	U 91	Walkerling	BD 1334	-D	6000+	Tf	HX.229s	17/	am -D	William Eustis(o.)	7196+	50.34 N/ 35.02 W	34)
17/1058 dt	U 228	Christo-phersen	BD 2142	-D	6000=?	T	HX.229			-----		40)
17/1157 dt	U 665	Haupt	BD 2113	-D	5000=	Tf	SC.122s	17/	br -D	Fort Cedar Lake	7134+	52.14 N/ 32.15 W	36)
17/1405 dt	U 384	v.Rosenberg-Gruszczynski	AK 8867	-D	6000=	T	HX.229	17/1305 br -D	Coracero	7252+	51.04 N/ 33.20 W	41)
17/1405 dt	U 384	v.Rosenberg-Gruszczynski	AK 8867	-D	4000+	T	HX.229			-----		41)
17/1405 dt	U 384	v.Rosenberg-Gruszczynski	AK 8867	-D	2500+	T	HX.229			-----		41)
17/1406 dt	U 631	Krüger	AK 8877	-T	7000+	T	HX.229	17/1305 nl -D	Terkoelei	5158+	51.45 N/ 31.15 W	41)
17/1452 dt	U 338	Kinzel	BD 2131	-D	10000+	T	SC.122	17/1354 pa -D	Granville	4071+	52.50 N/ 30.35 W	42)
17/1454 dt	U 338	Kinzel	BD 2131	-D	5000=	T	SC.122	17/		-----		42)

36) U 338 assumed to have hit with the first two-torpedo spread one ship. In reality the *Kingsbury* (pos.51) and *King Gruffydd* (pos.52) were hit. One torpedo from the second spread sank the *Alderamin* (pos.61). The stern shot missed the target but hit the *Fort Cedar Lake* in pos.124, which was later sunk by a coup de grâce from *U 665*.
37) *U 435* heard two detonations 8 min 19 sec after a FAT spread, and then two additional G7e detonations. But this must have been the two hits by *U 91* on the *H.Luckenbach*. A tanker sunk in 1 min by *U 435* cannot be identified.
38) *U 600* fired five FAT torpedoes, and heard four hits. Two hit the *I.du Pont*. The burning *S.Princess* sank at 1030 GCT, the *Nariva* and *I.du Pont* were sunk by coups de grâce from *U 91* after HMS *Mansfield* had failed to sink the ships.
39) *U 558* fired a four-torpedo spread against some ships and heard three detonations, but they must have been depth charges.
40) *U 228* heard two detonations after a 2-torpedo spread. -41) *U 384* fired three torpedoes and heard three detonations. At the same time *U 631* reported the sinking of one tanker with one torpedo. It is not probable that the *C.* and *T.* were hit by the same boat.
42) *U 338* observed one hit and heard three detonations, probably depth charges.

1	2	3	4	5	6	7	8	9	10	11	12	13	14	15
March 1943, cont.														
17/1608	dt	U 91	Walkerling	BD 1334	-D 4000+	Tf	HX.229s	17/	am	-D	Irenée Du Pont	6125+	50.34 N/ 35.02 W	38)
17/1608	dt	U 91	Walkerling	BD 1334	-D 7000+	Tf	HX.229s	17/	br	-D	Nariva (s.o.)	8714+	50.34 N/ 35.02 W	38)
17/2034	dt	U 167	Sturm	CF 5592	-D 8000=	T	UGS.6	17/	am	-D	Molly Pitcher(s.u.)	7200=	38.21 N/ 19.54 W	43)
17/2308	dt	U 305	Bahr	AK 9529	-D 8400+	T	SC.122	17/2214	br	-D	Port Auckland(s.u.)	8789+	52.25 N/ 30.15 W	44)
17/2309	dt	U 305	Bahr	AK 9529	-D 6000+	T	SC.122	17/2214	br	-D	Zouave	4256+	52.25 N/ 30.15 W	44)
18/0041	dt	U 305	Bahr	AK 9529	-D 8400+	Tf	SC.122s	18/	br	-D	Port Auckland(s.o)	8789+	52.25 N/ 30.15 W	44)
18/0550	dt	U 521	Bargsten	CF 5675	-D 10528+	Tf	UGS.6 s	18/	am	-D	Molly Pitcher(s.o)	7200+	38.21 N/ 19.54 W	43)
18/1540	dt	U 663	Schmid	AK 9655	-D 6000+	T	SC.122s	9/	br	-D	Clarissa Radcliffe	5754+	42. N/ 62. W	45)
18/1643	dt	U 221	Tröjer	AK 6897	-D 5495+	T	HX.229	18/1552	am	-D	Walter Q.Gresham	7191+	53.35 N/ 28.05 W	46)
18/1649	dt	U 221	Tröjer	AK 6897	-D 6843+	T	HX.229	18/1552	br	-M	Canadian Star	8293+	53.24 N/ 28.34 W	46)
19/0134	dt	U 666	Stengel	AL 4855	-D 4000=	T	SC.122					-----		47)
19/0550	dt	U 441	Hartmann	AL 4741	-D 7000+	T.	HX.229					-----		48)
19/0552	dt	U 441	Hartmann	AL 4741	-D 5000+	T.	HX.229					-----		48)
19/0600	dt	U 441	Hartmann	AL 4741	-D =	T	HX.229					-----		48)
19/0608	*dt*	*U 608*	*Struckmeier*	*AL 4746*	*DD 1350+*	*T*	*HX.229*	*19/0506*	*br*	*DD*	*Highlander*	------		*49)*
19/0642	dt	U 666	Stengel	AL 4869	-D 4000+	T	SC.122	19/0550	gr	-D	Carras (s.u.)	5234=	54.05 N/ 24.19 W	50)
19/0643	dt	U 666	Stengel	AL 4869	-D 7000+	T	SC.122	19/				-----		50)
19/0644	dt	U 666	Stengel	AL 4869	-D 4000=	T	SC.122	19/				-----		50)
19/1047	dt	U 527	Uhlig	AL 4835	-D 8000+	T	HX.229s	19/0954	am	-D	Mathew Luckenbach (s.u.)	5848=	54.23 N/ 23.34 W	51)

43) *U 167* reported one hit and sinking noises. The *M.Pitcher* was damaged and sunk by a coup de grâce from *U 521* in 8 min.
44) *U 305* hit the *P.Auckland* and *Zouave* with a 2-torpedo spread, the latter of which sank in 5 min. A third torpedo hit the *P.Auckland* which sank 2 hrs 8 min after a coup de grâce by *U 305*.
45) *U 663* reported three missing shots and one hit. The ship may have been the *Clarissa Radcliffe*, missing since a heavy storm on March 9th and possibly straggling behind the convoy SC.122. - 46) *U 221* hit the *W.Q.Gresham* with a stern shot, after which the ship sank in 1 h. Two torpedoes hit the *Canadian Star* which sank in 15 min. The FAT torpedo was an end-of-run detonator.
47) *U 666* heard one detonation after 5 min 11 sec. - 48) *U 441* fired three FAT- and two G7e-torpedoes and heard three detonations.
49) *U 608* fired a 3-torpedo spread and heard two hits without detonations after 5 min 34 sec. Then sinking noises and a very heavy explosion were heard. - 50) *U 666* observed three hits after 3 min 15 sec, 3 min 30 sec, and 3 min 20 sec. The second ship sank in 3 min. Only the *Carras* was hit. She remained afloat until sunk by a coup de grâce from *U 333*.
51) The *M.Luckenbach* was abandoned by the crew after deliberately straggling. She was torpedoed by *U 527* and sunk by *U 523*.

1	2	3	4	5	6	7	8	9	10	11	12	13	14	15
March 1943, cont.														
19/nm	it	DA VINCI	Gazzana	11s/01e	-D: 7628+	T	-	19/	br	-D	Lulworth Hill	7628+	10.10 S/ 01.00 E	
19/2008	dt	U 523	Pietsch	AL 4838	-D 6000+	Tf	HX.229s	19/	am	-D	Mathew Luckenbach	5848+	54.23 N/ 23.34 W	51)
19/2128	dt	U 333	Schwaff	AL 4854	-D 5000+	Tf	SC.122s	19/	gr	-D	Carras (s.o.)	5234+	54.05 N/ 24.19 W	50)
20/	dt	U 518	Wißmann	FJ 8883	-D: 7659+	T	-	20/0045	nl-D		Mariso	7659+	13.20 S/ 37.25 W	
25/	dt	U 518	Wißmann	FJ 9181	-D: 4861+	T	-	25/	sw	-M	Industria	1688+	11.40 S/ 35.55 W	52)
28/	dt	U 167	Sturm	DU 2723	-D 6500+	T	RS.3	28/	be	-M	Moanda	4621+	24.44 N/ 16.48 W	
28/	dt	U 159	Witte	DU 2723	-D 9000+	T	RS.3	28/	br	-D	Lagosian	5449+	25.35 N/ 15.43 W	
28/2202	it	FINZI	Rossetto	04n/15w	-D: 3689+	T	-	28/	gr	-D	Granicos	3689+	02.00 N/ 15.30 W	
29/0006	dt	U 172	Emmermann	DU 2722	-D 7000+	T	RS.3	28/	br	-M	Silverbeach	5319+	25.30 N/ 15.55 W	
29/21	dt	U 404	v.Bülow	BE 5653	-D 4500=	T	SL.126	29/	br	-D	Nagara	8791+	46.50 N/ 16.40 W	
29/2250	dt	U 662	Müller	BE 5635	-D 5000+	T.	SL.126	29/2300	br	-D	Ocean Viceroy	7174=	46.44 N/ 16.38 W	53)
29/2250	dt	U 662	Müller	BE 5635	-D =	T.	SL.126	29/2300	br	-D	Empire Whale	6159+	46.44 N/ 16.38 W	53)
29/2250	dt	U 662	Müller	BE 5635	-D 4000=	T	SL.126	29/2300	br	-D	Umaria	6852+	46.44 N/ 16.38 W	53)
29/2340	dt	U 610	v.Freyberg	AL 2950	-D 10000+	T	HX.230	29/	am	-D	William Pierce Frye	7176+	56.57 N/ 24.15 W	54)
30/0048	it	FINZI	Rossetto	04n/17w	-D: 5575+	T	-	30/	br	-D	Celtic Star	5575+	04.16 N/ 17.44 W	
30/0407	dt	U 662	Müller	BE 5635	-D 6000=	T	SL.126							55)
30/	dt	U 404	v.Bülow	BE 6146	-D 6000+	T	SL.126	30/	br	-D	Empire Bowman	7031+	47.26 N/ 15.53 W	
April 1943														
2/0441	dt	U 155	Piening	DM 4288	-D 3000+	T	-	1/	nw	-D	Lysefjord	1091+	23.09 N/ 83.24 W	
2/	dt	U 129	Witt	DD 9929	-M:12086+	T	-	2/	br	-M	Melbourne Star	12806+	28.05 N/ 57.30 W	

52) *U 518* assumed to have sunk the British freighter *Industrie* (4861 gross tons).
53) *U 662* fired a 4-torpedo spread and one G7e torpedo. On the first ship two hits were heard, and on the second, one, and the G7e was evaluated as a hit. It is not clear which ships were hit first, second, and third.
54) *U 610* sank the torpedoed *William Pierce Frye* on the morning of March 30th by a coup de grâce.
55) *U 662* reported one G7e-hit on a steamer, possibly one of the ships hit at 29/2250.

1	2	3	4	5	6	7	8	9	10	11	12	13	14	15
April 1943, cont.														
2/1855	dt	U 124	Mohr	CF 3628	--------	T	OS.45	2/	br	-D	Katha	4357+	41.02 N/ 15.39 W	
2/1855	dt	U 124	Mohr	CF 3628	--------	T	OS.45	2/	br	-D	Gogra	5190+	41.02 N/ 15.39 W	
3/	dt	U 155	Piening	DM 2883	-T 9973+	T	-	3/	am	-DT	Gulfstate	6882+	24.26 N/ 80.18 W	
4/	dt	U 635	Eckelmann	AK 0117	-D 7000+	T	HX.231		5/0015	br -M	Shillong	5529+	57.10 N/ 35.30 W	1)
4/	dt	U 635	Eckelmann	AK 0117	-D 6000+	T	HX.231							1)
5/0158	dt	U 630	Winkler	AK 0114	-T 6000+	T	HX.231		5/0105	br -D	Waroonga	9365+	57.10 N/ 35.30 W	2)
5/0158	dt	U 630	Winkler	AK 0114	-D +?	T	HX.231					-----		2)
5/0509	dt	U 229	Schetelig	AK 0193	-D 9500+	T	HX.231 s	5/	sw	-M	Vaalaren	3406+	58. N/ 34. W	3)
5/1145	dt	U 563	v.Hartmann	AK 1931	-T 7000=	T	HX.231 s	5/vorm	am	-MT	Sunoil (s.u.)	9005=	58.16 N/ 34.14 W	4)
5/1645	dt	U 706	v.Zitzewitz	AK 2722	-T 8000+	T	HX.231	5/1420	br	-DT	British Ardour	7124+	58.08 N/ 33.04 W	5)
5/2211	dt	U 530	Lange	AK 2521	-T 9000+	T	HX.231 s	5/	am	-MT	Sunoil (s.o.)	9005+	58.16 N/ 34.14 W	4)
6/	dt	U 185	Maus	DN 70	-D 5500+	T	.	5/	am	-D	John Sevier	7176+	20.49 N/ 74.00 W	
6/0136	dt	U 632	Karpf	AK 0354	-D 8000+	T	HX.231 s	5/	nl	-D	Blitar	7065+	57.45 N/ 27.30 W	6)
6/0142	dt	U 270	Otto	AK 2838	-D 4000=	T	HX.231					-----		7)
6/0142	dt	U 270	Otto	AK 2838	-D 6000=	T	HX.231					-----		7)
6/abds	*dt*	*U 632*	*Karpf*	*AK 3865*	*DD +*	*T*	*HX.231*	*6/*	*br*	*PE*	*Alisma*	-----		8)
8/	it	ARCHIMEDE?	Saccardo	-------	--------	T	-	8/	sp	-M	Castillo Monteallegre	3972+	09.46 N/ 16.50 W	9)
9/	dt	U 515	Henke	EK 4633	-D 3500+	T	.	9/	fr	-M	Bamako	2357+	14.57 N/ 17.15 W	

1) *U 635* reported two ships of 13,000 gross tons sunk.
2) *U 630* fired on a tanker and another ship and heard two detonations and sinking noises.
3) *U 229* reported the sinking of a freighter of the *Glennearn* type. The *Vaalaren* had left the convoy after the first attack.
4) *U 563* reported one hit on a tanker. The *Sunoil* was straggling because of machinery troubles. She was sunk by *U 530* with three torpedoes.
5) *U 706* fired a 2-shot spread and heard loud sinking noises. The second torpedo missed the flagship of the commodore, the *Tyndareus*.
6) *U 632* reported one freighter of the *Nardana* type sunk. The *Blitar* had left the convoy after the first attack.
7) *U 270* fired single torpedoes and heard two detonations.
8) *U 632* fired a G7e-torpedo and heard a detonation and sinking noises. The torpedo missed the corvette HMS *Alisma*.
9) There is no attack report about the *Castillo Monteallegre*. The *Archimede* didn't return from this area.

1	2	3	4	5	6	7	8	9	10	11	12	13	14	15
April 1943, cont.														
11/0446	dt	U 615	Kapitzky	AK 5415	-D 12000+	T	HX.232 s	10/		am -D	Edward B.Dudley	7177+	53. N/ 39. W	10)
11/0549	dt	U 188	Lüdden	AJ 9661	-T 8000+	T	ON.176	*11/*		*br DD*	*Beverley*	*1190+*	*52.19 N/ 40.28 W*	*11)*
11/0550	dt	U 188	Lüdden	AJ 9661	-D 5000+	T	ON.176							11)
11/0550	dt	U 188	Lüdden	AJ 9661	-D 5000+	T	ON.176							11)
11/0552	dt	U 188	Lüdden	AJ 9661	-D =	T	ON.176							11)
11/0735	dt	U 571	Möhlmann	AJ 9682	-D 7500+	T	ONS.2	11/		nw -D	Ingerfire	3835+	51.29 N/ 42.59 W	12)
11/0735	dt	U 571	Möhlmann	AJ 9682	-D 5000=	T	ONS.2							12)
11/0735	dt	U 571	Möhlmann	AJ 9682	-D 6000+	T	ONS.2							12)
11/0821	dt	U 84	Uphoff	AJ 98	-D 5000+	T	ONS.2							13)
11/0821	dt	U 84	Uphoff	AJ 98	-D 5000=	T	ONS.2							13)
(11. 4.)	dt	U 117	Neumann	DJ 25	---------	M	-	11/		am -D	Matt W.Ransom	7177=	33.55 N/ 07.52 W	
11/	dt	U 181	Lüth	ET 8881	-D: 5983+	T	-	11/		br -D	Empire Whimbrel	5983+	02.31 N/ 15.55 W	14)
11/2330	dt	U 613	Köppe	BC	-D 6000+	T	ON.176 s	11/						13)
12/	dt	U 195	Buchholz	DG 9284	-D 8000+	T	-	11/		am -D	James W.Denver	7200+	28.52 N/ 26.30 W	
12/0130	dt	U 404	v.Bülow	BC 3149	-D 10000=	T	ON.176	11/						15)
12/0130	dt	U 404	v.Bülow	BC 3149	-D 6000+	T	ON.176	11/						15)
12/0130	dt	U 404	v.Bülow	BC 3149	-D 8000+	T	ON.176	11/2340	br -D	Lancastrian Prince	1914+	50.18 N/ 42.48 W	15)
12/0202	dt	U 168	Pich	AK 6474	-D 5000=	T	HX.232							16)
12/0203	dt	U 168	Pich	AK 6474	-T =	T	HX.232	12/		fr PE	*Renoncule*	-----		16)
12/0438	dt	U 563	v.Hartmann	AK 6721	-D 13000+	T	HX.232	12/0245	br -M	Pacific Grove	7117+	54.10 N/ 30.00 W	16)
12/0440	dt	U 563	v.Hartmann	AK 6721	-D 8000+	T	HX.232	12/0245	br -M	Fresno City (s.u.)	7261=	54.15 N/ 30.00 W	16)
12/0445	dt	U 563	v.Hartmann	AK 6721	-D 5000+	T	HX.232	12/0245	nl -D	Ulysses	2666+	54.30 N/ 30.30 W	16)
12/0446	dt	U 563	v.Hartmann	AK 6721	-D =	T	HX.232							16)
12/1340	dt	U 706	v.Zitzewitz	AK 6485	-D 6000+	Tf	HX.232 s	12/1203	br -D	Fresno City	7261+	54.15 N/ 30.00 W	16)

10) The *E.B.Dudley* was hit at 10/1430 by a dud from *U 615* and sunk with three torpedoes on April 11th.

11) *U 188* observed a hit on a tanker after 94 sec which broke her back. She sank after 45 min. After 1 min 58 sec and 2 min 11 sec hits on two ships were heard. Two torpedoes after running 1 min 58 sec hit a fourth ship, which settled by the bow. From Allied sources, only the destroyer HMS *Beverley* was recorded sunk at this time. - 12) *U 571* fired a 3-torpedo spread and a stern shot at five ships. One broke in two, two detonations were heard, and one listing ship remained behind.

13) *U 84* heard two detonations; *U 613* reported one straggler sunk. There are no Allied reports.

14) *U 181* reported the *Empire Whimbrel* under her old name *Monasses*.

1	2	3	4	5	6	7	8	9	10	11	12	13	14	15
April 1943, cont.														
17/0747	dt	U 628	Hasenschar	AL 4615	−D 7000+	T	HX.233	17/		br	−D	Fort Rampart(s.u.)7134=	47.22 N/ 21.58 W	17)
17/0749	dt	U 628	Hasenschar	AL 4615	−D 5000=	T	HX.233					-----		17)
17/1130	dt	U 628	Hasenschar	AL 4615	−D 5000+	Tf	HX.233s	17/		br	−D	Fort Rampart(s.o.)7134+	47.22 N/ 21.58 W	17)
17/	dt	U 226	Borchers	BE 45	−D 7000+	Tf								
18/	*dt*	*U 123*	*v.Schroeter*	*ET 6537*	*SS 1090+*	*T*	*−*	*15/*		*br*	*SS*	*P.615*	*683+ 06.49 N/ 13.09 W*	*18)*
18/	dt	U 123	v.Schroeter	ET 6543	−D 5500+	T	−	18/		br	−D	Empire Bruce	7459+ 06.40 N/ 13.17 W	
19/0100	dt	U 732	Carlsen	AE 7792	−D 5000+	T	ONS.4J	19/						19)
19/	dt	U 108	Wolfram	BC 3223	−D 6100+	T	−	19/						20)
21/0807	dt	U 415	Neide	AJ 5358	−D 6000+	T	ON.178	21/		br	−D	Ashantian	4917+ 55.50 N/ 44.00 W	
21/0814	dt	U 415	Neide	AJ 5358	−D 6000+	T	ON.178	21/		br	−D	Wanstead	5486+ 55.46 N/ 45.14 W	
21/	dt	U 191	Fiehn	AJ 53	−D 5000+?	T	ON.178	21/		nw	−D	Scebeli	3025+ 56.07 N/ 44.26 W	
22/0155	dt	U 306	v.Trotha	AJ 2659	−D 12200+	T	HX.234	22/		br	−M	Amerika	10218+ 57.30 N/ 42.50 W	
23/1500	dt	U 306	v.Trotha	AK 24	−D 7800+	T	HX.234	22/		am	−D	Robert Gray	7176+ 57.30 N/ 43.00 W	
23/1600	dt	U 954	Loewe	AK 24	−D groß=	T	HX.234	23/		br	−M	Silvermaple	5313= 59.05 N/ 35.40 W	
24/	dt	U 129	Witt	DC 5693	−D 7000+	T	.	24/		am	−D	Santa Catalina	6507+ 30.42 N/ 70.58 W	
24/0635	dt	U 610	v.Freyberg	AK	−D =	T	HX.234	24/						21)
24/	dt	U 386	Kandler	AE 8472	−D 3500+	T	RU.71 s	24/		br	−D	Rosenborg	1997+ 61. N/ 15. W	
25/0817	*dt*	*U 404*	*v.Bülow*	*AK 4729*	*CV 14700=*	*T*	*ONS.4*	*25/*		*br*	*CVE*	*Biter*	*-----*	*22)*
25/1420	dt	U 413	Poel	AL 1478	−D groß3?	T	.	25/					-----	23)

15) *U 404* fired two FAT and two G7e torpedoes, and heard one premature and three other detonations after 6 min 12 sec, 7 min 45 sec, 3 min 45 sec.

16) *U 168* fired six torpedoes and heard detonations after 1 min 32 sec and 3 min 4 sec. *U 563* reported three ships sunk and one damaged. *U 168* observed a burning tanker at 0842 hrs, and *U 706* reported the sinking of a burning vessel by an escort. *U 706* sank the *Fresno City* by a coup de grâce.

17) *U 628* observed one hit on each of two ships. The *Fort Rampart* was sunk by coups de grâce from *U 628* and *U 228*.

18) *P.615* was the former submarine *Uluc Ali Reis* built for Turkey and taken over by the British.

19) *U 732* reported one munitions ship sunk.

20) *U 108* reported one Liberty ship loaded with munitions sunk. − 21) *U 610* heard one hit by a FAT torpedo.

22) *U 404* fired two FAT and 2 G7e-torpedoes against a carrier of the *Ranger* class, and heard four detonations. The detonations were observed by the British escort carrier *Biter* some distance away. − 23) *U 413* heard two probable end-of-run detonations.

1	2	3	4	5	6	7	8	9	10	11	12	13	14	15
April 1943, cont.														
(10. 4.) dt	U 455		Scheibe	DJ 25	---------	M	–	25/	fr	-D	Rouennais	3777+	34.04 N/ 07.23 W	
(11. 4.) dt	U 117		Neumann	DJ 25	---------	M	–	25/	br	-D	Empire Morn	7092=	33.52 N/ 07.50 W	
29/0514 dt	U 532		Junker	AD 7856	-D =	T	ONS.5					-----		24)
29/0517 dt	U 532		Junker	AD 7856	APC =	T	ONS.5	*29/*	*br*	*PE*	*Snowflake*	-----		24)
29/0924 dt	U 258		Mässenhausen	AD 7852	-D 4000=	T	ONS.5	29/				-----		25)
29/0924 dt	U 258		Mässenhausen	AD 7852	-D 5000=	T	ONS.5	29/				-----		25)
29/0924 dt	U 258		Mässenhausen	AD 7852	-D 7000+	T	ONS.5	29/0730	am	-D	McKeesport	6198+	60.52 N/ 34.20 W	25)
29/ dt	U 123		v.Schroeter	EJ 9788	-D 7000+	T	–	29/	sw	-M	Nanking	5931+	05.10 N/ 11.10 W	
29/1200 dt	U 752		Schroeter	BE 50	-D 20012=	T	–							26)
30/2102 dt	U 515		Henke	ET 6433	-D 6000+	T	TS.37	30/	br	-M	Corabella	5682+	07.15 N/ 13.49 W	27)
30/2102 dt	U 515		Henke	ET 6433	-T 7000+	T	TS.37							27)
30/2102 dt	U 515		Henke	ET 6433	-D 6000+	T	TS.37	30/	br	-D	Bandar Shahpur	5236+	07.15 N/ 13.49 W	27)
30/2102 dt	U 515		Henke	ET 6433	-D 7000+	T	TS.37	30/	nl	-M	Kota Tjandi	7295+	07.15 N/ 13.49 W	27)
30/2256 dt	U 515		Henke	ET 6433	-D 5000+	T	TS.37	30/	br	-D	Nagina	6551+	07.19 N/ 13.50 W	27)
30/2256 dt	U 515		Henke	ET 6433	-D 6000+?	T	TS.37							27)
May 1943														
1/0100 dt	U 107		Gelhaus	BE 4511	-D 12000+	T	–	30/	br	-M	Port Victor	12411+	47.49 N/ 22.02 W	
1/0230 dt	U 192		Happe	AJ 3797	-D 5000=	T	ONS.5							1)
1/0513 dt	U 515		Henke	ET 6128	-D 6000+	T	TS.37	1/	br	-D	Clan Macpherson	6940+	07.58 N/ 14.14 W	2)
1/0513 dt	U 515		Henke	ET 6128	-D 6000+	T	TS.37	1/	be	-M	Mokambo	4996+	07.58 N/ 14.14 W	2)
1/0540 dt	U 515		Henke	ET 6128	-D 7000+	T	TS.37	1/	br	-D	City of Singapore	6555+	07.55 N/ 14.16 W	2)

24) *U 532* fired a 4-torpedo spread and heard detonations after 7 min 30 sec and 7 min. HMS *Snowflake* observed missing shots.
25) *U 258* reported hits on three ships of 4-6000 gross tons. Later a damaged ship was sunk by two coups de grâce. The *McKeesport* was hit by only one torpedo, the others detonating outside the convoy.
26) *U 752* heard one detonation on a passenger liner of the *Winchester Castle* type.
27) *U 515* hit a freighter after 58 sec that sank immediately, one tanker after 59 sec that sank with a broken back, a freighter after 51 sec sinking fast, a freighter after 52 sec which exploded, a freighter after 60 sec that sank immediately, and another freighter after 90 sec, which was not observed sinking.
1) *U 192* heard one detonation. 2) *U 515* hit a freighter after 68 sec that burned fiercely, a freighter after 65 sec that burned, and a freighter after 35 sec that began to sink by the stern. The *Mokambo* was towed to Freetown roads, but sank on May 2nd.

1	2	3	4	5	6	7	8	9	10	11	12	13	14	15

May 1943, cont.

1	2	3	4	5	6	7	8	9	10 11	12	13	14	15
1/	dt	U 182	Clausen	FD 6884	-D: 5838+	TA	-	1/	gr -D	Adelfotis	5838+	03.32 S/ 21.33 W	
4/	dt	U 125	Folkers	AJ 6298	-D 4000+	T	ONS.5 s	4/	br -D	Lorient	4737+	54.04 N/ 44.18 W	
5/	dt	U 129	Witt	DC 12	-T 5000+	T	-	4/	pa -MT	Panam	7277+	34.11 N/ 76.12 W	
5/0222	dt	U 707	Gretschel	AJ 6434	-D 7500+	T	ONS.5 s	5/0024	br -D	North Britain	4635+	55.08 N/ 42.43 W	3)
5/0243	dt	U 628	Hasenschar	AJ 6436	-D 7000+	T	ONS.5	5/			-----		4)
5/0244	dt	U 628	Hasenschar	AJ 6436	-D 5000+	T	ONS.5	5/			-----		4)
5/0244	dt	U 628	Hasenschar	AJ 6436	-D 5000+	T	ONS.5	5/			-----		4)
5/0246	dt	U 628	Hasenschar	AJ 6436	-D =	T	ONS.5	5/0050	br -D	Harbury (s.u.)	5081=	55.01 N/ 42.59 W	4)
5/0251	dt	U 952	Curio	AJ 6432	-D 5000+	T	ONS.5	5/					5)
5/0302	dt	U 264	Looks	AJ 6514	-D 6000+	T	ONS.5	5/0106	am -D	West Maximus	5561+	55.00 N/ 42.58 W	6)
5/0303	dt	U 264	Looks	AJ 6514	-D 5000+	T	ONS.5	5/0110	br -D	Harperley	4586+	55.00 N/ 42.58 W	6)
5/0305	dt	U 264	Looks	AJ 6514	-D 4500=	T	ONS.5	5/			-----		6)
5/0422	dt	U 358	Manke	AJ 6517	-D 8700+	T	ONS.5	5/0225	br -D	Bristol City	2864+	54.00 N/ 43.55 W	7)
5/0428	dt	U 358	Manke	AJ 6517	-D 6000+	T	ONS.5	5/0230	br -D	Wentworth (s.u.)	5212=	53.59 N/ 43.55 W	7)
5/0506	*dt*	*U 628*	*Hasenschar*	*AJ 6436*	*PE +*	*T*	*ONS.5*				-----		8)
5/0707	dt	U 264	Looks	AJ 6465	-D 5000+	Tf	ONS.5 s	5/0507	br -D	Harbury (s.o.)	5081+	55.01 N/ 42.59 W	4)
5/	dt	U 123	v.Schroeter	EU 7251	-D: 4566+	T	-	5/	br -D	Holmbury	4566+	04.30 N/ 10.20 W	
5/	dt	U 638	Staudinger	-------	---------	T	ONS.5	5/1400	br -M	Dolius	5507+	54.00 N/ 43.35 W	8a)
5/1634	dt	U 584	Deecke	AJ 5965	-D 7000+	T	ONS.5 s	5/1453	am -D	West Madaket	5565+	54.47 N/ 44.12 W	8b)
5/1634	dt	U 584	Deecke	AJ 5965	-D 5000+	T	ONS.5 s				-----		8b)
5/1737	dt	U 628	Hasenschar	AJ 6436	-D: 5081+	TA	ONS.5 s	5/1540	br -D	Wentworth (s.o.)	5212+	53.59 N/ 43.55 W	7)

3) *U 707* reported the sinking of a freighter of the *City of Manchester* type 5nm behind the convoy. The *N.B.* sank in 2 min.
4) *U 628* reported one ship sunk, one ship probably sunk, one burning, and two detonations after 7 min 58 sec and 9 min 4 sec. Only the *Harbury* was hit. HMT *Northern Spray* took off the crew. The wreck was later sunk by *U 264*. - 5) *U 952* reported one hit with a magnetic pistol. It could have been the first detonation near the *West Maximus*. - 6) *U 264* observed the sinking of two ships with two hits each. *West Maximus* and *Harperley* were both hit by two torpedoes. - 7) *U 358* observed two ships sinking, but only the *B.C.* sank after 20 min. HMS *Loosestrife* failed to sink the *W*, which was finally sunk by gunfire by *U 628*.
8) *U 628* reported the sinking of a corvette. - 8a) The *Dolius* must have been hit by *U 638*, later sunk herself by the escorts.
8b) *U 584* reported the sinking of two ships. She attacked a straggler group escorted by the corvette HMS *Pink*, and sank only the *W.M.*

1	2	3	4	5	6	7	8	9	10	11	12	13	14	15
May 1943, cont.														
5/2150	dt	U 266	v.Jessen	AJ 8359	-D 5000+	T	ONS.5	5/	br	-D	Selvistan	5136+	53.10 N/ 44.40 W	9)
5/2150	dt	U 266	v.Jessen	AJ 8359	-D 5000+	T	ONS.5	5/	br	-D	Gharinda	5306+	53.10 N/ 44.40 W	9)
5/2150	dt	U 266	v.Jessen	AJ 8359	-D =	T	ONS.5	5/	nw	-D	Bonde	1570+	53.28 N/ 44.20 W	9)
7/	dt	U 195	Buchholz	FU 1615	-D 5000+	T	-	6/	am	-D	Samuel Jordan Kirkwood	7191+	15. S/ 07. W	
7/0646	dt	U 607	Jeschonnek	CF 3487	-D =	T.	SL.128					-----		10)
7/1200	dt	U 89	Lohmann	CF 34	-D 7000+	T	SL.128	7/	gr	-D	Laconikos	3803+	41.40 N/ 18.13 W	11)
8/0445	dt	U 154	Kusch	FK 6238	-T: 8917=?	T	-	8/	pa	-MT	Motocarline	-----	08.41 S/ 34.36 W	12)
9/0055	dt	U 123	v.Schroeter	EU 4792	-D 6000+	T	-	8/	br	-D	Kanbe	6244+	Liberian Coast	13)
9/	dt	U 515	Henke	EV 7356	-D: 4544+	T	-	9/	nw	-M	Corneville	4544+	04.50 N/ 01.10 W	
11/	dt	U 753	v.Mannstein	BE 5626	-D =?	T.	-					-----		14)
11/2000	dt	U 402	v.Forstner	CE 1547	-D 5000+	T	SC.129	11/	br	-D	Antigone	4545+	40.30 N/ 32.30 W	
11/2000	dt	U 402	v.Forstner	CE 1547	-D 4000+	T	SC.129	11/	nw	-D	Grado	3082+	40.30 N/ 32.30 W	
11/0441	dt	U 456	Teichert	BC 4714	-D 10000+	T	HX.237							15)
11/2220	dt	U 403	Clausen	BD 9474	-D 7000+	T	HX.237	11/	br	-D	Fort Concord	7138+	46.05 N/ 25.20 W	15)
12/	dt	U 221	Trojer	BE 1934	-T 8000+	T	HX.237 s	12/	nw	-MT	Sandanger	9432+	46. N/ 21. W	16)
12/	dt	U 603	Baltz	BE 4416	-D: 4819+	T	HX.237 s	12/	nw	-M	Brand	4819+	47.19 N/ 24.41 W	
13/1936	dt	U 640	Nagel	AD 8870	-D 4000+	T	.	13/						17)
13/1936	dt	U 640	Nagel	AD 8870	-D 6000+	T	.	13/						17)

9) *U 266* reported one ship sunk, one probably sunk and two detonations heard. The three ships were close to each other in pos. 91, 101 and 84 and were all hit (*Selvistan* 2 torpedoes) within about three minutes. So the torpedoes most probably all came from the same U-boat.

10) *U 607* heard one detonation after 10 min, probably an end-of-run detonation.

11) *U 89* observed a hit with a torpedo having magnetic detonation, so the *Laconikos* was probably hit by this attack.

12) *U 154* reported a hit without detonation (dud). The *Motocarline* observed two torpedoes that missed.

13) The *Kanbe* was reported missing after May 8th. She was probably the victim of *U 123*.

14) *U 753* fired two single FAT-torpedoes, and heard one loud detonation after 30 min. No hit.

15) *U 456* reported the sinking of a freighter, and *U 403* reported one hit on an armed ship and sinking noises. Because the time of the attack against the *Fort Concord* is unknown, both U-boats may have been responsible.

16) *U 221* reported one tanker sailing independently sunk. 17) *U 640* heard two hits and sinking noises.

1	2	3	4	5	6	7	8	9	10	11	12	13	14	15
May 1943, , cont.														
13/	dt	U 176	Dierksen	DM 69	-T: 2249+	T	.	13/		am -DT	Nickeliner	2249+	21.25 N/ 76.40 W	
13/	dt	U 176	Dierksen	DM 69	-T: 1983+	T	.	13/		cu -DT	Mambi	1983+	21.25 N/ 76.40 W	
15/	dt	U 105	Nissen	ET 5997	-D: 4669+	T	-	15/1835		gr -D	Maroussio Logothetis	4669+	05.28 N/ 14.28 W	
15/1331	dt	U 607	Jeschonnek	BD 6355	-D: 5589+	T	-	15/		ir -D	Irish Oak	5589+	47.51 N/ 25.53 W	
17/0237	dt	U 657	Göllnitz	AD 9725	-D 5000+	T	ONS.7	17/		br -D	Aymeric	5196+	59.42 N/ 41.39 W	
19/	dt	U 161	Achilles	-------	---------	A	-	19/		ca -S	Angelus	255+	38.40 N/ 64.00 W	
19/0930	dt	U 92	Oelrich	AK 5491	-D 6500+	T	SC.130	19/				-----		18)
19/0930	dt	U 92	Oelrich	AK 5491	-D =	T	SC.130	19/				-----		18)
20/	dt	U 197	Bartels	FM 2269	-T: 4763+	T	-	20/0728		nl -DT	Benakat	4763+	06.05 S/ 12.56 W	
25/	dt	U 190	Wintermeyer	CB 7569	-D =?	T	-	25/						19)
27/23	dt	U 154	Kusch	FB 9621	-T 8000=	T	BT.14	27/		am -MT	Florida	8580=	03.56 S/ 36.43 W	20)
27/23	dt	U 154	Kusch	FB 9621	-D 7500+	T	BT.14	27/		am -D	Cardinal Gibbons	7191=	03.56 S/ 36.43 W	20)
27/23	dt	U 154	Kusch	FB 9621	-T 6000+?	T	BT.14	27/		am -DT	John Worthington	8166+	03.52 S/ 36.48 W	20)
27/23	dt	U 154	Kusch	FB 9621	-D 7000+	T	BT.14	27/				-----		20)
27/23	dt	U 154	Kusch	FB 9621	-D 7000+	T	BT.14	27/				-----		20)
30/	dt	U 126	Kietz	ET 6243	-D 8000+	T	-	30/2157		am -D	Flora MacDonald	7177=§	07.15 N/ 13.20 W	21)
June 1943														
2/	dt	U 126	Kietz	ET 6246	-T +	T	TS.42s	2/0536		br -MT	Standella	6197=	07.25 N/ 13.26 W	
3/	dt	U 180	Musenberg	FL 3816	-D: 5166+	T	-	3/		gr -D	Boris	5166+	07.14 S/ 18.41 W	
(1. 6.)	dt	U 119	v.Kameke	BB 75	---------	M	-	3/		pa -M	Halma	2937+	44.17 N/ 62.23 W	1)

18) *U 92* reported one ship sunk, one torpedoed. But these probably were detonations of depth charges.
19) *U 190* fired a two shot-spread and heard one hit without detonating. 20) *U 154* fired six torpedoes, and reported one tanker torpedoed, one freighter sunk, one tanker probably sunk, and two freighters sunk. The *Florida* was towed into Fortaleza by USS *Saucy*; the *Cardinal Gibbons* arrived at Port of Spain, Trinidad, on June 5th.
21) The *Flora MacDonald* was beached in damaged condition and became a total loss.
 1) The xB-Dienst intercepted signals from the British S/S *Alva* (1584 gross tons) on June 7th, and from S/S *Highland Count* on June 10th concerning mine damage incurred off Halifax. But there is no data about these ships in Allied archives.

1	2	3	4	5	6		7	8	9	10	11	12	13	14	15
June 1943, cont.															
10/tags	dt	U 66	Markworth	DC 10	-T	8000+	T	-	10/	am	-MT	Esso Gettysburg	10173+	31.02 N/ 79.17 W	
(7. 6.)	dt	U 214	Graf v. Treuberg	EK 46	---------		M	-	20/	am	-D	Santa Maria	6507=	14.34 N/ 17.28 W	
21/	dt	U 513	Guggen-berger	GB 15	-D	5000+	T	-	21/	sw	-D	Venezia	1673+	25.50 S/ 38.38 W	
22/2046	dt	U 572	Kummetat	DR 4133	-D	10000+	T	UGS.10	22/	fr	-DT	Lot	4220+	32. N/ 43. W	
25/	dt	U 513	Guggen-berger	GB 15	-D	=	T	-	25/0350	am	-DT	Eagle	6003=	23.07 S/ 41.53 W	
27/	dt	U 199	Kraus	GB	-D	7176=	TA	-	27/	am	-D	Charles Willson Peale	-----	50m S Rio de Jan.	2)
28/0643	dt	U 172	Emmermann	FD 7458	-D:	4952+	T	-	28/0300	br	-D	Vernon City	4748+	04.30 S/ 27.30 W	3)
30/	dt	U 759	Friedrich	EC 3932	-S	+	A	-	30/						4)
July 1943															
1/	dt	U 513	Guggen-berger	GB 16	-D	3000+	T	.	2/0937	bz	-D	Tutóia	1125+	24.43 S/ 47.19 W	
2/	dt	U 66	Markworth	DB 62	-T	7000+	TA	-	2/	am	-DT	Bloody Marsh	10195+	31.33 N/ 78.57 W	
2/	dt	U 618	Baberg	ET 5498	-D	7000+	T	-	2/	br	-D	Empire Kohinoor	5225+	06.20 N/ 16.30 W	
3/	dt	U 513	Guggen-berger	GA 38	-D	7000+	T	.	3/	am	-D	Elihu B.Washburne	7176+	24.03 S/ 45.11 W	
4/	dt	U 199	Kraus	GA	-S	+	A	-	4/						1)
4/1745	dt	U 590	Krüer	FA 5322	-D	4000+	T	.	4/	bz	-D	Pelotaslóide	5228+	00.24 S/ 47.36 W	1)
5/	dt	U 759	Friedrich	EC 1253	-D	6000+	T	-	5/	am	-D	Maltran	3513+	18.11 N/ 74.57 W	
6/	dt	U 199	Kraus	GA	-S	+	A	-	6/						1a)

2) *U 199* reported two hits on a steamer named *Liberty Schjal*, but in reality the *Ch.W.Peale* was attacked and missed.
3) *U 172* reported this ship as the *Cornish City*.
4) *U 759* reported the sinking of one sailing freight vessel by gunfire.
1) The *Pelotaslóide* was escorted by the Brazilian sub-chasers (SC) *Jacuí* and *Jundiaí*.
1a) *U 199* reported the sinking of one sailing freight vessel by gunfire off Rio de Janeiro.

1	2	3	4	5	6	7	8	9	10	11	12	13	14	15
July 1943, cont.														
7/	dt	U 185	Maus	FC 7179	-T 8000+	T	BT.18	7/	am	-DT	William Boyce Thompson	7061+	04.05 S/ 35.58 W	2)
7/	dt	U 185	Maus	FC 7179	-D 8000+	T	BT.18	7/	am	-D	James Robertson	7176+	04.05 S/ 35.58 W	2)
7/	dt	U 185	Maus	FC 7179	-D 7000=	T	BT.18	7/						2)
7/	dt	U 185	Maus	FB 9396	-D 6000+	T	BT.18	7/	am	-DT	S.B.Hunt	6840=	03.51 S/ 36.22 W	2)
7/	dt	U 185	Maus	FB 9396	-D 6000+	T	BT.18	7/	am	-D	Thomas Sinnickson	7176+	03.51 S/ 36.22 W	2)
8/0520	dt	U 510	Eick	EP 4679	-T 10000=	T	TJ.1	8/0520	nw	-MT	B.P.Newton	10324+	05.50 N/ 50.20 W	3)
8/0521	dt	U 510	Eick	EP 4679	-D 6000=	T	TJ.1							3)
8/0720	dt	U 510	Eick	EP 4925	-D 6000+	T	TJ.1	8/	am	-D	Eldena	6900+	05.50 N/ 50.20 W	3)
9/	dt	U 508	Staats	EV 6729	-D 12000+	T	-	9/	fr	-D	De la Salle	8400+	05.50 N/ 02.22 E	
9/	dt	U 508	Staats	EV 6729	-D 6000+	T	-	9/	br	-D	Manchester Citizen	5343+	05.50 N/ 02.22 E	
10/0250	dt	U 510	Eick	EP 2984	-M: 2475+	T	-	10/	sw	-M	Scandinavia	1641+	08.21 N/ 48.30 W	4)
12/0656	dt	U 172	Emmermann	GB 5466	-D: 8200+	T	-	12/	am	-D	African Star	6507+	25.46 S/ 40.35 W	
12/1558	it	CAGNI	Roselli-Lorenzini	27n/21w	-D 5000=	T	-							5)
14/	dt	U 572	Kummetat	EO 1466	-S +	A	-	14/	br	-S	Harvard	114+	10.05 N/ 60.20 W	
15/2043	dt	U 172	Emmermann	GC 1613	-D: 4558+	T	-	15/	br	-D	Harmonic	4558+	23.00 S/ 33.00 W	
15/	dt	U 572	Kummetat	EO 1198	-S +	A	-	15/	br	-S	Gilbert B.Walters	176+	09.40 N/ 59.50 W	
15/	dt	U 135	Luther	-------	---------	T	OS.51	15/	br	-D	Twickenham	4762=	28.36 N/ 13.18 W	
16/	dt	U 306	v.Trotha	EK 79	-D 7000+	T	.	16/	br	-M	Kaipara	5882=	13.30 N/ 17.43 W	6)
16/	dt	U 306	v.Trotha	EK 79	-D 7000+	T	.	16/						6)
16/	dt	U 306	v.Trotha	EK 79	-D 7000+	T	.	16/						6)
16/	dt	U 306	v.Trotha	EK 79	-D 6000+	T	.	16/						6)
16/	dt	U 306	v.Trotha	EK 49	-D 5000+?	T	.	16/						6)

2) *U 185* probably made two attacks. In the first, hits on two ships were observed. The ships were left in sinking condition. One additional magnetic detonation was heard. In the second attack, one munitions ship exploded, and one other slowly sank.
3) *U 510* fired three torpedoes at 05.20, 05.21 and 05.22, and reported hits on a tanker of 10,000 tons, a ship of 6,000 tons, and a ship of 5,000 gross tons. In a second attack, at 07.19 and 07.20 two ships of 6,000 and 6,900 gross tons were hit. At 1307 a ship of 6,000 gross tons was sunk. Escorts were the USS *Somers* and 5 SCs. 4) The *Scandinavia* was stopped in accordance with prize regulations and sunk.
5) *Cagni* fired three torpedoes and reported one hit. 6) *U 306* shadowed a convoy from EK 79 to EK 49, and reported four ships with 27,000 gross tons sunk, and one additional ship probably sunk.

1	2	3	4	5	6	7	8	9	10	11	12	13	14	15
July 1943, cont.														
16/	dt	U 84	Uphoff	DL 6415	-D 6000+	T	-	16/						7)
16/	dt	U 513	Guggen-berger	-------	---------	T	-	16/1600	am	-D	Richard Caswell	7177+	28.10 S/ 46.30 W	
18/	dt	U 508	Staats	EV 9933	-D: 7369+	TA	-	18/	br	-M	Incomati	7369+	03.09 N/ 04.15 E	
20/	dt	U 455	Scheibe	CG 5832	-D =	T	.	20/						8)
21/	dt	U 84	Uphoff	DL 2618	-D 7000=?	T	-							9)
22/	dt	U 66	Markworth	DN 36	-T =	TA	-	22/	am	-TT	Cherry Valley	10172=	25.10 N/ 68.35 W	10)
24/	dt	U 199	Kraus	GB 4191	-D 10000+	T	-	24/0930	br	-D	Henzada	4161+	25.30 S/ 44.00 W	
24/2059	dt	U 172	Emmermann	FR 1517	-D: 6000+	T	-	24/	br	-D	Fort Chilcotin	7133+	15.03 S/ 32.35 W	
25/	it	CAGNI	Roselli-Lorenzini	07n/21w	*CV 23000=*	*T*	*Task F.*	25/	br	ACL	Asturias	22048=	06.52 N/ 20.45 W	11)
(1. 6.)	dt	U 119	v.Kameke	BB 75	---------	M	-	28/	am	-D	John A.Poor	7176=	42.51 N/ 64.55 W	12)
28/	dt	U 615	Kapitzky	EC 9626	-T 6000+	T	-	28/	nl	-DT	Rosalia	3177+	12.07 N/ 69.13 W	
August 1943														
1/	dt	U 185	Maus	FJ 8372	-D 5000+	T	TJ.2s	31/2105	bz	-D	Bagé	8235+	11.29 S/ 36.49 W	
2/	dt	U 732	Carlsen	DN 7361	-D 7000+	T	.	2/						1)
2/	dt	U 732	Carlsen	DN 7361	-D =	T	.	2/				-----		1)
2/	dt	U 732	Carlsen	DN 7361	-D =	T	.	2/				-----		1)
5/	dt	U 566	Hornkohl	CA 8152	DD 1850+	T	-	5/	am	APY	Plymouth	2265+	36.17 N/ 74.29 W	
6/	dt	U 185	Maus	FK 6272	-D 5000+	TA	-	6/0450	br	-D	Fort Halkett	7133+	09.30 S/ 25.50 W	

7) *U 84* reported one ship torpedoed and left burning.
8) *U 455* fired two two-shot spreads and one stern shot. Two detonations were heard.
9) *U 84* heard one detonation of a pistol with detonation, probably a dud.
10) *U 66* observed two hits during the first attack. A three-torpedo spread fired during a second attack missed. The ship escaped after a gunfire attack, with some list to port.
11) *Cagni* reported an attack against a carrier, escorted by three destroyers. In reality the big ship was an AMC.
12) The *John A.Poor* was probably not hit by a torpedo but by a mine, because there was no attack report.
1) *U 732* reported one ship sunk, one torpedoed, and two other hits heard.

1	2	3	4	5	6	7	8	9	10	11	12	13	14	15
August 1943, cont.														
7/	dt	U 757	Deetz	ET 4418	-D: 4116+	T	-	6/	nw	-M	Fernhill	4116+	06.58 N/ 19.15 W	
28/früh	dt	U 107 ?	Simmermacher	-------	---------	T	-	28/früh	am	-D	Albert Gallatin	7176=	near Savannah	2)
September 1943														
11/	dt	U 107 ?	Simmermacher	-------	---------	T	NG.385	11/1359	am	-DT	Rapidan (AO 18)	8246=	33.26 N/ 72.47 W	2)
18/	dt	U 260	Purkhold	AK 9553	-T	groß=?	T	HX.256	18/1645	am	-D	William Pepperell	(7176)	55.02 N/ 29.27 W	3)
20/	dt	U 161	Achilles	FR 52	-D: 5472+	T	-	20/	br	-D	St.Usk	5472+	16.30 S/ 29.28 W	
20/0457	dt	U 270	Otto	AK 0366	DD	+	T'	ON.202	20/0305	br	PF	Lagan	1370=	57.09 N/ 27.28 W	4)
20/	dt	U 260	Purkhold	AK 0321	-D	6800=?	T	ON.202					-----		5)
20/0932	dt	U 238	Hepp	AK 3939	-D	5000+	T	ON.202 ONS.18	20/0540	am	-D	Theodore Dwight Weld	7176+	57.03 N/ 28.08 W	6)
20/0932	dt	U 238	Hepp	AK 3939	-D	5000+	T	ON.202	20/0540	am	-D	Frederick Douglass (s.u.)	7176=	57.03 N/ 28.08 W	6)
20/2151	dt	U 305	Bahr	AK 0218	DD	+	T'	ON.202	20/1756	ca	DD	St.Croix (s.u.)	1190=	57.30 N/ 31.10 W	7)
20/2156	dt	U 645	Ferro	AK 3932	-D	5000+	Tf	ON.202	20/	am	-D	Frederick Douglass (s.o.)	7176+	57.03 N/ 28.08 W	6)
20/2250	dt	U 305	Bahr	AK 0218	DD	+	T'f	ON.202	20/	ca	DD	St.Croix (s.o.)	1190+	57.30 N/ 31.10 W	7)
20/2253	dt	U 305	Bahr	AK 0218	DD	+	T'	ON.202	20/	br	PF	Itchen	-----		7)
20/23	dt	U 229	Schetelig	AK 6232	DD	+	T'	ON.202	20/				-----		8)
21/0022	dt	U 952	Curio	AK 2962	DD	+	T'	ON.202	20/2236	br	PE	Polyanthus	925+	57.00 N/ 31.10 W	
21/0028	dt	U 229	Schetelig	AK 2889	DD	+	T'	ON.202	20/				-----		9)
21/0127	dt	U 641	Rendtel	AK 2936	DD	+	T'	ON.202	20/				-----		10)

2) The *A.Gallatin*, escorted by the blimp K-34, reported sighting three torpedoes. One hit but didn't detonate. The *Rapidan* reported damage from a near-by detonation. There is no attack report, but only *U 107* was in the area.

3) *U 260* heard one hit without a detonation. The *W.Pepperell* reported one torpedo hit her torpedo net.

4) These attacks by U-boats of the "Leuthen" group against the combined convoys ON.202 and ONS.18 were the first attacks with the acoustic torpedo "T-5" or "Zaunkönig" (Gnat). The *Lagan* was towed into port, but became a total loss.

5) *U 260* heard two or three hits without detonations. They may have been duds or depth charges.

1	2	3	4	5	6	7	8	9	10	11	12	13	14	15
September 1943, cont.														
21/0341 dt		U 377	Kluth	AK 2928	DD	=	T´	ON.202	21/			-----		11)
21/0435 dt		U 270	Otto	AK 2882	DD	+	T´	ON.202	21/			-----		12)
21/0610 dt		U 584	Deecke	AK 2949	DD	=	T´	ON.202	21/	ca	PE Chambly	-----		13)
21/tags dt		U 123	v.Schroeter	EP 44	-T	=	T	.						14)
21/tags dt		U 123	v.Schroeter	EO 44	-D	5000+?	T	.						14)
22/0550 dt		U 377	Kluth	AK 4585	-D	5000=	T´	ON.202	22/			-----		15)
22/2357 dt		U 952	Curio	AK 7156	DD	+	T´	ON.202	22/			-----		16)
23/0156 dt		U 666	Engel	AK 7147	DD	+	T´	ON.202	23/	br	PE Morden	-----		17)
23/0156 dt		U 666	Engel	AK 7147	DD	+	T´	ON.202	22/2155	br	PF Itchen	1370+	53.25 N/ 39.42 W	17)
23/0414 dt		U 238	Hepp	AJ 9522	-D	5000+	T	ON.202	23/0020	nw	-M Oregon Express	3642+	53.40 N/ 39.50 W	18)
23/0414 dt		U 238	Hepp	AJ 9522	-D	5000+	T	ON.202	23/0020	br	-D Fort Jemseg	7134+	53.18 N/ 40.24 W	18)
23/0414 dt		U 238	Hepp	AJ 9522	-D	5000+	T.	ON.202	23/0020	nw	-D Skjelbred	5096+	53.18 N/ 40.24 W	18)
23/0414 dt		U 238	Hepp	AJ 9522	-D	4000+	T.	ON.202				-----		18)
23/0414 dt		U 238	Hepp	AJ 9522	-D	=	T	ON.202				-----		18)
23/0428 dt		U 260	Purkhold	AK 7179	DD	+	T´	ON.202	23/	br	PE Chambly	-----		19)
23/0831 dt		U 952	Curio	AJ 9353	-D	10000=	T	ON.202	23/0045	am	-D Steel Voyager	6198+	53.18 N/ 40.24 W	20)
23/0838 dt		U 952	Curio	AJ 9353	-D	6000=	T.	ON.202	23/0045	am	-D James Gordon Bennett	7176=	53. N/ 40. W	20)
23/0947 dt		U 758	Manseck	AJ 9384	-D	7175+	T.	ON.202	23/					21)
23/0950 dt		U 758	Manseck	AJ 9384	DD	+	T´	ON.202	23/			-----		21)

11) *U 377* heard a Gnat detonation after 3 min 5 sec a miss. 12) *U 270* heard one Gnat detonation after 11 min, an end-of-run detonation.

13) *U 584* heard a Gnat detonation after 7 min 50 sec, the corvette HMCS *Chambly* evaded the torpedo, which detonated in the wake.

14) *U 123* heard two hits and three additional detonations on a tanker and one Liberty-ship.

15) *U 377* heard a Gnat detonation after 26 sec, misfunction. 16) *U 952* heard one Gnat detonation after 10 min 3 sec, end-of-run detonation.

17) *U 666* heard a Gnat detonation after 8 min 21 sec; the torpedo detonated in the wake of HMCS *Morden*. The second Gnat hit the *Itchen* after 1 min 10 sec; debris from the ship was later found on the conning tower of the U-boat.

18) *U 238* fired two T-3 torpedoes, two FAT, and one T-3. Four ships of 19,000 gross tons were reported sunk, and one damaged, but only three really sank.

19) *U 260* heard a Gnat detonation after 3 min 29 sec, really near HMCS *Chambly*.

20) *U 952* fired two T-3s which hit the *Steel Voyager*, one additional T-3, and one FAT. The *J.G.Bennett* was hit by a dud.

1	2	3	4	5	6	7	8	9	10	11	12	13	14	15
September 1943, cont.														
26/	dt	U 161	Achilles	FJ 6711	-D 8000+	T	-	26/1350	bz	-D	Itapagé	4998+	10.10 S/ 35.45 W	22)
October 1943														
7/2158	dt	U 758	*Manseck*	AK 6258	DD +	T'	SC.143	7/1900	po	DD	*Orkan*	-----		1)
8/0331	dt	U 610	*v.Freyberg*	AK 6371	DD =	T'	SC.143					-----		2)
8/0705	dt	U 378	*Müder*	AK 6328	DD +	T'	SC.143	8/	po	DD	*Orkan*	1920+	56.30 N/ 26.26 W	3)
9/0727	dt	U 645	Ferro	AL 0279	-D 6500+	T	SC.143	9/0645	am	-D	Yorkmar	5612+	56.38 N/ 20.30 W	
12/	dt	U 536	Schauenburg	CC 52	-D 9000+	T	-	12/						4)
15/2248	dt	U 426	Reich	AK 3739	-D 6000=	T	ONS.20s	16/	br	-D	Essex Lance	6625+	57.53 N/ 28.00 W	5)
17/	dt	U 309	Mahrholz	AK 24	-D =	T	ONS.20							6)
(9.10.)	dt	U 220	Barber	BB 63	---------	M	-	19/	am	-D	Delisle	3478+	47.49 N/ 52.27 W	
(9.10.)	dt	U 220	Barber	BB 63	---------	M	-	19/	br	-D	Penolver	3721+	47.19 N/ 52.27 W	
22/	dt	U 214	Stock	DP 6178	-D 7000+	T	-	22/						7)
22/	*dt*	*U 68*	*Lauzemis*	*EU 4762*	*PE +*	*T*	.	22/	br	APC	Orfasay	545+	05.58 N/ 11.30 W	
22/	dt	U 68	Lauzemis	EU 4762	-T 3000+	T	.	22/	nw	-DT	Litiopa	5356+	06.18 N/ 11.55 W	
23/1209	dt	U 170	Pfeffer	GA 3857	-D: 4663+	T	-	23/0800	bz	-D	Campos	4663+	25.07 S/ 45.40 W	
24/	dt	U 155	Piening	FB 3771	-M: 5393+	T	-	24/	nw	-M	Siranger	5393+	00.00 N/ 38.45 W	
26/2155	*dt*	*U 448*	*Dauter*	*BE 6549*	*DD +*	*T'*	-	26/				-----		8)
26/2219	*dt*	*U 448*	*Dauter*	*BE 6549*	*DD +*	*T'*	-	26/				-----		8)

21) *U 758* heard one FAT hit an auxiliary of the *Bridgeport*-type after 9 min 20 sec, and after 9 min 20 sec, a Gnat detonation on a destroyer. Then sinking noises were heard. Both torpedoes must have detonated at the end of the run.

22) *U 161* didn't sink the sailing vessel *Cisne Branco*; she was lost by grounding on the 26th at 04.24 S/37.45 W.

1) *U 758* heard one Gnat detonation after 1 min 30 sec, in the wake of ORP *Orkan*.

2) *U 610* heard one Gnat detonation after 8 min, most probably an end-of-run detonation. 3) *U 378* observed a hit after 3 min 48 sec.

4) *U 536* reported as sunk one Victory or Liberty freighter that had been on course 260°. 5) The boats of *Essex Lance* were reported sighted by *U 842*.

6) *U 309* fired a four-torpedo spread and heard two FAT-detonations after 13 min, probably end-of-run detonations.

7) *U 214* reported one independently steaming ship sunk. – 8) *U 448* heard one Gnat detonation after 10 min 20 sec and couldn't sight the destroyer after 3 min. One additional Gnat detonation was heard after 1 min 35 sec, a misfire.

1	2	3	4	5	6	7	8	9	10	11	12	13	14	15
October 1943, cont.														
30/1012	dt	U 405	Hopmann	BD 1647	-D	=	T.	.	30/			-----		9)
31/0925	*dt*	*U 262*	*Franke*	*BE 5715*	*DD*	+	*Tᵒ*	MKS.28				-----		10)
31/0925	dt	U 262	Franke	BE 5715	-D	7000+	T	SL.138	31/0833	nw	-D	Hallfried	2968+ 46.05 N/ 20.26 W	
31/0925	dt	U 262	Franke	BE 5715	-D	=	T					-----		
31/0942	*dt*	*'U 333*	*Cremer*	*BE 5714*	*DD*	+	*T*	*MKS.28*				-----		*11)*
31/2124	dt	U 68	Lauzemis	EW 7199	-D:	7422+	T	-	31/	br	-D	New Columbia	6574+ 04.25 N/ 05.03 W	12)
November 1943														
2/	dt	U 848	Rollmann	FD 60	-D	5000+	T	-	2/	br	-D	Baron Semple	4573+ 05. S/ 21. W	
4/	dt	U 218	Becker	EN 33	-S	+	A	-	4/					1)
9/o602	*dt*	*U 466*	*Hagenkötter*	*CF 2912*	*DD*	+	*T'*	*MKS.29A*	*9/*			-----		2)
9/1023	*dt*	*U 262*	*Franke*	*CF 2658*	*DD*	=?	*T'*	*MKS.29A*	*9/*			-----		3)
9/1109	dt	U 228	Christo-phersen	CF 2685	-D	5000+	T'	MKS.29A s	9/			-----		4)
11/	dt	U 516	Tillessen	EC 77	-D	+	T	-	12/	pa	-D	Pompoon	1082+ 11. N/ 75. W	
16/0854	*dt*	*U 542*	*Coester*	*BD 3917*	*DD*	=?	*T'*	*Esc.Gr.*	*16/*			-----		5)
17/	dt	U 516	Tillessen	EB 90	-S	+	A	-	17/	co	-S	Ruby	39+ 11.24 N/ 79.54 W	
18/	*dt*	*U 515*	*Henke*	*BE*	*DD*	+	*Tᵒ*	*MKS.30*	*18/1524*	*br*	*PS*	*Chanticleer*	*1350+ 40.06 N/ 19.48 W*	6)
19/2315	*dt*	*U 238*	*Hepp*	*BE 8737*	*PF*	+	*Tᵒ*	*MKS.30*	*19/*					6)
23/	dt	U 516	Tillessen	EB 80	-T	+	T	-	23/0600	am	-DT	Elizabeth Kellogg	5189+ 11.10 N/ 80.42 W	
24/	dt	U 516	Tillessen	EB 80	-D	+	T	-	24/0200	am	-D	Melville E.Stone	7176+ 10.36 N/ 80.19 W	

9) *U 405* heard two FAT end-of-run detonations after 12 min. - 10) *U 68* reported this ship as the *Troilus* (Brit.S/S).

11) *U 262* fired two T-3 and two FAT torpedoes, and heard four detonations. One Gnat hit on a destroyer was heard after 6 min 30 sec. Sinking noises were heard; in addition, the sinking of a second ship and a hit on a third were assumed.

12) *U 333* heard a Gnat detonation on a one-funnel-destroyer after 4 min 20 sec. The torpedo detonated near the ship.

1) *U 218* reported the sinking of a sailing freight vessel. - 2) *U 466* heard one Gnat detonation after 4 min 15 sec.

3) *U 262* heard one Gnat detonation after 13 min 20 sec.

4) *U 228* heard one Gnat detonation after 7 min 10 sec on a straggler, and sinking noises. Probably an end-of-run detonation.

5) *U 542* heard one Gnat end-of-run detonation after 7 min.

6) The *Chanticleer* was towed into port but was not repaired. The convoy was the combined MKS.30 and SL.139.

North Sea - Atlantic

1	2	3	4	5	6	7	8	9	10	11	12	13	14	15
November 1943, cont.														
28/0016	dt	U 764	v.Bremen	CF 6275	DD	+	T'	MKS.31				-----		7)
28/0523	dt	U 107	Simmermacher	CF	DD	=	T'	.				-----		7a)
28/0717	dt	U 262	Franke	CF 6223	-D	5000+	T	MKS.31	28/			-----		8)
28/0717	dt	U 262	Franke	CF 6223	-D	5000+	T	MKS.31	28/			-----		8)
28/0717	dt	U 262	Franke	CF 6223	-D	5000+	T	SL.140	28/			-----		8)
30/	dt	U 68	Lauzemis	ET 6643	-D	7500+	T	-	30/	fr	-D	Fort de Vaux	5186+ 06.32 N/ 12.20 W	
December 1943														
3/	dt	U 193	Pauckstadt	DL 26	-T	12000+	T	-	3/	am	-TT	Touchet	10172+ 25.50 N/ 86.30 W	
4/	dt	U 129	v.Harpe	DN 1362	-D	6000+	T	.	4/	cu	-D	Libertad	5441+ 24.30 N/ 74.32 W	
8/1200	dt	U 516	Tillessen	EL 3156	-D	5500+	T	-	8/	pa	-M	Colombia	1064+ 09.50 N/ 78.55 W	
13/	dt	U 129	v.Harpe	BC 4993	DD	+	T	.	13/				-----	1)
16/1021	dt	U 516	Tillessen	EC 9235	-T	10000+	T'	-	16/	am	-TT	McDowell	10195+ 13.08 N/ 70.02 W	
17/2020	dt	U 515	Henke	EV 7611	-D:	5080+	T	-	17/	br	-D	Kingswood	5080+ 05.57 N/ 01.43 E	
20/2000	dt	U 515	Henke	EV 8134	-D:	7400+	T	-	19/	br	-D	Phemius	7406+ 05.01 N/ 00.47 E	
23/1143	dt	U 471	Klövekorn	AK 0164	-D	8000=	T'	UT.3	23/	am	BB	Arkansas	----- 300m W Rockall	2)
24/0143	dt	U 415	Neide	BE 7343	DD	+	T'	TF.21.14	24/	am	DD	Decatur	-----	3)
24/0505	dt	U 275	Bork	BE 7343	DD	+	T'	TF.21.14	24/	am	DD	Leary	1090+ 45.15 N/ 21.40 W	4)
24/0521	dt	U 382	Zorn	BE 7319	DD	+	T'							4)
24/2057	dt	U 415	Neide	BE 7321	DD	+	T'	OS.62	24/	br	DD	Hurricane	1340+ 45.10 N/ 22.05 W	5)
24/	dt	U 515	Henke	EU 8372	-D	9000+	T	.	24/	br	-M	Dumana	8427+ 04.27 N/ 06.58 W	

7) U 764 heard a Gnat end-of-run detonation after 14 min 4 sec and sinking noises. The convoy was the combined MKS.31 and SL.140.
7a) U 107 heard one Gnat detonation. - 8) U 262 fired three torpedoes and heard three detonations; one Gnat was an end-of-run detonation.
1) U 129 heard one early Gnat detonation after 47 sec. - 2) U 471 heard one hit with no detonation. In reality the US battleship Arkansas in the convoy observed one torpedo that missed.
3) U 415 fired one three-torpedo FAT spread, and missed the CVE Card. The Gnat detonated after 8 min, but missed the USS Decatur.
4) The Leary belonged to US Task Group 21.14 (CVE Card). She was first hit by a Gnat from U 275, and sunk after one Gnat from U 382 missed.
5) The convoys OS.62 and KMS.36 were combined.

1	2	3	4	5	6	7	8	9	10	11	12	13	14	15
December 1943, cont.														
26/	dt	U 392	*Schümann*	AL 4592	DD	+	T	. 26/				-----		6)
26/	dt	U 392	Schümann	AL 4592	-D	=	T	. 26/				-----		6)
26/	dt	U 530	Lange	EB 97	-T	10000+	T	- 26/	am	-TT	Chapultepec	10195=	10.30 N/ 78.58 W	
29/0234	dt	U 629	*Bugs*	BE 5763	DD	+	T'	- 29/				-----		7)
29/2137	dt	U 541	*Petersen*	BE 7617	DD	+	T'	E.G. 29/				-----		8)
29/2202	dt	U 541	*Petersen*	BE 7536	DD	+	T'	E.G. 29/				-----		8)
30/0001	dt	U 541	*Petersen*	BE 7374	DD	+	T'	E.G. 29/				-----		8)
30/0027	dt	U 543	*Hellriegel*	BE 5880	DD	+	T'	E.G. 29/				-----		9)
30/0528	dt	U 421	*Kolbus*	BE 6592	DD	+	T'	E.G. 30/				-----		10)
30/1139	dt	U 129	*v.Harpe*	DC 2168	DD	+	T'	- 30/				-----		11)
30/	dt	U 545	Mannesmann	AL 1228	-D	6000+	T	ON.217 30/	br	-M	Empire Housman	7359=	60.30 N/ 24.35 W	12)
30/	dt	U 545	Mannesmann	AL 1228	-D	6000+	T	ON.217 30/			(s.u.)	-----		12)
30/	dt	U 545	Mannesmann	AL 1228	-D	6000+	T	ON.217 30/				-----		12)
30/	dt	U 545	Mannesmann	AL 1228	-T	=	T	ON.217 30/				-----		12)
30/	dt	U 744	Blischke	AL 1215	-D	9000=	T	ON.217 30/				-----		12)
31/2235	dt	U 541	*Petersen*	BE 8181	DD	+	T'	E.G. 31/				-----		13)
January 1944														
1/0232	dt	U 545	*Mannesmann*	AL 1248	DD	+	T'	ON.217 31/				-----		1)
1/1746	dt	U 382	*Zorn*	BE 8224	PE	+	T'	. 1/				-----		2)

6) *U 392* observed one hit under the bridge of a destroyer, and heard one detonation from a 3-torpedo spread of FAT after 3 min 1 sec.

7) *U 629* heard one Gnat detonation on an A/I-destroyer and sinking noises. - 8) *U 541* attacked a hunting-group and heard one Gnat end-of-run detonation after 12 min 51 sec, observed one Gnat-hit after 45 sec, and heard one Gnat detonation after 5 min 50 sec.

9) *U 543* heard one Gnat end-of-run detonation after 11 min 12 sec. - 10) *U 421* heard a Gnat end-of-run detonation after 10 min.

11) *U 129* fired a 4-torpedo spread and heard one Gnat end-of-run detonation after 12 min 35 sec.

12) *U 545* fired four torpedoes and heard four detonations. One ship observed sinking on Jan.1st. The damaged *Emp.Housman* was probably attacked by *U 744* also, but was not sunk until Jan.3rd by the latter. So *U 545* deserves only half the credit.

13) *U 541* reported one destroyer sunk by Gnat. - 1) *U 545* reported one destroyer sunk by Gnat.

2) *U 382* heard one Gnat end-of-run detonation on an auxiliary sub-chaser after 12 min 10 sec, and a boiler explosion.

1	2	3	4	5	6	7	8	9	10	11	12	13	14	15

January 1944, cont.

1	2	3	4	5	6	7	8	9	10 11	12	13	14	15
2/	dt	U 275	Bork	BE 8248	DD	+ T´		2/			——		3)
2/	dt	U 275	Bork	BE 8248	DD	+ T´		2/			——		3)
3/0029	dt	U 543	Hellriegel	BC 5489	DD	+ T´		2/			——		4)
3/	dt	U 270	Otto	BE 8559	DD	+ T´		3/			——		5)
3/	dt	U 744	Blischke	AE 7877	-D	6000+ T	ON.217s	3/	br -M	Empire Housman	7359+	60.50 N/ 22.07 W	6)
7/1711	dt	U 305	Bahr	BE 7655	DD +	+ T´	E.G.	7/	br PF	Tweed	1370+	48.18 N/ 21.19 W	
9/	dt					T	OS.64	9/	ca PE	Amelia	925=	50. N/ 18. W	6a)
11/1753	dt	U 953	Marbach	CF 2374	PE	+ T´	KMS.38	11/	ca PE	Lunenburg	(925)		6b)
13/0416	dt	U 471	Klövekorn	AL 6712	-D	9000= T´	−	13/			-----		7)
15/040.	dt	U 377	Kluth	BE 5748	DD	= T´	−	15/			-----		8)
16/2248	dt	U 960	Heinrich	AK 8518	-D	7000+ T	ON.219s	16/	am -D	Sumner I.Kimball	7176+	52.35 N/ 35.00 W	
18/	dt	U 571	Lüssow	AL 9845	DD	=? T´	.	18/			——		9)
19/0853	dt	U 390	Geissler	AL 3984	-D	7000= T´	.	19/					10)
19/0855	dt	U 390	Geissler	AL 3984	-D	8000= T´	.	19/					10)
23/2115	dt	U 386	Albrecht	AM 5370	APC:	+ T´		23/					11)
25/1230	dt	U 271	Barleben	AL 9846	DD	= T´		25/			——		12)

February 1944

1	2	3	4	5	6	7	8	9	10 11	12	13	14	15
5/	dt	U 845	Weber	BC 5184	-D	7800+? T´	.	5/			-----		1)
8/0145	dt	U 985	Kessler	AE 8688	-D	6000+ T	RA.56	7/	br -D	Margit	1735+	61.30 N/ 10.30 W	
9/	dt	U 845	Weber	BB 6386	-D	6000+ T	.	9/	br -D	Kelmscott	7039=	47.31 N/ 52.23 W	

3) *U 275* reported two destroyers sunk by Gnats. 4) *U 543* heard one Gnat end-of-run detonation after 11 min 45 sec. 5) *U 270* reported one destroyer sunk by a Gnat. 6) *Empire Housman* was torpedoed on Dec.30th by *U 545* and possibly by *U 744*.
6a) *Amelia* lost her rudder after being hit by a U-boat torpedo. 6b) *U 953* reported a hit on the corvette with the designation K.151.
7) *U 471* heard one Gnat detonation after 90 sec. 8) *U 377* heard one Gnat end-of-run detonation after 9 min.
9) *U 571* heard one Gnat end-of-run detonation after 12 min. 10) At 0830 *U 390* missed four ships with a 3-torpedo spread, and heard at 1143 one hit without a detonation (dud), and at 0853 and 0855 two Gnat detonations, after run times of 3 min 20 sec and 6 min 43 sec.
11) *U 386* heard one Gnat detonation after 2 min 47 sec on a trawler named *Horseflash (?)*.
12) *U 271* heard one Gnat end-of-run detonation after 11 min. 1) *U 845* heard one Gnat end-of-run detonation after 10 min.

1	2	3	4	5	6	7	8	9	10	11	12	13	14	15
February 1944, cont.														
10/0111 dt		U 256	Brauel	BE 2511	DD	+	T' HX.277	9/				-----		2)
11/0011 dt		U 731	Graf Keller	BE 2964	-D	5000+	T OS.67	10/				-----		3)
11/0012 dt		U 731	Graf Keller	BE 2996	DD	+	T' $\overline{KMS.41}$	10/				-----		3)
11/0424 dt		U 413	Poel	BE 6121	DD	+?	T' $\underline{OS.67}$	11/				-----		4)
11/0703 dt		U 413	Poel	BE 3779	DD	+	T' $\overline{KMS.41}$	11/				-----		4)
11/1802 dt		U 437	Lamby	BE 5436	DD	+	T' OS.67	11/				-----		5)
13/2020 dt		U 518	Offermann	DF 8567	CVE	+?	T'	13/				-----		6)
13/2056 dt		U 445	Graf Treuberg	AL 8245	DD	+	T' E.G.3	13/				-----		7)
15/0457 dt		U 984	Sieder	AL 6449	DD	+	T' −	15/				-----		8)
19/0422 dt		U 437	Lamby	BE 1976	DD	+	T'	19/				-----		9)
19/0424 dt		U 437	Lamby	BE 1976	DD	+	T'	19/				-----		9)
19/0730 dt		U 66	Seehausen	ET 6267	DD	1690=?	T'	19/				-----		10)
20/	dt	U 256	Brauel	BE 1834	DD	+	T' ON.224	20/				-----		11)
20/	dt	U 413	Poel	BF 24	DD	1100+	T −	20/	br		DD Warwick	1100+	50.27 N/ 05.23 W	
2o/2011 dt		U 256	Brauel	BE 1834	DD	+	T' ON.224	20/	br		PS Woodpecker	1300+	48.49 N/ 22.11 W	13)
20/2011 dt		U 256	Brauel	BE 1834	DD	+	T' ON.224	20/	br		PS Starling	-----	48.49 N/ 22.11 W	13)
26/	dt	U 66	Seehausen	EV 7154	-D	5000+	T .	26/	br		-M Silvermaple	5313+	04.44 N/ 03.20 W	14)
26/	dt	U 66	Seehausen	EV 7154	-D	5000=	T .							14)

---

2) *U 256* heard one Gnat end-of-run detonation after 12 min 30 sec.

3) *U 731* fired a spread and assumed two hits on a steamer, and heard one Gnat detonation after 2 min 30 sec.

4) *U 413* heard two Gnat end-of-run detonations after 11 min 25 sec and 12 min 24 sec. 5) *U 437* heard one end-of-run detonation after 11 min 47 sec.

6) *U 518* heard one Gnat end-of-run detonation after 13 min 45 sec on a seaplane tender similar to the German *Friesenland*.

7) *U 445* heard a Gnat end-of-run detonation after 13 min 5 sec. 8) *U 984* heard one Gnat end-of-run detonation after 12 min 30 sec.

9) *U 437* heard two Gnat detonations after 6 min and 8 min. 10) *U 66* heard one Gnat end-of-run detonation after 12 min.

13) *U 256* heard one Gnat detonation after 3 min 10 sec (a hit on *Woodpecker*, which sank during efforts to tow her in), and one probable end-of-run detonation (a detonation near *Starling*).

14) *U 66* reported one ship sunk and the captain captured. One additional detonation was heard.

1	2	3	4	5	6	7	8	9	10	11	12	13	14	15
March 1944														
1/0114	dt	U 441	Hartmann	BD 3929	DD	+	T′		1/				——		1)
1/	dt	U 66	Seehausen	EV 5877	-D	7000+	T	-	1/	fr	-D	Saint Louis	5202+	05.23 N/ 00.09 W	
1/	dt	U 358	Manke	———	————		T′	E.G.1	1/1920	br	DE	Gould	1600+	45.46 N/ 23.16 W	
2/	dt	U 744	Blischke	BE 5221	-T	1000+	T	SL.149	2/0259	br	LS	LST 362	1625+	48.00 N/ 17.23 W	2)
2/	dt	U 744	Blischke	BE 5221	-T	1000+	T	MKS.40	2/				———		2)
2/	dt	U 744	Blischke	BE 5221	-T	1000+	T		2/				———		2)
5/	dt	U 66	Seehausen	EW 8427	-D:	4975+	T	-	5/	br	-D	John Holt	4964+	03.56 N/ 07.36 E	
7/0140	dt	U 518	Offermann	EC 7470	-D	+	T	-	7/	pa	-DT	Valera	3401+	11.30 N/ 76.27 W	
9/2200	dt	U 255	Harms	AK 3862	DE	+	T′	CU.16	9/	am	DE	Leopold	1200+	58.44 N/ 25.50 W	
10/0154	dt	U 575	Boehmer	BE 5887	DD	+	T′	SL.150	9/	br	PE	Asphodel	1015+	45.24 N/ 18.09 W	3)
11/0030	dt	U 653	Kandler	BE 2451	DD	+	T′	SC.154	10/				———		4)
13/	dt	U 852	Eck	FF	-D:	4675+	T	-	13/	gr	-D	Peleus	4695+	02. S/ 10. W	5)
17/1259	dt	U 311	Zander	BE 2247	DD	+	T′	CU.17	17/				———		6)
19/1250	dt	U 311	Zander	AL 9775	-D	5000+	T.	CU.17	18/	am	-DT	Seakay	10342+	51.10 N/ 20.20 W	
20/2328	dt	U 621	Kruschka	AM 3469	DD	+	T′		20/				———		7)
21/	dt	U 66	Seehausen	EW 7183	-T	8400+	T	-	20/	br	-DT	Matadian	4275+	05.07 N/ 04.47 E	
21/2325	dt	U 413	Poel	BE 3585	DD	1000+	T′	.	21/				———		8)
21/232.	dt	U 413	Poel	BE 3585	-D	=?	T	.	21/				———		8)
22/	dt	U 802	Schmoeckel	BB 7537	-D	2000+	T	.	22/	ca	-D	Watuka	1621+	44.30 N/ 62.51 W	9)
22/	dt	U 802	Schmoeckel	BB 7537	-D	1500+	T	.	22/				———		9)
22/	dt	U 802	Schmoeckel	BB 7537	-D	1500+	T	.	22/				———		9)
22/	dt	U 802	Schmoeckel	BB 7537	-D	1500=	T	.	22/				———		9)
24/	dt	U 302	Sickel	BE 4178	DD	+	T′		24/				———		10)

1) U 441 heard one Gnat detonation after 2 min 25 sec. 2) U 744 reported three small tankers sunk (LSTs). 3) The convoy SL.150 was combined with MKS.41. 4) U 653 heard one Gnat end-of-run detonation after 11 min 35 sec. 5) U 852 tried to sink debris of the ship by gunfire; some survivors were hit and killed. 6) U 311 heard one Gnat end-of-run detonation after 13 min 5 sec. 7) U 621 heard one Gnat end-of-run detonation after 10 min 45 sec. 8) U 413 heard one Gnat end-of-run detonation after 2 min 35 sec and after firing a FAT-spread, one end-of-run detonation after 13 min. 9) U 802 reported the sinking of three small steamers of 5,000 gross tons and heard one Gnat detonation after 3 min 45 sec. 10) U 302 heard one Gnat end-of-run detonation after 11 min.

1	2	3	4	5	6	7	8	9	10	11	12	13	14	15
April 1944														
2/	dt	U 518	Offermann	DO 8211	-T 7000+	T´	.							1)
6/	dt	U 302	Sickel	-------	---------	T	SC.156	6/	nw	-MT	South America	6246+	45.05 N/ 35.11 W	
6/	dt	U 302	Sickel	-------	---------	T	SC.156	6/	nw	-D	Ruth I	3531+	45.05 N/ 35.11 W	
7/	dt	U 170	Pfeffer	DC 7265	-D 7000=	T	-	7/				-----		2)
8/	dt	U 843	Herwatz	FL 9171	-D: 7900+	T	-	8/	br	-D	Nebraska	8261+	11.55 S/ 19.52 W	
9/0928	dt	U 802	Schmoeckel	CB 2366	-D 10000+	T	HX.286	9/				-----		3)
9/0928	dt	U 802	Schmoeckel	CB 2366	-D 10000=	T	HX.286	9/				-----		3)
15/	dt	U 385	Valentiner	AL 2328	-D 16000=	T	.	15/				-----		4)
16/0753	*dt*	*U 667*	*Schroeteler*	*BE 4747*	*DE +*	*T´*	.	*16/*				------		*5)*
16/	dt	U 550	Hänert	CA 6231	-D =	T		16/	am	-DT	Pan Pennsylvania	11017+	40.07 N/ 69.24 W	
26/2046	dt	U 859	Jebsen	AK 6722	-D 4000+	T	SC.157s	26/	pa	-M	Colin	6255+	54.16 N/ 31.58 W	
27/0630	*dt*	*U 385*	*Valentiner*	*AM 4377*	*DD 1690+*	*T´*		*27/*				------		*6)*
May 1944														
1/0411	dt	U 181	Freiwald	FS 5931	-D 5872+	T	-	1/	br	-D	Janeta	5312+	18.14 S/ 20.00 W	7)
3/	*dt*	*U 765*	*Wendt*	*-------*	*---------*	*T´*	-	*3/*	*am*	*DE*	*Donnell*	*1400=*	*47.48 N/ 19.55 W*	*8)*
6/	dt	U 129	v.Harpe	FK 67	-D 4000+	T	-	6/	br	-D	Anadyr	5321+	10.55 S/ 27.30 W	
7/0432	*dt*	*U 548*	*Zimmermann*	*BB 6964*	*DD +*	*T´*	-	*7/*	*ca*	*PF*	*Valleyfield*	*1445+*	*46.03 N/ 52.24 W*	
11/	dt	U 129	v.Harpe	FR 45	-D: 6644+	T	-	11/	br	-D	Empire Heath	6643+	19. S/ 31. W	
12/2152	dt	U 190	Wintermeyer	EV 7916	-D 5500+	T	-	12/				-----		9)

1) *U 518* heard one Gnat end-of-run detonation after 13 min 25 sec near a tanker of the *Scottish American* class, and an explosion.
2) *U 170* heard two probable end-of-run detonations. 3) *U 802* fired two T-3 and two FAT, and heard one single and one double detonation.
4) *U 385* fired a T-3 3 torpedo spread, and heard two detonations and a boiler explosion. But the *Empreß*-class ship continued on course.
5) *U 667* heard one Gnat end-of-run detonation after 12 min 14 sec. 6) *U 385* heard a Gnat detonation after 1 min 47 sec.
7) This ship was reported as *Benavon*. 8) The *Donnell* was towed into harbor, but was a total loss.
9) *U 190* heard a Gnat end-of-run detonation after 13 min 5 sec.

1	2	3	4	5	6	7	8	9	10	11	12	13	14	15
May 1944, cont.														
14/0646	dt	U 541	Petersen	DC 5125	-D	=? T	.	14/				-----		10)
17/1310	dt	U 736	Reff	BE 5157	-D	= T´	.	17/				-----		11)
26/0820	dt	U 129	v.Harpe	FQ 5758	-D 5000=?	T´	-	26/				-----		12)
29/	dt	U 549	Krankenhagen	-------	--------	T.	Task F.	29/2013	am	CVE	Block Island	8600+	31.13 N/ 23.03 W	13)
29/	dt	U 549	Krankenhagen	-------	--------	T´	Task F.	29/2040	am	DE	Barr	1300=	31.14 N/ 23.00 W	13)
30/2118	dt	U 547	Niemeyer	ET 6115	-D 5000+	T.	-	30/						14)
June 1944														
5/	dt	U 539	Lauterbach-Emden	ED 1224	-D 3000+	T	.	5/	pa	-D	Pillory	1517+	18.26 N/ 67.17 W	
7/2136	dt	U 984	Sieder	BF 2769	DD	+? T´	E.G.12	7/	ca	DD	Saskatchewan	-----		1)
8/0945	dt	U 953	Marbach	BF 2739	DD 1350+	T´	E.G.12	8/	ca	DD	Qu´Appelle	-----		2)
8/0947	dt	U 953	Marbach	BF 2739	DD 1350+	T´	E.G.12	8/	ca	DD	Restigouche	-----		2)
8/0950	dt	U 953	Marbach	BF 2739	DD 1350+	T´	E.G.12	8/	ca	DD	Skeena	-----		2)
8/0044	dt	U 621	Struckmann	BF 2766	DD	=? T´	E.G.12					-----		3)
10/	dt	U 107 ?	Simmermacher			T	-	10/	pt	-D	Maria Amelia	1766=	CB 88	4)
10/2146	dt	U 539	Lauterbach	EC 9374	-T 9000=	T´	-	10/						5)
11/0738	dt	U 539	Lauterbach	EC 9617	-T 4000=	TÁ	-	11/	nl	-DT	Casandra	2701=		6)
11/0913	dt	U 275	Bork	BF 2639	DD	+ T´		11/				-----		7)
13/	dt	U 107	Simmermacher	BB 7758	-S	+ A	-	13/						4)

10) U 541 fired four T-3 and two Gnat, and heard two detonations after 13 min. Probable end-of-run detonations.
11) U 736 heard one Gnat detonation after 2 min 35 sec. 12) U 129 heard one Gnat detonation after 4 min 30 sec.
13) U 549 hit the CVE with three T-3 torpedoes and then the DE with one Gnat. The E.E.Elmore evaded one Gnat torpedo.
14) U 547 fired two FAT torpedoes, and heard one detonation after 9 min and a heavy explosion after 17 min.
1) U 984 fired three Gnats against the escort group 12; one detonated in the cat-gear of HMCS Saskatchewan.
2) U 953 fired four Gnats; three detonated in the wakes or near the ships. 3) U 621 heard one end-of-run detonation after 9 min 17 sec.
4) The xB-Dienst reported the torpedoing of the Maria Amelia, possibly the attack by U 107 on the 13th.
5) U 539 hit one tanker with a T-3 torpedo, and heard a Gnat detonate after 11 min 49 sec. The tanker listed by the stern following the hit.
6) U 539 fired two Gnats which detonated after 11 min 15 sec and 14 min 10 sec. The tanker fired its MGs and damaged U 539.
7) U 270 heard one Gnat detonation after 2 min 20 sec.

1	2	3	4	5	6		7	8	9	10	11	12	13	14		15

June 1944, cont.

1	2	3	4	5	6	7	8	9	10 11	12	13	14	15
14/0136	dt	U 547	Niemeyer	EU 4989	APC 1000+	T´	.	14/	br APC	Birdlip	750+	05. N/ 09. W	
14/	dt	U 547	Niemeyer	EU 4987	-D 6000+	T	.	14/	fr -D	Saint Basile	2778+	05.03 N/ 09.14 W	
15/0803	dt	U 621	Struckmann	BF 3615	LST +	T´	.	15/	am LS	LST 280	1490+	49.55 N/ 00.30 W	
15/	dt	U 767	Dankleff	-------	---------	T´	E.G.5	15/	br PF	Mourne	1370+	49.25 N/ 05.30 W	
15/	dt	U 764	v.Bremen	BF 2622	DE 1000+	T´	.	15/	br DE	Blackwood	1085+	50.07 N/ 02.15 W	8)
19/1257	dt	U 107	Simmermacher	BB 7551	DD =?	T´	-				-----		9)
25/1514	dt	U 984	Sieder	BF 2662	DD +	T´	E.G.5	25/	br DE	Goodson	1300=	50.00 N/ 02.49 W	10)
27/	dt	U 988	Dobberstein	-------	---------	T´		27/	br PE	Pink	925=§	49.48 N/ 00.49 W	11)
28/	dt	U 988 ?	Dobberstein	-------	---------	T	FXP.18	28/2130	br -D	Maid of Orleans	2385+	50.06 N/ 00.41 W	12)
29/15	dt	U 984	Sieder	BF 3532	-D 8000+	T:	EMC.17	29/1332	am -D	Henry G.Blasdel	7176=§	50.07 N/ 00.47 W	13)
29/15	dt	U 984	Sieder	BF 3532	-D 8000+	T:	EMC.17	29/1335	am -D	Edward M.House	7240=	50.07 N/ 00.47 W	13)
29/15	dt	U 984	Sieder	BF 3532	-D 8000+	T	EMC.17	29/1338	am -D	John A.Treutlen	7198=§	50.07 N/ 00.47 W	13)
29/1543	dt	U 984	Sieder	BF 3532	-D 9000+	T`	EMC.17	29/1337	am -D	James A.Farrell	7176=§	50.07 N/ 00.47 W	13)
29/	dt	U 988 ?	Dobberstein	-------	---------	T	FMT.22	29/16.	br -D	Empire Portia	7058+	50.33 N/ 00.35 W	12)

July 1944

1	2	3	4	5	6	7	8	9	10 11	12	13	14	15
2/0130	dt	U 547	Niemeyer	EU 7278	-D: 5593+	T	-	2/	nl -D	Bodegraven	5593+	04.14 N/ 11.00 W	
3/1153	dt	U 309	Mahrholz	BF 2564	DD 1100+	T:		3/			-----		1)
4/	dt	U 539	Lauterbach-	ED 2394	-T 9000+	T	.	4/	am -TT	Kittanig	10195=	09.55 N/ 79.27 W	2)
4/	dt	U 539	Emden	ED 2394	-T 6000=	T	.	4/			-----		2)
4/	dt	U 539	Lauterbach-	ED 2394	-T 6000=	T	.	4/			-----		2)
4/	dt	U 539	Emden	ED 2394	-T 5000=	T	.	4/	am -DT	Hollywood (?)	5498=		2)

8) The *Blackwood* sank on June 16th. 9) *U 107* assumed a Gnat hit after 16 min 5 sec; very doubtful.
10) The *Goodson* was hit in the stern and towed into Portland by HMS *Bligh*. 11/12) *U 988* didn't return, so there is some doubt if the *Pink* and *Maid of Orleans* were sunk by this boat or by mines.
13) *U 984* fired a spread of two LUT which hit the *H.G.Blasdel* and *E.M.House*, one coup de grâce which did not hit the damaged ships but instead the *A.A.Treutlen*, and one Gnat which hit the *J.A.Farrell*. *H.G.Blasdel* was towed into Southampton and beached and was a total loss; *E.M.House* reached the Tyne and was repaired; *J.A.Treutlen* was towed into Southampton but not repaired; *J.A.Farrell* was towed to Spithead and not repaired.
1) *U 309* heard one Gnat end-of-run detonation. 2) *U 539* reported four tankers totaling 26,000 gross tons torpedoed; one of the ships was, according to the xB-Dienst, the *Hollywood*.

1	2	3	4	5	6	7	8	9	10	11	12	13	14	15
July 1944, cont.														
5/	dt	U 390	Geissler	-------	--------	T	-	4/	br	APC	Ganilly	545+	49.36 N/ 00.57 W	3)
5/	dt	U 390	Geissler	-------	--------	T	.	5/	am	-D	Sea Porpoise	7934=	49.37 N/ 00.51 W	3)
5/080	dt	U 953	Marbach	BF 3196	-D 7000+	T:	.					-----		4)
5/0805	dt	U 953	Marbach	BF 3196	-D 4000+	T'	.	5/	br	-D	Glendinning	1927+	50.32 N/ 00.22 W	4)
5/	dt	U 247	Matschulat	AM 3682	APC: 207+	A	-	5/	br	-Df	Noreen Mary	207+	58.30 N/ 05.23 W	
5/1803	dt	U 763	Cordes	BF 3533	-D +	T:	ETC.26	4/	nw	-D	Ringen	1499+	50.12 N/ 00.46 W	
5/2145	dt	U 763	Cordes	BF 3533	-D 4000=	T'	.	5/				-----		5)
5/2148	dt	U 763	Cordes	BF 3533	-D 3000=	T:	.	5/				-----		5)
5/2200	*dt*	*U 763*	*Cordes*	*BF 3533*	*DD =?*	*T'*	*.*	*5/*				-----		*5)*
(1. 7.)	dt	U 218	Becker	BF 2189	---------	M	-	6/	br	-D	Empire Halberd	7177=	50.08 N/ 05.44 W	
7/0231	dt	U 516	Tillessen	EC 6741	-T 8000+	T'	-	6/	am	-DT	Esso Harrisburg	9887+	13.26 N/ 72.11 W	6)
8/0616	dt	U 516	Tillessen	EC 8263	-T 5000=?	T	-	8/	am	-MT	Point Breeze	-----		6)
11/1127	dt	U 953	Marbach	BF 3246	-D 9000+	T:	.	11/				-----		7)
11/1133	*dt*	*U 953*	*Marbach*	*BF 3193*	*DD +*	*T'*	*.*	*11/*				-----		*7)*
11/2057	*dt*	*U 763*	*Cordes*	*BF 2564*	*DD +*	*T'*	*E.G.*	*11/*				-----		*8)*
20/0454	dt	U 861	Oesten	GB 2154	-D: 1300+	T	*Javari*	19/2345	bz	AP	Vital de Oliveira	1737+	22.29 S/ 41.09 W	
20/1400	dt	U 309	Mahrholz	BF 3533	-D 6800=	T:	.	20/				-----		9)
24/0324	dt	U 861	Oesten	GA 6843	-D 7000+	T	JT.39	23/2230	am	-D	William Gaston	7177+	26.42 S/ 46.12 W	
24/2100	dt	U 309	Mahrholz	BF 3532	-D 7000+	T:	.	24/	br	-D	Samneva	7219=	50.14 N/ 00.47 W	10)
24/2100	dt	U 309	Mahrholz	BF 3532	-D 7000+	T:	.	24/				-----		10)

3) The *Ganilly* and *Sea Porpoise* may have been sunk or damaged by mines or by torpedoes from *U 390*, sunk on July 5th at 49.52 N/ 00.48 W. 4) *U 953* fired a spread of two LUTs and one Gnat, and observed the sinking of one ship and heard a detonation after 4 min 27 sec. 5) *U 763* heard a Gnat detonation after 6 min 28 sec, and a LUT detonation after 11 min 48 sec and one Gnat end-of-run detonation after 10 min 29 sec. 6) *U 516* hit the *Esso Harrisburg* with one Gnat and sank her with two coups de grâce. Against the *Point Breeze* she fired a 3-torpedo spread, and one Gnat, which were evaded.
7) *U 953* fired a spread of three LUTs and reported one ship sunk and one detonation of a Gnat after 3 min 5 sec.
8) *U 763* heard one Gnat end-of-run detonation after 9 min 28 sec. 9) *U 309* fired a spread of three LUTs and heard one detonation after 9 min 30 sec. 10) *U 309* fired three LUTs and heard detonations after 5 min 35 sec and 8 min 40 sec and sinking noises.

1	2	3	4	5	6	7	8	9	10	11	12	13	14	15
July 1944, cont.														
25/0212	dt	U 862	Timm	FT 8461	-D:	7000+	T	-	25/	am	-D	Robin Goodfellow	6885+	20.03 S/ 14.21 W	
29/	dt	U 621	Struckmann	BF 3533	-D	6000+	T´	.	29/	br	LSI	Prince Leopold	2938+	50.19 N/ 00.53 W	11)
29/	dt	U 621	Struckmann	BF 3533	-D	4000+	T:	.	29/				-----		11)
30/	dt	U 621	Struckmann	BF 3274	-D	9000+	T:	.	30/	br	-D	Ascanius	10048=	50.15 N/ 00.48 W	
August 1944														
2/	dt	U 621	Struckmann	BF 3613	-D	6000+	T:	.	2/				-----		1)
2/	dt	U 621	Struckmann	BF 3613	-D	7000+	T:	.	2/				-----		1)
2/1533	at	U 804	Meyer	BD 5513	DD	+	T´	TG.22.6	2/1235	am	DE	Fiske	1300+	47.11 N/ 33.29 W	2)
2/1536	dt	U 804	Meyer	BD 5513	DD	+	T´	TG.22.6	2/1240			"	"		2)
8/abds	dt	U 667	Lange	BF 22	-D	7000+	T	EBC.66	8/	am	-D	Ezra Weston	7176+	50.42 N/ 05.03 W	3)
8/abds	dt	U 667	Lange	BF 22	DD	+	T´	EBC.66	8/	ca	PE	Regina	925+	50.42 N/ 05.03 W	3)
14/	dt	U 667	Lange	AM 98	-T	+	T	EBC.72	14/	am	LS	LST 921	1653+	51.05 N/ 04.47 W	3)
14/	dt	U 667	Lange	AM 98	-T	+	T	EBC.72	14/	am	LC	LCI 99 (L)	246+	51.05 N/ 04.47 W	3)
18/1903	dt	U 480	Förster	BF 3278	-D	=	T:	.	18/				-----		4)
19/abds	dt	U 413	Sachse	BF 32	-D	8000+	T	ETC.72	19/	br	-D	Saint Enogat	2360+	50.16 N/ 00.50 W	
20/1708	dt	U 764	v.Bremen	BF 3199	-D	1500+	T´	ETC.72	20/	br	-D	Coral	638+	50.13 N/ 00.48 W	
21/1140	dt	U 480	Förster	BF 3274	PF	+	T´	.	21/	ca	PE	Alberni	925+	50.09 N/ 00.41 W	
22/1606	dt	U 480	Förster	BF 3278	PF	+	T´	.	22/	br	PM	Loyalty	850+	50.09 N/ 00.41 W	
23/	dt	U 480	Förster	BF 3270	-D	7000+	T	ETC.72	23/	br	-D	Fort Yale	7134+§	50.23 N/ 00.55 W	
23/1818	dt	U 989	Rodler v.Roithberg	BF 3511	-D	7000=	T	.	23/	am	-D	Louis Kossuth	7176=	50.14 N/ 01.41 W	
25/0705	dt	U 764	v.Bremen	BF 3617	LC	350+	T´	.	25/				-----		5)

11) *U 621* hit one ship with a Gnat after 1 min 50 sec. This ship sank. Two hours later, one ship was hit with a LUT after a run time of 53 sec.

1) *U 621* fired a spread of two LUTs and heard detonations after 8 min 48 sec and 9 min 13 sec and then sinking noises.

2) *U 804* fired three Gnats; the first missed, the second hit the *Fiske* after a run time of 3 min, and the third hit the *Fiske* after a run time of 4 min 30 sec.

3) *U 667* reported one destroyer and 15,000 gross tons of merchant shipping sunk. 4) *U 480* heard one LUT detonation after 9 min 20 sec.

5) *U 764* fired two Gnats against a convoy of landing vessels. The second detonated after 2 min 41 sec. Ten minutes later rescue boats were seen.

1	2	3	4	5	6	7	8	9	10	11	12	13	14	15
August 1944, cont.														
25/1443	dt	U 480	Förster	BF 3278	-D 7000+	T'	.	25/	br	-D	Orminister	5712+	50.09 N/ 00.44 W	
26/	dt	U 989	Rodler v.Roithberg	BF 3524	-D 5000+	T	.	26/	br	-D	Ashmun J.Clough	1791+	50.10 N/ 01.41 W	
27/2001	*dt*	*U 92*	*Brauel*	*BF 3189*	*LST 3000+*	*T'*	*.*	*27/*				*-----*		*6)*
30/1555	dt	U 482	Graf v. Matuschka	AM 5397	-T 7000+	T	CU.36	30/	am	-TT	Jacksonville	10448+	55.30 N/ 07.30 W	
September 1944														
1/0822	*dt*	*U 482*	*Graf v. Matuschka*	*AM 5612*	*DD +*	*T'*	*.*	*1/*	*br*	*PE*	*Hurst Castle*	*1010+*	*55.27 N/ 08.12 W*	
2/1106	dt	U 275	Wehrkamp	AM 7249	-D 12000=	T'	-	2/				-----		1)
3/0010	dt	U 482	Graf v. Matuschka	AM 5282	-D 5000+	T	ONS.251	2/	nw	-D	Fjordheim	4115+	55.55 N/ 09.28 W	
3/084	dt	U 541	Petersen	BB 5957	-T 7000+	T	ONS.251	3/0750	br	-D	Livingston	2140+	46.15 N/ 58.05 W	
8/0304	*dt*	*U 541*	*Petersen*	*BB 1947*	*DD +*	*T'*	*TG.*	*8/*				*-----*		*2)*
8/05	dt	U 482	Graf v.	AM 5387	-D 5000+	T	HXF.305	8/0600	br	-DT	Empire Heritage	15702+	55.27 N/ 08.01 W	3)
8/05	dt	U 482	Matuschka	AM 5387	-T 6000+	T	HXF.305	8/0634	br	-M	Pinto	1346+	55.27 N/ 08.01 W	3)
8/0559	*dt*	*U 482*	*Graf v. Matuschka*	*AM 5387*	*-D 5000+?*	*T'*	*HXF.305*	*8/*				*-----*		*3)*
12/0614	dt	U 518	Offermann	DC 1568	-D 7000=	T'	-	12/	am	-D	George Ade	7176=	33.30 N/ 75.40 W	4)
14/1602	*dt*	*U 802*	*Schmoeckel*	*BA 3693*	*DD +?*	*T'*	*.*	*14/*				*-----*		*5)*
15/2310	*dt*	*U 650*	*Zorn*	*AE 8664*	*PE +*	*T'*	*-*	*15/*				*-----*		*6)*

6) *U 92* heard one Gnat end-of-run detonation after 8 min 40 sec. 1) *U 275* heard one Gnat end-of-run detonation after 11 min 25 sec.

2) *U 541* heard one Gnat end-of-run detonation after 11 min 52 sec. 3) *U 482* fired a spread and hit both ships with one torpedo each. One Gnat detonated after 2 min 7 sec. The *Empire Heritage* was sunk by a coup de grâce.

4) The *George Ade* was damaged and sank during a towing operation in a hurricane.

5) *U 802* heard a Gnat premature detonation after 20 sec. 6) *U 650* heard one Gnat end-of-run detonation after 11 min 3 sec.

1	2	3	4	5	6	7	8	9	10	11	12	13	14	15
September 1944, cont.														
22/16	dt	U 979	Meermeier	AE 4752	-D	6000=	T	.	22/	am	-D	Yukon	5747=	64.07 N/ 22.50 W	7)
22/1853	dt	U 244	Fischer	AE 4756	DD	=	T'	.	22/				-----		8)
23/1516	dt	U 979	Meermeier	AE 4783	-D	=?	T	.	23/				-----		9)
28/	dt	U 248	Emde	AE 8493	-T	10000=	T	.	28/				-----		10)
October 1944														
4/2249	dt	U 1227	Altmeier	BD 3932	DD	1690+	T'	ONS.33	4/2205	ca	PF	Chebogue	1370=§	49.20 N/ 24.20 W	1)
14/1925	dt	U 1223	Kneip	BA 3589	-D	5000+?	T	GONS.33	14/1325	ca	PF	Magog	1370=	49.12 N/ 68.19 W	2)
14/1930	dt	U 1223	Kneip	BA 3589	DD	+	T'	.	14/				-----		2)
17/1656	dt	U 1004	Schimmel-pfennig	AN 1316	DD	1350+	T'		17/				-----		3)
21/	dt	U 1199	Nollmann	AN 0131	-D	8000+	T	.	21/				-----		4)
23/	dt	U 483	v.Morstein	AM 5396	BM	7200=	T	.	23/				-----		5)
28/1335	dt	U 170	Hauber	BE 4655	DD	+	T'		28/				-----		6)
31/1356	dt	U 170	Hauber	BE 1355	DD	+	T'		31/				-----		7)
November 1944														
1/02	dt	U 483	v.Morstein	AM 5397	-D	5000+	T	.	1/	br	PF	Whitaker	1300=§	55.30 N/ 07.39 W	8)
1/02	dt	U 483	v.Morstein	AM 5397	-D	+?	T	.							
2/	dt	U 1223	Kneip	BA 3829	-D	5000+	T	.	2/	br	-D	Fort Thompson	7134=	48.55 N/ 67.41 W	

7) *U 979* hit the *Yukon* with one torpedo out of a spread. A coup de grâce (a Gnat) missed, and she was towed into port.
8) *U 244* heard one Gnat detonation after 3 min. 9) *U 979* fired a spread against a convoy and heard detonations.
10) *U 248* fired a spread and heard two detonations. 1) The *Chebogue* was towed into Port Talbot, but was not repaired.
2) *U 1223* fired a two-torpedo spread; one hit the *Magog* after 2 min 5 sec, and the other, a Gnat, detonated behind the ship.
3) *U 1004* heard a Gnat detonation after 3 min 30 sec. 4) *U 1199* reported one freighter sunk.
5) *U 483* fired a 3-torpedo spread against a monitor of the *Erebus*-class, and heard two detonations (possibly end-of-run detonations).
6) *U 170* heard one Gnat end-of-run detonation after 13 min 4 sec. 7) *U 170* heard one Gnat end-of-run detonation after 12 min 40 sec.
8) The *Whitaker* was damaged and towed into port, but was declared a total loss.

North Sea - Atlantic

1	2	3	4	5	6	7	8	9	10	11	12	13	14	15
November 1944, cont.														
8/	dt	U 1227	Altmeier	CG	-T 8000+	T	UGS.58	8/1145				-----	36.16 N/ 07.35 W	9)
10/morg	dt	U 300	Hein	AE 4753	-D 1542+	T	UR.142	10/	is	-D	Godafoss	1542+	64.08 N/ 22.45 W	
10/	dt	U 300	Hein	AE 4753	-D 4000+	T	UR.142	10/	br	-DT	Shirvan	6017+	64.08 N/ 22.50 W	
10/	dt	U 300	Hein	-------	---------	T	UR.142	10/	br	-Dt	Empire World	260+	64.08 N/ 22.38 W	
19/1200	dt	U 978	Pulst	BF 3561	-D 7000+	T	.	19/				-----		10)
21/	dt	U 978	Pulst	BF 3562	-D 8000+	T	.	21/				-----	294° 700m Digne	11)
	11	-----	-----------	-------	---------	(M	.	21/	br	-D	Empire Cutlass	7177=	LT., Le Havre	11)
23/	dt	U 978	Pulst	BF 3617	-D 7000+	T	.	23/	am	-D	William D.Burnham	7176+	49.46 N/ 01.15 W	
25/0230	*dt*	*U 1228*	*Marienfeld*	*BB 5512*	*DD 900+*	*T'*	*-*	*25/*	*ca*	*PE*	*Shawinigan*	*900+*	*47.34 N/ 59.11 W*	
27/	dt	U 991	Balke	BF 3525	-D 14000=	T	.	27/				-----		12)
30/	*dt*	*U 1231*	*Lessing*	*BB 1486*	*DD +*	*T'*	*-*	*30/*				———		13)
December 1944														
3/	*dt*	*U 1231*	*Lessing*	*BA 3832*	*DD +?*	*T'*		*3/*				———		1)
3/	dt	U 1230	Hilbig	BA 9572	-D 5500+	T	-	3/	ca	-D	Cornwallis	5458+	43.59 N/ 68.20 W	
6/	*dt*	*U 775*	*Taschen-macher*	*AN 15*	*DD +*	*T'*	*-*	*6/*	*br*	*DE*	*Bullen*	*1300+*	*58.42 N/ 04.12 W*	
10/	*dt*	*U 1202*	*Thomsen*	*AM 9577*	*-D 7000+*	*T*	*.*	*10/*	*am*	*-D*	*Dan Beard*	*7176+*	*51.56 N/ 05.29 W*	2)
10/	*dt*	*U 1202*	*Thomsen*	*AM 9577*	*-D 7000+*	*T*	*.*	*10/*						2)
10/	*dt*	*U 1202*	*Thomsen*	*AM 9577*	*-D 6000+*	*T*	*.*	*10/*						2)
10/	*dt*	*U 1202*	*Thomsen*	*AM 9577*	*-D 6000+*	*T*	*.*	*10/*						2)
13/0940	dt	U 722	Reimers	AL	-D +	T'	.	13/				-----		3)

9) *U 1227* reported one tanker hit by a Gnat and sunk by two T-3 coups de grâce. There is only one A/C report of a radar detection near convoy UGS.58. 10) *U 978* observed a detonation after 5 min 55 sec and observed one burning ship sink.

11) *U 978* reported one ship sunk far to the west of the reported sinking position of the *Empire Cutlass*, which was probably also damaged by a mine near the position where the USS *Lee S.Overman* (7,716 gross tons) was damaged by a mine.

12) *U 991* fired a 3-torpedo spread and heard two detonations.

13) *U 1231* heard one Gnat end-of-run detonation after 10 min. 1) *U 1231* heard one Gnat end-of-run detonation after 9 min 27 sec.

2) *U 1202* reported sinking four ships totaling 26,000 gross tons out of a convoy. 3) *U 722* heard one Gnat end-of-run detonation.

1	2	3	4	5	6	7	8	9	10	11	12	13	14	15
December 1944, cont.														
15/	dt	U 991	Balke	AM 8883	-D 7000+	T	.	15/						4)
18/	dt	U 486	Meyer	BF 2516	-D 6000+	T	BTC.10	18/	br	-D	Silverlaurel	6142+	50.07 N/ 04.40 W	
20/	dt	U 870	Hechler	CF 2636	LST:3000+	T	.	20/	am	LS	LST 350 (?)			5)
20/	dt	U 870	Hechler	CF 2636	LST:3000+	T	.	20/	am	LS	LST 359	1490+	42.04 N/ 19.08 W	5)
20/	dt	U 870	Hechler	CF 2636	PE +	T´	.	20/	am	DE	Fogg	1400=	43.02 N/ 19.19 W	5)
21/	dt	U 486	Meyer	BF 3516	DD +	T´		21/				-----		6)
21/2004	dt	U 806	Hornbostel	BB 7551	-D 7176+	T´	.	21/	br	-D	Samtucky	7219=	44.22 N/ 63.23 W	7)
24/1437	dt	U 806	Hornbostel	BB 7527	PE +	T´	XB.139	24/1335	ca	PM	Clayoquot	672+	44.30 N/ 63.20 W	7)
24/1446	dt	U 806	Hornbostel	BB 7527	-D 4000=	T´	XB.139	24/1351	ca	PM	Transcona	-----	44.30 N/ 63.20 W	7)
23/0942	dt	U 772	Rademacher	-------	---------	T	WEG.14	23/	br	-D	Slemish	1536+	49.45 N/ 01.42 W	9)
23/1150	dt	U 772	Rademacher	-------	---------	T	MUS.71	23/	br	-D	Dumfries	5149+	50.23 N/ 01.43 W	9)
24/	dt	U 486	Meyer	BF 3553	-D:11000+	T	WEP.3	24/1754	be	-D	Leopoldville	11509+	49.45 N/ 01.34 W	
26/1414	dt	U 486	Meyer	BF 3528	DD +	T´	E.G.1	26/	br	DE	Capel	1085+	49.50 N/ 01.41 W	8)
26/1414	dt	U 486	Meyer	BF 3528	DD +	T´	E.G.1	26/	br	DE	Affleck	1085=	49.48 N/ 01.43 W	8)
26/	dt	U 486	Meyer	BF 3528	PE =	T´	E.G.1	26/				-----		8)
28/1538	dt	U 772	Rademacher	-------	---------	T	.	28/	br	LSI	Empire Javelin	7177+	50.04 N/ 01.00 W	9)
29/	dt	U 772	Rademacher	-------	---------	T	TBC.21	29/	am	-D	Black Hawk	7191=§	50.28 N/ 02.28 W	10)
29/	dt	U 772	Rademacher	-------	---------	T	TBC.21	29/	am	-D	Arthur Sewall	7176=	50.28 N/ 02.28 W	10)
31/0330	dt	U 1020	Eberlein	-------	---------	T´	.	31/	br	DD	Zephyr	1710=	58.57 N/ 04.00 W	

1	2	3	4	5	6	7	8	9	10	11	12	13	14	15
January 1945														
2/	dt	U 1232	Dobratz	BB 7564	DD 1850+	T	.	2/						1)

4) *U 991* reported one "Liberty"-type ship sunk. 5) *U 870* fired a spread and reported *LST 350* and *LST 369* sunk; in reality *LST 359* was sunk. *Fogg* was damaged by a Gnat hit in the stern, but was towed into port. 6) *U 486* heard a Gnat detonation after 1 min 9 sec.

7) The *Samtucky* was beached off Halifax and later repaired. On the 24th *U 806* first hit the *Clayoquot* with a Gnat after 1 min 9 sec, and then fired at a freighter in the convoy, but the Gnat detonated after 3 min in the cat gear of the *Transcona*.

8) *U 486* observed two hits by Gnats after 1 min 39 sec and 1 min 41 sec, and heard a third Gnat detonation after 7 min.

9) *U 772* did not report before being sunk, but the times were recorded by the xB-Dienst. 10) The *Black Hawk* was beached and became a total loss. 1) *U 1232* reported one destroyer of the *Somers*-class sunk.

1	2	3	4	5	6	7	8	9	10	11	12	13	14	15
January 1945, cont.														
3/	dt	U 870	Hechler	CG	-D	7000+	T	GUS.63	3/		am -D	Henry Miller	7207=	35.51 N/ 06.24 W	
3/	dt	U 1232	Dobratz	BB 75	-DP 20000=	T		3/				-----		2)
4/	dt	U 1232	Dobratz	BB 7535	-T	7500+	T	SH.194	4/		ca -MT	Nipiwan Park	2373=	44.30 N/ 63. W	
4/	dt	U 1232	Dobratz	BB 7535	-D	6000+	T	SH.194	4/		nw -D	Polarland	1591+	44.30 N/ 63. W	
8/	*dt*	*U 248*	*Loos*	*BD 52*	*PE*	*=?*	*T'*	*–*	*8/*				*-----*		*3)*
/	dt	U 278	Franze	AN 15	-D	=	T	.	/						4)
8/	dt	U 870	Hechler	CG 41	-T	6000+	T	.	8/						5)
8/	dt	U 870	Hechler	CG 41	-D	4000+	T	.	8/						5)
9/	*dt*	*U 870*	*Hechler*	*CG 41*	*PE*	*+*	*T'*	*.*	*9/*		*fr PC*	*L'Enjoue*	*335+*	*35.56 N/ 05.49 W*	*5)*
9/	dt	U 1055	Meyer	AM 9818	-D	7000+	T	ON.271	9/		am -D	Jonas Lie	7198+	51.45 N/ 05.27 W	6)
10/	dt	U 870	Hechler	CG	-D	6000=	T	.	10/		br -D	Blackheath	4637+	35.49 N/ 06.03 W	
11/	dt	U 1055	Meyer	AM 9252	-D	+	T	.	11/1510	jg -D	Senga	-----	53.19 N/ 04.48 W	7)
11/	dt	U 1055	Meyer	AM 9252	-D	4000+	T	.	11/1523	am -D	Roanoke	2606+	53.19 N/ 04.48 W	7)
11/	dt	U 1055	Meyer	AM 9252	-D	3000+	T	.	11/1538	br -D	Normandy Coast	1428+	53.19 N/ 04.48 W	7)
12/0012	*dt*	*U 427*	*Gudenus*	*AN 2338*	*DD*	*+*	*T'*	*Task F.*	*11/*				*-----*		*8)*
12/0045	*dt*	*U 427*	*Gudenus*	*AN 2338*	*CL ?*	*=*	*T'*	*Task F.*	*11/*				*-----*		*8)*
14/	dt	U 1232	Dobratz	BB 7527	-T	8000+	T	BX.141	14/		br -MT	British Freedom	6985+	44.28 N/ 63.28 W	
14/	dt	U 1232	Dobratz	BB 7527	-D	7000+	T	BX.141	14/		am -D	Martin Van Buren	7176=§	44.28 N/ 63.28 W	
14/	dt	U 1232	Dobratz	BB 7527	-T	9400+	T	BX.141	14/		br -MT	Athelviking	8779+	44.20 N/ 63.24 W	
14/	dt	U 1232	Dobratz	BB 7527	-D	6000+	T	BX.141	14/				-----		9)
15/	dt	U 482	Graf v.	AM 7429	-T:	7429=	T	.	15/		nw -MT	Spinanger	7429=	55.08 N/ 05.25 W	10)
15/	*dt*	*U 482*	Matuschka	-------	---------	*T*	*.*	*15/*		*br CVE*	*Thane*	*8300=§*	*55.08 N/ 05.25 W*	*10)*

2) *U 1232* fired a spread of two torpedoes and heard one detonation after 9 min 45 sec. 3) *U 348* heard one Gnat end-of-run
detonation after 12 min 14 sec. 4) *U 278* reported one ship torpedoed but gave no date. The xB-Dienst reported that at 1300
on Jan.8th in the Scapa Flow area the Norwegian S/S *Bestik* (2,684 gross tons) had anchored damaged, and that the British
S/S *Ashbury* (3,901 gross tons) was a total loss. 5) *U 870* reported detonations after 3 min 15 sec and sinking noises. The
xB-Dienst reported that at 1647 on Jan.9th a signal was received from the tanker *Sitala* (6,218 gross tons) from the
Gibraltar area, which may have had a connection with this attack.
6) The *Jonas Lie* drifted as a wreck until Jan.14th before she sank. 7) The first torpedo of *U 1055* exploded behind the *Senga*.
U 1055 reported two ships totaling 7,000 gross tons sunk. 8) *U 427* attacked a British cruiser force including HMS *Norfolk*
and *Bellona* and the destroyers HMS *Onslow*, *Orwell*, and *Onslaught* with a spread of three LUT torpedoes and two Gnats, and
heard detonations.

1	2	3	4	5	6	7	8	9	10	11	12	13	14	15
January 1945, cont.														
15/	dt	U 1055	Meyer	AM 98	-D	7000+	T	-	15/	br	-MT	Maja	8181+	53.40 N/ 05.14 W	
16/	dt	U 1055	Meyer	AM 9212	-D	+?	T	-	16/						11)
21/nm	dt	U 1199	Nollmann	-------	---------		T	TBC.43	21/	am	-D	George Hawley	7176=§	50. N/ 05.45 W	12)
21/	dt	U 1172	Kuhlmann	-------	---------		T		21/	nw	-D	Galatea	1152+	52.40 N/ 05.23 W	13)
23/	dt	U 1172	Kuhlmann	-------	---------		T	MH.1	23/	nw	-D	Vigsnes	1599+	53.33 N/ 04.17 W	13)
26/	*dt*	*U 1172*	*Kuhlmann*	-------	---------		*T*	.	*26/*	*br*	*DE*	*Manners*	*1300=*	*21m 280° from Skerries Isle of Man*	
26/14	dt	U 1017	Riecken	BF 35	-D:	7129+	T	.	26/	br	-D	Fort Douglas (?)	?		14)
27/0920	*dt*	*U 1017*	*Riecken*	*BF 35*	*PE*	*+?*	*T'*		*27/*				*?*		*15)*
27/	dt	U 825	Stölker	AM 9496	-D	+	T	HX.332	27/	nw	-MT	Solör	8262=§	52.35 N/ 05.18 W	16)
27/	dt	U 825	Stölker	AM 9496	-D	=	T	HX.332	27/	am	-D	Ruben Dario	7198=	52.35 N/ 05.18 W	16)
	dt	U 1051 ?	v.Holleben												16)
31/1230	*dt*	*U 869*	*Neuerburg*	*CG 9544*	*DD ?*	*+*	*T*								*17)*
February 1945														
5/2025	dt	U 245	Schumann-Hindenberg	AN 7960	-D	6000+	T	TAM.71	5/	am	-D	Henry B.Plant	7240+	51.22 N/ 02. E	
6/	dt	U 1017	Riecken	BF 3155	-D	6000+	T	TBC.60	6/	br	-D	Everleigh	5222+	50.30 N/ 01.48 W	
6/	dt	U 1017	Riecken	BF 3155	-D	6000+	T	TBC.60	6/				-----		1)
8/2057	dt	U 244	Fischer	BF 3256	-D	7000=	T	.	8/						2)
11/nm	dt	U 1017	Riecken	BF 2295	-D:	6000+	T	BTC.65	11/	be	-D	Persier	5382+	50.24 N/ 04.20 W	1)

9) *U 1232* reported four ships totaling 30,400 gross tons sunk. The *Martin van Buren* was damaged and beached but was declared a total loss.
10) *U 482* was sunk before she could report. The torpedoing of the *Spinanger* was established by the xB-Dienst. The *Thane* was damaged and towed into port, but was not repaired during the war.
11) The xB-Dienst reported an intercept of a signal about a torpedoing, perhaps from *U 1055*. 12) The *G.Hawley* probably was a total loss.
13) It is possible that these attacks were made by *U 1051*. 14) The xB-Dienst reported the sinking of *Fort Douglas* after an explosion. 15) *U 1017* reported one "Liberty" ship torpedoed, possibly the *Sibert*; the xB-Dienst reported this ship sunk near Portsmouth by an explosion. 16) *U 825* reported three detonations and one ship probably sunk. This attack was possibly made by *U 1051*, later sunk herself. 17) The xB-Dienst reported one SOS signal from the operational area of *U 869*. 1) *U 1017* reported two ships sunk. 2) *U 244* reported one ship sunk.

1	2	3	4	5	6	7	8	9	10	11	12	13	14	15
February 1945, cont.														
15/	dt	U 245	Schumann-Hindenberg	AN 79	-D 6000=	T	.	15/		nl -DT	Liseta	2628=	51.25 N/ 01.26 W	2a)
17/1100	dt	U 300	Hein	CG	-D =	T	UGS.72	17/1100		am -D	Michael J.Stone	7176=	35.56 N/ 05.45 W	3)
17/1100	dt	U 300	Hein	CG	--------	T	UGS.72	17/1100		br -MT	Regent Lion	9551=§	35.56 N/ 05.45 W	3)
/	dt	U 1058	Bruder	AM 9243	-D 9000+	T	.	/						4)
20/	*dt*	*U 1208*	*Hagene*	-------	---------	*T*	*HX.337*	*20/*		*br PE*	*Vervain*	*925+*	*51.47 N/ 07.06 W*	
21/	dt	U 1064	Schneidewind	AM 6547	-D 6000+	T	.	21/		is -D	Dettifoss	1564+	55.03 N/ 05.29 W	5)
21/	dt	U 1064	Schneidewind	AM 6547	-D 6000+	T	.	21/				-----		5)
21/	dt	U 1064	Schneidewind	AM 6547	-D 5000+	T	.	21/				-----		5)
22/	dt	U 1004	Hinz	BF 2289	-D 3000+	T	BTC.76	22/1320		br -D	Alexander Kennedy	1313+	50.06 N/ 04.50 W	
22/	dt	U 1004	Hinz	BF 2289	-D 5000+	T	BTC.76	*22/1329*		*ca PE*	*Trentonian*	*980+*	*50.06 N/ 04.50 W*	
22/	dt	U 1004	Hinz	BF 2289	-D 5000=	T:	BTC.76	22/				-----		6)
24/	dt	U 480	Förster	-------	---------	T	BTC.78	24/		br -D	Oriskany	1644+	50.05 N/ 05.51 W	
24/	dt	U 1203	Seeger	BF 2811	-D 5000+	T′	.	24/		br APC	Ellesmere	580+	49.04 N/ 05.31 W	
/	dt	U 1104	Perleberg	AM 3689	-D 7000+	T	.	/						7)
/	dt	U 1104	Perleberg	AM 3689	-T 3000+	T	.	/						7)
25/	dt	U 2322	Heckel	AN 5154	-D 1600+	T	FS.1739	25/		br -D	Egholm	1317+	55.50 N/ 01.32 W	
27/1013	dt	U 1018	Burmeister	BF 2511	-D =	T	BTC.81	27/		nw -D	Corvus	1317+	49.55 N/ 05.22 W	
/	dt	U 1203	Seeger	BF 2542	-D 7000+	T	.	/						8)
/	*dt*	*U 1203*	*Seeger*	*BF 2542*	*PE =*	*T′*	.	/				-----		*8)*
28/	dt	U 1022	Ernst	AE 4758	-D +	T	UR.155	28/		pa -D	Alcedo	1392+	64.07 N/ 23.17 W	
28/	dt	U 1022	Ernst	AE 4758	-D +	T	UR.155	28/				-----		9)
28/	dt	U 1302	Herwatz	-------	---------	T	–	28/0915		pa -D	Soreldoc	1926+	52.15 N/ 05.35 W	
28/	dt	U 1302	Herwatz	-------	---------	T	–	28/		br -M	Norfolk Coast	646+	51.58 N/ 05.25 W	

3) Survivors of *U 300* reported an attack against this convoy, also reported by the xB-Dienst. The *Regent Lion* was towed into Tangiers on Feb.19th but was declared a total loss. 4) *U 1058* reported one freighter sunk between Feb.13th and March 2nd.
5) *U 1064* reported three ships of 17,000 gross tons sunk. 6) *U 1004* reported one LUT detonation on the third ship after a run time of 11 min 43 sec.
7) *U 1104* reported one freighter and one tanker sunk between Feb.9th and Mar.12th, probably on about Feb.25th.
8) *U 1203* reported one "Liberty"-type ship torpedoed, and one Gnat end-of-run detonation after 8 min 26 sec, between Feb.24th and Mar.9th.
9) *U 1022* fired a 3-torpedo spread and heard detonations and sinking noises from two ships.

1	2	3	4	5	6	7	8	9	10	11	12	13	14	15
March 1945														
/	dt	U 1203	*Seeger*	BF 2432	DD +	T'		/				------		1)
2/	dt	U 775	Taschen-	AM 4769	-D 6000+	T	.	2/						2)
2/	dt	U 775	macher	AM 4769	-D 8000+	T	.	2/						2)
2/1812	dt	U 1302	Herwatz	-------	--------	T	SC.167	2/	br	-M	King Edgar	4536+	52.05 N/ 05.42 W	3)
2/1900	dt	U 1302	Herwatz	-------	--------	T	SC.167	2/	nw	-D	Novasli	3204+	52.01 N/ 05.41 W	3)
3/	dt	U 1022	Ernst	AE 4758	APC +	T		3/	br	-Df	Southern Flower	328+	64.05 N/ 23.15 W	
/	dt	U 1005	*Lauth*	AN 1542	DE +	T'		/						4)
6/	dt	U 775	Taschen-macher	-------	---------	T	.	6/	br	-D	Empire Geraint	6991=	51. N/ 05. W	**2)**
6/	dt	U 681	Gebauer	AM 73	APC =	T		6/				-----		5)
8/1055	dt	U 275	Wehrkamp	-------	--------	T	ONA.289	8/	br	-D	Lornaston	4934+	50.35 N/ 00.30 W	6)
10/	dt	U 714	Schwebke	-------	--------	T	.	10/	nw	APM	Nordhav II	425+	Dundee	
10/	dt	U 532	Junker	FL 44	-D 6000+	T	FS.1753d	10/	br	-D	Baron Jedburgh	3656+	10.02 S/ 25. W	
10/	dt	U 866	Rogowski	CA 3689	-D 7000=	T:	.	10/						7)
10/	dt	U 866	Rogowski	CA 3689	-T 7000=	T:	.	10/						7)
/	dt	U 1019	Rinck	BF 1356	-D 8000+	T	.	/						8)
14/	dt	U 714	Schwebke	-------	--------	T	.	14/	sw	-D	Magne	1226+	55.52 N/ 01.59 W	
16/0920	dt	U 722	Reimers	AM 3796	-D =	T	RU.156	16/	br	-D	Inger Toft	2190+	57.25 N/ 06.52 W	9)
16/	*dt*	*U 868*	*Turre*	-------	---------	*T'*	.	*17/1850*	*ca*	*PM*	*Guysborough*	*672+*	*46.43 N/ 09.30 W*	10)
17/	*dt*	*U 878*	*Rodig*											

1) *U 1203* heard one Gnat detonation after 6 min 48 sec. 2) *U 775* reported two ships of 6,000 and 8,000 gross tons torpedoed. The attack on *Sir Geraint* very probably was made by *U 775*. 3) *U 1302* couldn't report any attack.
4) *U 1005* reported one DE sunk between March 1st and 12th. 5) *U 681* heard one Gnat end-of-run detonation after 9 min 24 sec. 6) The sinking of *Lornaston* was reported by the xB-Dienst. 7) *U 866* heard LUT detonations after 58 sec and 3 min 30 sec.
8) *U 1019* reported one big freighter sunk between March 4th and 19th. 9) This success was reported by the xB-Dienst.
10) The *Guysborough* was hit by one Gnat and later sunk by a coup de grâce. It is impossible to determine with certainty whether *U 868* or *U 878* attacked.

1	2	3	4	5	6		7	8	9	10 11	12	13	14		15

March 1945, cont.

1	2	3	4	5	6		7	8	9	10 11	12	13	14		15
21/	dt	U 1202	Thomsen	BE 3446	DD	1350+	T	.	21/			————			11)
21/	dt	U 1202	Thomsen	BE 3446	CVE	+	T	.	21/			————			11)
21/	dt	U 399	Buhse	———————	————————		T	TBC.102	21/	am -D	John R.Park	7184+	49.56 N/ 05.26 W		12)
	dt	U 246 ?	Raabe	———————	————————		T								12)
21/1540	dt	U 1195	Cordes	———————	————————		T	BTC.103	21/	am -D	James Eagan Layne	7176=§	50.13 N/ 04.05 W		12)
22/	dt	U 315	Zoller	BF 2432	-D	8000+	T:	TBC.103	22/	br -D	Empire Kingsley	6996+	50.08 N/ 05.51 W		13)
22/	dt	U 315	Zoller	BF 2432	-D	=	T:	TBC.103	22/			—————			13)
22/	dt	U 315	Zoller	BF 2432	-D	=	T:	TBC.103	22/			—————			13)
26/0530	dt	U 399	Buhse	———————	————————		T	BTC.108	26/	nl -M	Pacific	362+	49.54 N/ 05.17 W		
28/	dt	U 532	Junker	EG 50	-D	12000+	T	.	28/0545	am -DT	Oklahoma	9298+	13.37 N/ 41.43 W		
29/0822	dt	U 246	Raabe	BF 2431	DD	+	T'	BTC.111	29/0624	ca PF	Teme	1370=§	50.07 N/ 05.45 W		14)
31/	dt	U 1202	Thomsen	BE 6123	-D	7000+	T	.	31/						15)
31/	dt	U 1202	Thomsen	BE 6123	-D	7000+	T	.	31/						15)

April 1945

1	2	3	4	5	6		7	8	9	10 11	12	13	14		15
1 ?	dt	U 1202	Thomsen	BE	-D	7000=	T	.	/						1)
1 ?	dt	U 1202	Thomsen	BE	PE	+	T'	.	/						1)
1 ?	dt	U 1202	Thomsen	BE	PE	+	T'	.	/						1)
4/0106	dt	U 299	Emde	AN 3513	DD	+	T.		4/			—————			2)
4/0106	dt	U 299	Emde	AN 3513	DD	=?	T.		4/			—————			2)
4/	dt	U 978	Pulst	AN 1520	-D	6000+	T		5/1859 br -D		Gasray				

---

11) *U 1202* reported one destroyer of the A/I-class sunk and two hits on a CVE, with sinking noises. The CVE was never seen again.
12) There were different attacks, but it is not clear which of the U-boats *U 399*, *U 246* or *U 1195* attacked the different ships.
13) *U 315* reported one ship sunk and heard two LUT detonations after run times of 8 min 27 sec and 8 min 35 sec.
14) The damage to the *Teme* was recognized by the xB-Dienst; the ship was towed into harbor but not repaired. *U 246* was lost.
15) *U 1202* reported two ships sunk. 1) *U 1202* heard hits on one ship and reported two corvettes sunk.
 2) *U 299* fired a spread of 3 FAT and heard detonations after run times of 1 min 35 sec and 1 min 36 sec. Sinking noises were heard from one ship.
 3) *U 978* reported one ship sunk.

1	2	3	4	5	6	7	8	9	10 11	12	13	14	15
April 1945, cont.													
5/	*dt*	*U 1024*	*Gutteck*	*AM 90*	*PE*	*+*	*T'*	*.*	*5/*		*-----*		*4)*
5/	dt	U 857	Premauer	-------	---------		T	.	5/2240 am -TT	Atlantic States	8537=	42.07 N/ 70. W	
6/	*dt*	*U 978*	*Pulst*	*AN 15*	*CV 23000=*		*T*	*Task F.*	*6/*		*-----*		*5)*
6/0613	dt	U 1195	Cordes	-------	---------		T	VWP.16	6/0413 br -D	Cuba	11420+	50.36 N/ 00.57 W	6)
7/1723	dt	U 1024	Gutteck	AM 9252	-D 8000+		T	HX.346	7/1531 am -D	James W.Nesmith	7176=	53.24 N/ 04.48 W	
9/1930	dt	U 1023	Schroeteler	AM 5310	-D 8000=		T	SC.171	*9/* *ca PF*	*Capilano*	-----	*North Channel*	7)
12/	dt	U 1024	Gutteck	AM 90	-D 8000+		T	.	12/1200 am -D	Will Rogers	7200=	53.48 N/ 04.46 W	8)
12/	dt	U 1024	Gutteck	AM 90	-D 12000+		T	.	12/		-----		8)
12/	dt	U 1024	Gutteck	AM 90	-D 6000=		T	.	12/		-----		8)
14/	dt	U 879	Manchen	-------	---------		T	−	14/1550 be -D	Belgian Airman	6959+	36.09 N/ 74.05 W	9)
16/	dt	U 2324	v.Rapprad	AN 5194	-D 5000+		T	.	16/1700 br -D	Monarch	1150+	52.08 N/ 01.52 W	
16/	dt	U 1274	Fitting	-------	---------		T	FS.1784	16/1732 br -MT	Athelduke	8966+	55.39 N/ 01.31 W	
16/	*dt*	*U 190*	*Reith*	*BB*	*---------*		*T'*	*.*	*16/1930 ca -PM*	*Esquimalt*	*590+*	*44.28 N/ 63.10 W*	
18/0555	dt	U 245	Schumann-	AN 7968	-D 5000+		T	TAM.142	18/0347 nw -M	Karmt	4991+	51.27 N/ 01.43 E	
18/0555	dt	U 245	Hindenberg	AN 7968	-T 5000+		T	TAM.142	18/0354 br -D	Filleigh	4856+	51.20 N/ 01.42 E	
18/	*dt*	*U 245*	*"*	*AN 7968*	*PE* *=*		*T'*	*TAM.142*	*18/*		*-----*		*10)*
18/	dt	U 1107	Parduhn	BF 5151	-D 6000+		T	HX.348	18/1015 am -D	Cyrus H.McCormick	7181+	47.47 N/ 06.26 W	
18/	dt	U 1107	Parduhn	BF 5151	-D 8000+		T	HX.348	18/1015 br -MT	Empire Gold	8028+	47.47 N/ 06.26 W	
18/	dt	U 548	Krempl	-------	---------		T	−	18/1330 am -DT	Swiftscout	8300+	37.30 N/ 73.03 W	
19/	dt	U 1023	Schroeteler	AM 88	-D 8000+		T	.	19/		-----		11)
(18. 4.)	dt	U 218	Stock	AM 65	---------		M	−	20/2109 br -Df	Ethel Crawford	200+	55.13 N/ 05.14 W	

4) *U 1024* reported one corvette sunk. 5) *U 978* fired a spread of three LUT against a carrier of the *Illustrious*-class, and heard detonations. 6) *U 1195* was herself sunk after the attack but the xB-Dienst reported this success.

7) *U 1023* fired a spread of three LUT and heard two detonations after more than 5 min; they were reported by HMCS *Capilano* of SC.171.

8) *U 1024* reported two ships of 7-8,000 BRT and 8,000 gross tons sunk and one ship of 7,000 gross tons damaged.

9) It is probable that this ship was sunk by *U 879*, but possibly it might have been *U 548*.

10) *U 245* heard one Gnat end-of-run detonation after 16 min. The success was reported by the xB-Dienst. 11) *U 1023* fired a spread of three LUT, heard and observed one detonation after about 50 sec, and heard one more detonation in a convoy.

North Sea – Atlantic

1	2	3	4	5	6	7	8	9	10	11	12	13	14	15
April 1945, cont.														
23/	dt	U 2329	Schlott	AN 7660	-D 5000+	T	.	23/		nw -D	Sverre Helmerson	7209=	51.28 N/ 01.55 W	
23/1535	dt	U 1023	Schroeteler	BF 2190	-D 10000=	T	TBC.135	23/1335		br -D	Riverton	7345=	50.25 N/ 05.25 W	12)
23/	dt	U 548	Krempl	-------	--------	T	.	23/		nw -MT	Katy	6825=	35.56 N/ 74.52 W	13)
23/	dt	U 853	Frömsdorf	-------	--------	T	.	23/		am PE	Eagle 56	430+	Portland/Maine	14)
24/	dt	U 546	Just	-------	--------	T'	Task Un.	24/0836		am DE	Frederick C.Davis	1200+	43.52 N/ 40.15 W	
24/	dt	U 956 ?	Mohs	AM 5542	--------	T	–	24/		br -D	Monmouth Coast	878+	80m off Sligo	15)
24/	dt	U 293 ?	Klingspor	AM 5427										
27/	dt	U 1105	Schwarz	AM 5723	---------	T'	–	27/		br DE	Redmill	1300=	54.23 N/ 10.36 W	
29/	dt	U 2322	Heckel	AN 76	-D +	T	.	29/				-----		16)
May 1945														
2/	dt	U 979	Meermeier	AE 77	--------	T	–	2/		br -Df	Ebor Wyke	348+	64.10 N/ 23.12 W	
4/	dt	U 979	Meermeier	AE 77	--------	T	.	4/		br -MT	Empire Unity	6386=	64.23 N/ 22.37 W	
5/	dt	U 853	Frömsdorf	-------	--------	T	–	5/1740		am -D	Black Point	5353+	41.19 N/ 71.23 W	
7/	dt	U 1023	Schroeteler	BF 35	PE +	T'	.	7/1952		nw PM	NYMS 382	335+	50.22 N/ 03.09 W	
7/	dt	U 2336	Klusmeyer	AN 51	-D +	T	.	7/		nw -D	Sneland I	1791+	56.10 N/ 02.31 W	
7/	dt	U 2336	Klusmeyer	AN 51	-D +	T	.	7/		br -D	Avondale Park	2878+	56.05 N/ 02.32 W	
July 1945														
(18. 8.) 1944	dt	U 218	Becker	BF 25	--------	M	–	10/		br -Df	Kned	352+	Lizard Head	1)

12) U 1023 fired a spread of two LUT and heard one detonation plus sinking noises. 13) The Katy was towed into Lynnhaven.
14) The Eagle 56 sank after an explosion. Probably U 853 operated in this area.
15) U 956 and U 293 both operated in this area; there is no report as to which of the two boats made this attack.
16) U 2322 reported one ship sunk by torpedo.
1) The Kned probably hit a mine laid by U 218 on August 18th, 1944.

1	2	3	4	5	6	7	8	9	10	11	12	13	14	15

July 1941

August 1941

1	2	3	4	5	6	7	8	9	10 11 12	13	14	15
6/1900 dt	U 652		Fraatz	AC 8947	APC 500+	T	−	6/	sj APC ^{x}SKR-70 Kapitan Voronin	558+	Cape Teriberka	
10/2112 dt	*U 451*		*Hoffmann*	*AW 2352*	*DD 1200+*	*T*	−	*10/*	*sj PE SKR-27 Žemčug*	*550+*	*W Kanin Nos*	*1)*
25/1041 dt	U 752		Schroeter	AW 2270	APC 800+	T	−	25/	sj APM TSC-898/T-44 ^{x}RT-45 Dvina	633+	NW Svyatoy Nos	2)
26/0459 dt	U 571		Möhlmann	AC 8915	-D 6000=	T	−	26/	sj -M Marija Uljanova	3870=§	N C.Retiberka	3)

September 1941

October 1941

1	2	3	4	5	6	7	8	9	10 11 12	13	14	15
18/1320 dt	U 132		Vogelsang	AW 2644	-D 5000+	T	.	18/	sj -D Argun	3487+	69.30 N/ 33.30 E	
18/2017 dt	U 132		Vogelsang	AW 2647	-D 1500+	T	.	18/			N Kackovskij	5)

November 1941

1	2	3	4	5	6	7	8	9	10 11 12	13	14	15
15/1808 dt	U 752		Schroeter	AW 2671	-D 4000=	T	.	15/				6)
15/1922 dt	U 752		Schroeter	AW 2647	APC 1000=	T	.	15/	sj APM T-34(^{x}RT 3)	...+		6)

December 1941

1	2	3	4	5	6	7	8	9	10 11 12	13	14	15
9/2104 dt	U 134		Schendel	AC 8148	-D 4000+	T	−	9/2106 dt -D (Steinbek)		2185+	71.09 N/ 29.25 E	7)

---

1) *U 451* reported one hit on a destroyer of the *Vojkov*-class, and later observed debris and two survivors.

2) *U 752* sighted a patrol vessel with the number 44 and sank this ship. At this time the RT-No. and the old minesweeper-No. were already changed. 3) The *M.Uljanova* was hit by two torpedoes, but remained afloat, was beached, and was declared a total loss.

4) *U 752* observed one hit on a patrol vessel after a run time of 1 min 37 sec. The identity of this ship is uncertain.

5) *U 132* sank the *Argun* with one hit and a coup de grâce. Then another ship was hit after a run time of 16 sec, and sank in 32 sec.

6) *U 752* hit a lumber-carrier with one torpedo, but the ship continued under way, listing. The coup de grâce missed, but hit a patrol vessel behind, which exploded with a big smoke column.

7) The *Steinbek* was a German ship attacked erroneously by *U 134*.

1	2	3	4	5	6		7	8	9	10	11	12	13	14	15

January 1942

2/0648 dt	U 134	Schendel	AB 6362	-D	6000+	T	PQ.7A	2/	br	-D	Waziristan	5135+	74.09 N/ 19.10 E	
10/0722 dt	U 584	Deecke	AC 8493	SS	920+	T	–	10/	sj	SS	M-175 ^{x}M-93	206+	70.09 N/ 32.50 E	
17/0632 dt	U 454	Hackländer	AW 2244	APC	800=	T	–	17/	sj	APM	TSC-68 ^{x}Enisej	557=	69.30 N/ 39.05 E	1)
17/1846 dt	U 454	Hackländer	AC 8952	-D	3500=	T	PQ.8	17/	br	-D	Harmatris	5395=	69.16 N/ 36.08 E	2)
17/1854 dt	U 454	Hackländer	AC 8952	DD	1120=	T	PQ.8	17/						2)
17/2221 dt	U 454	Hackländer	AC 8945	DD	1120=	T	PQ.8	17/	br	DD	Matabele	1870+	69.21 N/ 35.34 E	2)
17/2221 dt	U 454	Hackländer	AC 8945	-D	5000=	T	PQ.8	17/						2)
17/2222 dt	U 454	Hackländer	AC 8945	-D	2000+	T	PQ.8	17/						2)

February 1942

March 1942

1/1140 dt	U 436	Seibicke	AC 8948	-D	1500+	T	–	1/					NE Cape Teriberskij	3)
30/0807 dt	U 376	Marks	AC 8533	-D:	5086+	T	PQ.13	30/	br	-D	Induna	5086+	70.55 N/ 37.18 E	
30/1036 dt	U 456	Teichert	AC 8649	-D:	4000=	T	PQ.13	30/	ho	-DT	Mana (?)	3283 ?		4)
30/1219 dt	U 435	Strelow	AC 8646	-D:	6000+	T	PQ.13	30/	am	-D	Effingham	6421+	70.28 N/ 35.44 E	

April 1942

1/0059 dt	U 436	Seibicke	AC 5410	-D	4500+	T	–	1/	nw	-Df	Sulla (APC)	250+		5)
13/0129 dt	U 435	Strelow	AC 4662	-D:	6008+	T	QP.10	13/	pa	-D	El Occidente	6008+	73.28 N/ 28.30 E	
13/1535 dt	U 435	Strelow	AC 4521	-D	6000+	Tf	QP.10	13/	sj	-D	Kiev	5823+	73.22 N/ 28.48 E	6)
16/1445 dt	U 403	Clausen	AC 4157	-D	8000+	T	PQ.14	16/	br	-D	Empire Howard	6985+	73.48 N/ 21.32 E	
17/1737 dt	U 376	Marks	AC 5198	CL	10000=	T	PQ.14	17/				-----		7)

1) *U 454* observed the forepart of the ship going down, but the rest remained afloat.
2) *U 454* hit one ship amidship, which then burned heavily. After a miss, one destroyer was torpedoed at the stern and stopped. During a second attack a destroyer was hit at the stern (probably both on the *Matabele*), and after 6 min a water column was observed by a ship at a greater distance. Then after one torpedo hit another ship blew up in a 2-300m column of smoke and water.
3) *U 436* observed a hit after 47 sec and the subsequent sinking of the ship.

1	2	3	4	5	6	7	8	9	10	11	12	13	14	15
April 1942, cont.														
30/0603	dt	U 88	Bohmann	AC 5921	-D 5000=	T	QP.11	30/						1)
30/1618	*dt*	*U 456*	*Teichert*	*AC 5519*	*CL 10000=*	*T*	*QP.11*	*30/*	*br*	*CL*	*Edinburgh*	*11500=*	*73.18 N/ 33.00 E*	*2)*
May 1942														
1/0313	dt	U 589	Horrer	AC 4669	-D 6000=	T	QP.11	1/						3)
3/0014	dt	U 251	Timm	AB 6634	-D: 6153+	T	QP.11	2/	br	-D	Jutland	6153+	73.02 N/ 19.46 E	
26/0259	dt	U 703	Bielfeld	AB 5581	-D 8000+	T	PQ.16	26/	am	-D	Syros	6191+	72.35 N/ 05.30 E	
29/0318	dt	U 586	v.d.Esch	AC 5660	-D 5000=	T	PQ.16	29/				-----		4)
29/0318	dt	U 586	v.d.Esch	AC 5660	-D 6000=	T	PQ.16	29/				-----		4)
June 1942														
July 1942														
4/0808	dt	U 457	Brandenburg	AB 3683	-D: 7000+	Tf	PQ.17 s	4/	am	-D	Christopher Newport	7176+	75.49 N/ 22.25 E	5)
4/2259	dt	U 334	Siemon	AC 1681	-D 5000+	Tf	PQ.17 s	4/	am	-D	William Hooper	7177+	75.57 N/ 27.15 E	6)
5/0827	dt	U 703	Bielfeld	AC 2625	-D: 9000+	Tf	PQ.17 s	5/	br	-D	Empire Byron	6645+	76.18 N/ 33.30 E	6)
5/1015	dt	U 88	Bohmann	AC 2974	-D: 5162+	T	PQ.17 d	5/	am	-D	Carlton	5127+	76.14 N/ 40. E	
5/1431	dt	U 456	Teichert	AC 2933	-D: 6977+	T	PQ.17 d	5/	am	-D	Honomu	6977+	75.05 N/ 38.00 E	

4) *U 456* observed one hit after 55 sec following which the ship listed. The xB-Dienst reported this ship as the Hondurian tanker *Mana*.

5) *U 436* heard one hit after a run time of 48 sec and observed three rescue boats later.

6) The *Kiev* was damaged by bombs from a Ju-88 of the III./K.G.30 prior to the attack.

7) *U 376* fired a 3-torpedo spread against a cruiser of the *Belfast*-class or a destroyer-leader, and heard three detonations after 3 min 35 sec.

1) *U 88* fired a 3-torpedo spread and heard one detonation after 4 min 23 sec.

2) The damaged *Edinburgh* was under tow to the Kola Fjord when she was attacked by three German destroyers and hit by one torpedo from *Z 24*. Then she was sunk by a coup de grâce from the British destroyer *Foresight*.

3) *U 589* heard one end-of-run detonation after 5 min. 4) *U 586* fired a 4-torpedo spread and heard four detonations.

5) The *Chr.Newsport* was damaged earlier by a torpedo from a He-115 of the Küstenfliegergruppe 906.

6) The *Wm.Hooper* and *Empire Byron* were damaged by torpedoes from He-111s of the II./K.G.26.

1	2	3	4	5	6	7	8	9	10	11	12	13	14	15
July 1942, cont.														
5/1747	dt	U 334	Siemon	AC 2861	-D: 7000+	Tf	PQ.17	d	5/	br	-D	Earlston	7195+ 74.54 N/ 37.40 E	1)
5/2102	dt	U 703	Bielfeld	AC 3568	-D: 5479+	T	PQ.17	d	5/	br	-D	River Afton	5479+ 75.57 N/ 43.00 E	
5/2252	dt	U 88	Bohmann	AC 3769	-D: 8770+	Tf	PQ.17	d	5/	am	-D	Daniel Morgan	7177+ 75.08 N/ 45.06 E	1)
6/16	dt	U 255	Reche	AT 7216	-D:10900+	T	PQ.17	d	6/	am	-D	John Witherspoon	7191+ 70.30 N/ 52.30 E	
7/0927	dt	U 255	Reche	AT 4876	-D: 5120+	TA	PQ.17	d	7/	am	-D	Alcoa Ranger	5116+ 71.20 N/ 51.00 E	
7/1513	dt	U 457	Brandenburg	AC 3834	-T: 8402+	TA	PQ.17	d	7/	br	-MT	Aldersdale	8402+ 75. N/ 45. E	2)
7/1835	dt	U 355	La Baume	AT 4589	-D: 5082+	T	PQ.17	d	7/	br	-D	Hartlebury	5082+ 72.30 N/ 52.00 E	
8/0100	dt	U 255	Reche	AT 4827	-D: 6069+	TA	PQ.17	d	8/	am	-D	Olopana	6069+ 72.10 N/ 51.00 E	
10/0045	dt	U 251	Timm	AC 9554	-D 7000+	Tf	PQ.17	s	10/	pa	-D	El Capitan	5255+ 69.23 N/ 40.50 E	3)
10/0256	dt	U 376	Marks	AC 9843	-D: 6000+	Tf	PQ.17	s	10/	am	-D	Hoosier	5060+ 69.25 N/ 38.35 E	3)
13/0825	dt	U 255	Reche	AC 3437	-D: 7168+	Tf	PQ.17	d	13/	nl	-D	Paulus Potter	7168+ 70. N/ 52. E	4)
August 1942														
1/0023	dt	U 601	Grau	AT 7252	-D 2000+	T	-		1/	sj	-D	Krest'janin	2513+ W Mesduzarskij I.	
17/0710	dt	U 209	Brodda	AT 8761	-Dt 200+	A	-		17/	sj	-Dt	Kompleks	200+ W Yugor St.	5)
17/0715	dt	U 209	Brodda	AT 8761	-Bg 1000+	A	-		17/	sj	-Bg	B-III	+ W Yugor St.	
17/0810	dt	U 209	Brodda	AT 8761	-Dt 200+	A	-		17/	sj	-DT	Komsomolec	1250+ W Yugor St.	
17/0920	dt	U 209	Brodda	AT 8761	-Bg 800+	A	-		17/	sj	-Bg	P-IV	+ W Yugor St.	
24/1409	dt	U 601	Grau	AS 41	-D 5000+	T	-		24/	sj	-D	Kujbysev	2332+ E Yugor St.	6)

1) The *Earlston* and *D.Morgan* were damaged on July 5th by bombs from Ju-88s of III./K.G.30.
2) The *Aldersdale* was damaged earlier by bombs of a Ju-88 of III./K.G.30 and was sunk under tow by a coup de grâce from *U 457*.
3) The *El Capitan* and *Hoosier* belonged to the small convoy assembled at Novaya Zemlya by Commodore Dowding, and were already damaged by bombs from Ju-88s of III./K.G.30 on July 9th.
4) The *Paulus Potter* was damaged by bombs from Ju-88s of K.G.30 on July 6th, and was drifting abandoned. Important documents were taken off by the U-boat.
5) The name of this tug is sometimes given in Soviet publications as *Nord*.
6) It is not settled whether the *Kujbysev* was sunk in this attack or on Aug.27th 1943. On Aug.27th the xB-Dienst recorded the name *Kujbysev*, but assumed a connection with the attack by the pocket battleship *Admiral Scheer* on Port Dikson. It was then assumed to be the tanker *Valerian Kujbysev* (4,629 gross tons).

1	2	3	4	5	6	7	8	9	10	11	12	13	14	15
September 1942														
13/0952	dt	U 405	Hopmann	AB 2569	-D	7000+	T	PQ.18						1)
13/0954	dt	U 589	Horrer	AB 2566	-D	7000+	T	PQ.18						1)
13/0955	*dt*	*U 589*	*Horrer*	*AB 2566*	*CVE*	*=*	*T*	*PQ.18*	*13/0855*	*sj*	*-D Stalingrad*	*3559+*	*75.52 N/ 07.55 E*	*1)*
13/0957	dt	U 408	v.Hymmen	AB 2569	-D	7000+	T	PQ.18	13/0855	am	-D Oliver Ellsworth	7191+	75.52 N/ 07.55 E	1)
13/0957	dt	U 408	v.Hymmen	AB 2569	-D	=	T	PQ.18						1)
14/0400	dt	U 457	Brandenburg	AB 3643	-T	6000+	T	PQ.18	14/0330	br	-MT Atheltemplar	8992+	76.10 N/ 18.00 E	2)
14/0400	dt	U 457	Brandenburg	AB 3643	-T	4000+	T	PQ.18				-----		2)
14/0400	*dt*	*U 457*	*Brandenburg*	*AB 3643*	*DD*	*1690=*	*T*	*PQ.18*	*14/*			*------*		*2)*
16/1650	*dt*	*U 405*	*Hopmann*	*AT 4174*	*DD*	*1870=?*	*T*	*PQ.18*	*16/*			*---·---*		*3)*
16/1918	dt	U 377	Köhler	AC 6633	-D	7000=	T	PQ.18	16/			-----		4)
20/0625	dt	U 435	Strelow	AB 2272	-D	6000+	T	QP.14	20/			-----		5)
20/0626	dt	U 435	Strelow	AB 2272	-D	6000=	T	QP.14	20/			-----		5)
20/0629	dt	U 435	Strelow	AB 2272	-D	6000=?	T	QP.14	20/			-----		5)
20/0631	*dt*	*U 435*	*Strelow*	*AB 2272*	*DD*	*+*	*T*	*QP.14*	*20/0520*	*br*	*PM Leda*	*835+*	*76.30 N/ 05.00 E*	*5)*
20/1815	dt	U 255	Reche	AB 1648	-D	9000+	T	QP.14	20/1720	am	-D Silver Sword	4937+	75.52 N/ 00.20 W	
20/1955	*dt*	*U 703*	*Bielfeld*	*AB 1836*	*DD*	*1870+*	*T*	*QP.14*		*br*	*DD Somali*	*1870+*	*75.40 N/ 02.00 W*	*6)*
22/0718	dt	U 435	Strelow	AA 9286	-D	8000+	T	QP.14	22/	am	-D Bellingham	5345+	71.23 N/ 11.03 W	
22/0719	dt	U 435	Strelow	AA 9286	-D	12000+	T	QP.14	22/	br	-D Ocean Voice	7174+	71.23 N/ 11.03 W	
22/0719	dt	U 435	Strelow	AA 9286	-D	6000+	T	QP.14	22/	br	-DT Grey Ranger	3313+	71.23 N/ 11.03 W	
22/1016	*dt*	*U 408*	*v.Hymmen*	*AA 9227*	*DD*	*1870=*	*T*	*QP.14*	*22/*			*------*		*7)*
22/1016	dt	U 408	v.Hymmen	AA 9227	-D	8000=?	T	QP.14	22/			-----		7)

1) There is a possibility that *U 405* was credited by mistake for an attack by *U 408*. Both targets probably were hit by the same U-boat, but there is no other way of finding out which boat was successful. *U 589* reported one ship of 7,000 gross tons sunk and two detonations after 3 min 35 sec following the firing of a 2-torpedo spread against the CVE *Avenger*. *U 408* observed a hit after 5 min 27 sec with a fire column and boiler explosion, and one hit on a second ship behind.
2) *U 457* reported one tanker and one other ship sunk, and two hits on a destroyer of the *Javelin*-class. 3) *U 405* heard one detonation after 7 min 20 sec. 4) *U 377* heard one detonation after a run time of 4 min 25 sec. 5) *U 435* observed one hit after 46 sec, heard detonations after 4 min 10 sec and 4 min 30 sec, and observed the destroyer sinking. 6) *Somali* was taken in tow by HMS *Ashanti*, but was lost during a gale on September 24th.
7) *U 408* heard one detonation on a destroyer of the *Tribal*-class after a run time of 5 min 27 sec, and one more on a ship beyond.

1	2	3	4	5	6	7	8	9	10	11	12	13	14	15
October 1942														
(27. 8.)	dt	U 589	Horrer	AT 4612	---------	M	-	11/	sj	APC	SKR-23 Musson ×RT-54 Sudak	163+	W Matochkin-St.	1)
(13.10.)	dt	U 592	Borm	AT 8765	---------	M	-	14/	sj	-D	Shchors	3770=	69.45 N/ 60.45 E	
November 1942														
2/0118	dt	U 586	v.d.Esch	AA 9468	-D: 7000+	T	-	2/	br	-D	Empire Gilbert	6640+	70.15 N/ 13.50 E	
4/	dt	U 354	Herbschleb	AA 9513	-D 7000+	T	-	4/	am	-D	William Clark	7176+	71.02 N/ 13.05 E	2)
6/2224	dt	U 625	Benker	AB 3388	-D: 6670+	T	-	6/	br	-D	Empire Sky	7455+	76.20 N/ 17.30 E	3)
16/1558	dt	U 625	Benker	AB 3281	-D 4000+	Tf	-	6/	br	-D	Chulmleigh	5445+	South of Spitzberg	4)
23/0056	dt	U 625	Benker	AB 3692	-D: 5851+	T	QP.15	23/	br	-D	Goolistan	5851+	75.50 N/ 16.45 E	
23/0728	dt	U 601	Grau	AB 3569	-D: 3974+	T	QP.15	23/	sj	-D	Kusnec Lesov	3974+	75.30 N/ 08.00 E	
December 1942														
30/1642	dt	U 354	Herbschleb	AC 4182	-D 8000=	T	JW.51B	30/				-----		5)
30/1753	dt	U 354	Herbschleb	AC 4513	-D 8000=	T	JW.51B	30/				-----		5)
30/1753	dt	U 354	Herbschleb	AC 4513	-D 8000=?	T	JW.51B	30/				-----		5)
January 1943														
5/1510	dt	U 354	Herbschleb	AB 6342	-D 4000+	T	-	5/	sj	-D	Vanzetti	-----	Barents-Sea	6)
26/1100	dt	U 255	Reche	AC 6751	AG 4000+	T	-	26/	sj	-D	Ufa	1892+	Barents-Sea	7)
29/0547	dt	U 255	Reche	AB 6373	-D 3000+	T	-	29/	sj	-D	Krasnyj Partizan	2418+	Barents-Sea	8)

1) It is not clear if *SKR-23* and *Musson* were in fact the same. The sinking dates are given as Oct.11th, 13th and 23rd. It is possible that the ship was lost to a mine barrage laid by the heavy cruiser *Admiral Hipper*.
2) The *William Clark* was damaged earlier by bombs of a Ju-88 of II./K.G.30 on Nov.4th.
3) The *Empire Sky* was reported as *Bangalore* (6,067 gross tons) by *U 625*. The *Empire Sky* was reported missing after Nov.14th.
4) The *Chulmleigh* was beached south of Spitzbergen after damage by bombs of a Ju-88 of II./K.G.30. Then she was torpedoed by *U 625* and again bombs by a Ju-88 of II./K.G.30.
5) *U 354* heard one detonation during the first attack, and one more and possibly two during the second attack.
6) *U 354* missed the *Vanzetti*, which escaped. 7) *U 255* sank one ice-breaker-freighter with two torpedoes.
8) *U 255* reported one freighter of the *Manych*-class (2,274 gross tons) sunk with one torpedo.

1	2	3	4	5	6	7	8	9	10	11	12	13	14	15

February 1943

1	2	3	4	5	6	7	8	9	10 11	12	13	14	15
1/1850 dt	U 625	Benker	AB 6263	-D 10000=	T	RA.52	1/					1)
1/1850 dt	U 625	Benker	AB 6263	-D 7000=?	T	RA.52	1/			-----		1)
1/1850 dt	U 625	Benker	AB 6263	-D 7000=?	T	RA.52	1/			-----		1)
1/1853 dt	U 625	Benker	AB 6263	-D 7000=?	T	RA.52	1/			-----		1)
3/1412 dt	U 255	Reche	AB 7552	-D: 7460+	T	RA.52	3/	am -D	Greylock	7460+	70.52 N/ 00.21 W	2)
3/1413 dt	U 255	Reche	AB 7552	-D 5000=	T	RA.52	3/			-----		2)
16/2018 dt	U 302	Sickel	AC 1875	-D 4000=?	T		16/			-----		3)

March 1943

1	2	3	4	5	6	7	8	9	10 11	12	13	14	15
5/0926 dt	U 255	Reche	AB 5939	-D 6000+	T	RA.53	5/	am -D	Executive	4978+	72.44 N/ 11.27 E	
5/0926 dt	U 255	Reche	AB 5939	-D 6000+	T	RA.53	5/	am -D	Richard Bland(u.)	7191=	72.44 N/ 11.27 E	4)
9/ dt	U 586	v.d.Esch	AE 3574	-D 9000=	T	RA.53	9/	am -D	Puerto Rican	6076+	66.44 N/ 10.41 W	
10/1636 dt	U 255	Reche	AE 2824	-D 7000+	T	RA.53	10/	am -D	Richard Bland(o.)	7191+	66.53 N/ 14.10 W	4)

April 1943

May 1943

June 1943

1	2	3	4	5	6	7	8	9	10 11	12	13	14	15
24/ dt	U 302	Sickel	ÄG 75	Motorboot+	A	-	24/			+	Spitzbergen	5)

July 1943

1	2	3	4	5	6	7	8	9	10 11	12	13	14	15
(20. 7.) dt	U 625	Benker	AT 8810	---------	M		27/	sj APM	TSC-58 XSpartak	557+	Jugor-Strait	
27/1754 dt	U 255	Harms	AT 3513	AGS: 300+	A	-	27/	sj AGS	Akademik Sokalskij	300+	Sporyj Navolok	
30/1548 dt	U 703	Brünner	AT 7282	APC 500+	T	.	30/	sj APM	TSC-65	...+	WNW Cape Kostin	6)

1) *U 625* fired a 4-torpedo spread and a stern torpedo, observed one hit after 3 min, and heard three detonations between 190-225 sec after firing.

2) *U 255* observed two hits on one ship after a run time of 1 min 50 sec, and heard one additional detonation after 3 min 20 sec.

3) *U 302* heard one hit without a detonation after 1 min 20 sec (a dud) - 4) *U 255* fired a 3-torpedo spread and heard two detonations. U-boats and air-recon reported both ships sinking. But only *R.Bland* was damaged and sunk on March 10th, by 3 torpedoes.

5) *U 302* sank a small motorboat. 6) *U 703* hit a patrol craft after 90 sec, and the ship sank in 50 sec by the stern.

1	2	3	4	5	6		7	8	9	10	11	12	13	14	15

August 1943

(13. 8.) dt	U 625	Benker	AT 8580	---------		M	−	25/	sj	Dt	SKR-.. [x]Skval	572+	Yugor-Street	
27/2021 dt	U 354	Herbschleb	AS 2722	-D	4000+	T	.	27/					75.15 N/ 84.30 E	1)
27/2022 dt	U 354	Herbschleb	AS 2722	-D	5000+	T	.	/	sj	-D	Petrovskij	3771=		1)
28/1116 dt	U 302	Sickel	XA 7542	-D	2900+	T	.	/	sj	-D	Dikson	2900+	75.37 N/ 89.10 E	2)

September 1943

| (28. 8.) dt | U 636 | Hildebrandt | AS 4942 | --------- | | M | − | 7/ | sj | -D | Tbilisi | 7169+ | Enisej-Mündung | 3) |
| 30/0750 dt | U 960 | Heinrich | XA 4897 | -D | 6000+ | T | VA-18 | 30/ | sj | -D | Archangelsk | 2480+ | 72.30 N/ 62. E | |

October 1943

1/1310 dt	U 703	Brünner	AS 2426	-D:	4200+	T	VA-18	1/	sj	-D	Sergej Kirov	4146+	20m Izvestij-Ins.	
1/1314 dt	U 703	Brünner	AS 2426	-D	3000=	T	VA-18	1/	sj	-D	Mossovet	-----		4)
1/1713 dt	U 601	Grau	AS 24	-D	5100=	T	VA-18	1/	sj	AG	Murman	-----		5)
1/1806 dt	U 960	Heinrich	AS 2712	-D	2900+	T	VA-18	1/	sj	-D	A.Andreev	-----	Arktik Institute	6)
1/1806 dt	U 960	Heinrich	AS 2712	APC	500+	T	VA-18	1/	sj	APM	TSC-42 [x]Krasnyj Onezanin	611+	Arktik Institute	6)

November 1943

December 1943

| 28/2210 dt | U 957 | Schaar | AC 5637 | PE | | = | T′ | JW.55B | 28/ | | | | ------ | | 7) |
| 28/2243 dt | U 957 | Schaar | AC 5637 | DD | | = | T′ | JW.55B | 28/ | | | | ------ | | 7) |

---

1) *U 354* attacked a convoy of four ships and two patrol craft. A single detonation was heard 1 min 55 sec after a single shot was fired, and 5 min after a 3-torpedo spread was fired. Later only two ships and one patrol craft were observed. Possibly the *Petrovskij* was torpedoed at this time.
2) *U 302* fired a 4-torpedo spread and after a run time of 2 min 56 sec observed one hit on a ship of the *Dikson*-class which sank. However, Soviet sources give the date of the sinking of the *Dikson* as Aug.26th or 28th near the Luna Island.
3) Soviet sources say the *Tbilisi* was torpedoed, but there was no reported attack. It must have struck a mine.
4) *U 703* heard two detonations 3 min 14 sec after the second of two 2-torpedo spreads were fired. But the *Mossovet* was missed.
5) *U 601* missed the attacked icebreaker-steamer *Murman*, and assumed a hit on one other ship.
6) *U 960* reported erroneously the sinking of the *A.Andreev* and one patrol craft, but only the patrol-minesweeper sank.
7) *U 957* heard one Gnat end-of-run detonation after 11 min, and one Gnat detonation after 3 min 5 sec.

1	2	3	4	5	6	7	8	9	10	11	12	13	14	15
January 1944														
25/1128 dt	U	965	Ohling	AB 6683	DD	=	T'	JW.56A	25/			-----		1)
25/1410 dt	U	601	Hansen	AB 6931	DD	=	T'	JW.56A	25/			-----		2)
25/1720 dt	U	425	Bentzien	AC 4492	DD	=?	T'	JW.56A	25/			-----		3)
25/1833 dt	U	360	Becker	AC 4451	DD	+	T'	JW.56A	25/	br DD	Obdurate	1540=	73.25 N/ 25.16 E	
25/2012 dt	U	278	Franze	AC 4572	-D	7000+	T.	JW.56A	25/2015	am -D	Penelope Barker	7177+	73.22 N/ 22.30 E	4)
25/2012 dt	U	278	Franze	AC 4572	-D	7000+	T.	JW.56A	25/			-----		4)
25/2157 dt	U	957	Schaar	AC 4541	DD	+	T'	JW.56A	25/			-----		5)
26/0016 dt	U	360	Becker	AC 4529	-D	7000=	T.	JW.56A	26/0010	br -D	Fort Bellingham	7153=	73.25 N/ 25.10 E	6)
26/0016 dt	U	360	Becker	AC 4529	-D	7000=	T.	JW.56A	26/		(s.u.)	-----		6)
26/0016 dt	U	360	Becker	AC 4529	-D	7000=	T.	JW.56A	26/					
26/0020 dt	U	716	Dunkelberg	AC 4552	-D	7000=	T.	JW.56A	26/0200	am -D	Andrew G.Curtin	7200+	73.25 N/ 25.16 E	7)
26/0020 dt	U	716	Dunkelberg	AC 4552	-D	7000=	T.	JW.56A	26/			-----		7)
26/0240 dt	U	957	Schaar	AC 4543	-T	7000=	T'	JW.56A	26/			-----		8)
26/0250 dt	U	314	Basse	AC 4618	DD	=	T'	JW.56A	26/			-----		9)
26/0653 dt	U	957	Schaar	AC 4562	-D	7000+	T'	JW.56A	26/	br -D	Fort Bellingham(s.o.)	7153+	73.25 N/ 25.10 E	6)
30/0108 dt	U	737	Brasack	AB 6378	DD	+	T'	JW.56B	30/	br DD	Milne	-----		1o)
30/0346 dt	U	957	Schaar	AB 6381	DD	=	T'	JW.56B	30/			-----		11)
30/o354 dt	U	957	Schaar	AB 6381	DD	+	T'	JW.56B	30/	br DD	Hardy	-----		11)
30/0357 dt	U	278	Franze	AB 6391	DD	+	T'	JW.56B	30/	br DD	Hardy	1730+	73.40 N/ 24.30 E	11)
30/0357 dt	U	472	v.Forstner	AB 6297	DD	+	T'	JW.56B	30/	nw DD	Stord	-----		11)
30/0420 dt	U	957	Schaar	AB 6301	DD	=	T.	JW.56B	30/			-----		12)
30/0524 dt	U	601	Hansen	AB 6292	DD	+	T'	JW.56B	30/	br DD	Venus	-----		11)

1) Gnat end-of-run detonations were heard by U 965 after 10 min and by 2) U 601 after 12 min 48 sec and by 3) U 425.
4) U 278 fired a spread of three FAT and heard two detonations and sinking noises. 5) U 957 heard one Gnat end-of-run detonation after 13 min; the debris later observed was probably from the P.Parker. 6) U 360 fired a spread of three FAT and heard three hits. The torpedoed Fort Bellingham was later sunk by a T-3 from U 957. 7) U 716 fired a spread of three FAT and heard two hits.
8) U 957 heard one Gnat end-of-run detonation after 13 min 35 sec and observed a ship burning. 9) U 314 heard a Gnat detonation after 3 min 30 sec. 10) U 737 observed one Gnat detonation after a run time of 40 sec, in reality a wake detonation. 11) U 957 heard two Gnat end-of-run detonations after 11 min 45 sec and 12 min, and observed the hit by U 278 on Hardy. U 472 claimed this hit. The damaged Hardy was sunk by a torpedo from HMS Venus, which U 601 claimed as its Gnat-hit. 12) U 957 heard a Gnat detonation after 4 min.

1	2	3	4	5	6	7	8	9	10	11	12	13	14	15
January 1944, cont.														
30/0628	dt	U 313	Schweiger	AB 6532	DD	+ T′	JW.56B	30/				-----		13)
30/1256	dt	U 965	Ohling	AC 4273	DD	+ T′	JW.56B	30/				-----		14)
30/1801	dt	U 425	Bentzien	AC 4349	DD	+ T′	JW.56B	30/				-----		15)
30/2246	dt	U 737	Brasack	AC 4638	DD	+ T′	JW.56B	30/				-----		16)
31/0601	dt	U 990	Nordheimer	AC 5818	DD	+ T′	JW.56B	30/				-----		17)
February 1944														
25/2055	dt	U 990	Nordheimer	AB 9483	DD	+ T′	JW.57	25/	br	DD	Mahratta	1920+	71.12 N/ 13.30 E	
26/	dt	U 956	Mohs	AB	DD	=? T′	JW.57	26/				-----		1)
26/	dt	U 366	Langenberg	AB 6858	DD	=? T′	JW.57	26/				-----		2)
27/	dt	U 278	Franze	AC 4954	DD	= T′	JW.57	27/				-----		3)
27/	dt	U 312	Nicolay	AC 4588	DD	=? T′	JW.57	27/				-----		4)
27/1630	dt	U 362	Franz	AC 4951	DD	= T′	JW.57	27/				-----		5)
March 1944														
4/0425	dt	U 739	Mangold	AC 4359	DD	=? T′	RA.57	4/	br	DD	Swift	-----		6)
4/0555	dt	U 472	v.Forstner	AC 4680	DD	+ T′	RA.57	4/				-----		7)
4/	dt	U 703	Brünner	AC 4438	-D	7000+	T.	RA.57	4/	br	-D	Empire Tourist	7062+	73.25 N/ 22.11 E
4/1545	dt	U 703	Brünner	AC 4438	DD	= T′	RA.57	4/	br	DD	Milne	-----		8)
5/2129	dt	U 278	Franze	AB 8292	DD	=? T′	RA.57	5/				-----		9)
6/0629	dt	U 959	Weitz	AB 8571	DD	+ T′	RA.57	6/				-----		10)

13) Gnat detonations were heard by *U 313* after a run time of 8 min, by 14) *U 965* after 5 min 6 sec, by 15) *U 425* after 1 min 58 sec, by 16) *U 737* after 10 min 30 sec, and by 17) *U 990* after 13 min 9 sec. During some of the attacks sinking noises were heard but in reality, there were no hits.

1) Gnat detonations were heard by *U 956* after 13 min, by 2) *U 366* after 10 min, by 3) *U 278* after 4 min 13 sec, by 4) *U 312* after 9 min 43 sec, by 5) *U 362* after 4 min 13 sec, by 6) *U 739* after 12 min, by 7) *U 742* by 8) *U 703* after 3 min 10 sec, by 9) *U 278* after 5 min 46 sec, and by 10) *U 959* after 13 min 28 sec. The detonations after 5 to 6 min were end-of-run detonations.

1	2	3	4	5	6	7	8	9	10	11	12	13	14	15
April 1944														
1/0231	dt	U 968	Westphalen	AB 8110	DD	+?	T'	JW.58	1/			-----		1)
1/0448	dt	U 674	Muhs	AB 8121	DD	+	T'	JW.58	1/			-----		2)
1/1040	dt	U 968	Westphalen	AB 5874	DD	+	T'	JW.58	1/			-----		3)
1/2308	dt	U 711	Lange	AB 5637	DD	+	T'	JW.58	1/			-----		4)
1/2313	dt	U 354	Sthamer	AB 6442	DD	+	T'	JW.58	1/			-----		4)
2/1719	dt	U 990	Nordheimer	AC 4428	DD	+	T'	JW.58	2/			-----		5)
2/1847	dt	U 711	Lange	AC 4461	DD	1870+	T'	JW.58	2/			-----		6)
2/1848	dt	U 739	Mangold	AC 4452	DD	1870+	T'	JW.58	2/	br DD	Ashanti	-----		6)
2/1848	dt	U 739	Mangold	AC 4452	DD	1870+	T'	JW.58	2/			-----		6)
2/1858	dt	U 278	Franze	AC 4445	DD	+	T'	JW.58	2/			-----		7)
2/2338	dt	U 277	Lübsen	AC	DD	+	T'	JW.58	2/			-----		8)
3/00	dt	U 277	Lübsen	AC	DD	+?	T'	JW.58	2/			-----		8)
3/	dt	U 315	Zoller	AC	DD	+	T'	JW.58	3/			-----		9)
3/0125	dt	U 312	Nicolay	AB 1975	DD	+	T'	JW.58	3/			-----		10)
3/2130	dt	U 674	Muhs	AC 5912	DD	1700+	T'	JW.58	3/			-----		11)
10/0535	dt	U 361	Seidel	AB 6661	DE	=?	T'	RA.58	10/			-----		12)
10/0707	dt	U 703	Brünner	AB 6833	DD	1870=	T'	RA.58	10/			-----		13)
10/2236	dt	U 313	Schweiger	AB 63	DD	=?	T'	RA.58	10/			-----		14)

1) Gnat end-of-run detonations were heard by U 968 after 9 min 30 sec, by 2) U 674 after 12 min 56 sec, and by 3) U 968 after 10 min 42 sec.

4) U 711 heard one Gnat detonation after 2 min 6 sec and one explosion. U 354 heard one Gnat detonation after 3 min 58 sec.

5) U 990 heard one Gnat end-of-run detonation after 11 min 4 sec. 6) Gnat detonations were heard by U 711 after 2 min 5 sec, and by U 739 after 2 min 25 sec, and 1 min 35 sec. The last one was identified by both boats as an explosion. 7) U 278 reported a Gnat detonation after 1 min 20 sec, but in reality it was a depth charge. 8) U 277 heard two Gnat detonations after 2 min 20 sec and 3 min 18 sec. 9) Gnat detonations were heard by U 315 after 11 min (an end-of-run detonation), by 10) U 312 after 1 min 30 sec, by 11) U 674 after 5 min 45 sec (an end-of-run detonation), by 12) U 361 after 2 min 15 sec, by 13) U 703 after 1 min 38 sec, and by 14) U 313 after 1 min 30 sec. The detonations after 5-6 min were mostly end-of-run detonations, the others detonations in the wake or detonations after depth charges were dropped in defense against Gnat torpedoes.

Northern Theater

1	2	3	4	5	6		7	8	9	10	11	12	13	14	15
April 1944, cont.															
30/1956 dt	U 307	Herrle	AB 6373	-D	7000+	T.	RA.59	30/				-----			15)
30/1956 dt	U 307	Herrle	AB 6373	-D	4000+	T.	RA.59	30/				-----			15)
30/1956 dt	U 307	Herrle	AB 6373	-D	7000=	T.	RA.59	30/				--.--			15)
30/2138 dt	U 387	Büchler	AB 6347	DD	=	T'	RA.59	30/				-----			16)
30/2206 dt	U 711	Lange	AB 6346	DD	1600+	T'	RA.59	30/							17)
30/2212 dt	U 711	Lange	AB 6346	-D	7000+	T.	RA.59	30/	am	-D	William S.Thayer	7176+	73.52 N/ 18.26 E	17)
30/2214 dt	U 711	Lange	AB 6346	DD	+	T'	RA.59	30/				-----			17)
30/2245 dt	U 387	Büchler	AB 6347	DD	1600=	T'	RA.59	30/							17)
30/2347 dt	U 711	Lange	AB 6349	DD	1870+	T'	RA.59	30/				-----			18)
May 1944															
1/0013 dt	U 711	Lange	AB 6349	-D	5000=	T.	RA.59	30/				-----			18)
1/0947 dt	U 278	Franze	AB 6441	DD	+	T'	RA.59	1/				-----			1)
1/1206 dt	U 278	Franze	AB 5653	DD	=?	T'	RA.59	1/				-----			2)
1/1648 dt	U 307	Herrle	AB 5914	DD	+	T'	RA.59	1/				-----			3)
1/2230 dt	U 307	Herrle	AB 8228	DD	=?	T'	RA.59	1/				-----			4)
1/ dt	U 959	Weitz	AB 5888	DD	+	T.	RA.59	1/				-----			5)
1/ dt	U 959	Weitz	AB 5888	DD	+	T.	RA.59	1/				-----			5)
2/1015 dt	U 307	Herrle	AB 7692	DD	=?	T'	RA.59	2/				-----			6)
2/1351 dt	U 711	Lange	AB 8740	DD	=?	T'	RA.59	2/				-----			7)
30/2017 dt	U 957	Schaar	AB 4693	DD ?	=	T'	Task F.	30/				-----			8)

15) *U 307* fired a spread of three FAT and reported two ships sunk, one torpedoed. 16) *U 387* heard a Gnat detonation after 2 min 29 sec.
17) *U 711* observed after a run time of 4 min 3 sec a Gnat hit on a destroyer of the *Groznyj*-class, and after 5 min 7 sec, a FAT-hit on a "Liberty"-ship. One additional Gnat detonation was heard after 6 min 15 sec. *U 387* probably attacked the same *Groznyj*-class destroyer. Soviet destroyers of this class were often misidentified British ships of the *Black Swan*-class.
18) *U 711* heard after a run time of 7 min 20 sec a FAT detonation, and one Gnat end-of-run detonation after 11 min 26 sec.
1) There were Gnat end-of-run detonations heard by *U 278* after 11 min 24 sec and 2) after 12 min and by 3) *U 307* after 7 min 20 sec and 4) after 10 min 15 sec. 5) *U 959* reported two destroyers sunk by a FAT spread. 6) *U 307* heard a Gnat end-of-run detonation after 15 min 13 sec. 7) *U 711* heard a Gnat end-of-run detonation after 9 min 7 sec. 8) *U 957* heard a Gnat detonation in a task group after 4 min 30 sec.

1	2	3	4	5	6	7	8	9	10	11	12	13	14	15
June 1944														
July 1944														
August 1944														
12/1853	dt	U 365	Wedemeyer	AT 6434	-D	3560+	T.	BD-5	12/	sj	-D Marina Raskova	5685+	72.30 N/ 66.00 E	1)
12/1903	dt	U 365	Wedemeyer	AT 6434	PM	600+	T'	BD-5	12/	sj	PM TSC-118 ˣArmada	625+	72.30 N/ 66.00 E	1)
12/2345	dt	U 365	Wedemeyer	AT 6434	PM	600+	T	BD-5	12/	sj	PM TSC-114 ˣAlchemy	625+	72.30 N/ 66.00 E	1)
18/0028	dt	U 307	Herrle	ÄG 75	Mbt	100+	A	-	18/			+	Van Mijen Fjord	
21/0604	dt	U 344	Pietsch	AB 5456	CL	5450+	T.	JW.59	21/	br	PS Kite	1350+	73.01 N/ 03.57 E	2)
22/0	dt	U 354	Sthamer	AB 9333	CVE	+	T.	Task F.	22/	ca	CVE Nabob	11420=§	71.42 N/ 19.11 E	3)
22/0122	dt	U 354	Sthamer	AB 9333	"	+	Tf	Task F.	22/	br	DE Bickerton	1300+	71.42 N/ 19.11 E	3)
23/0720	dt	U 711	Lange	AC 2729	BB	=	T.	Task F.	23/	sj	BB Archangel'sk ˣRoyal Sovereign	-----		4)
23/0728	dt	U 711	Lange	AC 2729	DD	1190=	T'	Task F.	23/	sj	DD Žarkij ˣBrighton	-----		4)
24/0152	dt	U 997	Lehmann	AC 5499	DD	+	T'	JW.59	24/			-----		5)
24/0153	dt	U 997	Lehmann	AC 5499	DD	+	T'	JW.59	24/			-----		5)
24/0157	dt	U 668	v.Eickstedt	AC 5477	DD	+	T'	JW.59	24/			-----		5)
24/0201	dt	U 668	v.Eickstedt	AC 5477	DD	+	T'	JW.59	24/			-----		5)
24/0309	dt	U 363	Nees	AC 5491	DD	=?	T'	JW.59	24/			-----		6)
24/0311	dt	U 363	Nees	AC 5491	DD	+	T'	JW.59	24/			-----		6)
25/0158	dt	U 711	Lange	AC 5856	DD	+	T'	JW.59	25/	br	DD Keppel	-----		7)
25/0240	dt	U 354	Sthamer	AC	---------		T'	JW.59	25/	br	PS Mermaid	-----		7)
26/0641	dt	U 711	Lange	AC 4958	SS	840=	T'	-	26/	sj	SS S-	----		8)
26/	dt	U 957	Schaar	XA 7553	AGS:	200+	A	-	28/	sj	AGS Nord	200+	75.35 N/ 89.50 E	

1) *U 365* hit the *M.Raskova* with a FAT spread, the *TSC-118* by a Gnat, and the *TSC-114* by a T-3. The *M.Raskova* was sunk by two coups de grâce. 2) *U 344* hit the *Kite* by a FAT spread and identified the ship as a cruiser of the *Dido*-class. 3)*U 354* hit the *Nabob* with a FAT spread and tried to sink her with a Gnat, which hit the *Bickerton*. This ship was later sunk by a torpedo from HMS *Aylmer*. The *Nabob* was taken into port, and was rebuilt to a freighter for the NDL after the war.
4) It is improbable that the *Archangelsk* was hit by the torpedo, which detonated after a run time of 8 min 45 sec. A Gnat detonation reported heard by *U 711* after 8 min 32 sec was probably a depth charge dropped by the Soviet destroyer *Zharkij*.
5) *U 997* heard two Gnat detonations after 7 min and 9 min. 5) *U 668* after 1 min 35 sec and 3 min 25 sec. 6) *U 363* heard two Gnat end-of-run detonations after 10 min 15 sec and 11 min 1 sec. 7) *U 711* heard a Gnat detonation after 6 min 20 sec probably a detonation in the wake of HMS *Mermaid*.

1	2	3	4	5	6	7	8	9	10	11	12	13	14	15
September 1944														
23/0012	dt	U 957	Schaar	XA 7183	DD	1600+	T′	VD-1	23/		sj PC	SKR-29 *Brilliant*	550+	N *Krakovka*-I.	1)
24/0901	dt	U 739	*Mangold*	AS 2723	PM	600+	T′	–	24/		sj PM	TSC-120 *Assail*	625+	76.30 N/ 84.50 E	
29/1627	dt	U 310	Ley	AC 4526	-D	7000+	T.	RA.60	29/		am -D	Edward H.Crockett	7176+	72.59 N/ 24.26 E	
29/1627	dt	U 310	Ley	AC 4526	-D	7000+	T.	RA.60	29/		br -D	Samsuva	7219+	72.58 N/ 23.59 E	
October 1944														
26/2331	dt	U 956	Mohs	AC 8314	DD	=	T′	JW.61	26/			–––––		2)
27/	dt	U 365	Wedemeyer	AC 5898	DD	=	T′	JW.61	27/			–––––		3)
27/	dt	U 995	Hess	AC 8214	DD	+	T′	JW.61	27/			–––––		4)
27/	dt	U 995	Hess	AC 8214	DD	=	T′	JW.61	27/			–––––		4)
27/1415	dt	U 295	*Wieboldt*	AC 8356	DD	=?	T′	JW.61	27/			–––––		5)
November 1944														
2/	dt	U 295	*Wieboldt*	AC	DD	?	T′	RA.61	2/		br DE	Mounsey	1150=	69.20 N/ 36.44 E	
5/	dt	U 997	*Lehmann*	AC 80	DD	+	T′	–	5/		sj DD	Spokojnyj (?)	1686+?	?	6)
8/2030	dt	U 771	*Block*	AC 59	DD	+?	T′	–	8/			–––––		7)
December 1944														
2/	dt	U 363	Nees	AC 8578	-D	4500+	T	PK-20	2/		sj -D	Proletarij	1123+	15m N Zyp Navolok	
3/	dt	U 1163	Balduhn	AW 2163	APC	+	T	KB-35	3/		sj -D	Revoljucija	557+	N Cape Cernyj	
4/	dt	U 363	Nees	AC 8575	-D	10000=	T	KP-..	4/					8)
4/	dt	U 992	Falke	AC 8577	-D	10000=	T	KP-..	4/					8)
4/	dt	U 992	*Falke*	AC 8577	PM	600=	T′	KP-..	4/					8)
4/	dt	U 992	*Falke*	AC 8577	PM	600=?	T′	KP-..	4/					8)
4/	dt	U 995	Hess	AC 8733	-D	6000=	T	KP-..	4/					8)

8) *U 711* assumed to have damaged a submarine of the S-class. 1) The *Brilliant* was a former NKVD patrol vessel of the modified *Tral*-class. 2) *U 956* heard a Gnat proximity detonation after 56 sec. 3) Gnat detonations were heard by *U 365* after a run time of 9 min 40 sec, by 4) *U 995* after 2 min 19 sec and 4 min 50 sec, by 5) *U 295* after 11 min 50 sec and by 6) *U 997* after 2 min 13 sec. This may have been a newly built destroyer of the *Strozhevoj*-class which was transferred in 1941 and completed in 1944 but never heard of again.
7) *U 711* heard a Gnat end-of-run detonation after 11 min. 8) A west-bound Soviet convoy was attacked; one ship was of the "War Emergency"-type. No result known.

1	2	3	4	5	6	7	8	9	10	11	12	13	14	15
December 1944, cont.														
4/	dt	U 997	Lehmann	AW 2220	PC	+	T′	.	4/	sj	PC	BO-226 ^{x}SC 1485	105+		9)
5/	dt	U 995	Hess	AC 8577	-D	6000+	T.	PK-	5/	sj	-M	Reshitelnyj	...+	off Kola	10)
5/	dt	U 995	Hess	AC 8579	-D	7000=	T.	PK-	5/	sj	APM	TSC-107 ^{x}Vega	250+	off Kola	10)
5/	dt	U 365	Todenhagen	AC 8852	-D	4000=	T	.	5/						11)
6/	dt	U 365	Todenhagen	AC 8941	DD	+	T′	.	6/						9)
6/	dt	U 318	Will	AC 80	PC	=?	T′	.	6/						12)
6/1946	dt	U 293	Klingspor	AC 8853	DD	=?	T′	.	6/	sj	DD	Dejatelnyj	-----	Kildin I.	13)
7/	dt	U 997	Lehmann	AC 8864	PE	+	T′	-	7/1010	sj	PC	BO-229 ^{x}SC 1477	105+	N Kildin I.	9)
9/	dt	U 997	Lehmann	AC 80	DD	=	T.	-	9/	sj	DD	Zhivuchij	-----	off Kola	14)
10/	dt	U 365	Todenhagen	AC 8860	-T	7000+	T′	RA.62	10/				-----		15)
11/	dt	U 365	Todenhagen	AC 5763	DD	+	T′	RA.62	11/	br	DD	Cassandra	1710=	71.57 N/ 32.04 E	
20/	dt	U 956	Mohs	AC 8973	-D	3000+	T		20/						16)
20/	dt	U 956	Mohs	AC 8973	APC	+	T		20/						16)
21/	dt	U 997	Lehmann	AC 80	APC	+	T.		21/						17)
26/1833	dt	U 995	Hess	AW 2261	-D	+	T	.	26/	sj	-D	Som	417+		18)
29/1515	dt	U 995	Hess	AW 2297	-D	2000+	T		29/						18)
30/	dt	U 956	Mohs	AC 8812	-D	5000+	T	KP.24	30/	sj	-D	Tbilisi	7176=	Skorbeyevskij Bay	19)
30/	dt	U 956	Mohs	AC 8812	-D	=	T	KP.24	30/						19)
31/1845	dt	U 310	Ley	AC 8570	APC	=?	T	.	31/				-----		20)

9) There were two ex-USSCs sunk in early December; *BO-229* was sunk by *U 997*, and *BO-226* on either the 4th by *U 997* or the 6th by *U 365*.
10) *U 995* reported one ship damaged by FAT and later AC 8821 sunk by a Gnat, and a second ship damaged by a Gnat after a run time of 5 min 24 sec. There is some indication that the ship sunk at this occasion was the *Proletarij* (see page 209).
11) *U 365* reported one hit. 12) *U 318* heard one Gnat end-of-run detonation after 9 min 25 sec. 13) *U 293* reported a Gnat detonation after 10 min 40 sec; the *Dejazelnyj* reported a detonation in the wake. 14) *U 997* assumed a hit but missed in reality, and *Zivuchij* and *Razumnyj* dropped D/Cs on her. 15) *U 365* heard one Gnat end-of-run detonation after 10 min 58 sec.
16) *U 956* reported one ship and one patrol craft sunk. 17) *U 997* reported one auxiliary patrol craft sunk.
18) *U 995* observed a hit and the steamer exploding, only the bow later seen. 19) *U 956* reported one ship sunk, one probably sunk. The *Tbilisi (II)* was towed into Kildin and beached. 20) *U 310* heard one hit, possibly a ground detonation.

1	2	3	4	5	6	7	8	9	10	11	12	13	14	15
January 1945														
12/	dt	U 956	Mohs	AC 8989	APC	+	T.	–	12/				-----		1)
16/	dt	U 286	Dietrich	AC 8980	DD	+	T′	KB-1	16/2030	sj	DD	Dejatelnyj *Churchill	1190+	68.56 N/ 36.31 E	1a)
20/1055	dt	U 293	Klingspor	AC 8574	DD	1600+	T′	KP-	20/		sj	DD Razjarennyj	1658=	N.Rybachi-Penins.	2)
February 1945														
5/	dt	U 992	Falke	AC 8855	PE	+	T′	.	5/		sj	PM TSC-116 *Arcade ?	625+		3)
8/	dt	U 992	Falke	AC 8855	DD	=	T′						————		4)
9/	dt	U 995	Hess	AC 8754	-D	6000+	T	–	9/1715	nw	-D	Idefjord	-----	Kirkenes Hafen	5)
13/	dt	U 992	Falke	AC 88	-D	=	T	JW.64	13/00	br	PE	Denbigh Castle	1060+	69.20 N/ 33.33 E	6)
14/1039	dt	U 711	Lange	AC 8869	-D	7000+	T	BK-	14/	am	-D	Horace Gray	7200+	68.23 N/ 33.47 E	7)
14/1039	dt	U 711	Lange	AC 8869	-D	7000+	T	BK-	14/				-----		7)
14/1230	dt	U 968	Westphalen	AC 8559	-T:	8129+	T	BK-	14/	nw	-DT	Norfjell	8129=§	69.22 N/ 33.50 E	8)
14/1230	dt	U 968	Westphalen	AC 8559	-D	7000+?	T	BK-	14/				-----		8)
14/1230	dt	U 968	Westphalen	AC 8559	-D	7000=	T	BK-	14/				-----		8)
14/1230	dt	U 968	Westphalen	AC 8559	-D	7000=	T	BK-	14/				-----		8)
14/	dt	U 992	Falke	AC 8858	-T	7000+	T	BK-	14/						8)
16/0225	dt	U 286	Dietrich	AC 8972	-D	3000+	T	BK-	16/						9)
16/0225	dt	U 286	Dietrich	AC 8972	APC	=	T	BK-	16/				-----	Seleneckij-Ins.	9)
17/	dt	U 968	Westphalen	AC 8865	DD	1600+	T′	RA.64	17/1024	br	PS	Lark	1350=§	69.30 N/ 34.33 E	10)
17/	dt	U 968	Westphalen	AC 8865	-D	7000+	T	RA.64	17/1200	am	-D	Thomas Scott	7176+	69.30 N/ 34.42 E	11)
17/	dt	U 968	Westphalen	AC 8865	DD	1120+	T	RA.64	17/				————		11)
17/	dt	U 711	Lange	AC 8942	DD	+	T′	RA.64	17/1523	br	PE	Bluebell	925+	69.36 N/ 25.29 E	

1) *U 956* heard one FAT end-of-run detonation after 7 min 40 sec. 1a) There is no final proof of the attack by *U 286*; the destroyer might have struck a mine. 2) The *Razjarennyj* was towed into Liinahamaari. 3) *U 992* reported an escort destroyer sunk, perhaps the lost ex US-minesweeper *TSC-116*. 4) *U 992* heard one Gnat-detonation after 5 min 53 sec.
5) *U 995* missed the *Idefjord* tied up at a pier by 30 to 40 m. 6) The *Denbigh Castle* was towed by the HMS *Bluebell* into the Kola Fjord but was never repaired. 7) *U 711* reported two ships sunk; the *H.Gray* sank under tow by Soviet tugs.
8) *U 968* reported four ships hit. The *Norfejell* was beached and was declared a total loss. She might also have been hit by *U 992*.
9) *U 286* attacked a Soviet convoy consisting of a steamer and three escorts. The result was not accurately assessed.

1	2	3	4	5	6	7	8	9	10	11	12	13	14	15
March 1945														
2/1316 *dt*	U 995	*Hess*	AC 8858	PM	+	*T'*	-	3/		*sj PC*	*BO-223* ˣ*SC 1507*	105+		1)
20/0910 dt	U 995	Hess	AC 8947	-D	8000+	T	JW.65	20/0815 am -D			Horace Bushnell	7176=§	69.23 N/ 35.17 E	2)
20/0910 dt	U 995	Hess	AC 8947	-D	7000=	T	JW.65	20/				-----		2)
20/0910 dt	U 995	Hess	AC 8947	-D	7000=	T	JW.65	20/				-----		2)
20/1014 *dt*	*U 716*	*Thimme*	AC 8860	DD	1600+	*T*	*JW.65*	20/				------		3)
20/1232 dt	U 313	Schweiger	AC 8856	-D	7000+?	T.	JW.65	20/				-----		4)
20/1232 dt	U 313	Schweiger	AC 8856	-D	7000+?	T.	JW.65	20/				-----		4)
20/1232 dt	U 313	Schweiger	AC 8856	-D	7000+?	T.	JW.65	20/				-----		4)
20/mitt *dt*	*U 968*	*Westphalen*	AC 8867	DD	+	*T*	*JW.65*	20/1149 br PS			*Lapwing*	1350+	69.26 N/ 33.44 E	5)
20/mitt dt	U 968	Westphalen	AC 8867	-D	7000+	T	JW.65	20/1213 am -D			Thomas Donaldson	7210+	69.26 N/ 33.44 E	6)
20/mitt dt	U 968	Westphalen	AC 8867	-D	7000=	T	JW.65	20/				-----		6)
22/vorm dt	U 711	Lange	AC 8893	APC	=	*T'*	-	22/						6)
31/1427 dt	U 312	v.Gaza	AC 8311	APC	+	T	-	31/						7)

---

10) *U 968* reported one destroyer of the *Groznyj*-class sunk. The *Lark* was hit at the bow and towed into Kola Fjord and beached. She was never salvaged by the British, who later transferred her to the Soviets; she was probably never repaired.

11) The *Thomas Scott* was abandoned prematurely after the hit. She sank under tow of the Soviet destroyer *Zhestkij* and the tug *M-12*. *U 968* reported in addition a hit on a destroyer of the *Urickij*-class.

1) *U 995* reported one escort sunk, possibly the *BO-223* which was lost in 1945. 2) *U 995* reported one ship sunk and two torpedoed. The *H.Bushnell* was damaged and beached but never salvaged, and was declared a total loss. 3) *U 716* reported one destroyer of the *Groznyj*-class sunk, but this was probably a miss of a British escort of the *Black Swan*-class. 4) *U 313* fired a spread of three FAT and heard detonations on "Liberty" ships after run times of 3 min 30 sec, 3 min 32 sec and 7 min. 5) *U 968* reported one destroyer and one "Liberty" ship sunk, and one "Liberty" torpedoed. Probably the torpedoes hit the *Lapwing* and *Th.Donaldson*.

6) *U 711* observed one Gnat hit after a run time of 6 min 45 sec at the stern of an armed trawler.

7) *U 312* reported a large armed trawler sunk.

Northern Theater

1	2	3	4	5	6	7	8	9	10	11	12	13	14	15

April 1945

1	2	3	4	5	6	7	8	9	10 11	12	13	14	15
19/vorm	dt	U 481	Andersen	AC 4791	APC	500+	T	–	19/					1)
19/	dt	U 711	Lange	AC 8864	-D	3000+	T	KB-	19/					2)
22/0245	dt	U 481	Andersen	AC 8499	-D	= T:	PK-9	22/0618 sj DD	Karl Libknecht	-----			3)
22/0245	dt	U 481	Andersen	AC 8499	-D	= T:	PK-9	22/0618 sj DD	Derzkij	-----			3)
22/04	dt	U 997	Lehmann	AC 8852	DD	+ T′	PK-9	22/0823 sj DD	Karl Libknecht	-----			4)
22/04	dt	U 997	Lehmann	AC 8852	DD	+? T′	PK-9	22/0823 sj PC	BO-225	-----			4)
22/	dt	U 997	Lehmann	AC 8852	-D	7000=	T	PK-9	22/0841 nw -D	Idefjord	4287=	69.38 N/ 33.21 E	5)
22/	dt	U 997	Lehmann	AC 8852	-D	4000+	T	PK-9	22/0845 sj -D	Onega	1603+	69.38 N/ 33.21 E	5)
25/1200	dt	U 711	Lange	AC 8864	DD	+ T′	JW.66	25/			-----		6)
29/	dt	U 968	Westphalen	AC 88	DD	+ T′	RA.66	29/	br PE	Alnwick Castle	-----		7)
29/	dt	U 968	Westphalen	AC 88	DD	+ T′	RA.66	29/	br DE	Goodall	1150+	69.25 N/ 33.38 E	7)
29/	dt	U 427	Graf Gudenus	AC 8829	DD	= T′	RA.66	29/	ca DD	Haida	-----		8)
29/	dt	U 427	Graf Gudenus	AC 8829	DD	= T′	RA.66	29/	ca DD	Iroquois	-----		8)

May 1945

---

1) *U 481* reported one trawler heading east sunk.
2) *U 711* reported one steamer in an eastbound convoy sunk.
3) *U 481* fired a spread of three LUT and heard two detonations, which were observed by the Soviet destroyers *K.Libknecht* and *Derzkij*.
4) *U 997* reported one destroyer with a coastal convoy sunk, and another probably sunk. The detonations were observed by the Soviet destroyer *Karl Libknecht* and the SC *BO-225*.
5) *U 997* reported one big steamer damaged and a small one sunk, in the same convoy.
6) *U 711* reported one destroyer sunk.
7) *U 968* reported two destroyers sunk. The detonations were observed by HMS *Alnwick Castle*. A second Gnat hit the *Goodall*.
8) *U 427* reported two hits on two destroyers. In reality there were two near miss detonations near the Canadian destroyers *Haida* and *Iroquois*.

1	2	3	4	5	6	7	8	9	10	11	12	13	14	15
September 1939														
3/2210 dt	U 14		Wellner	AO 2345	SS	990+	T	–	3/	po	SS	------		1)
7/2309 dt	U 22		Winter	AO 23	SS	+	T	–	7/	po	SS	------		1)

October 1939 - November 1939

No U-boat-operations

December 1939 - March 1940

During the Finnish-Russian war the Finnish U-boats reported only one attack which was unsuccessful (*Vetehinen* off Liepaya) on Dec. 4th.

April 1940 - May 1941

No U-boat-operations

1	2	3	4	5	6	7	8	9	10	11	12	13	14	15
June 1941 [2)]														2)
23/	dt	U 144	v.Mittel-staedt	AO 6486	SS	206+	T	–	23/	sj	SS M-78	161+	W Windau	
26/	dt	U 149	Höltring	AO 2982	SS	206+	T	–	26/	sj	SS M-101 (?)	206+	59.20 N/ 21.12 E	3)
July 1941														
3/	fi	VETEHINEN	Pakkala	AO 3624	-D	=	A	–.	3/1130	sj	-D Viborg	-----	N Stenskär	4)
4/	fi	VESIKKO	Aittola	AO 3374	-D	4000+	T	–	4/1431	sj	-D Viborg	4100+	60.08 N/ 27.32 E	4)
(23. 6.)	fi	VESIHIISI	Kijanen	AO 3617	---------		M	–	5/	le	-D Rasma	3204=§	N Ekholm	5)
21/0655 dt		U 140	Hellriegel	AO 6139	SS	567+	T	–	21/	sj	SS M-94	206+	58.51 N/ 22.00 E	

1) These torpedoes were the first German torpedoes to have the magnetic proximity fuse. In the first part of the war many such torpedoes detonated some distance away from the target, but the U-boats considered the detonations to be hits.
2) The Finnish U-boats *Iku-Turso* (Pekkanen), *Vetehinen* (Pakkala) and *Vesihiisi* (Kijanen) laid 13 mine barrages from June 22nd to August 2nd. They may have been the causes for some otherwise unidentified losses of Soviet ships.

1 2 3   4   5   6   7 8   9   10 11 12   13   14   15

_____

August 1941 - November 1941

One attack reported by the Finnish U-boat *Vetehinen* (Pakkala) on 4 November 1941 failed. There may have been some mine successes; there are no other reports for this time.

December 1941 - September 1942

No U-boat operations in the Baltic

October 1942

1	2	3	4	5	6	7	8	9	10 11 12	13	14	15
21/	fi	VESIHIISI	Aittola	AO 2826	SS:	840+	T	–	21/	sj SS S-7	840+	59.56 N/ 19.38 E	
27/	fi	IKU-TURSO	Pakkala	AO 2380	SS	+	TA	–	27/	sj SS ŠČ-306 (?)	586+	Aaland Sea	1)

November 1942

1	2	3	4	5	6	7	8	9	10 11 12	13	14	15
5/	fi	VETEHINEN	Leino	AO 23	SS	+	AR	–	5/	sj SS ŠČ-305 (?)	586+	Aaland Sea	2)

December 1942 - June 1944

No U-boat operations in the Baltic

_____

3) *U 149* hit one submarine of the *M*-class after a run time of 34 sec. The submarine exploded. It probably belonged to the 8th division; was probably the *M-101 (?)*.

4) Soviet sources claim that the *Viborg* evaded 6 rounds fired by the *Vetehinen*'s gun, but was sunk on the next day by 3 torpedo hits.

5) The *Rasma* was beached after being hit by a mine. On July 10th the wreck was destroyed by 1 or 2 torpedoes from the German motor-torpedoboats *S 26* and *S 28*.

1) The *Iku-Turso* was sent to chase a Soviet submarine which she attacked the evening of Oct.26th. The submarine dived when taken under gunfire. Shortly after midnight on Oct.27th it was sunk while surfaced by gunfire and 1 torpedo. Probably it was the Soviet submarine *ŠČ-306* which was sunk by this attack, but it may have been *ŠČ-320* or *ŠČ-304*, which were also lost at about this time.

2) The *Vetehinen* destroyed one Soviet submarine after a long chase with gunfire, machine-guns, and finally by ramming the enemy. The submarine sunk must have been *ŠČ-305*, which was reported lost at this time in the Aaland Sea.

```
1    2   3       4          5       6    7    8   9       10 11 12       13    14                15

July 1944 1)                                                                                     1)
14/0016 dt  U 679   Breckwoldt  AO 3355 PT    =  A  -  14/                          60.27 N/ 28.28 E 2)
28/     dt  U 475   Stöffler    AO 3381 PR   80+ T  -  28/0318 sj PC  MO-304   56=  60.15 N/ 28.12 E 3)
30/1142 dt  U 250   Schmidt     AO 3356 PC    +  T  -  30/     sj PC  MO-105   56+  60.25 N/ 28.30 E
30/1736 dt  U 481   Andersen    AO 3666 PR    +  T' -  30/     sj                                   4)
30/1740 dt  U 481   Andersen    AO 3666 PR    =  T' -  30/                                          4)
31/0843 dt  U 370   Nielsen     AO 3391 PR   80+ T  -  31/     sj PC  MO-107   56=  60.15 N/ 28.48 E 5)

August 1944
25/     dt  U 242   Pancke      AO 3398 AG  600+ T  -  25/                          60.04 N/ 29.00 E 6)
25/     dt  U 242   Pancke      AO 3398 -Bg 500+ T  -  25/                          60.04 N/ 29.00 E 6)
26/     dt  U 745   v.Trotha    AO 3373 PC  300+ T  -  26/     sj                   60.15 N/ 28.00 E 7)

September 1944
10/     dt  U               AO          PM    +  T  -                                               8)

October 1944
8/      dt  U 370   Nielsen     AO 0253 PG    +  T  .  8/                                            9)
9/      dt  U 370   Nielsen     AO 0250 -Dt 250= A  -  9/      fi -Dt No.764  ----- Hangö-Odensholm
15/     dt  U 481   Andersen    AO 0267 -S  100+ AR -  15/     fi -S  Endla   68+   Odensholm
15/     dt  U 481   Andersen    AO 0267 -S  100+ AR -  15/     fi -S  Dan     47+   Odensholm
15/     dt  U 481   Andersen    AO 0267 -S  100+ AR -  15/     fi -S  Maria   +     Odensholm
```

1) Early in July 1944 the Finnish U-boats *Vesihiisi* and *Vetehinen* laid 3 mine barrages. No known successes resulted.
2) *U 679* fired her gun at two MTBs which were hit but escaped. One might have been the *MO-104* which sent a radio message.
3) *MO-304* lost its forepart; only the after part of this boat was towed into port and repaired.
4) *U 481* observed one Gnat-torpedo hit after a run time of 35 sec and observed one small minesweeping boat sinking. The second Gnat was heard to detonate after a run of 1 min 55 sec. The target was not observed to sink, but later at the place of the attack wreckage was found.
5) *MO-107* was only damaged by a torpedo according to Soviet sources.
6) *U 242* torpedoed and sank a stopped survey vessel with a barge alongside.
7) *U 745* reported one patroler sunk. 8) There is a report about the sinking of a minesweeper by a U-boat on Sept.10th.
9) *U 370* reported one gunboat sunk.

1	2	3	4	5	6	7	8	9	10	11	12	13	14	15
October 1944, cont.														
17/1136	*dt*	*U 1165*	*Homann*	*AO 3548*	*PR*	*+*	*T´*	*−*	*17/*				*59.27 N/ 24.10 E*	*1)*
19/	*dt*	*U 1165*	*Homann*	*AO 3571*	*PC*	*=? T*		*−*	*19/*				*59.26 N/ 24.00 E*	*2)*
19/	*dt*	*U 1165*	*Homann*	*AO 3571*	*PC ?*	*=? T*		*−*	*19/*				*59.26 N/ 24.00 E*	*2)*
24/	dt	U 958	Groth	AO 0283	−S	+	A	−	24/	fi	−S	Linnea	40+	Odensholm	
24/	dt	U 958	Groth	AO 0283	−S	+	A	−	24/	fi	−S	Piikiö	+	Odensholm	
25/	dt	U 1001	Blaudow	AO 02	−Dt	=	A	−	25/						3)
(21. 9.)	dt	U 242	Pancke	AO 3513	−−−−−−−−−		M	−	28/	fi	−D	Rigel	1495+	59.57 N/ 24.21 E	
31/	*dt*	*U 475*	*Stöffler*	*AO 0291*	*PC*	*150+*	*T´*	*−*	*31/*				*59.24 N/ 23.23 E*	*4)*
November 1944														
18/	*dt*	*U 679*	*Aust*	*AO 0269*	*PC*	*80+*	*T*	*−*	*18/*				*59.28 N/ 23.48 E*	*5)*
19/nm	dt	U 481	Andersen	AO 0285	−Bg	1000+	TA	−	19/				59.18 N/ 23.06 E	6)
27/	*dt*	*U 679*	*Aust*	*AO 3571*	*PM*	*441+*	*T.*	*−*	*27/*	*sj*	*PM*	*T.217 (?)*	*441+*	*off Baltijsk*	*7)*
28/1225	dt	U 481	Andersen	AO 3548	CM	+	T	.	28/	fi		ACM		59.34 N/ 24.06 E	8)
December 1944														
/	*dt*	*U 637*	*Riekeberg*	*AO*	*PC*	*+*	*T´*	*−*	*/*					*9)*
January 1945														
11/	dt	U 745	v.Trotha	AO 3528	−Dt	+	T	−	11/				59.45 N/ 24.47 E	10)
12/	dt	U					T	−	12/	fi		ACM Louhi	640+	59.41 N/ 23.07 E	11)

February 1945 May 1945   No successes, no operations by U-boats in the Baltic after March.

---

1) *U 1165* observed one hit and the explosion of one minesweeping boat. 2) *U 1165* heard 3 hits on one U-boat, two patrolers and one tug with a barge. No report confirming the hits was found. 3) *U 1001* observed gunfire hits on a tug with barges. 4) *U 475* reported a small destroyer sunk. 5) *U 679* reported one patroler sunk. 6) *U 481* reported one barge torpedoed and sunk by gunfire. 7) *U 679* fired a spread of 3 FAT torpedoes against a *Fugas*-class minesweeper, and heard one detonation. 8) *U 481* reported one Gnat-hit after 2 min on a Finnish minelayer which sank in 1 hour (probably *Louhi*?). 9) *U 637* heard one Gnat detonation. 10) *U 745* heard two detonations on two tugs and a towed floating crane. 11) The *Louhi* was possibly already sunk on November 28th, 1944 by *U 481*.

1	2	3	4	5	6	7	8	9	10	11	12	13	14	15

June 1941 - May 1942: During this time only the Rumanian U-boat *Delfinul* was in the Black Sea. Four patrols up to November, and
November 1941 ᵃ fifth patrol in May.

| 5/0845 ru | DELFINUL | Costachescu | 4m S Yalta-D | 12000+ | T | - | | 6/ | | sj -D Ural' | | 1975+ | S.Krim-coast | |

June 1942

| 15/1226 *it* | C.B.3 | *Sorrentino* | CL 5832 | SS | + | T | - | 15/ | | sj SS | ? | ? | 43.40 N/ 33.48 E | 1) |
| 18/0503 *it* | C.B.2 | *Russo* | CL 5546 | SS | 587+ | T | - | 18/ | | sj SS | SC-208 (?) | 586+? | 44.17 N/ 33.13 E | 1) |

July 1942 - October 1942
No U-boat-operations through October

November 1942

| 5/2137 dt | U 24 | Petersen | CL 9695 | -T | 2100=? | TA | - | 5/ | | sj -DT | | | 42.08 N/ 41.05 E | 2) |

December 1942

January 1943

February 1943

| 14/ | dt | U 19 | Gaude | CL 69 | -D: 4000+ | T | . | 14/ | | sj -D | Krasnyj Profintern | 4648+ | SW Tuapse | |

March 1943

| 23/1303 dt | U 19 | Gaude | CL 9445 | -DP 2000= | T | . | | 23/ | | | | | Gagry-Bucht | 3) |
| 31/1230 dt | U 24 | Schöler | CL 9447 | -T: 7000+ | T | - | | 31/ | | sj -MT Sovetskaja Neft | | 8228+ | Gagry-Bucht | |

April 1943

May 1943

| 5/ | dt | U 9 | Schmidt-Weichert | CL 9628 | -T | 7000=? | T | - | 5/ | | sj -DT Kreml' | ----- | 22m S Cape Koder | 4) |

---

1) There is no Soviet confirmation of the sinking of two submarines by Italian midgets. The only acknowledged losses were *ŠČ-214* sunk on June 19th by the Italian MTB *MAS-571* and *S-32* sunk by bombs from German a/c on June 26th. But there is a possibility that *ŠČ-208* was sunk by *C.B.2* on June 18th. 2) *U 24* heard one torpedo hit but not explode (dud). 3) *U 19* observed one hit aft. 4) *U 9* heard one detonation after 10 min, probably at the end of the run.

1	2	3	4	5	6	7	8	9	10	11	12	13	14	15
June 1943														
15/	dt	U 24	Petersen	CL	PG	800+	T	-	15/	sj	PM	Zaščitnik	441+	off Tuapse	1)
23/	dt	U 18	Fleige	CL 9179	-D	2000+	T	-	23/	sj	-D	Leningrad	1783+	43.50 N/ 39.15 E	2)
23/	dt	U 18	Fleige	CL 91	-T	1000=	T	-	23/	sj	-DT	Stalin	-----	near Suchumi	3)
28/	dt	U 18	Fleige	CL 9473	-Bg	800=	T	-	28/					Kap Pizunda	4)
July 1943														
17/	dt	U 18	Fleige	CL 9329	-D	2000+	T	-	17/	sj	-D	Vorošilov	3908+	20m SE Tuapse	5)
30/2007	dt	U 24	Petersen	CL 96	-T	7000+	Tf	-	30/	sj	-MT	Emba	7886+	Suchumi-Hafen	6)
August 1943														
22/	dt	U 24	Petersen	CL 94	-Dt	10+	A	-	22/	sj				SW Gagry-Bucht	7)
22/	dt	U 24	Petersen	CL 94	-Mbt	9+	S	-	22/	sj				SW Gagry-Bucht	7)
22/	dt	U 24	Petersen	CL 94	-Mbt	9+	S	-	22/	sj				SW Gagry-Bucht	7)
24/	dt	U 23	Wahlen	CL 8227	PC	+	T	-	24/	sj	PR		+	22m S Suchumi	8)
26/	it	C.B.4	Sibille	CL 5164	SS	+	T	-	26/	sj	SS	ŠČ-207 (?)	586+	S Tarchankut	
29/2158	dt	U 18	Fleige	CL 9665	APC	800+	T	-	29/	sj	APC		+	34m S Suchumi	9)
30/1943	dt	U 18	Fleige	CL 9660	PC	=	A	-	30/					NNW Poti	10)
September 1943														
18/0540	dt	U 18	Fleige	CL 6637	-D	800+	T	-	18/	sj				20m NW Tuapse	11)
30/	dt	U 20	Schöler	CL 7516	-Bg	800+	T	-	30/	sj				near Anapa	12)

1) *U 24* observed one hit on an escort vessel after a run time of 1 min 30 sec, which broke in two and sank. Soviet sources admit the loss of one minesweeper in 1943, very probably the *Zascitnik*. But she may have been sunk by *U 9* on May 11th, 1944.
2) *U 18* reported one hit after 2 min 30 sec. The ship sank. 3) *U 18* reported one hit but didn't observe the results.
4) *U 18* reported a barge damaged. 5) *U 18* reported one freighter sunk. 6) *U 24* hit a damaged tanker, lying at the quay, which sank. 7) *U 24* reported a small tug and two small landing boats sunk by gunfire and demolition charges. Soviet sources admit two motorboats lost in 1943. 8) *U 23* reported one patroler sunk. Soviet sources admit the loss of two minesweeping-boats in 1943 (see Oct.31st, 1943). 9) *U 18* reported one Q-ship with sonar sunk. 10) *U 18* hit an ASW-vessel with 20mm gunfire.
11) *U 18* reported one freighter sunk. 12) *U 20* reported one loaded supply vessel sunk.

1	2	3	4	5	6	7	8	9	10 11 12	13	14	15
October 1943												
15/2131	dt	U 23	Wahlen	CL 96	-D 2000=	T	–	15/	sj -D		near Poti	1)
23/	dt	U 23	Wahlen	CL 96	-D 1000+	T	–	23/	sj		20m NW Poti	2)
/	dt	U 23	Wahlen	CL 96	-Df +	A	–	/	sj		near Poti	3)
29/2130	dt	U 9	Klapdor	CL 9312	-T 3000+?	T	–	29/	sj		NW Soči	4)
31/0150	*dt*	*U 24*	*Petersen*	*CL 9470*	*PC +*	*T*	*–*	*31/*	*sj PR*	*+*	*40m WzN Suchumi*	*5)*
November 1943												
8/1116	dt	U 18	Fleige	CS 1743	-T 2000+	T	–	8/	sj		Batumi-Roads	6)
18/1715	dt	U 18	Fleige	CL 9179	-D 1500+	T	–	18/	sj -D		10m S Tuapse	7)
December 1943												
January 1944												
/	dt	U 23	Wahlen	CL 96	-D 1500+	T	–	/				8)
/	dt	U 23	Wahlen	CL 96	-T 2000+	T	–	/				8)
16/1635	dt	U 20	Grafen	CS 1672	-T 1500+?	T	–	16/	sj			9)
February 1944												
17/	dt	U 18	Fleige	CS 1743	-D 1500+	T	–	17/	sj		Batumi-Hafen	10)
March 1944												

1) *U 23* reported one freighter torpedoed and probably sunk. 2) *U 23* reported one coaster sunk. 3) *U 23* reported one fishing vessel sunk. 4) *U 9* reported one tanker probably sunk. 5) *U 24* observed one hit on a patroler or minesweeping boat after a run time of 24 sec. Soviet sources admit two minesweeping boats were lost in 1943 (see Aug.24th,1943.)
6) *U 18* reported one tanker sunk. 7) *U 18* reported one steamer sunk. 8) *U 23* reported one steamer and one tanker sunk during early January. 9) *U 20* reported one tanker probably sunk. 10) *U 18* fired through the opened net-barrage into the harbor and observed one steamer in sinking condition. Other hits on vessels or the quay probable.

1	2	3	4	5	6		7	8	9	10 11 12	13	14	15

April 1944

5/	dt	U 23	Wahlen	CS 1648	PR	+	TA	–	5/			10m NW Poti	1)
24/	dt	U 18	Fleige	CL 6650	-Dt	500+	T	–	24/	sj -Dt	+	22m SE Gelendžik	2)
24/	dt	U 18	Fleige	CL 6650	-Bg	600+?	T	–	24/				2)
24/	dt	U 18	Fleige	CL 6650	-Bg	600=	T	–	24/				2)

May 1944

5/	dt	U 9	Petersen	CL 91	-Df	50+	A	–	5/	sj -Df	+	near Tuapse	3)
11/1630	dt	U 9	Petersen	CL 9176	TB	700+	T'	.	11/	sj PM T-.../Storm (?)	?	20m SE Tuapse	4)
12/abds	dt	U 24	Landt-Hayen	CL 1670	PC	200+	T	⊤	12/			near Poti	5)
/	dt	U 24	Landt-Hayen	CL 1740	PC	50+	T	–	/			near Batumi	5)
17/mitt	dt	U 9	Petersen	CL 6620	-T	=	T	.	17/	sj		18m SE Gelendžik	6)
23/vorm	dt	U 23	Wahlen	CL 9366	-D	1500+?	T	.	23/	sj		8m SE Adler	7)
25/vorm	dt	U 9	Petersen	CL 9170	PC	=	T	–	25/		─────	S Tuapse	8)
27/früh	dt	U 24	Landt-Hayen	CL 1640	PC	=	A	–	27/			N Poti	9)
29/1256	dt	U 23	Wahlen	CL 9631	-T	1800+	Tf	–	29/	sj -DT		10m S Suchumi	10)
31/0828	dt	U 18	Arendt	CL 6627	-Dt	300+	T	–	31/	sj		12m SE Gelendžik	11)

June 1944

| 1/1434 | dt | U 18 | Arendt | CL 6651 | PG | 200+ | T' | – | 1/ | | | 14m NW Tuapse | 12) |
| 2/1006 | dt | U 23 | Wahlen | CL 1647 | -Df | + | S | – | 2/ | sj -Df | + | 13m NNW Poti | 13) |

1) U 23 reported one minesweeping boat sunk by gunfire. 2) U 18 fired a 3-torpedo spread against a tug convoy. Three detonations occurred. One tug sank, one barge was damaged, with more possibly. 3) U 9 reported a small fishing vessel sunk by 20 mm gunfire.
4) U 9 fired a Gnat and observed a large detonation after 2 min 31 sec in a convoy with one minesweeper, one torpedo boat and one tanker. A hit on the T-boat assumed. Heavy oil smell the next day. Possibly T-411/Zaščitnik was sunk (but see June 15th,1943) or torpedo Storm was damaged. 5) U 24 reported two patrolers sunk. 6) U 9 observed one torpedo hit after 46 sec at the bow.
7) U 23 heard hits on a tug convoy and one freighter which was not observed again later. 8) U 9 heard a detonation after 11 min 30 sec (probably end-of-run detonation). 9) U 24 set a beached patroler on fire with 20mm gunfire. 10) U 23 hit a beached tanker with one torpedo.
11) U 18 reported one tug sunk. 12) U 18 heard a Gnat detonation after a run time of 5 min 45 sec on a gunboat. 13) U 23 sank a small fishing vessel with hand grenades. Three prisoners were taken back.

1	2	3	4	5	6		7	8	9	10	11	12	13	14	15
June 1944, cont.															
3/2119	dt	U 23	Wahlen	CL 6690	PG	+	T'	−	3/					NNW Tuapse	1)
19/2028	dt	U 20	Grafen	CL 9932	-D: 2000+	T		−	19/	sj	-D	Pestel'	1850+	8m NE Trapezunt	
24/	dt	U 20	Grafen	CL 9470	-Mbt	+	A	−	24/				+	13m SSE Adler	2)
24/	dt	U 20	Grafen	CL 9470	-Mbt 15	+	A	−	24/				+	13m SSE Adler	2)
24/	dt	U 20	Grafen	CL 9470	-Mbt	+	A	−	24/				+	13m SSE Adler	2)
24/	dt	U 20	Grafen	CL 9470	-Mbt	+	A	−	24/				+	13m SSE Adler	2)
27/	dt	U 19	Ohlenburg	CL 6660	-Dt	+?	T	−	27/					NW Tuapse	3)
July 1944															
August 1944															
2/	dt	U 18	Fleige	CS 1648	APC	=	T	−	2/					10m NW Poti	4)
2/	dt	U 18	Fleige	CS 1648	-D 1500=	T		−	2/					10m NW Poti	4)
11/	dt	U 18	Fleige	CS 1640	-D 1500+	T		.	11/					10m NW Poti	5)
13/	dt	U 18	Fleige	CS 1716	PG	+	T	−	13/					20m S Poti	6)
September 1944															
1/0230	dt	U 23	Arendt	Konstanza	DD ?	T		−	1/	ru	-D	Oituz	2686=§	Konstanza-Hafen	7)
2/0522	dt	U 19	Ohlenburg	CL 1577	PM 441+	T		−	2/	sj	PM	Vzryv BTŠČ-410	441+	near Konstanza	

---

1) *U 23* reported a motor gunboat sunk. 2) *U 20* reported four small motorboats of 15 GRT sunk. 3) *U 19* reported one unit in a tug-convoy sunk. 4) *U 18* reported one hit each on a patroler and one freighter. 5) *U 19* reported one freighter sunk.
6) *U 18* reported one motor-gunboat sunk. 7) *U 23* fired three torpedoes into Constanza harbor and reported two detonations after a run time of 1 min 43 sec near the berth of the Rumanian destroyer *Regele Ferdinand* and one detonation near a steamer of 6,000 GRT. In reality only the steamer *Oituz* that was already damaged was hit. She became a total loss. The second torpedo only damaged the quay.

1	2	3	4	5	6	7	8	9	10 11	12	13	14	15
June 1940													
12/0059	it	BAGNOLINI	Tosoni-Pittoni	34.03 N/24.05 E	CL: 4180+	T	a	12/	br	CL Calypso	4180+	33.45 N/24.32 E	
12/0503	it	NEREIDE	Spano	32.57 N/26.05 E	-T 15000+	T	-	12/	nw	-MT Orkanger	8029+	31.42 N/28.50 E	1)
12/2157	it	NAIADE	Baroni	. N/ . E	-T +	T	-						
16/0610	it	DURBO	Acanfora	36.06 N/11.33 E	DD 2441+	T	b						2)
17/0712	it	ADUA	Roselli-Lorenzini	NW C.S.Antonio	-D groß=	T	c						3)
21/0335	it	MOROSINI	Criscuolo	65m C.Palos	-D 8000+	T	-						4)
22/0130	it	ASCIANGHI	Gelli	S Balearen	-D 15000=	A	-						5)
22/0135	it	CAPPONI	Romei	36.59 N/11.12 E	-D +	TA	-	22/	sw	-D Elgö	1888+	N Sfax	6)
26/0250	it	GLAUCO	Corvetti	C.Corbelin	-D -	A	-						7)
July 1940													
2/2330	it	MARCONI	Chial-amberto	Gibraltar	DD =	T	-	2/	br	DD Vortigern	-----	36.20 N/ 03.46 W 8)	
7/2341	it	BEILUL	Vagliasindi	32.40 N/28.1/ E	DD: 1100=	T	-	7/	br	DD (Whirlwind)	-----		9)
10/1930	it	SCIRÈ	Pini	54m 310°Asinara	-D: 1057+	T	-	10/	fr	-D Cheik	1058+	54m 310° Semaphore d'Asmare	
11/0300	it	MARCONI	Chial-amberto	36.20 N/03.46 W	DD +	T	-	11/	br	DD Escort	1375+	Western Med.	
11/2300	it	TARANTINI	Iaschi	Haifa	-T: 3039+	TA	-	11/	pa	-DT Beme	3039+	33.12 N/33.38 E	
18/0430	it	DELFINO	Aicardi	38.16 N/24.47 E	DD /?	T	-						10)

1) After a torpedo-hit from *Nereide* set the tanker ablaze, the *Naiade* sank the ship with two torpedoes.
2) The *Durbo* heard a heavy detonation after 2 min.
3) *Adua* heard a detonation after an attack against a convoy between Marseille and Toulon.
4) *Morosini* heard a detonation after a run time of 56 sec followed by a heavy explosion.
5) *Ascianghi* fired four torpedoes which missed, and had to break off a gun action after some hits.
6) *Capponi* first missed with one torpedo, then hit it with two rounds of 102mm gunfire, and finally sank the ship with torpedoes.
7) *Glauco* missed with one torpedo, but hit several times with gunfire, and assumed the ship to have been sunk.
8) *Marconi* was diving when there was a detonation heard in a destroyer force. The *Vortigern* was missed by one torpedo.
9) *Beilul* reported erroneously the sinking of the destroyer *Whirlwind*. This ship was sunk by *U 34* on July 5th west of the Channel.
10) *Delfino* fired against a destroyer and later observed an oil patch.

1	2	3	4	5	6	7	8	9	10	11	12	13	14	15
August 1940														
1/	it	MAMELI	Maiorana	34.00 N/26.00 E	-D:	1044+	A	−	1/	gr	-D Roula	1044+	34.06 N/26.30 E	1)
14/1358	it	*MICCA*	*Ginocchio*	*N Alexandria*	DD	+	T	−						2)
15/	it	DELFINO	*Aicardi*	*Tinos*	CL	+	T	−	15/	gr	CL *Helli*	2116+	off *Tinos/Crete*	3)
25/0603	it	BIANCHI	Giovannini	Gibraltar	APC	+	T	−						4)
September 1940														
19/2034	it	*SERPENTE*	*Tognelli*	*59m S M.di Leuca*	SS	=	T	−	19/	it	SS *Colonna*	-----		5)
October 1940														
6/	it	*TRICHECO*	*Avogadro di Cerrione*	*35.30 N/27.18 E*	SS	+	T	−	6/	it	SS *Gemma*	695+	*35.30 N/ 27.18 E*	5a)
15/0140	it	*TOTI*	*Bandini*	*38.16 N/17.37 E*	SS:	1475+	TA	−	15/	br	SS *Rainbow*	1475+	*38.15 N/ 17.37 E*	
November 1940														
10/0009	it	*CAPPONI*	*Romei*	*40m SE Malta*	BB	=	T	a	10/	br	BB *Ramillies*	-----		6)
11/0133	it	*TOPAZIO*	*Berengan*	*34.32 N/16.17 E*	-D	=	T	b						7)
11/0133	it	*TOPAZIO*	*Berengan*	*34.32 N/16.17 E*	-D	=	T	b						7)
27/2226	it	*TEMBIEN*	*Gozzi*	*36.00 N/14.47 E*	DD	?	T	c	27/	br	CA *York*	-----		8)
27/2333	it	*TEMBIEN*	*Gozzi*	*36.00 N/13.47 E*	DD	=	T	c	27/	br	CL *Gloucester*	-----		8)
28/0305	it	*DESSIÈ*	Pini	*36.30 N/12.59 E*	-D	=	T	d	28/	br	CL *Glasgow*	-----		9)
29/2320	it	*DELFINO*	*Avogadro di Cerrione*	*12m E Kalojeri*	DD	1329+	T	−	29/	gr	DD *Spetsai (?)*	-----	*Aegean*	10)

1) This sinking is not verified by Italian Navy records, but there is little doubt about the sinking of the *Boula* by the *Mameli*.
2) *Micca* reported a heavy detonation after a run time of 40 sec on the attacked destroyer.
3) The sinking was not officially verified, but it was established by historical research.
4) *Bianchi* reported the sinking of an armed patroler. 5) *Serpente* erroneously fired against the Italian U-boat *Colonna*, but luckily the torpedo didn't hit the target. 5a) *Tricheco* erroneously sank the Italian U-boat *Gemma*.
6) *Capponi* attacked a British naval task force and heard two torpedo detonations after run times of 3 min 15 sec and 3 min 21 sec.
7) *Topazio* attacked a force of two steamers, two cruisers and three destroyers, and heard two detonations after a run time of 2 min 50 sec.
8) *Tembien* attacked a warship and missed with the first shot. A detonation was heard after the second shot.
9) *Dessie* heard two detonations after a run time of 2 min. 10) *Delsino* attacked two Greek destroyers and assumed the first was sunk, but there was no loss. The torpedoes may have missed the destroyer *Spetsai*.

1	2	3	4	5	6	7	8	9	10	11	12	13	14	15
December 1940														
13/2036	it	NEGHELLI	Ferracuti	32.37 N/26.44 E	CL	9100+	T	a 13/	br	CL	Coventry	4290=	32.27 N/26.44 E	
20/0102	it	SERPENTE	Dotta	35.30 N/16.20 E	DD	+	T	- 20/	br	DD	Hyperion	1340+	Pantellaria	1)
January 1941														
9/0017	it	BEILUL	Vagliasindi	35.25 N/26.28 E	-D	=	T							2)
9/0017	it	BEILUL	Vagliasindi	35.25 N/26.28 E	-D	=	T							2)
10/2222	it	SETTIMO	Spano	35.22 N/16.15 E	CL	9100=	T	b	br	CL	Southampton	?		3)
19/	it	NEGHELLI	Ferracuti	--------------	---------		T	- 19/	br	-D	Clan Cumming	7264=	37.15 N/ 24.04 E	
February 1941														
March 1941														
30/2027	it	DAGABUR	Romano	33.30 N/25.20 E	CL	9100=	T	c						4)
31/0244	it	AMBRA	Arillo	33.20 N/26.35 E	CL	+	T	c 31/	br	CL	Bonaventure	5450+	90m S Crete	4)
31/0244	it	AMBRA	Arillo	33.20 N/26.35 E	DD	=	T	c 31/	au	DD	Stuart	------	"	4)
April 1941														
3/0400	it	MICCA	d'Alterio	34.10 N/25.24 E	-D	+	T	d)						5)
3/0400	it	MICCA	d'Alterio	34.10 N/25.24 E	-D	=	T	d)						5)
14/2327	it	SIRENA	Scarelli	36.07 N/24.15 E	DD	1870=	T							6)
May 1941														
21/0115	it	ONICE	Lovatelli	8m S Kaso	DD	=	T							7)

1) *Serpente* reported one hit and later a second detonation. This was the coup de grace of HMS *Ilex* which sank the *Hyperion*.
2) *Beilul* reported one hit each on two steamers out of a convoy after a run time of 2 min 55 sec.
3) *Settimo* fired a 3-torpedo spread against the cruiser *Southampton*, sinking after a German dive bomber attack. One detonation was heard. 4) *Dagabur* heard two detonations after a run time of 2 min 50 sec. *Ambra* observed one heavy explosion and assumed one ship was sunk, one damaged. In reality the first torpedo hit and sank the cruiser, the second missed the *Stuart*.
5) *Micca* reported the sinking of one ship and damage to a second ship.
6) 7) *Sirena* reported hits on two destroyers after run times of 1 min 30 sec and 1 min 42 sec.

1	2	3	4	5	6	7	8	9	10	11	12	13	14	15
June 1941														
20/2133	it	ONDINA	Dal Pozzo	36.08 N/34.44 E	-D groß+	T	-	20/	tü	-D	Refah	3805+	40m S Mersin	
27/0545	it	JANTINA	Politi	31.34 N/27.28 E	DD 1350=	T	-							1)
July 1941														
3/2005	it	MALACHITE	Zanni	32.25 N/24.40 E	CL 5450+	T		3/	br	CL	Phoebe	————		2)
16/0107	it	NEREIDE	Migliorini	37.25 N/25.52 E	SS =	TA		16/	gr	SS	Triton	————		3)
22/2305	it	DIASPRO	Dotta	38.10 N/05.30 E	CV =	T	a	22/	au	DD	Nestor	1690=	near Bougie	4)
24/2301	it	SQUALO	Grion	32.20 N/24.53 E	-T =	T								5)
August 1941														
September 1941														
10/2129	it	TOPAZIO	Berengan	33.27 N/34.54 E	-D 3000+	TA	-	10/	br	-D	Murefte	691+	33.12 N/34.35 E	
20/	it	SCIRÈ	Borghese	Gibraltar		ma	-	20/	br	-D	Fiona Shell	2444+	Strait of Gibralt.	6)
20/	it	SCIRÈ	Borghese	Gibraltar		ma	-	20/	br	-MT	Denbydale (AO)	8145=	Strait of Gibralt.	6)
20/	it	SCIRÈ	Borghese	Gibraltar		ma	-	20/	br	-M	Durham	10893=	Strait of Gibralt.	6)
21/2146	it	ASCIANGHI	Serio	8m NW Ras Beirut	-T +	T	-	21/	pl	-D	Antar	389+	33.57 N/35.04 E	
29/0617	it	DIASPRO	Dotta	37.32 N/06.45 E	DD =	T								7)
29/1642	it	SERPENTE	Ferrini	37.22 N/06.16 E	DD =	T								7)
30/0350	it	ADUA	Riccardi	36.50 N/00.55 E	DD =?	T								7)

1) *Jantina* heard one detonation on a destroyer of the *Hero*-class.
2) *Malachite* heard a detonation after a run time of 2 min on a cruiser of the *Dido*-class and assumed it sunk.
3) *Nereide* heard one detonation after a run time of 40 sec and then hit a submarine by gunfire.
4) *Diaspro* fired a 4-torpedo spread against a carrier in a task force and heard one detonation, but the carrier was not hit.
5) *Squalo* heard two hits on a tanker of the type *War*.
6) *Scirè* launched three "maialis" which were steered by Lt.Cdrs.Vesco, Visintini and Catalano.
7) The attacks were made against the escort of a carrier task force. The U-boats each heard one detonation.

Mediterranean Sea

1	2	3	4	5	6	7	8	9	10	11	12	13	14	15
October 1941														
10/0430	dt	U 331	v.Tiesen-hausen	31.10 N/26.42 E	-Bg: 500=	A	-	10/	br	-Bg	A.18	=		
12/0124	dt	U 75	Ringelmann	32.08 N/24.56 E	-Bg: 500+	TA	-	12/	br	-Bg	A.2	+		
12/0155	dt	U 75	Ringelmann	32.08 N/24.56 E	-Bg: 500+	A	-	12/	br	-Bg	A.7	+		
17/0325	dt	U 97	Heilmann	31.18 N/28.34 E	-D: 1208+	T	-	17/	gr	-D	Samos	1208+	31.14 N/ 28.50 E	
17/0400	dt	U 97	Heilmann	31.18 N/28.34 E	-T: 758+	T	-	17/	br	-DT	Pass of Balmaha	758+	31.14 N/ 28.50 E	
18/2144	dt	U 559	Heidtmann	32.40 N/24.34 E	DD +	T	-							1)
18/2354	dt	U 79	Kaufmann	32.10 N/24.18 E	-Bg 500=	T	-							2)
21/0334	dt	U 79	Kaufmann	32.08 N/25.22 E	PG: 625+	T	-	21/	br	PG	Gnat	625=	32.08 N/ 25.22 E	3)
November 1941														
4/0440	it	DANDOLO	Auconi	36.49 N/02.20 E	-T groß+	T	-	4/	fr	-DT	Tarn	4220=	36. N/ 02. E	4)
8/0720	it	DANDOLO	Auconi	Melilla	-D +	T	-	8/	sp	-D	Castillo Oropesa	6600+	near Melilla	4)
13/0506	dt	U 205	Reschke	CH 7623	DD =	T	a							5)
13/0506	dt	U 205	Reschke	CH 7623	CV 22600=	T	a							5)
13/1637	dt	U 81	Guggen-berger	CG 9652	BB 31100=	T	a	13/1541	br	CV	Ark Royal	22600+	36.03 N/ 4.45 W	5)
25/1629	dt	U 331	v.Tiesen-hausen	CO 6858	BB 31100+	T	b	25/	br	BB	Barham	31100+	32.34 N/ 26.24 E	
27/0046	dt	U 559	Heidtmann	CO 6774	DD 1600+	T	-	27/	au	PS	Parramatta	1060+	off Bardia	
30/1147	it	TRICHECO	Campanella	34.23 N/15.46 E	DD =	T	c							6)

1) *U 559* observed one hit on an escort vessel escorting 3 barges after a run time of 3 min 27 sec.
2) *U 79* observed a heavy detonation on a barge, which was never seen again. 3) The *Gnat* was heavily damaged by one torpedo but was towed into port. She was not repairable and stricken off the list. 4) The Vichy-French *Tarn* (damaged) and the Spanish *Castillo Oropesa* were not recognized as neutral in time.
5) *U 205* fired a 3-torpedo spread against the *Ark Royal* and observed a flash of fire after a run time of 3 min 29 sec. Two additional detonations were heard after 8 min 54 sec. A hit on the nearest destroyer and two hits on the carrier were assumed. *U 81* fired a 4-torpedo spread against the battleship *Malaya* in the force and heard two detonations after run times of 6 min 6 sec and 7 min 43 sec. In reality one torpedo from *U 81* hit the *Ark Royal*. She sank under tow 25 miles east of Gibraltar on Nov.14th at 0613 GMT.
6) *Tricheco* heard one detonation after a run time of 1 min 15 sec.

1	2	3	4	5	6	7	8	9	10	11	12	13	14	15
December 1941														
2/0119	dt	U 562	Hamm	CH 7761	-D	5000+	T	-	2/	br	-D Grelhead	4274+	2m N Pt.Negri, Morocco	
2/2033	dt	U 557	Paulshen	CG 9619	-D:	4032+	T	-	2/	nw	-D Fjord	4032+	Estepona, Spain	
2/2355	*dt*	*U 205*	*Reschke*	*CP 7186*	*DD*	*=?*	*T*	*-*						*1)*
5/2231	dt	U 81	Guggen-	CO 6786	-T	3000=	T	a						2)
5/2253	*dt*	*U 81*	*berger*	*CO 6786*	*DD*	*=*	*T*	*a*						*2)*
6/0252	dt	U 81	Guggen-berger	CO 5966	-D	4000=	T	a						3)
9/1401	dt	U 652	Fraatz	CH 9122	-D:	1595+	T	-	9/	fr	-D St.Denis	1595+	S Balearen	
10/1853	*dt*	*U 431*	*Dommes*	*CO 6789*	*DD*	*=?*	*T*	*-*						*4)*
11/	dt	U 374	v.Fischel	-------	---------		T	-	11/	br	PY Rosabelle	525+	Strait of Gibraltar	
11/	dt	U 374	v.Fischel	-------	---------		T	-	11/	br	APC Lady Shirley	477+	Strait of Gibraltar	
13/1805	dt	U 453	v.Schlip-penbach	CH 7434	-T:	4202+	T	-	13/	sp	-MT Badalona	4202+	36.43 N/03.30 W	
13/1915	dt	U 431	Dommes	CP 7423	-T:	3500=	T	-	13/	br	-DT Myriel	3560=	31.03 N/29.00 E	5)
14/1955	*it*	*DAGABUR*	*Torri*	*34.01 N/26.02 E*	*CL*	*=*	*T*	*b*						*6)*
15/	*dt*	*U 557*	*Paulshen*	*-------*	*CL*	*+*	*T*	*b*	*14/*	*br*	*CL Galatea*	*5220+*	*31.12 N/29.15 E*	*6)*
18/2244	*dt*	*U 371*	*Driver*	*CP 7274*	*CL*	*6900+*	*T*	*c*						*7)*
18/2244	*dt*	*U 371*	*Driver*	*CP 7274*	*DD*	*=?*	*T*	*c*						*7)*
19/0554	it	SCIRÈ	Borghese	Alexandria	---------		ma	-	19/0554	nw	-MT Sagona	7554=	Alexandria	8)
19/0554	*it*	*SCIRÈ*	*Borghese*	*Alexandria*	*---------*			*-*	*19/0554*	*br*	*DD Jervis*	*1695=*	*Alexandria*	*8)*
19/0600	*it*	*SCIRÈ*	*Borghese*	*Alexandria*	*---------*		*ma*	*-*	*19/0600*	*br*	*BB Valiant*	*32700=*	*Alexandria*	*9)*
19/0604	*it*	*SCIRÈ*	*Borghese*	*Alexandria*	*---------*		*ma*	*-*	*19/0604*	*br*	*BB Queen Elizabeth*	*32700=*	*Alexandria*	*10)*

1) *U 205* heard one detonation after a run time of 9 min 58 sec, probably an end-of-run detonation.
2) *U 81* heard hits on an overlapping tanker and destroyer after run times of 3 min 46 sec and 5 min 10 sec.
3) *U 81* heard one detonation after a run time of 4 min 45 sec.
4) *U 431* heard one detonation 5 min after firing a 3-torpedo spread.
5) *U 431* observed a hit and a 100m column of fire. The tanker reversed course after 5-6 hrs at a speed of 3 knots.
6) *Dagabur* heard two detonations after a run time of 1 min 45 sec. It's not clear if the *Galatea* had already been hit at the time of this attack. She was sunk by *U 557*.

Mediterranean Sea

1	2	3	4	5	6	7	8	9	10	11	12	13	14	15
December 1941, cont.														
19/2134	dt	U 652	Fraatz	CK 9284	-T	8000+	T	-	19/	sj	-MT	Varlaam Avanesov	6557+	39,27 N/26.05 E	
21/	dt	U 573	Heinsohn	CG 99	-D	8000+	T	a	21/	nw	-D	Hellen	5289+	4m Cape Negro	
23/1902	dt	U 559	Heidtmann	CO 6788	-D	3000+	T	b	23/	br	-D	Shuntien	3059+	32.06 N/24.46 E	
23/2013	dt	U 559	Heidtmann	CO 6788	-D	=	T	b							11)
23/2317	*dt*	*U 562*	*Hamm*	*CO 6790*	*DD*	*=*	*T*	*b*							*12)*
24/0135	*dt*	*U 568*	*Preuß*	*CO 6878*	*DD*	*1600+*	*T*	*b*	*24/*	*br*	*PE*	*Salvia*	*925+*	*31.46 N/28.00 E*	
26/1429	dt	U 559	Heidtmann	CO 6777	-D	3000=	T	c	26/	po	-D	Warszawa	2487+	32.10 N/24.32 E	13)
28/	dt	U 75	Ringelmann	CO 92	-D	4000+	T	d	28/	br	-D	Volo	1587+	31.45 N/26.48 E	14)
28/	dt	U 75	Ringelmann	CO 92	-D	5000+	T	d							14)
28/	dt	U 75	Ringelmann	CO 92	-D	=	T	d							14)
January 1942														
12/0236	*dt*	*U 77*	*Schonder*	*CO 5996*	*DD*	*1690+*	*T*	*.*	*11/*	*br*	*DD*	*Kimberley*	*1690=*	*near Tobruk*	
15/2336	dt	U 205	Reschke	CO 6797	-D	8000=	T	e							1)
16/0042	*dt*	*U 133*	*Hesse*	*CO 6789*	*DD*	*=*	*T*	*e*							*2)*
17/0735	*dt*	*U 133*	*Hesse*	*CO 9214*	*DD*	*+*	*T*	*f*	*17/*	*br*	*DD*	*Gurkha*	*1920+*	*31.50 N/26.15 E*	
29/2146	dt	U 431	Dommes	CO 6795	PY	1000+	T	g	29/	br	-Dw	Sotra	313+	Eastern Med.	3)
31/0044	*dt*	*U 375*	*Koenenkamp*	*CO 9373*	*DD*	*=*	*T*	*.*							*4)*

7) *U 371* fired a 4-torpedo spread against one cruiser and four destroyers. There were three detonations heard after 50 sec and another after 1 min 25 sec. 8) *Scirè* launched three "maialis". *SLC 222* under V.Martellotta was attached to the *Sagona* and damaged this ship.
9) In addition the destroyer *Jervis* was damaged. 9) The *SLC 221* under L.Durand de la Penne attacked the *Valiant*. 10) The *SLC 223* under A.Marceglia attacked the *Queen Elizabeth*. Both sank to the bottom and were later salvaged and repaired.
11) *U 559* heard one detonation. 12) *U 562* missed the target, a steamer of 8000 GRT, and heard one detonation after a run time of 7 min 30 sec, possibly on an escorting destroyer. 13) The *Warszawa* sank after a coup de grâce at 1930.
14) *U 75* reported two ships sunk and a third damaged.
1) *U 205* heard detonations after run times of 4 min 53 sec and 4 min 51 sec.
2) One detonation was heard 3 min after a 4-torpedo spread was fired, two of which detonated prematurely.
3) One hit was observed on a patrol-yacht which exploded.
4) One hit without a detonation was heard after a run time of 6 min 52 sec.

1	2	3	4	5	6	7	8	9	10	11	12	13	14	15
February 1942														
3/2257 dt		U 431	Dommes	CO 6877	-T	5000=?	T	a						1)
3/2305 dt		U 431	Dommes	CO 6877	DD	=	T	a						2)
3/2305 dt		U 73	Rosenbaum	CO 6798	DD	1400+	T	.						3)
4/0305 dt		U 561	Bartels	CO 9226	-D	3000=	T	–						4)
10/0436 dt		U 652	Fraatz	CO 9396	-T	2500=?	T	–						5)
13/05 dt		U 652	Fraatz	CO 6777	DD	2000=	T	–						6)
14/2336 dt		U 83	Kraus	CO 9347	-D	1200+	T	b						7)
14/2336 dt		U 83	Kraus	CO 9347	PE	+	T	b						7)
15/2359 dt		U 81	Guggen-berger	CO 7199	CL	=	T							8)
21/2043 dt		U 559	Heidtmann	CO 9124	-D	4000+	T	.						9)
22/0340 dt		U 83	Kraus	CO 9261	-D	3000=	T	.						10)
22/0341 dt		U 83	Kraus	CO 9256	DD	1690=	T	.						10)
25/1724 dt		U 652	Fraatz	CO 6771	PS	890=?	T	.						11)
March 1942														
11/2001 dt		U 565	Jebsen	CO 9221	CL	7200+	T	c	11/	br	CL Naiad	5450+		
13/									13/	gr	-S Zoodochos Pighi	48+		
14/0459 dt		U 83	Kraus	CO 6797	-D	1500=	T	.						1)

1) *U 431* heard one torpedo hit without detonating (dud). 2) *U 431* heard a double detonation after a run time of 2 min 17 sec. Probably depth charges.
3) *U 73* heard two detonations after run times of 2 min 17 sec and 2 min 58 sec. Four min later one of the attacked destroyers was not visible.
4) *U 561* heard one detonation after a run time of 57 sec. 5) *U 652* heard one end-of-run detonation after 9 min 30 sec.
6) *U 652* heard one detonation after a run time of 6 min 10 sec and 15 depth charges after 15 min.
7) *U 83* heard detonations after run times of 2 min 55 sec and 2 min 58 sec and observed bursts of smoke. 8) *U 81* observed detonations after run times of 4 min 30 sec and 4 min 33 sec.
9) *U 559* observed two hits by coups de grâce on a damaged steamer with two funnels. The ship then listed 45°.
10) *U 83* heard detonations on a steamer after a run time of 6 min 32 sec and a destroyer after a run time of 5 min 8 sec.
11) *U 652* heard one hit without a detonation (dud).
1) *U 83* heard one detonation after a run time of 68 sec. The steamer listed after a column of fire appeared. A coup de grâce missed.

1	2	3	4	5	6	7	8	9	10	11	12	13	14	15
March 1942 (cont.)														
14/2056		MOCENIGO	Monechi	37.16 N/05.05 E	-T 5000+	T	-	14/	fr	-S	Ste.Marcelle	1518+	25m C.Carbon.	
16/0143		GALATEA	Baroglio	35m W Beirut	-S big+	A	-							
17/2317	dt	U 83	Kraus	CO 6775	-T 8000+	T	a.	17/	br	-M	Crista	2590=	32.21 N/25. E	
20/1054	dt	U 652	Fraatz	CO 6795	DD 1690+	T	.	20/	br	DE	Heythrop	1050+	32.22 N/25.28 E	
23/1433	it	ONICE	Zelik	34.14 N/22.26 E	DD +	T	.							2)
26/0227	dt	U 652	Fraatz	CO 9214	DD 1690+	T	b	26/	br	DD	Jaguar	1690+	31.53 N/26.18 E	
26/0437	dt	U 652	Fraatz	CO 9229	-D 5000+	T	b	26/	br	-DT	Slavol	2623+	32.01 N/25.55 E	
26/0510	dt	U 205	Reschke	CO 9215	-T 6000=	T								3)
April 1942														
6/0317	it	ARADAM	Gran	36.47 N/11.05 E	DD: 1340+	Tf	-	6/	br	DD	Havock	1340+	near Kelibia	4)
7/1257	dt	U 453	v.Schlippenbach	CO 6896	-D 10000+	T	-	7/	br	-M	Somersetshire	9716=	32.13 N/26.34 E	5)
14/	dt	U 331	v.Tiesenhausen	Beirut	---------	M	-							6)
15/1833	dt	U 331		CP 6178	-D 3000+	T	-	15/	nw	-D	Lyder Sagen	-----	Beirut harbor	6)
16/0334	dt	U 331	v.Tiesenhausen	CP 5665	-D 4000=?	T	-							7)
16/2305	dt	U 331		CP 6171	-S 200+	A	-							8)
16/2326	dt	U 331	v.Tiesenhausen	CP 6171	-S 300+	A	-							8)
17/0616	dt	U 331		CP 5281	-S 100+	A	-							8)
16/21	dt	U 81	Guggenberger	CP 5639	APC 400+	T	c	16/	fr	-Df	Viking	1150+	Lebanon	9)
16/2148	dt	U 81		CP 5636	-T 8000+	T	c	16/	br	-DT	Caspia	6018+	10m S Beirut	9)

2) *Onice* heard one detonation after a run time of 3 min. 3) *U 205* heard one detonation after a run time of 5 min 26 sec without visual confirmation. Possibly the *Slavol?*
4) The *Havock* was beached on a shelf and was destroyed by a coup de grâce from *Aradam*.
5) The *Somersetshire* was used as a hospital ship, but was not recognized as such.
6) *U 331* laid a minefield off Beirut, three mines of which were swept on April 28th. A ship inside the harbor was attacked while barges were alongside. A large fire- and smoke-column was seen. The Norwegian ship, 3944 GRT, was not damaged.
7) *U 331* observed one torpedo running on the surface hit but not explode.
8) *U 331* reported three small fishing vessels sunk. 9) *U 81* reported one patroler and one tanker of the *Ahamo*-class sunk.

1	2	3	4	5	6	7	8	9	10	11	12	13	14	15
April 1942, cont.														
16/2250	dt	U 81	Guggen-berger	CP 5638	-S	80+	A	-	16/	äg	-S	Fatouh el Kher	97+	Palestine	10)
16/2250	dt	U 81	berger	CP 5638	-S	80+	A	-	16/	äg	-S	Bab el Farag	105+	Palestine	10)
16/2250	dt	U 81	"	CP 5638	-D	100+	A	-							10)
17/	dt	U 81	Guggen-berger	CP 5953	-S	80=	A	-							10)
19/	dt	U 81	berger	CP 5639	-S	80+	R	-	19/	äg	-S	Hefz el Rahman	90+	Palestine	10)
20/	dt	U 81	Guggen-	CP 5631	-S	80+	A	-							10)
22/	dt	U 81	berger	CP 5688	-S	80+	A	-	22/	äg	-S	El Saadiah	122+	Palestine	10)
22/	dt	U 81	"	CP 5688	-S	80+	A	-							10)
23/0255	dt	U 565	Franken	CO 9237	-D	5000+	T	a	23/	br	-D	Kirkland	1361+	31.51 N/26.37 E	11)
23/0301	dt	U 565	Franken	CO 9237	-D	4500+	T	a							11)
26/	dt	U 81	Guggen-berger	CP 5361	-S	80+	A	-	26/	äg	-S	Aziza	100+	Palestine	10)
28/0410	it	CORALLO	Andreani	37.01 N/11.09 E	-S	+	A	-	28/	tu	-S	Dar-el-Salam	138+	off Bone	
28/0410	it	CORALLO	Andreani	37.01 N/11.09 E	-S	+	A	-	28/	tu	-S	Tunis	41+	off Bone	
(13. 4.)	dt	U 562	Hamm	35.09 N/33.56 E	---------		M	-	29/	br	-S	Terpsithea	157+	Famagusta	
(13. 4.)	dt	U 562	Hamm	35.09 N/33.56 E	---------		M	-	29/	br	-Dt	Alliance	81+	Famagusta	
May 1942															
1/0947	dt	U 372	Neumann	CO 5999	APC	=?	T	b							1)
4/2131	dt	U 372	Neumann	CO 5996	APC	+	T	-							2)
(15. 4.)	dt	U 561	Bartels	31.27 N/32.27 E	---------		M	-	14/	gr	-D	Mount Olympos	6692+	31.21 N/32.21 E	
(15. 4.)	dt	U 561	Bartels	31.27 N/32.27 E	---------		M	-	14/	nw	-D	Hav	5062+	Port Said	
(15. 4.)	dt	U 561	Bartels	31.27 N/32.27 E	---------		M	-	14/	gr	-D	Fred	4043=	Port Said	
15/0513	*dt*	*U 83*	*Kraus*	*CO 9126*	*PS*	*1190+*	*T*	*c*							*3)*

10) *U 81* set afire by gunfire three sailing vessels on April 16th, one on April 20th, two on April 22nd, and one on April 26th, each of 80-100 GRT. One was damaged on April 17th, and one sunk by ramming on April 19th.

11) *U 565* observed an explosion of munitions on the ship first attacked. On the second, only a detonation was heard.

1) *U 372* heard one detonation after a run time of 7 min 52 sec. Could have been either a hit or an end-of-run detonation.

2) *U 372* heard one detonation after a run time of 2 min 8 sec and one explosion after 4 min. Later a smell of fuel was recorded.

3) *U 83* missed the targeted steamer and heard one detonation after 6 min, possibly on an escort vessel.

1	2	3	4	5	6	7	8	9	10	11	12	13	14	15
May 1942, cont.														
18/2000	dt	U 431	Dommes	CO 9121	-D	3000+	Tf	-						4)
20/2019	dt	U 431	Dommes	CO 9125	-T	3600+	T	.	20/	br	-DT	Eocene	4216+	31.56 N/ 25.14 E	
27/1237	dt	U 431	Dommes	CO 9112	-D	4500=	T	a							5)
27/1237	dt	U 431	Dommes	CO 9112	-D	3500=	T	a							5)
June 1942														
3/							T	-	3/	br	APC	Crocker	303+	32.06 N/24.12 E	
4/2140	dt	U 331	v.Tiesen-hausen	CO 9381	DE	1100=?	T	-							1)
4/2258	dt	U 453	v.Schlip-penbach	CO 9382	-D	2500=	T	b							2)
7/0200	it	CORALLO	Andreani	37.24 N/09.10 E	-S		+	A	-	7/	tu-S		Hady M'hammed	26+	
'7/2310	dt	U 83	Kraus	CP 5927	-D	2500+	T	-							3)
8/0511	dt	U 83	Kraus	CP 5973	-D	1500+	A	-							4)
8/	dt	U 83	Kraus	CP 5978	-S	1500+	A	-	8/	äg -S		Said	231+	15m SW Yaffo	
8/	dt	U 83	Kraus	CP 5978	-S	200+	A	-							5)
9/	dt	U 83	Kraus	CP 5639	-S	200+	A	-	9/	pl -S		Typhoon	175+	4m SW Sidon	
10/0456	dt	U 559	Heidtmann	CP 7179	-T	6000+	T	c	10/	nw -MT		Athene	4681+	31.12 N/28.10 E	
10/0456	dt	U 559	Heidtmann	CP 7179	-D	4000=	T	c	10/	br -DT		Brambleleaf	(AO) 5917=	31.12 N/28.10 E	
10/2241	dt	U 453	v.Schlip-penbach	CO 9385	-D	3000=	T	.							6)
10/2348	dt	U 431	Dommes	CO 9255	-D	6000+	T	.	10/	br -D		Havre	2073+	Alexandria - Marsa Matruh	

4) *U 431* fired one torpedo against a beached steamer and observed one hit aft of the bridge. A large flash was seen.
5) *U 431* heard two detonations on different targets after run times of 3 min 45 sec and 5 min 16 sec.
1) *U 331* heard two end-of-run detonations after a run time of 7 min 16 sec. 2) *U 453* heard one detonation.
3) *U 83* observed one hit after a run time of 1 min 48 sec. The ship was gone 20 min later. 4) *U 83* sank one ship by gunfire.
5) *U 83* sank two sailing vessels by gunfire on June 8th. 6) *U 453* heard one heavy detonation after 4 min 53 sec.

June 1942, cont.

1	2	3	4	5	6	7	8	9	10	11	12	13	14	15
11/0218	dt	U 81	Guggen-berger	CP 7421	-T	6000+	T	a						7)
11/0417	dt	U 83	Kraus	CP 5958	-D	6000=	T	.						8)
11/	dt	U 83	Kraus	CP 59	-S	400+	A	-	11/	br	-S Farouk	91+	Palestine	9)
12/	dt	U 97	Bürgel	CP 56	-D	+	T	-						10)
12/0537	dt	*U 77*	*Schonder*	*CO 9131*	DD	1000+	T	b	12/	br	DE *Grove*	1050+	32.05 N/25.30 E	
13/	dt	U 83	Kraus	CP 6151	-D	500+	A	-						11)
14/0152	*it*	*UARSCIEK*	*Allegri*	*38.02 N/05.06 E*	DD	? =	T	c						12)
14/0358	dt	U 205	Reschke	CO 6874	-D	? =	T	b						13)
14/0505	*it*	*GIADA*	*Cavallina*	*37.55 N/06.12 E*	CV	22600=	T	c						14)
15/	dt	U 97	Bürgel	CP 56	-T	+	T	-						15)
15/	dt	*U 431*	*Dommes*	*CO 59*	LCT	? +	A	-	15/	br	LCT *LCT 119*	296+	*Mediterranean*	16)
16/0019	dt	U 205	Reschke	CO 6572	CL	9100+	T	b	16/	br	CL *Hermione*	5450+	33.20 N/26.00 E	
21/2119	*it*	*ALAGI*	*Puccini*	*Cape Bon*	DD	*ital+*	Tf	-	21/	it	DD *A.Usodimare*	1943+	*Cape Bon*	17)
28/1316	dt	U 97	Bürgel	CP 5953	-T	2000+	T	-	28/	br	-D Zealand	1433+	32.27 N/34.43 E	
28/1324	dt	U 97	Bürgel	CP 5953	-D	3000+	T	-	28/	gr	-D Memas	1755+	14m SSW Haifa	
30/0824	dt	*U 372*	*Neumann*	*CP 9236*	AP	13000+	T	d	30/	br	AS *Medway*	14650+	31.03 N/30.35 E	

7) *U 81* missed an escort vessel and hit a tanker near the bow. There was a large flash, and the tanker was left burning.
8) *U 83* heard one end-of-run detonation after 7 min 42 sec. 9) From Italian records this U-boat sank a goelette. 10) *U 97* reported one steamer sunk SW of Beirut. 11) *U 83* sank a small steamer by gunfire. 12) *Uarsciek* heard one detonation after 2 min 15 sec. 13) *U 205* heard one detonation after a run time of 6 min 58 sec. 14) *Giada* attacked the carrier *Eagle* and heard three detonations after 2 min 7 sec. Possibly the tanker *Brown Ranger* (3417 GRT) was damaged (?).
15) *U 97* reported one tanker sunk SW of Beirut. 16) *U 431* sank one landing vessel by gunfire, possibly the *LCT 119*.
17) *Alagi* sank the *Usodimare* by mistake.

1	2	3	4	5	6		7	8	9	10	11	12	13	14	15

July 1942, cont.

1	2	3	4	5	6		7	8	9	10	11	12	13	14	15
1/1345	dt	U 97	Bürgel	CP 8258	-D	1800+	T	-	1/	br	-D	Marilyse Moller	786+	31.22 N/33.44 E	
6/0526	dt	U 375	Koenenkamp	CP 5157	-D	1500+	T	a	6/	nw	-D	Hero	1376+	32.23 N/34.35 E	
9/0500	it	PERLA	Ventura	Beirut	-D:	5600=?	T	b		br	-D	Manchester City	-----		1)
12/2004	it	ALAGI	Puccini	34.59 N/35.32 E	-T	+	T	-	12/	tü	-DT	Antares	3723+	34.35 N/35.39 E	
14/0046	dt	U 562	Hamm	CP 5663	-T	7000+	T	.	14/	nl	-MT	Adinda	3359=	33.33 N/35.10 E	
23/	dt	U 375	Koenenkamp	CP 5984	-D	800+	A	-	23/	br	APC	Vassiliki	190+	Beirut-Famagusta	
30/1216	*dt*	*U 77*	*Schonder*	*CP 2698*	*DD*	*905+*	*T*	*-*							*2)*
30/	dt	U 77	Schonder	CP	-S	+	A	-	30/	äg	-S	Ekbal	176+	Cypern/Lebanon	
/	dt	U 77	Schonder	CP	-S	+	A	-							3)
31/	dt	U 77	Schonder	CP	-S	+	A	-	30/	äg	-S	Fany	43+	Cypern/Lebanon	

August 1942

1	2	3	4	5	6		7	8	9	10	11	12	13	14	15
1/	dt	U 77	Schonder	CP	-S	+	A	-							3)
3/	dt	U 565	Franken	CP	-S	+	A	-							4)
/	dt	U 77	Schonder	CP	-S	+	A	-							3)
6/	dt	U 77	Schonder	CP	-S	+	A	-	6/	äg	-S	Ezzet	158+	Cypern/Lebanon	
6/	dt	U 77	Schonder	CP	-S	+	A	-	6/	äg	-S	Adnan	155+	Cypern/Lebanon	
9/	dt	U 77	Schonder	CP	-S	+	A	-	9/	pl	-S	Kharouf	158+	Cypern/Lebanon	
/	dt	U 77	Schonder	CP	-S	+	A	-							3)
11/0442	*it*	*UARSCIEK*	*Arezzo del-la Targia*	*37.52 N/01.48 E*	*CV*	*=*	*T*	*c*	*11/*	*br*	*CV*	*Furious*	*------*		*5)*
11/1315	*dt*	*U 73*	*Rosenbaum*	*CH 9119*	*CV:22600+*		*T*	*c*	*11/*	*br*	*CV*	*Eagle*	*22600+*	*38.05 N/03.02 E*	

1) This success of *Perla* was based on xB-Dienst reports. 2) *U 77* heard three hits without detonations after 61 sec. After 7 min there was a dull explosion. An interior explosion was assumed. 3) *U 77* sank ten sailing vessels by gunfire between 30th July to 13th Aug. 4) *U 565* sank one sailing vessel by gunfire.
5) *Uarsciek* heard two detonations after a run time of 50 sec and assumed to have hit the carrier.

1	2	3	4	5	6	7	8	9	10	11	12	13	14	15
August 1942, cont.														
12/1633	*it*	*EMO*	*Franco*	*37.52 N/09.21 E*	CL	=	T	c	12/1640	br DD	*Tartar*	-----		6)
12/1938	it	DESSIE	Scandola	37.38 N/10.25 E	-D	=	T	c	12/	br -M	Brisbane Star	12791=	Skuki-Kanal	
12/1938	it	DESSIE	Scandola	37.38 N/10.25 E	---------		T	c	12/	br -M	Deucalion	7516+		7)
12/1955	*it*	*AXUM*	*Perrini*	*37.26 N/10.22 E*	CL	=	T	c	12/	br CL	*Nigeria*	8000=	37.40 N/10.06 E	8)
12/1955	*it*	*AXUM*	*Perrini*	*37.26 N/10.22 E*	-D	=	T	c	12/	br CL	*Cairo*	4200+	37.40 N/10.06 E	8)
12/	*it*	*AXUM*	*Perrini*		---------		T	c	12/	br -D	Ohio	9514=	75m N Cap Bon	8)
12/2105	*it*	*ALAGI*	*Puccini*	*37.28 N/10.38 E*	CL	=	T	c	12/	br CL	*Kenya*	8000=	37.34 N/10.35 E	9)
12/2105	it	ALAGI	Puccini	37.28 N/10.38 E	-D	=	T	c	12/	br -D	Clan Ferguson	7347+	20m N Zemba	9)
12/2348	it	BRONZO	Buldrini	37.34 N/10.34 E	-D	=	T	c	12/	br -D	Empire Hope	12688+	near Galeta I.	10)
13/1848	*dt*	*U 73*	*Rosenbaum*	*CJ 7739*	DD	1335=	T	c						11)
14/0451	*it*	*GRANITO*	*Sposito*	*37.15 N/09.40 E*	CL	=	t	C	14/	br DD	*Ashanti*	-----		12)
17/1408	dt	U 83	Kraus	CP 8134	ACL	12500+	T	.	17/	ca -D	Princess Marguerite	5875+	32.03 N/32.47 E	
26/	dt	U 375	Koenenkamp	CP 8239	-D	4000+	T	d	26/	br -D	Empire Kumari	6288=§	31.58 N/34.21 E	13)
September 1942														
3/1504	dt	U 375	Koenenkamp	CP 3785	-D	1200+	TfA	-	3/	pl -D	Arnon	558+	34.48 N/35.54 E	
4/1453	*dt*	*U 205*	*Reschke*	*CP 5893*	DD	=	T	.						1)
6/	dt			CP	-S	+	A	-	6/	äg -S	Turkian	108+	20m Khan Yunis	
7/	dt			CP	-S	+	A	-	7/	pl -S	Salina	108+	35.31 N/35.42 E	

---

6) *Emo* heard three detonations after run times of 1 min 47 sec, 2 min 20 sec and 2 min 30 sec. The torpedoes missed the destroyer *Tartar* which dropped depth charges. 7) *Dessie* heard two detonations after a run time of 1 min 40 sec. Possibly the *Deucalion*, previously hit by German aircraft, was hit, or both torpedoes hit the *Brisbane Star*, with the *Deucalion* being sunk by A/C torpedoes only.

8) *Axum* heard three detonations between 63 and 90 sec. Hits were assumed on a cruiser and a transport.

9) *Alagi* heard three detonations and assumed hits on a cruiser or destroyer and a transport.

10) *Bronzo* observed one hit after 55 sec. The *Empire Hope* was sunk by an escort. 11) *U 73* heard one detonation after 61 sec.

12) *Granito* heard three detonations but missed the *Ashanti*, which dropped depth charges. 13) The *Empire Kumari* was heavily damaged but towed into Haifa. There she was declared a total loss. 1) *U 205* heard one detonation after a run time of 5 min 48 sec.

1	2	3	4	5	6	7	8	9	10	11	12	13	14	15
September 1942, cont.														
20/	dt			CP	-S	+	A							2)
20/	dt			CP	-S	+	A							2)
20/2351	dt	U 561	Schomburg	CP 3479	-S	500+	A	−						3)
24/	dt	U 561	Schomburg	CP	-S	+	A	−	24/	äg	-S Sphinx	39+	36m SW Tiros	
October 1942														
6/2109	*it*	*SCIESA*	*Galletti*	*34.41 N/19.21 E*	*SS*	+	*T*							4)
29/0140	*dt*	*U 565*	*Franken*	*CH*	*CV 22450/*		*T*	−						5)
29/1737	*dt*	*U 431*	*Dommes*	*CH 8153*	*CV 22450/*		*T*	−	*29/1638*	*br*	*CV Furious*	———		5)
November 1942														
							T	a	7/0537	am	-D Thomas Stone (AP) 9255=§		37.31 N/00.01 E	6)
7/2009	dt	U 205	Bürgel	CH 8333	-D 18000=		T	b						6)
8/2230	*dt*	*U 458*	*Diggins*	*CH 9145*	*CL 7200=*		*T*	*c*						7)
9/	*dt*	*U 605*	*Schütze*	*CH 8390*	*PS*	+	*T*	.						8)
9/1310	dt	U 331	v.Tiesenhausen	CH 8390	-D	=	T	a	9/1310	am	-D Leedstown	9135+	near Algiers	9)
10/0146	dt	U 81	Guggenberger	CH 8523	-D 4000=		T	.	10/	br	-D Garlinge	2012+	37.00 N/02.00 E	10)
10/0146	dt	U 81	Guggenberger	CH 8523	APC	=	T	.						10)
10/0354	*dt*	*U 431*	*Dommes*	*CH 9247*	*CL 7200+*		*T*	*d*	*10/*	*br*	*DD Martin*	*1920+*	*37.53 N/03.57 E*	11)
10/0354	*dt*	*U 431*	*Dommes*	*CH 9247*	*DD*	=	*T*	*d*						11)
10/1108	*dt*	*U 561*	*Schomburg*	*CH 9445*	*CV*	=?	*T*	*e*						12)

2) A German U-boat reported four sailing vessels sunk between 3 and 20 Sept. Two of them probably were the *Turkian* and *Salina*.
3) *U 561* sank one topsail-schooner. 4) *Sciesa* reported one submarine sunk. 5) *U 565* reported four hits without any detonating. *U 431* missed the *Furious* with four torpedoes. 6) The *Thomas Stone* was hit by one torpedo at the stern and towed into Algiers, where she became a hulk for the French navy. *U 205* probably attacked another convoy. 7) *U 458* heard one hit.
8) *U 605* reported one escort vessel sunk. 9) The *Leedstown* was hit by an aircraft-torpedo on Nov.11th at 1700 and was damaged by three near misses of bombs on Nov.9th at 1255. Then it was hit by two U-boat torpedoes and was abandoned at 1615.
10) *U 81* observed one hit on a steamer and a red flash on an escort vessel.

1	2	3	4	5	6	7	8	9	10	11	12	13	14	15

November 1942, cont.

1	2	3	4	5	6	7	8	9	10 11	12	13	14	15
10/2318 dt		*U 77*	*Hartmann*	*CH 9442*	*CV 22450=*	*T*	*a*						*13)*
11/0524 dt		U 407	Brüller	CH 7619	-D:19627+	T	b	11/	br -D	Viceroy of India	19627+	36.26 N/00.24 W	
11/1242 dt		U 380	Röther	CH 7472	-D 10000+	T	c	11/	nl -D	Nieuw Zeeland	11069+	35.57 N/03.58 E	
12/ dt		U 595	Quaet-Faslem	CH 7694	-D 11000+	T	.	12/	br -D	Browning	5332+	35.52 N/00.45 E	
12/0309 dt		*U 77*	*Hartmann*	*CH 7492*	*DD 1870+*	*T*	*.*	*12/*	*br PS*	*Stork*	*1190=*	*36.40 N/02.45 E*	
12/0601 it		ARGO	Gigli	36.42 N/05.10 E	-D 12000+	T	-	12/	br ACL	Tynwald	2376+	Bougie-Roads	14)
12/0601 it		ARGO	Gigli	36.42 N/05.10 E	-D 13000+	T	-	12/	br -D	Awatea	13482+	7m N Bougie-Roads	14)
12/1516 dt		U 593	Kelbling	CH 8456	-D 7000=	T	d						15)
12/1516 dt		U 593	Kelbling	CH 8456	-D 7000=	T	d						15)
13/0326 it		PLATINO	Rigoli	36.43 N/05.06 E	-D 10000+	T	-	13/	br -D	Narkunda	16632+	36.52 N/05.01 E	16)
13/0615 dt		*U 431*	*Dommes*	*CH 8324*	*DD 1870+*	*T*	*.*	*13/*	*nl DD*	*Isaac Sweers*	*1628+*	*37.23 N//2.12 E*	*17)*
13/0615 dt		U 431	Dommes	CH 8324	-T groß=	T	.						17)
13/0814 dt		*U 593*	*Kelbling*	*CH 8155*	*CV =? T*		*.*						*18)*
13/1555 dt		U 81	Guggen-berger	CH 7629	-D 6000+	T	e	14/	br -M	Maron	6487+	36.27 N/00.55 W	19)
13/1556 dt		U 81	Guggen-berger	CH 7629	-D 5000=	T	e						19)
14/0023 dt		U 380	Röther	CH 7476	-D 10000=	T	.						20)
14/0513 dt		U 73	Deckert	CH 7455	-D 6000+	T	.	14/	br -D	Lalande	7453=	36.08 N/03.46 W	21)

11) *U 431* observed three hits and the target, identified as a cruiser of the *Leander* class, blew up.
12) *U 561* heard one detonation near the target, identified as the escort carrier *Argus*. Probably it was a depth charge.
13) *U 77* heard one detonation after 2 min 45 sec near the target, identified as the carrier *Furious*.
14) The A/A-ship *Tynwald* and the transport *Awatea* were already damaged by air attacks and settled to the bottom.
15) *U 593* heard two detonations after two 2-torpedo spreads were fired after run times of 48 sec and 1 min 50 sec. Sinking noises were subsequently heard.
16) The *Narkunda* was sunk by air attacks on Nov. 14th.
17) *U 431* observed the sinking of one destroyer after two hits, and saw a tanker afire and stopped after one hit.
18) *U 593* heard one detonation after a run time of 1 min 4 sec on a target identified as a fleet carrier.
19) *U 81* heard one detonation and sinking noises after a run time of 3 min, and one additional detonation after 3 min 30 sec.
20) *U 380* heard one detonation after a run time of 3 min 1 sec without optical confirmation.
21) *U 73* observed one hit and saw 20 survivors. Possibly the *Maron* was hit during this attack and the *Lalande* was hit by *U 81*.

1	2	3	4	5	6		7	8	9	10	11	12	13	14	15

November 1942, cont.

1	2	3	4	5	6a	6b	7	8	9	10 11	12	13	14	15
15/0342	it	ASCIANGHI	Erler	36.45 N/05.11 E	CL	4180=	T	a						22)
15/0348	it	ASCIANGHI	Erler	36.45 N/05.11 E	CL	7200+	T	a	15/	br PM	Algerine	850+	near Bougie	22)
15/1132	dt	U 380	Röther	CH 7476	-D	10000=	T							23)
16/0514	it	ARADAM	Forni	3m SE Bone	-D	groß=	A							24)
19/0035	it	MOCENIGO	Longhi	37.14 N/06.54 E	-D	+	T							25)
19/0401	dt	U 617	Brandi	CH 8359	DD	1500=	T	b						26)
19/0402	dt	U 617	Brandi	CH 8359	-D	5500+	T	b						26)
19/0403	dt	U 617	Brandi	CH 8359	-D	5500=	T	b						26)
21/1127	dt	U 617	Brandi	CH 8474	BB	33950=	T	c						27)
23/1612	dt	U 617	Brandi	CH 7693	CL	6496=	T	d						28)
24/0154	it	AVORIO	Priggione	36.42 N/05.11 E	DD	+	T							29)
24/0411	it	MALACHITE	Cinti	37.11 N/07.05 E	-D	=	T	e						30)
24/0414	it	MALACHITE	Cinti	37.11 N/07.05 E	DD	=	T	e						30)

December 1942

1	2	3	4	5	6a	6b	7	8	9	10 11	12	13	14	15
1/1705	dt	U 375	Koenenkamp	CH 8198	CA	10000+	T	.	1/	br CM	Manxman	2650=	36.39 N/00.15 E	1)
9/	dt	U 562	Hamm	CH	DD	=	T							2)
9/2330	dt	U 602	Schüler	CH	DD	1690+	T	.	9/	br DD	Porcupine	1540=	36.40 N/00.04 W	3)

22) *Ascianghi* heard one detonation after 2 min 47 sec on a cruiser of the *Caledon* class, and observed the sinking of a target identified as a cruiser of the *Leander* class.
23) *U 380* heard one detonation. 24) *Argo* reported hits by gunfire on a steamer.
25) *Mocenigo* heard two detonations after 1 min 5 sec and reported the sinking of one steamer.
26) *U 617* observed one large flash after a run time of 3 min 45 sec on a probable destroyer, after having heard two detonations at 3 min 1 sec and 3 min 10 sec. Red and white lights were observed.
27) *U 617* heard detonations after run times of 2 min 24 sec, 2 min 45 sec, 3 min 16 sec and 6 min 21 sec. Probably three hits on one target.
28) *U 617* heard one detonation after a run time of 2 min 7 sec and later two heavy explosions. Target was identified as the cruiser *Jeanne d'Arc*.
29) *Avorio* heard one detonation after a run time of 40 sec. 30) *Malachite* fired two 2-torpedo spreads at a steamer and a tanker. One detonation was heard after 3 min, probably on an escort vessel and not on the target.
1) *U 375* identified the target as a cruiser of the *London* class.
2) *U 562* heard one detonation. 3) *U 602* heard two detonations after a run time of 2 min.

1	2	3	4	5	6	7	8	9	10	11	12	13	14	15

December 1942, cont.

1	2	3	4	5	6	7	8	9	10 11	12	13	14	15
10/1916	it	BRONZO	Buldrini	37.14 N/08.03 E	DD	+	T	.					4)
11/1625	dt	U 443	v.Puttkamer	CH 7675	DD	1500+	T	.	11/	br DE	Blean	1087+	11m 126° Oran	5)
11/1627	dt	U 443	v.Puttkamer	CH 7675	-D	=	T	.						5)
11/	it	AMBRA	Arillo	Bay of Algiers	-D	=	HM	-	11/	br -D	Empire Centaur	7041=	Bay of Algiers	6)
12/	it	AMBRA	Arillo	Bay of Algiers	-D	=	HM	-	12/	nw -D	Berto	1493+	36.48 N/03.04 E	6)
12/	it	AMBRA	Arillo	Bay of Algiers	-D	=	HM	-	12/	br -D	Harmattan	4558=	36.48 N/03.04 E	6)
12/	it	AMBRA	Arillo	Bay of Algiers	-D	=	HM	-	12/	br -D	Ocean Vanquisher	7174=	36.48 N/03.04 E	6)
12/	it	AMBRA	Arillo	Bay of Algiers	-D	=	HM	-						6)
14/0558	it	MOCENIGO	Longhi	37.30 N/08.13 E	DD	1870+	T	.	14/	br CL	Argonaut	5450=	W Galite I.	7)
14/2212	dt	U 443	v.Puttkamer	CH 7679	-D	6000+	T	.	14/	br -D	Edencrag	1592+	35.49 N/01.25 W	
17/							T							
18/	dt	U 565	Franken	CH 79	DD	+	T	.	18/	br DD	Partridge	1540+	35.50 N/01.35 W	
21/0223	dt	U 562	Hamm	CH 8171	-D	14000=	T	a	21/0231	br -D	Strathallan	23722+	36.52 N/00.34 W	9)
22/	dt	U 565	Franken	CH 95	-D	=	T	b	22/	br -D	Cameronia	16297=	37.03 N/o5.24 E	
28/0200	dt	U 617	Brandi	CO 4936	-Dt	1000+	T	.	27/	br -Dt	St.Issey	810+	32.37 N/20.22 E	
28/0336	dt	U 617	Brandi	CO 4934	-Bg	1000+	T	.						10)
28/0654	dt	U 617	Brandi	CO 4928	DD	+	T	.						11)
30/1546	dt	U 617	Brandi	CO 4697	-D	8000+	T	.						12)
30/1546	dt	U 617	Brandi	CO 4697	-D	7000=	T	.						12)
30/1546	dt	U 617	Brandi	CO 4697	-D	7000=	T	.						12)
31/	dt	U 561	Schomburg	CP 20	DD	1690+	T	.						13)

---

4) *Bronzo* heard one detonation after 1 min 25 sec and one explosion after 14 min. 5) *U 443* heard one hit on a destroyer of the type *Craven*. The second torpedo hit the destroyer *Blean*, too, and not the steamer. 6) *Ambra* discharged frogmen. They fastened "baulettis" (hollow charge) to five steamers. 7) *Mocenigo* heard two detonations after a run time of 1 min. The *Argonaut* was hit at the bow and the stern. 9) *U 562* heard two hits on a troop transport. 10) *U 617* attacked a tug towing two barges, sank the tug, and heard two detonations after a run time of 2 min 7 sec without optical confirmation.

11) *U 617* heard one hit on a destroyer, which exploded in a flash of 100m high. A corvette left the scene. 12) *U 617* fired four single torpedoes and heard three detonations after 2 min 3 sec, 2 min 25 sec and 2 min 25 sec followed by sinking noises. 13) *U 561* heard two Pi-2 (pistol-type) detonations on a destroyer of the *Jervis* class.

1	2	3	4	5	6	7	8	9	10	11	12	13	14	15

January 1943

1	2	3	4	5	6	7	8	9	10 11	12	13	14	15
1/0500	it	DANDOLO	Scani	37.14 N/05.14 E	-D	big =	T	-					1)
1/1428	dt	U 73	Deckert	CH 8474	-D	8000+	T	a	1/	am -D	Arthur Middleton	7176+	Mediterranean	2a)
3/1204	dt	U 73	Deckert	CH 8432	-D	+?	T	b						2b)
7/1204	dt	U 371	Mehl	CH 9467	APC	800+	T	c	7/	br APC	Jura	545+	36.58 N/03.48 E	
7/1831	dt	U 371	Mehl	CH 9466	-D	6000+	T	c	7/	br -D	Ville de Strasbourg	7159=	37.04 N/04.06 E	
13/0640	dt	U 617	Brandi	CO 5721	-D	4000+	T	d						3)
13/0640	dt	U 617	Brandi	CO 5721	-D	2000+	T	d						3)
15/1031	dt	U 617	Brandi	CO 5722	-D	big+	T	e	15/	gr -D	Annitsa	4324+	33.02 N/21.58 E	4)
15/1031	dt	U 617	Brandi	CO 5722	-D	med.+	T	e	15/	nw -M	Harboe Jensen	1862+	33.04 N/21.50 E	4)
18/	dt	U 83	Wörrishöfer	CH 7688	-D	3000=	T	.						5)
20/	dt	U 453	v.Schlippenbach	CH 85	-D	+	T	f	20/	be -D	Jean Jadot	5859+	Cape Tenes	6)
21/	dt	U 83	Wörrishöfer	CH 8179	-D	6000+	T	g						7)
21/	dt	U 83	Wörrishöfer	CH 8179	-D	4000+	T	g						7)
21/	dt	U 83	Wörrishöfer	CH 8179	-D	=	T	g						7)
22/0349	it	DANDOLO	Scano	37.25 N/06.06 E	-D	groß+	T	h						8)
22/0519	it	MALACHITE	Cinti	37.14 N/06.28 E	DD	1350+	T	h						9)
23/	dt	U 431	Schöneboom	CP 50	-S	+	A	-	23/	äg -S	Alexandria	100+	Cypern-Haifa	
23/1957	it	GIADA	Cavallina	36.58 N/00.43 E	-D	18000+	T	.						10)

1) *Dandolo* heard two detonations after a run time of 1 min 50 sec. 2a) *U 73* observed the target explode after 17 sec. Probably it was the *A.Middleton*. 2b) *U 73* heard two detonations and sinking noises. 3) *U 617* fired on three ships steaming some distance from a convoy, escorted by a corvette. Detonations were heard after 3 min 8 sec, 4 min 2 sec and 4 min 35 sec, two on a large steamer that sank. 4) *U 617* observed four hits on two ships that had great effect. 5) *U 83* reported one hit.
6) *U 453* fired a 4-torpedo spread against four ships and heard three detonations. One ship was observed sinking.
7) *U 83* reported two ships sunk out of a convoy, and one more damaged by a torpedo hit.
8) *Dandolo* heard two detonations after a run time of 1 min 51 sec. 9) *Malachite* heard two detonations after a run time of 1 min 20 sec on a destroyer of the A/I-class.
10) *Giada* heard detonations after run times of 57 sec and 1 min 1 sec.

1	2	3	4	5	6	7	8	9	10	11	12	13	14	15

January 1943, cont.

1	2	3	4	5	6	7	8	9	10 11	12	13	14	15
25/	dt	U 431	Schöneboom	CP 50	-S	+	A	-	25/	sy -S	Mouyassar	47+	Cypern-Haifa	
25/	dt	U 431	Schöneboom	CP 50	-S	+	A	-	25/	sy -S	Omar El Kattab	38+	Cypern-Haifa	
25/	dt	U 431	Schöneboom	CP 50	-S	+	A	-	25/	sy -S	Hassan	80+	Cypern-Haifa	
27/	dt	U 83	Wörrishöfer	CH 8289	-D	=	T							11)
30/0017	*it*	*PLATINO*	*Patrelli-*	*36.56 N/05.40 E*	*DD*		*= T*	*a*	*30/*	*br PE*	*Samphire*	*925+*	*37.07 N/05.32 E*	*12)*
30/0017	*it*	*PLATINO*	*Campagnano*	*36.56 N/05.40 E*	*DD*		*= T*	*a*						*12)*
30/0017	it	PLATINO	Patrelli-	36.56 N/05.40 E	-D		= T	a						12)
30/0023	it	PLATINO	Campagnano	36.56 N/05.40 E	-D	8000=	T	a						12)
30/0454	it	MOCENIGO	Longhi	37.16 N/06.08 E	-D	=	T	a						13)
30/0454	it	MOCENIGO	Longhi	37.16 N/06.08 E	-D	=	T	a						13)

February 1943

1	2	3	4	5	6	7	8	9	10 11	12	13	14	15
1/1745	*dt*	*U 617*	*Brandi*	*CO 6776*	*CL*	*5450+*	*T*	*-*	*1/*	*br CM*	*Welshman*	*2650+*	*32.12 N/24.52 E*	*1)*
5/0808	dt	U 617	Brandi	CO 6774	-D	3000+	T	b	5/	nw -D	Henrik	1350+	32.11 N/24.46 E	
5/0808	dt	U 617	Brandi	CO 6774	-D	4000+	T	b	5/	nw -D	Corona	3264+	32.11 N/24.46 E	
5/1003	dt	U 81	Krieg	CO 5834	-T	5000=	T	c						2)
6/0840	dt	U 596	Jahn	CH 8472	-D	5000=	T	d						4)
6/0842	dt	U 596	Jahn	CH 8472	-D	5000=	T	d						4)
6/0842	dt	U 596	Jahn	CH 8472	-D	5000=	T	d						4)
6/2302	dt	U 407	Brüller	CH 7677	-D	=?	T	e	6/	br PE	*Nasturtium*	-----		5)
7/	*dt*	*U 596*	*Jahn*	*CH 84*	*LC*	*+*	*T*	*-*	*7/*	*br LC*	*LCI 162*	*380+*	*Mediterranean*	
7/0200	dt	U 77	Hartmann	CH 8190	-D	+	T	d	7/0150	br -D	Empire Webster	7043+	36.47 N/01.37 E	**5b)**
7/0200	dt	U 77	Hartmann	CH 8190	-D	+	T	d	7/0150	br -D	Empire Banner	6699+	36.48 N/01.32 E	5b)

11) *U 83* reported one freighter of medium GRT torpedoed. It was not observed sinking. 12) *Platino* first fired a 4-torpedo spread and heard hits after run times of 54 sec and 68 sec on two destroyers, and after 85 sec on one other ship. Then she fired a 2-torpedo spread and hit a freighter after a run time of 85 sec. 13) *Mocenigo* heard three detonations on two ships after 65-70 sec.

1) *U 617* identified the target as a cruiser of the *Dido* class. Two hits, a boiler explosion, and the capsizing of the ship were observed. 2) *U 81* heard detonations after run times of 5 min 30 sec and 6 min 25 sec. 4) *U 596* heard three detonations on three steamers. 5) *U 596* reported one large landing vessel sunk, probably *LCI 162*, lost at this time in the Med.
5b) *U 77* hit the ships in pos.13 and 14 of convoy KMS.8 with a 4-torpedo spread. The *E.Webster* was hit by a coup de grâce at 0515 and was sunk by gunfire. The *E.Banner* was hit by a coup de grâce at 0612 and sank.

1	2	3	4	5	6	7	8	9	10 11	12	13	14	15

February 1943, cont.

1	2	3	4	5	6	7	8	9	10 11	12	13	14	15
7/	dt	U 205	Bürgel	CO 5839	-D 5000+	T	a						6)
7/	dt	U 205	Bürgel	CO 5839	-D 4000=	T	a						6)
7/	dt	U 205	Bürgel	CO 5839	-D 4000=	T	a						6)
7/2212	it	PLATINO	Patrelli-Campagnano	37.16 N/06.26 E	-D groß+	T	b						7)
7/2327	it	ACCIAIO	Beltrami	37.22 N/06.14 E	DD 1690+	T	b	7/	br APC	Tervani	409+	37.02 N/05.55 E	7)
8/	dt	U 596	Jahn	CH 84	PS 1045+	T						15m N Cape Ivi	8)
9/	dt	U 81	Krieg	CP 5713	-S 50+	A	-	9/	äg -S	El Kassbana	110+	35.02 N/34.35 E	
10/2325	dt	U 81	Krieg	CP 5636	-T 12000+	T	.	10/	nl -DT	Saroena	6671=	33.47 N/ 35.09 E	
11/	dt	U 81	Krieg	CP 5326	-S 150+	A	-	11/	lb -S	Husni	107+	40m W Tripoli	
11/	dt	U 81	Krieg	CP 5326	-S 200+	A	-	11/	pl -S	Dolphin	135+	40m W Tripoli	
11/	dt	U 81	Krieg	CP 5326	-S 150+	A	-						9)
11/	dt	U 81	Krieg	CP 2953	-S 150+	A	-						10)
18/0555	it	PLATINO	Patrelli-Campagnano	37.22 N/05.04 E	-D =	T	c						11)
23/	dt	U 371	Mehl	CH 94	-D 6000+	T	d	23/	br -D	Fintra	2089+	36.57 N/03.41 E	
24/	dt	U 565	Franken	CH 84	-D 8000+	T	.	24/	am -D	Nathanael Greene	7176=	40m OzN Oran	12)
27/1112	dt	U 565	Franken	CH 76	-T 10000+	T	e	27/	br -MT	Seminole	10389=	35.33 N/02.33 W	13)
28/1710	dt	U 371	Mehl	CH 9468	-D 5000=	T	f	28/	am -D	Daniel Carrol	7176=	37.03 N/03.58 E	14)
28/1718	dt	U 371	Mehl	CH 9468	-D 8000=?	T	f						14)

6) *U 205* reported one freighter of 5,000 GRT sunk and one each of 4-5,000 and 4,000 GRT torpedoed.

7) *Platino* heard one detonation after a run time of 3 min and observed the rescue operation for survivors. Probably they came from the *Tervani* which was probably sunk by *Acciaio*, that reported two hits on a destroyer of the *Jervis* class.

8) *U 596* observed an escort vessel of the *Bridgewater* class blow up after being hit by a Pi-2 torpedo.

9) 10) *U 81* sank three sailing vessels in convoy CP 5326 and one more in CP 2953. 11) *Platino* heard one detonation after a run time of 4 min.

12) The *Nathanael Greene* was later hit by an aircraft torpedo but was towed into harbor. She was a total loss.

13) *U 565* observed the sinking of a tanker by the stern. Italian sources reported one additional steamer damaged.

14) *U 371* observed the first hit and then heard one hit without a detonation after a run time of 35 sec, probably a dud.

1	2	3	4	5	6	7	8	9	10	11	12	13	14	15
March 1943														
2/0131	*it*	*ASCIANGHI*	*Erler*	*31.47 N/16.13 E*	*DD*		*=*	*T*	*.*					*1)*
2/0131	it	ASCIANGHI	Erler	31.47 N/16.13 E	-D		=	T	.					1)
3/2342	dt	U 593	Kelbling	CP 7436		-D	4000=	T	.					2)
7/0747	dt	U 596	Jahn	CH 8435		-D	6000=	T	a					3)
9/1843	dt	U 596	Jahn	CH 8428		-D	5000+	T	b	9/	br	-D	Fort Norman	7133= 36.51 N/01.09 E	4)
9/1843	dt	U 596	Jahn	CH 8428		-D	=	T	b						4)
9/1844	dt	U 596	Jahn	CH 8428		-D	6000+	T	b	9/	br	-D	Empire Standard	7047= 36.51 N/01.09 E	4)
15/1845	dt	U 380	Röther	CH 8374		-D	8000+	T	c	15/	br	-D	Ocean Seaman	7178+ 36.55 N/01.59 E	
16/mitt	dt	U 77	Hartmann	CH 8473		-D	5000=	T	c	16/	br	-D	Hadleigh	5222+ 36.10 N/00.30 W	
16/mitt	dt	U 77	Hartmann	CH 8473		-D	5000=	T	c	16/	br	-M	Merchant Prince	5229= 36.10 N/00.30 W	
18/0834	dt	U 593	Kelbling	CO 5811		-D	4000+	T	d	18/	br	-D	Dafila	1940+ 32.59 N/22.21 E	
18/0834	dt	U 593	Kelbling	CO 5811		-D	4000+	T	d	18/	br	-D	Kaying	2626+ 32.59 N/22.21 E	
18/1046	dt	U 431	Schöneboom	CH 9289		-D	2000=	T	e						5)
20/	dt	U 81	Krieg	CP 5359		-S	+	A	-	20/	sy	-S	Mawahab Allar	77+ 34.30 N/34.32 E	
20/	dt	U 81	Krieg	CP 5359		-S	+	A	-	20/	äg	-S	Bourghieh	244+ 32.32 N/34.30 E	
26/0042	dt	U 431	Schöneboom	CH 8264		-D	5000+	T	f	26/	br	-D	City of Perth	6415+ 35.50 N/01.41 W	6)
26/0043	dt	U 431	Schöneboom	CH 8264		-D	6000=	T	f						6)
26/0044	dt	U 431	Schöneboom	CH 8264		-D	8000=	T	f						6)
26/	dt	U 755	Göing	CH 7551		-D	4000+	T	-	26/	fr	-D	Sergeant Gouarne	1147+ N Ceuta	
26/	dt	U 755	Göing	CH 75		-D	=	T	g						7)

1) *Ascianghi* heard three detonations after a run time of 1 min, and assumed hits on a destroyer and a freighter.
2) *U 593* heard one hit but ASW operations prevented optical confirmation.
3) *U 596* heard one heavy detonation after a run time of 3 min 40 sec. 4) *U 596* observed one torpedo hit after a run time of 1 min 59 sec, then heard one additional detonation after 2 min 55 sec, probably on a more distant ship. A third torpedo detonation and a boiler explosion were also heard. 5) *U 431* heard one detonation after a run time of 1 min 59 sec.
6) *U 431* observed smoke columns rise above the target after the first torpedo hit, and heard two additional detonations after 5 min 49 sec and 6 min and observed additional smoke columns.
7) *U 755* heard one detonation after 12 min, probably an end-of-run detonation.

1	2	3	4	5	6	7	8	9	10	11	12	13	14	15
March 1943, cont.														
27/1524 dt	U 593		Kelbling	CO 5811	-D	4000+	T	a						8)
27/1524 dt	U 593		Kelbling	CO 5811	-D	5000+	T	a	27/	br	-D	City of Guildford 5157+	33.	N/22.50 E	8)
27/1850 dt	U 77		Hartmann	CH 7676	-D	6000=	.								9)
28/2202 dt	U 81		Krieg	CP 8341	-D	500+	T	-	28/	äg	-D	Roushdy	133+	31.46 N/34.23 E	
30/2015 dt	U 596		Jahn	CH 8292	-T	8000+	T	b	30/	nw	-MT	Hallanger	9551+	36.55 N/01.39 E	10)
30/2015 dt	U 596		Jahn	CH 8292	-D	=	T	b							10)
30/2015 dt	U 596		Jahn	CH 8292	-D	6000+	T	b	30/	br	-D	Fort a la Corhe	7133+	36.52 N/01.47 E	10)
April 1943														
2/0624 dt	U 755		Göing	CH 7566	-D	8000+	T	-	2/	fr	-D	Simon Duhamel II	928+	36.01 N/02.29 W	
10/1400 dt	*U 617*		*Brandi*	*CH 7546*	*CL*	*8000+*	*T*	*.*							*1)*
10/1400 dt	*U 617*		*Brandi*	*CH 7546*	*DD*	*1870=*		*.*							*1)*
11/0022 dt	U 593		Kelbling	CO 5957	-D	3500+	T	c	11/	br	-D	Runo	1858+	32.15 N/23.55 E	2)
11/0024 dt	U 593		Kelbling	CO 5957	-D	4000+	T	c							2)
13/0710 dt	*U 617*		*Brandi*	*CH 7466*	*DD*	*=*	*T*	*d*							*3)*
13/0710 dt	U 617		Brandi	CH 7466	-D	23500=	T	d							3)
20/0752 dt	U 565		Franken	CH 7682	-D	6000+	T	e	20/	fr	-D	Sidi-Bel-Abbès	4392+	35.59 N/01.25 W	
20/0752 dt	U 565		Franken	CH 7682	-D	12000+	T	e	20/	am	-D	Michigan	5594+	35.59 N/01.25 W	
20/2234 dt	U 453		v.Schlip- penbach	CH 8288	-D	groß+	T	e							4)
20/2234 dt	U 453			CH 8288	-D	=	T	e							4)
20/2234 dt	U 453			CH 8288	-D	=	T	e							4)
27/ dt	U 371		Mehl	CH 94	-D	4000+	T	.	27/	nl	-D	Merope	1162+	10m ENE C.Bengut	

8) *U 593* fired a 4-torpedo spread and heard three detonations after 3 min 40 sec, followed by loud sinking noises. She assumed hits on two ships.
9) *U 77* reported one ship torpedoed. 10) *U 596* reported five hits on two ships; the Italians reported hits on three ships.
1) *U 617* reported two hits on a cruiser of the *Uganda* class which sank, and one hit on a destroyer of the "Tribal" class which was damaged. 2) *U 593* observed one hit after 65 sec, one ship and one more hit after 63 sec.
3) *U 617* reported one hit on a destroyer and three hits on a transport of the *Orcades* type.
4) *U 453* reported one large freighter sunk and two ships torpedoed and damaged.

1	2	3	4	5	6	7	8	9	10	11	12	13	14	15
May 1943														
1/	dt	U 565	Franken	CH 74	-T		=	T	a				15m WNW Alboran	1)
12/	dt	U 616	Koitschka	CH 73	-D		=	T	b				63m N Oran	2)
18/	dt	U 414	Huth	CH 8430	-D	8000+	T	c	18/	br -D		Empire Eve	5979+	36.37 N/00.46 E
18/	dt	U 414	Huth	CH 8430	-D	8000+	T	c	18/	br -D		Fort Anne	7134=	36.35 N/01.01 E
June 1943														
10/2206	it	BRIN	Andreotti	37.10 N/05.30 E	-D		=	T	d					3)
10/2212	it	BRIN	Andreotti	37.10 N/05.30 E	-D		+	T	d					3)
12/	dt	U 97	Trox	CP 56	---------		T	.	12/	nl -D		Palima	1179+	33.36 N/35.15 E
13/	dt			CO 55	-D	6000+	T	e					10m NNE Apollonia	4)
15/	dt	U 97	Trox	CP 59	---------		T	.	15/	br -MT		Athelmonarch	8995+	32.20 N/34.39 E
17/	dt			CO 5499	-D	+	T	f	17/	br -D		Yoma	8131+	33.03 N/22.04 E	4)
19/0902	it	ARGO	Giliberti	36.54 N/05.25 E	-D	+	T	g						5)
19/0902	it	ARGO	Giliberti	36.54 N/05.25 E	-D	=	T	g						5)
21/früh	*dt*	*U 431*	*Schöneboom*	*CH 7490*	*CA*	*9860+*	*T*	*.*					*15m NNE*	6)
21/früh	*dt*	*U 431*	*Schöneboom*	*CH 7490*	*CL*	*=? T*		*.*					*Cape Tres Forcas*	6)
21/	dt	U 73	Deckert	CH 83	-D	3000+	T	h	21/	br -D		Brinkburn	1598+	36.53 N/02.22 E
26/	*dt*	*U 617*	*Brandi*	*CH 7578*	*DD*	*1350+*	*T*	*.*						7)
22/	*dt*	*U 593*	*Kelbling*	*CH 9546*	*-T*	*6000+*	*T*	*i*	*22/*	*br LST*		*LST 333*	*1625+*	*8m NE C.Corbelin*
22/	*dt*	*U 593*	*Kelbling*	*CH 9546*	*-T*	*6000+*	*T*	*i*	*22/*	*am LST*		*LST 387*	*1625+*	*9m NE C.Corbelin*

1) *U 565* reported one probable hit on a tanker in a tanker convoy.
2) *U 616* missed an escort vessel and heard one detonation on an other ship of the convoy.
3) *Brin* fired a 4-torpedo spread and heard two detonations after a run time of 1 min 20 sec. Sixty seconds after a 3-torpedo spread was fired there were two additional detonations. 4) It is not known which U-boat reported this attack.
5) *Argo* fired a 4-torpedo spread and heard two hits after a run time of 4 min and one after 4 min 7 sec.
6) *U 431* heard three detonations during an attack on a cruiser of the *Frobisher* class, and one possibly on a second cruiser.
7) *U 617* reported the sinking of a destroyer of the *H*-class.

1	2	3	4	5	6	7	8	9	10	11	12	13	14	15
June 1943, *cont.*														
26/	dt	U 81	Krieg	CP 3724	–D: 1667+	T	–	26/	gr	–D	Michalios	3742+	3m W Latakia	8)
26/	dt	U 81	Krieg	CP 3724	–S	+	A	–	26/		sy –S	Toufic Allah	75+	40m WSW Beirut
26/	dt	U 81	Krieg	CP 3724	–S	+	A	–						9)
26/	dt	U 81	Krieg	CP 3724	–S	+	A	–						9)
27/1704	dt	U 73	Deckert	CH 8343	–T 8000+	T	a	27/	br	–DT	Abbeydale	(AO) 8299=	36.53 N/01.55 E	
30/2257	dt	U 453	v.Schlip-penbach	CO 57	–D	=	T	b	30/		br –D	Oligarch	6894+	40m WzN Derna	10)
July 1943														
1/	dt			CP	–S	+	A	–	1/		sy –S	El Ghazala	24+	35m off Cyprus	1)
4/	dt	U 409	Massmann	CH 84	–D	+	T	c						
4/2140	dt	U 375	Koenenkamp	CH 8295	–D 8000+	T	c	4/	br	–M	St.Essylt	5634+	36.44 N/01.31 E	
4/2140	dt	U 375	Koenenkamp	CH 8295	–D	+	T	c	4/	br	–D	City of Venice	8762+	36.44 N/01.31 E	
5/1543	dt	U 593	Kelbling	CH 9544	–D 8000+	T	c	5/	br	–M	Davis	6054+	37.01 N/04.10 E	
6/1005	dt	U 453	v.Schlip-penbach	CO 5721	–D 8000+	T	d	6/	br	–D	Shahjeban	5454+	33.01 N/21.32 E	
10/1241	dt	U 371	Mehl	CH 95	–D 8000+	T	e	10/	am	–D	Matthew Maury	7176=	37.13 N/05.12 E	
10/1241	dt	U 371	Mehl	CH 95	–T 10000+	T	e	10/	am	–DT	Gulfprince	6561=	37.13 N/05.12 E	
11/1402	*it*	*ARGO*	*Giliberti*	*37.02 N/15.28 E*	*CL 9100=*	*T*	*.*							*2)*
12/2155	*it*	*BEILUL*	*Beltrami*	*36.54 N/15.35 E*	*DD*	*=*	*T*	*.*						*3)*
13/0113	*it*	*DIASPRO*	*Donato*	*37.05 N/07.40 E*	*–D 15000=*	*T*	*.*							*4)*
14/2230	*it*	*NICHELIO*	*Celli*	*Messina-Str.*	*MGB*	*'*	*A*	*–*	*14/*		*br MGB*	*MGB 641*	*90+*	*Messina Strait*	
16/0307	*it*	*Dandolo*	*Turcio*	*37.06 N/16.04 E*	*BB*	*=*	*T*	*.*	*16/*		*br CL*	*Cleopatra*	*5450=*	*37.13 N/16.oo E*	*5)*

1) *U 81* reported the ship sunk as the Greek steamer *Livathos* (1667 GRT). 9) *U 81* reported three sailing vessels sunk.
10) *U 453* reported one of three ships torpedoed. One more detonation was heard, possibly on a second ship.
1) There is no U-boat report about the sinking of the *Ghazala*. Possibly the ship was sunk earlier by *U 81*.
2) *Argo* heard one detonation 8 min after firing at a cruiser of the *Southampton* class.
3) *Beilul* heard two detonations 2 min 15 sec after an attack against several destroyers.
4) *Diaspro* fired one 4-torpedo spread which missed, followed by a 2-torpedo spread. She heard one detonation from the latter after 2 min 28 sec.
5) *Dandolo* assumed to have attacked a battleship, and heard two detonations after 1 min 40 sec.

1	2	3	4	5	6	7	8	9	10	11	12	13	14	15
July 1943, cont.														
16/0613	*it*	*ALAGI*	*Puccini*	*37.02 N/15.55 E*	*DD*		*=*	*T*	.					*6)*
18/1428	it	PLATINO	Patrelli-Campagnano	37.12 N/15.21 E	-D	8000	=	T	.					7)
19/1354	it	NICHELIO	Celli	36.40 N/15.13 E	-D	groß	+	T	.					8)
20/	dt			CP 56	-S		+	A	-	20/	br -S Panikos	21+	33.42 N/34.43 E	9)
21/	dt	U 81	Krieg	CN 3246	-D	12000	=	T	.					10)
22/	dt	U 81	Krieg	CN 3282	-D	5000	=	T	.	22/	br -D Empire Moon	7472=	36.43 N/15.20 E	
23/	*dt*	*U 407*	*Brüller*	*CN 3254*	*CL*	*8000*	*=*	*T*	.	*23/*	*br CL Newfoundland*	*8800=*	*37.03 N/15.24 E*	
August 1943														
5/1127	*dt*	*U 453*	*v.Schlippenbach*	*CN 32*	*DD*		*=*	*T*	.				*10m S Siracus*	*1)*
6/0955	dt	U 81	Krieg	CO 5474	-D		=	T	a					2)
7/	dt	U 371	Mehl	CJ 77	-D	5000	+	T	b	7/	br -D Contractor	6004+	37.15 N/07.21 E	
9/	dt	U 371	Mehl	CJ 77	-D		=?	T	c				Cape de Fer	3)
9/	dt	U 596	Jahn	CP 53	-S		+	A	-	9/	äg -S El Sayeda	68+	off Coast of Lebanon	
11/1943	*dt*	*U 73*	*Deckert*	*CJ 97*	*CL*	*10000*	*+?*	*T*	.	*11/*	*am CL Philadelphia*	-----	*N Brolo*	*4)*
15/	*dt*	*U 616*	*Koitschka*	*CH 95*	*CL*	*7200*	*=*	*T*	.					*5)*
15/	*dt*	*U 616*	*Koitschka*	*CH 95*	*DD*	*?*	*=*	*T*	.				*30m NNW Bougie*	*5)*
15/	*dt*	*U 616*	*Koitschka*	*CH 95*	*DD*	*?*	*=*	*T*	.				*40m N Bougie*	*5)*

6) *Alagi* heard one detonation after 1 min 45 sec. 7) *Platino* heard one detonation after a run time of 6 min.
8) *Nichelio* observed one hit after a run time of 42 sec, and observed one corvette engaged in rescue operations.
9) There are no U-boat reports about the sinking of the *Panikos*.
10) *U 81* observed one hit and two detonations in a net defense.
1) *U 453* attacked a battleship escorted by six destroyers, and heard two detonations after 8 min.
2) *U 81* heard four detonations. 3) *U 371* missed a cruiser but heard four detonations inside the convoy possibly end-of-run detonations.
4) *U 73* heard two hits on a cruiser of the *Brooklyn* class and assumed it to have been sunk.
5) *U 616* observed one hit on a cruiser of the *Leander* class, and heard two detonations on other ships.

1	2	3	4	5	6	7	8	9	10 11	12	13	14	15
August 1943, cont.													
19/0052	it	DIASPRO	Donato	38.55 N/15.00 E	DD	+	T	.					6)
19/2223	it	DIASPRO	Donato	38.42 N/15.20 E	DD	+	T	.					7)
19/2223	it	DIASPRO	Donato	38.42 N/15.20 E	DD	+	T	.					7)
20/	dt	U 596	Jahn	CP 53	−S	+	A	−	20/ br	−S Namaz	50+	33.42 N/34.43 E	
22/	dt	U 431	Schöneboom	CJ 86	CL	5220=	T	.				65m NNW Palermo	8)
23/1925	dt	U 380	Röther	CJ 8687	−D	6000+	T	a	23/ am	−D Pierre Soulé	7191=	38.19 N/12.55 E	
26/	dt	U 410	Fenski	CJ 78	−D	7000+	T	b	26/2030 am	−D John Bell	7242+	37.15 N/08.24 E	
26/	dt	U 410	Fenski	CJ 78	−D	7000+	T	b	26/2032 am	−D Richard Henderson	7194+	37.15 N/08.24 E	
26/	dt	U 410	Fenski	CJ 78	−D	=	T	b					9)
29/	dt	U 596	Jahn	CP 61	−D	4000+	T	.				30m N Beirut	10)
29/	dt	U 596	Jahn	CP 53	−S	+	A	−				20m NNW Beirut	11)
29/	dt	U 596	Jahn	CP 53	−S	+	A	−				20m NNW Beirut	11)
29/	dt	U 596	Jahn	CP 53	−S	+	A	−				20m NNW Beirut	11)
29/	dt	U 596	Jahn	CP 53	−S	+	A	−	30/ äg	−S Nagwa	183+	34.40 N/33.20 E	11)
30/	dt			CJ 78	−D	8000+	T	c	7 ? äg	−S Hamdiah	80+	34.02 N/33.05 E	11)
30/	dt			CJ 78	−D	=	T	c				30m E Bone	12)
September 1943													
3/				CH 80	DD			d	3/ am	DD Kendrick	1630=	Oran to Algiers	1)
6-7	dt			CP 56	−D	=	T	−					1a)
6/even.	dt	U 617	Brandi	CG 96	DD	+	T	−	6/ br	DE Puckeridge	1050+	40m E Gibraltar	

6) *Diaspro* fired a 2-torpedo spread and heard two detonations in a destroyer group, and 7) four detonations after a run time of 5 min 22 sec.
8) *U 431* observed one cruiser of the *Aurora* class stopped after one hit, and heard one more detonation after 5 min.
9) *U 410* reported two ships sunk and one more torpedoed. 10) *U 596* reported one ship sunk.
11) *U 596* reported four sailing vessels sunk. Possibly one was the *Hamdiah*, not reported as lost until Sept.7th.
1) There is no U-boat report on this attack. 1a) There is no U-boat known to have attacked this steamer and a sailing vessel.

1	2	3	4	5	6	7	8	9	10	11	12	13	14	15
September 1943, cont.														
11/	dt	U 617	Brandi	CG 9657	DD	1800+	T	.						2)
11/	dt	U 617	Brandi	CG 9657	DD	1600+	T	.						2)
12/	dt	U 565	Franken	CJ 68	LC	+	T	.					S Salerno	3)
12/								12/	am	−D	William B.Travis	7176=	37.17 N/09.54 E	4)
15/	dt			CJ 68	⌐T	=	T	.					near Salerno	5)
15/	dt			CJ 68	DD	=	T	.					near Salerno	5)
21/	dt	U 593	Kelbling	CJ 9130	−D	6000+	T	a	21/	am	−D	William W.Gerhard	7176+	40.05 N/14.43 E	6)
21/	dt	U 593	Kelbling	CJ 9130	−D	=	T	a							6)
22/							M	.	22/	am	−D	Richard Olney	7191=	37.25 N/09.54 E	7)
24/	dt	U 565	Franken	CJ 91	−D	=	T	b					65m S Salerno	8)
24/	dt	U 565	Franken	CJ 91	−D	=	T	b					65m S Salerno	8)
25/	dt	U 593	Kelbling	CJ 68	DD	1690+	T	.	25/	am	PM	Skill	815+	40.20 N/14.35 E	
26/	dt	U 410	Fenski	CJ 7794	−D	7886+	T	c	26/	nw	−D	Christian Michelsen	7176+	37.12 N/08.26 E	9)
26/	dt	U 410	Fenski	CJ 7794	−D	7000+?	T	c							9)
October 1943														
1/	dt	U 410	Fenski	CJ 7718	−D	8000+	T	d	30/o113	br	−D	Fort Howe	7133+	37.19 N/06.40 E	1)
1/	dt	U 410	Fenski	CJ 7718	−D	8000+	T	d	30/	br	−DT	Empire Commerce	3722+	37.19 N/06.40 E	1)
1/	dt	U 410	Fenski	CJ 7718	−D	8000=	T	d							1)
1/	dt	U 410	Fenski	CJ 7718	−D	7000=	T	d							1)

2) *U 617* reported the sinking of two destroyers based on acoustic data. 3) *U 565* reported two FAT-hits on landing vessels.
4) It is not known whether the *Wm.B.Travis* was damaged by a U-boat torpedo or a mine. 5) One U-boat (*U 616, U565, U...?*) reported one hit on a large tanker or an escort carrier which began to list, and heard two detonations and sinking noises after a 2-torpedo spread against four destroyers. 6) *U 593* reported one freighter probably sunk and one more torpedoed.
7) The *R.Olney* was damaged by a mine while in convoy KMS.26, and towed in to Bizerta by HMS *Landguard*.
8) *U 565* reported three hits in an attack against a convoy going south. 9) *U 410* reported the sinking of a munitions-freighter of the *Collegian* type, and the probable sinking of one more ship. 1) *U 410* fired five single shots, observed one ship sinking, and heard four more detonations. The resulting report assumed sinking or torpedoing of four ships of 31,000 GRT.

1	2	3	4	5	6		7	8	9	10	11	12	13	14	15

October 1943, cont.

1	2	3	4	5	6		7	8	9	10 11	12	13	14	15
2/0102	dt	U 223	Wächter	CH 8269	-D	10000=	T	.	2/	br -D	Stanmore	4970+	36.41 N/01.10 E	2)
2/0102	*dt*	*U 223*	*Wächter*	*CH 8269*	*DD*	*=*	*T*	*.*						2)
2/0102	dt	U 223	Wächter	CH 8269	-D	8000=	T	.						2)
4/	dt	U 596	Nonn	CO 57			T	.	4/	nw -DT	Marit	5542+	32.57 N/21.11 E	3)
5/	dt	U 380	Röther	CJ 91	-T	8000+	T	.					60m S Salerno	4)
6/	dt	U 596	Nonn	CO 5721	-D	=	T	.					60m W Derna	5)
6/	dt	U 596	Nonn	CO 5721	-D	=	T	.					60m W Derna	5)
9/0036	*dt*	*U 616*	*Koitschka*	*CJ 9126*	*DD*	*+*	*T*	*.*	*9/*	*am DD*	*Buck*	*1570+*	*39.57 N/14.28 E*	
10/0	dt	U 616	Koitschka	CJ 9443	-D	4000+	T	.						6)
11/0109	*dt*	*U 371*	*Mehl*	*CH 9553*	*DD*	*=*	*T*	*a*	*11/*	*br PM*	*Hythe*	*656+*	*37.04 N/05.00 E*	
11/0541	*dt*	*U 616*	*Koitschka*	*CJ 9194*	*LST*	*3000+*	*T*	*.*			*LCT 553 ?*			7)
11/0544	*dt*	*U 616*	*Koitschka*	*CJ 9194*	*LST*	*3000+*	*T*	*.*			*LCT 618 ?*			7)
13/0417	*dt*	*U 371*	*Mehl*	*CH 9631*	*DD*	*+*	*T*	*b*	*13/*	*am DD*	*Bristol*	*1630+*	*37.19 N/06.19 E*	
15/*1239*	dt	U 371	Mehl	CJ 7729	-D	5000+	T	c	15/	am -D	James	7176+	37.22 N/07.08 E	8)
15/*1239*	dt	U 371	Mehl	CJ 7729	-D	+	T	c			Russell Lowell			
18/	dt	U 73	Deckert	CH 85	-D	6000+	T	d					50m W Algier	9)
19/0306	dt	U 431	Schöneboom	CH 7496	-D	10000+	T	e						10)
19/0306	dt	U 431	Schöneboom	CH 7496	-D	8000+	T	e						10)
19/0306	dt	U 431	Schöneboom	CH 7496	-D	10000+?	T	e						10)
19/0306	dt	U 431	Schöneboom	CH 7496	-D	12000=	T	e						10)

---

2) *U 223* heard two detonations on the first freighter targeted and observed one hit on a destroyer and one T-5 hit (Gnat) on another ship.

3) The *Marit* was probably sunk by *U 596* operating in this area. (See note 5).

4) *U 380* reported the sinking of one tanker. 5) *U 596* fired four torpedoes against four ships, and heard three detonations. There is some uncertainty about the date.

6) *U 616* reported one ship torpedoed and left burning. 7) *U 616* heard one detonation after a run time of 9 min 33 sec, and one more detonation after 1 min 42 sec. The second LST was seen sinking by the stern. Probably either *LCT 553* or *LCT 618* was sunk. 8) *U 371* reported one freighter sunk and one more probably sunk.

9) *U 73* reported one freighter probably sunk. 10) *U 431* reported two ships sunk, one more probably sunk, and one torpedoed. Possibly an end-of-run detonation.

1	2	3	4	5	6	7	8	9	10	11	12	13	14	15
October 1943, cont.														
20/	dt	U 431	Schöneboom	CH 74	-D	8000+	T	.						11)
27/2112	dt	U 565	Henning	CJ 8845	DD	+	T	.						12)
November 1943														
2/	dt	U 73	Deckert	CH 83			T	a	3/0050	fr -D	Mont Viso	4531+	36.45 N/01.52E	1)
15/1729	dt	U 565	Henning	CO 3381	SS	+	T	.						2)
(11.11.)	dt	U 453	v.Schlip-penbach	41.08 N/16.51 E	---------		M	-	15/	br DD	Quail	1705=	near Bari	3)
16/	dt						A	-	16/	äg -S	Abis	63+	E.Mediterranean	4)
18/	dt	U 81	Krieg	CK 7180	-D	7500+	T	.	18/	br -D	Empire Dunstan	2887+	39.24 N/17.40 E	
20/0143	dt	U 565	Henning	CO 36	SS	+	T	-					NW Rhodos	2)
(11.11.)	dt	U 453	v.Schlip-penbach	41.08 N/16.51 E	---------		M	-	22/	br PM	Hebe	835+	near Bari	
27/							T	.	27/	br PR	ML 126	73+	off Salerno	5)
28/1117	dt	U 407	Brüller	CO 54	CL	=	T	.	28/	br CL	Birmingham	9100=	33.05 N/21.43 E	
December 1943														
1/							T	.	1/	am LC	LCT 242	126+	40.50 N/14.15 E	6)
4/2241	dt	U 223	Wächter	CH 85	DD	+	T	-				-----		7)

11) *U 431* heard one Gnat detonation after a run time of 7 min 20 sec. 12) *U 565* heard one Gnat detonation after a run time of 1 min 22 sec and sinking noises.

1) It is possible but not certain whether the Mont Viso was attacked by *U 73*. 2) *U 565* heard first a Gnat detonation after 3 min 42 sec, and a second after 13 min. The latter was an end-of-run detonation. The first may have sunk the British submarine *Simoon* (715 ts), reported missing about this time.

3) The *Quail* was towed into port, but the damage was too heavy to allow reconstruction.

4) It is not known which U-boat sank this sailing vessel. 5) It is unknown which U-boat made this attack.

6) It is not known which U-boat made this attack. 7) *U 223* heard one detonation after 12 min 45 sec (an end-of-run detonation).

1	2	3	4	5	6	7	8	9	10	11	12	13	14	15
December 1943, cont.														
8/0300	dt	U 616	Koitschka	CJ 7712	-D	8000+	T	a						8)
8/0300	dt	U 616	Koitschka	CJ 7712	-D	8000+	T	a						8)
8/0301	dt	U 616	Koitschka	CJ 7712	-D	8000=	T	a						8)
9/1317	dt	U 596	Nonn	CK 7445	-D	7600+	T	b	9/	br	-D	Cap Padaran	8009+	39.15 N/17.30 E
9/1955	*dt*	*U 616*	*Koitschka*	*CJ 7428*	*DD*	*+*	*T*	*.*				*-----*		*9)*
11/1304	*dt*	*U 223*	*Wächter*	*CH 8518*	*DD*	*+*	*T*	*c*	*11/*	*br*	*PF*	*Cuckmere*	*1300=*	*36.55 N/03.01 E*	*10)*
12/	*dt*	*U 593*	*Kelbling*	*------*	*---------*		*T*	*c*	*12/0710*	*br*	*DE*	*Tynedale*	*1000+*	*37.10 N/06.05 E*
12/	*dt*	*U 593*	*Kelbling*	*------*	*---------*		*T*	*c*	*12/1445*	*br*	*DE*	*Holcombe*	*1087+*	*37.20 N/05.30 E*
13/1037	dt	U 596	Nonn	CJ 9953	-D	7000+	T	.						11)
13/1037	*dt*	*U 596*	*Nonn*	*CJ 9953*	*DD*	*+*	*T*	*.*						*11)*
13/	dt	U 73	Deckert	CH 76	---------		T	.	13/	am	-D	John S.Copley	7176=	35.54 N/00.53 W
23/	*dt*	*U 380*	*Brandi*	*CH 8355*	*DD*	*=*	*T*	*.*	*23/2330*	*fr*	*DL*	*Le Fantasque*	*------*	*off Algiers*	*12)*
January 1944														
3/	dt	U 642	Brünning	CJ 8395	-D	7000+	T	.						1)
9/1124	*dt*	*U 616*	*Koitschka*	*CH 9525*	*SS*	*+*	*T*	*-*				*-----*		*2)*
9/1124	*dt*	*U 616*	*Koitschka*	*CH 9525*	*SS*	*+*	*T*	*-*				*-----*		*2)*
11/0034	*dt*	*U 380*	*Brandi*	*CH 7585*	*DD*	*=*	*T*	*d*				*-----*		*3)*
11/0728	dt	U 380	Brandi	CH 75	-D	=	T	d				-----		3)
13/0047	dt	U 616	Koitschka	CH 9394	-D	=	T	e				-----		4)
13/0047	dt	U 616	Koitschka	CH 9394	-D	=	T	e				-----		4)
13/0047	*dt*	*U 616*	*Koitschka*	*CH 9394*	*DD*	*=*	*T*	*e*				*-----*		*4)*

8) *U 616* reported two ships sunk and one Gnat hit after a run time of 6 min 55 sec on a steamer, left burning.

9) *U 616* reported a Gnat detonation after 12 min 52 sec on a destroyer (*Kedar ?*). But it was probably an end-of-run detonation.

10) The *Cuckmere* was damaged and towed into harbor, but never repaired.

11) *U 596* reported one steamer and one destroyer sunk by a 4-torpedo spread.

12) *U 380* heard one Gnat detonation after 10 min, probably an end-of-run detonation. 1) *U 642* reported one steamer sunk.

2) *U 616* observed one Gnat hit with a water-column after 8 min 27 sec, and heard one Gnat detonation after 10 min 9 sec (an end-of-run detonation).

3) *U 380* heard Gnat-detonations after 14 min 6 sec and 15 min (probably end-of-run detonations). 4) *U 616* heard three end-of-run detonations.

1	2	3	4	5	6	7	8	9	10	11	12	13	14	15
January 1944, cont.														
25/0415	dt	U 223	Gerlach	CJ 8160	PE	+	T	.				-----		5)
25/1109	dt	U 230	Siegmann	CJ 5941	DD	+	T	.				-----		6)
25/1110	dt	U 230	Siegmann	CJ 5941	DD	÷	T	.				-----		6)
28/0410	dt	U 223	Gerlach	CJ 81	DD	=	T	.				-----		7)
29/1645	dt	U 223	Gerlach	CJ 5912	LCF	+	T	.						8)
30/1700	dt	U 223	Gerlach	CJ 5912	LST	+	T	.						9)
30/1700	dt	U 223	Gerlach	CJ 5912	LST	+	T	.						9)
30/1714	dt	U 223	Gerlach	CJ 5912	DD	=	T	.						9)
February 1944														
1/	dt	U 453	Lührs	CP 34	-S	+	R	-	1/	1b -S	Salem	81+	E.Mediterranean	
1/	dt	U 453	Lührs	CP 34	-S	+	R	-	1/	sy -S	Yahia	64+	6m W Bassit	
4/	dt	U 453	Lührs	CP 5244	-S	+	R	-						1)
4/	dt	U 453	Lührs	CP 5244	-S	+	R	-						1)
15/	dt	U 410	Fenski	CJ 6768	-D 7000+	T	.	15/	br -D	Fort St.Nicolas	7154+	40.34 N/14.37 E		
16/1511	dt	U 230	Siegmann	CJ 5678	LST 3000+	T	.	16/	br LS	LST 418	1625+	Anzio		
16/1540	dt	U 230	Siegmann	CJ 5678	PE	=?	T	.				-----		2)
17/0907	dt	U 410	Fenski	CJ 5951	DD	+	T	.				-----		3)
18/	dt	U 410	Fenski	CJ 5934	CL 5220+	T	.	18/	br CL	Penelope	5270+	40.55 N/13.25 E		
19/2310	dt	U 410	Fenski	CJ 5951	DD	+	T	.				-----		4)
20/0200	dt	U 410	Fenski	CJ 5950	LST 3000+	T	.	20/	am LS	LST 348	1625+	40.57 N/13.14 E		
20/1755	dt	U 230	Siegmann	CJ 5678	LST 3000+	T	.	20/	br LS	LST 305	1625+	41.14 N/12.31 E		

5) *U 223* heard one Gnat end-of-run detonation after 13 min 12 sec. 6) *U 230* heard one T-3 detonation after a run time of 5 min 11 sec and one Gnat end-of-run detonation after 11 min 55 sec, then sinking noises. 7) *U 223* heard one Gnat end-of-run detonation after 14 min 5 sec.

8) *U 223* reported the sinking of one LCT or LCF. 9) *U 223* fired a 3-torpedo spread and heard three detonations, and one more Gnat detonation after 3 min 45 sec.

1) *U 453* reported a third and fourth sailing vessel sunk on Feb.4th. 2) *U 230* probably missed this time.

3) *U 410* heard one Gnat end-of-run detonation after 12 min 38 sec. 4) *U 410* heard one Gnat end-of-run detonation after 13 min 28 sec.

1	2	3	4	5	6	7	8	9	10	11	12	13	14	15

February 1944, cont.

1	2 3	4	5	6	7	8	9	10 11	12	13	14	15
22/1213 dt	U 969	Dobbert	CJ 77	-D 8000+	T	a	22/	am -D	George Cleeve	7176=§	37.22 N/07.17 E	5)
22/1213 dt	U 969	Dobbert	CJ 77	---------	T	a	22/	am -D	Peter Skene Ogden	7176=§	37.22 N/07.17 E	5)
23/0950 dt	U 596	Nonn	CJ 9942	DE +	T	.						6)
26/2111 dt	U 952	Curio	CJ 60	DD +	T	.				-----		7)
27/ dt	U 407	Korndörfer	CP 56	-S +	A	-	27/	äg -S	Rod el Farag	55+	33.48 N/34.15 E	
29/1704 dt	U 407	Korndörfer	CP 34	-T: 6207=	T	.	29/	br -MT	Ensis	6207=	35.36 N/35.33 E	

March 1944

1	2 3	4	5	6	7	8	9	10 11	12	13	14	15
2/1350 dt	U 616	Koitschka	CJ 5955	DD +	T	.				-----		1)
3/0012 dt	U 565	Henning	CO 5714	PE +	T	.				-----		2)
3/0900 dt	U 565	Henning	CO 5714	CL 7200=	T	.				-----		3)
4/1607 dt	U 952	Curio	CJ 8328	PE =	T	.				-----		4)
6/2115 dt	U 616	Koitschka	CJ 5952	DD +	T	.				-----		5)
10/1615 dt	U 952	Curio	CJ 9472	-D 7000+	T	.	10/	am -D	William B. Woods	7176+	38.36 N/13.45 E	
17/0938 dt	U 371	Mehl	CH 9566	-D 8000+	T	b	17/	am -D	Maiden Creek	5031+	37.08 N/05.27 E	6)
17/0938 dt	U 371	Mehl	CH 9566	-D 8000+	T	b	17/	nl -M	Dempo	17024+	37.08 N/05.27 E	6)
17/0938 dt	U 371	Mehl	CH 9566	-D 8000=	T	b						6)
18/ dt	U 453	Lührs	CK 7441	-D 8000=	T	c						7)
18/ dt	U 453	Lührs	CK 7441	-D 5000=	T	c						7)
18/ dt	U 453	Lührs	CK 7441	-D 5000=	T	c						7)
30/ dt	U 223	Gerlach	-------	--------	T	.	30/	br DD	Laforey	1935+	38.54 N/14.18 E	

5) The *George Cleeve* and *Peter Skene Ogden* were damaged and although beached, were total losses.
6) *U 596* heard one Gnat end-of-run detonation after 3 min 50 sec. 7) *U 952* heard one Gnat end-of-run detonation after 13 min 26 sec.
1) *U 616* heard one Gnat end-of-run detonation after 12 min 16 sec. 2) *U 565* heard one Gnat end-of-run detonation after 11 min 20 sec.
3) *U 565* observed two detonations after 9 min on a cruiser of the *Leander* class.
4) *U 952* heard one Gnat end-of-run detonation after 14 min 48 sec. 5) *U 616* heard one Gnat end-of-run detonation after 12 min 20 sec.
6) *U 371* observed one hit on a first, and two hits on the second ship. One more detonation was heard on a third ship. The first one was sunk by a coup de grâce. 7) *U 453* heard one hit on each of three ships.

1	2	3	4	5	6	7	8	9	10	11	12	13	14	15

April 1944

13/2251	dt	U 596	Nonn	CK 4811	PE	=	T	.						1)
16/1827	dt	U 407	Korndörfer	CO 5822	-D	+	T	a	16/	am -D	Thomas G.Masaryk	7176=§	32.51 N/23.00 E	2)
16/1827	dt	U 407	Korndörfer	CO 5822	-D	+	T	a	16/	am -D	Meyer London	7210+	32.51 N/23.00 E	
26/0020	dt	U 967	Brandi	CH 7549	DD	+	T	.				------		3)

May 1944

2/	dt	U 371	Fenski	--------	---------	T	b	2/0110	am DE	Menges		1200=	37.01 N/05.29 E	
2/	dt	U 453	Lührs	CN 35	-D	=	T	c					140m ENE Malta	4)
4/	dt	U 371	Fenski	--------	---------	T	b	4/0300	fr DE	Sénégalais		1300=	37.49 N/05.39 E	
5/0354	dt	U 967	Brandi	CH 7542	-D	5000+	T	b				-----		5)
5/0441	dt	U 967	Brandi	CH 7542	DD	+	T	b	5/0441	am DE	Fechteler	1300+	36.07 N/02.40 W	
8/0255	dt	U 967	Brandi	CH 74	DD	+	T	.				------ N Alboran		6)
9/0456	dt	U 230	Siegmann	CJ 8693	PE	+	T	.	9/	am PC	PC 558	335+	38.41 N/13.43 E	
14/	dt	U 616	Koitschka	-------	---------	T	d	14/	am -MT	G.S.Walden		10627=	36.45 N/00.55 E	
14/	dt	U 616	Koitschka	-------	---------	T	d	14/	br -D	Fort Fidler		7127=	36.45 N/00.55 E	
17/	dt	U 960	Heinrich	CG 90	DD	=	T	.	17/	am DD	Ellyson		------	7)
19/	dt	U 453	Lührs	CJ 99	-D	7000+	T	e	19/	br -D	Fort Missanabie	7147+	38.20 N/16.28 E	

1) *U 596* heard one detonation after a run time of 7 min.
2) The *Thomas G.Masaryk* was damaged and towed into Alexandria but was declared a total loss.
3) *U 967* heard one detonation after a run time of 9 min 12 sec.
4) It is not clear whether the report of one hit against a west-bound convoy came from *U 453*.
5) *U 967* reported one hit on a ship of medium size after 11 min 58 sec, but it was probably an end-of-run detonation.
6) *U 967* heard one Gnat end-of-run detonation after 12 min 12 sec.
7) The *Ellyson* was missed by a 3-torpedo spread.

1	2	3	4	5	6	7	8	9	10	11	12	13	14	15
June 1940														
16/1500	it	GALILEI	Nardi	12n/45e	-T: 8215+	T	.	16/	nw	-MT	James Stove	8215+	12.35 N/ 45.03 E	
22/0535	it	TORRICELLI	Pelosi	13n/43e	---------	A	-	22/	br	PS	Shoreham	1105=	N Perim	1)
22/0600	it	TORRICELLI	Pelosi	13n/43e	---------	A	-	22/	br	DD	Khartoum	1690+	N Perim	1)
23/	it	GALVANI	Spano	24n/60e	---------	T	-	23/	in	PC	Pathan	661+	Gulf of Oman	

July 1940

Only one cancelled patrol (*Archimede*, Signorini) and one patrol without success (*Guglielmotti*, Tucci).

August 1940

Only one unsuccessful attack (*Ferraris*, Piomarta, 2355 August 14th against warships) and three unsuccessful patrols (*Gugliel-motti* (2) and *Farrasis* (1).

September 1940

1	2	3	4	5	6	7	9	10	11	12	13	14
6/1500	it	GUGLIEL-MOTTI	Tucci	16n/42e	-T: 4008+	T	6/	gr	-DT	Atlas	4008+	15.50 N/ 41.50 E

October 1940 - February 1941

From September 1940 to February 1941 the Italian submarines made fourteen patrols without successes: *Archimede* (6). *Ferraris* (6) and *Guglielmotti* (2). From March to May 1941 these three boats and *Perla* transitted around Africa to Bordeaux.

March 1941 − October 1941

No U-boat operations.

November 1941

1	2	3	4	5	6	7	8	9	10	11	12	13	14
17/0429	fr	LE HÉROS	Lemaire	33s/29e	-D: 4500+	T	-	17/	nw	-D	Thode Fagelund	5757+	60m E East London 2)

1) *Torricelli* was intercepted N of Perim by the destroyers HMS *Kandahar*, *Kingston* and *Khartoum*, and the sloops HMS *Shoreham* and HMS *Indus*. In a 40-minute gun battle, during which the British ships evaded a 4-torpedo spread, the *Shoreham* was hit by one 10cm round. On *Khartoum* splinters caused a torpedo to explode, following which the ship burned and was lost.
2) The French submarines *Le Héros* and *Le Glorieux* were ordered by the Vichy-government to attack Allied shipping as a reprisal for the capture of a Vichy-French convoy off South Africa on November 3rd,1941. *Le Glorieux* attacked one ship without success on November 15th.

1	2	3	4	5	6	7	8	9	10	11	12	13	14	15
December 1941														
10/	jp	I-124	Kishigami	15n/120e	-D	+	T -	10/	br	-D	Hareldawins	1523+	W Luzon	
11/1830	jp	I-156	Ohashi	05n/104e	-D	+	T -	11/					05.08 N/104.32 E	1)
(8.12.)	jp	I-124	Kishigami	Manila	---------		M -	17/	am	-D	Corregidor	1881+	Manila Bay	
24/	*jp*	*I-166*	*Yoshitome*	*01n/110e*	*DD*	*+*	*T -*	*24/*	*nl*	*SS*	*K-XVI*	*759+*	*N Api*	
January 1942														
3/0145	jp	I-158	Kitamura	05s/112e	-D	+	TA -	1/	nl	-D	Langkoeas	7395+	N Bawean I.	
5/0500	jp	I-156	Ohashi	09s/111e	-D	+	A -	4/	br	-D	Kwantung	2626+	09.12 S/111.10 E	
6/0300	jp	I-156	Ohashi	09s/111e	-D	+	A -	6/	nl	-M	Tanimbar	8169=	40m S Tjilatjap	
7/1800	jp	I-157	Nakashima	07s/116e	-D	+	A -	7/	nl	-DT	Djirak	3077+	07.15 S/116.23 E	
8/0716	jp	I-156	Ohashi	10s/111e	-D	+	T -	8/	nl	-D	Van Rees	3000+	80m S Tjilatjap	
8/2100	jp	I-156	Ohashi	08s/109e	-D	+	A -	8/	nl	-D	Van Riebeeck	2263+	08.11 S/108.47 E	
9/	jp	I-158	Kitamura	05s/112e	-D	+	TA -	9/	nl	-D	Camphuijs	2380+	04.40 S/111.47 E	
9/0957	jp	I-165	Harada	05s/112e	-T	8000=	TA -	9/					Java See	2)
9/1513	jp	I-165	Harada	05s/112e	-T:	5000+	TA -	9/	nl	-D	Benkoelen	1003+	04.50 S/112.20 E	
(8.12.)	jp	I-124	Kishigami	Manila	---------		M -	10/	pa	-D	Daylite	1976+	Manila Bay	
11/0415	jp	I-166	Yoshitome	08s/116e	-D	15000+	T .	11/	am	-D	Liberty Glo	4979+	10m SW Lombok	3)
13/	jp	I-156	Ohashi		-D	?	A -	13/	nl	-D	Patras	2065=	SW Bali	4)
15/0217	jp	I-165	Harada	00s/ 97e	-D:	8000+	TA -	14/	in	-D	Jalarajan	5102+	00.12 S/ 97.00 E	
18/	jp	I-121	Yendo	07s/126e	-D	10000+	T -	15/	nl	-M	Bantam	9312+	07.15 S/126.30 E	5)

1) The Japanese fleet submarines *I-53* - *I-75* were renumbered in May 1942 and became *I-153* - *I-175*. To avoid confusion with war-built submarines these submarines are here referred to by their later numbers. *I-156* reported one transport sunk by gunfire, possibly a ship named *Hydra II (?)*.

2) *I-165* attacked one tanker with two torpedoes and 28 rounds of 100mm. The ship was set afire but escaped.

3) The *Liberty Glo* was beached in damaged condition by the destroyers USS *Paul Jones* and HNeMS *Van Ghent* off the SE corner of Bali, but capsized on Jan.14th.

4) There is no report from *I-156*, but among the boats of the 4th squadron only this boat was operating in the Bali area.

1	2	3	4	5	6	7	8	9	10	11	12	13	14	15
January 1942, cont.														
20/2026	jp	I-159	Yoshimatsu	10s/106e	-D: 8000+	T	-	20/	nw	-M	Eidsvold	4184+	Christmas I.	1)
21/0825	jp	I-166	Yoshitome	15n/ 95e	-D: 4000+	TA	-	22/	br	-D	Chak Sang	2358+	15.42 N/ 95.02 E	
21/1816	jp	I-166	Yoshitome	15n/ 95e	-D 5000+	T	-	21/	pa	-D	Nord	3193+	15.28 N/ 94.36 E	
22/1940	jp	I-164	Ogawa	01n/ 90e	-D: 4500+	TA	-	22/	nl	-D	Van Overstraten	4482+	01.40 N/ 90.13 E	
25/1816	jp	I-159	Yoshimatsu	06n/ 95e	-D 7000+	T	-	25/	br	-D			Sabang-Roads	2)
28/1950	jp	I-164	Ogawa	10n/ 80e	-D: 1500+	A	-	28/	br	-D	Idar	391=	10.12 N/ 80.13 E	
29/1330	jp	I-164	Ogawa	13n/ 80e	-T: 5300+	T	-	29/	am	-D	Florence Luckenbach	5049+	12.55 N/ 80.33 E	
30/2233	jp	I-164	Ogawa	13n/ 80e	-T: 7000+	TA	-	30/	in	-D	Jalatarang	2498+	12.59 N/ 81.00 E	
31/0626	jp	I-164	Ogawa	12n/ 80e	-D 7000+	TA	-	30/	in	-D	Jalapalaka	4215+	13.00 N/ 81.08 E	
31/1055	jp	I-162	Kinashi	07n/ 79e	-T 10000+	T	-	31/	br	-MT	Longwood	9463=	20m W Colombo	
February 1942														
3/2145	jp	I-162	Kinashi	06n/ 79e	-T:10000=	TA	-	3/	br	-MT	Spondilus	7402=	06.16 N/ 79.38 E	
4/	jp	I-155	Nakajima	06s/119e	-D +	T	-	4/	nl	-D	Van Lansberge	1937+	S Makassar	
4/	jp	I-156	Ohashi	10s/123e	-D +	A	-	4/	nl	-M	Togian	979=§	near Koepang	3)
5/	*jp*	*Ro-34*	*Ota*	*06s/106e*	*DD +*	*T*	*-*	*5/*	*nl*	*DD*			*Sunda Strait*	*4)*
7/1430	jp	I-155	Nakajima	06s/113e	-D +	TA	-	7/	nl	-D	Van Cloon	4519+	S Bawean I.	
9/2043	jp	I-165	Harada	05n/ 81e	-D 2000+	T	.	9/	nl	-D	Meroendoeng	2464+	05.30 N/ 81.10 E	5)
11/	jp	I-156	Ohashi	07s/105e	-D +	T	-	11/					S Sunda Strait	6)

5) The *Bantam* was reported missing after Jan.18th. It is not clear if this ship was of 9,312 GRT or of 3,322 GRT. The target could also have been another unknown ship. *I-121* reported only one transport sunk.
1) The *Eidsvold* was hit by the sixth shot, broke in two parts, and sank to the bottom in shallow water.
2) *I-159* entered the roads of Sabang, sank one freighter and captured a part of the crew.
3) The *Togian* was probably only damaged and later scuttled by the crew off Koepang on Feb.22nd.
4) *Ro-34* reported one Dutch destroyer sunk. 5) *I-165* reported one ship from a 6-ship convoy sunk.
6) *I-156* reported one transport sunk.

1	2	3	4	5	6	7	8	9	10	11	12	13	14	15
February 1942, cont.														
13/2225	jp	I-155	Nakajima	05s/106e	-D +	T	-	13/						1)
14/1117	jp	I-166	Yoshitome	08n/ 82e	-D: 4000+	TA	-	14/	br	-D	Kamuning	2076+	08.35 N/ 81.44 E	
15/1850	jp	I-165	Harada	09n/ 76e	-T: 2000+	T	-	15/	br	-D	Johanne Justesen	4681+	09.04 N/ 75.58 E	
18/0300	jp	I-155	Nakajima	05s/106e	-D +	T	-	18/						2)
20/1840	jp	I-165	Harada	08n/ 73e	-T: 8000+	T	-	20/	br	-M	Bhima	5280+	07.47 N/ 73.31 E	
22/	jp	I-158	Kitamura	S Java	-D +	T	-	22/	nl	-D	Pijnacker Hordijk	2982+	S Tjilatjap	
25/	jp	I-158	Kitamura	S Java	-D +	T	-	25/	nl	-D	Boero	7135+	S Sunda Strait	
27/	jp	I-153	Nakamura	08s/114e	-D +	T	-	27/	nl	-M	Moesie	913+	25m Banjoewangi	
28/0544	jp	I-153	Nakamura	08s/109e	-D groß+	TA	.	28/	br	-D	City of Manchester	8917+	08.16 S/108.52 E	
28/0544	jp	I-153	Nakamura	08s/109e	-D groß+	T	.	1/	nl	-D	Parigi	1172+	Tjilatjap/Colombo	3)
28/	jp	I-158	Kitamura	06s/105e	-T 15000+	T	-	28/	br	-DT	British Judge	6735=	10m S Sunda Strait	
28/1745	jp	I-4	Nakagawa	S Bali	-D +	T	-	28/	nl	-D	Ban Ho Guan	1693+	Padang/Tjilatjap	4)
March 1942														
1/0150	jp	I-159	Yoshimatsu	00n/ 87e	-D: 7000+	T	-	28/	nl	-D	Rooseboom	1035+	00.15 N/ 86.50 E	
1/	jp	I-154	Kobayashi	13s/106e	-D +	TA	-	1/	nl	-M	Modjokerto	8806+	12.40 S/106.40 E	
1/	jp	I-3	Tonozuka	32s/113e	-D mittl+	T	-	1/						5)
3/	jp	I-1	Ankyu	21s/109e	-D +	TA	-	3/	nl	-M	Siantar	8667+	21.20 S/108.45 E	
4/1300	jp	I-7	Koizumi	08s/ 95e	-DP +	A	-	4/	nl	-D	Le Maire	3271+	Tjilatjap -Austr.	6)

1) *I-155* reported one transport sunk north of Sunda Strait. 2) *I-155* reported one additional transport sunk.
3) The *Parigi* was reported missing after March 1st between Tjilatjap and Colombo.
4) The *Ban Ho Guan* was expected at Tjilatjap from Padang on March 1st, but never arrived.
5) *I-3* reported one ship of medium size sunk at 31-50 S/113-30 E.
6) The *Le Maire* was lost between Tjilatjap and Australia. *I-7* reported one combined freight-passenger-steamer sunk at a
   position bearing 330° at 250 miles from the Cocos Islands.

1	2	3	4	5	6	7	8	9	10	11	12	13	14	15
March 1942, cont.														
10/	jp	I-162	Kinashi	12n/ 85e	-S: 400+	A	-	10/	br	-S	Lakshimi Govinda	235+	13.22 N/ 87.27 E	
11/	jp	I-2	Inada	01S/100e	-D +	A	-	11/	br	-D	Chilka	4360+	near Padang	
13/	jp	I-164	Ogawa	14n/ 81e	-D: 5000+	TA	-	13/	nw	-D	Mabella	1513+	14.00 N/ 81.47 E	
16/2311	jp	I-162	Kinashi	08n/ 73e	-D 7000+	T	-	/	nl	-M	Merkus (?)	865+	Tjilatjap/Bombay	1)
21/1432	jp	I-162	Kinashi	06n/ 79e	-T:15000+	T	-	21/	br	-MT	San Cirilo	8012=	06.40 N/ 79.40 E	
22/1537	jp	I-162	Kinashi	10n/ 84e	-D 10000=	T	-	22/					10.50 N/ 83.59 E	2)
April 1942														
2/1714	jp	I-6	Inaba	16n/ 68e	-D: 6000+	T	-	2/	br	-D	Clan Ross	5897+	15.58 N/ 68.24 E	
3/0740	jp	I-7	Koizumi	01s/ 78e	-D: 9500+	TA	-	2/	br	-M	Glenshiel	9415+	01.00 S/ 78.11 E	
6/1900	jp	I-5	Utsuki	07n/ 73e	-D: 7000+	T	-	6/	am	-D	Washingtonian	6617+	07.25 N/ 73.05 E	
7/0540	jp	I-3	Tonozuka	07n/ 79e	-D: 5000+	A	-	6/	br	-D	Elmdale	4872=	06.52 N/ 78.50 E	
7/1020	jp	I-2	Inada	01n/ 82e	-D mittl+	T	-	7/					00.48 N/ 82.18 E	3)
7/2220	jp	I-6	Inaba	20n/ 68e	-D: 6000+	TA	-	7/	br	-D	Bahadur	5424+	19.44 N/ 68.28 E	
8/0450	jp	I-3	Tonozuka	07n/ 77e	-D +	T	-	7/	br	-M	Fultala	5051+	06.52 N/ 76.54 E	
10/0400	jp	I-5	Utsuki	07n/ 79e	-S 200+	A	-	10/		-S			near Colombo	4)
10/1115	jp	I-6	Inaba	20n/ 68e	-S 150+	A	-	11/		-S			near Bombay	5)
10/1115	jp	I-6	Inaba	20n/ 68e	-S 150+	A	-	11/		-S			near Bombay	5)
May 1942														
30/	*jp*	*I-20*	*Yamada, T.*	*D.Suarez CL*	*5440+*	*KU*	*-*	*30/2025*	*br*	*BB*	*Ramillies*	*29150=*	*Diego-Suarez*	*6)*
30/	*jp*	*I-20*	*Yamada, T.*	*D.Suarez*	*--------*	*KU*	*-*	*30/2125*	*br*	*-MT*	*British Loyalty*	*6993=*	*Diego-Suarez*	*6)*

1) The *Merkus* was reported missing after March 4th between Tjilatjap and Bombay. According to Japanese sources she was sunk by *I-162*.

2) *I-162* observed two torpedo hits on a freighter-passenger-steamer, but the listing vessel escaped.

3) *I-2* reported one ship of medium size sunk. 4) *I-5* sank a sailing vessel with seven rounds of 14cm. 5)*I-6* sank two sailing vessels with eight rounds of 14cm. 6) A midget submarine launched by *I-20* penetrated the roads of Diego Suarez and torpedoed both ships. The tanker sank to the bottom, but was salvaged and repaired. During operations off Madagaskar the Vichy-French submarine *Monge* (Delort) unsuccessfully attacked the carrier HMS *Indomitable* at midday on May 8th.

1	2	3	4	5	6	7	8	9	10	11	12	13	14	15
June 1942														
5/0831	jp	I-10	Kayahara	21s/ 38e	-D	+	TA	-	5/	pa	-D	Atlantic Gulf	2639+	21.03 S/ 37.36 E	
5/1245	jp	I-20	Yamada, T.	13s/ 42e	-D	+	T	-	5/	pa	-M	Johnstown	5086+	13.12 S/ 42.06 E	
5/1644	jp	I-10	Kayahara	22s/ 37e	-D	+	T	-	5/	am	-M	Melvin H.Baker	4999+	21.44 S/ 36.38 E	
6/	jp	I-16	Yamada, K.	16s/ 41e	-D	+	TA	-	6/	jg	-D	Susak	3889+	15.42 S/ 40.58 E	
8/	jp	I-18	Otani	20s/ 37e	-D	+	A	-	8/	nw	-D	Wilford	2158+	20.20 S/ 36.47 E	
8/	jp	I-16	Yamada, K.	16s/ 41e	-D	+	A	-	8/	gr	-D	Agios Georgios IV.	4847+	16.12 S/ 41.00 E	
8/1253	jp	I-10	Kayahara	20s/ 40e	-D	+	T	-	8/	br	-M	King Lud	5224+	20.00 S/ 40.00 E	
8/2351	jp	I-20	Yamada, T.	05s/ 41e	-D	+	T	-	8/	gr	-D	Christos Markettos	5209+	05.05 S/ 40.53 E	
11/2343	jp	I-20	Yamada, T.	15s/ 41e	-D	+	T	-	11/1730	br	-D	Mahronda	7926+	14.37 S/ 40.58 E	
12/0030	jp	I-20	Yamada, T.	15s/ 41e	-D	+	A	-	11/	pa	-D	Hellenic Trader	2052+	14.40 S/ 40.53 E	
12/	jp	I-16	Yamada, K.	22s/ 36e	-D	+	TA	-	12/	jg	-D	Supetar	3748+	21.49 S/ 35.50 E	
12/1933	jp	I-20	Yamada, T.	16s/ 40e	-D	+	T	-	12/	br	-M	Clifton Hall	5063+	16.25 S/ 40.10 E	
28/	jp	I-10	Kayahara	21s/ 40e	-D	+	T	-	28/	br	-M	Queen Victoria	4937+	21.15 S/ 40.30 E	
30/0415	jp	I-20	Yamada, T.	13s/ 42e	-D	+	T	-	29/	nw	-D	Goviken	4854+	13.25 S/ 41.53 E	
30/0700	jp	I-10	Kayahara	23s/ 37e	-D	+	T	-	30/	am	-D	Express	6736+	23.30 S/ 37.30 E	
30/0905	jp	I-20	Yamada, T.	09s/ 42e	-T	+	T	-	1/	br	-DT	Steaua Romana	5311+	09. S/ 42. E	
July 1942														
1/	jp	I-18	Otani	25s/ 35e	-D	=	TA	-	1/	nl	-D	Alchiba (s.u.)	-----	25.25 S/ 34.49 E	1)
1/	jp	I-16	Yamada, K.	17s/ 40e	-D	+	T	-	1/	sw	-M	Eknaren	5243+	17.00 S/ 40.00 E	
1/	jp	I-18	Otani	25s/ 36e	-D	+	A	-	1/	nl	-D	De Weert	1805+	25.12 S/ 35.56 E	
6/1615	jp	I-10	Kayahara	16s/ 41e	-D	+	T	-	6/	gr	-D	Nymphe	4504+	15.48 N/ 40.42 E	
8/	jp	I-18	Otani	29s/ 32e	-D	+	TA	-	6/	br	-D	Mundra	7341+	28.45 S/ 32.20 E	

1) According to Japanese sources the *Alchiba* was damaged on July 1st and sunk by *I-10*. According to Dutch sources she
   was not damaged on July 1st. According to British sources, she already been reported sunk on July 1st.

1	2	3	4	5	6	7	8	9	10 11	12	13	14	15
July 1942, cont.													
8/0748	jp	I-10	Kayahara	18s/ 41e	-D	+	TA	-	8/	br -D	Hartismere	5498+	18.00 S/ 41.22 E	
9/0029	jp	I-10	Kayahara	18s/ 42e	-D	+	TA	-	8/	nl -D	Alchiba (s.o.)	4427+	18.30 S/ 41.40 E	1)
August 1942													
25/1248	jp	I-165	Torisu	02n/ 77e	-D	+	T	-	25/	br -D	Harmonides	5237+	01.47 N/ 77.27 E	
September 1942													
2/früh	jp	I-29	Izu	13n/ 51e	-D	+	T	-	1/	br -D	Gazcon	4224+	13.01 N/ 50.41 E	
10/nm	jp	I-29	Izu	13n/ 54e	-D	+	T	-	9/	br -D	Haresfield	5299+	13.05 N/ 54.35 E	
16/	jp	I-29	Izu	13n/ 51e	-D	+	TA	-	16/	br -D	Ocean Honour	7174+	12.48 N/ 50.50 E	
23/	jp	I-29	Izu	10n/ 64e	-D	+	T	-	22/1430	am -D	Paul Luckenbach	6606+	10.03 N/ 63.42 E	
24/0957	jp	I-165	Torisu	08n/ 74e	-D	+	T	-	24/	am -D	Losmar	5549+	07.40 N/ 74.15 E	
25/	jp	I-165	Torisu	07n/ 74e	-D	+	T	-	25/					2)
October 1942													
1/	jp	I-166	Tanaka	08n/ 77e	-D	+	A	-	30/	pa -D	Camila	1201=§	08.01 N/ 77.07 E	3)
1/1610	jp	I-166	Tanaka	07n/ 76e	-D	=	T	-	1/				07.34 N/ 75.52 E	4)
3/1724	jp	I-162	Shimose	19n/ 85e	-D	+	T	-	3/	sj -D	Mikojan	2332+	19.24 N/ 85.24 E	
7/0502	dt	U 172	Emmermann	GR 5593	-D: 6200+		T	-	7/	am -D	Chickasaw City	6196+	34.15 S/ 17.11 E	
7/0926	dt	U 172	Emmermann	GR 5671	-D: 6000+		T	-	7/	pa -M	Firethorn	4700+	34.13 S/ 17.21 E	
7/1924	jp	I-162	Shimose	15n/ 80e	-D	+	T	-	7/	br -D	Manon	5597+	15.00 N/ 80.30 E	
7/2355	dt	U 159	Witte	GR 5881	-D: 8482+		T	-	7/	br -D	Boringia	5821+	35.09 S/ 16.32 E	5)

1) See note 1, p.262. 2) *I-165* reported one transport sunk by torpedo.
3) The *Camila* was heavily damaged at 08-10 N/77-41 E and was beached and abandoned. She was a total loss.
4) *I-166* reported one transport damaged by one torpedo hit.
5) *I-159* reported the ship sunk to be the motor-freighter *Selandia* of 8,482 GRT.

1	2	3	4	5	6	7	8	9	10	11	12	13	14	15
October 1942, cont.														
8/0140	dt	U 172	Emmermann	GR 5649	-D	3500+	T	-	8/	gr	-D	Pantelis	3845+	34.20 S/ 17.50 E	
8/0231	dt	U 68	Merten	GR 5689	-D	5000+	T	-	8/	gr	-D	Koumoundouros	3598+	34.10 S/ 17.07 E	
8/0346	dt	U 68	Merten	GR 5932	-D	8000+	T	-	8/	nl	-D	Gaasterkerk	8679+	34.20 S/ 18.10 E	
8/0905	dt	U 159	Witte	GR 5856	-D	5300+	T	-	8/	br	-D	Clan Mactavish	7631+	34.53 S/ 16.45 E	
8/1731	dt	U 179	Sobe	-------	---------		T	-	8/	br	-D	City of Athens	6558+	33.40 S/ 17.03 E	
8/2051	dt	U 68	Merten	GR 5939	-T:	8207+	T	-	8/	am	-DT	Swiftsure	8207+	34.40 S/ 18.25 E	
8/2202	dt	U 68	Merten	GR 5963	-D	6000+	T	-	8/	br	-D	Sarthe	5271+	34.50 S/ 18.40 E	
9/0344	dt	U 68	Merten	GR 5965	-D:	4981+	T	-	9/	am	-D	Examelia	4981+	34.52 S/ 18.30 E	
9/0454	dt	U 68	Merten	GR 5965	-D	6000+	T	-	9/	be	-D	Belgian Fighter	5403+	35.00 S/ 18.30 E	
9/1154	dt	U 159	Witte	GR 8144	-D:	6557+	T	-	9/	am	-D	Coloradan	6557+	35.47 S/ 14.34 E	
10/1028	dt	U 172	Emmermann	GR 7335	-D:	23456+	T	-	10/	br	-D	Orcades	23456+	31.51 S/ 14.40 E	
13/1337	dt	U 159	Witte	GR 8996	-D:	10133+	T	-	13/1449	br	-D	Empire Nomad	7167+	37.50 S/ 18.16 E	
13/1920	jp	I-162	Shimose	06n/ 82e	-D	+	T	-	13/	br	-D	Martaban	4161=	06.31 N/ 82.03 E	
17/0615	dt	U 504	Poske	JJ 1313	-D	5000+	T	-	17/	br	-D	Empire Chaucer	5970+	40.20 S/ 18.30 E	
22/	jp	I-27	Kitamura	22n/ 60e	-D	+	T	-	22/	br	-D	Ocean Vintage	7174+	21.37 N/ 60.06 E	
23/2312	dt	U 504	Poske	KZ 1972	-D:	5600+	T	-	23/	br	-D	City of Johannesburg	5669+	33.20 S/ 29.30 E	
26/1843	dt	U 504	Poske	KZ 1864	-D	12000+	T	-	26/	am	-D	Anne Hutchinson	7176=§	33.10 S/ 28.30 E	1)
29/1226	dt	U 159	Witte	JJ 2511	-M:	4978+	T	-	29/	br	-M	Ross	4978+	38.51 S/ 21.40 E	
29/2118	dt	U 159	Witte	JJ 2795	-D:	7327+	T	-	29/	br	-D	Laplace	7327+	40.35 S/ 21.35 E	
31/0903	dt	U 504	Poske	KP 9787	-D:	8000+	T	-	31/	br	-D	Empire Guidon	7041+	30.10 S/ 33.50 E	
31/1718	dt	U 504	Poske	KP 9843	-D:	5113+	T	-	2/	br	-D	Reynolds	5113+	29. S/ 41. E	2)
31/2223	dt	U 172	Emmermann	GP 3211	-D:	4891+	T	-	31/	br	-M	Aldington Court	4891+	30.20 S/ 02.10 W	

1) After breaking in two as a result of the attack, the after part of this ship sank on Oct.29th. The fore part was towed into Port Elizabeth by HMSAS *David Haigh* on Nov.1st but was a loss.
2) The *Reynolds* sank in a few seconds after two hits. It was assumed she was sunk by a German raider.

Indian Ocean

1	2	3	4	5	6	7	8	9	10	11	12	13	14	15
November 1942														
1/1533 dt		U 178	Ibbeken	KP 8611	-D: 8400+	T	-	1/	br	-D	Mendoza	8233+	29.20 S/ 32.13 E	
2/2143 dt		U 172	Emmermann	GG 4769	-D: 4966+	T	-	2/	br	-D	Llandilo	4966+	27.03 S/ 02.59 W	
2/2159 dt		U 177	Gysae	GR 1715	-D 8000+	T	-	31/	gr	-D	Aegeus	4538+	32.30 S/ 16.00 E	1)
3/1622 dt		U 181	Lüth	GR 7835	-M: 8159+	T	-	3/	am	-M	East Indian	8159+	37.23 S/ 13.34 E	
3/1642 dt		U 504	Poske	KZ 4589	-D: 5187+	T	-	3/	bz	-D	Porto Alegre	5187+	35.27 S/ 28.02 E	
4/1142 dt		U 178	Ibbeken	KP 5355	-D: 3600+	T	-	4/	nw	-D	Hai Hing	2561+	25.55 S/ 33.10 E	
4/1446 dt		U 178	Ibbeken	KP 5355	-D: 5244+	T	-	4/	br	-D	Trekieve	5244+	25.46 S/ 33.48 E	
6/2136 dt		U 68	Merten	GF 3811	-D: 8034+	T	-	6/	br	-D	City of Cairo	8034+	23.30 S/ 05.30 W	
7/2250 dt		U 159	Witte	GR 7599	-D: 8500+	T	-	29/	am	-D	La Salle	5462+	40.00 S/ 21.30 E	2)
8/2055 dt		U 181	Lüth	KY 6982	-D 6000+	TA	-	8/	pa	-D	Plaudit	5060+	36.00 S/ 26.32 E	
10/0827 dt		U 181	Lüth	KZ 4681	-D: 3799+	T	-	10/	nw	-D	K.G.Meldahl	3799+	34.59 S/ 29.45 E	
13/0620 dt		U 178	Ibbeken	KP 9885	-D: 3764+	T	-	13/	br	-D	Louise Moller	3764+	30.50 S/ 35.54 E	
13/0801 dt		U 181	Lüth	KZ 1914	-D: 4969+	T	-	13/	am	-D	Excello	4969+	32.23 S/ 30.07 E	
13/	dt	U 159	Witte	GG 5811	-S: 2290+	A	-	13/	am	-S	Star of Scotland	2290+	26.30 S/ 00.20 W	
15/0145 dt		U 178	Ibbeken	KZ 2385	-D 6000+	T	-	15/	br	-D	Adviser	6348=	32.03 S/ 33.52 E	
19/2125 dt		U 181	Lüth	KP 1324	-D 2000+	T	-	19/	nw	-D	Gunda	2241+	25.40 S/ 33.53 E	
19/2307 dt		U 177	Gysae	KP 9780	-T 10000+	T	-	19/	br	-DT	Scottish Chief	7006+	30.39 S/ 34.41 E	
20/0124 dt		U 181	Lüth	KP 5322	-D: 3562+	T	-	20/	gr	-D	Corinthiakos	3562+	25.42 S/ 33.27 E	
20/1140 dt		U 177	Gysae	KP 9910	-D: 7191+	T	-	20/	am	-D	Pierce Butler	7191+	29.40 S/ 35.35 E	
22/0033 dt		U 181	Lüth	KP 5372	-D: 6700+	T	-	21/	am	-D	Alcoa Pathfinder	6797+	26.45 S/ 33.10 E	
23/1153 jp		I-166	Tanaka	08n/ 77e	-D +	T	-	23/	br	-D	Cranfield	5332+	08.26 N/ 76.42 E	
23/	jp	I-29	Izu	07n/ 61e	-D +	T	-	23/	br	-D	Tilawa	10006+	07.36 N/ 61.08 E	

1) The ship hit by *U 177* with two torpedoes sank after a big explosion. It must have been the reported missing after Oct.31st.
2) The ship identified by *U 159* as the munitions freighter *Umtali* sank after a big explosion. It was probably the munitions-freighter *La Salle*, reported missing after Oct.29th.

1	2	3	4	5	6	7	8	9	10	11	12	13	14	15
November 1942, cont.														
24/0737	dt	U 181	Lüth	KP 6455	−D: 5000+	TA	−	24/	gr	−D	Mount Helmos	6481+	26.38 S/ 34.59 E	
24/2034	dt	U 181	Lüth	KP 6158	−D: 5280+	TA	−	24/	br	−D	Dorington Court	5281+	27.00 S/ 34.45 E	
27/1436	dt	U 178	Ibbeken	JJ 2557	−D: 8000+	T	−	27/	am	−D	Jeremiah Wadsworth	7176+	39.25 S/ 22.23 E	
28/0715	dt	U 177	Gysae	KP 8325	ACL:6796+	T	−	28/	br	−D	Nova Scotia	6796+	28.30 S/ 33.00 E	1)
28/2250	dt	U 181	Lüth	KP 3719	−D: 3551+	TA	−	28/	gr	−D	Evanthia	3551+	25.13 S/ 34.00 E	
29/2000	it	CAGNI	Liannazza	35s/ 17e	−D: 5550+	T	−	29/	gr	−D	Argo	1995+	34.53 S/ 17.54 E	
30/0511	dt	U 181	Lüth	KP 3523	−D: 4153+	TA	−	30/	gr	−D	Cleanthis	4153+	24.29 S/ 35.44 E	
30/1729	dt	U 177	Gysae	KP 5925	−D:10799+	T	−	30/	br	−D	Llandaff Castle	10799+	27.20 S/ 33.40 E	
December 1942														
2/1740	dt	U 181	Lüth	KP 3583	−D: 4000+	T	−	2/	pa	−D	Amarylis	4328+	28.14 S/ 33.24 E	
3/1230	jp	I-29	Izu	11n/ 55e	−D +	TA	−	3/	nw	−MT	Belita	6323+	11.29 N/ 55.00 E	
7/1720	dt	U 177	Gysae	KP 6155	−D: 3548+	T	−	7/	gr	−D	Saronikos	3548+	24.46 S/ 35.30 E	
12/2050	dt	U 177	Gysae	KP 6267	−D: 6000+	T	−	12/	br	−D	Empire Gull	6408+	26. S/ 35. E	
14/1636	dt	U 177	Gysae	KP 8990	−D: 3085+	T	−	14/	nl	−D	Sawahloento	3085+	31.02 S/ 34.00 E	
January 1943														
12/0351	jp	I-165	Torisu		−D =	A	−	12/					near Pt.Gregory	2)
February 1943														
10/0219	dt	U 509	Witte	GR 6844	−D 5000+	T	−	10/	br	−M	Queen Anne	4937+	34.53 S/ 19.51 E	
11/0652	dt	U 516	Wiebe	KY 6267	−D 6000+	T.	−	11/	br	−D	Helmsprey	4764+	34.22 S/ 24.54 E	
17/0224	dt	U 516	Wiebe	KZ 4113	−D: 6187+	T	−	17/	am	−D	Deer Lodge	6187+	33.46 S/ 26.57 E	

1) On board the troop transport *Nova Scotia* there were 765 Italian civilian internees.
2) *I-165* reported one transport damaged by gunfire near Point Gregory.

1	2	3	4	5	6	7	8	9	10	11	12	13	14	15
February 1943, cont.														
17/tags	dt	U 182	Clausen	KZ 42	-D:	4836+	T	-	17/	br	-D	Llanashe	4836+	34.22 S/ 24.54 E
27/1141	dt	U 516	Wiebe	KZ 1791	-D	10000+	T	-	27/	nl	AS	Colombia	10972+	near Dimonstown
March 1943														
3/2322	dt	U 160	Lassen	KZ 1336	-D	7000+	T	DN.21	3/	am	-D	Harvey W.Scott	7176+	31.54 S/ 30.37 E
3/2322	dt	U 160	Lassen	KZ 1336	-D	5000+	T	DN.21	3/	br	-D	Nirpura	5961+	32.47 S/ 30.48 E
3/2322	dt	U 160	Lassen	KZ 1336	-T	10000+	T	DN.21	3/	nl	-MT	Tibia	10356=	32. S/ 30.21 E	1)
4/0110	dt	U 160	Lassen	KZ 2411	-D	5000+	T	DN.21	4/	br	-D	Empire Mahseer	5087+	32.01 S/ 30.48 E
4/0110	dt	U 160	Lassen	KZ 2411	-D	5000+?	T	DN.21	4/				-----		1)
4/0346	dt	U 160	Lassen	KZ 2442	-D	5000+	T	DN.21	4/	br	-D	Marietta E.	7628+	31.49 S/ 31.11 E
4/0346	dt	U 160	Lassen	KZ 2442	-D	5000+	T	DN.21	4/	br	-D	Sheaf Crown	4868=	31.49 S/ 31.11 E	1)
7/früh	dt	U 506	Würdemann	KY 5399	-D	6000+	T	-	7/	br	-D	Sabor	5212+	34.30 S/ 23.10 E
8/abds	dt	U 160	Lassen	KP 9174	-D	6000+	T	-	8/	am	-D	James B.Stephens	7176+	28.53 S/ 33.18 E
9/morg	dt	U 506	Würdemann	KY 9415	-D:	4581+	TA	-	9/	nw	-D	Tabor	4768+	37.30 S/ 23.15 E	2)
10/	dt	U 182	Clausen	KP 6827	-D:	10000+	TA	-	10/	am	-D	Richard D.Spaight	7177+	28. S/ 37. E
11/abds	dt	U 160	Lassen	KP 9178	-D:	6452+	T	-	11/	br	-D	Aelybryn	4986+	28.30 S/ 34. E	3)
20/	jp	I-27	Fukumura	09n/ 71e	-D	+	T	-	20/	br	-D	Fort Mumford	7132+	10. N/ 71. E	4)
20/	dt	U 516	Wiebe	GJ 7395	-D	7000+	T	-	20/	pa	-D	Nortun	3663+	27.35 S/ 14.22 E
April 1943														
2/2200	dt	U 509	Witte	GJ 8144	-D	=	T	.	2/	br	-D	City of Baroda	7129=§	26.56 S/ 15.21 E	5)

1) The *Tibia* reached Durban under her own power. During the second attack *U 160* reported hits on two ships; one was reported sunk, the other left in sinking condition. In reality the *Empire Mahseer* was hit by two torpedoes and sank in 2 min. The *Sheaf Crown* was damaged and towed into East London.
2) *U 506* reported this ship erroneously as the British S/S *Pearlmoor*. 3) *U 160* reported this ship as American *Arian*.
4) The *Fort Mumford* was reported missing. Wreckage was found on the shore near Cape Comorin.
5) The *City of Baroda* was heavily damaged and was beached at Lüderitz Bay. She was a total loss.

1	2	3	4	5	6	7	8	9	10	11	12	13	14	15
April 1943, cont.														
5/	dt	U 182	Clausen	JA 1470	-D: 5047+	T	-	5/	br	-D	Aloe	5047+	32.37 S/ 37.50 E	
17/	it	DA VINCI	Gazzana	32s/ 35e	-D: 6566+	T	-	17/	nl	-D	Sembilan	6566+	31.30 S/ 33.30 E	
18/früh	dt	U 180	Musenberg	KZ 6568	-T: 8132+	T	-	18/	br	-MT	Corbis	8132+	34.56 S/ 34.03 E	
18/	it	DA VINCI	Gazzana	31s/ 34e	-D: 7242+	TA	-	18/	br	-D	Manaar	8007+	30.59 S/ 33.00 E	
21/	it	DA VINCI	Gazzana	33s/ 34e	-D: 6800+	TA	-	21/	am	-D	John Drayton	7177+	32.10 S/ 34.50 E	
25/	it	DA VINCI	Gazzana	37s/ 23e	-T: 8078+	TA	-	25/	br	-MT	Doryssa	8078+	37.03 S/ 24.03 E	
May 1943														
7/0556	jp	I-27	Fukumura	04n/ 75e	-D: 6600+	TA	-	7/	nl	-M	Berakit	6608+	03.40 N/ 75.20 E	
11/0408	dt	U 181	Lüth	KP 4777	-D: 5232+	T	-	11/	br	-D	Tinhow	5232+	25.15 S/ 33.30 E	
11/23	dt	U 196	Kentrat	KZ 1383	-D 6000+	T	-	11/	br	-D	Nailsea Meadow	4962+	32.04 S/ 29.13 E	
12/	dt	U 195	Buchholz	GG 1656	-D 8000+	T	-	12/	am	-D	Cape Neddick	6797=	23.21 S/ 01.22 W	
17/1412	dt	U 198	Hartmann	KP 8441	-D 6000+	T	LMD.17	17/	br	-D	Northmoor	4392+	28.27 S/ 32.43 E	
17/1412	dt	U 198	Hartmann	KP 8441	-D 6000+?	T	LMD.17	17/						1)
20/morg	dt	U 181	Lüth	KP 3578	-D: 1633+	T	-	27/	sw	-M	Sicilia	1633+	24.31 S/ 35.12 E	2)
28/2353	dt	U 177	Gysae	GR 6769	-D 8000+	T	CD.20	28/	am	-D	Agwimonte	6679+	34.57 S/ 19.33 E	
28/2354	dt	U 177	Gysae	GR 6769	-T 8000+	T	CD.20	28/	nw	-MT	Storaas	7886+	34.57 S/ 19.33 E	
29/1937	dt	U 198	Hartmann	JA 1223	-D: 5231+	T	-	29/	br	-M	Hopetarn	5231+	30.50 S/ 39.32 E	
June 1943														
1/0939	dt	U 178	Dommes	KP 8779	-D 5000+	T	CD.20	1/	nl	-D	Salabangka	6586+	31.08 S/ 31.18 E	3)
3/0735	jp	I-27	Fukumura	18n/ 59e	-D +	T	-	3/	am	-D	Montanan	4898+	17.54 N/ 58.09 E	
5/morg	dt	U 198	Hartmann	KP 5989	-D: 2304+	T	-	5/	br	-D	Dumra	2304+	28.15 S/ 33.20 E	

1) *U 198* heard detonations and sinking noises after the second 2-torpedo spread.
2) *U 181* sank this ship after stopping it by gunfire and giving the crew time to abandon ship.
3) The *Salabangka* was damaged and sank during a storm in the evening while under tow.

1	2	3	4	5	6	7	8	9	10	11	12	13	14	15
June 1943, cont.														
6/tags	dt	U 198	Hartmann	KP 9754	-D:10000+	T	-	6/	am	-D	William King	7176+	30.25 S/ 34.15 E	
7/früh	dt	U 181	Lüth	KP 53	-D 1000+	T	-	6/	sa	-D	Harrier	193+	29. S/ 34. E	
16/früh	jp	I-37	Otani		-T +	TA	-	15/	br	-MT	San Ernesto	8078+	09.18 S/ 80.20 E	1)
19/1350	jp	I-37	Otani	00n/ 70e	-D +	T	-	19/	am	-D	Henry Knox	7176+	00.00 N/ 70.15 E	
24/0500	jp	I-27	Fukumura	25n/ 58e	-T +	T	-	24/	br	-DT	British Venture	4696+	25.13 N/ 58.02 E	
27/	dt	U 511	Schneewind	KR 4869	-D: 7000+	T	-	27/	am	-D	Sebastiano Cermeno	7194+	29. S/ 50.10 E	
28/0405	jp	I-27	Fukumura	Muscat	-D +	T	-	28/	nw	-D	Dah Pu	1974+	Muscat Harbor	2)
July 1943														
2/2315	dt	U 181	Lüth	KG 5937	-D: 2798+	T	-	2/	br	-D	Hoihow	2798+	19.30 S/ 55.30 E	
4/1410	dt	U 178	Dommes	KE 7471	-D: 2669+	T	DN.50 s	4/	nw	-D	Breiviken	2669+	21.50 S/ 37.50 E	
4/1830	dt	U 178	Dommes	KD 9985	-D: 4774+	T	-	4/	gr	-D	Michael Livanos	4774+	22.52 S/ 36.47 E	
5/0610	jp	I-27	Fukumura	24n/ 59e	-D +	T	PA.44	5/	am	-D	Alcoa Prospector	6797=	24.21 N/ 59.04 E	
6/0825	dt	U 177	Gysae	JA 2577	-D: 5000+	T	-	6/	ca	-D	Jasper Park	7129+	32.52 S/ 42.15 E	
6/2030	dt	U 198	Hartmann	KP 3810	-D: 4476+	T	-	6/	gr	-D	Hydraios	4476+	24.44 S/ 35.12 E	
7/0645	dt	U 198	Hartmann	KP 3810	-D: 4742+	TA	-	7/	br	-D	Leana	4742+	25.06 S/ 35.33 E	
9/	dt	U 511	Schneewind	LY 26	-D 7000+	T	-	9/	am	-D	Samuel Heintzelmann	7176+	09. S/ 81. E	3)
10/1205	dt	U 177	Gysae	KQ 5388	-D 7000+	TA	-	10/	am	-D	Alice F.Palmer	7176+	26.30 S/ 44.20 E	
11/0915	dt	U 178	Dommes	KE 2168	-D: 4771+	T	-	11/	gr	-D	Mary Livanos	4771+	15.40 S/ 40.45 E	
12/0922	jp	I-29	Izu	14n/ 52e	-D +	T	-	12/	br	-D	Rahmani	5463+	14.52 N/ 52.06 E	
14/0034	dt	U 178	Dommes	KE 2274	-D: 6000+	T	-	14/	am	-D	Robert Bacon	7191+	15.25 S/ 41.13 E	

1) The wreck, hit by two torpedoes and many rounds of artillery was abandoned in sinking condition. Wreckage was seen on Aug. 16th at 01-28N/78-31E and on Aug.19th at 01-07N/79-31E. On Aug.30th a wreck was sighted at 09-18S/8020E. It is not clear whether the position reported is correct or whether in fact it was the wreck of the ship attacked by U 511 on July 9th. (See note 3.)

2) The "special service vessel" *Dah Pu* sank inside the harbor, and was a total loss. 3) The *Samuel Heintzelman* left Fremantle on July 1st and was reported missing after July 4th at 20 S/103 E. Her destination was Colombo. The attack by U 511 was made at her plotted position for July 9th.

1	2	3	4	5	6	7	8	9	10	11	12	13	14	15
July 1943, cont.														
15/	dt	U 181	Lüth	KF 9169	-D: 2852+	T	-	15/	br	-D	Empire Lake	2852+	21.27 S/ 51.47 E	
16/1200	dt	U 181	Lüth	KF 9759	-D: 7000+	T	-	16/	br	-D	Fort Franklin	7135+	22.36 S/ 51.22 E	
16/2207	dt	U 178	Dommes	LT 6591	-D: 6692+	T	-	16/	br	-D	City of Canton	6692+	13.52 S/ 41.10 E	
22/	jp	I-10	Tonozuka	03s/ 68e	-D: +	T	-	22/	nw	-M	Alcides	7634+	03. S/ 68. E	1)
24/2205	dt	U 197	Bartels	KQ 4770	-D: 9583+	T	-	24/	sw	-MT	Pegasus	9583+	28.05 S/ 37.40 E	
29/0600	dt	U 177	Gysae	KR 5726	-D: 4950+	T	-	29/	br	-M	Cornish City	4952+	27.20 S/ 52.10 E	
30/	dt	U 197	Bartels	KP 98	-D =	T	-	30/	am	-D	William Ellery	7181=	32. S/ 36. E	
August 1943														
1/	dt	U 198	Hartmann	KP 3755	-D 7000+	T	BC.2	1/	nl	-D	Mangkalibat	8457+	25.06 S/ 34.14 E	
2/	dt	U 196	Kentrat	LT 8582	-D 10000+	T	CB.21	2/	br	-D	City of Oran	7323+	13.45 S/ 41.16 E	
2/	dt	U 196	Kentrat	LT 8582	-D 10000=	T	CB.21	2/						2)
4/	dt	U 181	Lüth	KG 8555	-D: 4458+	T	-	4/	br	-D	Dalfram	4558+	20.53 S/ 56.43 E	
5/	dt	U 177	Gysae	KR 1543	-D: 4195+	T	-	5/	gr	-D	Efthalia Mari	4195+	24.21 S/ 48.55 E	
7/	dt	U 181	Lüth	KG 5878	-D 4000+	T	-	7/	br	-D	Umvuma	4419+	20.18 S/ 57.14 E	
11/	dt	U 181	Lüth	KR 2213	-D:10528+	T	-	11/	br	-D	Clan Macarthur	10528+	23. S/ 53.11 E	
17/	dt	U 197	Bartels	KQ 6676	-D: 6900+	T	-	17/	br	-M	Empire Stanley	6921+	27.08 S/ 48.15 E	
19/	dt	U 183	Schäfer	GZ 2478	-D =?	T	-	19/						3)
September 1943														
7/	jp	I-27	Fukumura	o4n/ 75e	-D =	TA	-	7/0435	am	-D	Lyman Stewart	7176=	03.30 N/ 75.00 E	4)
10/	jp	I-27	Fukumura	o8n/ 74e	-D +	T	-	9/1700	br	-M	Larchbank	5151+	07.38 N/ 74.00 E	

1) *I-10* reported the delivery of prisoners from a Norwegian ship. The *Alcides* left Abadan on July 14th for Fremantle and was scheduled to arrive there on Aug.8th. She was reported missing. The sinking was credited to a German raider, but there is no report of such an attack.
2) *U 196* attacked a north-bound convoy of three ships with four escorts. She reported one ship sunk, one left in sinking condition and burning. 3) *U 183* heard two hits without detonation after firing a 3-shot spread at a ship steaming independently on course 275°. 4) *I-27* fired five torpedoes but observed only one hit without an explosion. The gunfire attack caused only minor damage. One more attack was evaded by the *Lyman Stewart* on Sept.9th at 0400.

1	2	3	4	5	6	7	8	9	10	11	12	13	14	15
September 1943, cont.														
14/	jp	I-10	Tonozuka	06n/ 67e	-D	+	T	-	14/		nw -MT	Bramora	6361+	Pers.Gulf-Melb	1)
19/	dt	U 532	Junker	LW 62	-D: 7128+	T	-	19/		br -D	Fort Longueuil	7128+	10. S/ 68. E	
21/	dt	U 188	Lüdden	MZ 8916	-D	8000+	T	-	21/		am -D	Cornelia P.Spencer	7176+	02.08 N/ 50.10 E	
24/	jp	I-10	Tonozuka	11n/ 46e	-D	7000+	T	-	24/0320		am -D	Elias Howe	7176+	11.37 N/ 45.46 E	
28/	dt	U 188	Lüdden	MF 7826	-D	=?	T	.	28/						2)
29/	dt	U 532	Junker	LC 1224	-D	6000+	T	.	29/		nw -D	Banffshire	6479+	09.26 N/ 71.20 E	
October 1943														
1/	jp	I-10	Tonozuka	12n/ 48e	-D	+	T	-	1/		nw -D	Storviken	4836+	11.43 N/ 48.07 E	
1/	dt	U 168	Pich	MH 7743	-S	+	A	-	1/		-S		+		3)
1/	dt	U 168	Pich	MH 7743	-S	+	A	-	1/		-S		+		3)
1/	dt	U 168	Pich	MH 7743	-S	+	A	-	1/		-S		+		3)
1/	dt	U 532	Junker	LD 1760	-D	6000+	TA	-	1/1530		br -M	Tahsinia	7267+	06.51 N/ 74.38 E	
2/	dt	U 168	Pich	MH 7789	-D	4000+	T	-	2/0020		br -D	Haiching	2183+	18.46 N/ 71.55 E	
2/	dt	U 168	Pich	MH 77	-S	+	A	-	2/		-S		+		3)
2/	dt	U 168	Pich	MH 77	-S	+	A	-	2/		-S		+		3)
2/	dt	U 168	Pich	MH 77	-S	+	A	-	2/		-S		+		3)
5/	jp	I-10	Tonozuka	14n/ 51e	-T	+	T	AP.47	5/0237		nw -MT	Anna Knudsen	9057=	14.20 N/ 50.47 E	
5/	dt	U 188	Lüdden	MF 2642	-T: 9977+	T	-	5/2230		nw -MT	Britannia	9977=	24.21 N/ 58.02 E	
11/	dt	U 532	Junker	MS	-D	9000+	T	-	11/1530		in -D	Jalabala	3610+	11.40 N/ 75.19 E	
20/	dt	U 532	Junker	MS 8330	-D	6000+	T	.	20/1730		br -MT	British Purpose	5845+	11.49 N/ 74.54 E	
23/	jp	I-37	Otani	16s/ 40e	-D	+	T	-	23/0625		gr -D	Faneromeni	3404+	16.21 S/ 40.04 E	
24/	jp	I-10	Tonozuka	LN 1220	-D	+	A	-	24/		br -M	Congella	4533+	01.02 N/ 71.14 E	

1) *I-10* sank one ship at 06-10N/67-37E. Probably it was the *Bramora*, reported missing en route from the Persian Gulf to Melbourne.
2) *U 188* fired six torpedoes against a convoy and heard six detonations after 8-10min. Probably end-of-run detonations.
3) *U 188* reported six sailing freight vessels sunk by gunfire.

1	2	3	4	5	6	7	8	9	10	11	12	13	14	15
November 1943														
10/	jp	I-27	Fukumura	12n/ 43e	-D	+	T -	10/	br	-D	Sambo	7219+	12.28 N/ 43.31 E	
18/	jp	I-27	Fukumura	11n/ 47e	-D	+	T -	18/1525	br	-D	Sambridge	7219+	11.25 N/ 47.25 E	
27/	jp	I-37	Otani	03s/ 69e	-D	+	T -	27/1240	nw	-MT	Scotia	9972+	03.00 S/ 69.03 E	
29/1630	jp	I-27	Fukumura	12n/ 44e	-D	+	T -	29/1630	gr	-D	Athina Livanos	4824+	12.20 N/ 44.00 E	
December 1943														
2/	jp	I-27	Fukumura	12n/ 45e	-D	+	T -	2/	gr	-D	Nitsa	4732+	11.42 N/ 45.32 E	
3/	jp	I-27	Fukumura	11n/ 46e	-D	+	T -	3/	br	-D	Fort Camosun	7126=	11.23 N/ 46.03 E	
14/	jp	Ro-110	Ebato	16n/ 82e	-D:	4000+	T -	13/	br	-D	Daisy Moller	4087+	16.21 N/ 82.13 E	1)
23/	jp	Ro-111	Nakamura	11n/ 80e	-D:	8000+	T .	23/	br	-D	Peshawur	7934+	11.11 N/ 80.11 E	
27/	dt	U 178	Spahr	LC 2197	-D	6500+	T -	26/	am	-D	José Navarro	7244+	08.20 N/ 73.55 E	
28/	jp	I-26	Kusaka	20n/ 60e	-D	+	T -	28/	am	-D	Robert F.Hoke	7176=§	20.00 N/ 59.25 E	2)
31/	jp	I-26	Kusaka	20n/ 60e	-T	+	TA -	31/	br	-MT	Tornus	8054=	19.45 N/ 59.10 E	
January 1944														
2/	jp	I-26	Kusaka	21n/ 6/e	-D	+	T -	2/0452	am	-D	Albert Gallatin	7176+	21.21 N/ 59.58 E	
11/	dt	U 532	Junker	LO 52	-D	=?	T -	11/	br	-D	Triona	7283=	00.03 N/ 80.43 E	3)
16/0537	jp	I-165	Shimizu	12n/ 80e	-D:	10000+	T -	16/0537	br	-D	Perseus	10286+	12.00 N/ 80.14 E	
20/	dt	U 188	Lüdden	LB 2616	-D	7000+	T -	20/	br	-D	Fort Buckingham	7122+	08.19 N/ 66.40 E	
25/	dt	U 188	Lüdden	MQ 5474	-D	8422+	T -	25/	br	-D	Fort la Maune	7130+	13.04 N/ 56.30 E	
26/	dt	U 532	Junker	MS 79	-D	7500+	T -	25/2332	am	-D	Walter Camp	7176+	10.00 N/ 71.49 E	
26/vorm	dt	U 188	Lüdden	MQ 4658	-D	9000+	T -	26/	br	-D	Samouri	7219+	13.13 N/ 55.56 E	

1) Fifty-five of the 127 crew members of the *Daisy Moller* were killed by the ramming and strafing of their rafts and boats.
2) The *Robert F.Hoke* was beached with heavy damage and was a total loss after Jan.5th, 1944.
3) *U 532* observed the detonation of two torpedoes in the anti-torpedo nets. The ship was damaged.

1	2	3	4	5	6		7	8	9	10 11	12	13	14	15

January 1944, cont.

1	2	3	4	5	6		7	8	9	10 11	12	13	14	15
26/	dt	U 188	Lüdden	MQ 4565	-D: 5427+		T	-	26/1900	br -D	Surada	5427+	13.00 N/ 55.15 E	
29/	dt	U 188	Lüdden	MP 5979	-D: 5728+		T	-	29/2100	gr -D	Olga E.Embiricos	4677+	12.30 N/ 50.10 E	1)

February 1944

1	2	3	4	5	6		7	8	9	10 11	12	13	14	15
3/	dt	U 188	Lüdden	MO 4456	-D	7000+	T	-	3/	cn -D	Chung Cheng	7176+	13.00 N/ 54.20 E	
7/	dt	U 188	Lüdden	MQ 6747	-S	+	AR	-	8/	in -S		+	270m E Sokotra	2)
7/	dt	U 188	Lüdden	MQ 6747	-S	+	AR	-	8/	in -S		+	270m E Sokotra	2)
7/	dt	U 188	Lüdden	MQ 6747	-S	+	AR	-	8/	in -S		+	270m E Sokotra	2)
7/	dt	U 188	Lüdden	MQ 6747	-S	+	AR	-						2)
9/	dt	U 188	Lüdden	MQ 5868	-D	7500+	T	-	9/1800	nw -D	Viva	3798+	12.30 N/ 57.50 E	
11/	jp	Ro-110	Ebato	17n/ 83e	---------		T	JC.36	11/0219	br -D	Asphalion	6274=	17.28 N/ 83.32 E	3)
12/	jp	I-27	Fukumura	01n/ 72e	---------		T	KR.8	12/0905	br -D	Khedive Ismail	7513+	00.57 N/ 72.16 E	
12/	dt	U 188	Lüdden	LA 3613	-S	+	A	-	12/			+		2)
12/	dt	U 188	Lüdden	LA 3613	-S	+	A	-	12/			+		2)
12/	dt	U 188	Lüdden	LA 3613	-S	+	A	-	12/			+		2)
14/	*dt*	*U 168*	*Pich*	*LC 9519*	*-D*	*5000+*	*T*	*-*	*14/1620*	*br AR*	*Salviking*	*1440+*	*03.30 N/ 76.30 E*	
15/	dt	U 168	Pich	LC 8777	-D: 4385+		TA	-	15/	gr -D	Epaminondas C.Embiricos	4385+	01.30 N/ 73.　　E	
21/	dt	U 168	Pich	LM 2824	-T 10000=		T	-	21/	nw -MT	Fenris	9804=	08.32 N/ 65.35 E	
22/	dt	U 510	Eick	MP 5511	-T	8000+	T	PA.69	22/03.26	br -MT	San Alvaro	7385+	13.46 N/ 48.49 E	4)
22/	dt	U 510	Eick	MP 5511	-T	10000+	T	PA.69	22/03.28	nw -MT	Erling Brovig	9970=	13.50 N/ 48.49 E	4)
22/	dt	U 510	Eick	MP 5511	-D	7000+	T	PA.69	22/03.34	am -D	E.G.Seubert	9181+	13.50 N/ 48.49 E	4)
22/	dt	U 510	Eick	MP 5511	-D	7000+?	T	PA.69	22/03.38					4)
22/	dt	U 510	Eick	MP 5435	-D	7000=	T	PA.69						4)
22/	jp	I-37	Nakagawa	01s/ 68e -D		+	T	-	22/	br -DT	British Chivalry	7118+	00.50 S/ 68.00 E	5)

1) *U 188* reported this ship as the *Georgios M.Embiricos*. 2) *U 188* reported on Feb.7th four and on Feb.12th three sailing freight vessels sunk by 20mm gunfire and ramming. According to British sources three vessels were sunk on Feb.18th. They carried cotton. 3) The *Asphalion* was damaged and towed into port. The attacking submarine was sunk by the escort.
4) *U 510* reported in two attacks two tankers and one freighter sunk, one freighter left burning and sinking, and one freighter damaged by one torpedo. It is not clear if one ship was hit by two torpedoes.

1	2	3	4	5	6	7	8	9	10	11	12	13	14	15
February 1944														
26/	jp	I-37	Nakagawa	08s/ 70e -D		+	T	-	26/		br -M	Sutlej	5189+	08.00 S/ 70.00 E	
29/	jp	I-37	Nakagawa	05s/ 63e -D		+	TA	-	29/1205		br -D	Ascot	7005+	05.00 S/ 63.00 E	
29/	dt	U 183	Schneewind	LD 4379	-T 12000+	T		-	29/1530		br -M	Palma	5419+	05.51 N/ 79.58 E	
March 1944														
3/	jp	I-162	Doi	02n/ 77e -D		+	TA	-	3/1650		br -D	Fort McLeod	7127+	02.01 N/ 77.06 E	
7/	dt	U 510	Eick	MQ 6751	-D 6000+	T		-	7/0720		nw -M	Tarifa	7229+	12.48 N/ 58.44 E	
9/	dt	U 183	Schneewind	LN 2726	-T 5000+	T		-	9/0800		br -MT	British Loyalty	6993=§	Addu Atoll	1)
13/	jp	I-26	Kusaka	22n/ 66e -T		+	TA	-	13/1315		am -MT	H.D.Collier	8298+	21.30 N/ 66.11 E	2)
16/	jp	Ro-111	Nakamura	21n/ 90e -D:	4000+	T		HC.44	16/1000		in -D	El Madina	3962+	20.54 N/ 89.36 E	
18/	jp	I-165	Shimizu	02n/ 78e -D		+	T	-	18/0200		br -D	Nancy Moller	3916+	02.14 N/ 78.25 E	
18/	jp	I-162	Doi	S Ceylon -D		+	T	-	18/						3)
19/	dt	U 510	Eick	MR 6398	-D 7000+	T		-	19/1615		am -D	John A.Poor	7176+	13.58 N/ 70.30 E	
21/	jp	I-26	Kusaka	21n/ 60e -D		+	TA	-	21/0909		nw -MT	Grena	8117+	20.48 N/ 59.38 E	
24/	dt	U 510	Eick	MS 5864	-S	+	A	-	24/		-S		+		4)
26/	jp	I-8	Ariizumi	02s/ 78e -D		+	T	-	26/		nl -D	Tjisalak	5787+	02.30 S/ 78.40 E	5)
27/	dt	U 510	Eick	LC 6659	-D 5000+	T		-	26/		nw -Dw	Maaloy	249+	05.25 N/ 77.32 E	
27/	dt	U 532	Junker	LY 57	-D: 4734+	T		-	27/		br -M	Tulagi	2281+	11.00 S/ 78.40 E	6)

5) According to survivors' reports, the crew on rafts and in boats was machine-gunned by the submarine.
1) The *British Loyalty* was anchored off the SW entrance to the Addu Atoll and sank burning to the bottom. Later salvaged and hulked. 2) The wreck of the *H.D.Collier* sank on March 16th. 3) *I-162* reported one transport sunk south of Ceylon.
4) *U 510* sank one sailing vessel on a westerly course by gunfire.
5) Ninety-eight survivors of this attack were killed by the submarine crew.
6) *U 532* reported this ship as the Australian steamer *Age* of 4,734 GRT.

1	2	3	4	5	6	7	8	9	10 11	12	13	14	15
March 1944, cont.													
29/	jp	I-26	Kusaka	17n/ 64e	-D	+	TA	-	29/	am -D	Richard Hovey	7176+	16.40 N/ 64.30 E	1)
30/	jp	I-8	Ariizumi	12s/ 80e	-D	+	TA	-	30/	br -D	City of Adelaide	6589+	12.01 S/ 80.27 E	
April 1944													
1/	dt	U 852	Eck	GR 5699	-D	7000+	T	-	1/	br -D	Dahomian	5277+	34.25 S/ 18.19 E	
16/	jp	I-8	Ariizumi	Addu	-S	+	A	-	16/	-S		+		2)
May 1944													
June 1944													
5/	dt	U 183	Schneewind	LN 4931	-D	5000+	T	-	5/	br -D	Helen Moller	5259+	04.28 S/ 74.45 E	
16/	dt	U 198	Heusinger v.Waldegg	GR 2978	-D	5000+	T	-	16/	sa -D	Columbine	3268+	32.44 S/ 17.22 E	
19/	dt	U 181	Freiwald	LW 7346	-D:	7118+	T	-	19/1953	nl -D	Garoet	7118+	12.30 S/ 64. E	
29/	jp	I-8	Ariizumi	08s/ 75e	-D	+	T	-	29/	br -D	Nellore	6942+	07.51 S/ 75.20 E	
July 1944													
2/	jp	I-8	Ariizumi	03s/ 74e	-D	+	TA	-	2/	am -D	Jean Nicolet	7176+	03.28 S/ 74.30 E	3)
8/1200	dt	U 537	Schrewe	LD 4636	-T	7000=	T.	-	8/			-----		4)
8/1333	dt	U 537	Schrewe	LD 4636	DD	1690=	T'	-	8/			------		4)
9/	dt	U 196	Kentrat	MR	-D	6000+	T	-	9/	br -D	Shahzada	5454+	15.30 N/ 65.30 E	
15/	dt	U 198	Heusinger v.Waldegg	KP 3568	-D:	5107+	T	-	14/	br -D	Director	5107+	24.30 S/ 35.44 E	

1) The crew of the *Richard Hovey* in boats and on rafts was machine-gunned by the submarine. Some of the survivors were rescued after 16 days by British merchant ships.
2) *I-8* reported one sailing vessel sunk by gunfire off Addu Atoll. 3) Ninety-six survivors of the *Jean Nicolet* who were picked up by the submarine were wounded by running the gauntlet of the crew, and 23 of them survived when the submarine had to dive and they were rescued by an Indian warship on July 4th. The c/o responsible committed harakiri when a later command, the large submarine *I-400*, was taken over by the U.S. Navy in August 1945.

1	2	3	4	5	6	7	8	9	10	11	12	13	14	15
July 1944, cont.														
15/	dt	U 181	Freiwald	MS 5569	-D	6000+	T	-	15/2213	br	-D	Tanda	7174+	13.22 N/ 74.09 E	
19/	dt	U 198	Heusinger v.Waldegg	KP 3332	-D	groß=	T	-	19/						1)
19/	dt	U 181	Freiwald	MS 7974	-D:	5265+	T	-	19/1703	br	-D	King Frederick	5265+	09.29 N/ 71.45 E	
August 1944														
6/	dt	U 198	Heusinger v.Waldegg	KP 5839	-M:	7295+	T	-	5/	br	-M	Empire City	7295+	11.33 S/ 41.25 E	
7/	dt	U 198	Heusinger v.Waldegg	-------	---------		T	-	7/	br	-M	Empire Day	7242+	07.06 S/ 42. E	
13/	dt	U 862	Timm	KQ 2158	-D	5500+	T	-	13/	br	-D	Radbury	3614+	24.20 S/ 41.45 E	
16/	dt	U 862	Timm	KE 3277	-D	8000+	T	-	16/	br	-D	Empire Lancer	7037+	15. S/ 45. E	
18/	dt	U 862	Timm	KE 2342	-D	5500+	T	-	18/	br	-D	Nairung	5414+	15. S/ 45. E	
19/	dt	U 862	Timm	LT 8946	-D:	5900+	T	-	19/	br	-D	Wayfarer	5068+	14.30 S/ 42.20 E	
20/	dt	U 861	Oesten	JA 1215	-D	8000+	T	-	20/0038	br	-D	Berwickshire	7464+	30.58 S/ 38.50 E	
20/	dt	U 861	Oesten	JA 1125	-T	8465+	T	DN.68	20/1941	br	-MT	Daronia	8139=	31.10 S/ 38. E	
27/	dt	U 859	Jebsen	MQ 41	-T	10000+	T	.	27/						2)
28/	dt	U 859	Jebsen	MQ 1891	-D	10492+	T	-	28/	am	-D	John Barry	7176+	15.10 N/ 55.18 E	
September 1944														
1/	dt	U 859	Jebsen	MQ 6249	-D	7000+	T	-	31/	br	-D	Troilus	7422+	14.10 N/ 61.04 E	
5/	dt	U 861	Oesten	LJ 91	-D	5000+	T	-	5/	gr	-D	Ioannis Fafalios	5670+	04.20 S/ 43.57 E	
October 1944														

---

4) *U 537* heard one FAT-detonation after a run time of 8 min 2 sec and one Gnat end-of-run detonation after 6 min 45 sec.

1) *U 198* heard one detonation after a shot at a big freighter and three escorts.

2) *U 859* reported one tanker escorted by two corvettes sunk.

Indian Ocean

1	2	3	4	5	6	7	8	9	10	11	12	13	14	15
November 1944														
2/	dt	U 181	Freiwald	KU 49	-T:10000+	T	-	2/	am	-TT	Fort Lee	10198+	27.35 S/ 83.11 E	
6/	jp	Ro-113	Harada	11n/ 81e	-D: 4000+	T	-	5/	br	-D	Marion Moller	3827+	10.40 N/ 81.10 E	
December 1944														
19/	jp	Ro-113	Harada		-D	+	T	-	18/					Bengalen Gulf	1)
19/	jp	Ro-113	Harada		-D	=	T	.	18/					Bengalen Gulf	1)
January 1945														
February 1945														
6/	dt	U 862	Timm	JF 6245	-D	7176+	T	-	5/2351	am	-D	Peter Silvester	7176+	34.19 S/ 99.37 E	2)
23/	dt	U 510	Eick		-D	6000+	T	-	23/	ca	-D	Point Pleasant Park	7136+	29.42 S/ 09.58 E	3)

1) *Ro-113* reported one freighter sunk and one more damaged and listing after one torpedo hit.
2) *U 862* was on a patrol, off the SE coast of Australia.
3) *U 510* was returning to Europe and reported one ship of 6,000 GRT sunk.

March 1945 to August 1945

At the end of December 1944 the Japanese subs *Ro-113* and *Ro-114* returned from antishipping operations in the Gulf of Bengal. These were the last Japanese operations in the Indian Ocean. German U-boats did not conduct operations there after January 1945. Between December 1944 to January 1945 *U 843*, *U 510*, *U 532*, *U 861* and *U 195* began their return voyages. Of the other boats only *U 510* and *U 532* sank one or two ships, the last two in the Atlantic (see under Atlantic).

December 1941

Date		Sub	Commander	Position					Date			Ship	Tonnage	Location	
8/	jp	I-26	Yokota	34n/145w	-D	3000+	A	-	7/	am	-D	Cynthia Olson	2140+	1000m NE Hawaii	
10/	jp	I-10	Kayahara	S Hawaii	-D		+	A	-	9/	pa	-M	Donerail	4473+	08. N/152. W	
12/	jp	I-9	Fujii	N Hawaii	-D		+	TA	-	11/	am	-D	Lahaina	5645+	27.42 N/147.38 W	
15/	jp	I-4	Nakagawa	Hawaii	-D		+	T	-	14/	nw	-M	Hoegh Merchant	4858+	29m Cape Makapuu	
18/	jp	I-175	Inoue	Hawaii	-D		+	T	-	17/	am	-D	Manini	3253+	180m S Hawaii	1)
19/	jp	I-172	Togami	Hawaii	-D		+	T	-	19/	am	-D	Prusa	5113+	150m S Hawaii	
21/0731	jp	I-17	Nishino	40n/125w	-D		+	TA	-	20/	am	-DT	Emidio	6912+	40.30 N/125.00 W	
21/	jp	I-23	Shibata	37n/122w	-D		=	A	-	20/	am	-DT	Agwiworld	6771=	37. N/122. W	
23/	jp	I-19	Narahara	34n/121w	-T		=	A	-	22/	am	-DT	H.M.Storey	10763=	34.35 N/120.45 W	
24/	jp	I-17	Nishino	40n/125w	-T		=	A	-	23/	am	-DT	Larry Doheny	7038=	40. N/125. W	
24/	jp	I-21	Matsumura	35n/121w	-T		+	T	-	23/0545	am	-DT	Montebello	8272+	35.30 N/121.15 W	
24/	jp	I-21	Matsumura	35n/121w	-T		=	A	-	23/	am	-DT	Idaho	6418=	35. N/121. W	
25/0324	jp	I-19	Narahara	34n/121w	-D		=	T	-	24/	am	-D	Absaroka	5695=	California	
25/	jp	I-23	Shibata	37n/122w	-D: 2119=	A		-	24/	am	-D	Dorothy Philips	2119=	Monterey Bay	
28/	jp	I-25	Tagami	46n/124w	-T		=	T	-	27/	am	-DT	Connecticut	8684=	10m W Columbia R.	

January 1942

Date		Sub	Commander	Position					Date			Ship	Tonnage	Location	
8/	jp	I-25	Tagami		AV		+	T	-	8/						2)
11/	jp	I-6	Inada	19n/165w	CV	33000=	T	Task F.	11/	am	CV	Saratoga	33000=	500m SW Oahu	3)
23/	jp	I-172	Togami	Hawaii	-T		+	T	-	23/	am	AO	Neches	7383+	21.01 N/160.06 W	
29/	jp	I-171 ?	Kawasaki				TA	-	28/	am	-D	Royal T.Frank	244+	2m W Maui	4)

1) The Japanese fleet submarines *I-53* to *I-75* were renumbered in May 1942 to *I-153* to *I-175*. To avoid confusion these numbers are used in this list from the beginning. When numbers *I-53ff* are used, they designate the large submarines built during the war.
2) *I-25* reported an American seaplane-carrier sunk between Johnston and Marshall Islands by a 4-torpedo spread.
3) *I-6* assumed to have sunk the carrier *Lexington* at a position bearing 60° 270 miles from Johnston Island.
4) There is no report about the sinking of this small U.S. Army transport; possibly this ship was sunk by *I-171*.

1	2	3	4	5	6	7	8	9	10	11	12	13	14	15
February 1942														
13/	jp	I-25	Tagami	05s/166e	-D	+	T	–	13/	br	-D	Derrymore	4799+	05.18 S/166.20 E	
March 1942														
1/	jp	I-17	Nishino	37n/123w	-T 10000+	TA	–		28/2215	am	-DT	William H.Berg	-----	37.25 N/123.28 W	1)
May 1942														
5/	jp	I-21	Matsumura	22s/164e	-D	+	T	–	5/	am	-D	John Adams	7180+	22.30 S/164.35 E	
6/	jp	I-21	Matsumura	23s/166e	-D	+	TA	–	6/	gr	-D	Chloe	4641+	22.59 S/166.29 E	
16/	jp	I-29	Izu		-D	=	A	–	16/2034	sj	-D	Uélen	5135=	50m SE Newcastle	
31/	*jp*	*I-24*	*Hanabusa*	*Sydney*	*BB 30600=*	*KU*	–		*31/2325*	*au*	*-Bg*	*Kuttabul*	+	*Garden I.,Sydney*	*2)*
June 1942														
3/2009	jp	I-24	Hanabusa	E Sydney	-D	=	A	–	3/2110	au	-D	Age	-----	E Sydney	3)
3/2138	jp	I-24	Hanabusa	E Sydney	-D	+	T	–	3/2242	au	-D	Iron Chieftain	4812+	33.55 S/151.50 E	
4/	jp	I-27	Yoshimura	39s/151e	-D	=	TA	–	4/	au	-D	Barwon	4239=	45m SE Gabo I.	4)
4/	jp	I-27	Yoshimura	38s/149e	-D	+	T	–	4/	au	-D	Iron Crown	3353+	38.17 S/149.44 E	
7/1331	*jp*	*I-168*	*Tanabe*	*31n/176w DD*		+	*T*	*Task F.*	*7/*	*am*	*DD*	*Hammann*	*1570+*	*30.36 N/176.34 W*	*5)*
7/1331	*jp*	*I-168*	*Tanabe*	*31n/176w CV*	*19000+*		*T*	*Task F.*	*7/*	*am*	*CV*	*Yorktown*	*19000+*	*30.36 N/176.34 W*	*5)*
7/	jp	I-26	Yokota	48n/126w	-D	+	TA	–	7/	am	-D	Coast Trader	3286+	48.15 N/125.40 W	
9/	jp	I-24	Hanabusa	S Sydney	-D	=	A	–	9/0050	br	-M	Orestes	7748=	SE Jervis Bay	
12/	jp	I-21	Matsumura	34s/152e	-D	+	T	CO.2 s	11/0115	pa	-D	Guatemala	5527+	33.40 S/152.04 E	
20/	jp	I-25	Tagami	47n/125w	-D	+	T	–	20/	br	-D	Fort Camosun	7126=	47.22 N/125.30 W	

1) The tanker *Wm.H.Berg* was attacked by gunfire but escaped undamaged. The submarine was forced to dive by the destroyer USS *King*. A Japanese account stating that *I-16* attacked a tanker of 7,000 GRT on March 2nd off Cape Mendocino, must have been in error.

2) Two of the midgets launched by *I-22*, *I-24* and *I-27* reached the harbor at Sydney. They attacked the U.S. cruiser *Chicago*, reported as the battleship HMS *Warspite*, but the torpedoes detonated against the quay and damaged an accommodation-hulk, which was a total loss.

3) The *Age* escaped the gunfire attack undamaged. 4) The *Barwon* was only slightly damaged by the torpedo hit.

1	2	3	4	5	6	7	8	9	10	11	12	13	14	15
July 1942														
15/	jp	I-7	Koizumi	54n/158w	-D	+	AT -	15/	am	-D	Arcata	2722+	53.41 N/157.45 W	
20/	jp	I-11	Hichiji	Sydney	-D	+	T -	20/2300	gr	-D	G.S.Livanos	4835+	35.00 S/151.00 E	1)
21/	jp	I-11	Hichiji	Sydney	-D	+	T -	21/0200	am	-D	Coast Farmer	3290+	35.23 S/151.00 E	1)
22/	jp	I-24	Hanabusa	Sydney	-D	+	T -	22/0530	am	-D	William Dawes	7176+	35.45 S/150.20 E	1)
23/	jp	I-174	Kusaka	Sydney	-D	=	T -	23/0515	au	-D	Allara	3279=	33.03 S/152.22 E	1)
24/	jp	I-175	Uno	Sydney	-D	=	T -	24/0745	au	-D	Murada	-----	Crowdy Island	1)
25/	jp	I-169	Watanabe	Noumea	-D	+	T -	25/	nl	-M	Tjinegara	9227+	23.10 S/165.00 E	
26/	jp	I-11	Hichiji	Sydney	-D	=	A -	26/0445	au	-D	Coolana	-----	60m NE Gabo I.	1)
28/	jp	I-175	Uno	NE Sydney	-D	+	T -	28/	fr	-D	Cagou	2795+	NE Sydney	1)
August 1942														
3/	jp	I-175	Uno	Sydney	-D	+	A -	2/0045	au	-Df	Dureenbee	233+	35.55 S/150.33 E	1)
4/	jp	Ro-34	Morinaga		-D	+	A -	4/	au	-D	Katoomba	9424=	300m ESE Albany	
6/	jp	Ro-33	Kuriyama		-D	+	A -	6/1034	br	-M	Mamutu	300+	09.11 S/144.12 E	
29/	jp	Ro-33	Kuriyama		-D	+	T -	29/	au	-M	Malaita	3310=	09.50 S/142.55 E	
_30/_	_jp_	_Ro-61_	_Tokutomi_	_Adak_	_CA_	_9100=_	_T -_	_30/_	_am_	_AVP_	_Casco_	_1695=_	_Nazan Bay, Atka_	_2)_
_31/_	_jp_	_I-26_	_Yokota_	_10s/164e_	_CV_	_33000=_	_T Task F._	_31/_	_am_	_CV_	_Saratoga_	_33000=_	_10.34 S/164.18 E_	
September 1942														
_15/_	_jp_	_I-19_	_Kinashi_	_12s/164e_	_CV_	_14700+_	_T Task F._	_15/1445_	_am_	_CV_	_Wasp_	_14700+_	_12.25 S/164.08 E_	_3)_
_15/_	_jp_	_I-19_	_Kinashi_	_12s/164e_		_+_	_T Task F._	_15/1452_	_am_	_BB_	_North Carolina_	_35000=_	_12. S/164. E_	_3)_
_15/_	_jp_	_I-19_	_Kinashi_	_12s/164e_		_/_	_T Task F._	_15/1454_	_am_	_DD_	_O'Brien_	_1570=$_	_12. S/164. E_	_3)_

5) The Yorktown was damaged by three bomb and two torpedo hits from planes of the Japanese carrier Hiryu on June 4th. When I-168 attacked, the destroyer Hammann was alongside. One torpedo hit the destroyer, two hit the carrier. The D/C's of the sinking Hammann exploded and damaged the carrier, which sank on June 7th. 1) Of the Japanese submarines off Sydney I-11 reported three ships sunk and one damaged, I-175 two sunk and one damaged. In addition there were attacks by I-24 and I 174. These are the most probable assessments from Japanese and Australian sources. The Murada and Coolana escaped undamaged. 2) Ro-61 reported one cruiser of the Northampton class sunk. The Casco was beached and later salvaged and repaired. 3) I-19 fired a 4-torpedo spread against the Wasp Task Group. Two of the long-range-torpedoes sank the Wasp, the two missing shots hitting the O'Brien and North Carolina in a more distant task group. The N.C. was not heavily damaged. The O'B was repaired temporarily in Samoa, but sank on Oct.19th during transfer to the U.S.

1	2	3	4	5	6	7	8	9	10	11	12	13	14	15
September 1942, cont.														
29/	jp	I-4	Kawasaki	11s/161e -D		+	T	-	29/		am AK	Alhena	7440=	10.47 S/161.16 E	
October 1942														
4/	jp	I-25	Tagami	44n/125w -D		+	T	-	4/		am -DT	Camden	6653+	43.43 N/124.54 W	
6/	jp	I-25	Tagami	41n/125w -D		+	T	-	6/		am -DT	Larry Doheny	7038+	41.30 N/125.22 W	
11/	jp	I-25	Tagami	46n/139w SS		+	T	-	11/1115 sj SS			L-16	1039+	46.41 N/138.56 E	1)
20/	jp	I-176	Tanabe	13s/163e BB		=	T	Task F.	20/		am CA	Chester	9200=	13.31 S/163.17 E	2)
27/0126	jp	I-24	Hanabusa	15s/159w BB		/	T	Task F.	27/				------	15.05 S/159.45 W	3)
27/0338	jp	I-21	Matsumura	15s/160w BB 32500+		T	Task F.	27/		am BB	Washington	------	15.30 S/160.22 W	3	
November 1942														
7/	jp	I-20	Yoshimura	Lunga Pt -D		+	KU	-	7/		am -D	Majaba	2227=	Lunga Point	
9/	jp	I-21	Matsumura	Nouméa -D		+	T	-	9/		am -D	Edgar Allen Poe	7176=	56m SE Amedée Pt.	
13/	jp	I-26	Yokota	10s/164e CA		+	T	Task F.	13/1101		am CL	Juneau	6000+	10.34 S/164.04 E	5)
														6)
15/	jp	I-16	Yamada	Lunga Pt DD		+	KU	-	15/				------		6)
15/	jp	I-20	Yoshimura	Lunga Pt -D		+	KU	-	15/				-----		
29/	jp	I-16	Yamada	Lunga Pt -D		+	KU	-	29/		am AK	Alchiba	6198=	Lunga Point	7)
29/	jp	I-20	Yoshimura	Lunga Pt DD		+	KU	-	29/				------		7)
December 1942														

1) The two Soviet submarines L-15 and L-16 were transiting from Dutch Harbor to San Francisco. I-25 assumed the submarines were U.S.
2) I 176 attacked a task group containing the battleship Washington and assumed a hit on her.
3) The detonations I-24 heard were depth charges. I-21 assumed to have hit a battleship of the Colorado class, but the torpedo detonated 350 yds from the battleship Washington, which was not the target but was reported attacked by I-15 (Ishikawa). On Sept.15th I-15 attacked the task group containing the battleship North Carolina, but its torpedoes missed. The hits came from an attack of I-19 some minutes earlier. 4) The Majaba was beached and was later salvaged and repaired.

1	2	3	4	5	6	7	8	9	10	11	12	13	14	15
January 1943														
18/	jp	I-21	Matsumura	Sydney	-D	+	T	-	18/0100	au	-D	Kalingo	2051+	34.07 S/153.15 E	
18/	jp	I-21	Matsumura	Sydney	-D	+	T	-	18/2250	am	-DT	Mobilube	10222=§	33.56 S/152.09 E	1)
22/	jp	I-21	Matsumura	Sydney	-D	+	T	-	22/2155	am	-D	Peter H.Burnett	7176=§	32.54 S/159.32 E	1)
/	jp	I-21	Matsumura	Sydney	-D	+	T	-	/						1)
29/	jp	I-10	Yamada	Nouméa	-D	+	T	-	29/	am	-D	Samuel Gompers	7176+	24.21 S/166.12 E	
February 1943														
8/	jp	I-21	Matsumura	Sydney	-D	+	T	OC.68	8/0225	br	-D	Iron Knight	4812+	30.51 S/150.38 E	
10/	jp	I-21	Matsumura	Sydney	-D	+	T	-	9/0948	am	-D	Starr King	7176+	34.15 S/154.20 E	1)
March 1943														
1/	jp	I-10	Yamada	N.Hebr.	-T	+	T	-	1/	am	-DT	Gulfwave	7141=	20.30 S/174.45 E	
April 1943														
11/	jp	I-26	Yokota	37s/150e	-D	+	T	OC.86	11/1400	jg	-D	Recina	4732+	37.24 S/150.19 E	
24/	jp	I-26	Yokota	24s/153e	-D	+	T	BT.54	24/1900	au	-D	Kowarra	2125+	24.26 S/153.44 E	
25/	jp	I-177	Nakagawa	29s/153e	-D	+	T	GP.48	26/0104	br	-M	Limerick	8724+	28.54 S/153.54 E	
27/	jp	I-178	Utsuki	33s/153e	-D	+	T	-	27/0655	am	-D	Lydia M.Childs	7176+	33.08 S/153.24 E	
29/	jp	I-180	Kusaka	31s/153e	-D	+	T	-	29/1036	au	-D	Wollongbar	2239+	31.17 S/153.07 E	
30/	jp	I-19	Kinashi	Fiji-Ins	-D	+	T	-	30/	am	-D	Phoebe A.Hearst	7176+	20.07 S/177.35 W	

5) The *Juneau* was damaged during battle off Guadalcanal the night of Nov.13th and was retiring to the south. *I-26* missed the damaged cruiser *San Francisco* with a spread, but hit the *Juneau* which sank.

6) The Japanese submarines *I-16*, *I-20* and *I-24* launched midgets. Only one returned. The sinking of one destroyer and one transport was assumed.

7) The Japanese submarine *I-16* and possibly also *I-20* launched midgets. The sinking of one transport and one destroyer was assumed. The transport *Alchiba* was damaged and beached, but later salvaged and returned to service on April 14th, 1943.

1) *I-21* reported during this patrol the sinking of six ships. The *Mobilube* and *P.H.Burnett* were towed into port, but were total losses. The *Starr King* sank on Feb.10th.

1	2	3	4	5	6	7	8	9	10	11	12	13	14	15
May 1943														
2/	jp	I-19	Kinashi	Fiji-Ins	-D	+	T	-	2/	am	-D	William Williams	7181=	20.09 S/178.04 W	
5/	jp	I-180	Kusaka	Coffs Hb.	-D	+	T	.	5/1345	nw	-D	Fingal	2137+	30.35 S/153.29 E	
12/	jp	I-180	Kusaka	Coffs Hb	-D	+	T	PG.50	12/1412	au	-D	Ormiston	5832=	30.16 S/153.23 E	
12/	jp	I-180	Kusaka	Coffs Hb	-D	+	T	PG.50	12/1412	au	-D	Caradale	1881=	WNW Coffs Harbor	1)
13/	*jp*	*I-31*	*Inoue*	*Attu*	*BB*	*=*	*T*	*Task F.*	*13/*	*am*	*BB*	*Pennsylvania*	*------*	*Horotu/Attu*	*2)*
14/	*jp*	*I-31*	*Inoue*	*Attu*	*BB*	*+*	*T*	*Task F.*	*14/*	*am*	*BB*	*Pennsylvania*	*------*	*Attu*	*2)*
14/	jp	I-177	Nakagawa	27s/154e	-D	+	T	-	14/0410	br	AH	Centaur	3222+	27.17 S/154.05 E	3)
16/	*jp*	*I-35*	*Yamamoto*	*N Attu*	*CL*	*+*	*T*	*Task F.*	*16/1031*	*am*	*CL*	*Santa Fé*	*------*	*53.06 N/172.19 E*	*4)*
16/	jp	I-19	Kinashi	19s/175e	-D	+	T	-	16/	am	-D	William K.Vanderbilt	7181+	18.41 S/175.07 E	
17/	jp	I-25	Tagami	17s/173e	-T	+	T	-	17/	am	-DT	H.M.Storey	10763+	17.20 S/173.30 E	
23/	jp	I-17	Harada	Noumea	-T 15000+		T	-	23/	pa	-DT	Stanvac Manila	10169+	23.45 S/166.30 E	
23/	*jp*	*I-17*	*Harada*	*--------*	*---------*		*"*	*-*	*23/*	*am*	*PT*	*PT 165*	*38+*	*alongside Stanv.M.*	
23/	*jp*	*I-17*	*Harada*	*--------*	*---------*		*"*	*-*	*23/*	*am*	*PT*	*PT 173*	*38+*	*alongside Stanv.M.*	
June 1943														
4/	jp	I-174	Nanbu	Brisbane	-M	=	A	-	4/	am	-M	Edward Chambers	-----	20m E C.Moreton	5)
16/	jp	I-174	Nanbu	Coffs-H	-D	5551+	T	GP.55	16/	am	-D	Portmar	5551+	60m SE Coff's Hb.	
16/	*jp*	*I-174*	*Nanbu*	*Coffs-H*	*-D*	*+*	*T*	*GP.55*	*16/*	*am*	*LS*	*LST 469*	*1625=*	*60m SE Coff's Hb.*	
23/	jp	Ro-103	Ichimura	11s/162e	-D	+	T	.	23/	am	AK	Aludra	7440+	11.26 S/162.00 E	
23/	jp	Ro-103	Ichimura	11s/162e	-D	+	T	.	23/	am	AK	Deimos	7440+	11.26 S/162.00 E	
July 1943														
18/	*jp*	*Ro-106*	*Nakamura*	*Salomon.*	*-T*	*+*	*T*	*-*	*18/*	*am*	*LS*	*LST 342*	*1625+*	*09.03 S/158.11 E*	
20/	*jp*	*I-11*	*Tagami*	*15s/163e*	*CL*	*+*	*T*	*Task F.*	*20/*	*au*	*CL*	*Hobart*	*6890=*	*15.07 S/163.34 E*	

1) The *Caradale* was lightly damaged by a dud torpedo. 2) On May 13th *I-31* reported two hits on a battleship, and on May 14th, reported one more battleship heavily damaged and possibly sunk. The *Pennsylvania* recorded both attacks.
3) The *Centaur* was marked as hospital ship and lighted. Two hundred sixty-eight were killed. 4) *I-35* reported one cruiser sunk.
5) The *Edward Chambers* evaded 9 rounds of 12cm and escaped undamaged.

1	2	3	4	5	6	7	8	9	10	11	12	13	14	15
August 1943														
11/	jp	I-11	Tagami	Nouméa	-D	+	T	-	11/		am -D	Matthew Lyon	7176=	22.30 S/166.30 E	
13/	jp	I-19	Kinashi	Fiji	-D	+	T	-	13/		am -D	M.H.de Young	7176=§	21.50 S/175.10 E	1)
31/	jp	I-20	Otsuka	N.Hebr.	-T	+	T	-	31/		am -DT	W.S.Rheem	10872=	15.51 S/167.02 E	
September 1943														
11/	jp	I-39	Tanaka	N.Hebr.	CL	6890+	T	-	11/		am -Dt	Navajo	1280+	E New Hebrides	2)
October 1943														
3/	jp	Ro-108	Arai	Huon-B.	DD	+	T	Task F.	3/0819	am DD	Henley	1500+	07.40 S/148.06 E	3)
3/	jp	Ro-108	Arai	Huon-B.	DD	+	T	Task F.	3/0819	am DD	Reid, Smith	------	07.40 S/148.06 E	3)
November 1943														
1/	jp	I-2	Itakura	Amchitka	-D	+	T	-	1/						4)
11/	jp	I-21	Inada	22s/178w	-D	+	T	-	11/		am -D	Cape San Juan	6711+	22.08 S/178.06 W	
16/	jp	I-176	Yamaguchi	S Truk	SS	+	T	-	16/		am SS	Corvina	1525+	S Truk	
24/	jp	I-175	Tabata	Gilbert	CV	+	T	Task F.	24/		am CVE	Liscome Bay	7800+	02.54 N/172.30 E	
December 1943														
January 1944														
14/	jp	Ro-42	Wada	S Noumea	-D	+	T	-	14/		am YP	YO 159	+	15.27 S/171.28 E	
23/	jp	Ro-37	Sato	Salomon.	-T	+	T	-	23/		am AO	Cache	12000=	12.08 S/164.33 E	
February 1944														
1/	jp	Ro-39	Tachigami	Wotje	CA	+	T	Task F.	1/						5)

1) The *M.H.De Young* was damaged and towed into port but was a total loss. 2) *I-39* reported a cruiser of the *Achilles* class sunk.
3) *Ro-108* reported two of three destroyers sunk. The destroyers *Reid* and *Smith* reported several torpedo wakes.
4) *I-2* reported one transport sunk. 5) *Ro-39* reported one heavy cruiser sunk.

Pacific Ocean

1	2	3	4	5	6	7	8	9	10 11 12	13	14	15
March 1944												
April 1944												
28/	jp	I-36	Teramoto	12n/178w	CV	+	T	Task F.	28/	-----		1)
May 1944												
June 1944												
16/	jp	Ro-114	Ata	Guam	BB 45000+		T	Task F.	16/	-----		2)
19/	jp	I-185	Arai	E Saipan	CV ?	+	T	Task F.	19/	-----		3)
19/	jp	Ro-115	Koreeda	50m W Rota	CV 14700+		T	Task F.	19/	-----	50m W Rota	4)
30/	jp	I-6	Fumon	E Saipan	CV	+?	T	Task F.	30/	-----	20m E Saipan	5)
July 1944												
2/	jp	I-38	Shimose	E Saipan	?	+	T	Task F.	2/	-----	E Saipan	6)
2/	jp	I-10	Nakajima	E Saipan	?	+	T	Task F.	2/	-----	70m NE Saipan	7)
August 1944												
14/	jp	I-165 (?)	Ono					14/	au PC ML 430	150+	off Biak	7a)
October 1944												
2/	jp	I-177	Watanabe	Peleliu	DD	+	T	Task F.	2/	-----		8)
2/	jp	I-177	Watanabe	Peleliu	DD	+	T	Task F.	2/	-----		8)
3/	jp	Ro-41	Shiizuka	Morotai	CV	+	T	Task F.	3/0807 am DE Shelton	1350+	02.32 N/129.13 E	9)
3/	jp	Ro-41	Shiizuka	Morotai	CV	=	T	Task F.		-----		9)

1) I-36 reported one carrier sunk. 2) Ro-114 reported attacking one battleship of the *Iowa* class which exploded after being torpedoed. 3) I-185 reported one success against a carrier force. 4) Ro-115 reported one carrier of the *Wasp* class sunk. 5) I-6 reported one carrier probably sunk. 6) I-38 reported one success against a task force. 7) I-10 reported one warship sunk. 7a) The ML was sunk by an underwater detonation; I-165 may have been in the area. 8) Coast watchers on Peleliu reported the torpedoing and sinking of two destroyers, which were credited by the CinC 6th fleet to I-177 and Ro-47, but the latter was already sunk at the time.

1	2	3	4	5	6	7	8	9	10	11	12	13	14	15
October 1944, cont.														
24/AM	jp	I-56	Morinaga	E Leyte	-D	+	T	.	24/	am	LS	LST 695	1653=	08.31 N/128.34 E	1)
25/	jp	I-56	Morinaga	E Leyte	CV	+	T	Task F.	25/	am	CVE	Santee	12000=	09.45 N/126.42 E	2)
25/	jp	I-56	Morinaga	E Leyte	DD	+	T	Task F.	25/				-----		2)
27/	jp	I-56	Morinaga	E Leyte	-D	+	T	.	27/				-----		3)
27/	jp	I-56	Morinaga	E Leyte	-D	+	T	.	27/				-----		3)
27/	jp	I-56	Morinaga	E Leyte	-D	+	T	.	27/				-----		3)
28/	jp	I-45	Kawashima	-------	---------		T	Task F.	28/	am	DE	Eversole	1350+	10.10 N/127.28 E	
30/	jp	I-12	Kudo	27n/142w	-D	+	T	-	30/	am	-D	John A.Johnson	7176+	29.55 N/141.25 W	4)
30/	jp	I-12	Kudo	27n/142w	-D	+	T	-	30/				-----		4)
(31/	jp	(I-26)	Nishiuchi	E Leyte	CL	+	T	Task F.	31/				------		5)
November 1944														
3/	jp	I-41	Kondo	E Luzon	CV	+	T	Task F.	3/	am	CL	Reno	6000=	13.46 N/131.27 E	6)
20/0415	jp	I-47	Orita/Nishina	Ulithi	CV	+	KT	-	20/0547	am	AO	Mississinewa	11316+	10.06 N/139.43 E	7)
20/0425	jp	I-47	" /Fukuda	Ulithi	CV	+	KT	-	20/				-----		7)
20/0440	jp	I-47	" /Sato	Ulithi	BB	+	KT	-	20/	am	CL	Mobile	-----	Ulithi-Atoll	7)
20/0510	jp	I-47	" /Watanabe	Ulithi	BB	+	KT	-	20/	am	CL	Biloxi	-----	Ulithi Atoll	7)
20/0454	jp	I-36	Teramoto/ Imanishi	Ulithi	CV	+	KT	-	20/				-----		7)
25/	jp	Ro-50	Kimura	E Luzon	CV	+	T	Task F.	25/				-----	150m NE Lamon Bay	8)
25/	jp	Ro-50	Kimura	E Luzon	DD	+	T	Task F.	25/				-----	150m NE Lamon Bay	8)

1) *I-56* reported one transport sunk by a 3-shot spread during the early morning of Oct.24th. One torpedo may have hit *LST 695* (?).
2) *I-56* fired five torpedoes and heard three detonations, two on a carrier, one on a destroyer. The *Santee* had already been hit by a kamikaze.
3) *I-56* reported three transports in a convoy sunk. There are also some reports of a transport sunk by *I-41* (?). 4) The assumption of two sunk transports came from Japanese radio intelligence. Only the *John A.Johnson* was sunk, and her lifeboats and survivors were machine-gunned by the submarine.
5) According to air-recce-reports one success of *I-26* was credited, but this submarine was already sunk.
6) *I-41* reported the sinking of one carrier of the *Essex* class. In reality the cruiser *Reno* was hit and damaged.
7) The successes of the Kaitens were only assumptions by the Japanese staff. There was no possibility of confirmation.
8) *Ro-50* reported one carrier and one destroyer sunk. The U.S. task group was attacked at the same time by kamikazes which hit four carriers. There were no ships damaged by underwater hits.

1	2	3	4	5	6	7	8	9	10	11	12	13	14	15
December 1944														
8/	jp	*Ha-..*		*Ormoc*	DD	+	T	*8/*				——		*2)*
9/	dt	U 862	Timm	37s/139e	-D	=?	A -	9/1210	gn	-D	*Ilissos*	4724=?	37.11 S/139.35 E	*3)*
18/	jp	*Ha-..*		*Ormoc*	-D	+	T .	*18/*						*4)*
18/	jp	*Ha-..*		*Ormoc*	-D	+	T .	*18/*						*4)*
24/	dt	U 862	Timm	VD 8222	-D	7176+	T -	25/0218	am	-D	Robert J.Walker	7180+	36.45 S/150.43 E	
January 1945														
3/	jp	*Ha-..*		*Mindanao*	DD	+	T .	*3/*				-----		*5)*
3/	jp	*Ha-..*		*-See*	-D	+	T .	*3/*				-----		*5)*
3/	jp	*Ha-..*		"	-D	+	T .	*3/*				-----		*5)*
5/	jp	*Ha-..*			DD	+	T .	*5/*				——		*5)*
5/	jp	*Ha-..*			CVS ?	+	T .	*5/*				——		*5)*
5/	jp	*Ha-..*			CL	+	T .	*5/*	am	CL	*Boise*	——		*5)*
10/	jp			Lingayen			T .	10/	am	AP	War Hawk	7907=	Lingayen Gulf	*6)*
11/	jp	*I-36*	*Teramoto*	*Ulithi*	BB	+	*KT* -	*11/*	am	AE	Mazama	-----	Ulithi Atoll	*7)*
11/	jp	*I-36*	*Teramoto*	*Ulithi*	BB ?	+	*KT* -	*11/*	am	LC	*LCI 600*	——	*Ulithi Atoll*	*7)*
11/	jp	*I-36*	*Teramoto*	*Ulithi*	CV ?	+	*KT* -	*11/*				——	*Ulithi Atoll*	*7)*
11/	jp	I-36	Teramoto	Ulithi	AO	+	KT -	11/				-----	Ulithi Atoll	*7)*
12/	jp	*I-47*	*Orita*	*Hollandia* AK ?		+	*KT* -	*12/0610*	am	-D	Pontus H.Ross	-----	01.33 S/140.46 E	*8)*
12/	jp	I-47	Orita	Hollandia AK ?		+	KT -	12/0615	am	-D	Pontus H.Ross	-----	01.33 S/140.46 E	*8)*
12/	jp	I-47	Orita	Hollandia AK ?		+	KT -	12/0655	am	-D	Pontus H.Ross	-----	01.33 S/140.46 E	*8)*
12/	jp	I-47	Orita	Hollandia AK ?		+	KT -	12/				-----	Humboldt Bay	*8)*

2) Between December 1944 to March 20th, 1945 Japanese midget submarines from Cebu reported a total of two cruisers, one seaplane carrier, five destroyers and five transports sunk. The other successes might have been reported by other midgets from other bases.

3) The *Ilissos* was attacked by a submarine with gunfire. Only *U 862* was in the area.

4) On Dec.18th one midget submarine reported two transports sunk (Cebu boats). 5) Cebu midgets reported one destroyer and two transports sunk. On Jan.5th they reported one destroyer and one other warship (CVS?) sunk. One of the missing midgets was credited with a cruiser sunk. This boat was sunk after missing the cruiser *Boise* with a torpedo.

1	2	3	4	5	6		7	8	9	10	11	12	13	14	15

January 1945, cont.

1	2	3	4	5	6		7	8	9	10	11	12	13	14	15
12/	jp	I-53	Toyomasu	Palau	AK	?	+	KT	−	12/				-----	Kossol Passage	9)
12/	jp	I-53	Toyomasu	Palau	AK	?	+	KT	−	12/				-----	Kossol Passage	9)
12/	jp	*I-58*	*Hashimoto*	*Guam*	*CVE*	?	+	*KT*	−	12/				——	*10m v LT Guam*	10)
12/	jp	*I-58*	*Hashimoto*	*Guam*	*CL*	?	+	*KT*	−	12/				——	*Guam*	10)
12/	jp	I-58	Hashimoto	Guam	AK	?	+	KT	−	12/				-----	Guam	10)
12/	jp	I-58	Hashimoto	Guam	AK	?	+	KT	−	12/				-----	Guam	10)
12/	jp	*Ro-49*	*Sugayoshi*	*Lingayen*	BB	33000+	+	*T*	*Task F.*	12/				——	*Lingayen-Gulf*	11)
20/	jp	*(I-48)*	*Toyama*	*Ulithi*	*CV*		+	*KT*	−	——				——		12)
20/	jp	*(I-48)*	*Toyama*	*Ulithi*	*CV*		+	*KT*	−	——				——		12)
20/	jp	*(I-48)*	*Toyama*	*Ulithi*	*AK*	?	+	*KT*	−	——				——		12)
20/	jp	*(I-48)*	*Toyama*	*Ulithi*	*AO*	?	+	*KT*	−	——				——		12)
24/	jp	*Ha-..*		*Mindoro*	*DD*	?	+	*T*	.	24/				——	*Mindoro-Strait*	13)
25/	jp	Ha-..		Mindoro	-D		+	T	−	25/				-----	Mindoro-Strait	13)
25/	jp	Ha-..		Mindoro	-D		+	T	.	25/				-----	Mindoro-Strait	13)
29/	jp	Ro-46	Tokunaga	W Iba	-T		+	T	.	29/				-----		14)
29/	jp	Ro-46	Tokunaga	W Iba	-D		+	T	.	29/	am	AP	Cavalier	7800=	14.48 N/119.18 E	14)
29/	jp	Ro-46	Tokunaga	W Iba	-D		+	T	.	29/				-----		14)

February 1945

1	2	3	4	5	6		7	8	9	10	11	12	13	14	15
1/	jp	Ro-50	Kimura	E Leyte	-D		+	T	.	1/				-----	SE Surigao-Strait	1)
10/	jp	*Ro-50*	*Kimura*	*E Leyte*	*-D*		+	*T*	.	11/	*am*	*LS*	*LST 577*	1653+	*08.01 N/130.37 E*	2)

6) The *War Hawk* was temporarily beached after a midget submarine attack but was later salvaged and repaired. 7) *I-36* launched four kaitens. One detonated a few yards from the munitions ship *Mazama*, the second near the *LCI-600*. *I-36* heard the detonations and was credited with four successes. 8) *I-47* launched four Kaitens. Three of them in succession detonated near the steamer *P.H.Ross*. *I-47* heard the detonations, observed smoke columns, and intercepted a SSS-warning. It was credited with four successes.

9) *I-53* heard the detonation of two Kaitens in the Kossol Passage.

10) *I-58* had to dive and could observe nothing. Nevertheless she was credited with four successes.

11) *Ro-49* reported the sinking of a battleship of the *Idaho* class. 12) According to an air-recce-report on the wreck of the *Mississinewa* (p.286), *I-48* was credited with four successes. But this submarine was sunk before launching the Kaitens.

13) Midget submarines reported one warship and two transports sunk in the Mindoro Strait.

1	2	3	4	5	6	7	8	9	10	11	12	13	14	15
February 1945														
/	jp	Ha-..		v.Cebu	DD	+	T	.		/				3)
/	jp	Ha-..		v.Cebu	-D	+	T	.		/				3)
17/	jp	Ro-109	Masuzawa	Lingayen	CV	+	T	Task F.	17/			-----	60m W Lingayen	4)
17/	jp	Ro-109	Masuzawa	Lingayen	CL	+	T	Task F.	17/			-----	60m W Lingayen	4)
17/	jp	Ro-109	Masuzawa	Lingayen	DD	+	T	Task F.	17/			-----	60m W Lingayen	4)
21/	jp	Ro-43	Tsukigata		DD	+	T	Task F.	21/	am DD	Renshaw	2050=	24.36 N/141.48 E	
March 1945														
/	jp	Ha-..		v.Cebu	-D	+	T	.		/				5)
/	jp	Ha-..		v.Cebu	-D	+	T	.		/				5)
/	jp	Ha-..		v.Cebu	-D	+	T	.		/				5)
26/	jp	Ro-49 ?	Go	-------	---------		T	TG.54.3	26/0940	am CA	Wichita	------	near Kerama Retto	6)
26/	jp	Ro-49 ?	Go	-------	---------		T	TG.54.3	26/0940	am CL	St.Louis	------	Okinawa	6)
27/	jp	Ro-56 ?	Nagamatsu	-------	---------		T	TG.54.4	27/	am CA	Pensacola	------	near Kerama Retto	6)
April 1945														
/	jp	(I-44)	Masuzawa	Okinawa	?	+	KT			/		-------		7)
/	jp	(I-56)	Masada	Okinawa	?	+	KT			/		-------		7)
27/	jp	I-38	Sugamasa	zwisch.	DD	+	KT	SON.2	27/	am APD	Ringness	-----	24.03 N/132.39 E	8)
27/	jp	I-36	Sugamasa	Saipan	-D	+	KT	SON.2	27/			-----		8)
27/	jp	I-36	Sugamasa	und	-D	+	KT	SON.2	27/			-----		8)
27/	jp	I-36	Sugamasa	Okinawa	-D	+	KT	SON.2	27/			-----		8)

1) *Ro-50* reported one transport sunk on Feb.1st and 2) one more on Feb.10th. This one may have been *LST 577*.
3) During February midget submarines reported one destroyer and one transport sunk.
4) *Ro-109* reported an attack against a carrier force west of the Lingayen Gulf with one carrier, one cruiser and one destroyer sunk. 5) During March 1945 midget submarines from Cebu reported three transports sunk. Exact dates are unknown.
6) Three U.S. cruisers reported torpedo wakes. They must have been attacks by *Ro-49* and *Ro-56*, which did not return and report. *I-8* last reported on March 28th, but gave no success report. 7) *I-44* and *I-56* were lost before they could launch their Kaitens. The Japanese staff assumed successes. 8) *I-38* launched four Kaitens against a convoy and 10 min later heard four detonations. APD *Ringness*, escorting a convoy of landing vessels, observed two Kaitens, one of which was sunk and the other detonated. The other detonations probably were depth charges.

1	2	3	4	5	6		7	8	9	10	11	12	13	14	15

May 1945

1	2	3	4	5	6		7	8	9	10 11	12	13	14	15
1/	jp	I-47	Orita	Ulithi-	-D	+	T	.	1/			-----		1)
1/	jp	I-47	Orita	Okinawa	-D	+	T	.	1/			-----		1)
2/0930	jp	I-47	Orita	Ulithi-	-D	+	KT	.	2/			-----		2)
2/0930	jp	I-47	Orita	Okinawa	-D	+	KT	.	2/			-----		2)
2/0955	jp	I-47	Orita	"	DD	+	KT	.	2/			-----		2)
6/1100	jp	I-47	Orita	Okinawa-Guam	CL	+	KT	-	6/			-----		3)
27/	jp	I-367	Taketomi	E Okina-	DD	+	KT	.	28/	am DE	Gilligan	1275=	26.47 N/127.47 E	4)
27/	jp	I-367	Taketomi	wa	DD	+	KT	.	28/			-----		4)

June 1945

22/	jp	I-36	Sugamasa	Saipan	-T	+	T	-	20/1945 am ARL Endymion ^LST 513			1653=	12.41 N/156.20 E	5)
28/1329	jp	I-36	Sugamasa	Saipan	-D	?	KT	-	28/1329 am AKS Antares			-----	13.10 N/154.57 E	6)
28/1418	jp	I-36	Sugamasa	Saipan	DD	+	KT	-	28/1418			-----		6)
28/	jp	(I-165)	Ono	Saipan	?	+	KT	-				-----		6)

July 1945

21/	jp	I-47 ?	Suzuki	3-400m	--------		KT	-	21/	am APA	Marathon	7607=	26.13 N/127.50 E	7)
	jp	I-367 ?	Imanishi	E Okin.										
24/	jp	I-53	Oba	Philip-	-D	+	KT	.	24/	am DE	Underhill	-----		8)
24/	jp	I-53	Oba	pinen S.	-D	+	KT	.	24/	am DE	Underhill	1400+	19.20 N/126.42 E	8)
27/	jp	I-58	Hashimoto	Guam-Leyte	-T	+	KT	.	26/	am DD	Lowry	2200=	19.30 N/128.00 E	9)
30/	jp	I-58	Hashimoto	"	BB 33000+		T	-	30/	am CA	Indianapolis	9950+	12.02 N/134.48 E	10)

1) I-47 fired a 4-torpedo spread against a convoy and heard three detonations. Two transports were assumed sunk.
2) I-47 launched two Kaitens against two transports and heard two detonations after 25 min. Twenty-two min after launching two additional Kaitens against the escorts one detonation was heard. The U.S. transport Carina (AK-74) (7,740 GRT) was slightly damaged by a Kaiten at 26-30 N/127-30 E on May 4th. If this report is correct, the Kaiten must have been launched by I-47.
3) I-47 launched one Kaiten against a cruiser, and heard one detonation after 24 min.
4) I-367 launched two Kaitens and heard two detonations. It was credited with the sinking of two destroyers. Probably the damage to the Gilligan was caused by this attack.
5) I-36 fired a 4-torpedo spread against a tanker and heard several detonations (June 22nd). Possibly the torpedo hit on an ARL/LST on June 20th was a result of this attack.

1	2	3	4	5	6		7	8	9	10 11	12	13	14	15
August 1945														
4/00	jp	I-53	Oba	Phil.-	PC ?	+	KT		4/			————		11)
4/00	jp	I-53	Oba	See	PC ?	+	KT		4/			————		11)
10/0815	jp	I-58	Hashimoto	Okinawa-	DD	+	KT		10/			————		12)
10/0815	jp	I-58	Hashimoto	Leyte	-D	+	KT		10/			-----		12)
11/abds	jp	I-366	Tokioka	500m	-D	+	KT	.	11/			-----		13)
11/abds	jp	I-366	Tokioka	N	-D	+	KT	.	11/			-----		13)
11/abds	jp	I-366	Tokioka	Palau	-D	+	KT	.	11/			-----		13)
12/1800	jp	I-58	Hashimoto	E Oki-	CV 15000+		KT	.	12/	am LS	LSD-7 Oak Hill	————	Okinawa-Leyte	14)
12/1800	jp	I-58	Hashimoto	nawa	DD	+	KT	.	12/	am DE	Thomas F. Nickel	————	Okinawa-Leyte	14)

6) *I-36* first launched one Kaiten against a freighter. *Antares* (AKS-3) turned away and fired on the Kaiten astern and sank him. To defend itself against the counter-attack by the escorts, *I-36* launched two more Kaitens. One detonation was heard and one destroyer assumed sunk. Japanese radio-intelligence assumed from intercepted traffic successes of the Kaiten of *I-165*, but this submarine was already sunk.

7) The *Marathon* (APA 200) was damaged by a torpedo. Only *I 47* and *I-367* operated in this area. Both submarines returned but gave no success reports.

8) *I-53* launched two Kaitens against a convoy and assumed the sinking of two transports. But the DE *Underhill* sank the first Kaiten by D/Cs but was hit by the second and sunk.

9) *I-58* launched two Kaitens on July 27th against a tanker, and heard two detonations after 50-60 min. Possibly the damage to the DE *Lowry* was related to this attack.

10) *I-58* fired a six-torpedo spread against the cruiser transiting from Tinian to Leyte. At Tinian the cruiser had unloaded material for the first atomic bombs. After two or three hits the cruiser sank, 883 men perished. *I-58* reported sinking a battleship of the *Idaho* class.

11) *I-53* launched two Kaitens in defense against two escort vessels 400 miles east of Formosa. The detonations were heard about three hours later.

12) *I-58* launched two Kaitens against a convoy about 260 miles NE of North Luzon, and heard two detonations.

13) *I-366* launched three Kaitens against a convoy 500 miles N of Palau and heard three detonations.

14) *I-58* launched two Kaitens against a seaplane carrier. It was really the LSD *Oak Hill*, which was scraped by a Kaiten which was detonated by depth charges from a DE. The second Kaiten scraped the DE, then detonated about 2500m away. The submarine heard the detonations and assumed two hits.

Dohrn, Erwin (38) OL *U 325* 194
Doi, Y. (jp) KL *I-162* 271, 274
Dommes, Wilhelm (31) KK R *U 431, U 178* 68, 228, 229, 230,
    233, 234, 237, 238, 268, 269, 270
Donato, Alberto (it) TV *Diaspro* 247, 249
Dotta, Antonio (it) TV *Serpente, Diaspro* 225, 226
v.Dresky, Hans-Wilhelm (29) KL *U 33* 1, 2, 3, 6, 7, 9, 10
Drewitz, Hans-Joachim (33) KL *U 525* 149
Driver, Heinrich (33) KL *U 371* 56, 57, 61, 228
Dunkelberg, Hans (37b) OL *U 716* 204
Durand de la Penne, Luigi (it) TV *S.L.C.221*   229

Ebato, Kazuro (jp) KL   *Ro-110* 272, 273
Eberlein, Otto (I/38) OLdR *U 1020* 188
Eck, Heinz-Wilhelm (34) KL *U 852* 179, 275
Eckelmann, Heinz (37a) OL *U 635* 161
Eckermann, Hans (25) KK *UA* 45
Eckhardt, Hermann (36) KL *U 432* 156
Eick, Alfred (37) KL R *U 510* 169, 273, 274, 277
v.Eickstedt, Wolfgang (35) KL *U 668* 208
Emde, Bernhard (37) OL *U 248* 186, 193
Emmermann, Carl (34) KL RE *U 172* 99, 100, 101, 103, 104,
    105, 108, 139, 141, 263, 264, 265, 153, 157, 160,
    168, 169, 170
Endrass, Engelbert (35) KL RE *U 46, U 567* 19, 21, 25, 26,
    27, 30, 33, 34, 47, 48, 54, 55, 56, 71, 73
Engel, Herbert (VII/39) KL *U 666* 172, 159
Engelmann, Kurt-Eduard (23) KK *U 163* 134, 136, 139, 140
Enrici, Aldo (it) CC *Faa'di Bruno*   28, 29
Erler, Rino (it) TV *Ascianghi*   239, 244
Ernst, Hans-Joachim (37b) KL *U 1022, U 246* 191, 192, 193
v.d.Esch, Dietrich (34) KL *U 586* 198, 201, 202, 77
Ewerth, Klaus (25) KL *U 26* 2, 4, 6, 7
Ey, Hans ( ) KL   *U 433* 65

Fahr, Theodor (30) KL   *U 567* 63
Falke, Hans (39a) OL   *U 992* 209, 211

Fechner, Otto (24) KK 118, 120, 145 *U 164*
Fecia di Cossato, Carlo (it) CF R 49, 51, 62, 62, 83, 84, 85,
    112, 113, 141, 142 *Tazzoli*
Feiler, Gerhard (34) KL *U 653* 82, 96, 101, 152, 156
Fenski, Horst-Arno (X/37) OL R *U 410, U 371* 153, 249, 250,
    254, 256
Ferracuti, Carlo (it) CC *Neghelli* 225
Ferrini, Renato (it) TV *Serpente, Axum* 226, 236
Ferro, Otto (40) OLdR *U 645* 171, 173
Fiehn, Helmut (35) KL *U 191* 163
v.Fischel, Unno (34) OL *U 374* 71, 228
Fischer, Hans-Georg (26) KK *U 109* 53
Fischer, Ruprecht (37a) KL *U 244* 186, 190
Fischler Graf v.Treuberg, Rupprecht (39) OL *U 214, U 445*   168
    178
Fitting, Hans-Hermann (39) OL *U 1274* 194
Flachsenberg, Walter ( ) KK *U 71* 86, 87, 88
Fleige, Karl (24) KL (KrO) R *U 18* 219, 220, 221, 222
Förster, Hans-Joachim (38) OL *U 480* 184, 185, 191
Förster, Heinz (40) OLdR *U 359* 156
Förster, Hugo (24) KK *U 501* 63
Folkers, Ulrich (34) KL R *U 125* 76, 91, 93, 94, 95, 96, 97,
    120, 125, 126, 127, 165
Forni, Carlo (it) TV *Aradam* 239
Forster, Ludwig (36) OL *U 654* 77, 89, 91
Frhr.v.Forstner, Siegfried (30) KK R *U 402* 74, 90, 92, 132,
    148, 149, 166
Frhr.v.Forstner, Wolfgang-Friedrich (37a) KL *U 472* 204, 205
Fraatz, Georg-Werner (35) KL *U 652* 196, 63, 64, 228, 229, 230,
    231
Frahm, Peter (32) KL *U 15* 9
Franco, Giuseppe (it) TV *Emo* 236
Franke, Heinz (36) KL R *U 262* 137, 138, 139, 148, 174, 175
Franken, Wilhelm (35) KL R *U 565* 232, 235, 237, 240, 243, 245,
    246, 250
Franz, Johannes (26) KL *U 27* 1, 2
Franz, Ludwig (37a) OL *U 362* 205

Loeser, Paul-Karl (35) KL *U 373* 86, 87, 103, 105, 124
Loewe, Axel-Olaf (28) KK *U 505* 83, 88, 106, 107, 110
Loewe, Odo (34) KL *U 254, U 954* 127, 163
Lohmann, Dietrich (30) KK *U 89* 110, 111, 133, 134, 166
Lohmeyer, Peter (32) KL *U 651* 57, 58
Longanesi-Cattani, Luigi (it) *Brin, Da Vinci* 56, 81, 82,
        100, 101, 102, 103 CC
Longhi, Alberto (it) TV *Mocenigo* 239, 240, 242
Longobardo, Primo (it) CF *Torelli* 41
Looff, Hans-Günther (25) KK *U 122* 20
Looks, Hartwig (36) KL *U 264* 137, 138, 165
Loos, Johann (XII/39) OL *U 248* 189
Lorentz, Günther (32) OL *U 63* 15
Lott, Werner (26) KL *U 35* 2, 4
Lovatelli, Gustavo (it) CC *Onice* 225
Lübsen, Robert (37a) KL *U 277* 206
Lüdden, Siegfried (36) KL R *U 188* 162, 271, 272, 273
Lührs, Dierk (38) OL *U 453* 254, 255, 256
Lüssow, Gustav (37a) OL *U 571* 177
Lüth, Wolfgang (33) FK RESB *U 9, U 138, U 43, U 181*
        10, 13, 17, 18, 29, 32, 38, 39, 55, 57, 72, 73,
        162, 265, 266, 268, 269, 270
Luther, Otto (37b) OL *U 135* 169
Mäder, Erich (36) KL *U 378* 173
v.Mässenhausen, Wilhelm (35) KL *U 258* 125, 164
Mahn, Bruno (11) KzS *UD 5* 131
Mahrholz, Hans-Gert (38) OL *U 309* 173, 182, 183
Maiorana, Nicola (it) CC *Mameli* 224
Makowski, Kurt (36) OL *U 619* 125, 126
Manchen, Erwin (36) KL *U 879* 194
Mangold, (X/35) OL *U 739* 205, 206, 209
Manhardt v.Mannstein, Alfred (25) KK *U 753* 97, 98, 99,
        138, 150, 166
Manke, Rolf (35) KL *U 358* 147, 165, 179
Mannesmann, Gert ( ) KLdR *U 545* 176
Manseck, Helmut (34) KL *U 758* 140, 157, 172, 173
Marbach, Karl-Heinz (IV/37) KL *U 953* 181, 183
Marceglia, Antonio (it) Cap.GN *S.L.C.223* 229

Marienfeld, Friedrich-Wilhelm (38) OL *U 1228* 187
Marks, Friedrich-Karl (34) KL *U 376* 197, 199
Markworth, Friedrich (34) KL R *U 66* 108, 111, 112, 113, 119,
        121, 148, 152, 168, 170
Martellotta, Vincenzo (it) CapAN *S.L.C.222* 229
Masada, K. (jp) KL *I-56* 289
Maßmann, Hanns-Ferdinand (36) KL *U 409* 131, 155
Masuzawa, Seiji (jp) KL *Ro-109, I-44* 289
Mathes, Ludwig (28) KL *U 44* 10, 11, 12
Matschulat, Gerhard (XI/38) OL *U 247* 183
Matsumura, K. (jp) KK *I-21* 278, 279, 281, 282
Graf v.Matuschka, Frhr.v.Toppolczan und Spaetgen, Hartmut (34)
        KL *U 482* 185, 189
Matz, Joachim (32) KL *U 59, U 70* 24, 25, 27, 31, 32, 44, 45
Maus, August (34) KL *U 185* 140, 142, 155, 161, 169, 170
Meckel, Hans (28) KL *U 19* 5
Meermeier, Johannes (37a) KL *U 979* 186, 195
Mehl, Waldemar (33) KL R *U 371* 241, 243, 245, 247, 248, 251,
        255
Mellina, Giuseppe (it) CF *Glauco* 31
Mengersen, Ernst (33) KL R *U 18, U 101, U 607* 6, 11, 37, 43,
        55, 56, 69, 111, 113, 128, 147, 149, 166, 167
Merten, Karl-Friedrich (26) FK *U 68* RE 60, 66, 70, 71, 82, 83,
        85, 86, 88, 101, 102, 104, 105, 122, 123, 264, 265
Metzler, Jost (32) KL R *U 69* 43, 47, 48, 53, 54, 55, 57, 58
Meyer, Fritz (34) OL *U 207* 65
Meyer, Gerhard (35) OLdR *U 486* 188
Meyer, Herbert (III/37) OLdR *U 804* 184
Meyer. Rudolf (38) OL *U 1055* 189, 190
Michalowski, Hans-Bernhard (33) KL *U 62* 18, 21, 23
Migliorini, Augusto (it) TV *Nereide* 226
v.Mittelstaedt, Gert (32) KL *U 144* 214
Moehle, Karl-Heinz (30) KL R *U 20, U 103* 7, 8, 9, 31, 32, 33,
        34, 36, 41, 42, 43, 44, 49
Möhlmann, Helmut (33) KL R *U 571* 196, 87, 88, 90, 108, 109,
        146, 162
Mohr, Johann (34) KK RE *U 124* 66, 67, 72, 85, 86, 87, 94, 102,
        103, 104, 141, 143, 145, 161

A.B. Aden - Bombay From November 1942	*B.C. Beira - Capetown* *From* July to September 1943, then A.K.D.	*B.T.C. U.K.coastal* From June 1944

A.C.   Aden - Colombo

BC.2   270

BTC.10	188	BTC.81	191
BTC.65	190	BTC.103	193
BTC.76	191	BTC.108	193
BTC.78	191	BTC.111	193

A.H.   Aruba - Halifax
From July to September 1942   4 convoys

B.C.   Bombay - Colombo
From September 1943

B.X.   Boston - Halifax
From 1942

A.K.D.   Aden - Kilindini - Durban
From September 1943 for all former
East African coastal convoys.

B.D.   White Sea - Dikson (Soviet)
From summer 1943, new numbering annually

BD.5   208 (1943)

BX.141   189

A.P.   U.K. - Middle East via Cape
Summer 1940, fast military convoys
with war material for the Near East.

B.H.X.   Bermuda - Halifax (feeder)
From May 1940 to March 1941

C.A.   Colombo - Aden

A.P.   Aden - Persian Gulf
From late 1942

AP.47   271

B.K.   White Sea - Kola Fjord (Soviet)
From summer 1941, new numbering annually

C.B.   Capetown - Beira
From July to September 1943, then D.K.A.

B.R.N.   Brazilian coastal
From late 1942

BRN.3   139

A.S.   U.S.A. - Freetown
From March 1942, military convoys

AS.4   109

C.B.   Colombo - Bombay
From September 1943

CB.21   270

A.T.   New York - U.K.
From March 1942, military convoys,
combined with former N.A.convoys.

B.S.   Brest - Casablanca (French)
From September 1939 to June 1940

14.BS   7

C.D.   Capetown - Durban
From November 1942

CD.20   268

B.A.   Bombay - Aden/Red Sea
From May 1941 to November 1942, military
convoys, then merchant convoys.

BA.2   107

B.T.   Sydney (NSW) to U.S.A.
From January 1943, military convoy

BT.54   282

C.E.   St.Helen's (Wight) - Southend
From September 1940, U.K.coastal

C.F.   Capetown - Freetown - U.K.
From May 1941

B.B.   U.K.coastal

B.T.   Bahia - Trinidad
From November 1942 to July 1943, then J.T.

BT.1	145	BT.14	167
BT.6	153,154	BT.18	169

C.G.   Casablanca - Gibraltar
From January 1943 for F.T.

C.H.   Colombo - Calcutta

C.J.	*Colombo - Chittagong*		

C.M.   *Capetown - (Durban - Kilindini) -*
         Red Sea - Middle East
From June 1940, military convoys

CO.2   279

C.T.   *U.K. - North America*
From August 1941, military convoys

C.U.   *Caribbean - U.K. (tankers)*
From February 1943, tanker convoys

CU.16   179

C.W.   *U.K.coastal - Channel coast*

C.X.   *Colombo - Maledives (Addu) -*
         Chagos
From April 1943

C.Z.   *Curacao - Panama canal*
From August 1942

D.B.   *Dikson - White Sea (Soviet)*
From summer 1942, new numbering annually

D.C.   *Durban - Capetown*
From December 1942

D.K.A. *Durban - Kilindini - Aden*
From September 1943 for all former
East African coastal convoys.

D.N.   *Durban - North*

D.N.   *Durban - North*

| DN.21 | 267 | DN.68 | 276 |
| DN.50 | 269 | | |

E.B.C.   *Channel*
From June 1944 eastern feeder for
Operation "Neptune"

| EBC.66 | 184 | EBC.72 | 184 |

E.B.M.   *Channel*
From June 1944 western feeder for
Operation "Neptune"

E.C.   *Southend - Loch Ewe - Clyde*
From March to October 1941

E.C.P.   *Channel*
From June 1944, Invasion convoys

ECP.7   182

E.M.C.   *Channel*
From June 1944, Invasion convoys

EMC.17   182

E.N.   *Methil - Loch Ewe - (Clyde)*
From August 1940 to Clyde, from July 1941
to Loch Ewe only.

E.T.   *North African ports - Gibraltar*
From November 1942

ET.16   245

E.T.C.   *Channel*
From June 1944 eastern feeder for Operation
"Neptune"

| ETC.26 | 183 | ETC.72 | 184 |

E.W.   *U.K.coastal - Channel area   west*

F.C.   *Freetown - Caoetown*
From May 1941

F.N.   *Southend - Methil*
From September 1939

| FN.43 | 7 | FN.81 | 12 |

F.N.   *Freetown - Natal (?)*
From summer 1942

FN.20   111

F.P.   *Brest-U.K.*
From March to June 1940

F.S.   *Methil - Southend*
From September 1939

| FS.56 | 8 | FS.1753 | 192 |
| FS.1739 | 191 | FS.1784 | 194 |

F.S.S.   *Bizerta - Salerno*
From September 1939 to the end of 1943
feeder convoy for Operation "Avalanche"

K.S.   *Oran/Casablanca – Brest/St.Nazaire*
From September 1939 to June 1940 (French)

27.KS	6	56.KS	11

K.X.   *U.K. – Gibraltar*
From October to November 1942. special
convoy for Operation "Torch"

L.E.   *Port Said/Alexandria – Famagusta-*
         Haifa/Beirut
From July 1941

L.M.D. Laurenço Marques – Durban
From November 1942 to September 1943,
then A.K.D.

LMD.17	268

L.S.   *Lagos – Freetown*
From April to August 1942, then T.S.

M.C.   *Middle East – Kilindini –*
         Capetown
From June 1940, military convoys

M.E.   *Mediterranean – East*
From June 1940

M.G.   *Malta – Gibraltar*
From July 1941 to August 1942, military
convoys

M.H.   *U.K.coastal*

MH.1	190

M.K.F. Mediterranean – U.K. (fast)

M.K.F. Mediterranean – U.K. (fast)
From November 1942, military convoys

MKF.1	136	MKF.3	139
MKF.1Y	136		

M.K.S. Mediterranean – U.K. (slow)
From November 1942 in place of HG. From
May 1943 from Gibraltar combined with
S.L.convoys.

MKS.3Y	142	
MKS.7	149	
MKS.26	250	
MKS.27	251	
MKS.28	174	(see also SL.137)
MKS.29	174	(see also SL.138)
MKS.30	174	(see also SL.139)
MKS.31	175	(see also SL.140)
MKS.40	179	(see also SL.149)

M.T.   *Methil – Tyne*
From 1939

M.W.   *Mediterranean West / Alexandria*
         – Malta
From July 1940 to 1941. Resumed beginning
November 1942. July 1943 MWF.36, 37 and
MWS.36 and 37 for Operation Husky.

MWS.36	247

N.A.   *North America – U.K.*
From January to February 1942, military
convoys, then combined with A.T.

N.C.   *Oran/Algier – Sicily*
July 1943, invasion concoys for operation Husky.

N.E.   *New Zealand – Panama*

N.G.   *New York – Guantanamo*
From August 1942

NG.385	171

N.K.   *New York – Key West*
From May to August 1942 from Hampton Roads
only, from August from New York.

N.P.   *Clyde/Scapa Flow – Narvik*
April 1940, military convoy.

N.S.   *North African – Naples*

O.A.   *Southend – Outward (North America)*
From September 1939 to July 1940 south of
Ireland, from July 1940 to October 1940 from
North Channel. Gibraltar section until July
1940 O.A.G. From October 1940 O.B.only.

OA.7	2	OA.200	26
OA.17	4	OA.204	27
OAG.80	12	OA.207	28
OA.180	23	OA.210	28

O.B.   *Liverpool – Outward (North America)*
From September 1939 to July 1940 from Bristol
Channel, from July 1940 from North Channel.
In July 1941 merged with ON(F) and ONS. Gib-
raltar section O.B.G. until June/July 1940.

OB.4	2	OB.84	13
OB.17	4	OB.188	24
OB.46	7	OB.193	24,25
OB.48	8	OB.197	25
OB.71	10	OB.202	26
OB.74	10	OB.205	27

O.B. (cont.)

OB.216	29,30	OB.279	42
OB.217	30	OB.287	43
OB.218	30	OB.288	43,44
OB.223	32	OB.289	44
OB.227	32	OB.290	44
OB.228	32	OB.293	45
OB.229	34	OB.302	47
OB.244	36	OB.306	49
OB.251	37,38	OB.310	51
OB.252	38	OB.318	51,52,53
OB.259	39	OB.327	54
OB.260	40	OB.328	56
OB.262	40	OB.329	56
OB.263	40	OB.336	57

O.C.   *Australian coastal*
1943

OC.68	282	OC.86	282

O.G.   *U.K. - Gibraltar*

From October 1939 to August 1942 and again from May to October 1943, then KMS. Until July 1940 south of Ireland, then from North Channel. Combined with KMS in July 1943. In 1940 for a time also OGF (fast).

OG.7	6	OG.60	50
OG.16	12	OG.63	55
OG.18	14	OG.64	56
OGF.19	15	OG.67	ʃ 59
OG.43	30	OG.68	59
OG.46	37	OG.69	60
OG.47	40	OG.71	62,63
OG.52	42	OG.74	66
OG.56	47	OG.75	68
OG.57	49		

·O.L.   *Mersey - Clyde - Outward*

From September 1940 to October 1940, large passenger liners only, 9 convoys.

O.N.   *Methil - Bergen*

From November 1939 to April 1940

O.N.(F)   *U.K. - North America*

From July 1941 fast convoys for former OB. Always designated by ON. only. From September 1944 south of Ireland. From August 1942 final destination shifted from Halifax to New York.

ON.14	65	ON.	127
ON.5	61	ON.137	129
ON.19	68	ON.139	129
ON.28	71	ON.143	135
ON.54	75	ON.145	138
ON.52	74	ON.146	140
ON.53	75	ON.153	141,142
ON.55	73,74	ON.156	144
ON.56	75,76	ON.166	150-2
ON.60	78	ON.170	156
ON.61	77	ON.168	154
ON.67	80,81	ON.176	162
ON.77	87	ON.178	163
ON.87	92	ON.202	171-2
ON.93	97	ON.217	176-7
ON.113	111	ON.219	177
ON.115	112,113	ON.224	178
ON.122	118	ON.251	185
ON.127	121-123	ON.271	189
ON.129	124	ON.	191
ON.131	124,125	ONA.289	192
ON.130	124	ON.293	193

O.N.S.   *U.K. - North America*

From July 1941, slow convoy for former OB.

O.N.S. (cont.)

From September 1942 to 1943 final destination shifted to New York. From September 1944 south of Ireland. From March 1943 new numbering to avoid confusion with ON.

ONS.54	75	ONS.152	142
ONS.61	77	ONS.154	142-144
ONS.63	77	ONS.156	144
ONS.67	80,81	ONS.165	149
ONS.68	84	ONS.167	150
ONS.92	94,95	ONS.169	156
ONS.76	86	ONS.2	162
ONS.100	102,103	ONS.3	163
ONS.102	104	ONS.4	163
ONS.136	127-129	ONS.5	164-166
ONS.142	135	ONS.7	167
ONS.144	136-138	ONS.18	171-172
ONS.146	140	ONS.20	173
		ONS.33	186

O.S.   *U.K. - Freetown*

From July 1941 to September 1942, then again from February 1943. From April 1943 off Gibraltar together with KMS.

OS.1	60	OS.36	118
OS.4	63	OS.44	156
OS.10	71	OS.45	161
OS.12	72	OS.51	169
OS.28	97	OS.62	175
OS.33	108-109	OS.64	177
OS.34	110	OS.67	178

O.T.   *New York - Caribbean - North West Africa*

From February 1943 to June 1944, tanker c.

OT.1	97

P.A.		Persian Gulf – Aden	

From September 1943

| PA 44 | 269 | PA.69 | 273 |

P.G.		Panama – Guantanamo	

From July 1942 to September 1942,
then ZG.

| PG.6 | 116 | | |

P.G.		Australian coastal	
1943

| PG.150 | 283 | | |

P.K.		Pilottotown (Mississippi) – Key West	

From August 1942

P.K.		Petsamo (Kirkenes) – Kola Fj.	

From November 1944. New numbering annually. soviet convoys.

PK.20	209 (1944)
PK.	210 (1944)
PK.9	213 (1945)

P.Q.		Iceland – North Russia	

From September 1941 to December 1942,
then continued as JW.

PQ.7A	197	PQ.16	198
PQ.8	197	PQ.17	198–199
PQ.13	197	PQ.18	199–200
PQ.14	197		

P.W.		Portsmouth – Bristol Channel	

From July 1941

Q.P.		North Russia – Iceland	

From September 1941 to December 1942,
then continued as RA.

QP.10	197	QP.14	200
QP.11	198	QP.15	201

Q.S.		Quebec – Sydney	

From 1942

QS.15	107–108	QS.33	120
QS.	110		

R.A.		Kola Fjord – Loch Ewe	

From December 1942 for former QP. Ships
coming from Arkhangelsk with Soviet
feeder convoys BK.

RA.52	202	RA.60	209
RA.53	202	RA.61	209
RA.56	177	RA.62	210
RA.57	205	RA.64	211
RA.58	206	RA.66	213
RA.59	207		

R.B.		St.Lawrence – U.K.	

September 1942, transfer of passenger
ships from the Great Lakes to England.

| RB.1 | 125,126 | | |

R.S.		Gibraltar – Brest (french)	

From October 1939 to June 1940.

| 10.RS | 14 | | |

R.S.		Gibraltar – Sierra Leone	

From February 1943

| RS.3 | 160 | | |

R.U.		Reykjavik – U.K.	

| RU.71 | 163 | RU.156 | 192 |

S.		Brest – Casablanca (french)	

From 1939 to June 1940.

S.B.		Malta – Sicily	

From July 1943 as invasion convoys for
operation Husky. Subdivided into SBF (Malta)
SBM and SBS (Sfax).

S.C.		Sydney – U.K.	

From August 1940 to May 1944, again from
October 1944. From September 1942 to March
1943 assembly port New York, then Sydney
again.

SC.1	26	SC.67	78
SC.2	28	SC.94	113–115
SC.3	28	SC.95	116
SC.6	31	SC.97	119–120
SC.7	32–34	SC.100	124–125
SC.11	36	SC.101	126
SC.15	39	SC.104	128
SC.19	41,42	SC.107	131–134
SC.21	43	SC.109	138
SC.24	46	SC.117	147
SC.26	48	SC.118	148–149
SC.30	52	SC.121	154–155
SC.41	63	SC.122	156–160
SC.42	64–66	SC.130	167
SC.44	66	SC.143	173
SC.48	69	SC.154	179
SC.52	71–72	SC.156	180
SC.53	72	SC.157	180
SC.57	72	SC.167	192
SC.63	74	SC.171	194
		SC.194	189

S.G.	U.K.coastal		

S.G.	Sydney - Greenland		

From 1942

SG.6	119	SG.19	148

S.L.	Sierra Leone (Freetown) - U.K.		

From September 1939 to October 1942
and again from March 1943. From May 1943
off Gibraltar together with MKS.

SL.7A	6	SL.76	56-57
SL.8B	7	SL.78	57-58
SL.40	24	SL.81	61
SLS.46	28	SL.87	66-67
SLS.53	36	SL.89	70
SLS.56	39	SL.93	76
SL.61	41	SL.109	95
SL.64	43	SL.118	116-118
SLS.64	44	SL.119	118-119
SL.67	45	SL.125	129-131
SL.68	46-47	SL.126	160
SL.73	52	SL.129	166

SL.137	174 (see also MKS.28)
SL.138	174 (see also MKS.29)
SL.139	174)see also MKS.30)
SL.140	175 (see also MKS.31)
SL.149	179 (see also MKS.40)
SL.150	179

S.N.	Napoli - North African ports	

From 1943. Also fast convoys SNF.

SNF.17	255

S.Q.	Sydney - Quebec		

From 1942

SQ.30	121	SQ.36	123

S.R.	Sierra Leone - Gibraltar		

From February 1943

S.T.	Freetown - Takoradi		

From December 1941. Later FL and FT.

S.W.	Suez - Durban/Capetown		

From 1940, WS convoys returning

T.A.	U.K. - U.S.A.		

From March 1942, military convoys, combined
with AN.

TA.5	102

T.A.G.	Trinidad - Aruba - Guantanamo		

From August 1942 for former TAW.

TAG.5	123	TAG.20	136
TAG.18	133-134		

T.A.M.		

TAM.71	190	TAM.142	194

T.A.W.	Trinidad - Aruba - Key West		

July to August 1942, then TAG.

TAW.12	115-116	TAW (S)	117
TAW.13	117	TAW.15	118-119

T.B.	U.S.A. - Sydney (Australia)		

From January 1942, military convoys.

T.B.	Trinidad - Bahia		

From December 1942 to July 1943, then TJ.

TB.1	145

T.B.C.	U.K.coastal		

From 1944, invasion convoys

TBC.1	188	TBC.102	193
TBC.21	188	TBC.103	193
TBC.43	190	TBC.135	194
TBC.60	190		

T.C.	Canadian Troop Convoy		

From 1939 to 1940

T.E.	Trinidad - eastward		

From Bovember 1942

T.F.	Trinidad - Freetown		

From November 1942 to July 1943

T.E.	Gibraltar - North African ports		

From November 1942

T.G.	U.K.coastal		

T.J.	Trinidad - Rio de Janeiro		

From July 1943, former TB.

TJ.1	169	TJ.2	170

T.J.	Tunisia - Sicily		

July 1943, invasion convoy for operation
"Husky". with TJF, TJM and TJS.

T.M.	*U.K.coastal*

T.M.   *Trinidad - Gibraltar*
From January 1943, tanker convoy for
operation "Torch".

TM.1   145-146

T.O.   *NW Africa - Caribbean - U.S.A*
From February 1943 to June 1944, tanker

T.R.   *Trinidad - Recife*
November 1942, only one convoy, then TB.

T.S.   *Takoradi - Freetown*
From August 1942 (from April 1942 LS)

TS.23   133   TS.42   167
TS.37   164

T.S.   *Tripolis - Termini*
September 1943. Invasions-convoys
for operation "Avalanche". With TSF
and TSS.

T.U.   *U.K. - U.S.A.*
From September 1943, Military convoys.

T.X.   *Tripolis - Alexandria*
From February 1943.

U.C.   *U.K. - Caribbean*
From February 1943, special tanker convoys.

UC.1   151-152

U.G.F.   *U.S.A. - Gibraltar (fast)*
From October 1942, initially invasion

U.G.F. (cont.)
convoys for operation "Torch"m then destination ports in Northwest Africa.

UGF.1   135-136

U.G.S.   *U.S.A. - Gibraltar (slow)*
From October 1942, as U.G.F.

UGS.3	146	UGS.14	249
UGS.4	147	UGS.17	250
UGS.6	157-159	UGS.37	256
UGS.7	245	UGS.58	187
UGS.10	168	UGS.72	191

U.R.   *U.K. - Reykjavik*

UR.59	147	UR.155	191
UR.142	187		

U.S.   *Australia - Middle East*
From January 1940, military convoys

U.T.   *U.S.A. - U.K.*
From August 1943, military convoys.

UT.3   175

V.A.   *Vilkizky - Dikson (Soviet)*
From July 1943 during summer months.
New numbering annually.

VA.18   *203 (1943)*

V.D.   *Vilkitsky Strait - Dikson*
same as V.A.

VD.1   *209*

W.A.T.   *Key West - Aruba - Trinidad*
From July to August 1942, then GAT.

W.A.T. (cont.)

WAT.13   113

W.E.P.

WEP.3   188

W.N.   *Loch Ewe - Methil*
From July 1940

W.P.   *Bristol Channel - Portsmouth*
From July 1941

W.S.   *"Winstons Specials": U.K. -
            Middle East*
From June 1940 to August 1943. Mainly via
Capetown. A few, e.g. WS.11X, WS.19Z, WS.21S
(Sept.1941, June 1942, Aug.1942), via the Me-
diterranean.

WS.13   72

X.   *Le Verdon - Casablanca (french)*
From September 1939 to June 1940

65.X   20

X.B.   *Halofax - Boston*
From April 1942

XB.25   104   XB.139   188

X.C.   *Chagos - Maldives (Addu) -
            Colombo*
From May 1940

X.K.   *Gibraltar - U.K.*
From October 1942 to

Special convoys for operation "Torch".
XK.2   153

X.S.   Le Verdon - Mediterranean (French)
From September 1939 to June 1940.

X.T.   Alexandria - Tripolis
From January 1943

X.T.G.   Alexandria - Tripolis - Gibraltar
From June 1943.

Z.C.   Panama Canal - Curaçao
From August 1942.

Z.G.   Panama Canal - Guantanamo
From September 1942 for former PG.

Various U.K. coastal convoys

MVS.71   188

VWP.16   194

WEG.14   188

Index D. – Ships Attacked

1	2	3	4	5	6	7
Ashcrest	br	-D	20	5652	Lon	38
ex Zrinski (40)						
Ashmun J.Clough	br	-D	43	1791	Lon	185
Ashworth	br	-D	20	5227	New	128
Askö	dä	-D	20	1299	Kop	---
s. Foxen (40)						
Askol'd (RT 42)	sj	-Df	31	611	Mur	---
xx s. TSC-42						
Aspasia	gr	-D	14	4211	Chi	25
Asphalion	br	-D	24	6274	Liv	273
Asphodel (K.56)	*br*	*PE*	*40*	*925*	*RN*	*179*
Assail (AM 147)	*am*	*PM*	*42*	*625*	*USN*	*---*
s. TSC-120 (43)						
Assyrian	br	-D	14	2962	Liv	33
Asta	fi	-D	00	1854	Mar	---
s. Nimba (41)						
Astra	dä	-D	20	2398	Kop	---
s. Astra II (40)						
Astra II	br	-D	20	2393	Lon	27
ex Astra (40)						
Astral	am	-DT	16	7542	NYo	72
Astrea	nl	-D	21	1406	Rot	83
Astrell	nw	-MT	25	7595	Ris	134
Astronomer	br	-D	17	8401	Liv	18
Asturias (F.71)	br	ACL	25	22048	RN	170
ex -DP (39)						
Atalaya	sp	-D	21	3309	Bil	---
s. Cabo Tortosa (39)						
Atenas	am	-D	09	4639	NYo	99
Athelbeach	br	-MT	31	6568	Liv	45
Athelcrest	br	-MT	40	6825	Liv	26
Athelcrown	br	-MT	29	11999	Liv	75
Athelduke	br	-MT	29	8966	Liv	194
Athelempress	br	-MT	30	8941	Liv	92
Athelknight	br	-MT	30	8940	Liv	99
Athellaird	br	-MT	30	8999	Liv	22
Athelmonarch	br	-MT	28	8995	Liv	34
"	"	"	"	"	"	246

1	2	3	4	5	6	7
Athelprince	br	-MT	26	8782	Liv	19
"	"	"	"	"	"	47
Athelprincess	br	-MT	29	8882	Liv	151
Athelqueen	br	-MT	28	8780	Liv	85
Athelsultan	br	-MT	29	8882	Liv	124
Atheltemplar	br	-MT	30	8992	Liv	200
Athelviking	br	-MT	26	8779	Liv	189
Athelviscount	br	-MT	29	8882	Liv	86
Athene	nw	-MT	28	4681	Kri	233
Athenia	br	-DP	23	13581	Gla	1
Athenic	br	-D	37	5351	Hul	48
Athina Livanos	gr	-D	36	4824	Chi	272
Atik	am	AG	12	3209	USN	87
ex Carolyn (42)						
Atlantic	br	-D	04	3016	Hul	---
s. Margareta (39)						
Atlantic City	br	-D	41	5133	Bid	60
Atlantic Gulf	pa	-DP	19	2639	Pan	262
Atlantic States	am	-DT	43	8537	Phi	194
Atlantic Sun	am	-MT	41	11355	Phi	86
"	"	"	"	"	"	149
Atlas	it	-DT	98	2005	Gen	---
s. Las Choapas (41)						
Atlas	fi	-D	01	1082	Mar	---
s. Pompoon (42), ex Atlas II (41)						
Atlas	gr	-D	09	4008	Pir	257
Atlas	am	-DT	16	7137	NYo	89
Atlas	nl	-D	22	1277	Cur	---
s. Quiberon (39)						
Atlas II	pa	-D	01	1082	Pan	---
s. Pompoón (42)						
Atos	sw	-D	02	2161	Hel	24
Auckland Star	br	-M	39	13212	Bel	24
Auctoritas	it	-D	18	5228	Gen	---
s. Pelotasloide (42)						
Audacity (D.10)	*br*	*CVE*	*39*	*11000*	*RN*	*73*
ex Empire Audacity (39), ex Hannover						

1	2	3	4	5	6	7
Auditor	br	-D	24	5444	Liv	59
August	nw	-D	11	5254	Ber	---
s. Dimitris (40)						
Augvald	nw	-D	20	4811	Hau	45
Aurania (F.28)	br	ACL	24	13984	RN	70
ex -DP (39)						
Aurillac	br	-D	21	4733	Car	49
Auris	br	-MT	35	8030	Lon	58
Aurora	am	-MT	20	7050	NYo	94
Australia	am	-MT	28	11628	Wmt	85
Avelona Star	br	-D	27	13376	Lon	22
Avenger (D.14)	*br*	*CVE*	*42*	*8200*	*RN*	*136*
ex am CVE 2, ex Rio Hudson (40)						
Aviemore	br	-D	20	4060	Liv	2
Avila Star	br	-DP	27	14443	Lon	107
Avoceta	br	-DP	23	3442	Liv	67
Avondale Park	ca	-D	44	2878	Mon	195
Awatea	nz	-D	36	13482	Wel	238
Aylesbury	br	-D	32	3944	Lon	23
Aymeric	br	-D	19	5196	Gla	167
Axtell J.Byles	am	-DT	27	8955	Wmt	90
Azalea City	am	-D	20	5529	Mob	79
Aziza	äg	-S			100	232
B-III	sj	-Bg				199
B.P.Newton	nw	-MT	40	10324	Osl	169
BO-2..	*sj*	*PC*	*43*	*105*	*SNF*	*210*
ex SC 1507 (43)						
BO-2..	*sj*	*PC*	*43*	*105*	*SNF*	*211*
ex SC 1485 (43)						
BO-225	*sj*	*PC*	*43*	*105*	*SNF*	*213*
ex SC (43)						
BO-229	*sj*	*PC*	*43*	*105*	*SNF*	*210*
ex SC 1477 (43)						

1	2	3	4	5	6	7
BTSČ-410 Vrzyv	*sj*	*PM*	*38*	*441*	*SSF*	*222*
BTSČ-411 Zaŝĉitnik		*PM*	*38*	*441*	*SSF*	*221*
Bab el Farag	äg	-S		105		232
Badalona	sp	-MT	22	4202	Bar	228
Baependy	bz	-D	99	4801	Rio	116
Bagé	bz	-D	12	8235	Rio	170
Baghdad	nw	-M	36	2161	Osl	99
Bahadur	br	-D	29	5424	Lon	261
Bainbridge	*am*	*DD*	*20*	*1190*	*USN*	*104*
(DD 246)						
Baja California	ho	-D	14	1649	PCo	110
Balingkar	nl	-D	21	6318		117
ex Werdenfels (40)						
Balkis	nw	-M	39	2161	Osl	89
Balladier	am	-D	19	3279	NYo	116
ex Namarib (42), ex Marsodak (41)						
Balmoralwood	br	-D	37	5834	Mid	19
Baltallinn	br	-D	20	1303	Lon	66
Baltanglia	br	-D	21	1523	Lon	11
Baltistan	br	-D	37	6803	Lon	44
Baltonia	br	-D	25	2013	Lon	149
Baluchistan	br	-D	40	6992	Lon	83
Bamako	fr	-M	30	2357	Mar	161
Ban Ho Guan	nl	-D	08	1693	Ban	260
Bandar Shahpur	br	-D	27	5236	Lon	164
Banderas	sp	-D	99	2140	Bil	14
Banffshire	nw	-D	12	6479	Gla	271
Bangu	am	-D	19	4945	NYo	---
s. Empire Antelope (41)						
Bantam	nl	-M	29	3322	Bat	258
Baoulé	fr	-D	21	5874	Hav	5
Barbacena	bz	-D	09	4772	Rio	111
Barbana C.	it	-D	15	6561	Gen	---
s. Empire Airman (40)						
Barbara	am	-D	13	4637	NYo	83
Barbara Marie	br	-D	28	4223	New	19
Barbara Robertson	br	APC	19	325	RN	9
ex -Df (39)						

1	2	3	4	5	6	7
Barberrys	br	-D	20	5170	Lon	139
Barbro	fi	-D	02	2155	Mar	---
s. Margareta (39)						
Barbro	nw	-MT	34	6325	Osl	66
Barham (04)	*br*	*BB*	*14*	*31100*	*RN*	*9*
"	"	"	"	"	"	*227*
Barfonn	nw	-MT	31	9739	Sta	69
Barnby	br	-D	40	4813	Whi	53
Barnegat	am	-Bg		914		88
Baron Blythswood	br	-D	29	3668	Ard	29
Baron Cochrane	br	-D	27	3385	Ard	143
Baron Dechmont	br	-D	29	3675	Ard	145
Baron Erskine	br	-D	30	3657	Ard	73
Baron Jedburgh	br	-D	36	3656	Ard	192
Baron Kelvin	br	-D	24	3081	Ard	69
Baron Kinnaird	br	-D	27	3355	Ard	156
Baron Loudoun	br	-D	25	3164	Ard	20
Baron Lovat	br	-D	26	3395	Ard	55
Baron Nairn	br	-D	25	3164	Ard	55
Baron Newlands	br	-D	28	3386	Ard	85
Baron Ogilvy	br	-D	26	3391	Ard	126
Baron Pentland	br	-D	27	3410	Ard	64
"	"	"	"	"	"	66
Baron Semple	br	-D	39	4573	Ard	174
Baron Vernon	br	-D	29	3642	Ard	131
Barr (DE 576)	*am*	*DE*	*43*	*1300*	*USN*	*181*
Barrdale	br	-D	25	5072	Gla	96
Barrwhin	br	-D	29	4998	Gla	131
Barwon	**au**	-D	39	4239	Mel	279
Bassa	br	-D	18	5267	Liv	31
Bassano	br	-D	37	4843	Hul	41
Batavier III	nl	-D	97	1406	Rot	---
s. El Sonador (39)						
Bath	*nw*	*DD*	*18*	*1060*	*RNo*	*62*
ex Hopewell (DD 181) (40)						
Batna	br	-D	28	4399	Lon	95
Bayard	nw	-M	36	2160	Osl	108
Bayonet (Z.05)	*br*	*PN*	*38*	*605*	*RN*	*9*

1	2	3	4	5	6	7
Bayou	pa	-D	19	2605	Pan	82
ex Lake Fairfax (40)						
Beacon Grange	br	-M	38	10160	Lon	50
Beaconlight	pa	-DT	20	6926	Pan	109
Beatrice	am	-D	17	3451	NYo	98
Beatus	br	-D	25	4885	Car	32
Beaverburn	br	-D	27	9874	Lon	13
Beaverdale	br	-DT	28	9957	Lon	48
Bedfordshire	br	APC	35	913	RN	94
ex -Df (39) (FY.141)						
Beduin	nw	-MT	36	8136	Osl	46
Beechwood	br	-D	40	4897	Lon	118
Beignon	br	-D	39	5218	Lon	22
Belaes	pt	-Mf		415		121
Belcrest	br	-D	25	4517	Lon	43
ex Treherbert (39)						
Belfast (35)	*br*	*CL*	*38*	*11500*	*RN*	*6*
Belgia	sw	-D	30	1744	Göt	---
s. Empire Bell (42)						
Belgian Airman	be	-D	42	6959	Ant	194
ex Empire Ballantyne (42)						
Belgian Captain	be	-D	42	7041	Ant	---
s. Empire Centaur (43)						
Belgian Fighter	be	-D	21	5403	Ant	264
ex Empire Albatross (42), ex						
Black Condor (41)						
Belgian Soldier	be	-D	41	7167	Ant	112
ex Empire Selwyn (42)						
"	"	"	"	"	"	113
Belgravian	br	-D	37	3136	Liv	61
Belita	nw	-MT	33	6323	Tön	266
Belize	nw	-M	19	2153	Osl	75
Bellflower	pa	-D	19	6085	Pan	---
s. Victoria (40)						
Bellingham	am	-D	20	5345	Mob	200
Bello	nw	-MT	30	6125	Tön	141

1	2	3	4	5	6	7
Belmoira	nw	-D	28	3214	Osl	21
Belmont (H.46)	*br*	*DD*	*18*	*1190*	*RN*	*76*
ex Satterlee (DD 190) (40)						
Belpamela	nw	-D	28	3215	Osl	15
Beme	pa	-DT	04	3039	Pan	223
Ben and Josephine	am	-Mf	41	102	Glo	100
Ben Brush	pa	-MT	28	7691	Pan	90
ex Caroline Maersk (41)						
Benakat	nl	-DT	35	4763	Pal	167
Benalder	br	-D	19	5161	Lei	135
Bengore Head	br	-D	22	2609	Bel	51
Benjamin Brewster	am	-DT	17	5950	Wmt	108
Benjamin Franklin	nw	-M	27	7034	Osl	43
Benjamin Harrison	am	-D	42	7191	Bal	157
Benjamin Smith	am	-D	42	7177	Wmt	147
Benkoelen	nl	-D	21	1003	Bat	258
Benlawers	br	-D	30	5943	Lei	31
Benlomond	br	-D	22	6630	Lei	139
Benmohr	br	-D	28	5920	Lei	83
Bennekom	nl	-DP	17	5998	Ams	71
Bennestvet	nw	-D	37	2438	Far	104
Bensalem	am	-D	19	5513	Phi	---
s. Alcoa Partner (41)						
Benvenue	br	-D	27	5920	Lei	52
Benvrackie	br	-D	22	6434	Lei	52
ex Darian (39)						
Benwyvis	br	-D	29	5920	Lei	47
Berakit	nl	-M	24	6608	Bat	268
ex Vogtland (40)						
Berenice	nl	-D	19	1177	Ams	21
Berganger	nw	-M	32	6826	Ber	100
Berhala	nl	-M	27	6622	Bat	53
Berto	nw	-D	18	1493	Osl	240
Berwickshire	br	-D	12	7464	Gla	276
Besholt	nw	-M	36	4977	Osl	139
Beth	nw	-MT	30	6852	Osl	96
Betta	dä	-D	35	1570	Esb	---
s. Vespasian (40)						
Betty	br	-D	18	2339	Sha	25
ex cn (40)						
Beverley (H.64)	*br*	*DD*	*19*	*1190*	*RN*	*162*
ex Branch (DD 197) (40)						
Bhima	br	-M	39	5280	Lon	260
Biarritz	nw	-D	22	1752	Osl	11
Bibury	br	-D	29	4616	Lon	27
Bic Island	ca	-D	17	4000	Mon	130
ex Capo Noli (40)						
Bickerton (K.466)	*br*	*DE*	*43*	*1300*	*RN*	*208*
ex am DE 75						
Bidewind	nw	-M	38	4956	Por	92
Bidwell	am	-MT	20	6837	Phi	88
Biela	br	-D	18	5298	Liv	78
Bilderdijk	nl	-D	22	6856	Rot	34
Bill	nw	-D	39	2445	Osl	111
Biloxi (CL 80)	*am*	*CL*	*43*	*10000*	*USN*	*286*
Binnendijk	nl	-D	21	6873	Rot	4
Bintang	nl	-M	16	6481	Bat	139
Birdlip (T.218)	br	APC	41	750	RN	182
Birmingham (19)	*br*	*CL*	*36*	*9100*	*RN*	*252*
Birmingham City	am	-D	20	6194	NYo	145
Biscaya	dt	-MT	27	6369	Hbg	---
s. Empire Unity (40)						
Biscaya	nw	-D	39	1323	Osl	148
Bisp	nw	-D	89	1000	Hau	11
Bissen	sw	-D	20	1514	Sto	22
Biter	*br*	*CVE*	*42*	*8200*	*RN*	*163*
ex am CVE 3 (42), ex Rio Parana (40)						
Black Condor	am	-D	21	5403	NYo	---
s. Belgian Fighter (42), ex Empire						
Albatross (41)						
Black Eagle	am	-D	20	5060	NYo	---
s. Hoosier (41)						
Black Hawk	am	-D	43	7191	NOr	188
Black Heron	am	-D	19	4926	NYo	---
s. Empire Barracuda (40)						
Black Osprey	br	-D	18	5589	Lon	43
Black Point	am	-D	18	5353	Bos	195
Black Tern	am	-D	19	5032	NYo	---
s. Empire Hawk (41)						
Blackheath	br	-D	36	4637	Lon	189
Blackwood (K.313)	*br*	*DE*	*42*	*1085*	*RN*	*182*
ex am DE 4 (42)						
Blairangus	br	-D	30	4409	Gla	29
Blairbeg	br	-D	17	3509	New	---
s. Fellside (40)						
Blairlogie	br	-D	29	4425	Gla	1
Blairmore	br	-D	28	4141	Gla	26
Blairspey	br	-D	29	4155	Gla	33
Blakely (DD 150)	*am*	*DD*	*18*	*1190*	*USN*	*99*
Blankaholm	sw	-M	30	2845	Göt	117
Blean (L.47)	*br*	*DE*	*42*	*1087*	*RN*	*240*
Blink	nw	-D	20	2701	Osl	78
Blitar	nl	-D	23	7065	Bat	161
Block Island	*am*	*CVE*	*42*	*9800*	*USN*	*181*
(CVE 21)						
Bloody Marsh	am	-DT	43	10195	Phi	168
Bluebell (K.80)	*br*	*PE*	*40*	*925*	*RN*	*211*
Bluefields	ni	-D	17	2063	Blu	109
ex Jupiter (41)						
Bodegraven	nl	-D	29	5593	Wil	182
Boekolo	nl	-D	30	2118	Ams	33
Boero/ex Dupleix	nl	-D	14	7135	Bat	260
Bogö	dä	-D	20	1214	Kop	8
Boise (CL 47)	*am*	*CL*	*36*	*10000*	*USN*	*287*
Boka	pa	-D	20	5560	Pan	29
Bold Venture	pa	-D	20	3222	Pan	69
ex Alssund (41)						
Boma	br	-D	20	5408	Liv	24
Bombay	br	-Df	07	229	Gri	112
Bonaventure (31)	*br*	*CL*	*39*	*5450*	*RN*	*225*

1	2	3	4	5	6	7
Bonde	nw	-D	36	1570	Osl	166
Bonheur	br	-D	20	5327	Liv	32
Bonneville	nw	-M	29	4665	Osl	155
Bor	jg	-D	10	3614	Sus	---
s. Radbury (41)						
Boren	sw	-D	21	4528	Göt	---
s. Skane (41)						
Borgland	nw	-M	18	3636	Osl	44
Boringia	br	-D	30	5821	Gla	263
Boris	gr	-D	17	5166	Pir	167
Borkum	dt	-D	22	3670	Bre	7
Borthwick	br	-D	20	1097	Lei	16
Bosnia	br	-D	28	2407	Liv	1
Boston	br	-D	24	4989	?	125
ex am (42)						
Bothal	dä	-D	20	2109	Kop	16
Botwey	br	-D	16	5106	Man	60
ex Manchester Producer (39)						
Bourgieh	äg	-S		244		244
Brabant	be	-M	38	2438	Ant	95
Braddock	am	-D	19	6615	NYo	---
s. Empire Redshank (41)						
Bradford City	br	-M	36	4953	Bid	71
Bradfyne	br	-D	28	4740	Bid	36
Brageland	sw	-M	37	2608	Göt	145
Brambleleaf	br	-DT	17	5917	Lon	233
Bramora	nw	-MT	28	6361	Osl	271
Bramwell	br	-D	21	1927	New	---
s. Glendinning (40)						
Branch (DD 197)	*am*	*DD*	*19*	*1190*	*USN*	*---*
s. Beverley (40)						
Brand	nw	-M	27	4819	Por	166
Brandanger	nw	-M	26	4624	Ber	31
Brandenburg	br	-D	10	1473	Lei	42
Brandon	br	-D	17	6668	Lon	8
Brant County	nw	-D	15	5001	Ber	156

1	2	3	4	5	6	7
Brasiloide	bz	-M	36	6075	Rio	149
ex Montevideo (42)						
Brask	nw	-D	11	4079	Osl	41
Brave Coeur	am	-D	19	6408	Sea	---
s. Empire Gull (41)						
Brazos	am	-D	99	4497	NYo	74
Brazza	fr	-MP	23	10387	Hav	18
Bredon (T.223)	br	APC	41	750	RN	149
Breedijk	nl	-D	22	6861	Rot	123
Breiviken	nw	-D	11	2669	Ber	269
Brenas	nw	-M	33	2687	Osl	113
Brerury	br	-D		4924		65
Bretagne	fr	-DP	22	10108	Hav	4
Bretwalda	br	-D	39	4906	New	142
Bright Wings	br	-D	10	4539	Lon	---
s. Everoja (39)						
Brighton (I.08)	*br*	*DD*	*18*	*1060*	*RN*	*---*
ex Cowell (DD 167) (40),						
s. Zarkij (44)						
Brilliant	am	-DT	30	9132	NYo	138
Brinkburn	br	-D	24	1598	Sun	246
Bris	nw	-D	38	2027	Osl	91
Brisbane Star	br	-M	37	12791	Lon	236
Bristol (DD 453)	*am*	*DD*	*41*	*1630*	*USN*	*251*
Bristol City	br	-D	20	2864	Bri	165
Britannia	nw	-MT	39	9977	Osl	271
British Ardour	br	-DT	28	7124	Lon	161
British Chivalry	br	-DT	29	7118	Lon	273
British Colony	br	-DT	27	6917	Lon	95
British Consul	br	-DT	24	6940	Lon	79
"	"	"	"	"	"	117
British Corporal	br	-DT	22	6972	Lon	---
s. Empire Corporal (42)						
British Dominion	br	-DT	28	6983	Lon	146
British Endeavour	br	-DT	27	4580	Lon	15
British Fame	br	-MT	36	8406	Lon	25

1	2	3	4	5	6	7
British Fortitude	br	-MT	37	8482	Lon	151
British Freedom	br	-MT	28	6985	Lon	106
"	"	"	"	"	"	189
British General	br	-DT	22	6989	Lon	31
British Glory	br	-MT	28	6993	Lon	32
British Grenadier	br	-MT	22	6857	Lon	53
British Gunner	br	-DT	22	6894	Lon	44
British Influence	br	-MT	39	8431	Lon	2
British Judge	br	-DT	21	6735	Lon	260
British Loyalty	br	-MT	28	6993	Lon	261
"	"	"	"	"	"	274
British Mariner	br	-DT	22	6996	Lon	69
British Merit	br	-MT	42	8093	Lon	111
British Monarch	br	-D	23	5661	Gla	20
British Premier	br	-DT	22	5872	Lon	40
British Promise	br	-MT	42	8443	Lon	138
British Prudence	br	-MT	39	8620	Lon	87
British Purpose	br	-MT	43	5845	Lon	271
British Reliance	br	-MT	28	7000	Lon	48
British Renown	br	-MT	28	6997	Lon	138
British Resource	br	-MT	31	7209	Lon	85
British Security	br	-MT	37	8470	Lon	52
British Splendour	br	-MT	31	7138	Lon	89
British Venture	br	-DT	30	4696	Lon	269
British Vigilance	br	-MT	42	8093	Lon	
"	"	"	"	"	"	147
British Viscount	br	-DT	21	6895	Lon	48
British Workman	br	-DT	22	6994	Lon	92
British Yeoman	br	-DT	23	6990	Lon	109
British Zeal	br	-MT	37	8532	Lon	40
Britta	dä	-D	21	1146	Esb	16
Britta	nw	-MT	28	6214	Osl	8
Britany	br	-M	28	4772	Liv	131
Broad Arrow	am	-DT	18	7718	NYo	145
Broadwater (H.81)	*br*	*DD*	*19*	*1190*	*RN*	*69*
ex Mason (DD 191) (40)						

Index D. - Ships Attacked

Index D. - Ships Attacked

1	2	3	4	5	6	7
Cheik	fr	-D	20	1058	Mar	223
Chelsea (I.35)	*br*	*DD*	*19*	*1090*	*RN*	*---*
ex Crowninshield (DD 134) (40)						
s. Derzkij (44)						
Chelsea	br	-D	25	4804	Hul	27
Chenango	pa	-D	18	3014	Pan	91
ex Kurikka (41)						
Chepo	pa	-D	19	5582	Pan	73
ex West Pocasset (41)						
Cherokee	am	-D	25	5896	NYo	104
Cherry Valley	am	-DT	42	10172	Phi	170
Cheshire (F.18)	br	ACL	27	10552	RN	32
ex -MP (39)						
"	"	"	"	"	"	117
Chester (CA 27)	*am*	*CA*	*29*	*9200*	*USN*	*281*
Cheyenne	br	-MT	30	8825	New	2
Chickasaw City	am	-D	20	6196	NYo	263
Chief Ouray	am	-D	42	7176		---
s. Deimos (42)						
Chile	br	-M	15	6956	Lon	101
Chilka	br	-D	22	4360	Gla	261
Chilore	am	-D	22	8310	NYo	109
China Arrow	am	-DT	20	8403	NYo	77
Chinese Prince	br	-M	26	8593	Lon	56
Chloe	gr	-D	28	4641	Arg	279
Chr.Knudsen	nw	-M	25	4904	Por	89
Chr.J.Kampman	ca	-D	24	2260	Mon	133
Christian Krohg	nw	-D	17	1992	Ber	56
Christian Michelsen	nw	-D	43	7176	Osl	250
ex John M.T.Finney (43)						
Christiansborg	dä	-M	22	3270	Kop	16
Christopher Newport	am	-D	42	7191	Bal	198
Christos Markettos	gr	-D	19	5209	Arg	262

1	2	3	4	5	6	7
Chulmleigh	br	-D	38	5445	Lon	201
Churchill (I.45)	*br*	*DD*	*19*	*1190*	*RN*	*---*
ex Herndon (DD 198) (40)						
s. Dejatel'nyj (44)						
Chung Cheng	cn	-D	43	7176		273
ex Murat Halstead (43)						
Ciltvaira	le	-D	05	3779	Rig	74
Cingalese Prince	br	-M	29	8474	Lon	66
Circe Shell	br	-MT	31	8207	Lon	80
Ciscar	br	-D	19	1809	Lon	62
Cisne Branco	br	-S		300		173
Cissy	nw	-D	20	2166	Ber	---
s. Inger Elisabeth (39)						
Cities Service Empire	am	-DT	18	8103	NYo	80
Cities Service Missouri	am	-DT	20	7506	NYo	157
Cities Service Toledo	am	-DT	18	8192	NYo	103
City of Adelaide	br	-D	20	6589	Liv	275
City of Alma	am	-D	20	5446	Mob	100
City of Athens	br	-D	23	6558	Liv	264
City of Atlanta	am	-D	04	5269	Sav	74
City of Baroda	br	-D	18	7129	Liv	267
City of Bath	br	-D	26	5079	Liv	139
City of Benares	br	-DP	36	11081	Gla	29
City of Birmingham	am	-D	23	5861	Sav	107
City of Bombay	br	-D	37	7140	Liv	141
City of Cairo	br	-D	15	8034	Liv	265
City of Canton	br	-D	16	6692	Liv	270
City of Cardiff	br	-D	18	5661	Liv	119
City of Corinth	br	-D	18	5318	Liv	136
City of Guildford	br	-D	19	5157	Liv	245
City of Flint	am	-D	20	4963	Phi	147
City of Johannesburg	br	-D	20	5669	Liv	264

1	2	3	4	5	6	7
City of Kobe	br	-D	24	4373	Liv	8
City of Manchester	br	-D	35	8917	Liv	260
City of Mandalay	br	-D	25	7028	Gla	5
City of Manila	br	-D	16	7452	Liv	118
City of Melbourne	br	-D	19	6630	Liv	95
City of Nagpur	br	-D	22	10146	Gla	50
City of New York	am	-M	30	8272	NYo	87
City of Oran	br	-D	15	7323	Gla	270
City of Oxford	br	-D	26	2759	Liv	103
City of Paris	br	-DP	22	10902	Gla	2
City of Perth	br	-D	13	6415	Shi	244
City of Pretoria	br	-D	37	8049	Lon	153
City of Ripon	br	-D	15	6368	Hul	135
City of Shanghai	br	-D	17	5828	Liv	52
City of Simla	br	-D	21	10138	Gla	29
City of Singapore	br	-D	23	6555	Liv	164
City of Venice	br	-D	24	8762	Gla	247
City of Wellington	br	-D	25	5733	Liv	118
City of Winchester	br	-D	17	7120	Liv	51
Clairton	am	-D	19	6259	Nwk	---
s. Empire Reindeer (41)						
Clan Alpine	br	-D	18	5442	Gla	156
Clan Chisholm	br	-D	37	7256	Gla	5
Clan Cumming	br	-D	38	7264	Gla	225
Clan Ferguson	br	-D	38	7347	Gla	236
Clan Grant	br	-D	12	5804	Gla	---
s. Stangrant (39)						
Clan Macarthur	br	-D	36	10528	Gla	270
Clan Macdougall	br	-M	29	6843	Gla	54
Clan Macfadyen	br	-D	23	6191	Gla	139
Clan Maciver	br	-D	21	4500	Gla	46
Clan Macnaughton	br	-D	21	6088	Gla	112
Clan Macphee	br	-D	11	6628	Gla	25
Clan Macpherson	br	-D	29	6940	Gla	164

1	2	3	4	5	6	7
Clan Macquarrie	br	-D	13	6471	Gla	103
Clan Mactaggart	br	-D	20	7622	Gla	136
Clan Mactavish	br	-D	21	7631	Gla	264
Clan Macwhirter	br	-D	18	5941	Gla	118
Clan Menzies	br	-D	38	7336	Gla	24
Clan Ogilvy	br	-D	14	5802	Gla	22
"	"	"	"	"	"	47
Clan Ross	br	-D	14	5897	Gla	261
Clan Skene	br	-D	19	5214	Gla	94
Clara	it	-D	22	6131	Tri	---
s. Stone Street (41)						
Clare	am	-D	15	3372	NYo	98
Clarissa Radcliffe	br	-D	15	5754	Lon	156
Clayoquot (J.174)	*ca*	*PM*	*40*	*672*	*RCN*	*188*
Clea	br	-MT	38	8074	Lon	42
Cleanthis	gr	-D	11	4153	Pir	266
Clearton	br	-D	19	5219	New	22
Cleopatra (33)	*br*	*CL*	*40*	*5450*	*RN*	*247*
Cliftonhall	br	-M	38	5063	Har	262
Clintonia	br	-D	17	3106	Shi	34
Clonlara	br	-D	26	1203	Lim	62
Coamo	am	-DP	25	7057	NYo	139
Coast Farmer	am	-D	20	3290	Ptl	280
Coast Trader	am	-D	20	3286	Ptl	279
Coaxet	am	-M	19	6082	Ptl	---
s. Empire Kingfisher (41)						
Cockaponset	br	-D	19	5995		53
ex am (40)						
Cocker	br	APC	36	303	RN	233
ex Kos XIX (41)						
Cocle	pa	-D	20	5630	Pan	94
ex Jacob Ruppert (41)						
Coimbra	br	-DT	37	6768	Lon	74
Colabee	am	-D	20	5617	Wmt	85
Cold Harbor	pa	-D	20	5010	Pan	103

1	2	3	4	5	6	7
Colin	pa	-M	21	6255	Pan	180
ex Villarperosa (42)						
Collamer	am	-D	20	5112	Phi	82
Collegian	br	-D	23	7886	Liv	30
Collingsworth	am	-D	20	5101	Phi	145
Colombia	nl	AS	30	10782	RNe	267
ex nl -MP (40)						
Colombia	pa	-M	39	1064	Pan	175
Colonial	br	-D	26	5108	Liv	53
Colonna	*it*	*SS*	*28*	*791*	*RIt*	*224*
Coloradan	am	-D	20	6557	NYo	264
Columbia (I.49)	*ca*	*DD*	*18*	*1060*	*RCN*	*131*
ex Haraden (DD 183)						
Columbia	dä	-M	28	6049	Kop	---
s. Sir Huon (41)						
Columbine	sa	-D	21	3268	Cap	275
ex Suriyothai Nawa (42), ex Admiral Laws (40)						
Comandante Lyra	bz	-D	19	5052	Rio	97
ex Southland (40)						
Comayagua	ho	-D	21	2493	PCo	95
Cometa	nw	-M	21	3794	Ber	16
Commander Horton	br	APC	15	227	RN	50
ex br -Df (39)						
Commercial Bostonian	am	-D	19	2730	NYo	---
s. Ozorio (40)						
Commercial Trader	am	-D	20	2606	NYo	124
ex Delaware River (39)						
Comol Rico	am	-DT	19	5034	NYo	88
ex Kisha-Coquillas (39)						
Comrade	br	-S		110		109
Conch	br	-MT	31	8376	Lon	37
"	"	"	"	"	"	38
Condylis	gr	-D	14	4439	And	115
Confield	br	-D	40	4956	New	31
Congella	br	-M	14	4533	Lon	271

1	2	3	4	5	6	7
Congonian	br	-MT	36	5056	Liv	36
Connecticut	am	-DT	38	8684	Wmt	278
Contractor	br	-D	30	6004	Liv	248
Conus	br	-MT	31	8132	Lon	48
Convallaria	sw	-D	21	1996	Hel	33
Coolana	au	-D	21	2197	Mel	280
Coquina	am	-D	19	2140	LAn	---
s. Cynthia Olsen (40)						
Corabella	br	-M	37	5682	Lon	164
Coracero	br	-D	23	7252	Gla	158
Coral	br	-D	19	638	Gla	184
Corbis	br	-MT	31	8132	Lon	268
Cordelia	br	-MT	32	8190	Liv	148
Corilla	nl	-MT	39	8096	Wil	77
Corinaldo	br	-D	21	7131	Gla	131
Corinthiakos	gr	-D	10	3562	And	265
Corinthic	br	-D	24	4823	Hul	49
Cornelia P. Spencer	am	-D	43	7176	Wmt	271
Corneville	am	-M	30	4544	Osl	166
Cornish City	br	-M	36	4952	Bid	270
Cornwallis	ca	-D	21	5458	Van	122
"	"	"	"	"	"	187
Corona	nw	-D	20	3264	Hau	242
Corregidor	am	-D	11	1881	Mnl	258
Corrientes	br	-D	20	6863	Gla	30
Corte Real	pt	-D	22	2044	PDe	68
Cortes	br	-D	19	1374	Lon	67
Cortona	br	-D	21	7093	Gla	108
Corvina (SS 226)	*am*	*SS*	*43*	*1525*	*USN*	*284*
Corvus	nw	-D	21	1317	Ber	191
Cossack (F.03)	*br*	*DD*	*37*	*1870*	*RN*	*70*
Cotati	am	-D	19	6015	SFr	---
s. Empire Avocet (42)						
Cotmarsum	nl	-D	20	3628	Ams	36
Coulmore	br	-D	36	3670	Gla	155

1	2	3	4	5	6	7
Coultarn	br	-D	38	3759	Gla	47
Counsellor	br	-D	26	5068	Liv	16
Courageous	*br*	*CV*	*16*	*22500*	*RN*	*2*
Courland	br	-D	32	1325	Lei	42
Coventry (I.43)	*br*	*CL*	*17*	*4290*	*RN*	*225*
Cranfield	br	-D	19	5332	Gla	265
Cranford	am	-D	20	6096	LCh	112
Cree	br	-D	20	4791	Lon	36
Creekirk	br	-D	12	3917	Lon	33
Creofield	br	-DT	28	838	New	12
Cressington Court	br	-M	29	4971	Lon	117
Cresswell	br	-Df	17	275	Mil	6
Crijnssen	nl	-D	19	4282	Ams	102
Cripple Creek	am	-D	19	6347	Tmp	115
Crispin (OBV-40)	br	-D	35	5051	RN	42
Crista	br	-MT	38	2590	Lon	231
Cristales	br	-D	26	5389	Liv	94
Crocus (K.49)	*br*	*PE*	*40*	*925*	*RN*	*127*
Crown Arun	br	-D	38	2372	Lon	29
ex Hannah Böge (39)						
Crowninshield	*am*	*DD*	*19*	*1090*	*USN*	*---*
(DD 134),						
s. *Derzkij (44), ex Chelsea (40)*						
Crusader	pa	-D	16	2946	Pan	72
ex Brosund (41)						
Crux	nw	-M	23	3828	Ber	21
Cuba	br	-D	23	11420	Liv	194
Cubano	nw	-D	21	5810	Tön	34
Cuckmere (K.299)	*br*	*PF*	*42*	*1370*	*RN*	*253*
Culebra	br	-D	19	3044	Liv	76
Culver (Y.87)	*br*	*PS*	*28*	*1546*	*RN*	*76*
ex Mendota (40)						
Cumberland	br	-D	19	10939	Lon	26
Cumberland	am	-D	19	2599	Por	---
s. Western Head (39)						
Cuzco	am	-D	19	5496	NYo	---
s. Carmona (40)						

1	2	3	4	5	6	7
Cyclops	br	-D	06	9076	Liv	73
Cygnet	pa	-D	17	3628	Pan	84
ex Mirach (39)						
Cynthia Olsen	am	-D	19	2140	SFr	278
ex Coquina (40)						
Cyrus H.McCormick	am	-D	42	7181	SFr	194
Cythera (PY.26)	am	PY	07	602	USN	92
ex -MY (41)						
D'Entrecasteaux	br	-D	22	7291		135
ex fr (40)					Hav	
Dafila	br	-D	27	1940	Liv	244
Daghestan	br	-MT	21	5742	New	15
"	"	"	"	"	"	16
Daghild	nw	-MT	27	9272	Osl	122
"	"	"	"	"	"	148
"	"	"	"	"	"	149
Dagomba	br	-M	28	3845	Liv	133
Dagrun	nw	-M	28	4562	Osl	32
Dah Pu	nw	-D	22	1974	Ber	269
Dahomian	br	-D	29	5277	Liv	275
Daisy Moller	br	-D	11	4087	Lon	272
Dalarö	sw	-D	11	3927	Sto	13
Dalblair	br	-D	26	4608	New	27
Dalcairn	br	-D	27	4608	New	29
Dalcroy	br	-D	30	4558	New	132
Dalfram	br	-D	30	4558	New	270
Dan	fi	-S				
				47		216
Dan Beard	am	-D	43	7176	SFr	187
Daniel Carrol	am	-D	42	7176	Hou	243
Daniel Morgan	am	-D	42	7177	Wmt	199
Danmark	br	-M	25	8391	Liv	112
ex dä (40)						

1	2	3	4	5	6	7
Danmark	dä	-MT	31	10517	Kop	9
Daphne	sw	-D	90	1513	Sto	38
ex Eos (40)						
Daphne	fi	-D	20	1939	Bra	48
Darcoila	br	-D	28	4084	Gla	30
Darian	br	-D	24	4281	Liv	---
s. Benvrackie (39)						
Darina	br	-MT	39	8113	Lon	97
Daring (H.16)	*br*	*DD*	*32*	*1375*	*RN*	*14*
Darino	br	-D	17	1351	Liv	6
Darkdale	br	AO	40	8145	RN	70
Darlington Court	br	-M	36	4974	Lon	52
Daronia	br	-MT	39	8139	Lon	276
Dartford	br	-D	30	4093	Lon	103
Davanger	nw	-MT	22	7102	Ber	31
Davara	br	-Df	12	291	Fle	1
Davenport	am	-D	20	5491	Phi	---
s. Alcoa Shipper (40)						
David H.Atwater	am	-D	19	2438	FRi	88
David McKelvy	am	-DT	21	6821	Wmt	95
Daydawn	br	-D	40	4768	Car	36
Daylite	pa	-D	17	1976	Pan	258
ex pa -S (41)						
Dayrose	br	-D	28	4113	Car	74
Daytonian	br	-D	22	6434	Liv	85
De la Salle	fr	-D	21	8400	Hav	169
De Weert	nl	-D	12	1805	Bat	262
Decatur (DD 341)	*am*	*DD*	*21*	*1190*	*USN*	*175*
Deer Lodge	am	-D	19	6187	Ptl	266
Defacto	am	-D	19	4800	NYo	---
s. Empire Caribou (40)						
Deimos (AK 78)	am	AK	42	7440	USN	283
ex Chief Ouray (42)						
Dejatel'nyj	*sj*	*DD*	*19*	*1190*	*SNF*	*211*
ex *Churchill (44), ex Herndon (40)*						

1	2	3	4	5	6	7
E.G.Seubert	am	-D	18	9181	Wmt	273
E.J.Sadler	am	-DT	21	9639	Wmt	105
E.M.Clark	am	-DT	21	9647	Wmt	86
E.P.Theriault	br	-S	19	326	Bdg	97
Eagle	am	-DT	17	6003	NYo	168
Eagle (94)	*br*	*CV*	*18*	*22600*	*RN*	*235*
Eagle 56	*am*	*PC*	*19*	*430*	*USN*	*195*
Earlspark	br	-D	29	5250	Gre	19
Earlston	br	-D	41	7195	New	199
East Indian	am	-M	18	8159	Dea	265
East Wales	br	-D	25	4358	Car	142
Eastern Glade	br	-D	19	5057	Lon	---
s. Empire Jaguar (40)						
Eastern Star	nw	-D	20	5658	Ber	51
Eastern Sword	am	-D	20	3785	NYo	93
Eastern Trader	br	-D	20	5117	Lon	---
s. Empire Razorbill (40)						
Eastlea	br	-D	24	4267	New	47
Eastmoor	br	-D	22	5812	Lon	88
Ebb	am	-Mf	29	260	Bos	111
Ebor Wyke	br	-Df	29	348	Hul	195
Eclipse	br	-DT	31	9767	Lon	93
Edencrag	br	-D	40	1592	Har	240
Edgar Allen Poe	am	-D	42	7176	Ptl	281
Edgehill (SSV)	br	-D	28	4724	RN	21
ex Willamette Valley (39)						
Edinburgh (16)	*br*	*CL*	*38*	*11500*	*RN*	*198*
Edisto	am	-D	43	11420		---
s. *Nabob (43)*						
Edith	am	-D	15	3382	NYo	101
Edward B.Dudley	am	-D	43	7177	Wmt	162
Edward Blyden	br	-M	30	5003	Liv	67
Edward Chambers	am	-M	09	4203	Mob	283
Edward H.Crockett	am	-D	44	7176	Ptl	209
Edward M.House	am	-D	43	7240	Jac	182
Edward Rutledge	am	AP	31	9360	USN	136
(AP.52) ex Exeter (42)						

1	2	3	4	5	6	7
Edwin Joseph O'Hara	am	-D	43	7219		---
s. Sambo (43)						
Edwy R.Brown	br	-MT	38	10455	Lon	43
Effingham	am	-D	19	6421	NOr	197
Effna	br	-D	19	6461	Sea	44
ex am (40)						
Efploia	gr	-D	11	3867	Chi	27
Efthalia Mari	gr	-D	19	4195	And	270
Egda	nw	-MT	40	10068	Ber	79
Egholm	br	-D	24	1317	Lon	191
Eglantine	am	-D	19	6404	NOr	---
s. Empire Buffalo (40)						
Egyptian	br	-D	20	2868	Liv	154
Eibergen	nl	-D	14	4801	Rot	54
Eidanger	nw	-MT	38	9432	Ber	81
Eidsvold	nw	-M	34	4184	Osl	259
Eika	nw	-D	39	1503	Kra	12
Einvik	nw	-D	18	2000	Tro	63
Eirini Kyriakides	gr	-D	22	3781	And	56
Ekatontarchos Dracoulis	gr	-D	18	5329	Ith	10
Ekbal	äg	-S		176		235
Eknaren	sw	-M	22	5243	Göt	262
El Capitan	pa	-D	17	5255	Pan	199
El Capitan	am	-D	19	2227	SFr	---
s. Majaba (42)						
El Dia	am	-D	01	4570	NYo	---
s. Pan York (41)						
El Ghazala	äg	-S		24		247
El Kassbana	äg	-S		110		243
El Lago	pa	-D	20	4221	Pan	127
El Madina	in	-D	37	3962	Bom	274
El Occidente	pa	-D	10	6008	Pan	197
El Oso	br	-DT	21	7267	Lon	9
El Saadiah	äg	-S		122		232
El Sayeda	äg	-S		68		248

1	2	3	4	5	6	7
El Sonador	pa	-D	97	1406	Pan	14
ex Batavier III (39)						
Elba	br	-D	18	1974	Gla	---
s. Aldergrove (40)						
Eldena	am	-D	19	6900	Sea	169
Electra (AK 21)	am	AK	41	8113	USN	136
ex Meteor (41)						
Elena R.	gr	-D	17	4576	Syr	7
Eleni Stathatos	gr	-D	19	5625	Ith	12
Eli Knudsen	nw	-MT	25	9026	Hau	20
Elias Howe	am	-D	42	7176	Ptl	271
Elihu B.Washburne	am	-D	42	7176	LAn	168
Elin K.	nw	-M	37	5214	Ber	157
Elios	it	-D	12	5202	Nea	---
s. Empire Brigade (40)						
Elisabeth van Belgie	be	-D	09	4241	Ant	121
Elizabeth	am	-D	18	4727	NYo	98
Elizabeth Kellogg	am	-DT	21	5189	NYo	174
Ellaroy	br	-D	05	712	Gla	23
ex Sagenite (40)						
Elle	fi	-D	13	3868	Was	26
Ellen M.	br	-D	38	498	Lon	12
Ellesmere (FY.204)	br	APC	37	580	RN	191
ex Kos XXIV (39)						
Ellin	gr	-D	38	4917	And	14
Ellinico	gr	-D	04	3059	Pir	57
Ellyson (DD 454)	*am*	*DD*	*41*	*1630*	*USN*	*256*
Elmbank	br	-D	25	5156	Gla	29
Elmdale	br	-D	41	4872	New	261
"	"	"	"	"	"	132
Elmdene	br	-D	39	4853	Lon	55
Elmwood	br	-D	42	7167	Lon	111
Elpis	gr	-D	12	3651	And	19
Elusa	nl	-MT	36	6235	Haa	53
Elwyn C.Hale	am	-D	18	2084	SFr	---
s. Alcoa Transport (40)						
Emanuel	fa	-Df	31	166		51

1	2	3	4	5	6	7
Empire Hartlebeeste	br	-D	18	5676	Lon	124
ex West Gambo (41)						
Empire Hawk	br	-D	19	5032	Lon	141
ex Black Fern (41)						
Empire Hawksbill	br	-D	20	5724	Lon	110
ex Delawarean (40)						
Empire Heath	br	-D	41	6643	Sun	180
Empire Heritage	br	-DT	30	15702	Car	185
ex Tafelberg (43)						
Empire Heron	br	-D	20	6023	Lon	69
ex Mosella (41)						
Empire Housman	br	-M	43	7359	Sun	176
"	"	"	"	"	"	177
Empire Hope	br-	-M	41	12688	Bel	236
Empire Howard	br	-D	41	6985	Gre	197
Empire Hudson	br	-D	41	7465	Sun	64
Empire Impala	br	-D	20	6116	Lon	154
ex Oakman (41)						
Empire Jaguar	br	-D	19	5186	Lon	38
ex Eastern Glade (40)						
Empire Javelin	br	LSI	43	7177	RN	188
ex -D Cape Lobos (43)						
Empire Johnson	br	-D	42	7168		---
s. Paulus Potter (42)						
Empire Kingfisher	br	-M	19	6082	Lon	74
ex Coaxet (41)						
Empire Kingsley	br	-D	41	6996	Gre	193
Empire Kite	br	-M	22	7965		---
ex Californian (40), s. Empire Seal (40)						
Empire Kohinoor	br	-D	19	5225	Lon	168
ex Caboto (41)						
Empire Kumari	br	-D	20	6288	Lon	236
ex Sturmfels (41)						
Empire Lake	br	-D	41	2852	Har	270
Empire Lakeland	br	-D	42	7015	Shi	154
Empire Lancer	br	-D	42	7037	Gre	276
Empire Leopard	br	-D	17	5676	Lon	132
ex Onomea (40)						
Empire Light	br	-MT	25	6537	Liv	156
ex Lumen (42)						
Empire Lugard	br	-M	41	7241	Sun	123
Empire Lynx	br	-D	17	6379	Lon	133
Empire Lytton	br	-DT	42	9807	Mid	145/6
Empire Mahseer	br	-D	20	5087	Lon	267
ex Liberty Bell (41)						
Empire Marvell	br	-DT	42	9812	Sun	151
Empire Merchant	br	-M	38	4864	Lon	25
ex Pomona (39)						
Empire Merlin	br	-D	19	5763	Lon	26
ex West Isleta (40)						
Empire Mersey	br	-D	20	5791	Liv	128
ex Ramon de Larrinaga (42)						
Empire Mica	br	-DT	41	8032	Mid	106
Empire Miniver	br	-D	18	6055	Lon	33
ex West Cobalt (40)						
Empire Moat	br	-D	41	2922	Gre	66
Empire Moon	br	-D	41	7472	Sun	248
Empire Moonbeam	br	-D	41	6849	Hon	122
Empire Moose	br	-D	20	6103	Lon	27
ex Oakwood (40)						
Empire Mordred	br	-D	42	7024	Gla	149
Empire Morn	br	-D	41	7092	Bar	164
Empire Nomad	br	-D	42	7167	Sun	264
Empire Norseman	br	-DT	42	9811	Mid	151
Empire Oak	br	-Dt	41	484		62
Empire Ocelot	br	-D	19	5759	Lon	30
ex San Marcos (40)						
Empire Oil	br	-DT	41	8029	Lon	121
Empire Onyx	br	-MT	41	8221		---
s. Nortind (42)						
Empire Piet	br	-MT	41	8134		---
s. Norland (42)						
Empire Portia	br	-D	42	7058	New	182
Empire Prairie	br	-D	41	7010	Gre	89
Empire Progress	br	-D	18	5249	New	90
ex Mugnone (40)						
Empire Protector	br	-D	21	6181	Lei	54
ex Pamia (40)						
Empire Rainbow	br	-M	41	6942	Gre	111
Empire Razorbill	br	-D	20	5118	Lon	39
ex Eastern Trader (40)						
Empire Redshank	br	-D	19	6615	Gla	150
ex Braddock (41)						
Empire Reindeer	br	-D	19	6259	Lon	115
ex Clairton (41)						
Empire Rennie	br	-D	41	6626		---
s. Frans Hals (42)						
Empire Ridge	br	-D	41	2922	Gre	52
Empire Sailor	br	-M	26	6140	Lon	138
ex Cellina (40)						
Empire Seal	br	-M	22	7965	Lon	79
ex Empire Kite (40), ex Californian (40)						
Empire Selwyn	br	-D	41	7167		---
s. Belgian Soldier (42)						
Empire Shackleton	br	-D	41	7068	Gre	143
"	"	"	"	"	"	144
Empire Sky	br	-D	41	7455	Sun	201
Empire Spenser	br	-MT	42	8194	Bel	140
Empire Spring	br	-M	41	6946	Gre	78
Empire Springbuck	br	-D	18	5591	Lon	64
ex San Angelo (40)						
Empire Standard	br	-D	42	7047	New	244
Empire Stanley	br	-M	41	6921	Gre	270
Empire Star	br	-M	35	12656	Bel	129
Empire Starling	br	-D	19	6060	Lon	139
ex Nockum (41)						
Empire Statesman	br	-D	20	5306	Lon	39
ex Pellice (40)						
Empire Steel	br	-MT	41	8138	Liv	87

1	2	3	4	5	6	7
Empire Storm	br	-D	41	7290	Shi	53
Empire Stream	br	-D	41	2922	Gre	67
Empire Sun	br	-D	41	6952	Sun	77
Empire Sunrise	br	-D	41	7459	Sun	132
Empire Surf	br	-D	41	6641	Sun	73
Empire Tennyson	br	-D	42	2880	Har	126
Empire Thrush	br	-D	19	6160	Lon	90
ex Lorain (42)						
Empire Thunder	br	-D	40	5965	Sun	40
Empire Toucan	br	-D	20	4421	Lon	21
ex Freeport Sulphur No.5 (40)						
Empire Tourist	br	-D	43	7062	Sun	205
Empire Turnstone	br	-D	18	6113	Lon	129
ex Western City (42)						
Empire Tower	br	-D	35	4378	Lon	153
ex Tower Field (42)						
Empire Trader	br	-D	08	9990	Lon	150
ex Tainui (40)						
Empire Unity	br	-MT	27	6386	Lon	195
ex Biscaya (40)						
Empire Union	br	-D	24	5952	Gla	142
ex Myrica (41), ex Sistiana (40)						
Empire Volunteer	br	-D	21	5319	Lon	28
ex Procida (40)						
Empire Wagtail	br	-D	19	4893	Lon	143
ex Point Lobos (41)						
Empire Wave	br	-D	41	7463	Sun	68
Empire Webster	br	-D	42	7043	Sun	242
Empire Whale	br	-D	19	6159	Lon	160
Empire Whimbrel	br	-D	19	5983	Lon	162
ex Monasses (41)						
Empire Wildebeeste	br	-D	18	5631	Lon	76
ex West Ekonk (41)						
Empire World	br	-Dt	42	260	Sun	187
Empire Zeal	br	-D	42	7009	Gre	132
Empreß of Britain	br	-DP	31	42348	Lon	35

1	2	3	4	5	6	7
Empreß of Canada	br	-DP	22	21517	Lon	157
Ena de Larrinaga	br	-D	25	5200	Liv	48
Endla	fi	-S			68	216
Endymion (ARL 9)	am	ARL	43	1653	USN	290
ex LST 513						
England	dä	-D	30	2319	Kop	11
Enid	nw	-D	24	1140	Tro	10
Enisej (RT.68)	sj	-Df	32	557	Mur	---•
s. TSC-68 (42)						
Ensis	br	-MT	37	6207	Lon	56
"	"	"	"	"	"	255
"	"	"	"	"	"	88
Eocene	br	-DT	22	4216	Lon	233
Eos	es	-D	90	1513	Tal	---
s. Daphne (40)						
Epaminondas C.Embiricos	gr	-D	27	4385	And	273
Equipoise	pa	-D	06	6210	Pan	87
ex Pietro Campanella (41)						
Erato	br	-D	23	1335	Hul	60
Erie (PG 50)	am	PG	36	2000	USN	136
Erica Reed	br	-D	20	5117		---
s. Empire Razorbill (40), ex Eastern Trader (39)						
Erik Boye	dä	-D	24	2238	Kop	19
Erik Frisell	sw	-M	26	5066	Sto	18
Erling Brövig	nw	-MT	37	9970	Far	273
Erna	dä	-D	30	1590	Esb	---
s. Erna III (40)						
Erna III	br	-D	30	1590	Lon	67
ex Erna (40)						
Ernani	it	-D	10	6619	Gen	58
Erodona	br	-MT	37	6207	Lon	46
Eros	br	-D	36	5888	Bel	19
Erviken	nw	-D	21	6595	Ber	69
Escort (H.66)	br	DD	34	1375	RN	223
Eskdene	br	-D	34	3829	Lon	7
"	"	"	"	"	"	49

1	2	3	4	5	6	7
Esmond	br	-D	30	4976	SJo	51
Esparta	am	-D	04	3365	NYo	89
Esquimalt (J.272)	ca	PM	41	590	RCN	194
Esquimaux	br	-Df	39	520		---
s. Alouette (39)						
Essex Lance	br	-D	18	6625	Lon	123
"	"	"	"	"	"	173
Esso Aruba	am	-DT	31	8773	Wmt	119
Esso Augusta	am	-MT	40	11237	Wmt	104
Esso Baton Rouge	am	-DT	38	7989	Wmt	89
"	"	"	"	"	"	151
Esso Bolivar	pa	-DT	37	10389	Pan	83
Esso Boston	am	-DT	38	7699	Wmt	90
Esso Concord	am	-DT	40	7698	Wmt	117
Esso Copenhagen	pa	-MT	39	9245	Pan	81
Esso Gettysburg	am	-MT	42	10173	Wmt	168
ex Gettysburg (42)						
Esso Harrisburg	am	-DT	42	9887	Wmt	183
Esso Houston	am	-DT	38	7699	Wmt	95
Esso Nashville	am	-DT	40	7934	Wmt	86
Esso Williamsburg	am	-MT	41	11237	Wmt	124
Eston	br	-D	19	1487	Lon	12
Estrellano	br	-D	20	1983	Liv	42
Ethel Crawford	br	-Df	19	200	Abe	194
Etna	sw	-D	18	2619	Hel	141
Etrib	br	-D	19	1943	Liv	103
Ettrick (AP)	br	-DP	38	11279	Lon	136
Eugene V.R.Thayer	am	-DT	20	7138	Wmt	89
Eulima	br	-MT	37	6207	Lon	151
Eulota	nl	-M	36	6236	Haa	16
Eumaeus	br	-DP	21	7472	Liv	41
Euphorbia	br	-D	24	3380	Shi	39
Eurymedon	br	-DP	24	6223	Liv	30
Eva	nw	-D	29	1599	Ber	26
Evanthia	gr	-D	15	3551	And	266
Evdoxia	gr	-D	03	2018	Pir	23
Everalda	le	-D	12	3950	Rig	107

1	2	3	4	5	6	7
Forfar	br	ACL	20	16402	RN	37
ex -DP (39)						
Fort a la Corhe	br	-D	42	7133	Lon	245
Fort Anne	br	-D	43	7134	Lon	246
Fort Battle River	br	-D	42	7133	Lon	153
Fort Bellingham	br	-D	43	7153	Lon	204
Fort Binger	br	-D	19	5671	Lon	96
Fort Buckingham	br	-D	43	7122	Lon	272
Fort Camosun	br	-D	42	7126	Lon	272
"	"	"	"	"	"	279
Fort Cedar Lake	br	-D	42	7134		157
"	"	"	"	"	"	158
Fort Chilcotin	br	-D	42	7133	Lon	170
Fort Concord	br	-D	42	7138	Lon	166
Fort de Vaux	fr	-D	18	5186	Hav	175
Fort Douglas	br	-D	42	7129	Lon	190
Fort Fidler	br	-D	43	7127	Lon	256
Fort Franklin	br	-D	42	7135	Lon	270
Fort Good Hope	br	-D	42	7130	Lon	102
Fort Halkett	br	-D	42	7133	Lon	170
Fort Howe	br	-D	42	7133	Lon	250
Fort Jemseg	br	-D	43	7134	Lon	172
Fort la Maune	br	-D	42	7130	Bri	272
Fort la Reine	br	-D	42	7133	Lon	116
Fort Lamy	br	-D	19	5242	Npt	154
Fort Lee	am	-DT	43	10198	Phi	277
Fort Longueuil	br	-D	42	7128	Lon	271
Fort McLeod	br	-D	42	7127	Lon	274
Fort Missanabie	br	-D	43	7147	Lon	256
Fort Mumford	br	-D	42	7132	Lon	267
Fort Norman	br	-D	42	7133	Lon	244
Fort Paskoyac	br	-D	42	7134	Lon	153
Fort Qu'Appelle	br	-D	42	7127	Lon	96
Fort Rampart	br	-D	42	7134	Lon	163
Fort Richepanse	br	-M	36	3485		63
ex Belfast (40)						
Fort St.Nicolas	br	-D	43	7154	Lon	254

1	2	3	4	5	6	7
Fort Thompson	br	-D	42	7134	Lon	186
Fort Yale	br	-D	42	7134	Lon	184
Fortune (H.70)	*br*	*DD*	*34*	*1375*	*RN*	——
s. Saskatchewan (43)						
Fortunstella	it	-D	12	4864	Gen	---
s. Rio Tercero (41)						
Fostat	äg	-D	18	5298	Ale	---
s. Star of Luxor (39)						
Foxen	sw	-D	20	1304	Kar	10
ex Askö (39)						
Foxhound (H.69)	*br*	*DD*	*34*	*1375*	*RN*	——
s. Qu+Appelle (44)						
Fram	sw	-D	97	2491	Sto	12
Frances Massey	br	-D	27	4212	Hul	19
Frances Salman	am	-D	19	2609	Hou	74
ex James River (39)						
Franche Comte	br	-MT	36	9314	Car	46
ex fr (40)	fr				Hav	---
ex Loosdrecht (39)						
Francis E.Powell	am	-DT	22	7096	Phi	76
Frangoula Goulandris	gr	-D	18	6701	And	21
Frank B.Baird	br	-D	23	1748	SCa	98
Frank Seamans	nw	-D	28	4271	Osl	93
Franken	dt	-D	26	7789	Hbg	---
s. Wangi-Wangi (40)						
Franklin K.Lane	am	-DT	20	6589	Wmt	102
Frans Hals	nl	-D	41	6626		133
ex Empire Rennie (42)						
Fred	gr	-D	07	4043	Pir	232
Fred W.Green	br	-D	18	2292	Lon	99
Fredensburg	dä	-D	22	2094	Kop	11
Frederic R.Kellogg	am	-DT	17	7127	Wmt	140
Frederick C.Davis	*am*	*DE*	*43*	*1200*	*USN*	*195*
(DE 136)						

1	2	3	4	5	6	7
Frederick Douglass	am	-D	43	7176	Bal	171
Frederick S.Fales	br	-DT	39	10525	Lon	30
Frederika Lensen	br	-D	12	4367	Lon	110
Fredville	nw	-D	17	1150	Are	9
Freeport Sulphur	am	-D	20	4127	NYo	---
No.5 (s. Empire Toucan (40)						
Fresno City	br	-M	42	7261	Bid	162
Friar Rock	pa	-D	21	5427	Pan	73
ex Arsa (41)						
Frimaire	fr	-DT	29	9242	Rou	104
(pt Charter)						
Frisco	nw	-D	39	1582	Por	73
Frodi	is	-Df		97		46
Frontenac	nw	-DT	28	7350	Osl	130
Fröya	*nw*	*CM*	*16*	*595*	*RNo*	*17*
Fultala	br	-M	40	5051	Lon	261
Furious (47)	*br*	*CV*	*16*	*22450*	*RN*	*235*
G.C.Brövig	nw	-MT	30	9718	Far	44
G.S.Livanos	gr	-D	37	4835	Chi	280
G.S.Walden	br	-MT	35	10627	Lon	112
"	"	"	"	"	"	256
Gaasterkerk	nl	-D	22	8679	Haa	264
Gairsoppa	br	-D	19	5237	Gla	43
Galatea (71)	*br*	*CL*	*34*	*5220*	*RN*	*228*
Galatea	nw	-D	12	1152	Ber	190
Gand	be	-D	19	5086	Ant	52
Ganda	pt	-D	07	4333	Loa	57
Gandia	be	-D	07	9626	Ant	75
Ganilly (T.376)	br	APC	43	545	RN	183
Gannet (AVP 8)	*am*	*AVP*	*19*	*840*	*USN*	*101*
Garlinge	br	-D	18	2012	Lon	237

1	2	3	4	5	6	7
Garm	sw -D	12	1231	Sto	65	
Garoet	nl -D	17	7118	Wil	275	
Garoufalia	gr -D	14	4708	Chi	8	
Gartavon	br -D	21	1777	Gla	1	
Garmula	br -D	20	5254	Gla	110	
Gasray	br -D	19	1406	Lon	193	
ex Springfal (40), ex Uhti (39)						
Gazcon	br -D	32	4224	Gla	263	
Geir ex dä (40)	fr -Dt	08	323		149	
Gemma	*it SS*	*36*	*622*	*RIt*	*224*	
Genoano	it -D	14	6067	Gen	---	
s. Faja de Oro (40)						
George Ade	am -D	44	7176	Pen	185	
George Calvert	am -D	42	7191	Bal	97	
George Cleeve	am -D	43	7176	Por	255	
George G.Meade	am -D	42	7176	LAn	154	
Geo.H.Jones	br -DT	19	6914	Lon	102	
George Hawley	am -D	44	7176	Por	190	
George J. Goulandris	gr -D	13	4345	And	58	
George L.Torain	ca -D	26	1754	SCa	80	
Georges Mabro	äg -D	18	2555	Ale	30	
Geo.R.Donovan	ca -D	26	1780	FWm	---	
s. Kenordoc (40)						
George Thacher	am -D	42	7176	LAn	132	
Geo.W.McKnight	br -MT	33	12502	Lon	92	
Georgios Kyriakides	gr -D	11	4201	And	22	
Ger-y-Bryn	br -D	41	5108	Lon	153	
Geraldine Mary	br -D	24	7244	SJo	24	
Germaine	gr -D	11	5217	Pir	8	
Germanic	br -D	36	5352	Hul	47	
Gertrud	fi -D	14	3396	Hsk	---	
s. Wilja (39)						
Gertrud Bratt	sw -D	27	1510	Göt	3	
Gertrude	am -Df		16		109	
Gettysburg	am -MT	42	10173	Wmt	---	
s. Esso Gettysburg (42)						
Gharinda	br -D	19	5306	Gla	166	
Gilbert B.Waters	br -S	19	176	Brd	159	
Gilligan (DE 508)	*am DE*	*44*	*1350*	*USN*	*290*	
ex Donaldson						
Gimle	nw -D	16	1271	Are	7	
Gioacchino Lauro	it -D	21	5345	Nea	---	
s. Empire Engineer (40)						
Glacier	br -S		130		109	
Gladiolus (K.34)	*br PE*	*40*	*925*	*RN*	*69*	
Glen Albyn	br APC	09	82	RN	9	
ex -Df (39)						
Glen Farg	br -D	37	876	Abe	4	
Glendene	br -D	29	4412	Whi	127	
Glendinning	br -D	21	1927	Lei	183	
ex Bramwell (40)						
Glenlea	br -D	30	4252	New	135	
Glenmoor	br -M	28	4393	Lon	37	
Glenroy	br -MP	38	9809	Liv	227	
Glenshiel	br -M	24	9425	Bel	261	
Glittree	nw -MT	28	6409	Sta	150	
"	"	"	"	"		151
Glittrefjell	nw -D	34	1568	Osl	8	
Gloria	br -D	17	5896		---	
ex Mount Pentelikon (39), s. Empire Conveyor (40)						
Gnat (T.60)	*br PG*	*15*	*625*	*RN*	*227*	
Godafoss	is -D	21	1542	Rey	187	
Gogovale	br -D	27	4586	Gla	24	
Gogra	br -D	19	5190	Gla	161	
Goncalves Dias	bz -D	20	4996	Rio	98	
ex Mormacsun (40)						
Goodall (K.479)	*br DE*	*43*	*1085*	*RN*	*213*	
ex am DE 275 (43)						
Goodleigh	br -D	38	5448	Lon	38	
Goodson (K.480)	*br DE*	*43*	*1085*	*RN*	*182*	
ex am DE 276						
Goodwood	br -D	37	2796	Lon	1	
Goolistan	br -D	29	5851	New	201	
Göteborg	sw -D	93	820	Göt	44	
Gothia	sw -M	37	1640	Göt	11	
Gould (K.476)	*br DE*	*43*	*1085*	*RN*	*179*	
ex am DE 272 (43)						
Goviken	nw -D	17	4854	Ber	262	
Gracia	br -D	21	5642	Gla	10	
Grado	nw -D	18	3082	Osl	166	
Grafton ((H.89)	*br DD*	*35*	*1335*	*RN*	*18*	
Graigwen	br -D	26	3697	Car	31	
Grangepark	br -D	19	5132	Gre	138	
Granicos	gr -D	16	3689	Pir	160	
Granville	pa -D	13	4071	Pan	158	
Gravelines	br -D	25	2491	Bri	54	
Grayburn	br -D	38	6342	Lon	58	
Green Island	am -M	37	1946	Det	93	
Greer (DD 145)	*am DD*	*18*	*1190*	*USN*	*63*	
Gregalia	br -D	29	5802	Gla	51	
Grelhead	br -D	15	4274	Lon	228	
Gretafield	br -DT	28	10191	New	13	
Grena	nw -MT	34	8117	Ber	274	
Grenager	nw -M	39	5393	Ber	89	
Gretaston	br -D	24	5008	Gla	---	
s. Sheaf Mead (40)						
Gretavale	br -D	28	4586	Gla	71	
Grey Ranger	br AO	41	3313	RN	200	
Greylock	am -D	21	7460	NYo	94	
"	"	"	"	"	"	202
Griffin (H.31)	*br DD*	*35*	*1375*	*RN*	----	
s. Ottawa (43)						
Gro	nw -D	17	4211	Ber	28	
Grootekerk	nl -D	23	8685	Haa	44	
Grove (L.77)	*br DE*	*41*	*1050*	*RN*	*234*	
Grutto	nl -D	25	920	Rot	16	
Gryfevale	br -D	29	4434	Gla	9	
Guatemala	pa -D	20	5527	Pan	279	
ex Valiente (41)						

1	2	3	4	5	6	7
Guayaquil	am	-D	19	2592	NYo	---
s. Caribstar (40)						
Gudveig	nw	-D	19	1300	Osl	11
Guelma	br	-D	28	4402	Swa	59
Guido	br	-D	20	3921	Hul	154
Guidonia	it	-D	13	5091	Nea	---
s. Plaudit (41)						
Gulfamerica	am	-DT	42	8081	Phi	89
Gulfbelle	am	-DT	36	7104	Phi	107
Gulfoil	am	-D	12	5189	Phi	96
Gulfpenn	am	-DT	21	8862	Phi	95
Gulfprince	am	-DT	21	6561	Phi	247
Gulfstate	am	-DT	20	6882	Phi	161
Gulftrade	am	-DT	20	6676	Phi	84
Gulfwave	am	-DT	37	7141	Phi	282
Gun	sw	-D	91	1198	Göt	3
Gunborg	sw	-D	30	1572	Göt	33
Gunda	nw	-D	19	2241	Osl	265
Gundersen	nw	-M	27	1841	Osl	107
Gunny	nw	-D	20	2362	Ber	82
Gurkha (F.63)	*br*	*DD*	*40*	*1920*	*RN*	*229*
ex Larne						
Gurney E.Newlin	am	-DT	42	8225	LAn	130
Gustaf Adolf	sw	-D	20	925	Göt	5
Gustaf E.Reuter	sw	-MT	28	6336	Göt	7
Guysborough (J.52)	*ca*	*PM*	*41*	*672*	*RCN*	*192*
Gwalia	sw	-D	07	1258	Göt	37
Gyda	nw	-D	20	1591	Ber	23
Gypsum Empress	br	-DP	29	4034	Mid	133
Gypsum Queen	br	-D	27	3915	Mid	65
H.Berg	am	-DT	37	8297	SFr	279
H.D.Collier	am	-MT	38	8298	SFr	274

1	2	3	4	5	6	7
H.H.Rogers	pa	-DT	16	8807	Pan	150
ex br					Lon	
H.M.Storey	am	-DT	21	10763	SFr	278
"	"	"	"	"	"	283
Haakon Hauan	nw	-MT	35	6582	Osl	98
Hadleigh	br	-D	30	5222	Lon	244
Hagan	am	-DT	19	6401	Wmt	102
Hahira	am	-DT	20	6855	Phi	133
Hai Hing	nw	-M	29	2561	Dra	265
Haiching	br	-D	98	2183	Hon	271
Haida (G.63)	*ca*	*DD*	*42*	*1927*	*RCN*	*213*
Hainaut	be	-D	05	4312	Ant	107
Halcyon	pa	-D	17	3531	Pan	77
ex Sirrah (39)						
Hallanger	nw	-MT	28	9551	Ber	245
Hallfried	nw	-D	18	2968	Osl	174
ex Fairfield (39)						
Halma	pa	-M	40	2937	Pan	167
ex Nora (41)						
Halo	am	-DT	20	6986	NYo	76
"	"	"	"	"	"	84
"	"	"	"	"	"	97
Halonia	ca	-Dy	31	358		---
s. Raccoon (40)						
Halsey	am	-DT	20	7088	Wmt	93
Hambleton (DD 455)	*am*	*DD*	*41*	*1630*	*USN*	*135*
Hamdiah	äg	-S		80		249
Hameln	dt	-D	21	4351	Bre	---
s. Oaxaca (41)						
Hamla	br	-D	29	4416	Lon	118
Hamlet	nw	-MT	34	6578	Dra	99
Hammann (DD 412)	*am*	*DD*	*39*	*1570*	*USN*	*279*
Hammaren	sw	-M	30	3220	Göt	118
Hampton Roads	am	-D	20	2689	Wmt	100
Handy	*br*	*DD*	*39*	*1340*	*RN*	*---*
ex Jurua (39),						
s. Harvester (40)						

1	2	3	4	5	6	7
Hannah Böge	dt	-D	38	2372	Hbg	---
s. Crown Arun (39)						
Hanne	dä	-D	05	1080	Kop	9
Hannover	dt	-M	39	5537	Hbg	---
s. Empire Audacity (39)						
Hanö	fi	-D	00	1781	Hsk	---
s. Hanonia (39)						
Hanonia	es	-D	00	1781	Kur	3
ex Hanö (39)						
Hanover	am	-D	19	7466	PAr	---
s. Adamastos (40)						
Hans Egede	gö	-D	05	900	Kop	83
Hanseat	pa	-MT	29	8241	Pan	84
Har Zion	br	-DP	07	2508	Fam	27
Haraden (DD 183)	*am*	*DD*	*18*	*1060*	*USN*	*---*
s. Columbia (40)						
Harbledown	br	-D	33	5414	Lon	48
Harboe Jensen	nw	-M	29	1862	Osl	241
Harborough	br	-D	32	5415	Lon	123
Harbury	br	-D	33	5081	Lon	165
Hardwicke Grange	br	-D	21	9005	Lon	103
Hardy (II)(R.08)	*br*	*DD*	*43*	*1730*	*RN*	*204*
Harelda	br	-D	01	1523	Liv	---
s. Hareldawins (39)						
Hareldawins	br	-D	01	1523	Hon	258
ex Harelda (39)						
Haresfield	br	-D	19	5299	Gla	263
Harlingen	br	-D	33	5415	Lon	61
Harmala	br	-D	35	5730	Lon	148
Harmatris	br	-D	32	5395	Lon	197
Harmattan	br	-D	30	4558	Lon	240
Harmodius	br	-D	19	5229	Liv	45
Harmonic	br	-D	30	4558	Lon	169
Harmonides	br	-D	20	5237	Liv	263
Harpagon	br	-D	35	5719	Lon	91
Harpagus	br	-D	40	5173	Lon	52
Harpalyce	br	-D	40	5169	Lon	26

1	2	3	4	5	6	7	1	2	3	4	5	6	7	1	2	3	4	5	6	7
							Hebe (N.24)	*br*	*PM*	*36*	*835*	*RN*	*252*							
Harpathian	br	-D	30	4671	Lon	49	*Hecla (F.20)*	*br*	*AS*	*40*	*10850*	*RN*	*135*	*Hermione (74)*	*br*	*CL*	*39*	*5450*	*RN*	*234*
Harpenden	br	-D	30	4678	Lon	28	Hector	nl	-M	39	1828	Ams	98	Hermis	pa	-D	19	5234	Pan	101
Harperley	br	-D	30	4586	Lon	165	Hedrun	sw	-D	20	2325	Sto	25	ex Ada O. (42)						
Harraton	br	-D	30	2795	New	---	Heemskerk	nl	-DP	19	6516	Haa	41	Hero	nw	-D	18	1375	Dra	235
s. Cagou (39)							Hefz el Rahman	äg	-S		90		232	Heronspool	br	-D	29	5202	Har	4
Harrier	sa	-D	92	193	Cap	269	Heina	nw	-M	25	4028	Ber	78	Hertford	br	-D	17	10923	Lon	87
Harry F.	am	-DT	31	6151	Wmt	89	Heinrich	pa	-MT	30	11020	Pan	90							
Sinclair,Jr.							v.Riedemann							*Heythrop (L.85)*	*br*	*DE*	*40*	*1050*	*RN*	*231*
Harry G.Seidel	pa	-MT	30	10354	Pan	91	Hekla	is	-D	07	1215	Rey	58	Highland Patriot	br	-MP	32	14172	Bel	31
Harry Luckenbach	am	-D	19	6366	NYo	158	Hektoria	br	-DW	99	13797	Lon	122	*Highlander (H.44)*	*br*	*DD*	*39*	*1340*	*RN*	*159*
Hartington	br	-D	32	5496	Lon	132	Helen Forsey	ca	-S	29	167	Lun	120	*ex Jaguaribe (39)*						
"	"	"	"	"	"	133	Helen Moller	br	-D	18	5259	Lon	275	Hilda	fi	-D	15	1144	Ram	20
Hartismere	br	-D	33	5498	Lon	27	Helena Margareta	br	-D	15	3316	Lon	49	Hindanger	nw	-M	29	4884	Ber	121
"	"	"	"	"	"	263	Helenus	br	-D	13	7366	Liv	82	Hindpool	br	-D	28	4897	Har	45
Hartlebury	br	-D	34	5082	Lon	199	Helle	nw	-D	18	2467	Por	48	Hird	nw	-M	24	4950	Osl	28
Harvard	br	-S	91	114	Geo	169	Hellen	nw	-D	21	5289	Dra	229	*Hobart (I.63)*	*au*	*CL*	*34*	*6890*	*RAN*	*283*
Harvester (H.19)	*br*	*DD*	*39*	*1340*	*RN*	*156*	Hellenic Pioneer	gr	-M	24	3838	Arg	---	Hobbema	nl	-DT	18	5507		133
ex Handy (40), ex Jurua (39)							s. Maro (40), ex Maro Y. (39)							ex Empire Cheetah (42), ex Kalani (40)						
Harvey W.Scott	am	-DD	42	7176	Ptl	267	Hellenic Trader	pa	-D	07	2052	Pan	262	Höegh Giant	nw	-MT	37	10990	Osl	100
Hassan	äg	-S		80		242	ex Catherine G.Sudden (39)							Höegh Merchant	nw	-M	34	4858	Osl	278
Hastings	am	-D	20	5401	Mob	151	*Helli*	*gr*	*CL*	*12*	*2115*	*RHN*	*224*	Holmpark	br	-D	27	5780	Gre	129
Hatarana	br	-D	17	7522	Lon	117	Helmspey	br	-D	31	4764	Car	266	Hoihow	br	-D·	33	2798	Lon	269
Hatasu	br	-D	21	3198	Liv	68	Heminge	br	-D	19	2499	New	31	*Holcombe (L.56)*	*br*	*DE*	*42*	*1087*	*RN*	*253*
Hatimura	br	-D	18	6690	Lon	133	Hengist	br	-D	28	984	Lei	83	Hollinside	br	-D	30	4172	New	120
"	"	"	"	"	"	134	*Henley (DD 391)*	*am*	*DD*	*37*	*1500*	*USN*	*284*	Hollywood	am	-DT	20	5498	SFr	182
Haulerwijk	nl	-D	24	3278	Rot	31	Henrik	nw	-D	20	1350	Dra	242	Holmbury	br	-D	25	4566	Liv	165
Hav	nw	-D	39	5062	Osl	232	Henry B.Plant	am	-D	44	7240	Jac	190	Holmelea	br	-D	28	4223	New	44
Havbör	nw	-MT	30	7614	Osl	35	Henry G.Blasdel	am	-D	43	7176	SFr	182	Holmside	br	-D	30	3433	New	96
Havildar	br	-D	40	5407	Lon	26	Henry Gibbins	am	-D	18	5766		105	Holmsteinn	is	-Df		16		54
Havock (H.43)	*br*	*DD*	*36*	*1340*	*RN*	*231*	Henry Knox	am	-D	42	7176	LAn	269	Holystone	br	-D	27	5462	New	43
Havre	br	-D	05	2073	Lon	233	Henry Miller	am	-D	43	7207	LAn	189	Honolulan	am	-D	21	7493	NYo	110
Havsten	nw	-MT	30	6161	Tön	112	Henri Mory	br	-D	20	2564	Swa	50	Honomu	am	-D	19	6977	SFr	198
"	"	"	"	"	"	113	Henry R.Mallory	am	-D	16	6063	NYo	149	Hoosier	am	-D	20	5060	NYo	199
Havtor	nw	-D	30	1624	Osl	56	Henry Stanley	br	-M	29	5026	Liv	140	·Hop	nw	-D	16	1365	Ber	12
Hawkinge	br	-D	24	2475	Lon	60	Henzada	br	-D	34	4161	Gla	170	Hopecastle	br	-M	37	5178	New	130
Hazelside	br	-D	28	4646	New	3	Heredia	am	-D	08	4732	NYo	97	Hopetarn	br	-M	39	5231	New	268
Hazelside	br	-D	40	5297	New	71	Hermes	nl	-MT	14	3768	Haa	26							

1	2	3	4	5	6	7
Hopewell (DD 181)	am	DD	18	1060	USN	---
s. Bath (40)						
Horace Bushnell	am	-D	43	7176	Bal	212
Horace Gray	am	-D	43	7200	Bal	211
Hörda	nw	-D	20	4301	Ber	47
Horn Shell	br	-MT	31	8272	Lon	60
Hororata	br	-D	42	13945	Ply	141
Hosanger	nw	-D	11	1591	Ber	11
Hugh L.Scott	am	AP	20	12479	USN	136
(AP 43), ex President Pierce (42)						
Hugoton	am	-DT	19	6943	Wmt	---
s. Tamaulipas (41)						
Humber Arm	br	-D	25	5758	SJo	22
Huncliffe	br	-D	36	4511	Lon	---
s. Stancliffe (40)						
Huntingdon	br	-D	20	10946	Lon	43
Hurricane (H.06)	br	DD	39	1340	RN	175
ex Japarua (39)						
Hurst Castle	br	PE	44	1010	RN	185
(K.416)						
Hurunui	br	-D	20	9331	Ply	32
Husni	lb	-S		107		243
Hvosleff	nw	-D	27	1630	Osl	84
Hydraios	gr	-D	02	4476	Hyd	269
Hylton	br	-D	37	5197	New	47
Hyperion (H.97)	br	DD	36	1340	RN	225
Hythe (J.194)	br	PM	41	656	RN	251
I.C.White	pa	-D	20	7052	Pan	67
ex am (40)					Wmt	---
Ia	gr	-D	17	4860	Syr	23
Icarion	gr	-D	12	4013	Arg	76
Ida Knudsen	nw	-MT	25	8913	Hau	59
Idaho	am	-DT	19	6418	Wmt	278

1	2	3	4	5	6	7
Idar	br	-D		391		259
Idefjord	nw	-D	21	4287	Osl	211
"	"	"	"	"	"	213
Ila	nw	-D	39	1583	Osl	69
Ile de Batz	br	-D	18	5755	Swa	86
ex West Hobomac (40)						
Ilissos	gr	-D	15	4724	Chi	287
Illinois	am	-D	20	5447	Tac	100
Ilorin	br	-D	20	815	Liv	120
Ilvington Court	br	-D	19	5187	Lon	26
Imperial Transport	br	-MT	31	8022	Lon	13
"	"	"	"	"	"	87
Inanda	br	-D	25	5345	Liv	---
s. Empire Explorer (41)						
Incomati	br	-M	34	7369	Bel	170
India Arrow	am	-DT	21	8327	NYo	77
Indianapolis	am	CA	31	9950	USN	290
(CA 35)						
Indier	be	-DP	18	5409	Ant	48
Indra	pa	-D	00	2032	Pan	69
Indra	nw	-M	23	5041	Hau	139
Induna	br	-D	25	5086	Gla	197
Industria	sw	-M	40	1688	Göt	160
Inga I	nw	-D	21	1304	Ber	60
Inger	nw	-D	30	1418	Tro	63
Inger Elisabeth	nw	-D	20	2166	Ber	123
ex Cissy (39)						
Inger Toft	br	-D	20	2190	Lon	192
Ingerfenn	nw	-D	12	3987	Ber	144
Ingerfire	nw	-D	05	3835	Ber	162
Ingerto	nw	-D	20	3089	Ber	84
Inglefield (D.02)	br	DD	36	1530	RN	6
Ingria	nw	-M	31	4391	Ber	152
Inneröy	nw	-MT	36	8260	Osl	75
Inverarder	br	-DT	19	5578	Lon	81
Inverdargle	br	-MT	38	9456	Gla	10

1	2	3	4	5	6	7
Inverielen	br	-MT	38	9456	Gla	148
Inverlee	br	-MT	38	9158	Gla	68
Inverliffey	br	-MT	38	9456	Dub	1
Inverness	br	-D	40	4897	New	59
Invershannon	br	-MT	38	9154	Gla	29
Inversuir	br	-MT	38	9456	Gla	54
Ioanna	gr	-D	07	950	Pir	18
Ioannis Fafalios	gr	-D	19	5670	Chi	276
Ionian	br	-D	38	3114	Liv	7
Irene	am	-D	19	3482	NYo	---
s. Nidarholm (39)						
Irene Maria	br	-D	22	1860	Lon	36
Irénée Du Pont	am	-D	41	6125	Wmt	158
"	"	"	"	"	"	159
Irish Oak	ir	-D	19	5589	Dub	167
ex West Neris (42)						
Irish Pine	ir	-D	19	5621	Dub	136
ex West Hematite (41)						
Iron Chieftain	au	-D	37	4812	Mel	279
Iron Drown	au	-D	22	3353	Syd	279
Iron Knight	au	-D	37	4812	Mel	282
Isaac Sweers	nl	DD	40	1628	RNe	238
Isabela	am	-D	11	3110	NYo	97
Itagiba	bz	-D	13	2169	Rio	116
Italia	nw	-MT	39	9973	Osl	19
Itapagé	bz	-D	27	4998	Rio	173
Itchen (K.227)	br	PF	42	1370	RN	171
"	"	"	"	"	"	172
Ivo Racic	jg	-D	07	3723	Dub	---
s. Yewcrest (39)						
Iroquois (G.89)	ca	DD	41	1927	RCN	213
Ixion	br	-DP	12	10263	Liv	51

1	2	3	4	5	6	7
Joseph M.Cudahy	am	-DT	21	6950	Wmt	93
Joseph Rodman Drake	am	-D	42	7181	SFr	154
Josephine	am	-D	19	2609		---
ex Stella Lykes (41), s. Leslie (41)						
Julia Ward Howe	am	-D	42	7176	Por	147
Julien	fr	-Df		177		18
Juneau (CL 52)	*am*	*CL*	*41*	*6000*	*USN*	*281*
Jupiter	ho	-D	17	2063	PCo	---
s. Bluefields (41)						
Jura (T.169)	*br*	*APC*	*41*	*545*	*RN*	*241*
Jurua	*bz*	*DD*	*39*	*1340*	*BzN*	*---*
s. Harvester (39), ex Handy (39)						
Justitia	br	-D	35	4562	Lon	36
Jutland	br	-D	28	6153	Gla	198
K-XVI	*nl*	*SS*	*33*	*759*	*RNe*	*258*
K.G.Meldahl	nw	-D	38	3799	San	265
Kabalo	be	-D	17	5186	Ant	32
Kafiristan	br	-D	24	5193	New	2
Kahuku	am	-D	20	6062	SFr	104
Kaimoku	am	-D	19	6367	SFr	114
Kaipara	br	-M	38	5882	Ply	169
Kalani	am	-D	18	5507	SFr	---
s. Hobbema (42), ex Empire Cheetah (42)						
Kalingo	au	-D	27	2051	Syd	282
Kalliopi	gr	-D	10	4965	Chi	149
Kalypso Vergotti	gr	-D	18	5686	Arg	58
Kamuning	br	-D	16	2076	Sin	260
Kanbe	br	-D	41	6244	Gla	166
Kapitan Voronin	sj	-Df	32	558	Mur	---
(RT 70), s. SKR-70 (41)						

1	2	3	4	5	6	7
Karamea	br	-D	28	10530	Sou	4
Karl Libknecht	*sj*	*DD*	*16*	*1399*	*SNF*	*213*
Karmt	nw	-M	38	4991	Hau	194
Kars	br	-MT	39	8888	Lon	80
Kasongo	be	-D	18	5254	Ant	44
Kassandra Louloudis	gr	-D	19	5106	And	86
Kastor	gr	-D	21	5497	Ith	112
Katha	br	-D	38	4357	Gla	161
Katoomba	au	-D	13	9424	Mel	280
Katvaldis	br	-D	07	3163	PTa	118
Katy	nw	-MT	31	6825	Osl	195
Kaunas	li	-D	31	1521	Sve	6
Kavak	br	-D	29	2782	Liv	37
Kayeson	br	-D	29	4606	Lon	31
Kaying	br	-D	22	2626	Lon	244
Kearny (DD 432)	*am*	*DD*	*40*	*1630*	*USN*	*69*
Kelet	un	-D	13	4295	Bud	25
Kellwyn	br	-D	20	1459	Swa	60
Kelmscott	br	-D	43	7039	Lon	177
Kelvinbank	br	-M	21	3872	Gla	154
Kelso	br	-D	24	3956	Hul	114
Kennebec	br	-DT	19	5548	Lon	1
Kenordoc	ca	-D	26	1780	FWm	28
ex Geo.R.Donovan (39)						
Kensington Court	br	-D	27	4863	Lon	2
Kentar	nl	-D	20	5878	Bat	112
Kenya (14)	*br*	*CL*	*39*	*8000*	*RN*	*236*
Keppel (D.84)	*br*	*DD*	*20*	*1480*	*RN*	*208*
Keramiai	gr	-D	17	5085	Arg	12
Keret	nw	-D	27	1718	Ber	26
Keystone	am	-D	19	5565	NYo	157
ex Sage Brush (41)						
Kharouf	*pl*	*-S*		*158*		*235*
Khartoum (F.45)	*br*	*DD*	*39*	*1690*	*RN*	*257*
Khedive Ismail	br	-D	22	7513	Lon	273
Kiev	sj	-D	17	5823	Ode	197

1	2	3	4	5	6	7
Kimberley (F.50)	*br*	*DD*	*39*	*1690*	*RN*	*229*
King Alfred	br	-D	19	5272	Sun	24
King Arthur	br	-M	28	5224	Lon	136
King Edgar	br	-M	27	4536	Lon	192
King Edward	br	-D	19	5224	Lon	142
King Erik	br	-Df	99	228	Gri	63
King Frederick	br	-D	20	5265	Lon	276
King Gruffydd	br	-D	19	5072	Lon	157
King Idwal	br	-D	20	5115	Lon	36
King James	br	-M	25	5122	Lon	145
King Lud	br	-M	28	5224	Lon	262
King Malcolm	br	-D	25	5120	Lon	71
King Robert	br	-D	20	5886	Lon	41
Kingsbury	br	-D	37	4898	Lon	157
"	"	"	"	"	"	158
Kingston Ceylonite	br	APC	35	448	RN	104
(FY.214), ex -Df (39)						
Kingston Hill	br	-D	40	7628	Lon	55
Kingston Sapphire	br	APC	29	356	RN	31
ex -Df (39)						
Kingswood	br	-D	29	5080	Mid	175
Kinross	br	-M	35	4956	New	57
Kioto	br	-D	18	3297	Liv	123
Kirkland	br	-D	34	1361	Lei	232
Kirnwood	br	-D	28	3829	Mid	72
Kishacoquillas	am	-DT	19	5034	NYo	---
s. Comol Rico (39)						
Kisnop	am	-D	19	6089	Por	---
s. Empire Dabchink (41)						
Kite (U.87)	*br*	*PS*	*42*	*1350*	*RN*	*208*
Kittaning	am	-DT	43	10195	Wmt	182
Kittiwake (L.30)	*br*	*PC*	*36*	*530*	*RN*	*2*
Kittys Brook	br	-D	07	4031	SJo	94
ex Sirio (41), ex Santa Catharina (41)						
Kned I	br	-Df		352		195
Knoxville City	am	-D	21	5686	NYo	100
Koenjit	nl	-M	29	4551	Bat	95

1	2	3	4	5	6	7
Kohinur	br	-D	22	5168	Lon	35
Kolchis	gr	-D	09	2219	Pir	36
Koll	nw	-MT	30	10044	Osl	88
Kollbjörg	nw	-MT	37	8259	Osl	147
Kollskegg	nw	-MT	40	9858	Osl	89
Kompleks	sj	-Dt	15	136		199
ex Nord						
Komsomolec	sj	-Dt				199
Kongsgaard	nw	-MT	37	9467	Sta	58
"	"	"	"	"	"	80
Konstantinos	gr	-D	13	5962	Chi	5
Hadjipateras						
Korana	br	-D	29	5407	Lon	---
s. Oakcrest (40)						
Koranton	br	-D	20	6695	New	47
Korshamn	sw	-M	20	6673	Sto	46
ex Vigeo (39)						
Korsholm	sw	-M	25	2647	Göt	90
Korthion	gr	-D	09	2116	And	90
Kos XIX	nw	-Dw	36	303	San	---
s. Cocker (41)						
Kos XXIV	nw	-Dw	39	560	San	---
s. Ellesmere (40)						
Kosmos II	nw	-DW	31	16966	San	130
Kota Tjandi	nl	-M	30	7295	Bat	164
Koumoundouros	gr	-D	25	3598	And	264
Kowarra	au	-D	16	2125	Mel	282
Krasnyj Profin-tern	sj	-D	02	4648	Ode	218
Krasnyj Partizan	sj	-D	27	2418	Vla	201
Kreml'	sj	-DT	32	7666	Tua	218
Krestjanin	sj	-D	28	2513	Len	199
Kronprinsen	nw	-M	42	7073	Osl	102
Kujbyšev	sj	-D	29	2332	Len	199
(= Kuibishev)						
Kumasian	br	-D	35	4922	Liv	61
Kumsang	br	-D	20	5447	Hon	126
Kupa	jg	-D	17	4382	Sus	96

1	2	3	4	5	6	7
Kurdistan	br	-D	28	5844	New	72
Kurikka	fi	-D	18	3106	Was	---
s. Chenango (41)						
Kuznec Lesov	sj	-M	33	3974	Vla	201
(= Kusnetz Lesov)						
Kuttabul	au	-Bg			Syd	279
Kvernaas	nw	-D	18	1819	Are	14
Kwantung	br	-DP	21	2626	Lon	258
Kyleclare	br	-D	32	700	Lim	151
Kyleglen	br	-D	17	3670	Liv	39
Kyma	gr	-D	12	3994	And	18
Kyno	br	-D	24	3946	Hul	27

1	2	3	4	5	6	7
L-16	sj	SS	39	1039	SPF	281
LCI 99 (L)	am	LC	42	246	USN	184
LCI 600	am	LC	43	246	USN	287
LCT 242	am	LC	42	126	USN	252
LCT 2239	br	LC	42	143	RN	147
LCT 2267	br	LC	42	143	RN	147
LCT 2335	br	LC	43	143	RN	148
LCT 2341	br	LC	43	143	RN	155
LCT 2344	br	LC	43	143	RN	147
LCT 2480	br	LC	43	143	RN	154
LSD 7	am	LS	43	4500	USN	---
s. Oakhill						
LST 280	am	LS	42	1490	USN	182
LST 305	br	LS	43	1625	RN	254
LST 333	br	LS	43	1625	RN	246
LST 342	am	LS	43	1625	USN	283
LST 348	am	LS	43	1625	USN	254
LST 350	am	LS	42	1490	USN	188
LST 359	am	LS	42	1490	USN	188
LST 362	br	LS	43	1625	RN	179

1	2	3	4	5	6	7
LST 387	am	LS	43	1625	USN	246
LST 418	br	LS	43	1625	RN	254
LST 469	am	LS	43	1625	USN	283
LST 513	am	LS	43	1653	USN	---
s. Endymion						
LST 577	am	LS	43	1653	USN	288
LST 695	am	LS	43	1653	USN	286
LST 921	am	LS	43	1653	USN	184
L.A.Christensen	nw	-M	25	4362	Tön	102
L.J.Drake	am	-DT	18	6693	Wmt	101
L'Enjoue	fr	PC	43	335	FFN	189
ex PC 482 (43)						
La Brea	br	-DT	16	6666		26
ex am (40)					LAn	---
La Carriere	br	-DT	38	5685	Lon	81
La Cordillera	br	-M	40	5185	Lon	134
La Dieppoise	fr	PE	40	925	RFN	---
s. Fleur de Lys (40)						
La Estancia	br	-D	40	5185	Lon	34
La Paz	br	-M	20	6548	Liv	92
La Salle	am	-D	20	5462	Mob	265
Labud	jg	-D	18	5334	Sus	20
Lackenby	br	-D	28	5112	Har	147
Laconia (F.42)	br	AP	22	19695	RN	122
ex br ACL (39), ex -DP						
Laconikos	gr	-D	14	3803	And	166
Lady Drake	ca	-D	28	7985	Hal	93
Lady Glanely	br	-M	38	5497	Car	37
Lady Hawkins	ca	-DP	28	7988	Hal	74
Lady Nelson	ca	-D	28	7970	Hal	84
Lady Shirley	br	APC	37	477	RN	228
ex -Df (39)						
Lady Somers (OBV)	br	-D	29	8194	RN	59
ex ca -DP (40)					Mon	
Ladylove	br	-Df	03	230	Lon	63
Laertes	nl	-D	19	5825	Ams	92
Laertes (T.137)	br	APC	40	545	RN	111

1	2	3	4	5	6	7
Lise	nw	-MT	31	6826	Osl	95
Liseta	nl	-DT	27	2628	Wil	191
Lissa	br	-D	27	1511	Gla	66
Lister	sw	-D	28	1366	Söl	8
Litiopa	nw	-DT	17	5356	Far	173
Liverpool Packet	ca	-D	26	1188	Lvp	99
rx Sonia (41)						
Livingston	br	-D	28	2140	SJo	185
Ljubica Matkovic	jg	-D	19	3289	Spl	105
Llanarth	br	-D	29	5053	Lon	21
Llanashe	br	-D	36	4836	Lon	267
Llandaff Castle	br	-D	26	10799	Lon	266
Llandilo	br	-D	28	4966	Lon	265
Llanfair	br	-D	28	4966	Lon	25
Llangibby Castle	br	-M	29	12053	Lon	74
Llanover	br	-D	28	4959	Lon	94
Loch Don	br	-M	37	5249	Gla	88
Loch Doon	br	APM	37	534	RN	9
ex -Df (39)						
Loch Lomond	br	-D	34	5452	Gla	34
Loch Maddy	br	-D	34	4996	Gla	15
Loch Ranza	br	-D	34	4958	Gla	38
Lochavon	br	-M	38	9205	Lon	4
Lochgoil	br	-D	22	9462	Lon	4
Lochkatrine	br	-M	22	9419	Lon	112
Longtaker	pa	-D		1700	Pan	62
ex						
Longwood	br	-MT	30	9463	Lon	259
Loosdrecht	nl	-MT	36	9314		---
s. Franche Comté (40)						
Lorain	am	-D	19	6160	Nwk	---
s. Empire Thrush (42)						
Lord Lonsdale	br	-Df	29	292		---
s. Tor II (39)						
Lord Minto	br	-Df	14	295	Fle	2
Lord Strathcona	ca	-D	15	7335	Hal	120
Lorient	br	-D	21	4737	Car	165
ex Fr (40)						
Lornaston	br	-D	25	4934	Gla	192
Losmar	am	-D	19	5549	NYo	263
Lot	fr	AO	39	4220	RFN	168
Lotos	nw	-D	19	1327	Ber	28
Lotta	dä	-D	38	1858	Esb	---
s. Tolten (41)						
Louhi	fi	ACM		640	FiN	217
Louis Kossuth	am	-D	43	7176	Bal	184
Louise Lykes	am	-D	41	6155	NOr	146
Louise Moller	br	-D	07	3764	Sha	265
Louisiana	am	-MT	37	8587	Wmt	116
Louisiane	fr	-D	05	6903	Hav	4
Lowry (DD 770)	am	DD	44	2200	USN	290
Loyalty (J.217)	br	PM	42	850	RN	184
ex Rattler (42)						
Lubrafol	pa	-MT	24	7138	Pan	94
Lucerna	br	-MT	30	6556	Liv	24
Lucifero	it	-DT	12	4000	Gen	---
s. Potrero del Llano (41)						
Lucille M.	ca	-Mf		54		111
Luciston	br	-D	24	5017	Gla	---
s. Sheaf Mount (39)						
Lucrecia	nl	-DT	28	2584	Wil	22
Luimneach	br	-D	15	1074	Lim	28
Lulworth Hill	br	-D	40	7628	Lon	160
Lumen	br	-MT	25	6537	Liv	---
s. Empire Light (42)						
Luna	nw	-D	11	959	Ber	9
Lundby	dä	-D	26	4150	Kal	---
s. Pink Star (41)						
Lutz	nw	-D	33	1416	Osl	148
Luxembourg	be	-D	15	5809	Ant	20
Lycaon	br	-DP	13	7350	Liv	50
Lydia M.Child	am	-D	43	7176	LAn	282
Lyman Stewart	am	-D	43	7176	LAn	270
Lynton Grange	br	-D	37	5029	Lon	143
Lynx II	br	-Df	06	250	Gri	5
Lysefjord	nw	-D	15	1091	Sta	160
M-78	sj	SS	35	161	SBF	214
M-93	sj	SS	38	206	SBF	---
s. M-175 (40)						
M-94	sj	SS	38	206	SBF	214
M-101	sj	SS	40	206	SBF	214
M-175	sj	SS	38	206	SNF	197
ex M-93 (40)						
ML. 1003	br	PC	40	46	RN	49
ML. 1037	br	PC	40	46	RN	49
MO-105	sj	PC		56	SBF	216
MO-107	sj	PC		56	SBF	216
MO-304	sj	PC		56	SBF	216
MTB.339	br	PT	41	32	RN	112
MTB.342	br	PT	41	32	RN	112
M.F.Elliott	am	-DT	21	6940	Wmt	100
M.H.de Young	am	-D	43	7176	SFr	284
Maalöy	nw	-Dw		249		274
Maas	nl	-D	20	1966	Rot	28
Maasdam	nl	-DP	21	8812	Rot	58
Mabella	nw	-D	26	1513	Dra	261
Mabriton	br	-D	20	6694	New	30
McCalla (DD 253)	am	DD	19	1190	USN	---
s. Stanley (40)						
McCook (DD 252)	am	DD	19	1190	USN	---
s. St.Croix (40)						
McDowell	am	-DT	43	10195	Phi	175
McKeesport	am	-D	19	6198	Nwk	164
Macabi	pa	-D	21	2802	Blb	130
Macedonier	be	-DP	21	5227	Ant	39
Macgregor	br	-D	19	2498	Ard	82

1	2	3	4	5	6	7
Macon	br	-D	19	5135	Liv	59
ex Point Ancha (40)						
Madoera	nl	-M	22	9382	Bat	152
Mae	am	-D	18	5607	NYo	123
Magdala	nl	-MT	31	8248	Wil	157
Magdalena	br	-D	23	3118	Har	29
Magdapur	br	-D	21	8641	Liv	1
Magne	sw	-D	12	1226	Sto	192
Magnus	dä	-D	06	1339	Mdf	8
Magog (K.673)	*ca*	*PF*	*43*	*1370*	*RCN*	*186*
Magog	ca	-D	23	2053	Mon	22
Mahratta (G.23)	*br*	*DD*	*42*	*1920*	*RN*	*205*
ex Marksman (41)						
Mahronda	br	-D	25	7926	Liv	262
Mahukona	am	-D	47	2512	SFr	47
Maid of Orleans	br	-D	18	2386	Lon	182
Maiden Creek	am	-D	19	5031	Mob	255
Maine	am	-D	17	6379	NYo	---
s. Empire Lynx (40)						
Maja	br	-MT	31	8181	Lon	190
Majaba (AG 43)	am	AG	19	2227	USN	281
ex El Capitan (42)						
Major Wheeler	am	-D	18	3431	Bal	77
Maks Hoelts	sj	-D	30	3972	Len	---
s. Castillo Montealegre (39)						
Malabar	br	-D	38	7976	Liv	5
Malaita	au	-D	33	3310	Syd	280
Malamton	am	-D	18	4554	Wmt	---
s. Minotaur (41)						
Malantic	am	-D	29	3837	Wmt	155
Malay	am	-DT	21	8207	Wmt	74
Malaya (01)	*br*	*BB*	*15*	*31100*	*RN*	*46*
Malaya II	br	-M	21	8651	Gla	58
ex dä Malaya (40)						
Malchace	am	-D	20	3516	Wmt	89
Maldonaldo	ur	-D	19	5285	Mtv	112
ex Fausto (41)						

1	2	3	4	5	6	7
Malmanger	nw	-DT	20	7078	Ber	114
Maloja	nw	-M	30	6400	Osl	135
Maltran	am	-D	20	3513	Wmt	168
Malygin	sj	AG	92	1571	Arc	201
Mambi	cu	-DT	83	1983	Hvn	167
Mamura	nl	-MT	32	8245	Wil	81
Mamutu	br	-M	38	300	Hon	280
Mana	ho	-DT	20	3283	PCo	197
Manaar	br	-D	42	8007	Liv	268
Manaar	br	-D	17	7242	Liv	1
Managua	ni	-D	19	2220	Blu	104
ex Neptuno (41)						
Manaqui	br	-D	21	2802	Lon	85
Manasseh Cutler	am	-D	43	7219		---
s. Samouri (43)						
Manchester Brigade	br	-D	18	6042	Man	30
Manchester Citizen	br	-D	25	5343	Man	169
Manchester City	br	-D	37	5600	Man	235
Manchester Merchant	br	-D	40	7264	Man	152
Manchester Post	br	-D	35	7071	Man	52
Manchester Producer	br	-D	16	5106	Man	---
s. Botwey (39)						
Mandalika	nl	-D	30	7750	Bat	46
Mangen	sw	-D	22	1253	Kar	40
Mangkalihat	nl	-D	28	8457	Bat	270
ex Lindenfels (40)						
Manini	am	-D	20	3253	SFr	278
Manipur	br	-D	20	8652	Liv	23
Manistee (F.104)	br	-D	20	5360	RN	43
ex -D (40) (OBV)						
Manners (K.568)	*br*	*DE*	*43*	*1085*	*RN*	*190*
ex am DE 523 (43)						
Manon	br	-D	01	5597	Mom	263

1	2	3	4	5	6	7
Mansepool	br	-D	28	4894	Har	44
Manuela	am	-D	34	4772	NYo	105
Manx	nw	-D	16	1343	Frs	9
Manxman (M.70)	*br*	*CM*	*40*	*2650*	*RN*	*239*
Manzanillo	cu	-D	15	1025	Hvn	115
Maplecourt	ca	-D	94	3388	Mon	42
Marathon (APA 200)	am	AP	44	7607	USN	290
Marcella	br	-D	28	4592	Lon	156
Marconi	br	-D	17	7402	Liv	53
Marcus Whitman	am	-D	42	7176	Ptl	135
Mardinian	br	-D	19	2434	Liv	28
Margaret	am	-D	16	3352	NYo	90
Margareta	fi	-D	02	2155	Lov	19
ex Barbro (39)						
Margareta	fi	-D	04	3103	Bor	68
ex Atlantic (39)						
Margit	br	-D	24	1735	Lon	177
Margot	br	-D	26	4545	Lon	98
Maria	fi	-S				216
Maria	pa	-D	28	4919	Pan	---
s. Santa Margarita (40)						
Maria Amelia	pt	-D	13	1766	Lis	181
Maria da Gloria	pt	-S	19	270	Ave	101
Maria Rosa	it	-D	14	4211	Gen	15
ex Triton (39)						
Mariana	am	-D	15	3110	NYo	82
Marie José	fr	-D	25	2477	Alg	18
Marietta E.	br	-D	40	7628	Lon	267
Marija Uljanova	sj	-MP	28	3870	Len	196
Marilyse Moller	br	-D	15	786	Sha	235
ex Tseang Tah (41)						
Marina	br	-D	35	5088	Lon	29
Marina Raskova	sj	-D		5685		208
Marion Moller	br	-D	09	3827	Lon	277
Marionga	gr	-D	12	4236	Pir	53
Marisa	nl	-MT	37	8029	Haa	52

1	2	3	4	5	6	7
Munger T.Ball	am	-DT	20	5104	Bal	93
Munster	br	-MP	38	4305	Dub	13
Murat Halstead	am	-D	43	7176		---
s. Chung Cheng (43)						
Murefte	br	-D		691		226
Murena	nl	-MT	31	8252	Wil	151
Murjek	sw	-M	25	5070	Sto	45
Murman	sj	ACM			SNF	203
Muskeget (AG 48)	am	PY	22	1827	USN	121
ex Cornish (41)						
Muskogee	am	-DT	13	7034	Wmt	87
Musson (RT.)	sj	APC	21	163	SNF	---
s. SKR-23 (41)						
Myrica	br	-D	24	5952		---
ex Sistiana (40),						
s. Empire Union (41)						
Myriel	br	-DT	13	3560	Lon	228
Myrmidon	br	-M	30	6278	Liv	120
Myrmidon (G.90)	br	DD	42	1920	RN	----
s. Orkan (42)						
NYMS 382	nw	PM	43	335	RNo	195
ex am (43)						
N.T.Nielsen Alonso	nw	-MW	00	9348	Lar	150
Nabob (D.77)	ca	CVE	43	8600	RCN	208
ex CVE 41, ex Edisto (42)						
Naeco	am	-DT	18	5373	Wmt	87
Naftilos	gr	-D	04	3531	And	23
Nagara	br	-D	19	8791	Sou	160
Nagina	br	-D	21	6551	Gla	164
Nagpore	br	-D	20	5283	Hul	130
Nagwa	äg	-S		183		249

1	2	3	4	5	6	7
Naiad (93)	br	CL	39	5450	RN	230
Nailsea Court	br	-D	36	4946	Car	155
Nailsea Lass	br	-D	17	4289	Liv	44
Nailsea Manor	br	-D	37	4926	Car	68
Nailsea Meadow	br	-D	37	4962	Car	268
Nairung	br	-D	42	5414	Lon	276
Nalgora	br	-D	22	6579	Gla	40
Namarib	am	-D	19	3279	NYo	---
ex Marsodak (41),						
s. Balladier (42)						
Namaz	br	-S		50		249
Nancy Moller	br	-D	07	3916	Lon	274
Nanking	sw	-M	24	5931	Göt	164
Napier Star	br	-D	27	10116	Lon	39
Narcissus	am	-D	20	6065	SFr	---
s. Potlatch (40)						
Nardana	br	-D	19	7974	Gla	45
Nariva	br	-D	20	8714	Sou	158
"	"	"	"	"	"	159
Narkunda	br	-D	20	16632	Bel	238
Narragansett	br	-MT	36	10389	Lon	87
Nathanael Greene	am	-D	42	7176	Wmt	243
Nathaniel Hawthorne	am	-D	42	7176	Ptl	134
Navajo (AT 64)	am	AT	39	1280	USN	284
Navarra	nw	-D	20	2118	Osl	17
Navasota	br	-D	17	8795	Sou	7
Navemar	sp	-D	21	5473	Sev	75
Nea Hellas	br	-D	22	16991	Gla	127
ex Tuscania (39)						
Nebraska	br	-D	20	8261	Lon	180
Neches (AO 5)	am	AO	20	7383	USN	278
Nedmac	am	-D	19	5698		---
s. Antares (AKS 3)						
Neion	gr	-D	18	5154	Pir	21
Nellie	gr	-D	13	4826	Pir	128
Nellore	br	-D	13	6942	Gre	275

1	2	3	4	5	6	7
Nelson	br	BB	25	33950	RN	7
Nemanja	jg	-D	18	5226	Dbr	89
Nemea	gr	-D	19	5101	Ith	41
Neptunia	br	-Dt	38	798	Lon	1
Neptunian	br	-D	25	5155	New	28
Neptuno	ho	-D	19	2220	PCo	---
s. Managua (41)						
Nerissa	br	-DP	26	5583	Ham	50
Nestor (G.02)	au	DD	40	1690	RAN	226
Neva (RT.44)	sj	-Df	31	633	Mur	---
s. TSČ-44 (41)						
Neva	sw	-D	28	1456	Hel	147
Nevada	dä	-D	17	3766	Kop	---
s. Apaloide (42)						
New Brunswick	br	-D	19	6529	Liv	97
New Columbia	br	-D	20	6574	Liv	174
New Foundland (59)	br	CL	41	8800	RN	248
New Jersey	am	-DT	21	6414	Wmt	99
New Sevilla	br	-DW	00	13801	Jer	29
New Toronto	br	-D	19	6568	Liv	134
New Windsor	am	-D	19	5590	NYo	---
s. Alcoa Mariner (40)						
New York	br	-D	24	4989		125
ex am (42)					Ptm	---
Newbury	br	-D	27	5102	Lon	65
Newton Ash	br	-D	25	4625	New	149
Newton Pine	br	-D	25	4212	Car	128
Nicarao	am	-D	20	1445	NYo	96
Niceto Larrinaga	br	-D	16	5591	Liv	67
Nicholas Cuneo	ho	-D	07	1051	PCo	108
Nickeliner	am	-DT	38	2249	NYo	167
ex Dolomite (40)						
Nicolaos Angelos	gr	-D	12	4351	Chi	42
Nicolaos Filinis	gr	-D	04	3111	Pir	41
Nicolas Pateras	gr	-D	10	4362	Chi	57
Nicoya	br	-D	29	5364	Gla	94

1	2	3	4	5	6	7
Nidarholm	nw	-D	19	3482	Osl	13
ex Irene (39)						
Nidarland	nw	-D	19	6132	Osl	135
ex Wisconsin (39)						
Nidarnes	nw	-D	20	2647	Osl	100
ex Santa Isabel (40)						
Niel Maersk	dä	-M	31	5086	Kop	---
s. Johnstown (41)						
Nieuw Zeeland	nl	-D	28	11069	Bat	238
Nigeria (60)	*br*	*CL*	*39*	*8000*	*RN*	*236*
Nigerian	br	-D	36	5423	Liv	140
Nikolina Matkovic	jg	-D	18	3672	Spl	128
Nikoklis	gr	-D	21	3576	And	59
Nils Gorthon	sw	-D	21	1787	Hel	25
Nimba	pa	-D	00	1854	Pan	123
ex Asta (41)						
Nina Borthen	nw	-MT	30	6123	Osl	31
Nipiwan Park	ca	-MT	43	2373	Mon	189
Niritos	gr	-D	07	3854	Ith	33
Nirpura	br	-D	21	5961	Gla	267
Nisus	br	-Df	17	210	Abe	47
Nitsa	gr	-D	15	4732	Syr	272
Nockum	am	-D	19	6060	SFr	---
s. Empire Starling (41)						
Nora	es	-D	02	1186	Pär	32
Nora	dä	-M	40	2937		---
s. Halma (41)						
Nord	pa	-D	04	3193	Pan	259
Nord	sj	-Dt	15	136	Len	---
s. Kompleks						
Nord	sj	AGS		200		208
Nordal	pa	-D	39	3845	Pan	105
Norden	dä	-M	37	4700	Kop	---
s. Firethorn (41)						
Nordhav II	nw	APM	13	425	RNo	192
ex -Df					Kri	---
Nordhval	dä	-M	24	4473	Kop	---
s. Donerail (41)						
Nordvangen	nw	-D	29	2400	Osl	79
Noreen Mary	br	-Df	16	207	Grt	183
Norfjell	nw	-DT	42	8129	Osl	211
Norfolk	ca	-D	23	1901	Mon	224
Norfolk	br	-D	18	10948	Lon	57
Norfolk	*br*	*CA*	*28*	*9975*	*RN*	*7*
Norfolk Coast	br	-M	37	646	Liv	191
Norita	sw	-D	24	1516	Hög	60
Norland	nw	-MT	41	8134	Osl	97
ex Empire Pict (42)						
Norlandia	am	-D	19	2689	Bal	107
ex Wyoming (41)						
Norlantic	am	-D	20	2606	Bal	95
Norlavore	am	-D	19	2713	Bal	81
ex Quantico (41)						
Norlindo	am	-D	20	2686	Bal	93
ex Volusia (41)						
Norman Monarch	br	-D	37	4718	Gla	52
Norman Prince	br	-D	40	1913	Lon	99
Normandy Coast	br	-D	16	1428	Liv	189
Norna	sw	-D	14	1022	Kar	13
Norne	nw	-M	30	3971	Ber	27
Norness	pa	-MT	39	9577	Pan	74
Norse King	nw	-D	20	5701	Osl	143
"	"	"	"	"	"	144
North Britain	br	-D	40	4635	New	165
North Carolina	*am*	*BB*	*40*	*35000*	*USN*	*280*
(BB 55)						
North Gaspe	ca	-M	38	888	Que	75
Northern Pride	br	APC	36	655	RN	40
ex -Df (39)					Lon	
Northern Princess	br	APC	36	655	RN	83
ex -Df (39)					Lon	
Northern Rover	br	APC	36	655	RN	5
ex -Df (39)					Lon	
Northern Spray	br	-Df	36	655	Lon	131
Northmoor	br	-M	28	4392	Lon	268
Nortind	nw	-MT	41	8221	Osl	105
ex Empire Onyx (42)						
"	"	"	"	"	"	147
Nortun	pa	-D	40	3663	Pan	267
Norvana	am	-D	20	2677		75
Norvik	pa	-MT	38	10034	Pan	145
"	"	"	"	"	"	146
Nottingham	br	-M	41	8532	Lon	72
Notts Country	br	APC	38	541	RN	83
ex -Df (39)						
Nova Scotia	br	-D	26	6796	Liv	266
Novasli	nw	-D	20	3204	Far	192
Nueva Alta Gracia	do	-S		30		103
Nurmahal	br	-D	23	5419	Lon	135
Nyggjaberg	fa	-Df	16	272	Mdv	83
ex St.Hubert (39)						
Nyholt	nw	-MT	31	8087	Hau	74
Nyland	sw	-D	09	3378	Göt	3
Nymphe	gr	-D	21	4504	Pir	262
O.A.Brodin	sw	-D	21	1960	Sto	23
O.A.Knudsen	nw	-MT	38	11007	Hau	82
Oak Hill (LSD 7)	*am*	*LS*	*43*	*4500*	*USN*	*291*
Oakbank	br	-M	26	5154	Gla	142
Oakcrest	br	-D	29	5407	Lon	36
ex Korana (40)						
Oakdene	br	-D	36	4255	Lon	51
Oakman	am	-D	20	6116	LCh	---
s. Empire Impala (41)						
Oakmar	am	-D	20	5766	NYo	86
Oakton	ca	-D	23	1727	Mon	120

1	2	3	4	5	6	7
Oakwood	am	-D	20	6071	Hou	---
s. Empire Moose (40)						
Oaxaca	me	-D	21	4351	Ver	111
ex Hameln (41)						
Obdurate (G.39)	*br*	*DD*	*42*	*1540*	*RN*	*204*
Oberon	nl	-DP	11	1996	Ams	58
O'Brien (DD 415)	*am*	*DD*	*39*	*1570*	*USN*	*280*
Observer	br	-D	28	5881	Liv	142
Ocana	nl	-MT	38	6256	Wil	87
Ocean Courage	br	-D	42	7173	Liv	147
Ocean Crusader	br	-D	42	7178	Liv	139
Ocean Honour	br	-D	42	7174	Liv	263
Ocean Justice	br	-D	42	7173	Car	134
Ocean Might	br	-D	42	7173	Liv	120
Ocean Seaman	br	-D	42	7178	Liv	244
Ocean Vagabond	br	-D	42	7174	Bri	126
"	"	"	"	"	"	146
Ocean Vanguard	br	-D	42	7174	Car	123
Ocean Vanquisher	br	-D	42	7174	Hul	240
Ocean Venture	br	-D	41	7174	Lon	77
Ocean Venus	br	-D	42	7174		92
Ocean Victory	br	-D	42	7174	Liv	160
Ocean Vintage	br	-D	42	7174	Mid	264
Ocean Voice	br	-D	41	7174	Gla	200
Octavian	nw	-M	38	1345	Ber	74
Ogontz	am	-D	19	5037	Jun	97
Ohio	br	-D	40	9514	Lon	236
Ohioan	am	-D	19	6078	NYo	94
Oilfield	br	-MT	38	8516	New	50
Oituz	ru	-D	05	2686	Kon	222
Oklahoma	am	-DT	40	9264	Wmt	89
"	"	"	"	9298	"	193
Olaf Fostenes	nw	-M	36	2994	Hau	124
Olancho	ho	-D	21	2493	PCo	156
Olean	am	-DT	19	7118	NYo	85
Olga	am	-D	19	2496	Wmt	84
Olga E.Embiricos	gr	-D	22	4677	And	273

1	2	3	4	5	6	7
Oligarch	br	-D	18	6894	Lon	247
Olinda	bz	-D	05	4053	Rio	79
Olivegrove	br	-D	29	4060	Gla	1
Oliver Ellsworth	am	-M	42	7191	Bal	200
Olney	am	-DT	20	7294	Wmt	76
Olopana	am	-D	20	6069	SFr	199
Oltenia	ru	-DT	28	6394	Kon	---
s. Oltenia II (41)						
Oltenia II	br	-DT	28	6394	Mom	145
ex Oltenia (41)						
Olympic	pa	-DT	07	5335	Pan	75
ex am (40)					LAn	---
Omar El Kattab	sy	-S		38		242
Ombilin	nl	-D	15	5658	Bat	141
Onega	sj	-D	24	1603	Arc	213
Oneida	am	-D	20	2309	Dea	109
Onomea	am	-D	17	5676	SFr	---
s. Empire Leopard (40)						
Onondaga	am	-D	20	2310	Dea	110
Ontario	am	-Bg		490		88
Ontario	ho	-D	04	3099		93
Onto	fi	-D	18	1333	Hsk	11
Opalia	br	-MT	38	6195	Lon	79
Opawa	br	-M	31	10354	Ply	77
Oporto	br	-D	28	2352	Liv	156
Orangemoor	br	-D	23	5775	Lon	18
Orania	sw	-D	19	1854	Sto	13
Oranjestad	br	-DT	27	2396	Lon	78
Orao	jg	-D	19	5135	Sus	31
Orari	br	-M	31	10350	Ply	39
"	"	"	"	"	"	84
Orcades	br	-D	37	23456	Lon	264
Oregon	am	-DT	19	7017	Wmt	88
Oregon	br	-D	20	6008	Lon	115
Oregon Express	nw	-M	33	3642	Osl	172
Orestes	br	-M	26	7748	Liv	279
Orfasay (T.204)	br	APC	42	545	RN	173

1	2	3	4	5	6	7
Orfor	br	-D	21	6578	Lon	141
Oriskany	br	-D	24	1644	Lon	191
Orkan (G.90)	*po*	*DD*	*42*	*1920*	*ORP*	*173*
ex Myrmidon (42)						
Orkanger	nw	-MT	28	8029	Ber	223
Orminster	br	-D	14	5712	Npt	185
Ormiston	au	-D	22	5832	Mel	283
Oronsay	br	-DP	25	20043	Gla	127
Oropesa	br	-DP	20	14118	Liv	41
Oropos	gr	-D	13	4474	And	142
Orsa	br	-D	25	1478	Gla	5
Oscilla	nl	-MT	39	6341	Wil	85
Osmed	sw	-D	03	1526	Hel	14
Otaio	br	-M	30	10298	Ply	63
Otho	am	-D	20	4839	NYo	88
Otina	br	-MT	38	6217	Lon	142
Ottawa (H.31)	*ca*	*DD*	*35*	*1375*	*RCN*	*122*
ex Griffin (43)						
"	"	"	"	"	"	123
Otterpool	br	-D	26	4876	Har	20
Oued Grou	br	-D	21	792	Lon	134
ex fr (40)						
Ove Toft	dä	-D	21	2135	Kop	7
Ozorio	bz	-D	19	2730	Rio	126
ex Commercial Bostonian (40)						
P-IV	sj	-Bg				199
P.615	*br*	*SS*	*40*	*683*	*RN*	*163*
ex Uluc Ali Reis (40)						
PC.482	*am*	*PC*	*43*	*335*	*USN*	---
s. L'Enjoue (43)						
PC.558	*am*	*PC*	*43*	*335*	*USN*	*256*
P.L.M.15	fr	-D	21	3754	Rou	14

1	2 3	4	5	6	7
P.L.M.22	br -D	21	5646	New	58
ex fr (40)				Roc	
P.L.M.27	br -D	22	5633	Gla	132
ex fr (40)				Roc	
PT 85	*am PT*	*42*	*35*	*USN*	*-—*
s. RPT 1 (43)					
PT 87	*am PT*	*42*	*35*	*USN*	*——*
s. RPT 3 (43)					
PT 165	*am PT*	*42*	*38*	*USN*	*283*
PT 173	*am PT*	*42*	*38*	*USN*	*283*
P.Margaronis	gr -D	13	4979	Pir	16
Pacific	nl -M	38	362	Gro	193
Pacific	br -D	15	6034		45
ex am (40)				NYo	
Pacific Grove	br -M	28	7117	Lon	162
Pacific Pioneer	br -M	28	6734	Lon	111
Pacific President	br -M	28	7113	Lon	38
Pacific Ranger	br -M	29	6895	Lon	32
Pacific Reliance	br -M	27	6717	Lon	15
Pacific Star	br -D	20	7951	Lon	130
ex Stanfleet (39)					
Paderewski	po -D	20	4426	Gdy	144
ex Trieste (41)					
Paimpol	fr -DP	18	9807	Hav	---
s. Winnipeg II (41), ex Winnipeg (40)					
Pajala	sw -M	24	6873	Sto	10
Palima	nl -D	22	1179	Bat	246
Palma	br -M	41	5419	Lon	59
"	" "	"	"	"	274
Palmella	br -D	20	1578	Liv	37
Pan Massachusetts	am -DT	19	8202	NYo	79
Pan New York	am -DT	38	7701	Wmt	130
Pan Norway	nw -MT	31	9231	Osl	76
Pan Pennsylvania	am -DT	41	7294	NYo	---
s. Petrofuel (41)					
Pan Pennsylvania	am -DT	43	11017	Wmt	180
Pan York	am -D	01	4570	Wmt	123
ex El Dia (41)					
Panachandros	gr -D	15	4661	And	10
Panam	pa -MT	25	7277	Pan	165
Pandia	fi -D	03	2368	Mar	---
s. Desert Light (42)					
Pandias	gr -D	12	4981	Pir	56
Panikos	br -S		21		248
Panna	it -D	21	6245	Gen	---
s. Empire Protector (40)					
Pantelis	gr -D	11	3845	Chi	264
Papalemos	gr -D	10	3748	Chi	53
Papoose	am -DT	21	5939	Wmt	86
Paracury	bz -S	09	265	Par	101
Parigi	nl -D	22	1172	Bat	260
Parismina	am -D	08	4732	NYo	137
Parkhill	br -D	15	500	Met	6
Parnahyba	bz -D	13	6692	Rio	92
Parramatta (L.44)	*au PS*	*39*	*1060*	*RAN*	*227*
Parthenon	gr -D	08	3189	Pir	133
Partridge (G.30)	*br DD*	*41*	*1540*	*RN*	*240*
Pass of Balmaha	br -DT	28	758	Lon	227
Pathan (PC.69)	*in PC*	*18*	*661*	*RIN*	*257*
Patras	nl -D	26	2065	Bat	258
Patria	sw -D	15	1188	Göt	10
Patrick J.Hurley	am -DT	41	10865	Wmt	122
Patroclus	br ACL	23	11314	RN	35
ex -DP (39)					
Paul H.Harwood	am -DT	18	6610	Wmt	108
Paul Luckenbach	am -D	13	6606	NYo	263
Paula	dä -D	34	1549	Esb	---
s. Montana (41)					
Paulus Potter	nl -D	42	7168		199
ex Empire Johnson (42)					
Pearlmoor	br -D	23	4581	Lon	23
Pecten	br -MT	27	7468	Lon	26
Peder Bogén	br -DT	25	9741	Lei	87
Pedernales	br -DT	38	4317	Lon	78
Pedrinhas	bz -D	35	3666	Per	106
Peeter	es -M	39	2437	Tal	---
ex Muncove (40),					
s. Cathrine (41)					
Pegasus	gr -D	20	5762	And	65
Pegasus	sw -MT	30	9583	Göt	270
Peiping	sw -M	31	6390	Göt	121
Peisander	br -M	25	6225	Liv	96
Pelayo	br -M	27	1346	Liv	103
Peleus	gr -D	28	4695	Syr	179
Pellice	it -M	20	5360	Gen	---
s. Empire Statesman (40)					
Pelotasloide	bz -D	18	5228	Rio	168
ex Auctoritas (42)					
Pennington Court	br -D	24	6098	Lon	127
Pendrecht	nl -M	39	10746	Rot	39
"	" "	"	"	"	56
Penelope	pa -MT	25	8436	Pan	85
Penelope (97)	*br CL*	*35*	*5270*	*RN*	*254*
Penelope Barker	am -D	42	7177	Wmt	204
Pennmar	am -D	20	5868	NYo	125
Pennsylvania (BB 38)	*BB*	*15*	*33100*	*USN*	*283*
Pennsylvania Sun	am -MT	38	11394	Phi	109
Penolver	br -D	12	3721	Fal	173
Penrose	br -D	28	4393	Fal	120
Pensacola (CA 24)	*am CA*	*29*	*9100*	*USN*	*289*
Pensilva	br -D	29	4258	Swa	6
Penteli	gr -D	19	5287	And	---
s. Brockley Hill (39)					
Penzance (L.28)	*br PS*	*30*	*1025*	*RN*	*26*
Persephone	pa -MT	25	8426	Pan	99
Perseus	br -D	23	10286	Liv	272
Persier	be -D	18	5382	Ant	190
Perth	br -D	15	2259	Dde	138
Peru	br -M	16	6961	Sou	72
Peshawur	br -D	19	7934	Gla	272
Pestel'	sj -D	90	1850	Ode	222

1	2	3	4	5	6	7
Peter H.Burnett	am	-D	42	7176	LAn	282
Peter Maersk	br	-M	32	5476	Hul	140
ex dä (40)					Kop	
Peter Silvester	am	-D	42	7176	LAn	277
Peter Skene Ogden	am	-D	42	7176	Ptl	255
Peterton	br	-D	19	5221	New	124
Petrel	br	-D	20	1354	Lon	67
Petrofina	nw	-MT	37	10095	Mos	---
s. Tankexpress (39)						
Petrofuel	am	-DT	41	7294	Wmt	124
ex Pan Pennsylvania (41)						
Petroheat	am	-MT	40	2469	NYo	---
s. Arriaga (40)						
Petrovskij	sj	-D	21	3771	Ode	203
Petrusey	is	-Df		91		46
Petsamo	fi	-D	07	4596	Hgö	23
Petunia (K.79)	*br*	*PE*	*40*	*925*	*RN*	*127*
Phemius	br	-D	21	7406	Liv	175
Phidias	br	-D	13	5623	Liv	56
Philadelphia	*am*	*CL*	*36*	*9700*	*USN*	*248*
(CL 41)						
Phoebe (43)	*br*	*CL*	*39*	*5450*	*RN*	*129*
Phoebe A.Hearst	am	-D	43	7176	LAn	282
Phryné	fr	-D	38	2660	Cae	3
Piako	br	-D	20	8286	Ply	52
Piave	bz	-D	12	2347	Rio	111
Picotee (K.63)	*br*	*PE*	*40*	*925*	*RN*	*61*
Pierce Butler	am	-D	42	7191	Bal	265
Pierre Soulé	am	-D	43	7191	NOr	249
Pietro Campanella	it	-D	06	6210	Gen	---
s. Equipoise (41)						
Piikiö	fi	-S				217
Pijnacker Hordijk	nl	-D	14	2982	Bat	260
Pilcot	br	-D	13	4549	Har	---
s. Vapper (39)						
Pillory	pa	-D	33	1516	Pan	181
ex Jonna (42)						

1	2	3	4	5	6	7
Pindos	gr	-D	08	4360	Arg	24
Pink (K.137)	*br*	*PE*	*42*	*925*	*RN*	*182*
Pink Star	pa	-D	26	4150	Pan	66
ex Lundby (41)						
Pinto	br	-M	28	1346	Liv	185
Pipestone County	am	-D	19	5102	NYo	91
Pizarro	br	-D	23	1367	Lon	42
Plaudit	pa	-D	13	5091	Pan	265
ex Guidonia (41)						
Planter	br	-D	27	5887	Liv	35
Pleasantville	nw	-M	29	4549	Osl	101
Plow City	am	-D	20	3282	NYo	98
Pluto	fi	-D	07	3496	Mar	58
Pluto	nw	-D	18	1598	Hau	11
Plymouth (PG.57)	am	PG	31	2265	USN	170
ex -DY (41)						
Poelau Roebiah	nl	-M	28	9251	Bat	168
Point Ancha	pa	-D	19	4727	Pan	---
s. Macon (40)						
Point Brava	am	-D	19	4834	NYo	---
s. Alcoa Guide (40)						
Point Breeze	am	-MT	18	4756	Phi	183
Point Lobos	am	-D	19	4893	SFr	---
s. Empire Wagtail (41)						
Point Pleasant Park	ca	-D	43	7136	Mon	277
Polarland	nw	-D	23	1591	Hau	189
Polyana	nw	-D	19	2267	Osl	50
ex Skjoldheim (39)						
Polyanthus (K.47)	*br*	*PE*	*40*	*925*	*RN*	*171*
Polybius	am	-D	19	7041	Sea	106
Polycarp	br	-D	18	3577	Liv	18
Polydorus	nl	-D	24	5922	Ams	139
Polyktor	gr	-D	14	4077	Ith	148
Polyphemus	nl	-M	30	6269	Ams	99

1	2	3	4	5	6	7
Polzella	br	-D	29	4751	PZc	10
Pomona	dt	-M	38	4864	Hbg	---
s. Empire Merchant (39)						
Pompoon	pa	-D	01	1082	Pan	174
ex Atlas II (42), ex Atlas (41)						
Pontus H.Ross	am	-D	44	7247	Hou	287
Pontypridd	br	-D	24	4458	Lon	102
Porcupine (G.93)	*br*	*DD*	*41*	*1540*	*RN*	*239*
Port Antonio	nw	-D	13	1266	Osl	110
Port Auckland	br	-D	22	8789	Lon	159
Port Gisborne	br	-M	27	8390	Lon	31
Port Hardy	br	-D	23	8897	Lon	50
Port Hunter	br	-D	22	8826	Lon	108
Port Jackson	br	-D	37	9687	Lon	119
Port Montreal	br	-M	37	5882	Lon	102
Port Nicholson	br	-D	19	8402	Lon	104
Port Victor	br	-M	42	12411	Lon	164
Portadoc	ca	-D	24	1746	FWm	49
ex James B.Foote (39)						
Portelet	br	-D	18	1064	Gue	12
Porter (DD 356)	*am*	*DD*	*35*	*1850*	*USN*	*281*
Portland	pa	-D	19	2648	Pan	149
Portmar	am	-D	19	5551	NYo	283
Porto Alegre	bz	-D	21	5187	Rio	265
Portugal	be	-D	06	1550	Ant	41
Poseidon	nl	-D	21	1928	Ams	100
Poseidonia	gr	-D	39	3702	Syr	---
s. Samir (39)						
Possidon	gr	-D	09	3840	Pir	28
Potlatch	am	-D	20	6065	Tac	106
ex Narcissus (40)						
Poughkeepsie	am	-D	19	5588	NYo	---
s. Alcoa Carrier (41)						
Potrero del Llano	me	-DT	12	4000	Tam	95
ex Lucifero (41)						
Preradović	jg	-D	07	5341	Spl	---
s. Fircrest (40)						

1	2	3	4	5	6	7
Rosario	am	-D	20	4659	NYo	150
Rose Castle	ca	-D	15	7803	Hal	129
"	"	"	"	"	"	132
Rose Schiaffino	br	-D	20	3349	Car	71
Rosemonde	br	APC	10	364	RCN	124
ex fr -Df (40)						
Rosenborg	br	-D	19	1512	Trn	101
Rosenborg	br	-D	14	1997	Bel	163
Rosewood	br	-DT	31	5989	Lon	155
Ross	br	-M	36	4978	New	264
Rosthern (K.169)	*ca*	*PE*	*40*	*925*		*124*
Rothermere	br	-D	38	5356	SJo	53
Rothley	br	-M	36	4996	New	129
Rotorua	br	-DP	11	10890	Ply	39
Rotterdam	nl	-MT	25	8968	Haa	119
Rouennais	fr	-D	11	3777	Dun	164
Roumanie	be	-D	06	3563	Ant	125
Roushdy	äg	-S		133		245
Roxborough Castle	br	-M	37	7801	Lon	150
Roxby	br	-D	23	4252	Har	135
Royal Archer	br	-DP	28	2266	Lei	15
Royal Oak (o8)	*br*	*BB*	*14*	*29150*	*RN*	*4*
Royal Sceptre	br	-D	37	4853	New	1
Royal Sovereign	*br*	*BB*	*15*	*29150*	*RN*	*---*
(05) *s. Archangel'sk (44)*						
Royal T.Frank	am	-D		244		278
Royston Grange	br	-D	18	5144	Lon	7
Rozewie	po	-D	38	766	Gdy	113
Ruben Dario	am	-D	44	7198	Sav	190
Ruby	co	-S		39		174
Ruckinge	br	-D	39	2869	Car	73
Rudolf	nw	-D	93	924	Osl	8
Rudolf	sw	-D	22	2119	Göt	7
Rudyard Kipling	br	-Df	21	333	Fle	2
Runa	br	-D	30	1575	Gla	66
Runo	br	-D	20	1858	Hul	245
Ruperra	br	-D	25	4548	Car	34
Rupert de Larrinaga	br	-D	30	5358	Liv	59
Rushpool	br	-D	28	5125	Har	42
Roula	gr	-D	99	1044		224
Ruth	am	-D	19	4833	NYo	107
Ruth I	nw	-D	00	3531	Hau	180
Ruth Lykes	am	-D	19	2612	Gal	96
Rutland	br	-D	35	1437	Lei	35
Rydboholm	sw	-M	33	3197	Göt	44
Rym	nw	-D	19	1369	Ber	69
S-7	*sj*	*SS*	*37*	*840*	*SBF*	*215*
ŠČ-207	*sj*	*SS*	*37*	*586*	*SSF*	*219*
ŠČ-208	*sj*	*SS*	*37*	*586*	*SSF*	*218*
ŠČ-214	*sj*	*SS*	*38*	*587*	*SSF*	*218*
ŠČ-305	*sj*	*SS*	*33*	*586*	*SBF*	*215*
ŠČ-306	*sj*	*SS*	*34*	*586*	*SBF*	*215*
SC 1477	am	PC	43	105	USN	—
s. BO-229 (43)						
SC 1485	am	PC	43	105	USN	---
s. BO- (43)						
SC 1507	am	PC	43	105	USN	---
s. BO- (43)						
SKR-	sj	APC			SNF	209
ex RT-						
SKR-23	sj	APC		163	SNF	201
ex Musson (41)						
SKR-29 Žemčug	*sj*	*PC*	*37*	*441*	*SNF*	*196*
SKR-70	sj	APC	32	558	SNF	196
ex RT-70 Kapitan Voronin (41)						
S.B.Hunt	am	-DT	19	6840	Wmt	169
Sabor	br	-D	20	5212	Lon	267
Sacramento Valley	br	-D	24	4573	Bid	55
Saganaga	br	-D	35	5454	Lei	120
Sagadahoc	am	-D	18	6275	NYo	72
Sage Brush	am	-D	19	5565	Por	---
s. Keystone (41)						
Sagenite	br	-D	05	712	Gla	---
s. Ellaroy (40)						
Sagona	nw	-MT	29	7554	Kri	228
Saguenay (D.79)	*ca*	*DD*	*30*	*1337*	*RCN*	*37*
Said	äg	-S		231		233
Saint Agnes	br	-D	18	5199	Lon	28
St.Anselm	br	-D	19	5614	Liv	58
Saint Basile	fr	-D	20	2778	Hav	182
St.Clair II	br	-D	29	3753	Car	67
ex Saint Clair (40)					Nan	---
St.Croix (I.81)	*ca*	*DD*	*19*	*1190*	*RCN*	*171*
ex McCook (40)						
St.Denis	fr	-D		1598		228
ex						
Saint Dunstan	br	-D	19	5681	Liv	26
St.Elwyn	br	-D	38	4940	Npt	37
Saint Enogat	br	-D	18	2360	Ply	184
St.Essylt	br	-M	41	5634	Npt	247
Saint Germain	br	-M	24	1044	Lon	35
St.Helena	br	-D	36	4313	Npt	49
St.Hubert	br	-Df	16	272		---
s. Nyggjaberg (39)						
St.Issey	br	AT	18	810	RN	240
St.Lindsay	ca	-D	21	5370	Nwp	56
Saint Louis	fr	-D	13	5202	Hav	179
St.Louis (CL 49)	*am*	*CL*	*38*	*10000*	*USN*	*289*
Saint Malo	fr	-D	17	5779	Dun	32
St.Margaret	br	-D	36	4312	Npt	152
St.Nidan	br	-Df	37	565	Hul	5
St.Usk	br	-S	09	5472	Npt	171
Ste.Clair	br	-Df		67		6
Ste.Marcelle	fr	-D	35	1518		231
ex Vigör (40)						

1	2	3	4	5	6	7
Sarcoxie	am	-D	19	5116	Phi	---
s. Alcoa Ranger (40)						
Sarita	nw	-DT	14	5824	Grm	23
Sarmatia	fi	-D	01	2417	Koi	19
Sarniadoc	ca	-D	29	40	FWm	85
Saroena	nl	-DT	39	6671	Haa	243
Saronikos	gr	-D	12	3548	And	266
Sarthe	br	-D	20	5271	Lon	264
Saskatchewan (H.70	*ca*	*DD*	*34*	*1375*	*RCN*	*181*
ex Fortune (43)						
Satterlee (DD 190)	*am*	*DD*	*18*	*1190*	*USN*	*---*
s. Belmont (40)						
Saturnus	nl	-D	09	2741	Ams	123
Saugor	br	-D	28	6303	Lon	63
Savia	it	-D	10	3454		---
s. Radhurst (41)						
Sawahloento	nl	-D	21	3085	Bat	266
Scandinavia	sw	-M	37	1641	Göt	169
Scania	sw	-D	34	1629	Göt	141
Scania	sw	-D	01	1980	Ari	65
Scanmail	am	-D	19	5152	NYo	---
s. Cayrú (40)						
Scanpenn	am	-D	19	5152	NYo	---
s. Buarque (40)						
Scapa Flow	pa	-D	14	4836	Pan	136
ex Anja (41)						
Scebeli	nw	-M	37	3025	San	163
Schie	nl	-D	22	1967	Rot	57
Schodack	am	-D	19	5041	Phi	---
s. Alcoa Leader (40)						
Scholar	br	-D	22	3940	Liv	29
Scoresby	br	-D	23	3843	Whi	32
Ščors (Shchors)	sj	-D	21	3770	Ode	201
Scorton	br	-D	39	4813	New	155
Scotia	nw	-MT	39	9972	Osl	272
Scotia	dä	-D	24	2400	Kop	8
Scotstoun	br	ACL	25	17046	RN	19
ex Caledonia (39)						
Scottish American	br	-DT	20	6999	Lon	17
Scottish Chief	br	-DT	28	7006	Lon	265
Scottish Heather	br	-DT	28	7087	Lon	143
Scottish Maiden	br	-MT	21	6993	Lon	35
Scottish Minstrel	br	-MT	22	6998	Lon	23
Scottish Monarch	br	-D	38	4719	Gla	54
Scottish Prince	br	-M	38	4917	Lon	86
Scottish Standard	br	-MT	21	6999	Lon	43
Scottish Star	br	-D	17	7224	Lon	79
Scottish Trader	br	-D	38	4016	Lon	72
Scottsburg	am	-D	19	8001	Gal	103
Sea Glory	br	-D	19	1964	Dov	22
Sea Porpoise	am	-D	44	7934	NOr	183
Sea Sweeper	br	-Df	15	329	Fle	6
Sea Thrush	am	-D	20	5447	Por	106
Sea Venture	br	-D	30	2327	Dov	5
Seabank Spray	br	-D	19	2465	Car	---
s. Jeanne M. (39)						
Seaforth	br	-M	39	5459	Liv	43
Seagull D.	br	-S		75		118
Seakay	am	-DT	42	11400		---
s. Santee (42)						
Seakay	am	-DT	42	10342	Wmt	179
Seattle Spirit	am	-D	19	5627	Sea	104
Sebastiano Cermeno	am	-D	43	7194	SFr	269
Sedgepool	br	-D	18	5556	Har	33
Segovia	nw	-M	22	1387	Osl	11
Segundo	nw	-M	25	4414	Osl	63
Selvistan	br	-D	24	5136	New	166
Sembilan	nl	-D	22	6566	Bat	268
Sembilangan	nl	-D	23	4990		156
Seminole	br	-MT	36	10389	Lon	243
Sénégalais	*fr*	*DE*	*43*	*1300*	*FFN*	*256*
ex am DE 106 (43)						
Senga	jg	-D	13	5164	Sus	189
Senta	nw	-D	17	3785	Osl	128
ex Sirehav (39)						
Serbino	br	-D	19	4099	Liv	70
Sergej Kirov	sj	-D	25	4146	Vla	203
Sergeant Gouarne	fr	-Df	28	1147	Roc	244
Serooskerk	nl	-D	22	8456	Haa	140
Sesostris	äg	-D	15	2962	Ale	41
Severn Leigh	br	-D	19	5242	Bri	26
Sfax	*fr*	*SS*	*34*	*1379*	*RFN*	*39*
Shaftesbury	br	-D	23	4284	Gla	109
Shahjeban	br	-D	42	5454	Lon	247
Shahristan	br	-D	38	6935	Lon	61
Shakespear	br	-D	26	5029	Lon	40
Shahzada	br	-D	42	5454	Lon	275
Shawinigan (K.136)	*ca*	*PE*	*41*	*925*	*RCN*	*187*
Sheaf Crown	br	-D	29	4868	New	267
Sheaf Mead	br	-D	24	5008	New	18
ex Gretaston (40)						
Sheaf Mount	br	-D	24	5017	New	118
ex Luciston (39)						
Sheherazade	pa	-MT	35	13467	Pan	102
ex fr (40)						
Shekatika	br	-D	36	5458	Lei	33
Shelton (DE 407)	*am*	*DE*	*43*	*1350*	*USN*	*285*
Shillong	br	-M	39	5529	Lon	161
Shirak	br	-MT	26	6023	Lon	34
Shirvan	br	-DT	25	6017	Lon	187
Shoreham (L.32)	*br*	*PS*	*30*	*1105*	*RN*	*257*
Shropshire	br	-D	39	10549	Lon	---
s. Salopian (39)						
Shuntien	br	-D	34	3059	Lon	229
Siam II	br	-D	13	6637	Bri	126
Siamese Prince	br	-M	29	8456	Lon	43
Siantar	nl	-M	21	8667	Bat	260
Sicilia	sw	-M	34	1633	Göt	268
Sicilien	am	-M	38	1654		101

1	2	3	4	5	6	7
Theodore Dwight Weld	am	-D	43	7176	LAn	171
Theodoros T.	gr	-D	12	3409	Pir	26
Thetis A.	gr	-D	10	4111	Chi	23
Thiara	br	-MT	39	10364	Lon	24
Thirlby	br	-D	28	4887	Har	75
Thistle	*br*	*SS*	*39*	*1090*	*RN*	*17*
Thistlegarth	br	-D	29	4747	Sun	32
Thistleglen	br	-D	29	4748	Sun	64
Thode Fagelund	nw	-D	20	5757	Tön	257
Thomas B.Schall	am	-D		62		141
Thomas Donaldson	am	-D	44	7210	Bal	212
Thomas F.Nickel (DE 587)	*am*	*DE*	*44*	*1450*	*USN*	*291*
Thomas G.Masaryk	am	-D	43	7176	LAn	256
Thomas Hankins	br	-Df	18	276	Lon	6
Thomas McKean	am	-D	42	7191	Bal	107
Thomas Ruffin	am	-D	42	7191	Bal	154
Thomas Scott	am	-D	42	7176	NOr	211
Thomas Sinnickson	am	-D	42	7176	NOr	169
Thomas Stone (AP 59) ex President Van Buren (41)	am	AP	20	9255	USN	237
Thomas Walton	br	-D	17	4460	New	8
Thornlea	br	-D	29	4261	New	27
Thornliebank	br	-D	39	5569	Gla	72
Thorshavet	nw	-MT	38	11015	San	133
Thorsholm	nw	-MT	37	9937	San	150
Thorstrand	nw	-M	38	3041	San	153
Thrasyvoulos	gr	-D	12	3693	And	5
Thurso	br	-D	19	2436	Hul	103
Thursobank	br	-D	40	5575	Gla	87
Thurston	br	-D	18	3072	Har	15
Tia Juana	br	-D	28	2395	Lon	78
Tibia	nl	-MT	39	10356	Haa	57
"	"	"	"	"	"	267
Tielbank	br	-D	37	5084	Gla	45

1	2	3	4	5	6	7
Tiger	am	-DT	17	5992	NYo	88
Tiiu	es	-D	07	1865	Tal	23
Tilawa	br	-D	24	10006	Gla	265
Tilia Gorthon	sw	-D	30	1776	Hel	20
Tillie Lykes	am	-D	20	2572	Gal	105
Tinhow	br	-D	13	5232	Gla	268
Tisnaren	sw	-M	18	5747	Göt	97
Titan	br	-DP	06	9035	Liv	28
Titus	nl	-D	30	1712	Ams	133
Tjileboet	nl	-D	18	5760	Bat	139
Tjinegara	nl	-M	31	9227	Bat	280
Tjisalak	nl	-D	17	5787	Bat	274
Togian	nl	-M	30	979	Bat	259
Togimo	br	-Df	19	290	Lon	13
Tolken	sw	-D	22	4471	Sto	95
Tolosa	nw	-D	30	1974	Osl	77
Tolten ex Lotta (41)	cl	-D	38	1858	Val	85
Tönsbergfjord	nw	-M	30	3156	Osl	83
Toorak	br	-DT	27	8627	Lon	74
Topa Topa	am	-D	20	5356	Mob	119
Tor II ex Lord Lonsdale (39)	fa	-Df	24	292	Tho	120
Torinia	br	-MT	39	10364	Lon	29
Tornus	br	-MT	36	8054	Lon	272
Torny	nw	-D	19	2424	Ber	94
Torondoc	ca	-D	27	1927	FWm	98
Toronto City	br	-D	25	2486	Bri	58
Tortugas	nw	-M	23	4697	Tön	138
Torungen	nw	-D	31	1948	Are	80
Torvanger	nw	-D	20	6568	Ber	105
Tosca	nw	-M	20	5128	Hau	17
Touchet	am	-DT	43	10172	Mob	175
Toufic Allah	sy	-S		75		247
Touraine	nw	-M	25	5811	Tön	31
Tourny	fr	-D	20	2769	Brd	11

1	2	3	4	5	6	7
Towa	nl	-D	30	5419	Rot	39
Toward	br	-D	23	1571	Gla	148
Tower Field s. Empire Tower (42)	br	-D	35	4378	Lon	---
Tower Grange	br	-M	40	5226	Lon	138
Trafalgar	nw	-M	38	5542	Tön	128
Transcona (J.271)	*ca*	*PM*	*41*	*590*	*RCN*	*188*
Transylvania ex -DP (39)	br	ACL	25	16923	RN	25
					Gla	---
Traveller	br	-D	22	3963	Liv	76
Trecarrell	br	-D	19	5271	SIv	55
Tredinnick	br	-D	21	4589	SIv	87
Trefusis	br	-D	18	5299	SIv	153
Tregantle s. Annitsa (39)	br	-D	18	4324	SIv	---
Tregarthen	br	-D	36	5201	Lon	55
Tregenna	br	-D	19	5242	SIv	29
Trehata	br	-D	28	4817	Lon	114
Treherbert s. Belcrest (39)	br	-D	25	4517	Lon	---
Trekieve	br	-D	19	5244	SIv	265
Treminnard	br	-D	22	4694	SIv	112
Tremoda	br	-D	28	4736	Lon	63
Trentonian (K.368)	*ca*	*PE*	*43*	*980*	*RCN*	*191*
Trepca	jg	-D	30	5042	Dub	85
Tresillian	br	-D	25	4743	Lon	56
Trevalgan	br	-M	37	5299	Lon	139
Trevarrack	br	-D	19	5270	SIv	56
Treverbyn	br	-D	20	5218	SIv	70
Trevilley	br	-M	40	5296	Lon	122
Trevisa	ca	-D	15	1813	Mon	32
Treworlas	br	-D	22	4692	SIv	143
Tricula	br	-MT	36	6221	Lon	112
Trieste s. Paderewski (41)	it	-D	20	4426		---
Triglav	jg	-D	29	6363	Dub	108

1	2	3	4	5	6	7
Tringa	br	-D	25	1930	Liv	17
Trinidad	pa	-M	39	434	Pan	63
ex Johan (41)						
Triona	br	-D	43	7283	Lon	272
Triton	nl	-D	28	2078	Ams	100
Triton	nw	-M	30	6607	Tön	116
Triton	gr	-D	14	4211	_th	---
s. Maria Rosa (39)						
Troilus	br	-D	21	7422	Liv	276
Trolla	nw	-D	23	1598	Tro	118
Tropic Star	nw	-M	26	5088	Osl	91
Truro	br	-D	22	974	Hul	2
Tseang Tah	cn	-D	15	786	Sha	---
s. Marilyse Moller (41)						
Tuapse	sj	-MT	31	6320	Tua	107
Tucurinca	br	-D	26	5412	Gla	155
Tudor	nw	-M	30	6607	Tön	19
Tuira	pa	-D	12	4397	Pan	25
ex Andriotis (39)						
Tulagi	br	-M	39	2281	Hon	274
Turkian	äg	-S		108		236
Tuscaloosa City	am	-D	20	5687	NYo	93
Tuscan Star	br	-M	30	11449	Lon	120
Tuscania	br	-DP	22	16991	Gla	---
s. Nea Hellas (39)						
Tutoya	bz	-D	13	1125	Rio	168
Tuva	nl	-M	35	4652	Rot	68
Tuxpam	me	-DT	03	7008		106
ex Americano (41)						
Tweed (K.250)	*br*	*PF*	*42*	*1370*	*RN*	*177*
Tweed	br	-D	26	2697	Lon	49
Twickenham	br	-D	40	4762	Lon	169
Tymeric	br	-D	19	5228	Gla	36
Tynedale (L.96)	*br*	*DE*	*40*	*907*	*RN*	*253*
Tynwald (D.69)	br	ACL	36	2376	RN	238
ex -DP (40)					Dou	---
Typhoon	pl	-S		175		233
Tyr	nw	-M	26	4265	Osl	84
Tysa	nl	-M	38	5327	Rot	107
Ufa	sj	-D	17	1892	Len	201
Uganda	br	-D	27	4966	Gla	34
Uhenfels	dt	-D	31	7603	Bre	---
s. Empire Ability (40)						
Uelen	sj	-D	13	5135	Vla	279
s. auch Wellen						
Uhti	es	-D	19	1406	Tal	---
s. Gasray (40), ex Springfal (39)						
Ulea	br	-D	36	1574	Gla	71
Ulster Prince	br	-DP	30	3791	Bel	18
Uluc Ali Reis	*tü*	*SS*	*40*	*863*	*T.N.*	---
s. P.615 (41)						
Ulva	br	-D	12	1401	Lon	28
Ulysses	br	-D	13	14647	Liv	89
Ulysses	nl	-D	18	2666	Ams	162
Umaria	br	-D	42	6852	Lon	160
Umtata	br	-D	35	8141	Lon	84
"	"	"	"	"	"	108
Umona	br	-DP	10	3767	Lon	47
Umwuma	br	-D	14	4419	Lon	270
Underhill (DE 682)	*am*	*DE*	*43*	*1400*	*USN*	*290*
Union Jack	fa	-Df		81		30
Uniwaleco	sa	-DT	05	9755	Dur	83
Upwey Grange	br	-M	25	9130	Lon	24
Uralles	sj	-D	27	1975	Ode	218
Urbi	it	-D	20	2008		---
s. Duero (39)						
Urla	br	-D	24	5198	Lon	41
Uruguay	ar	-D	21	3425	BAi	18
Uskbridge	br	-D	40	2615	Npt	32
Uskmouth	br	-D	28	2483	Npt	7
Uskvalley	br	-D	29	2480	Npt	---
s. Archangel'sk (39)						
Vaalaren	sw	-M	36	3406	Göt	161
Vaclite	br	-MT	28	5026	Lon	12
Vàlera	pa	-MT	43	3401	Pan	179
Valiant (02)	*br*	*BB*	*14*	*32700*	*RN*	*228*
Valiente	pa	-D	20	5527	Pan	---
s. Guatemala (40)						
Valleyfield (K.329)		*PF*	*43*	*1370*	*RCN*	*180*
Valparaiso	sw	-M	17	3760	Sto	40
Van Cloon	nl	-D	11	4519	Bat	259
Van Lansberge	nl	-D	13	1937	Bat	259
Van Overstraten	nl	-D	11	4482	Bat	259
Van Rees	nl	-D	13	3000	Bat	258
Van Riebeeck	nl	-D	02	2263	Bat	258
Vancouver City	br	-M	30	4955	Bid	1
Vancouver Island	ca	-M	29	9472	Mon	69
ex Weser (40)						
Vanja	nw	-MT	29	6198	Osl	146
Vapper	es	-D	13	4543	Tal	22
ex Pilcot (39)						
Varangberg	nw	-D	15	2842	Osl	67
ex Varangfjell (39)						
Varanger	nw	-MT	25	9305	Ber	76
Varangfjell	nw	-D	15	2842	Osl	---
s. Varangberg (39)						
Vardaas	nw	-MT	31	8176	Are	119
Varild	nw	-D	10	1085	Hau	11
Varlaam Avanesov	sj	-MT	32	6557	Tua	229
Vassiliki	br	APC	79	190	RN	235
Vassilios A.Polemis	gr	-D	07	3429	And	75

1	2	3	4	5	6	7
Vecht	nl	-D	17	1965	Rot	16
Veerhaven	nl	-D	30	5291	Rot	135
Vega	fi	-D	13	1073	Hsk	2
Velma Lykes	am	-D	20	2572	Hou	101
Vendia	dä	-D	24	1150	Kop	3
Venezia	sw	-D	38	1673	Göt	168
Venetia	br	-DT	27	5728	Gla	46
Venezuela	sw	-MP	39	6991	Sto	49
Venore	am	-D	21	8017	NYo	75
Venus (R.50)	*br*	*DD*	*43*	*1710*	*RN*	*204*
Vermont	fr	-D	19	5186	Hav	4
Vernon City	br	-D	29	4748	Bid	168
Veronica	sw	-D	18	1316	Hel	35
Vervain (K.190)	*br*	*PE*	*41*	*925*	*RN*	*191*
ex Broom (41)						
Vespasian	nw	-D	35	1570	Ber	41
ex Betta (40)						
Vestfold	pa	-DW	31	14547	Pan	147
Vestvard	nw	-D	25	4319	Osl	30
Veteran (D.72)	*br*	*DD*	*19*	*1120*	*RN*	*125*
Viborg	sj	-D		4100		214
ex						
Vibran	nw	-M	35	2993	Hau	124
Viceroy of India	br	-DP	29	19627	Gla	238
Victolite	ca	-MT	28	11410	Mon	78
Victor Ross	br	-MT	33	12247	Lon	38
Victoria	sp	-D	17	6600		---
s. Castillo Oropesa (39)						
Victoria	gr	-D	19	6085	Pir	36
ex Bellflower (40)						
Victoria	ar	-MT	41	7417	BAi	90
ex Carlantic (41)						
Victoria City	br	-D	29	4739	Bid	38
Vid	jg	-D	10	3547	Sus	12
Vid		-D	10	3701		---
s. Radchurch (41)						
Vidar	dä	-D	15	1353	Esb	12

1	2	3	4	5	6	7
Vigeo	nw	-D	20	6683	Tön	---
s. Korshamn (39)						
Vigilant	nw	-M	23	4765	Osl	---
s. Ringstad (40)						
Vigor	it	-DT	23	6511	Gen	---
s. Amatlan (41)						
Vigör	nw	-D	35	1518	Osl	---
s. Ste.Marcelle (40)						
Vigrid	nw	-M	23	4765	Osl	57
Vigsnes	nw	-D	30	1599	Ber	190
Viiu	es	-D	17	1908	Tal	17
Viking	dä	-D	93	1153	Aab	16
Viking Star	br	-D	20	6445	Lon	118
Vilja	nw	-MT	28	6672	Osl	123
Villarperosa	it	-D	21	6255	Gen	---
s. Colin (42)						
Ville d'Arlon	be	-DP	20	7555	Ant	37
ex American Traveler (40)						
Ville de Gand	be	-DP	20	7590	Ant	25
ex American Importer (40)						
Ville de Hasselt	be	-DP	20	7461	Ant	27
ex American Trader (40)						
Ville de Liège	be	-DP	20	7430	Ant	49
ex American Palmer (40)						
Ville de Mons	be	-DP	21	7463	Ant	27
ex American Shipper (40)						
Ville de Namur	be	-DP	20	7463	Ant	20
ex American Merchant (40)						
Ville de Rouen	br	-D	19	5083	Liv	143
"	"	"	"	"	"	144
Ville de Stras-bourg	br	-D	20	7159	Lon	241
Vimeira	br	-DT	27	5728	Gla	115
Vineland	br	-D	19	5587	Liv	
ex Sapinero (40)						
Vinemoor	br	-D	24	4359	Lon	24
Vinga	sw	-D	23	1974	Göt	8
Vingaland	sw	-M	35	2734	Göt	35

1	2	3	4	5	6	7
Violando N. Goulandris	gr	-D	19	3598	And	19
Virginia	am	-DT	41	10731	Wmt	95
Virginia Sinclair	am	-DT	30	6151	Wmt	155
Vistula	sw	-D	19	1018	Göt	4
Vital de Oliveira	bz	AP	10	1737	BzN	183
Viva	nw	-D	38	3798	Are	273
Vivian P.Smith	br	-S		130		115
Vogtland	dt	-M	24	6608	Hbg	---
s. Berakit (40)						
Vojvoda Putnik	jg	-D	16	5879	Spl	154
Volendam	nl	-DP	22	15434	Rot	27
Volo	br	-D	38	1587	Hul	229
Volusia	am	-D	20	2686	Bal	---
s. Norlindo (41)						
Vorošilov	sj	-D	24	3908	Ode	219
(= Voroshilov)						
Vortigern (D.37)	*br*	*DD*	*17*	*1090*	*RN*	*223*
Vrzyv (BTŠČ-41o)	*sj*	*PM*	*38*	*441*	*SSF*	*222*
Vulcain	br	-D	11	4362	Car	53
ex Rouen (40)						
W.B.Walker	br	-DT	35	10468	Lon	41
W.C.Teagle	pa	-DT	17	9552	Pan	69
W.D.Anderson	am	-DT	21	10227	Phi	80
W.E.Hutton	am	-DT	20	7076	Bal	86
W.L.Steed	am	-DT	18	6182	Wmt	77
W.S.Rheem	am	-DT	21	10872	SFr	284
Wade Hampton	br	-D	42	7176	NOr	153
Wahehe	dt	-D	22	4709	Hbg	---
s. Empire Citizen (40)						
Waiotira	br	-M	39	12823	Sou	40
Waiwera	br	-M	34	12435	Sou	107
Wallsend	br	-D	37	3157	New	139
Walma	fi	-D	08	1361	Hsk	3
Walter Camp	am	-D	42	7176	SFr	272

1	2	3	4	5	6	7
Walter Q.Gresham	am	-D	43	7191	NOr	159
Wandby	br	-D	40	4947	Har	34
Wangi-Wangi	nl	-D	26	7789	Bat	53
ex Franken (40)						
Wanstead	br	-D	28	5486	Lon	163
War Hawk (AP 168)	am	AP	43	7906	USN	287
Waroonga	br	-D	14	9365	Ply	161
Warrior	am	-D	20	7551	Mob	107
Warszawa	po	-DP	16	2487	Gdy	229
Warwick (D.25)	*br*	*DD*	*17*	*1100*	*RN*	*178*
Warwick Castle	br	-M	30	20107	Lon	136
Washington	br	APM	19	209	RN	8
ex -Df (39)					Gri	---
Washington (BB 56)	*am*	*BB*	*40*	*35000*	*USN*	*281*
Washingtonian	am	-D	19	6617	NYo	261
Wasp (CV 7.)	*am*	*CV*	*39*	*14700*	*USN*	*280*
Waterton	br	-D	28	2140	SJo	127
Watsonville	pa	-D	18	2220	Pan	98
Watuka	ca	-D	18	1621	Pic	179
Wawaloam	am	-S		342		113
Wayfarer	br	-D	25	5068	Liv	276
Waynegate	br	-D	31	4260	Lon	44
Waziristan	br	-D	24	5135	New	197
Weirbank	br	-M	25	5150	Gla	111
Wellcombe	br	-D	30	5122	Lon	48
Wellen	sj	-D	13	5135	Vla	---
s. Uelen						
Wellfield	br	-MT	24	6054	New	55
Wellington Star	br	-M	39	13212	Bel	19
Welshman (M.84)	*br*	*CM*	*40*	*2650*	*RN*	*242*
Wentworth	br	-D	19	5212	New	165
Werdenfels	dt	-D	21	6318	Bre	---
s. Balingkar (40)						
Weser	dt	-M	29	9472	Bre	---
s. Vancouver Island (40)						
West Amargosa	am	-D	19	5462	LAn	---
s. Empire Crossbill (40)						

1	2	3	4	5	6	7
West Campgaw	am	-D	20	5625	NYo	---
s. Capira (41)						
West Cawthon	am	-D	19	5611	NYo	---
s. Empire Bison (40)						
West Celina	am	-D	19	5722	Ptl	117
West Chetac	am	-D	19	5627	NYo	125
West Cobalt	am	-D	18	6055	Gal	---
s. Empire Miniver (40)						
West Ekonk	am	-D	18	5631	Hou	---
s. Empire Wildbeeste (41)						
West Gambo	am	-D	18	5676	NOr	---
s. Empire Hartlebeeste (41)						
West Hardaway	am	-D	19	5702	Ptl	104
West Hematite	am	-D	19	5621	Sea	---
s. Irish Pine (41)						
West Hobomac	am	-D	18	5755	NOr	---
s. Ile de Batz (40)						
West Humhaw	am	-D	18	5527	NYo	135
West Imboden	am	-D	19	5751	NYo	91
West Ira	am	-D	19	5681	SFr	105
West Irmo	am	-D	19	5775	NYo	88
West Isleta	am	-D	19	5680	NYo	---
s. Empire Merlin (40)						
West Ivis	am	-D	19	5666	SFr	76
West Kebar	am	-D	20	5620	NYo	130
West Kedron	am	-D	20	5620	NYo	---
s. Empire Eland (40)						
West Lashaway	am	-D	18	5637	NYo	119
West Madaket	am	-D	18	5565	Mob	165
West Maximus	am	-D	19	5561	Sea	165
West Neris	am	-D	19	5589	NOr	---
s. Irish Oak (42)						
West Notus	am	-D	20	5492	SFr	100
West Pocasset	am	-D	19	5707	Ptl	---
s. Chepo (41)						
West Portal	am	-D	20	5376	SFr	148
ex Emergency Aid (39)						

1	2	3	4	5	6	7
Western City	am	-D	18	6113	Sea	---
s. Empire Turnstone (42)						
Western Prince	br	-MP	29	10926	Lon	39
West Wales	br	-D	25	4353	Car	41
West Zeda	am	-D	18	5658	Ptl	80
Western Chief	br	-D	18	5759		46
ex am (41)					Ptl	---
Western Head	br	-D	19	2599	Nas	99
ex Cumberland (39)						
Westmoreland	br	-D	17	8967	Lon	100
Westpool	br	-D	18	5724		48
ex am (41)					Sea	---
Weyburn (K.173)	*ca*	*PE*	*41*	*925*	*RCN*	*151*
Whirlwind (D.30)	*br*	*DD*	*17*	*1100*	*RN*	*22*
Whitaker (K.580)	*br*	*DE*	*43*	*1300*	*RN*	*186*
ex am DE 571						
White Crest	br	-D	28	4365	New	81
Whitford Point	br	-D	28	5026	Lon	34
Wichita (CA 45)	*am*	*CA*	*37*	*10000*	*USN*	*289*
Wichita	am	-M	20	6174	NOr	124
Widestone	br	-D	20	3192	Lon	137
Wigmore	br	-Df	28	345	Gri	6
Wilford	nw	-D	21	2158	Tön	262
Wilhelmina	br	-D	09	6725	Gla	38
Wilja	fi	-D	14	3396	Hsk	14
ex Gertrud (39)						
Will Rogers	am	-D	42	7200	Bal	194
Willamette Valley	br	-D	28	4724	Bid	---
s. Edgehill (39)						
William A. McKenney	am	-D	16	6153	Bos	127
William B.Travis	am	-D	42	7176	Hou	250
William B.Woods	am	-D	43	7176	Bru	255
William Blackstone	am	-D	43	7219		---
s. Samtucky (43)						

1	2	3	4	5	6	7
William Boyce Thompson	am	-DT	21	7061	Wmt	98
"	"	"	"	"	"	169
William C.Gorgas	am	-DT	43	7197	Mob	155
"	"	"	"	"	"	156
William C. McTarnahan	am	-DT	41	7302	Wmt	96
William Clark	am	-D	42	7176	Ptl	201
William Cullen Bryant	am	-D	42	7176	Ptl	110
William D.Burnham	am	-D	43	7176	SFr	187
William Dawes	am	-D	42	7176	Ptl	280
William Ellery	am	-D	42	7181	SFr	270
William Eustis	am	-D	43	7196	Hou	157
William Gaston	am	-D	42	7177	Wmt	183
William Hansen	nw	-D	39	1344	Osl	75
William Hodson	am	-D	44	7209		---
s. Sverre Helmersen (44)						
William Hooper	am	-D	42	7177	Wmt	198
William Humphries	br	-Df	18	276	Lon	7
William J.Salman	am	-D	19	2616	Hou	97
William K. Vanderbilt	am	-D	42	7181	SFr	283
William King	am	-D	42	7176	Por	269
William Pierce Frye	am	-D	43	7176	Por	160
William Rockefeller	am	-DT	21	14054	Wmt	106
William S.Thayer	am	-D	42	7176	Ptl	207
William W.Gerhard	am	-D	43	7176	Bal	250
William Wilberforce	br	-M	30	5004	Liv	146
William Williams	am	-D	42	7181	SFr	283
Willimantic	br	-D	18	4857		105
ex am						
Willmoto	am	-D	19	4999	Phi	---
s. Melvin H.Baker (41)						

1	2	3	4	5	6	7
Willowbank	br	-M	39	5041	Har	19
Willowpool	br	-D	25	4815	Har	8
Winamac	pr	-DT	26	8621	Lon	119
Windsorwood	br	-D	36	5395	Mid	21
Winkleigh	br	-D	27	5055	Lon	1
Winkler	pa	-MT	30	6907	Pan	150
"	"	"	"	"	"	151
Winnipeg	br	-D	18	9807		---
s. Winnipeg II (41), ex Paimpol (39)						
Winnipeg II	br	-D	18	9807	Liv	129
ex Winnipeg (41), ex Paimpol (39)						
Winona	am	-D	19	6197	Eve	129
Winona County	am	-D	19	6159	Npt	---
s. Empire Whale (41)						
Winooski (AO 38)	am	AO	41	10600	USN	135
ex Calusa (41)						
Winterswijk	nl	-D	14	3205	Rot	64
Wisconsin	am	-D	19	6132	Ptl	---
s. Nidarland (39)						
Wivern (D.66)	br	DD	19	1120	RN	150
Woensdrecht	nl	-MT	26	4668	Rot	122
Wollongbar	au	-D	22	2239	Syd	282
Woodbury	br	-D	36	4434	Lon	23
Woodpecker (U.08)	br	PS	42	1300	RN	178
Worcestershire	br	ACL	31	11402	RN	48
ex -MP (39) (F.29)						
Worden	ni	-M	03	555	Blu	92
Wray Castle	br	-D	38	4253	Liv	50
Wrotham	br	-D	27	1884	Sun	60
Wyoming	am	-D	19	2689	Bal	---
s. Norlandia (41)						
Wyoming	fr	-D	30	8062	Hav	157

1	2	3	4	5	6	7
YO 159	am	YO			USN	284
YP 389	am	YP			USN	105
Yaka	am	-D	20	5432	Mob	137
"	"	"	"	"	"	138
Yahia	sy	-S			64	254
Yarraville	br	-DT	28	8627	Hon	20
Yewcrest	br	-D	07	3774	Lon	26
ex Ivo Racic (40)						
Yoma	br	-D	28	8131	Gla	246
Yorkmar	am	-D	19	5612	NYo	173
Yorkmoor	br	-D	25	4457	Lon	99
Yorkshire	br	-DP	20	10183	Liv	5
Yorktown	br	-D	28	1547		126
ex am (42)					Bal	---
Yorktown (CV 5)	am	CV	36	19900	USN	279
Yorkwood	br	-D	36	5401	Mid	145
Yselhaven	nl	-D	21	4802	Rot	55
Yngaren	sw	-M	21	5246	Göt	73
Yukon	am	-D	99	5747	NYo	186
Zaandam	nl	-M	39	10909	Rot	133
Zaanland	nl	-D	21	6813	Ams	157
Zagloba	po	-D	38	2864	Gdy	148
ex Robur VIII (40)						
Zannes Gounaris	gr	-D	07	4407	And	31
Zarian	br	-D	38	4871	Fre	22
"	"	"	"	"	"	143
Žarkij	sj	DD	18	1190	SNF	208
ex Brighton (44), ex Cowell (40)						
Zaščitnik	sj	PM	38	441	SSF	---
s. BTŠČ-411						
Zealand	br	-D	36	1433	Lei	234

1	2	3	4	5	6	7	1		2	3	4	5	6	7	1		2	3	4	5	6	7

```
Zealandic            br -M  28 10578 Sou  41
Zebra (AKN 5)        am AKN 43  7176 USN ---
  s. Matthew Lyon
Žemčug               sj PC  37   441 SNF ----
  s. SKR-29
Zenobia              br PE  41   925 RN  ---
  s. Snowflake (41)
Zeus                 gr -D  20  5961 Syr 149
Zephyr (R.19)        br DD  43  1710 RN  188
Zinnia (K.98)        br PE  40   925 RN   63
Zoodochos Pighi      gr -S         48     230
Zouave               br -D  30  4256 Lon 159
Zuiderkerk           nl -D  22  8424 Haa 119
Zurichmoor           br -D  25  4455 Lon  98
Zrinski              jg -D  20  5652     ---
  s. Ashcrest (40)


No.764               fi -Dt        216
```

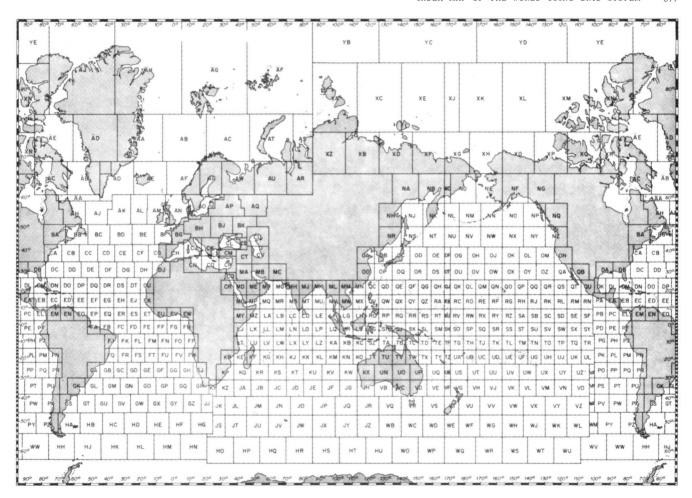

QUADRANT 41

54 sm

6 sm 18 sm

AB   AD   AL

AA   AK   AL   AM

AT   AJ

BB   BC   BD   BE   BF

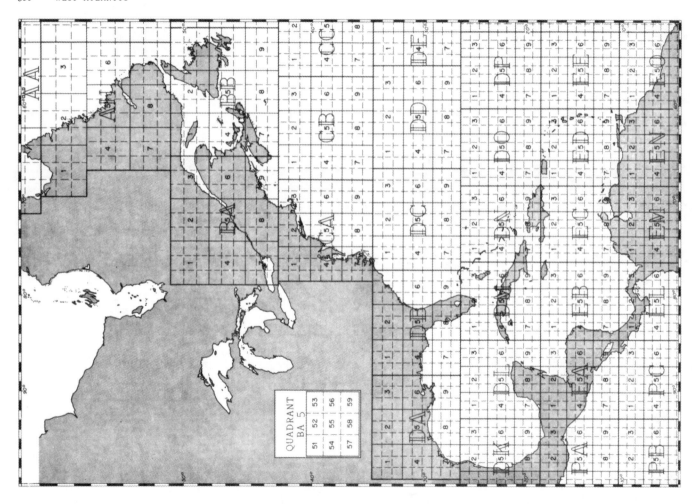

QUADRANT
BA 5

51	52	53
54	55	56
57	58	59

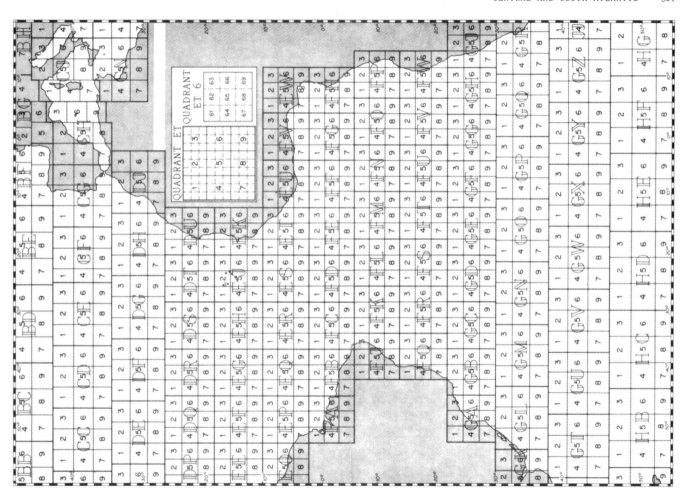

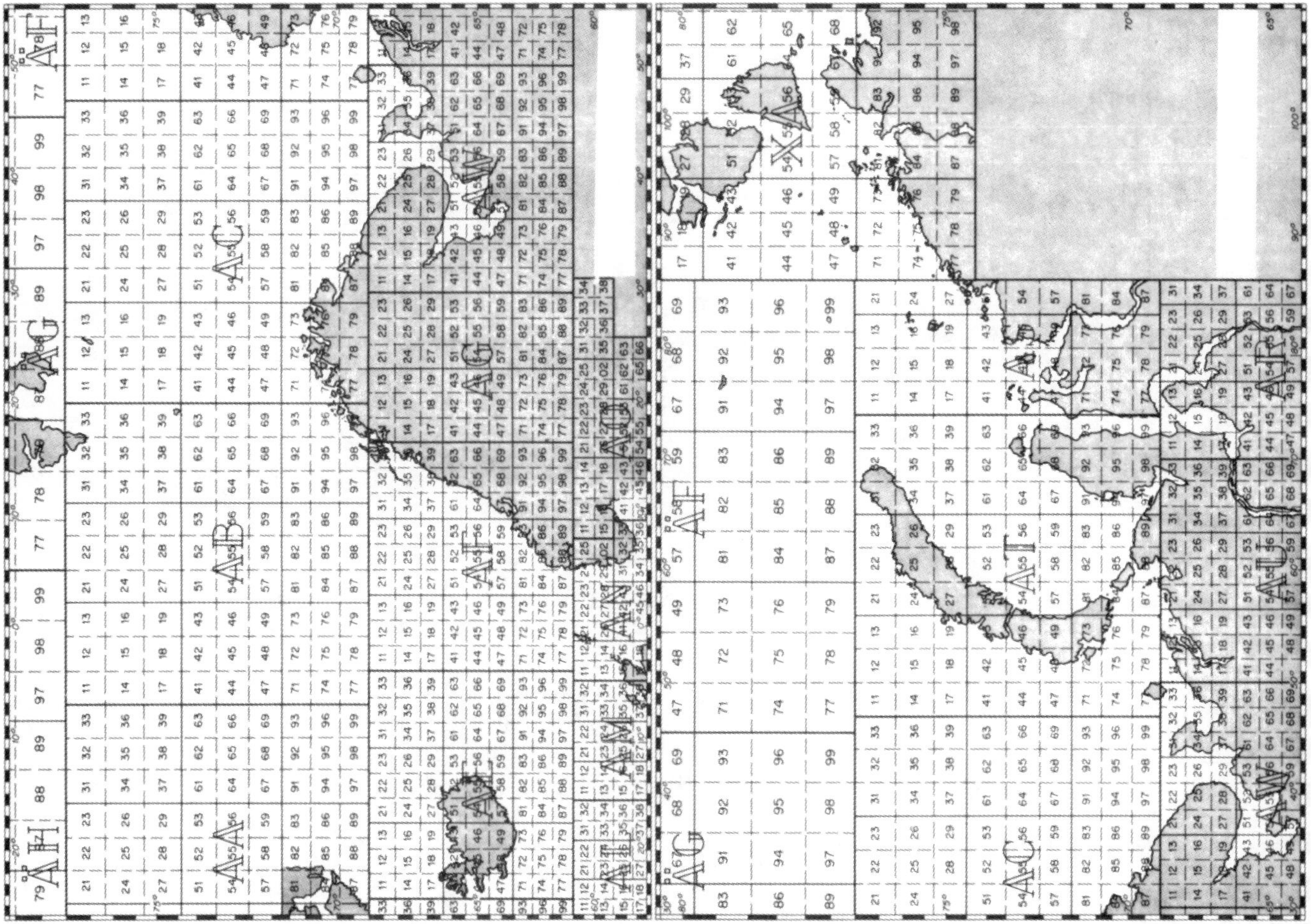

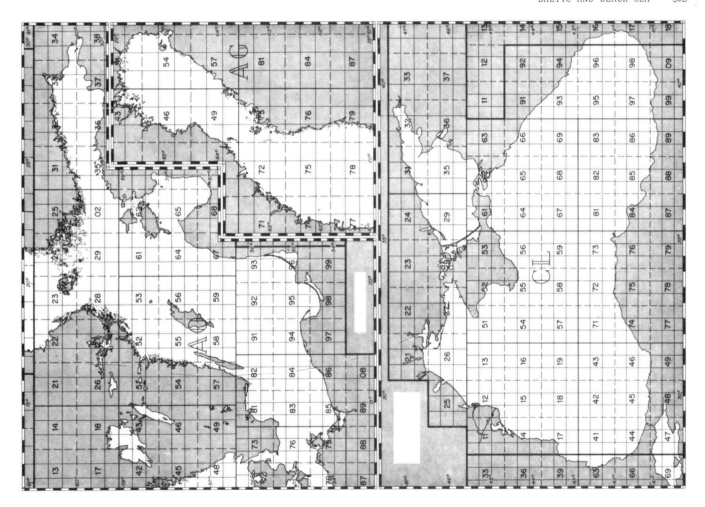

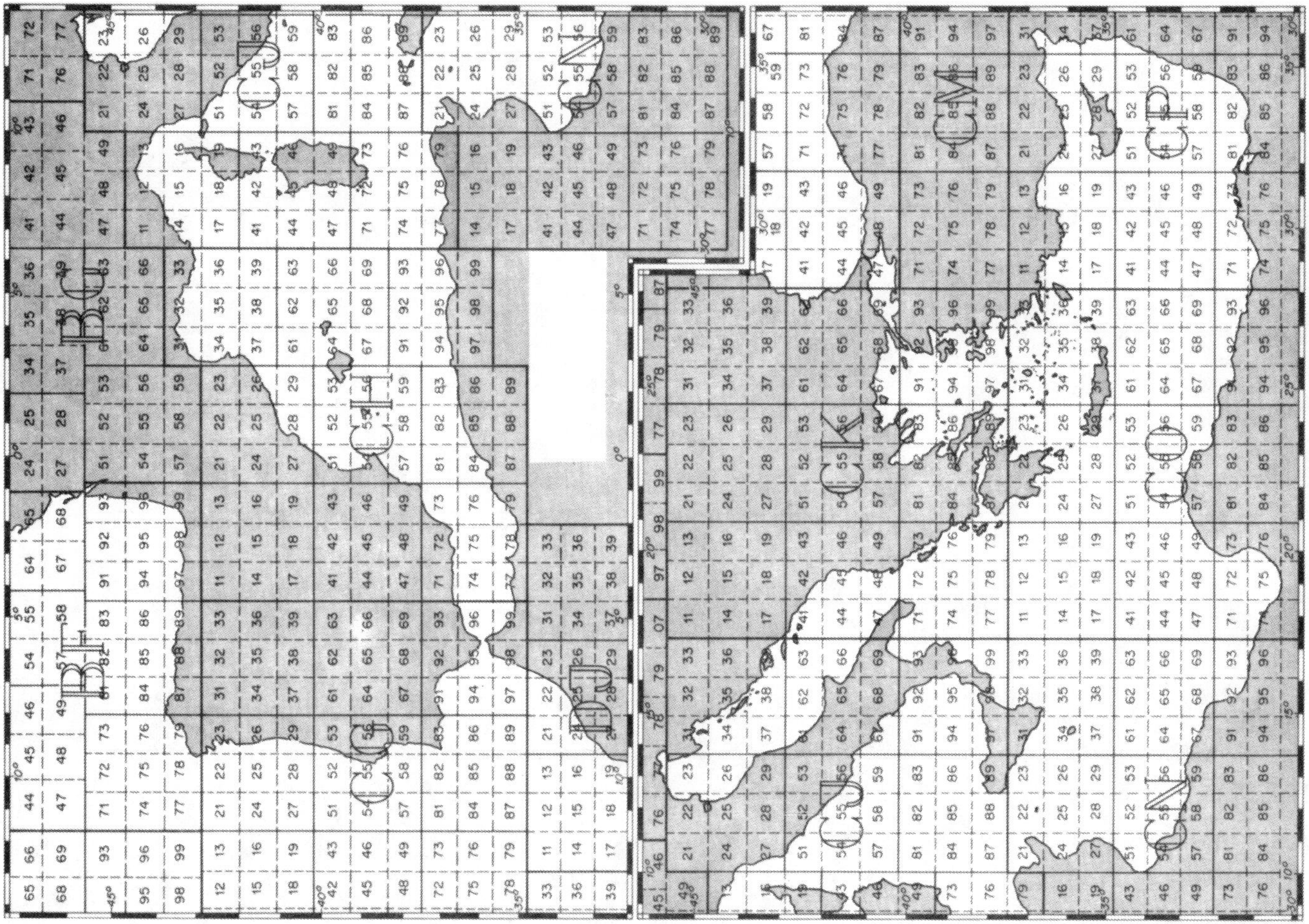

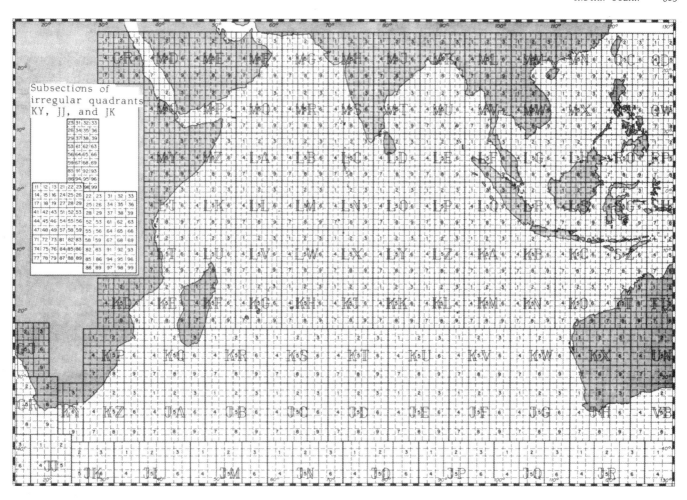

Subsections of
irregular quadrants
KY, JJ, and JK

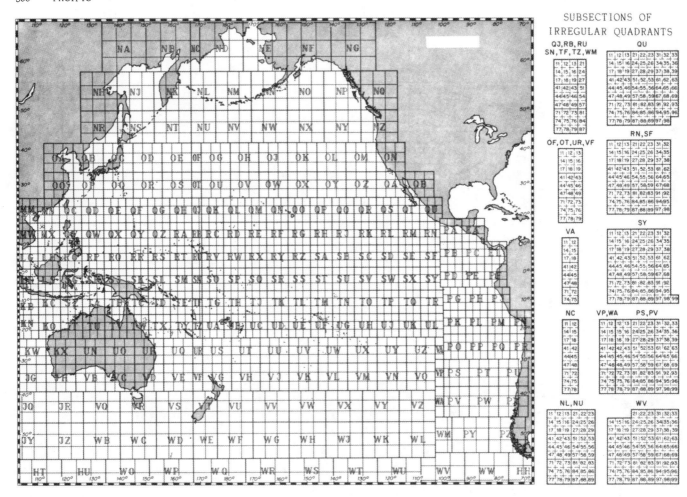